W9-BFT-929

Katakana

ア	イ	ウ	エ	オ			
カ	キ	ク	ケ	コ	キャ	キュ	キョ
サ	シ	ス	セ	ソ	シャ	シュ	ショ
タ	チ	ツ	テ	ト	チャ	チュ	チョ
ナ	ニ	ヌ	ネ	ノ	ニャ	ニュ	ニョ
ハ	ヒ	フ	ヘ	ホ	ヒャ	ヒュ	ヒョ
マ	ミ	ム	メ	モ	ミャ	ミュ	ミョ
ヤ	(イ)	ユ	(エ)	ヨ			
ラ	リ	ル	レ	ロ	リャ	リュ	リョ
ワ	(イ)	(ウ)	(エ)	ヲ			
ン							

ガ	ギ	グ	ゲ	ゴ	ギャ	ギュ	ギョ
ザ	ジ	ズ	ゼ	ゾ	ジャ	ジュ	ジョ
ダ	ヂ	ヅ	デ	ド			
バ	ビ	ブ	ベ	ボ	ビャ	ビュ	ビョ
パ	ピ	プ	ペ	ポ	ピャ	ピュ	ピョ

Yookoso!

ようこそ

Yookoso!

An Invitation to Contemporary Japanese

MEDIA EDITION

Yasu-Hiko Tohsaku
University of California, San Diego

ようこそ

Boston Burr Ridge, IL Dubuque, IA Madison, WI New York
San Francisco St. Louis Bangkok Bogotá Caracas Kuala Lumpur
Lisbon London Madrid Mexico City Milan Montreal New Delhi
Santiago Seoul Singapore Sydney Taipei Toronto

This is an EBI book.

Yookoso!
An Invitation to Contemporary Japanese, Media Edition

Published by McGraw-Hill, an imprint of The McGraw-Hill Companies, Inc., 1221 Avenue of the Americas, New York, NY 10020. Copyright © 2004 by The McGraw-Hill Companies, Inc. All rights reserved. No part of this publication may be reproduced or distributed in any form or by any means, or stored in a database or retrieval system, without the prior written consent of The McGraw-Hill Companies, Inc., including, but not limited to, in any network or other electronic storage or transmission, or broadcast for distance learning.

This book is printed on acid-free paper.

2 3 4 5 6 7 8 9 0 WCK WCK 0 9 8 7 6 5 4

ISBN 0-07-286213-0

Vice president and Editor-in-chief: *Thalia Dorwick*
Publisher: *William R. Glass*
Director of development: *Scott Tinetti*
Executive marketing manager: *Nick Agnew*
Lead project manager: *David M. Staloch*
Senior production supervisor: *Richard DeVitto*
Design manager: *Cassandra Chu*
Interior designer: *Adriane Bosworth*
Cover designers: *Francis Owens/Glenda King*
Cover art: *Sally Vitsky*
Art director: *Jeanne M. Schreiber*
Senior supplements producer: *Louis Swaim*
Photo researcher: *Nora Agbayani*
Compositor: *Interactive Composition Corporation*
Typeface and paper: *Shinsei kaisho on 45# Publisher's Matte*
Printer and binder: *Quebecor World*

Because this page cannot legibly accommodate all the copyright notices, credits are listed after the index and constitute an extension of the copyright page.

Library of Congress Cataloging-in-Publication Data

Tohsaku, Yasu-Hiko
Yookoso! / Yasu-Hiko Tohsaku.—Media ed.
p. cm.
Contents: An invitation to contemporary Japanese
ISBN 0-07-286213-0
1. Japanese language—Textbooks for foreign speakers—English. 2. College readers.
I. Title: Yookoso II. Title.

PL539.5.E5T64 2004
495.6'82421—dc22 2003060018

www.mhhe.com

Contents

Preface xiii
Dear Student xxiv

GETTING STARTED 1

Part One

Meeting Others and Introducing Yourself 2
Everyday Greetings 7
Classroom Expressions 10
The Japanese Writing System (1): Introduction 14

Part Two

Numbers up to 20 17
Asking and Giving Telephone Numbers 18
Asking and Telling Time 20
Asking What Something Is 24
The Japanese Writing System (2): Hiragana (1) 26

Part Three

Talking About Daily Activities 34
Talking About Future Activities and Events 39
Talking About Likes and Dislikes 40
The Japanese Writing System (3): Hiragana (2) 43

Part Four

Talking About Activities and Events in the Past 51
Inviting Someone to Do Something 54
Talking About Weekly Schedules 56
Talking About the Weather 56
The Japanese Writing System (4): Katakana (1) 58

Part Five

Asking Location 63
Numbers from 21 to 10,000 66
Asking About Existence 67
Asking About Price 68
Talking More About Likes and Dislikes 71
The Japanese Writing System (5): Katakana (2) 72
Introduction to Kanji 75
Introduction to ***Yookoso!*** 80

Language Notes and Culture Notes are not listed here.

Topics / Vocabulary	Grammar
CHAPTER 1 CLASSMATES 82	
Nationalities and Languages 83 Personal Information 91 Around Campus 105 Vocabulary 120 Study Hint: Learning New Vocabulary 122	1. Identification: The Copula です 86 2. Possessive Particle の 90 3. Personal Pronouns and Demonstratives 101 4. Asking Questions: Interrogatives 108 Particles は and が 111
Chapter 1 Review 125	
CHAPTER 2 MY TOWN 127	
Commuting 128 Cities and Neighborhoods 138 Buildings and Places Around Town 143 Vocabulary 172	5. Adjectives and Adverbs 130 6. Expressing Existence: The Verbs あります and います 140 7. Indicating Location 146 8. Positional Words 147 9. Numerals and Counters 155 10. Expressing Likes and Dislikes: 好き and きらい 161 Sentence-Final よ 151 Study Hint: Learning Grammar 136 Polite Form Versus Plain Form 140
Chapter 2 Review 177	
CHAPTER 3 EVERYDAY LIFE 179	
Schedules 180 Daily Activities 191 Weekends and Holidays 213 Vocabulary 234	11. The Basic Structure of Japanese Verbs 185 12. The Nonpast, Polite Form of Verbs 192 13. The Past, Polite Form of Verbs 201 14. Particles Showing Grammatical Relationships 207 15. Making Suggestions: ～ましょう 218 16. Conjoining Nouns: と and や 224 Adverbs Used in Negative Sentences 205 Connecting Disjunctive Sentences 216 Approximate Numbers 226
Chapter 3 Review 237	

Culture Notes	Reading and Writing	Skills Practice
出身(しゅっしん) *Origins* 92 Japanese Universities and Colleges 93 Asking Personal Questions 99	Reading 1: フランス人(じん)のクラスメート 114 Study Hint: Learning Kanji 115 Reading 2: ペン・パルをさがしています! 116 Kanji 123 The Six Types of Kanji 123	Language Functions and Situations 117 Introducing Friends 117 Introducing Yourself 119 Listening Comprehension 120
Long Commutes 137 交番(こうばん) *Police Boxes* 144 Japanese Addresses 145	Reading 1: ブラウンさんのアパートの近所(きんじょ) 165 Reading 2: 林(はやし)さんのふるさと 167 Kanji 176	Language Functions and Situations 169 Making Communication Work 169 Showing Location on a Map 170 Listening Comprehension 172
Part-Time Jobs for College Students 181 年号(ねんごう) 184 国民(こくみん)の祝日(しゅくじつ) *National Holidays* 217	Reading 1: ブラウンさんの日常生活(にちじょうせいかつ) 225 Reading 2: ブラウンさんの週末(しゅうまつ) 227 Kanji 236	Language Functions and Situations 229 Making a Phone Call 229 Extending an Invitation 231 Listening Comprehension 233

Topics / Vocabulary	Grammar

CHAPTER 4 WEATHER AND CLIMATE 239

Weather Reports 240
Enjoying the Four Seasons 270
Forecasting 282
Vocabulary 297

17. Conjugating Adjectives 243
18. Comparatives and Superlatives 249
19. The Past, Plain Forms of Verbs 259
20. Explaining a Reason: ...のだ 264
21. The Te-Form of Adjectives and the Copula 273
22. The Te-Form of Verbs 277
23. Expressing Probability and Conjecture 283

Adverbs Used with Comparatives 251
Linking Disjunctive Clauses with けれども 272
Conjoining Sequential Actions 279

Chapter 4 Review 301

CHAPTER 5 HOBBIES AND LEISURE ACTIVITIES 303

Hobbies and Pastimes 304
Sports 314
Family 334
Vocabulary 366

24. Interrogative ＋か／も／でも 305
25. Describing Abilities 316
26. Nominalizers: こと and の 322
27. More Uses of the Particle も 326
28. Potential Form of Verbs 328
29. The Te-Form of Verbs ＋います 342
30. Relative Clauses 348
31. Describing a Change in State: なる 354

Nominal Verbs 312
か *or* 333
Words Expressing Respect and Politeness 336
Have You Already Eaten? 344
Some Time Expressions 345

Chapter 5 Review 371

Culture Notes

Reading and Writing

Skills Practice

Culture Notes

°C 242
Types of Rain 257
How to Write a Letter in Japanese 291

Reading and Writing

Reading 1: ブラウンさんへの手紙 289
Reading 2: トラベル・ガイド：いろは町の気候 293
Kanji 299

Skills Practice

Language Functions and Situations 295
- Asking Questions About the Japanese Language 295
- Asking for Assistance with **Kanji** 295

Listening Comprehension 297

Culture Notes

碁、将棋、マージャン、パチンコ: Japanese Games 311
When You Are Praised 320
日本のスポーツ: Japanese Sports 321
The Japanese Family 338

Reading and Writing

Reading 1: サンライズ・カルチャーセンターのお知らせ 356
Reading 2: 学生とサラリーマンの余暇調査 360
Kanji 369

Skills Practice

Language Functions and Situations 362
- Responding to Compliments 362
- Introducing a Family Member 363

Listening Comprehension 366

Topics / Vocabulary | Grammar

CHAPTER 6 FOOD 373

Foods and Beverages 374
Flavors and Tastes 394
Cooking Terms 408
Vocabulary 432

32. Expressing Experience: The Ta-Form of Verbs ＋ことがある 380
33. Expressing a Desire: ほしい, ほしがる, 〜たい, and …たがる 385
34. Expressing an Opinion: …と思う 395
35. 〜すぎる 398
36. Quoting Speech: …という 402
37. Expressing Intention: つもり and the Volitional Form of Verbs 410
38. The Te-Form of Verbs ＋ みる, しまう, いく, and くる 416
39. Expressing Simultaneous Actions: 〜ながら 422

〜がる 387
そう 396
Quote Marker と 403
Study Hint: How to Remember Verb Conjugations 415
もう and まだ 417

Chapter 6 Review 436

CHAPTER 7 SHOPPING 438

Shops and Stores 439
Shopping 453
Clothes 462
Vocabulary 494

40. When Something Happens: Temporal Clauses Ending in 時 442
41. Indefinite Pronoun の 449
42. Making If-Then Statements: The たら Conditional 457
43. Going Somewhere with a Purpose: Using the Particle に to Express Purpose 467
44. Reporting Hearsay: …そうだ 470
45. Saying Whether or Not Something Is True: …かどうか 473
46. Giving Reasons with …し, …し 478

だけ 450
〜やすい、〜にくい 480

Chapter 7 Review 498

Culture Notes | **Reading and Writing** | **Skills Practice**

Culture Notes

お茶 376
What Do Japanese Eat? 379

Reading and Writing

Reading 1: バイキング料理「むらさき」 424
Reading 2: あなたの食事チェック 427
Kanji 435

Skills Practice

Language Functions and Situations 429
- Asking and Expressing Opinions 429
- At a Restaurant 429

Listening Comprehension 431

Culture Notes

色 *Colors* 448
Handling Japanese Money 455
Metric System 477

Reading and Writing

Reading 1: 「サン・ロード」グランド・オープニング・セール 482
Reading 2: マイ・ファッション 485
Kanji 497

Skills Practice

Language Functions and Situations 487
- Shopping 487
- Saying Whether Two Things Are the Same or Different 493
- Listening Comprehension 494

APPENDICES 501

1. Verb Conjugation 502
2. Adjective and Copula Conjugation 506
3. Numbers 508
4. Counters 510
5. Time, Days, Months, and Years 515
6. **Ko-so-a-do** Words 518
7. Japanese Accent 519
8. Kanji List 521

Japanese-English Glossary 526

English-Japanese Glossary 544

Index 561

Preface

Welcome to ***Yookoso! An Invitation to Contemporary Japanese,*** a complete package of instructional materials for beginning language study. When the first edition published a decade ago, the response was overwhelmingly positive. It was clear that the program had struck a chord with instructors around the world who were looking for a text that matched what they were actually doing in the classroom. A pioneer among Japanese language materials, ***Yookoso!*** is the first program to integrate the teaching of all four language skills (listening, speaking, reading, writing) and to promote interaction in the classroom. In addition, ***Yookoso!*** integrates grammar in a more useful and flexible way to accommodate various approaches to teaching and different learning styles. Grammar is used as a tool for developing language proficiency rather than as the focal point of learning. This approach continues to characterize ***Yookoso!*** today.

Recognizing the changing role of multimedia in and out of language classrooms today, this special **Media Edition** of the Second Edition includes an interactive CD-ROM with each new copy of the textbook. This powerful learning tool provides students opportunities to review and practice grammar and vocabulary in a fun, interactive, and effective way. Integrated video clips from the ***Yookoso!*** video help further develop comprehension skills. The **Media Edition** is additionally enhanced by a new Online Learning Center, which includes Internet resources for instructors and students. What follows is the original Preface to the Second Edition of ***Yookoso!***

Changes in the Second Edition

In responding to feedback about the first edition of ***Yookoso!,*** our goal has been to make suggested changes that will enhance instruction, while at the same time retaining the key features that were praised by reviewers and that set ***Yookoso!*** apart from other beginning and intermediate-level Japanese programs. The visual *Guided Tour Through* ***Yookoso!*** explains all major features, some of which are new.

Enhancements to the Second Edition of Book 1 include the following:

- The text has been streamlined by reducing slightly the amount of content with no loss in the number of vocabulary and grammar topics and activities.
- The presentation of vocabulary and grammar has been reorganized so that related vocabulary and grammar are grouped together in sections. Each chapter now has three such Vocabulary and Grammar sections.
- Certain oral activities now appear after the grammar explanations to which they are related. Students and instructors will find grammar-related oral activities in a logical sequence.
- **Hurigana** now appears on new **kanji** for a total of three chapters.
- Some grammar points have been revised to provide more clarity.

- Some oral and written activities have been either revised or replaced in order to make them more accessible to students.
- Many cultural notes have been updated.
- A list of functional objectives appears at the beginning of every chapter. A similar checklist appears at the end of each chapter so students can check their progress.
- Chapter vocabulary lists and **kanji** lists have been moved to the end of each chapter and now follow the Language Skills section of Reading and Writing, Language Functions and Situations, and Listening Comprehension.
- The first edition's review chapters, which appeared only twice in the book, have been replaced by a two-page review section following each chapter.
- The font size for Japanese characters has been increased for easier readability.
- The exercise answer key formerly in the Appendices has been moved to the Instructor's Manual.

Objectives of the *Yookoso!* Program

- To teach the listening skills needed to understand basic everyday conversations
- To teach the oral skills needed to express oneself in a variety of everyday situations in Japanese
- To teach skimming, scanning, and intensive reading skills
- To teach basic writing skills, including descriptions and some functional writing tasks, such as letter writing
- To provide grammar explanations that help students acquire functional skills more readily
- To provide sociocultural information useful to beginning and intermediate-level Japanese language students

Methodology

Yookoso! was developed based on the results of recent research into second language acquisition and language pedagogy. All activities and exercises have been designed so that students develop proficiency in Japanese rather than simply acquiring grammatical knowledge.

- The main purpose of ***Yookoso!*** is to teach students how to use Japanese in real-life situations for different communicative purposes. Since activities involving interaction promote communicative abilities, ***Yookoso!*** includes a variety of activities that serve as a starting point for communicative interaction in the classroom.
- Current research has shown that the role of explicit grammar instruction in language learning is less important than previously believed. The study of grammar is neither a sufficient nor a necessary condition for learning to communicate, and it is best learned through self-study outside of class. For this reason, grammar is presented in simple terms and via charts whenever possible. Easily understood explanations and abundant examples make it

possible for students to study grammar on their own. Thus, instructors can devote precious class time to more meaningful communicative, interactive activities.

- The ***Yookoso!*** approach to orthography expects students to master the reading and writing of **hiragana** and **katakana** while working with the chapter called Getting Started. All texts in Getting Started are romanized to provide students who are still in the process of learning **hiragana** and **katakana** with an aid for preparing and reviewing class activities outside the classroom. Students should learn the reading and writing of **hiragana** and **katakana** as soon as possible and avoid using romanization, which has been known to retard the learning of **hiragana** and **katakana** and to promote poor pronunciation. We recommend that instructors avoid the use of romanization in the classroom and in tests as much as possible. In the textbook, romanization is limited to Getting Started. Throughout the text, **hurigana** accompany a **kanji** in the chapter in which it is first presented and in the following two chapters. The materials in the grammar exercises also follow this principle, but students need not use **kanji** that have not yet been presented for active learning, and they may write these words in **hiragana.**
- In each chapter, all activities are related to the main theme, and students can practice listening, speaking, reading, and writing about this theme in an integrated way.
- Topics and content in the textbook have been selected for their relevance to the life and interests of college students. Topically based organization presents meaningful contexts for language learning and raises students' motivation for learning the language.
- For successful language acquisition, learners must be exposed to meaningful input. Activities throughout the text are designed to encourage instructors and students to engage in meaningful interactions.
- The acquisition of vocabulary is of great importance for achieving proficiency, especially at the early stage of language learning. For this reason, a relatively large number of vocabulary items is presented throughout the text.
- Language acquisition takes place when learners attempt to comprehend a conveyed message. Also, students must be able to comprehend before they can produce language of their own. Priority is given to the development of comprehension abilities over production abilities. In order to facilitate students' language acquisition, the activities are carefully sequenced from comprehension activities to simple production activities to creative, personalized production activities. Since Total Physical Response (TPR) is a proven and effective technique in helping beginning-level language students develop their comprehension abilities, it is used to introduce new vocabulary and expressions in *Getting Started.*
- Reintroduction of vocabulary, grammar, and language functions at regular intervals facilitates the development of students' proficiency. The cyclical organization of this textbook helps students review materials consistently and repeatedly.
- Group work encourages interaction and communication. For this reason, ***Yookoso!*** includes a variety of pair work, small-group work, and interviews, during which students can practice using Japanese in a stress-free, non-threatening atmosphere.

Guided Tour Through *Yookoso!* Book 1

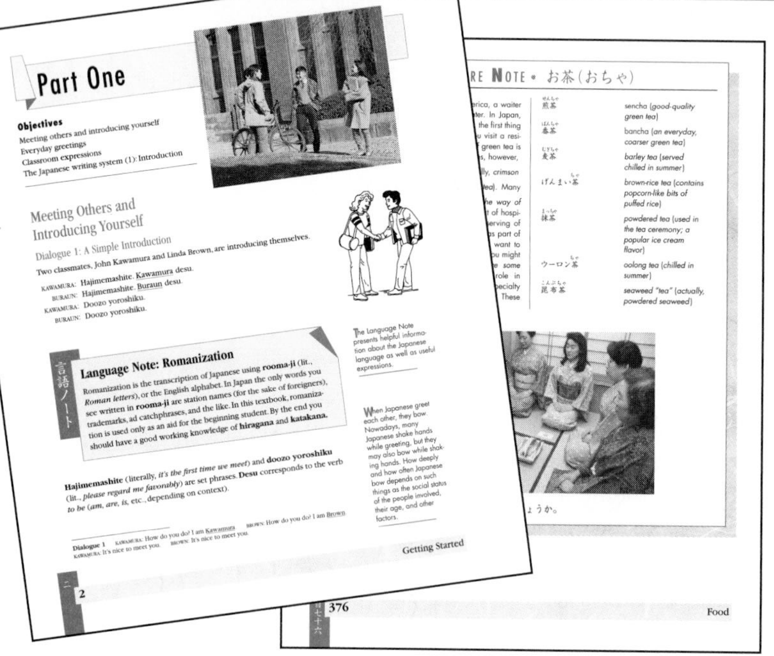

Part One

Objectives
Meeting others and introducing yourself
Everyday greetings
Classroom expressions
The Japanese writing system (1): Introduction

Meeting Others and Introducing Yourself

Dialogue 1: A Simple Introduction

Two classmates, John Kawamura and Linda Brown, are introducing themselves.

KAWAMURA: Hajimemashite. Kawamura desu.
BURAUN: Hajimemashite. Buraun desu.
KAWAMURA: Doozo yoroshiku.
BURAUN: Doozo yoroshiku.

Language Note: Romanization

言語ノート

Romanization is the transcription of Japanese using **rooma-ji** (lit., *Roman letters*), or the English alphabet. In Japan the only words you see written in **rooma-ji** are station names (for the sake of foreigners), trademarks, ad catchphrases, and the like. In this textbook, romanization is used only as an aid for the beginning student. By the end you should have a good working knowledge of **hiragana** and **katakana**.

The Language Note presents helpful information about the Japanese language as well as useful expressions.

When Japanese greet each other, they bow. Nowadays, many Japanese shake hands while greeting, but they may also bow while shaking hands. How deeply and how often Japanese bow depends on such things as the social status of the people involved, their age, and other factors.

Hajimemashite (literally, *it's the first time we meet*) and **doozo yoroshiku** (lit., *please regard me favorably*) are set phrases. **Desu** corresponds to the verb *to be* (*am, are, is*, etc., depending on context).

Dialogue 1 KAWAMURA: How do you do? I am Kawamura. BROWN: How do you do? I am Brown. KAWAMURA: It's nice to meet you. BROWN: It's nice to meet you.

Getting Started

二 2

RE NOTE • お茶(おちゃ)

...rica, a waiter ... In Japan, the first thing ... visit a resi... green tea is ...s, however, ...ly, crimson ...tea). Many ...he way of ...t of hospi... serving of ...s part of ... want to ...u might ...e some ...role in ...pecialty ... These

煎茶	sencha (good-quality green tea)
番茶	bancha (an everyday, coarser green tea)
麦茶	barley tea (served chilled in summer)
げんまい茶	brown-rice tea (contains popcorn-like bits of puffed rice)
抹茶	powdered tea (used in the tea ceremony; a popular ice cream flavor)
ウーロン茶	oolong tea (chilled in summer)
昆布茶	seaweed "tea" (actually, powdered seaweed)

三百七十六 376 Food

Organization of the Textbook

Getting Started

Yookoso! An Invitation to Contemporary Japanese, Second Edition, begins with a preliminary chapter called Getting Started. The five parts of this chapter are a functional introduction to the Japanese language. In them, students learn to express themselves in a variety of situations without formally studying grammar. At the same time, students learn to read and write hiragana and katakana and are introduced to the basic concepts and uses of **kanji.**

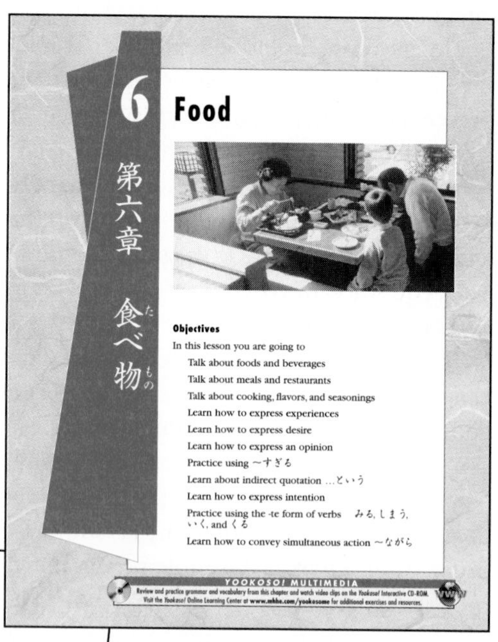

6 第六章 食べ物

Food

Objectives

In this lesson you are going to

Talk about foods and beverages
Talk about meals and restaurants
Talk about cooking, flavors, and seasonings
Learn how to express experiences
Learn how to express desire
Learn how to express an opinion
Practice using 〜すぎる
Learn about indirect quotation ...という
Learn how to express intention
Practice using the -te form of verbs みる, しまう, いく, and くる
Learn how to convey simultaneous action 〜ながら

YOOKOSO! MULTIMEDIA

Review and practice grammar and vocabulary from this chapter and watch video clips on the *Yookoso!* Interactive CD-ROM. Visit the *Yookoso!* Online Learning Center at **www.mhhe.com/yookoso** for additional exercises and resources.

CHAPTERS 1–7

The opening page of each chapter lists the functional goals of the chapter and contains a photo related to the theme of the chapter. This can be used as a starting point for oral activities or class discussion.

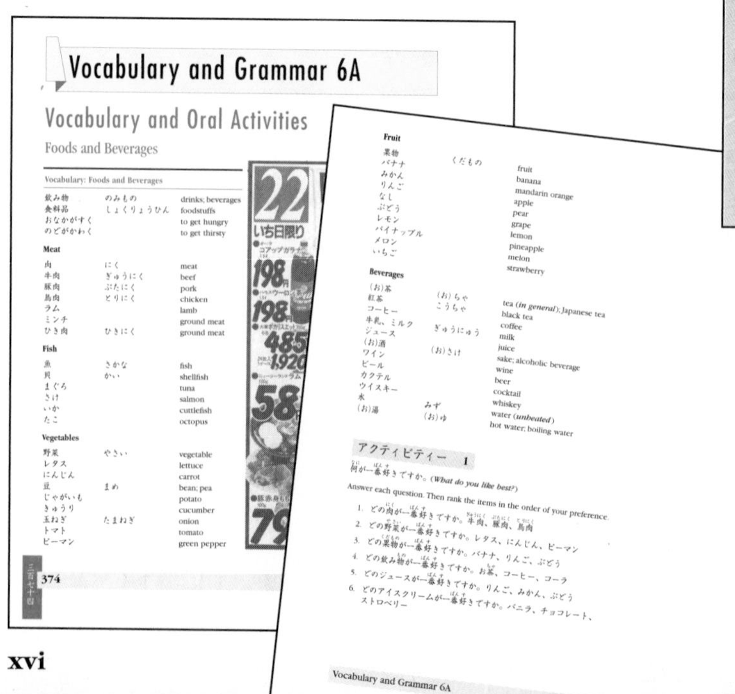

Vocabulary and Grammar 6A

Vocabulary and Oral Activities

Foods and Beverages

Vocabulary: Foods and Beverages

飲み物	のみもの	drinks; beverages
食料品	しょくりょうひん	foodstuffs
おなかがすく		to get hungry
のどがかわく		to get thirsty
Meat		
肉	にく	meat
牛肉	ぎゅうにく	beef
豚肉	ぶたにく	pork
鳥肉	とりにく	chicken
ラム		lamb
ミンチ		ground meat
ひき肉	ひきにく	ground meat
Fish		
魚	さかな	fish
貝	かい	shellfish
まぐろ		tuna
さけ		salmon
いか		cuttlefish
たこ		octopus
Vegetables		
野菜	やさい	vegetable
レタス		lettuce
にんじん		carrot
豆	まめ	bean; pea
じゃがいも		potato
きゅうり		cucumber
玉ねぎ	たまねぎ	onion
トマト		tomato
ピーマン		green pepper

三百七十四 374

Fruit		
果物	くだもの	fruit
バナナ		banana
みかん		mandarin orange
りんご		apple
なし		pear
ぶどう		grape
レモン		lemon
パイナップル		pineapple
メロン		melon
いちご		strawberry
Beverages		
(お)茶	(お)ちゃ	tea (*in general*); Japanese tea
紅茶	こうちゃ	black tea
コーヒー		coffee
牛乳、ミルク	ぎゅうにゅう	milk
ジュース		juice
(お)酒	(お)さけ	sake; alcoholic beverage
ワイン		wine
ビール		beer
カクテル		cocktail
ウイスキー		whiskey
水	みず	water (*unheated*)
(お)湯	(お)ゆ	hot water; boiling water

アクティビティー 1

何が一番好きですか。(*What do you like best?*)

Answer each question. Then rank the items in the order of your preference.

1. どの肉が一番好きですか。牛肉、豚肉、鳥肉
2. どの野菜が一番好きですか。レタス、にんじん、ピーマン
3. どの果物が一番好きですか。バナナ、りんご、ぶどう
4. どの飲み物が一番好きですか。お茶、コーヒー、コーラ
5. どのジュースが一番好きですか。りんご、みかん、ぶどう
6. どのアイスクリームが一番好きですか。バニラ、チョコレート、ストロベリー

Vocabulary and Grammar 6A

1. Vocabulary and Oral Activities is intended for vocabulary building and oral communication practice in the classroom. Activities in this section are designed so that students can build up their knowledge of vocabulary and practice using it in natural communicative situations in an integrated fashion.

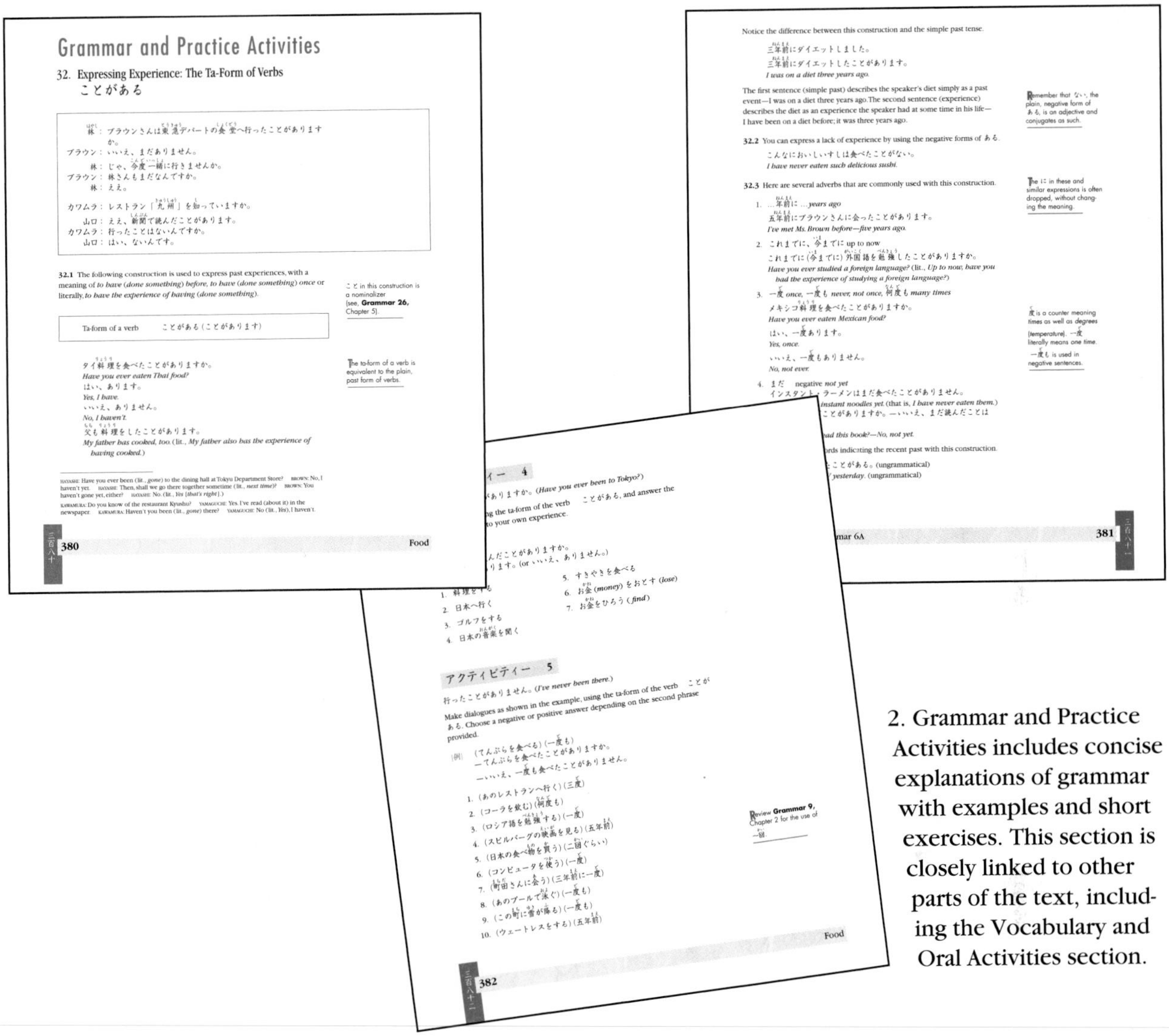

Grammar and Practice Activities

32. Expressing Experience: The Ta-Form of Verbs ことがある

林：ブラウンさんは東急デパートの食堂へ行ったことがありますか。
ブラウン：いいえ、まだありません。
林：じゃ、今度一緒に行きませんか。
ブラウン：林さんもまだなんですか。
林：ええ。

カワムラ：レストラン「九州」を知っていますか。
山口：ええ、新聞で読んだことがあります。
カワムラ：行ったことはないんですか。
山口：はい、ないんです。

32.1 The following construction is used to express past experiences, with a meaning of *to have (done something) before, to have (done something) once* or literally, *to have the experience of having (done something)*.

こと in this construction is a nominalizer (see, **Grammar 26**, Chapter 5).

Ta-form of a verb　　ことがある（ことがあります）

The ta-form of a verb is equivalent to the plain, past form of verbs.

タイ料理を食べたことがありますか。
Have you ever eaten Thai food?
はい、あります。
Yes, I have.
いいえ、ありません。
No, I haven't.
父も料理をしたことがあります。
My father has cooked, too. (lit., *My father also has the experience of having cooked.*)

HAYASHI: Have you ever been (lit., gone) to the dining hall at Tokyu Department Store? BROWN: No, I haven't yet. HAYASHI: Then, shall we go there together sometime (lit., *next time*)? BROWN: You haven't gone yet, either? HAYASHI: No. (lit., *Yes [that's right]*.)
KAWAMURA: Do you know of the restaurant Kyusho? YAMAGUCHI: Yes. I've read (about it) in the newspaper. KAWAMURA: Haven't you been (lit., gone) there? YAMAGUCHI: No (lit., *Yes*), I haven't.

Notice the difference between this construction and the simple past tense.

三年前にダイエットしました。
三年前にダイエットしたことがあります。
I was on a diet three years ago.

The first sentence (simple past) describes the speaker's diet simply as a past event—I was on a diet three years ago. The second sentence (experience) describes the diet as an experience the speaker had at some time in his life—I have been on a diet before; it was three years ago.

Remember that ない, the plain, negative form of ある, is an adjective and conjugates as such.

32.2 You can express a lack of experience by using the negative forms of ある.

こんなにおいしいすしは食べたことがない。
I have never eaten such delicious sushi.

32.3 Here are several adverbs that are commonly used with this construction.

The に in these and similar expressions is often dropped, without changing the meaning.

1. ...年前に ...*years ago*
五年前にブラウンさんに会ったことがあります。
I've met Ms. Brown before—five years ago.
2. これまでに、今までに up to now
これまでに（今までに）外国語を勉強したことがありますか。
Have you ever studied a foreign language? (lit., *Up to now, have you had the experience of studying a foreign language?*)
3. 一度 *once*, 一度も *never, not once*, 何度も *many times*
メキシコ料理を食べたことがありますか。
Have you ever eaten Mexican food?
はい、一度あります。
Yes, once.
いいえ、一度もありません。
No, not ever.
4. まだ　negative *not yet*
インスタント・ラーメンはまだ食べたことがありません。
...*instant noodles yet.* (that is, *I have never eaten them.*)
...ことがありますか。—いいえ、まだ読んだことは...
...*ad this book?—No, not yet.*
...ords indicating the recent past with this construction.
...ことがある。(ungrammatical)
...*yesterday.* (ungrammatical)

度 is a counter meaning times as well as degrees (temperature). 一度 literally means one time. 一度も is used in negative sentences.

アクティビティー 4

...ありますか。(*Have you ever been to Tokyo?*)
...g the ta-form of the verb　ことがある, and answer the ...to your own experience.

...んだことがありますか。
...ります。(or いいえ、ありません。)

1. 料理をする
2. 日本へ行く
3. ゴルフをする
4. 日本の音楽を聞く
5. すきやきを食べる
6. お金 (*money*) をおとす (*lose*)
7. お金をひろう (*find*)

アクティビティー 5

行ったことがありません。(*I've never been there.*)

Make dialogues as shown in the example, using the ta-form of the verb　ことがある. Choose a negative or positive answer depending on the second phrase provided.

[例]（てんぷらを食べる）（一度も）
—てんぷらを食べたことがありますか。
—いいえ、一度も食べたことがありません。

1. （あのレストランへ行く）（三度）
2. （コーラを飲む）（何度も）
3. （ロシア語を勉強する）（一度）
4. （スピルバーグの映画を見る）（五年前）
5. （日本の食べ物を買う）（二回ぐらい）
6. （コンピュータを使う）（一度）
7. （町田さんに会う）（三年前に一度）
8. （あのプールで泳ぐ）（一度も）
9. （この町に雪が降る）（一度も）
10. （ウェートレスをする）（五年前）

Review **Grammar 9**, Chapter 2 for the use of ―回.

2. Grammar and Practice Activities includes concise explanations of grammar with examples and short exercises. This section is closely linked to other parts of the text, including the Vocabulary and Oral Activities section.

The sequencing of Vocabulary and Oral Activities directly before related Grammar and Practice Activities makes it possible to use *Yookoso!* in linear fashion.

The Language Skills part of each chapter includes instruction and practice with reading, writing, speaking, and listening.

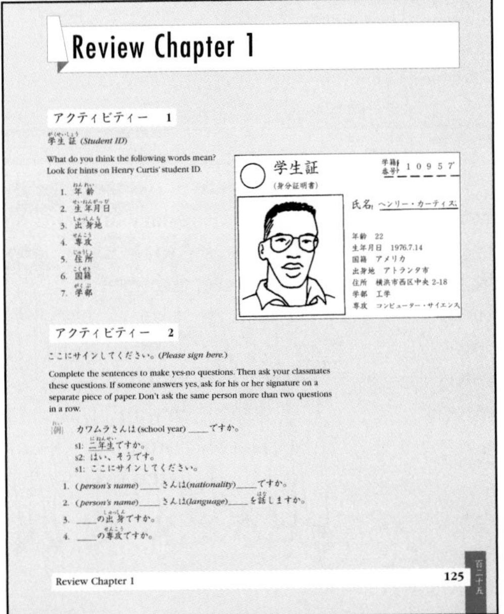

Review Chapter 1

アクティビティー 1

学生証 (*Student ID*)

What do you think the following words mean? Look for hints on Henry Curtis' student ID.

1. 年齢
2. 生年月日
3. 出身地
4. 専攻
5. 住所
6. 国籍
7. 学部

学生証（身分証明書）　学籍番号 10957
氏名 ヘンリー・カーティス
年齢 22
生年月日 1976.7.14
国籍 アメリカ
出身地 アトランタ市
住所 横浜市西区中央 2-18
学部 工学
専攻 コンピューター・サイエンス

アクティビティー 2

ここにサインしてください。(*Please sign here.*)

Complete the sentences to make yes-no questions. Then ask your classmates these questions. If someone answers yes, ask for his or her signature on a separate piece of paper. Don't ask the same person more than two questions in a row.

[例] カワムラさんは (school year) ____ですか。
s1: 二年生ですか。
s2: はい、そうです。
s1: ここにサインしてください。

1. (*person's name*) ____さんは(*nationality*)____ですか。
2. (*person's name*) ____さんは(*language*)____を話しますか。
3. ____の出身ですか。
4. ____の専攻ですか。

Review Chapter 1　125 百二十五

A two-page Review follows each chapter. Each review includes oral and written activities that combine, recycle, and review vocabulary, grammar, and language functions presented in the preceding chapter.

CULTURE

Culture notes provide information on Japanese culture that is important or pertinent for understanding vocabulary and facilitating oral or written activities.

文化ノート

CULTURE NOTE • Japanese Names

When Japanese give their full names, they say their family name first and given name last (Japanese do not have middle names). Japanese typically introduce themselves with their family name alone and address others (except close friends and family members) by family name followed by a respectful title. For now, the only titles you need to know are **-san** (*Mr./Ms.*) for your friends or classmates and **-sensee** (*Professor*) for your instructor. *Never attach these titles to your own name.*

Some of the marginal notes offer sociolinguistic information, and many language notes provide linguistic information that can help students use the language more effectively and communicate smoothly in a variety of real-life situations.

Note that it is rude to ask your superior's intention using …つもりですか。You should use …おつもりですか, as in 何をするおつもりですか。

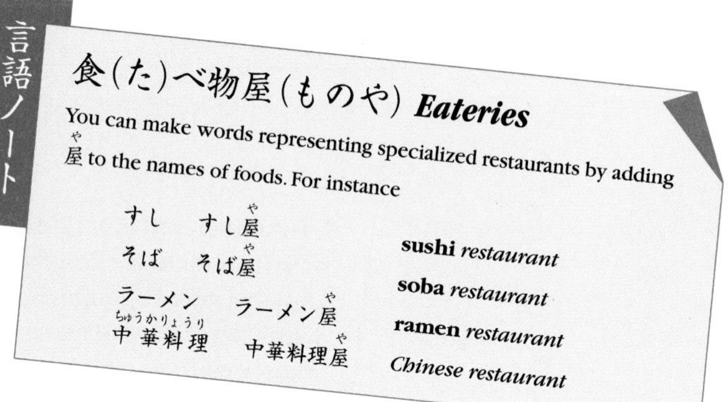

言語ノート

食(た)べ物屋(ものや) *Eateries*

You can make words representing specialized restaurants by adding 屋(や) to the names of foods. For instance

すし	すし屋(や)	**sushi** *restaurant*
そば	そば屋(や)	**soba** *restaurant*
ラーメン	ラーメン屋(や)	**ramen** *restaurant*
中華料理(ちゅうかりょうり)	中華料理屋(や)	*Chinese restaurant*

96

お弁当　スパゲッティチーズチキン弁当 (園)

酒蒸しにした鶏肉小¼枚は厚みに切り込みを入れてチーズをはさみ、両面を油焼きにする。ゆでたスパゲッティは炒めて塩、胡椒、ケチャップで調味する。スパゲッティの上にチキンをのせ、グリーンアスパラと生椎茸のソテー、キーウィを添える。

Realia, photos, and line drawings may serve as a starting point for oral and written activities, and all are intended to expose students to real culture.

A cast of characters appears throughout the text. The main characters are foreign students who are studying Japanese language and culture at the University of Tokyo. These people reappear in dialogues, grammar examples, reading materials, and listening comprehension activities. The characters are meant to illustrate the social relationships in Japanese culture that determine speech style and the use of honorifics. They also help students better understand the contexts in which the conversations take place.

LANGUAGE SKILLS

The series of activities in Vocabulary and Grammar begins with contextualized mechanical drills and proceeds through meaningful, communicative exercises to creative, free-answer sequences. This enables students to begin with the basics and move gradually on to more thoughtful communication as they gain skill and confidence with the vocabulary and grammar being learned.

Many language notes present brief information on grammar that is helpful for conducting oral activities or understanding reading materials. Study hints provide advice about how to acquire language skills: how to learn vocabulary, **kanji,** verb conjugations, and so forth.

The Reading and Writing section contains two sets of reading materials and writing tasks.

- Reading selections are based on authentic materials such as magazine articles, personal messages, and advertisements. They are preceded by activities that facilitate students' comprehension and help develop good reading strategies. Post-reading activities are mostly comprehension-oriented; in some cases, students apply their reading skills to related materials.
- Writing exercises are extensions of the preceding reading activities. Students write a response to the content of the reading selection, write a similar passage on their own, or write about their own lives and ideas by using the chapter vocabulary and grammatical structures.

In the Language Functions and Situations section, students learn how to express themselves in specific real-life situations. They study dialogues that illustrate functional language and situations related to chapter themes, then practice interacting in role plays that engage them in real communication in meaningful contexts.

In the Listening Comprehension section, students practice comprehending the general content of conversations or narratives related to chapter themes. They receive training in listening for meaning and perform tasks based on what they have heard. The section is the basis for a variety of interactive oral activities in class. The audio for these sections is provided on the Listening Comprehension Audio Program, packaged free with every new copy of the textbook. A transcript of the selections appears in the Instructor's Manual.

Program Components

Available to adopters *and* to students:

- *Main text.*
- *Workbook/Laboratory Manual to accompany* ***Yookoso! An Invitation to Contemporary Japanese.*** The *Workbook/Laboratory Manual* is intended to (1) help students review the grammar, vocabulary, and language functions presented in the main text and (2) practice writing **hiragana, katakana,** and **kanji.** There are three sections for each of the seven main chapters.

  1. *Listening Comprehension Activities* (coordinated with the *Audio Program*). The activities in this section develop listening comprehension through dialogues, interviews, and narratives. Pronunciation exercises are also included.
  2. *Kanji practice and Exercises.* This section consists of a list of newly introduced **kanji,** including the pronunciations, meanings, examples of use, and stroke order, followed by exercises. This section also includes some interesting and useful notes about **kanji** and the writing systems of Japanese (for example, the radicals, the principles of stroke order).
  3. *Writing Activities.* This section provides additional vocabulary and grammar practice through a variety of activities, from controlled, mechanical exercises to creative, free-response activities. Several activities in this section are realia-based, and many of them can also be used for speaking practice.

- *Listening Comprehension Audio Program to accompany* ***Yookoso! An Invitation to Contemporary Japanese.*** The *Listening Comprehension Audio Program* for the textbook available in audio CD format and packaged free with each new copy of the textbook, contains recordings of the dialogues from the main text as well as vocabulary lists and passages for extensive and intensive listening practice.
- *Audio Program to accompany the Workbook/Laboratory Manual.* Corresponding to the laboratory portion of the *Workbook/Laboratory Manual,* this *Audio Program* contains the listening passages for every laboratory exercise. Available free to adapting institutions, this Audio Program is also available for student purchase.
- *CD-ROM.* A new CD-ROM, developed for ***Yookoso!*** provides students with a wealth of additional vocabulary and grammar practice, video clips, and other resources.
- *Online Learning Center.* This new Web site, developed exclusively for ***Yookoso!,*** allows students to complete online activities that practice the vocabulary and structures of each chapter. Visit the site at **www.mhhe.com/yookosome.**

Available to adopters only:

- *Instructor's Manual/Testing Program/Tapescript*. Revised for ***Yookoso! An Invitation to Contemporary Japanese***, Second Edition, this practical guide includes a general introduction to the communicative approach to language teaching and learning, general guidelines for using the textbook, a sample lesson plan and syllabus, sample semester and quarter schedules, suggestions for using and expanding the text materials, additional exercises, models for vocabulary introduction and expansion, other teaching hints and techniques, sample tests and quizzes, listening comprehension materials, and scripts for the Listening Comprehension section of each chapter. A transcript of the listening comprehension activities from the *Audio Program* for the *Workbook/Laboratory Manual* is also included.
- *Video to accompany* ***Yookoso!*** This 30-minute video includes some of the situations and dialogues presented in the textbook and others related to chapter topics. The majority of segments were filmed in Japan and include a variety of interactions in natural settings.

Acknowledgments

Many people have contributed to the process of developing the second edition of ***Yookoso!*** First of all, I would like to thank the following language-teaching professionals and friends whose valuable suggestions and feedback contributed to the preparation of this revised edition. The appearance of their names does not necessarily constitute an endorsement of this textbook or its pedagogical approach.

Tom Abbott
(*California State University, Monterey Bay*)
Mako Beecken
(*Colorado State University*)
Mark Blum
(*Florida Atlantic University*)
Minako Brunelle
(*Seattle Central Community College*)
Amy Christiansen
(*Wittenberg University*)
Lydia Coyle
(*Northern Kentucky University*)
Yoko Collier-Sanuki
(*University of British Columbia*)
Tamaye Csyionie
(*Scottsdale Community College*)
Janet Fair
(*Southern Illinois University at Carbondale*)
Carl Falsgraf
(*University of Oregon*)
Fumiko Foard
(*Arizona State University*)
Jeff Fox
(*College of Southern Idaho*)
M. Fuke
(*University of Tulsa*)
Yumiko Guajardo
(*U.S. Air Force Academy*)
Suzuko Hamasaki
(*University of California, Irvine*)
Jean Hanna
(*Windward Community College*)
Lawrence Herzberg
(*Calvin College*)
Kyoko Hijirida
(*University of Hawaii at Manoa*)
Junko Hondo
(*Philadelphia College of Textile and Science*)

Fumiko Ishii
(*Irvine Valley College*)
Yasuko Ito-Watt
(*Indiana University*)
Akiko Jones
(*Bowling Green State University*)
Akiko Kakutani
(*Earlham College*)
Akiko Kamo
(*Episcopal School, Baton Rouge, Louisiana*)
Yoko Kano
(*University of North Carolina at Wilmington*)
Hiroko Kataoka
(*California State University, Long Beach/Japan Foundation and Language Center*)
Akiko Kowano Jones
(*Bowling Green State University*)
Mieko Kimura Philips
(*Lansing Community College*)
Toshiko Kishimoto
(*Clemson University*)
Ryuko Kubota
(*University of North Carolina*)
Junko Kumamoto-Healey
(*University of Melbourne*)
Toshiyumi Kumashiro
(*University of California, Irvine*)
Yoko Maruyama Wong
(*Case Western Reserve University*)
Yukari McCagg
(*American School in Japan*)
Akemi Morioka
(*University of California, Irvine*)
Mutsuko Motoyama
(*Illinois Wesleyan University*)
Hiromi Muranaka
(*University of Western Sydney, Nepean*)
Emi Ochiai Ahn
(*Mesa Community College*)
Toyoko Okawa
(*Punaho School, Honolulu*)
Yoshiko Ozeki
(*James Madison University*)
Tamae Prindle
(*Colby College*)
Yoko Pusavat
(*California State University, Long Beach*)
Joe Ree
(*Florida State University*)
Christopher M. Rich
(*Northern Arizona University*)
Kyoko Saegusa
(*University of Colorado, Boulder*)
Yoshiko Saito
(*California State University, Monterey Bay*)
Kazuki Sawanoi
(*Southern University A&M College*)
Nobuko Sugamoto
(*Monterey Institute of International Studies*)
Naoki Takei
(*Tokyo Institute of Technology*)
Akira R. Takemoto
(*Whitman College*)
Yuzuru Takigawa
(*Western Washington University*)
Roger Thomas
(*Illinois State University*)
Chizuko Uema
(*Lewis and Clark College*)
Noriko Vergel
(*American School in Japan*)
Yuko Yamada
(*Nebraska Weslyan University at Lincoln*)
Hilofumi Yamamoto
(*University of Tsukuba*)
Toshiko Yokota
(*University of California, Irvine*)

Student feedback played a crucial role for the revision, too. My thanks go to all the students who sent me their comments while using the first edition.

I also would like to express my appreciation to many people at McGraw-Hill and their associates for their excellent work on this complicated project, their patience, and perseverance: Peggy Potter, Patricia Murray, Karen Sandness, Karen Judd, Francis Owens, Margaret Metz, Natalie Durbin, Pam Augspurger, Sally Vitsky, Rick Hackney, Chris de Heer, Cristene Burr, Bill Glass, and Leslie Oberhuber. In particular, I owe much to Gregory Trauth for his tireless work and insightful ideas for this project. Special thanks are due to Chieko Altherr, who checked the linguistic accuracy and cultural authenticity of the text.

This project could not have been completed without the generous support, assistance, and encouragement of the people at the University of California, San Diego: all of my colleagues at the Graduate School of International Relations and Pacific Studies, especially, Peter Gourevitch and Miles Kahler, Sherman George, Ron Quilan, Gary Hoffman, Hifumi Ito, Dennis Kelliher, Masao Miyoshi, Christena Turner, Jennifer Schroeder, Linda Murphy, Masato Nishimura, Noriko Kameda, Yutaka Kunitake, Noriko Knickerbockers, and Mayumi Mochizuki. I especially thank my former and current assistants, Sheri Brusch and Alejandrina Quintero-McCluskey, without whose daily help and encouragement I could not have finished this project.

I would also like to acknowledge and thank the following individuals from the University of Oregon for their work on the new Yookoso! interactive CD-ROMs: Yoshiko Shioya, Yoko O'Brien, and Miiko Suzuki.

A word of warmest thanks is due to Hiroko Kataoka for her steadfast friendship, patient criticism, helpful advice, insightful suggestions, and constant encouragement, all of which were indispensable to me at various stages of the development of this text.

I would like to extend my deepest gratitude and appreciation to Thalia Dorwick, for her constant support for ***Yookoso!,*** her enthusiasm for and commitment to developing an innovative Japanese language text, her encouragement, generosity, patience, thoughtfulness, and care. Her insights, creativity, dedication, wisdom, expertise have been a constant source of inspiration to me and have been my guiding light throughout this project.

I thank Umechiyo and Takechiyo for their unconditional affection and positive spirit.

A final simple but very sincere appreciation goes to my wife, Carol, for her inspiring love, spirit, understanding, patience, and support beyond the call of duty. I thank you for giving so much of you as well as putting up with me during the revision of *Yookoso!* This text is dedicated to Carol as well as to my parents, Morio and Ritsuko Tohsaku.

Yasu-Hiko Tohsaku
ytohsaku@ucsd.edu

Dear Student,

Yookoso means *welcome* in Japanese, and I am delighted to welcome you to this program for learning contemporary Japanese. You'll be able to listen with understanding, speak, read, and write Japanese by the time you finish the program if you take to heart the hints below.

- Your classroom is probably the only place you have to interact with other people in Japanese. Your instructor is your major resource and your classmates are your other contacts. Attend class regularly and make an effort to interact as much as possible with all of them.
- Keep up with daily assignments. They are essential if you are to be able to participate and learn in class.
- Use all of the supplementary materials that accompany the text. Use the Workbook/Laboratory Manual to review vocabulary and grammar in listening, speaking, reading, and writing, and to practice kanji. Use the Audiotape, Videotape, and CD for listening and speaking practice and to develop a stronger cultural knowledge. Regularly check the *Yookoso!* home page (http://www.mhhe.com/yookosome) for study hints, additional activities, and cultural information.
- Don't force yourself to memorize all the vocabulary words at the start. Learn and use vocabulary necessary to express yourself first. Then, since the acquisition of vocabulary is of great importance for achieving proficiency at the early stage of language learning, learn as much as you can of the other vocabulary as well, to broaden your ability to express ideas.
- Before starting each chapter, review the learning objectives found on the opening page. At the end of each chapter, use the checklist on the last page to check your progress.
- Familiarize yourself with the organization of the text.

  The Characters: You will meet a cast of characters who will appear throughout the text. Some of them are students at the university and others are their neighbors and families.

  Vocabulary and Grammar: Every chapter has three sections that start by introducing and practicing new vocabulary and then present grammar explanations and activities that use the grammar in meaningful context with previously-presented vocabulary.

  Language Skills: Once you have learned the grammar and vocabulary of the chapter, you can practice them as you strengthen your abilities with the four language skills. In Reading and Writing, you will learn to read for content, guess contextually, and understand the gist of what you read. Then you'll build on what you have read as you write. Language Functions and Situations help you develop your ability to cope with many daily contexts and situations through speaking. The activities in Listening Comprehension help you develop listening abilities for everyday contexts.

  Vocabulary and Kanji: At the end of each chapter is a list of vocabulary and kanji (Chinese characters). Use this list as a reference for review, reading, and writing activities.

  Review Activities: These activities offer a final review of the chapter's vocabulary and grammar.
- Keep studying little by little every day, don't wait until just before a test. Language learning takes time and is a gradual process. If you work at it day by day, you will become a proficient user of Japanese.

Now, let's get started.

Yasu-Hiko Tohsaku

About the Author

Yasu-Hiko Tohsaku is a Professor at the University of California, San Diego, where he is Director of the Language Program at the Graduate School of International Relations and Pacific Studies and Coordinator of the Undergraduate Japanese Language Program. He received his Ph.D. in Linguistics from the University of California, San Diego, in 1983. He is the author of numerous articles on second-language acquisition and Japanese-language pedagogy. In addition, he has been involved with the development of Japanese-language teaching videos, computer-assisted language-learning programs, and a Web-based training program for language teachers.

Getting Started

Getting Started

In **Getting Started** you are going to

- Learn how to greet others and introduce yourself
- Talk about your classroom
- Learn numbers up to 10,000
- Learn to ask and tell telephone numbers and time
- Learn to ask what something is
- Talk about daily activities
- Talk about future activities and events
- Talk about activities and events in the past
- Learn to express what you like and dislike
- Learn to invite someone to do something
- Learn to talk about weekly schedules
- Learn to talk about the weather
- Learn to ask about location, existence, and price

YOOKOSO! MULTIMEDIA

Review and practice grammar and vocabulary from this chapter and watch video clips on the *Yookoso!* Interactive CD-ROM. Visit the *Yookoso!* Online Learning Center at **www.mhhe.com/yookosome** for additional exercises and resources.

Part One

Objectives

Meeting others and introducing yourself
Everyday greetings
Classroom expressions
The Japanese writing system (1): Introduction

Meeting Others and Introducing Yourself

Dialogue 1: A Simple Introduction 

Two classmates, John Kawamura and Linda Brown, are introducing themselves.

KAWAMURA: Hajimemashite. Kawamura desu.
BURAUN: Hajimemashite. Buraun desu.
KAWAMURA: Doozo yoroshiku.
BURAUN: Doozo yoroshiku.

言語ノート

Language Note: Romanization

Romanization is the transcription of Japanese using **rooma-ji** (lit., *Roman letters*), or the English alphabet. In Japan the only words you see written in **rooma-ji** are station names (for the sake of foreigners), trademarks, ad catchphrases, and the like. In this textbook, romanization is used only as an aid for the beginning student. By the end you should have a good working knowledge of **hiragana** and **katakana.**

The Language Note presents helpful information about the Japanese language as well as useful expressions.

When Japanese greet each other, they bow. Nowadays, many Japanese shake hands while greeting, but they may also bow while shaking hands. How deeply and how often Japanese bow depends on such things as the social status of the people involved, their age, and other factors.

Hajimemashite (literally, *it's the first time we meet*) and **doozo yoroshiku** (lit., *please regard me favorably*) are set phrases. **Desu** corresponds to the verb *to be* (*am, are, is,* etc., depending on context).

Dialogue 1 KAWAMURA: How do you do? I am Kawamura. BROWN: How do you do? I am Brown. KAWAMURA: It's nice to meet you. BROWN: It's nice to meet you.

Study Hint

Working in Pairs or in Groups

Because most of you do not have many opportunities to speak regularly with native or near-native speakers of Japanese, your Japanese class is the most important place to practice speaking Japanese. This textbook includes many activities in which you practice using Japanese with your classmates in pairs or in groups. When working in pairs or groups, first find out the objective of a given activity (getting specific information, giving information, creating a dialogue, solving a problem, etc.) and then work together to accomplish that objective by using Japanese. Try to express yourself as much as possible using what you already know. If you have any questions, ask your partner(s) or your instructor. If a partner has difficulties, help out. Pair or group activities in the classroom probably present the most important opportunities for you to practice speaking Japanese. Try to avoid chatting in English.

The Study Hint offers useful strategies for learning Japanese. Review and use these hints often to maximize your study of Japanese.

Activity 1

Using Dialogue 1 as a model, introduce yourself and meet as many classmates as you can. Circulate throughout the classroom and write down their names.

Dialogue 2: Meeting Someone and Then Introducing Yourself

Linda Brown is introducing herself to Mei Lin Chin, another classmate.

BURAUN: Sumimasen. Chin-san desu ka.
CHIN: Hai, soo desu.
BURAUN: Buraun desu. Hajimemashite. Doozo yoroshiku.
CHIN: Chin desu. Hajimemashite. Doozo yoroshiku.

Sumimasen is an expression of apology, corresponding to the English *I'm sorry* or *excuse me.* It is also frequently used to attract someone's attention or to express appreciation (in the latter case *thank you* is a closer English equivalent). To form a simple yes/no question in Japanese, add **ka** to the end of a statement (with a raising intonation). **Ka** takes the place of a question mark.

Dialogue 2 BROWN: Excuse me. Are you Ms. Chin? CHIN: Yes, I am. (lit., *Yes, that's right.*) BROWN: I am Brown. How do you do? It's nice to meet you. CHIN: I am Chin. How do you do? It's nice to meet you.

文化ノート

CULTURE NOTE • Japanese Names

When Japanese give their full names, they say their family name first and given name last (Japanese do not have middle names). Japanese typically introduce themselves with their family name alone and address others (except close friends and family members) by family name followed by a respectful title. For now, the only titles you need to know are **-san** (*Mr./Ms.*) for your friends or classmates and **-sensee** (*Professor*) for your instructor. *Never attach these titles to your own name.*

Dialogue 3: Inquiring About Someone's Name 

John Kawamura is looking for Masao Hayashi.

KAWAMURA: Sumimasen. Hayashi-san desu ka.
TANAKA: Iie.
KAWAMURA: Shitsuree shimashita.
TANAKA: Iie.

The Culture Note presents interesting information about Japanese culture, society, and modes of interaction.

Activity 2

Practice Dialogues 2 and 3 with several classmates using your own names. (Do you remember your classmates' names from doing Activity 1?)

Dialogue 4: Asking for Someone's Name 

Linda Brown and Mei Lin Chin are getting acquainted.

BURAUN: Hajimemashite. Buraun desu. Onamae wa?
CHIN: Chin desu. Hajimemashite.

言語ノート

Language Note: Informal Questions

Notice that the question **onamae wa?** does not end in **ka.** In formal Japanese, questions end in **ka,** but in an informal, colloquial style of speech questions are often abbreviated. **Onamae wa?** is short for **Onamae wa nan desu ka** (lit., *As for your name, what is it?*). Here is a very literal translation of Dialogue 4.

Note that the subject may be left unexpressed in Japanese when it can be figured out from the context.

Dialogue 3 KAWAMURA: Excuse me. Are you Mr. Hayashi? TANAKA: No. KAWAMURA: I'm sorry. (lit., *I committed a rudeness.*) TANAKA: Not at all.

Dialogue 4 BROWN: How do you do? I am Brown. May I have your name? CHIN: I am Chin. How do you do?

BURAUN: Onamae wa? *Your name?*
CHIN: Chin desu. *Is Chin.*

Notice how Brown began the sentence and Chin finished it. This is common in Japanese conversation. Being an active listener when speaking Japanese is important.

Dialogue 5: Using a Name Card 

Linda Brown is meeting her neighbor, Yooichi Takada.

BURAUN: Hajimemashite, Tookyoo Daigaku no Buraun desu.
TAKADA: Hajimemashite, Sonii no Takada desu.
BURAUN: Kore, watashi no meeshi desu.
TAKADA: Doomo arigatoo gozaimasu. Kore, watashi no meeshi desu.
BURAUN: Doomo arigatoo gozaimasu.

When you introduce yourself in Japan, it is common to state your affiliation. Japanese tend to identify strongly with the group they belong to (their "in-group") and are more interested in knowing someone's affiliation and rank. You can tell a lot about someone from his/her affiliation and rank. Stating affiliation also helps get a conversation going by giving your conversational partner something more to ask you about. To clarify your affiliation, say

> (*Company/school*) no (*last name*) desu.
> *I am* (*name*) *of* (*institution*).

> Tookyoo Daigaku no Kawamura desu.
> *I am Kawamura of the University of Tokyo.*

You may also hand your name card in silence while lightly bowing.

Japanese tend to stand farther apart during a conversation than North Americans do. Some Japanese also consider it rude to look directly into another person's eyes, especially if that person has a higher social status.

文化ノート

CULTURE NOTE • Name Cards

Name cards (**meeshi**) play an important role in Japan because they contain the following pieces of information essential to developing a relationship:

- company or school affiliation
- rank in the company or school
- the correct written form and pronunciation of the person's name
- address, telephone, and fax numbers, and often e-mail address

A few people also put their photographs on the card, and those who deal with international visitors usually have their information in English on the reverse side. Some Japanese personal names are written in such unusual ways that even native speakers have trouble figuring out their correct written form and pronunciation, so this notation is an important part of the **meeshi.** The information about the person's rank is significant because it helps you figure out what level

Dialogue 5 BROWN: How do you do? I am Brown of the University of Tokyo. TAKADA: How do you do? I am Takada of SONY. BROWN: This is my name card. TAKADA: Thank you very much. This is my name card. BROWN: Thank you very much.

of politeness you should use in speaking to him or her.

Since the **meeshi** represents the person, you should treat it with respect, receiving it with both hands while bowing slightly and studying it for a few moments before putting it away, preferably in a card holder, or **meeshi-ire.** (Never put it in your back pocket.) If you receive a **meeshi** during a business meeting, you may want to keep it on the table in front of you for handy reference.

山村商事
営業部

部長　山口健次

〒120東京都千代田区三番町
二ー六ー七山村ビル
Tel (03) 3334-4561

東京大学工学部三年

ジョン・カワムラ

〒118 東京都文京区本郷三丁目 2－11
TEL (03) 3212-2118

KENJI YAMAGUCHI
General Manager
Sales and Marketing Department

YAMAMURA TRADING CO., LTD.
Yamamura Building
2-6-7, Sanbanchō, Chiyoda-ku
Tokyo 120 Japan
Telephone (03) 3334-4561

JOHN KAWAMURA
Junior
Faculty of Engineering
University of Tokyo

2-11, Hongō 3-chōme, Bunkyō-ku
Tokyo 118 Japan
TEL. (03) 3212-2118

Activity 3

Now make your own English name card including all the information discussed in Culture Note: Name Cards. Then practice Dialogue 5 with your classmates, using your name card. Be sure to offer and receive the name cards properly.

言語ノート

Language Note: Expressing Gratitude

Japanese express gratitude and apologize frequently as ways of maintaining harmonious relationships. Among the many ways to express gratitude in Japanese are these common expressions, listed from formal to informal.

Doomo arigatoo gozaimasu.
Arigatoo gozaimasu.

Doomo arigatoo.
Arigatoo.
Doomo.

Among these, **doomo** (lit., *very*) is commonly used in everyday conversation when speaking to social equals or subordinates. Among students, **sankyuu** (from English *thank you*) is also often used. Note that such an expression of apology as **(doomo) sumimasen (deshita)** is also used as a polite expresson of gratitude. When someone expresses gratitude and you would like to say *you're welcome,* say **doo itashimashite** or **iie, doo itashimashite.**

Everyday Greetings

Dialogue 6: Morning Greetings 

Linda Brown runs into Professor Yokoi in the morning.

BURAUN: Yokoi-sensee, ohayoo gozaimasu.
YOKOI: Aa, Buraun-san, ohayoo.
BURAUN: Ii otenki desu ne.
YOKOI: Ee, soo desu ne.

Notice that Brown says **ohayoo gozaimasu** to her professor, who simply says **ohayoo** to her student. This is because students are expected to speak politely to their professors, while professors have the option of speaking informally to their students.

Activity 4

Using Dialogue 6 as a model, with a partner play the roles of student and professor greeting one another in the morning. Then exchange roles.

Vocabulary: Common Greetings and Leave-Taking 

Greetings

Ohayoo gozaimasu.	Good morning. (*formal*)
Ohayoo.	Good morning. (*informal*)
Konnichi wa.	Good afternoon.
Konban wa.	Good evening.
Ogenki desu ka.	How are you?
Ee, genki desu.	(Yes,) I am fine.
Okagesama de, genki desu.	Thanks to you, I'm fine.
Ee, okagesama de,...	(Yes,) thanks to you . . . (I'm fine). (*informal*)
Ohisashiburi desu ne.	I haven't seen you for a long time.
Shibaraku desu ne.	I haven't seen you for a long time. (*informal*)

Dialogue 6 BROWN: Professor Yokoi, good morning. YOKOI: Ah, Ms. Brown, good morning. BROWN: It's fine weather, isn't it? YOKOI: Yes, it is.

Leave-Taking

Shitsuree shimasu.	Goodbye. (lit., *Excuse me.*)
Ja (or **Dewa**), **mata.**	See you later (lit., *again*).
Ja (or **Dewa**).	See you. (*very informal*)
Sayo(o)nara.	Goodbye.
Oyasuminasai.	Good night. (*informal*)

Shitsuree shimasu is commonly used among business associates, and as a polite way of taking leave of one's superior.

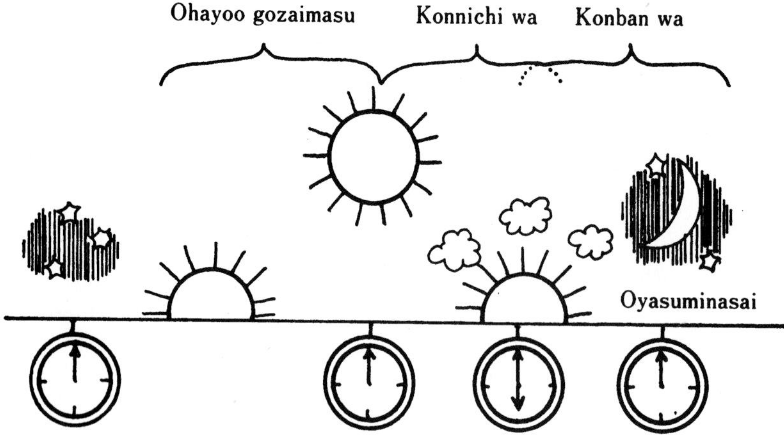

言語ノート

Language Note: Greetings

In America, *How are you?* is not an inquiry about your health as much as an idiomatic way of saying *hello.* In Japan, commenting on the weather serves much the same function. If someone greets you with **Ii otenki desu ne,** do not feel compelled to give your opinion on the matter. Just be agreeable: **Soo desu ne** (*Yes, it is, isn't it*).

So what about **Ogenki desu ka?** This *How are you?* really means *How have you been lately?*, so don't say it to anyone you have seen recently. If you haven't seen someone for some time, or if you are sincerely concerned about his or her health, **Ogenki desu ka** is appropriate. The proper response when asked **Ogenki desu ka** is **Okagesama de** (lit., *Thanks to you*). The implication is that the questioner's concern has contributed to your physical and spiritual health.

Also, be careful with **sayo(o)nara.** It has a sense of finality, so don't say it to someone you expect to see later in the day or in a couple of days in most situations. In this case, say **ja mata** or **dewa mata.** (School children say **sayo(o)nara** at the end of a day.)

Activity 5

Review the following greetings and phrases and then go to step 1.

1. Konnichi wa.
2. Ogenki desu ka.
3. Ja, mata.
4. Konban wa.
5. Arigatoo gozaimasu.
6. Hajimemashite.
7. Shibaraku desu ne.
8. Ohayoo gozaimasu.
9. Ii otenki desu ne.
10. Oyasuminasai.

Step 1 (in pairs)

Ask a classmate to respond appropriately to the ten greetings and phrases. Then, that classmate will quiz you on the same greetings and phrases. Note: there may be more than one response to a greeting or phrase. (Do not read the greetings or phrases as you say them.)

Step 2 (instructor and students)

Your instructor will say a greeting or phrase to a selected student. That student will in turn say the same greeting or phrase to another student, who will then give the appropriate response.

Example:

Instructor to Student 1: Hajimemashite.
Student 1 to Student 2: Hajimemashite.
Student 2: Hajimemashite, doozo yoroshiku.

Activity 6

Practice the following situations with your classmates.

1. It's 8:00 A.M. on a fine day and you see one of your friends, Mr. Sawai. Greet him.
2. It's 10:00 P.M. You see your friend Mr. Kawai, who is on his way home from work. Greet him.

Activity 7

Interaction: Turn to the classmate sitting next to you and do the following.

- Greet him or her appropriately.
- Ask how he or she is.
- Find out his or her name.
- Give a book to him or her.
  Useful expression: Doozo. (*Please* [*accept this*]. or *Here you are.*)

Classroom Expressions

Activity 8

You will have many opportunities in class to ask your instructor or a classmate how to say something in Japanese as in this example.

> Desk wa Nihongo de nan to iimasu ka.
> *How do you say desk in Japanese?*
>
> Tsukue to iimasu.
> *(You) say tsukue.*

Now practice asking your instructor to identify items in the classroom, following the example.

In informal speech, **Desk wa Nihongo de nantte iimasuka.—Tsukuette iimasu** is more common.

言語ノート

Language Note: Japanese Nouns

Japanese nouns do not have different singular and plural forms. One word means both *book* and *books*; another means *person* and *people*; another, *idea* and *ideas.* Context determines which is meant. Later you will learn how to indicate a specific number of items in cases where you need to make a plural/singular distinction. Remember that although their English equivalents are given in the singular, Japanese nouns in vocabulary lists throughout this book assume the plural too, unless otherwise stated. Note, too, that unlike nouns in such languages as Spanish and French, Japanese nouns have no gender (i.e., they are not masculine or feminine). In addition, Japanese nouns keep the same form whether they are the subject or the object of a sentence.

Vocabulary: Classroom Expressions 

Here are some useful expressions that you will hear and use frequently in class. Learn to understand your instructor's commands and to make the appropriate responses. Other useful expressions, which you will learn gradually as you hear them repeated, are presented in Vocabulary Library: More Classroom Expressions.

Student

Practice saying these aloud, as your instructor models them for you.

Shitsumon ga arimasu.	I have a question.
Moo ichido onegai shimasu.	Please say that again.
Wakarimasen.	I don't understand.
Wakarimashita.	I understood.
Chotto matte kudasai.	Please wait a moment.
Book wa Nihongo de nan to iimasu ka.	How do you say book in Japanese?
Hon to iimasu.	(You) say hon.

A verb accompanied by **kudasai** is used to ask someone politely to do something.

Instructor

Listen carefully as your instructor says these expressions.

Hon o tojite kudasai.	Please close your book.
Hon o akete kudasai.	Please open your book.
Hon o mite kudasai.	Please look at your book.
Hon wa minai de kudasai.	Don't look at your book.
Kiite (ite) kudasai.	Please listen.
Mite kudasai.	Please look at (me, it, this).
Itte kudasai.	Please say it.
Moo ichido itte kudasai.	Please repeat again.
Yonde kudasai.	Please read (it).

Nihongo de itte kudasai.	Please say it in Japanese.
Kurikaeshite kudasai.	Please repeat.
Kaite kudasai.	Please write.
Renshuu shite kudasai.	Please practice.
Pea o tsukutte kudasai.	Pair off with a classmate.
Nooto o dashite kudasai.	Please take out your notebook.
Nooto ni kaite kudasai.	Please write in your notebook.
Nani mo kakanai de kudasai.	Please don't write anything down.
Wakarimasu ka.	Do you understand?
Hai, wakarimasu.	Yes, I understand.
Iie, wakarimasen.	No, I don't understand.
Shitsumon ga arimasu ka.	Do you have any question(s)?
Hai, arimasu.	Yes, I do (have questions).
Iie, arimasen.	No, I don't (have any questions).

Vocabulary Library 

More Classroom Expressions

Hajimemashoo.	Let's begin.
Moo ichido.	Once again, please.
Minasan, issho ni.	Everyone (do it) together.
Ii desu ka.	Is that all right?
Ii desu ne.	That's fine.
Yoku dekimashita.	Well done.
Dewa mata kono tsugi.	See you next time.

The Vocabulary Library presents additional, optional vocabulary for use in activities.

 Activity 9

Follow your instructor's commands.

a. b.

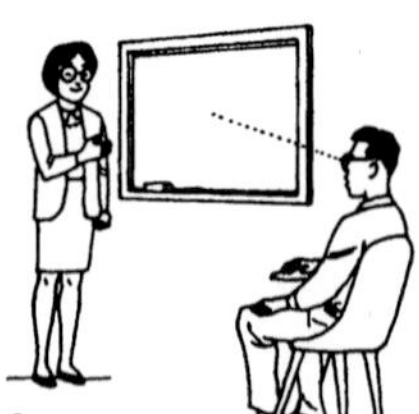
c.

d.

e. f.

g.

h.

Study Hint

Listening

The first step in learning Japanese is to acquire good listening skills. Though it may sound like a contradiction, you have to listen to a lot of Japanese in order to speak Japanese fluently. So when you listen to your instructor, pay close attention to what is said. Try to understand the meaning based on the context. Take note of your instructor's gestures and the pictures or photos that he/she uses, and draw on your own experiences with the Japanese language. Focusing on the meaning of what you hear will help build your grammar and vocabulary knowledge base. It is also important for you to react to what you hear and to demonstrate your understanding. In Activity 9, your instructor may ask you to follow his/her commands or to point to appropriate illustrations in order to check your understanding. Throughout this textbook many listening activities are presented in order to help you acquire good listening skills.

言語ノート

Language Note: Japanese Accentuation

Japanese has pitch accent, which is very different from stress accent in English. In English, accented syllables are pronounced louder than nonaccented syllables. In Japanese, accented syllables are pronounced at a higher pitch than other syllables. In English, only one sound (or syllable) can be primarily accented but in Japanese more than one syllable in a word can be accented and pronounced at the same pitch. Generally speaking, Japanese has only two pitches—high and low.

$\mathrm{i}^{\mathrm{chi}}$ (*one*)	$^{\mathrm{yo}}\mathrm{n}$ (*four*)
$\mathrm{Ni}^{\mathrm{hongo}}$ (*Japanese language*)	$\mathrm{wa}^{\mathrm{karima}}\mathrm{su}$ (*understand*)

Ichi has the accent pattern low-high, and **yon** has the accent pattern high-low. In **Nihongo,** the pitch rises after the first syllable. In **wakarimasu,** the pitch rises after the first syllable and falls after the fourth syllable. Sometimes pitch is the only way (other than context) to distinguish between two homonyms in spoken Japanese.

$\mathrm{ha}^{\mathrm{shi}}$ (*bridge*)	$^{\mathrm{ha}}\mathrm{shi}$ (*chopsticks*)
$\mathrm{ha}^{\mathrm{na}}$ (*flower*)	$\mathrm{ha}^{\mathrm{na}}$ (*nose*)

Both **hana** (*flower*) and **hana** (*nose*) have the same pitch pattern (low-high) when they are pronounced independently. However, there is a fall in pitch after **na** in **hana** (*flower*). This means that when a particle follows that word, the particle is pronounced with low pitch. In contrast, a particle following **hana** (*nose*) is pronounced with high pitch.

ha^{na} ga^{ooki}i (*the flower is big*)   ha$^{\text{na ga ooki}}$i (*the nose is big*)

The primary function of Japanese accentuation is to show the unity of words in a phrase more than to distinguish the meanings of words. For this reason, no accent is indicated in the vocabulary lists in this textbook. Just listen to your instructor and the tape very carefully and try your best to mimic them. Rather than paying too much attention to the accent pattern of each word, you should accurately articulate the overall intonation of the sentence in order to communicate effectively in Japanese.

The Japanese Writing System (1)

Introduction

Modern Japanese is written by combining three different writing systems: **hiragana, katakana,** and **kanji. Hiragana** and **katakana,** like the Roman alphabet, are composed of symbols that represent sounds. **Kanji,** or Chinese characters, are ideographs that represent sound and meaning. You will study **hiragana** and **katakana** in the next parts. The textbook introduces only the basics of these writing systems; you will need to complete the extensive exercises in the workbook to master them.

Hiragana and **katakana** are called *syllabaries,* which means each letter represents one syllable (a vowel, a consonant, or a consonant + vowel). Native speakers of Japanese spell words in terms of syllables and describe a word's length in terms of the number of syllables it contains. For example, **sushi** is a two-syllable word (**su-shi**), **Honda** is a three-syllable word (**Ho-n-da**), and **Tookyoo** (*Tokyo*) is a four-syllable word (**To-o-kyo-o**). Each syllable is held for one beat, so **Tookyoo** (four syllables) takes twice as long to say as **sushi** (two syllables).

With the forty-six basic symbols of the **hiragana** or **katakana** syllabary and two diacritical marks, you can transcribe all standard Japanese sounds. In theory you could write Japanese using just **hiragana** or **katakana,** but in practice the result would be too hard to read and understand.

Katakana is used primarily to transcribe foreign loanwords (e.g., **hottodoggu** for English *hot dog*) and onomatopoeic words (e.g., **zaa zaa,** meaning *raining hard*).

Vocabulary

This is a list of words that you have used or heard in Part 1 of this textbook. Before beginning Part 2, make sure that you know the words listed under the categories **Greetings and Polite Expressions, Questions, Classroom,** and **Other Useful Words.** These are considered active vocabulary, which means you will need not only to recognize them when you see or hear them, but also to use them yourself.

For your reading practice this list is rendered in **hiragana** and **katakana.** In authentic writing, **kanji** would be used in many words.

Greetings and Polite Expressions

Arigatoo.	ありがとう。	Thank you.
Arigatoo gozaimasu.	ありがとうございます。	Thank you. (*formal*)
Doomo.	どうも。	Thanks. (*very informal*)
Doomo arigatoo.	どうもありがとう。	Thank you very much.
Doomo arigatoo gozaimasu.	どうもありがとうございます。	Thank you very much. (*most formal*)
Doozo yoroshiku.	どうぞよろしく。	Nice meeting you.
Genki desu.	げんきです。	I am fine.
Hajimemashite.	はじめまして。	How do you do?
Ii otenki desu ne.	いいおてんきですね。	It's fine weather, isn't it?
Ja (dewa).	じゃ(では)。	See you.
Ja (dewa) mata.	じゃ(では)また。	See you. (*formal*)
Kekkoo desu.	けっこうです。	No thanks.
Konban wa.	こんばんは。	Good evening.
Konnichi wa.	こんにちは。	Good afternoon.
Ogenki desu ka.	おげんきですか。	How are you?
Ohayoo.	おはよう。	Good morning. (*informal*)
Ohayoo gozaimasu.	おはようございます。	Good morning. (*formal*)
Ohisashiburi desu ne.	おひさしぶりですね。	I haven't seen you for a long time.
Okagesama de genki desu.	おかげさまでげんきです。	Thanks to you, I am fine.
Onegai shimasu.	おねがいします。	Please (give me)…
Oyasuminasai.	おやすみなさい。	Good night.
Sayo(o)nara.	さよ(う)なら。	Goodbye. (*formal*)
Shitsuree shimasu.	しつれいします。	Goodbye.
Sumimasen.	すみません。	Excuse me, thank you.

Questions

Onamae wa.	おなまえは。	May I have your name?

Classroom

booru-pen	ボールペン	ballpoint pen
chooku	チョーク	chalk

denki	でんき	light, lamp
doa	ドア	door
enpitsu	えんぴつ	pencil
gakusee	がくせい	student
hon	ほん	book
isu	いす	chair
jisho	じしょ	dictionary
kaaten	カーテン	curtain
kaban	かばん	bag; briefcase
kabe	かべ	wall
kami	かみ	paper
keshigomu	けしゴム	eraser
kokuban	こくばん	chalkboard
kokuban-keshi	こくばんけし	eraser (for blackboard)
kyookasho	きょうかしょ	textbook
kyooshitsu	きょうしつ	classroom
mado	まど	window
mannenhitsu	まんねんひつ	fountain pen
nooto	ノート	notebook
sensee	せんせい	teacher, professor
shaapu penshiru	シャープ・ペンシル	mechanical pencil
teeburu	テーブル	table
tenjoo	てんじょう	ceiling
tsukue	つくえ	desk
yuka	ゆか	floor

Other Nouns

daigaku	だいがく	university
meeshi	めいし	name card, business card

Other Useful Words

desu	です	to be (copula)
doozo	どうぞ	please
Hai, soo desu.	はい、そうです。	Yes, that's right.
iie	いいえ	no
ka	か	(*question marker*)
kore	これ	this (*thing*)
no	の	(*possessive marker*)
watashi	わたし	I

Part Two

Objectives

Numbers up to 20
Asking and giving telephone numbers
Asking and telling time
Asking what something is
The Japanese writing system (2): **Hiragana** (1)

Numbers up to 20

Here's how to count to 20.

0	ree, zero
1	ichi
2	ni
3	san
4	yon, shi
5	go
6	roku
7	shichi, nana
8	hachi
9	ku, kyuu
10	juu
11	juu-ichi
12	juu-ni
13	juu-san
14	juu-yon, juu-shi
15	juu-go
16	juu-roku
17	juu-shichi, juu-nana
18	juu-hachi
19	juu-ku, juu-kyuu
20	ni-juu (*i.e., 2 tens*)

There are two different ways to say zero, four, seven, and nine. As you continue studying Japanese, you will learn which forms are used in different contexts.

Two common numbers are considered unlucky by Japanese: 4 and 9.

Activity 1

What number(s) between 0 and 20 do you associate with the following? Answer in Japanese.

1. baseball
2. unlucky
3. twin
4. rainbow
5. rectangle
6. a week
7. a watch
8. fingers
9. lucky
10. circle

Asking and Giving Telephone Numbers

Dialogue 1: Asking for Someone's Telephone Number

Linda Brown asks her classmate, Hitomi Machida, for her telephone number.

BURAUN: Machida-san no denwa bangoo wa?
MACHIDA: 675-8941 desu.
BURAUN: 675-8941 desu ne.
MACHIDA: Hai, soo desu.

Hai, soo desu indicates the speaker's agreement or assurance.

You can ask for a telephone number by saying

(Place or person) **no denwa bangoo wa?**
What is _____'s telephone number?

The particle **no** in **Machida-san no denwa bangoo** denotes possession and roughly corresponds to the English *of* or the possessive apostrophe *s*.

Activity 2

Practice Dialogue 1 with several classmates, substituting your real names and telephone numbers.

文化ノート

CULTURE NOTE • Telephone Numbers in Japan

Telephone numbers in Japan are usually four-digit numbers preceded by a prefix of one to four digits. The larger the town, the longer its prefix is. For example, the prefixes for Tokyo, the largest city, have four digits, but the prefix for a remote island may have only one digit. Area codes begin with zero and have at least two digits. When saying a telephone number out loud, substitute the particle **no** for the hyphens. For example, the number 03-3521-0987 is read **zero-san no san-go-ni-ichi no zero-kyuu-hachi-nana.**

Dialogue 1 BROWN: Ms. Machida, what is your telephone number? MACHIDA: It's 675-8941. BROWN: 675-8941, right? MACHIDA: Yes, that's right.

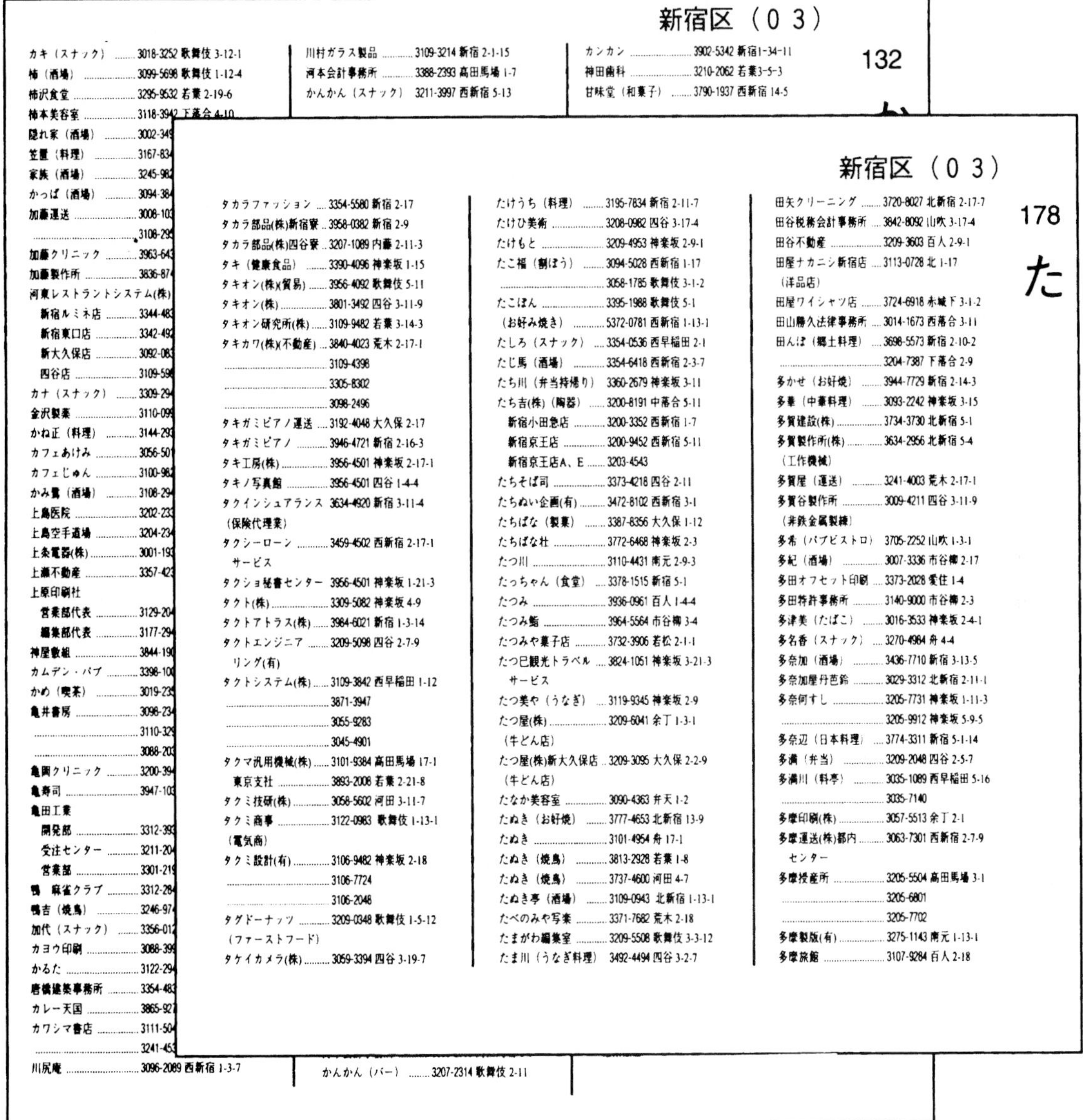

新宿区（０３）

132

カキ（スナック） .... 3018-3252 歌舞伎 3-12-1
柿（酒場） .... 3099-5698 歌舞伎 1-12-4
柿沢食堂 .... 3295-9532 若葉 2-19-6
柿本美容室 .... 3118-3942 下落合 4-10
隠れ家（酒場） 3002-349
笠置（料理） 3167-834
家族（酒場） 3245-982
かっぱ（酒場） 3094-384
加藤運送 3008-103
.... 3108-295
加藤クリニック 3963-643
加藤製作所 3836-874
河東レストラントシステム(株)
新宿ルミネ店 3344-483
新宿東口店 3342-492
新大久保店 3092-083
四谷店 3109-59
カナ（スナック） 3309-294
金沢製薬 3110-099
かね正（料理） 3144-293
カフェあけみ 3056-501
カフェじゅん 3100-982
かみ鶴（酒場） 3108-294
上島医院 3202-233
上島空手道場 3204-234
上条電器(株) 3001-193
上瀬不動産 3357-423
上原印刷社
営業部代表 3129-204
編集部代表 3177-294
神屋敷組 3844-190
カムデン・パブ 3398-100
かめ（喫茶） 3019-235
亀井書房 3098-234
.... 3110-329
.... 3088-203
亀岡クリニック 3200-394
亀寿司 3947-103
亀田工業
開発部 3312-393
受注センター 3211-204
営業部 3301-219
鴨 麻雀クラブ 3312-284
鴨吉（焼鳥） 3246-974
加代（スナック） 3356-012
カヨウ印刷 3088-399
かるた 3122-294
唐橋建築事務所 3354-483
カレー天国 3865-927
カワシマ書店 3111-504
.... 3241-453
川尻庵 .... 3096-2089 西新宿 1-3-7

川村ガラス製品 .... 3109-3214 新宿 2-1-15
河本会計事務所 .... 3388-2393 高田馬場 1-7
かんかん（スナック） 3211-3997 西新宿 5-13
かんかん（バー） .... 3207-2314 歌舞伎 2-11

カンカン 3902-5342 新宿1-34-11
神田歯科 3210-2062 若葉3-5-3
甘味堂（和菓子） .... 3790-1937 西新宿 14-5

新宿区（０３）

178

た

タカラファッション .... 3354-5580 新宿 2-17
タカラ部品(株)新宿寮 .... 3958-0382 新宿 2-9
タカラ部品(株)四谷寮 .... 3207-1089 内藤 2-11-3
タキ（健康食品） .... 3390-4096 神楽坂 1-15
タキオン(株)(貿易) .... 3956-4092 歌舞伎 5-11
タキオン(株) .... 3801-3492 四谷 3-11-9
タキオン研究所(株) .... 3109-9482 若葉 3-14-3
タキカワ(株)(不動産) .... 3840-4023 荒木 2-17-1
.... 3109-4398
.... 3305-8302
.... 3098-2496
タキガミピアノ運送 .... 3192-4048 大久保 2-17
タキガミピアノ .... 3946-4721 新宿 2-16-3
タキ工房(株) .... 3956-4501 神楽坂 2-17-1
タキノ写真館 .... 3956-4501 四谷 1-4-4
タクインシュアランス 3634-4920 新宿 3-11-4
(保険代理業)
タクシーローン .... 3459-4502 西新宿 2-17-1
サービス
タクショ秘書センター 3956-4501 神楽坂 1-21-3
タクト(株) .... 3309-5082 神楽坂 4-9
タクトアトラス(株) .... 3984-6021 新宿 1-3-14
タクトエンジニア .... 3209-5098 四谷 2-7-9
リング(有)
タクトシステム(株) .... 3109-3842 西早稲田 1-12
.... 3871-3947
.... 3055-9283
.... 3045-4901
タクマ汎用機械(株) .... 3101-9384 高田馬場 17-1
東京支社 .... 3893-2008 若葉 2-21-8
タクミ技研(株) .... 3058-5602 河田 3-11-7
タクミ商事 .... 3122-0983 歌舞伎 1-13-1
(電気商)
タクミ設計(有) .... 3106-9482 神楽坂 2-18
.... 3106-7724
.... 3106-2048
タグドーナッツ .... 3209-0348 歌舞伎 1-5-12
(ファーストフード)
タケイカメラ(株) .... 3059-3394 四谷 3-19-7

たけうち（料理） .... 3195-7834 新宿 2-11-7
たけひ美術 .... 3208-0982 四谷 3-17-4
たけもと .... 3209-4953 神楽坂 2-9-1
たこ福（割ぽう） .... 3094-5028 西新宿 1-17
.... 3058-1785 歌舞伎 3-1-2
たこぽん .... 3395-1988 歌舞伎 5-1
（お好み焼き） .... 5372-0781 西新宿 1-13-1
たしろ（スナック） .... 3354-0536 西早稲田 2-1
たじ馬（酒場） .... 3354-6418 西新宿 2-3-7
たち川（弁当持帰り） 3360-2679 神楽坂 3-11
たち吉(株)（陶器） .... 3200-8191 中落合 5-11
新宿小田急店 .... 3200-3352 西新宿 1-7
新宿京王店 .... 3200-9452 西新宿 5-11
新宿京王店A、E 3203-4543
たちそば司 .... 3373-4218 四谷 2-11
たちぬい企画(有) .... 3472-8102 西新宿 3-1
たちばな（製菓） .... 3387-8356 大久保 1-12
たちばな社 .... 3772-6468 神楽坂 2-3
たつ川 .... 3110-4431 南元 2-9-3
たっちゃん（食堂） .... 3378-1515 新宿 5-1
たつみ .... 3936-0961 百人 1-4-4
たつみ鮨 .... 3964-5564 市谷柳 3-4
たつみや菓子店 .... 3732-3906 若松 2-1-1
たつ巳観光トラベル .... 3824-1051 神楽坂 3-21-3
サービス
たつ美や（うなぎ） .... 3119-9345 神楽坂 2-9
たつ屋(株) .... 3209-6041 余丁 1-3-1
（牛どん店）
たつ屋(株)新大久保店 .... 3209-3095 大久保 2-2-9
（牛どん店）
たなか美容室 .... 3090-4363 弁天 1-2
たぬき（お好焼） .... 3777-4653 北新宿 13-9
たぬき .... 3101-4954 舟 17-1
たぬき（焼鳥） .... 3813-2928 若葉 1-8
たぬき（焼鳥） .... 3737-4600 河田 4-7
たぬき亭（酒場） .... 3109-0943 北新宿 1-13-1
たべのみや写楽 .... 3371-7682 荒木 2-18
たまがわ編集室 .... 3209-5508 歌舞伎 3-3-12
たま川（うなぎ料理） 3492-4494 四谷 3-2-7

田矢クリーニング .... 3720-8027 北新宿 2-17-7
田谷税務会計事務所 .... 3842-8092 山吹 3-17-4
田谷不動産 .... 3209-3603 百人 2-9-1
田屋ナカニシ新宿店 .... 3113-0728 北 1-17
（洋品店）
田屋ワイシャツ店 .... 3724-6918 赤城下 3-1-2
田山勝久法律事務所 .... 3014-1673 西落合 3-11
田んぼ（郷土料理） .... 3698-5573 新宿 2-10-2
.... 3204-7387 下落合 2-9
多かせ（お好焼） .... 3944-7729 新宿 2-14-3
多華（中華料理） .... 3093-2242 神楽坂 3-15
多賀建設(株) .... 3734-3730 北新宿 5-1
多賀製作所(株) .... 3634-2956 北新宿 5-4
（工作機械）
多賀屋（運送） .... 3241-4003 荒木 2-17-1
多賀谷製作所 .... 3009-4211 四谷 3-11-9
（非鉄金属製練）
多希（パブビストロ） 3705-2252 山吹 1-3-1
多紀（酒場） .... 3007-3336 市谷柳 2-17
多田オフセット印刷 .... 3373-2028 愛住 1-4
多田特許事務所 .... 3140-9000 市谷柳 2-3
多津美（たばこ） .... 3016-3533 神楽坂 2-4-1
多名香（スナック） .... 3270-4984 舟 4-4
多奈加（酒場） .... 3436-7710 新宿 3-13-5
多奈加屋丹芭鈴 .... 3029-3312 北新宿 2-11-1
多奈何すし .... 3205-7731 神楽坂 1-11-3
.... 3205-9912 神楽坂 5-9-5
多奈辺（日本料理） .... 3774-3311 新宿 5-1-14
多満（弁当） .... 3209-2048 四谷 2-5-7
多満川（料亭） .... 3035-1089 西早稲田 5-16
.... 3035-7140
多摩印刷(株) .... 3057-5513 余丁 2-1
多摩運送(株)都内 .... 3063-7301 西新宿 2-7-9
センター
多摩授産所 .... 3205-5504 高田馬場 3-1
.... 3205-6801
.... 3205-7702
多摩製版(有) .... 3275-1143 南元 1-13-1
多摩旅館 .... 3107-9284 百人 2-18

言語ノート

Language Note: Sentence-Final Particle *ne*

The sentence-final particle **ne,** as in **675-8941 desu ne,** is very common in Japanese. When said with a high or rising intonation, **ne(e)** is used to ask for someone's agreement (*don't you think?*), to confirm that your knowledge is correct (*that's right, isn't it?*), and to check that the listener is following you (*you see?*). When said with a falling intonation and extended to **nee,** the particle indicates your agreement with others or your hesitation.

> **Ne(e)** is just one of a variety of sentence-final particles that reveal the speaker's emotion and introduce subtle shades of meaning to an utterance. Spoken Japanese uses many different sentence-final particles in order to express one's different emotions and intentions. You will learn more such particles later.

Dialogue 2: Asking for Clarification 

Practice this variation of Dialogue 1 with another student, substituting the names and places in the art that follows the dialogue for those underlined in the dialogue.

Linda Brown asks John Kawamura for Professor Toshiko Yokoi's telephone number.

BURAUN: Yokoi-sensee no denwa bangoo wa?
KAWAMURA: 0134-76-9328 desu.
BURAUN: 0134-67-9328 desu ne.
KAWAMURA: Iie, 0134-76-9328 desu.

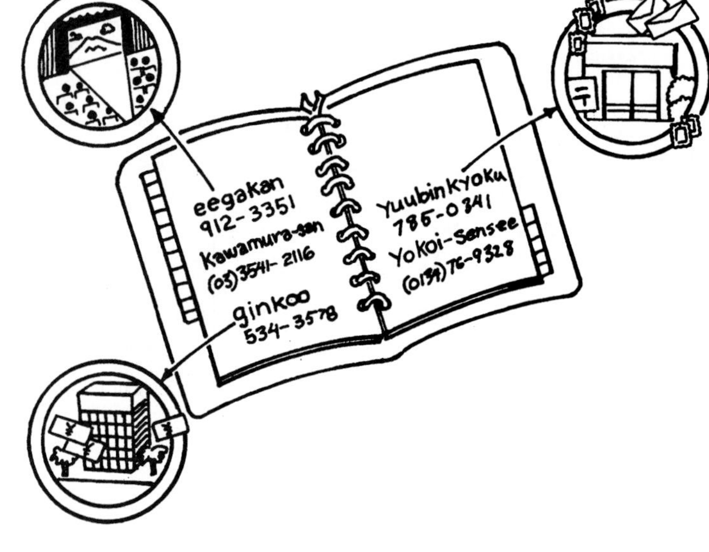

Asking and Telling Time

Dialogue 3: Asking What Time It Is 

John Kawamura asks a classmate, Masao Hayashi, what time it is.

KAWAMURA: Sumimasen. Ima nan-ji desu ka.
HAYASHI: Hachi-ji desu.
KAWAMURA: Arigatoo gozaimasu.
HAYASHI: Doo itashimashite.

✹ Activity 3

Practice Dialogue 3 with your classmates by changing the underlined time.

Telling Time

To tell time, add **-ji** (*o'clock*) to the appropriate numeral.

ichi-ji	*one o'clock*
ni-ji	*two o'clock*
san-ji	*three o'clock*

Dialogue 2 BROWN: What is Professor Yokoi's telephone number? KAWAMURA: It's 0134-76-9328. BROWN: It's 0134-67-9328, right? KAWAMURA: No, it's 0134-76-9328.

Dialogue 3 KAWAMURA: Excuse me. What time is it now? HAYASHI: It's eight o'clock. KAWAMURA: Thank you very much. HAYASHI: You are welcome.

yo-ji (*not* yon-ji *or* shi-ji)	*four o'clock*
go-ji	*five o'clock*
roku-ji	*six o'clock*
shichi-ji (*some people say* nana-ji)	*seven o'clock*
hachi-ji	*eight o'clock*
ku-ji (*not* kyuu-ji)	*nine o'clock*
juu-ji	*ten o'clock*
juu-ichi-ji	*eleven o'clock*
juu-ni-ji	*twelve o'clock*
ni-ji han	*2:30* (**han** means *half*)
Nan-ji desu ka.	*What time is it?*
Ni-ji han desu.	*It's 2:30.*

Activity 4

Practice this short dialogue, substituting the times that follow.

STUDENT 1:* Ima nan-ji desu ka.
STUDENT 2: ______ -ji desu.

Dialogue 4: Asking About the Time in Other Places

Two classmates, Takeshi Mimura and Heather Gibson, are talking about the time in the United States.

MIMURA: Ima nan-ji desu ka.
GIBUSON: Juu-ji desu.
MIMURA: Shikago wa ima nan-ji desu ka.
GIBUSON: Eeto, shichi-ji desu.
MIMURA: Gozen shichi-ji desu ka.
GIBUSON: Hai, soo desu. Amerika wa ima asa desu.

Dialogue 4 MIMURA: What time is it now? GIBSON: It's ten o'clock. MIMURA: What time is it now in Chicago? GIBSON: Uh. . . it's seven o'clock. MIMURA: Do you mean 7 A.M.? (lit., *Is it 7 A.M.?*) GIBSON: That's right. It's morning in the States now.

---

*In later activities, STUDENT 1 and STUDENT 2 will be abbreviated S1 and S2, respectively.

言語ノート

Language Note: Speech Fillers

When English speakers are trying to think of what to say next or are stalling for time in answering a question, they use so-called speech fillers such as *uh, let me see,* or *you know.* Japanese speakers also use certain words and phrases as speech fillers. The following can be used for this purpose.

Eeto desu nee (↓)	*Well, let me see…*
Soo desu nee (↓)	*Well, let me see…*
Anoo (↓)	*Well,…*
Eeto(*o*)	*Well,…*

When you are speaking Japanese, you should avoid English speech fillers, such as *uh,* and make an effort to use the Japanese ones.

Vocabulary: Time of Day 

gozen	A.M.
gogo	P.M.
asa	morning
hiru	noon, around noontime
yuugata	evening
yoru	night

Activity 5

Your instructor will point out a place on the map and ask you the time at that place.

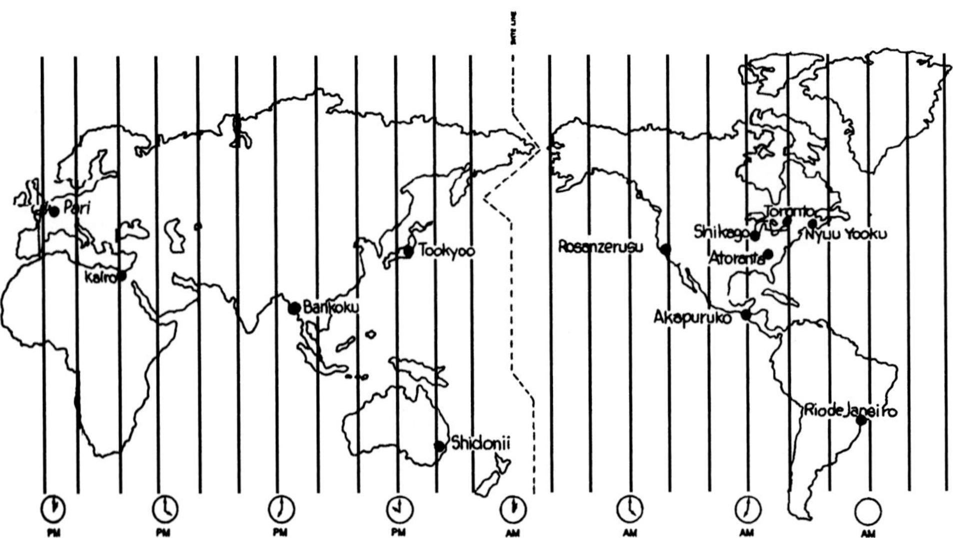

Dialogue 5: Asking When Something Is Taking Place 

Two classmates, John Kawamura and Mei Lin Chin, are relaxing in the student lounge.

KAWAMURA: Ima nan-ji desu ka?
CHIN: Eeto, ni-ji desu.
KAWAMURA: Miitingu no jikan desu ne.
CHIN: Ee, soo desu ne.

Activity 6

Step 1: Practice Dialogue 5 with another classmate, substituting times and activities from John Kawamura's schedule in the following illustration.

Step 2: Referring to John's schedule, ask a classmate what time each activity occurs.

Example:

s1: Nihongo no kurasu wa nan-ji desu ka.
s2: Gozen hachi-ji desu.

JOHN'S SCHEDULE

Dialogue 5 KAWAMURA: What time is it now? CHIN: Uh…it's two o'clock. KAWAMURA: It's time for the meeting, isn't it? CHIN: Yes, that's right.

Activity 6 s1: What time is Japanese class? s2: It's at 8 A.M.

Vocabulary Library

Daily Activities

asagohan	breakfast
hirugohan	lunch
bangohan	dinner, supper
kurasu	class
Nihongo no kurasu	Japanese language class
miitingu	meeting
deeto	date
eega	movie
paatii	party
kaimono/shoppingu	shopping
sanpo	a stroll, strolling
undoo	(physical) exercise
benkyoo	study, studying

Vocabulary Library sections present additional vocabulary that will help you express yourself more freely. If you need a Japanese word that is not listed, ask your teacher by using _____ **wa Nihongo de nan to iimasu ka.**

Asking What Something Is

In Japan, you may encounter many things you have never seen before. Here's how to ask people what things are.

Dialogue 6: Asking for Clarification

Linda Brown is at a restaurant.

BURAUN: Sumimasen. Are wa nan desu ka.
UEETAA: Soba desu.
BURAUN: Nihon ryoori desu ka.
UEETAA: Hai, soo desu.
BURAUN: Jaa, are o onegai shimasu.

In Dialogue 6, **sumimasen** (*excuse me*) is used to attract the waiter's attention. You can also use **anoo** to attract someone's attention.

Language Note: *Ko-so-a-do* Words

To refer to objects, the pronouns **kore, are,** and **sore** are used. They mean *this one, that one over there,* and *that one near you,* respectively. Thus **kore** refers to objects near the speaker, **are** to objects away from both the speaker and the hearer, and **sore** to objects near the hearer.

Dialogue 6 BROWN: Excuse me. What's that? WAITER: It's soba noodles. BROWN: Is it Japanese food? WAITER: Yes, it is. BROWN: Well then, I would like some.

Kore wa soba desu.	*This (near me) is soba.*
Sore wa nan desu ka.	*What is that (near you)?*
Are wa jisho desu.	*That (over there) is a dictionary.*

When you are not sure which item the speaker is referring to, you can use **dore.**

Are wa nan desu ka.	*What is that (over there)?*
Dore desu ka.	*Which one?*
Hora, are desu.	*Look. That one.* (while pointing)
Aa, are desu ka. Jisho desu yo.	*Oh, that one. That's a dictionary.*

Activity 7

With a classmate, play the roles of a foreign student who is in Japan for the first time and a waiter/waitress in a restaurant. When the student asks what a certain dish is, the waiter/waitress will respond using the answer in the first column. The student will then ask for more information, as indicated in the second column. Finally, the waiter/waitress must decide which of the following ways to end the exchange.

	Hai, soo desu.	*Yes, it is.*
or	Iie, chigaimasu. ____ desu.	*No, it's not. It's ____.*

Useful Word: kudamono *fruit*

WAITER/WAITRESS	STUDENT
1. sushi	Nihon ryoori desu ka.
2. marugariita	O-sake (*alcoholic beverage*) desu ka.
3. tenpura	Amerika ryoori desu ka.
4. kiui	Yasai (*vegetable*) desu ka.

Chigaimasu (lit., *it's different*) is used to correct someone's information or assumption. It's also one way to say no without using **iie**. Be careful because **chigaimasu** might sound so strong that some people may be offended by this response.

言語ノート

Language Note: Devoiced Vowels

When Japanese vowels [i] and [u] fall between voiceless consonants (i.e., [k], [s], [sh], [t], [ch], [ts], [h], and [p]) or when these vowels, preceded by one of these consonants, ends a word, these vowels sound whispered. Vowels are normally pronounced by vibrating the vocal cords but no vibration of the vocal cords accompanies pronunciation of these whispered, or devoiced, vowels. The devoiced vowels are underlined in the romanization.

すし	sushi	*sushi*
くつ	kutsu	*shoe*
えんぴつ	enpitsu	*pencil*
スペイン	Supein	*Spain*
ふたり	hutari	*two people*
あのひとはやまぐちさんです。	Ano hito wa Yamaguchi-san desu.	*That person is Mr. Yamaguchi.*

In standard, everyday Japanese spoken at a normal or fast speed, the devoicing of vowels occurs naturally in the aforementioned contexts. However, when people enunciate words slowly or emphatically or when they are nervous when speaking, devoicing may not take place.

The Japanese Writing System (2)

Hiragana (1)

Following is the basic **hiragana** syllabary chart. Under each symbol is the romanization used in this book to remind you of the Japanese pronunciation. Remember, you must listen closely to your instructor and the tapes to learn correct pronunciation. (Writing exercises for **hiragana** are included in your Workbook.)

あ a	い i	う u	え e	お o
か ka	き ki	く ku	け ke	こ ko
さ sa	し shi	す su	せ se	そ so
た ta	ち chi	つ tsu	て te	と to
な na	に ni	ぬ nu	ね ne	の no
は ha	ひ hi	ふ hu	へ he	ほ ho
ま ma	み mi	む mu	め me	も mo
や ya		ゆ yu		よ yo
ら ra	り ri	る ru	れ re	ろ ro
わ wa				を o
ん n				

を falls on the *w* line because historically it was pronounced **wo.**

The addition of two diacritical marks adds twenty-five more sounds (see the following list) to the basic **hiragana** chart. The ゛ (**dakuten**) turns the unvoiced consonants (*k*, *s*, *t*, and *h*) into voiced consonants (*g*, *z/j*, *d/j*, and *b*, respectively). The ゜ (**handakuten**) changes *h* to *p*.

が ga	ぎ gi	ぐ gu	げ ge	ご go
ざ za	じ ji	ず zu	ぜ ze	ぞ zo
だ da	ぢ ji	づ zu	で de	ど do
ば ba	び bi	ぶ bu	べ be	ぼ bo
ぱ pa	ぴ pi	ぷ pu	ぺ pe	ぽ po

言語ノート

Language Note: *a-i-u-e-o* order

In Japanese dictionaries, words are listed in the same order as the **hiragana** syllabary: **a, i, u, e, o, ka, ki, ku, ke, ko, sa, shi,** and so on. You might think of this as the Japanese alphabetical order. Since you cannot use a Japanese dictionary without knowing it, it is important to learn the order of the **hiragana** syllables. In addition, knowing the **hiragana** syllabary makes it easier to remember Japanese verb conjugations. By the way, listings in address books, encyclopedias, and the Japanese-English Glossary at the end of this book are ordered in the same way. Note that words starting with voiced sounds (e.g., **ga, gi, gu, ge, go**) are listed along with words starting with the corresponding voiceless sounds (e.g., **ka, ki, ku, ke, ko**). The listings in telephone directories are in **a-i-u-e-o** order, but when names are homonyms, other rules governing **kanji** order come into play.

The first line of **hiragana** consists of five symbols representing the five Japanese vowels.

あ	a	pronounced roughly as in English *father,* but the mouth is not so wide open as in English
い	i	as in English *see,* but shorter
う	u	as in English *doodle,* but it is short and does not require lip rounding
え	e	as in English *egg,* but the mouth is not open so wide
お	o	as in English *comb,* but it does not require so much lip rounding

The rest of the symbols (except ん **n** and を **o**) consist of a consonant or a semivowel (**y** or **w**) followed by one of the five vowels. Most Japanese consonants are easy for English speakers to pronounce, but note the following differences.

sh in し	as in *she,* but less lip-rounding
ch in ち	as in *cheese,* but with no lip-rounding
ts in つ	as in *cats*
h in は、へ、ほ	is similar to English *h*
h in ひ	as in *he,* but with friction as the air is expelled
h in ふ	articulated by bringing both lips close together without any rounding and then forcing air out between them
r in ら	Japanese **r,** very similar to the *t/d* in *water* or *rider,* is articulated by tapping the tip of the tongue very quickly against the gum just behind the upper teeth
w in わ	as in English *we,* but with less tension
g in が	as in *gate* but some speakers pronounce this sound like *ng* in *sing* when it occurs in the middle of a word
j in じ、ぢ	as in English *jeep*

Some Japanese pronounce ひ **hi** like English *he* but shorter and with no friction.

Hu ふ is sometimes transcribed as **fu.** You will notice this especially in common words like **futon** and Japanese personal names and places that begin with the ふ syllable: **Fuji-san** (*Mt. Fuji*), **Fukushima, Fujiwara, Fukuoka,** and so on.

ん **(n)** represents a nasal sound with the length of one full syllable. (Thus, it is called syllabic nasal.) The actual sound represented by this symbol depends on the context. Before [m], [p], or [b], it is pronounced [m]; before [s], [sh], [t], [ts], [ch], [n], [r], [z], [d], or [j], it is pronounced [n]; and before vowels, before [k], [y], [w], [g], or [ng], or at the end of a word, it is pronounced [ng]. In this book, however, ん is represented as **n** regardless of where it appears.

enpitsu	えんぴつ	*pencil*
kanji	かんじ	*Chinese character*
Nihongo	にほんご	*Japanese language*
hon	ほん	*book*
kin'en	きんえん	*no smoking*
cf. kinen	きねん	*commemoration*

Note that ん can never begin a word.

言語ノート

Language Note: The Origins of *Hiragana* and *Katakana*

Chinese characters (**kanji**) were imported to Japan around the fifth century A.D., before which time Japan had no writing system. The use of **kanji** to transcribe the Japanese language was inconvenient, to say the least, because **kanji** were designed to transcribe a completely different language. To remedy this problem, **hiragana** symbols were created by simplifying **kanji.**

以 → い
I → i

礼 → れ
REE → re

Katakana was originally created by Japanese priests to annotate Buddhist books written in **kanji. Katakana** symbols were created from parts of **kanji.**

伊 → イ
I → i

礼 → レ
REE → re

Hiragana and **katakana** spelling does not always conform to the **rooma-ji** spelling in *Yookoso!* For example, **sensee** (*teacher*) is the **rooma-ji** spelling, but it is written with the **hiragana** letters **se-n-se-*i*** せんせい; **doozo** (*please*) is written as **do-*u*-zo** どうぞ. These and other differences are explained in Parts 3 to 5.

Vocabulary

This is a list of words that you have used or heard in Part 2 of this textbook. Before beginning Part 3, make sure that you know the words listed under the categories **Greetings and Polite Expressions, Questions, Classroom, Numbers, Time Expressions,** and **Other Useful Words.** These are considered active vocabulary.

For your reading practice this list is rendered in **hiragana** and **katakana.** In authentic writing, **kanji** would be used in many words.

Greetings and Polite Expressions

Arigatoo.	ありがとう。	Thank you
Arigatoo gozaimasu.	ありがとうございます。	Thank you. (*formal*)
Doo itashimashite.	どういたしまして。	You are welcome.
Onegai shimasu.	おねがいします。	Please (give me)…
Sumimasen.	すみません。	Excuse me, thank you.

Questions

Nan desu ka.	なんですか。	What is it?
Nan-ji desu ka.	なんじですか。	What time is it?
____ wa Nihongo de nan to iimasu ka.	____はにほんごでなんと いいますか。	How do you say ____ in Japanese?

Classroom

enpitsu	えんぴつ	pencil
hiragana	ひらがな	cursive syllabary
hon	ほん	book
jisho	じしょ	dictionary
katakana	かたかな	square syllabary
kanji	かんじ	Chinese characters
kurasu	クラス	class
Nihongo no kurasu	にほんごのクラス	Japanese language class
sensee	せんせい	teacher, professor

Numbers

ree, zero	れい、ゼロ	zero
ichi	いち	one
ni	に	two
san	さん	three
yon, shi	よん、し	four
go	ご	five
roku	ろく	six

shichi, nana	しち、なな	seven
hachi	はち	eight
ku, kyuu	く、きゅう	nine
juu	じゅう	ten
juu-ichi	じゅういち	eleven
juu-ni	じゅうに	twelve
juu-san	じゅうさん	thirteen
juu-yon, juu-shi	じゅうよん、じゅうし	fourteen
juu-go	じゅうご	fifteen
juu-roku	じゅうろく	sixteen
juu-shichi, juu-nana	じゅうしち、じゅうなな	seventeen
juu-hachi	じゅうはち	eighteen
juu-ku, juu-kyuu	じゅうく、じゅうきゅう	nineteen
ni-juu	にじゅう	twenty

Time Expressions

ichi-ji	いちじ	one o'clock
ni-ji	にじ	two o'clock
san-ji	さんじ	three o'clock
yo-ji	よじ	four o'clock
go-ji	ごじ	five o'clock
roku-ji	ろくじ	six o'clock
shichi-ji, nana-ji	しちじ、ななじ	seven o'clock
hachi-ji	はちじ	eight o'clock
ku-ji	くじ	nine o'clock
juu-ji	じゅうじ	ten o'clock
juu-ichi-ji	じゅういちじ	eleven o'clock
juu-ni-ji	じゅうにじ	twelve o'clock
. . . han	～はん	. . . thirty (*when telling time*)
ni-ji-han	にじはん	2:30
asa	あさ	morning
gogo	ごご	P.M.
gozen	ごぜん	A.M.
hiru	ひる	noontime
jikan	じかん	time
yoru	よる	night
yuugata	ゆうがた	evening

Foods/Beverages

Nihon ryoori	にほんりょうり	Japanese food
o-sake	おさけ	alcoholic beverage
soba	そば	soba, buckwheat noodles
sushi	すし	sushi

Other Nouns

asagohan	あさごはん	breakfast
bangoo	ばんごう	number (*as in* **denwa bangoo** [*telephone number*])
bangohan	ばんごはん	dinner, supper
benkyoo	べんきょう	study, studying
denwa	でんわ	telephone
eega	えいが	movie
hirugohan	ひるごはん	lunch
kaimono	かいもの	shopping
sanpo	さんぽ	strolling
undoo	うんどう	exercise

Language

Nihongo	にほんご	Japanese

Place and Personal Names

Akapuruko (Mekishiko)	アカプルコ（メキシコ）	Acapulco (Mexico)
Atoranta	アトランタ	Atlanta
Bankoku (Tai)	バンコク（タイ）	Bangkok (Thailand)
Kairo (Ejiputo)	カイロ（エジプト）	Cairo (Egypt)
Nyuu Yooku	ニューヨーク	New York
Pari (Huransu)	パリ（フランス）	Paris (France)
Rosanzerusu	ロサンゼルス	Los Angeles
Riodejaneiro (Burajiru)	リオデジャネイロ（ブラジル）	Rio de Janeiro (Brazil)
Shidonii (Oosutoraria)	シドニー（オーストラリア）	Sydney (Australia)
Shikago	シカゴ	Chicago
Tookyoo	とうきょう	Tokyo
Toronto (Kanada)	トロント（カナダ）	Toronto (Canada)

Other Useful Words

aa	ああ	Oh
anoo	あのう	Well…
Chigaimasu.	ちがいます。	That's not right.
desu	です	to be (*copula*)
eeto	ええと	uhh, well (*used when pausing to think*)
eeto desu nee	ええとですねえ	well, let me see…
Hai, soo desu.	はい、そうです。	Yes, that's right.
Hontoo desu ka.	ほんとうですか。	Really? (lit., *Is that true?*)
hora	ほら	Look!

ima	いま	now
jaa	じゃあ	well, then
ne(e)	ね(え)	Right? (Isn't that so?)
no	の	(*possessive marker*)
wa	は	(*particle topic marker* [*pronounced* わ])
yo	よ	(*emphatic sentence-final particle*)
are	あれ	that (thing over there)
kore	これ	this (thing)
sore	それ	that (thing)
dore	どれ	which (thing)

Part Three

Objectives

Talking about daily activities
Talking about future activities and events
Talking about likes and dislikes
The Japanese writing system (3):
Hiragana (2)

Talking About Daily Activities

Dialogue 1: Talking About One's Schedule

Two classmates, Masao Hayashi and Linda Brown, are talking about what time they get up in the morning.

HAYASHI: Buraun-san wa nan-ji ni okimasu ka.
BURAUN: Go-ji desu.
HAYASHI: Waa, hayai desu ne.
BURAUN: Hayashi-san wa?
HAYASHI: Ku-ji desu.

Activity 1

First, listen to your teacher or CD while looking at the following schedule.

JOHN KAWAMURA'S DAY

6:00 A.M.	okimasu (*get up*)
7:00 A.M.	asagohan o tabemasu (*eat breakfast*)
8:00 A.M.	gakkoo e ikimasu (*go to school*)
Noon	hirugohan o tabemasu (*eat lunch*)
1:00 P.M.	koohii o nomimasu (*drink coffee*)

Dialogue 1 HAYASHI: What time do you get up in the morning, Ms. Brown? BROWN: Five o'clock. HAYASHI: Wow, that's early. BROWN: How about you, Mr. Hayashi? HAYASHI: (I get up at) nine o'clock.

3:00 P.M.	toshokan e ikimasu (*go to the library*)
7:00 P.M.	bangohan o tabemasu (*eat dinner*)
8:00 P.M.	terebi o mimasu (*watch TV*)
9:00 P.M.	hon o yomimasu (*read a book*)
Midnight	nemasu (*go to sleep*)

Now answer the following questions in Japanese.

Useful Word: mainichi *every day*

Example:

Kawamura-san wa mainichi nan-ji ni okimasu ka. (*What time does Mr. Kawamura get up every day?*) →
Gozen 6-ji desu.

1. Nan-ji ni asagohan o tabemasu ka.
2. Nan-ji ni gakkoo e ikimasu ka.
3. Nan-ji ni hirugohan o tabemasu ka.
4. Nan-ji ni toshokan e ikimasu ka.
5. Nan-ji ni bangohan o tabemasu ka.
6. Nan-ji ni hon o yomimasu ka.
7. Nan-ji ni nemasu ka.

Vocabulary: Daily Activities

	(*I, you, he, she, we, they*)…
okimasu	get up/wake up
asagohan o tabemasu	eat breakfast
hirugohan, bangohan	
gakkoo e ikimasu	go to school
kurasu, toshokan (*library*), **shigoto** (*work*)	
o-cha o nomimasu	drink tea
koohii, wain, koocha (*tea*)	
uchi e kaerimasu	go back home
undoo o shimasu	(do) exercise
jogingu, earobikusu	
terebi o mimasu	watch TV
eega (*movie*), **dorama, nyuusu**	
hon o yomimasu	read a book
shinbun (*newspaper*), **zasshi** (*magazine*)	
ongaku o kikimasu	listen to music
rajio (*radio*), **shiidii** (*CD*)	
Nihongo o benkyoo shimasu	study Japanese
suugaku (*math*), **Huransugo** (*French*)	
nemasu	go to sleep; go to bed
kara… made	from, beginning at… until

There is no subject-verb agreement in Japanese. In other words, Japanese verbs take the same form irrespective of the person and number of the subject.

言語ノート

Language Note: Basic Sentence Structure of Japanese

You may have already noticed that the sentence structure of Japanese is different from that of English. In English, the basic sentence structure is Subject-Verb-Object, as in *Mr. Kawamura watches TV*. In Japanese, the basic structure is Subject-Object-Verb (as in **Kawamura-san wa terebi o mimasu** (*Mr. Kawamura TV watch*). Thus, Japanese verbs (e.g., **okimasu**) come toward the end of a sentence.

In English, you can tell whether a noun is a subject or an object by its position in the sentence. If a noun comes at the beginning of a sentence, it is the subject. If it comes after a verb, it is an object. In Japanese, both the subject noun and object noun come before a verb. The roles of the nouns are differentiated by the use of particles (small words) that follow the word they mark. Notice, for instance, that the particle **o** marks the direct object. In **bangohan o tabemasu** (*I eat supper*), **o** marks **bangohan** as the object of the verb **tabemasu**.

Unlike English prepositions, Japanese particles are short words that occur after other words and thus are often called *postpositions*. Particles help identify the relationship of the word they follow to other parts of the sentence.

More Time Expressions

2:05	ni-ji go-hun
2:10	ni-ji jup-pun
	ni-ji jip-pun
2:15	ni-ji juu-go-hun
2:20	ni-ji ni-jup-pun
	ni-ji ni-jip-pun
2:25	ni-ji ni-juu-go-hun
2:30	ni-ji han
	ni-ji san-jup-pun
	ni-ji san-jip-pun
2:35	ni-ji san-juu-go-hun
2:40	ni-ji yon-jup-pun
	ni-ji yon-jip-pun
2:45	ni-ji yon-juu-go-hun
2:50	ni-ji go-jup-pun
	ni-ji go-jip-pun
2:55	ni-ji go-juu-go-hun

Activity 2

Practice this short dialogue with a classmate, substituting the times that follow.

s1: Ima nan-ji desu ka.
s2: ___ desu.

1.

2.

3.

4.

5.

6.

7.

8.

言語ノート

Language Note: Telling Time Politely

Japanese people think it is more polite to express themselves vaguely rather than clearly and directly. This tendency extends to unexpected areas like telling time. When you would like to tell time politely or give an approximate time, use **goro** (*about*).

> Nan-ji ni uchi o demasu ka.
> *What time do you leave home?*
>
> Hachi-ji goro demasu.
> *I leave about 8:00.*
>
> Nan-ji goro ikimasu ka.
> *Around what time will you go?*
>
> Ni-ji goro ikimasu.
> *I'll go around 2:00* (lit., *at about 2:00*).

Note that the particle indicating a point of time, **ni,** may be dropped when **goro** is used.

Don't be fooled by the use of **goro.** Some Japanese are extremely punctual and expect the same of others.

Activity 3

Step 1: Write down your daily schedule (choose, for instance, Friday) in English.

Step 2: Work in pairs. Explain your schedule to your partner in Japanese.

Dialogue 2: Asking How Often Someone Does Something 

Two classmates, Masao Hayashi and Heather Gibson, are talking about how often they go to the movies or watch television.

HAYASHI: Gibuson-san wa yoku eega ni ikimasu ka.
GIBUSON: Uun, amari ikimasen ne. Hayashi-san wa?
HAYASHI: Tokidoki ikimasu. Demo, terebi no eega wa yoku mimasu.
GIBUSON: Watashi wa terebi mo amari mimasen.

Mo is a particle meaning *too, either.*

言語ノート

Language Note: Indicating Frequency

Yoku, tokidoki, amari, and **zenzen** are some adverbs indicating frequency.

Yoku terebi o mimasu ka?	*Do you often watch TV?*
Hai, yoku mimasu.	*Yes, I watch it often.*
Hai, tokidoki mimasu.	*Yes, I watch it sometimes.*
Iie, amari mimasen.	*No, I don't watch it so often.*
Iie, zenzen mimasen.	*No, I don't watch it at all.*

Amari and **zenzen** are used only in negative sentences.

言語ノート

Language Note: Conjugation

Japanese verbs conjugate (change their form) based on three factors: tense, affirmative/negative, and politeness or formality of speech. Japanese has two tenses, past and nonpast. Such verb forms as **ikimasu** and **mimasu** are nonpast forms used to describe actions that you do habitually or in the future. **Ikimasen** and **mimasen** (see Dialogue 2) are nonpast forms, but they are the negative counterparts of **ikimasu** and **mimasu.** The verb forms you have been studying so far are all polite forms used to convey the speaker's politeness toward the addressee. The students in Professor Yokoi's class have just met, so they have been using polite forms. As they become more familiar with each other and their relationship gets closer, they will begin using informal forms.

Dialogue 2 HAYASHI: Ms. Gibson, do you often go to movies? GIBSON: Well, I don't go very much. How about you, Mr. Hayashi? HAYASHI: I go (to movies) sometimes, but I often watch movies on TV. GIBSON: I don't watch TV very much, either.

Activity 4

Talk with one or more classmates about your daily schedules using the following questions.

1. ___ san wa mainichi nan-ji ni okimasu ka.
2. Nan-ji ni uchi o demasu ka.
3. Nan-ji ni uchi e kaerimasu ka.
4. Nan-ji ni yuugohan o tabemasu ka.
5. Yoku terebi o mimasu ka.
6. Yoku hon o yomimasu ka.
7. Yoku ongaku o kikimasu ka.
8. Nan-ji ni nemasu ka.

Vocabulary Library 

More Daily Activities

	(I, you, he, she, we, they)…
tegami o kakimasu	write a letter
deeto (o) shimasu	have a date
yakyuu o shimasu	play baseball
kaimono ni ikimasu	go shopping
ichinichi-juu nemasu	sleep all day
tomodachi ni aimasu	see/meet a friend
tomodachi to hanashimasu	talk with a friend
Nihongo o renshuu shimasu	practice Japanese
denwa o shimasu	make a phone call

Activity 5

Step 1: The purpose of this activity is to find out the habits of one of your classmates. Write five questions that will help you understand his or her habits.

Step 2: Work in pairs. Ask your partner the five questions.

Step 3: Explain your partner's habits to the class.

Talking About Future Activities and Events

Dialogue 3: Asking About Someone's Weekend Plans 

Two classmates, Hitomi Machida and John Kawamura, are talking about activities for a coming weekend.

KAWAMURA: Machida-san wa konshuu no shuumatsu, nani o shimasu ka.
MACHIDA: Tomodachi to kaimono ni ikimasu. Kawamura-san wa?
KAWAMURA: Mochiron, Nihongo o benkyoo shimasu.
MACHIDA: Majime desu ne.

Vocabulary: Days and Weeks

kyoo	today
ashita	tomorrow
asatte	the day after tomorrow
konshuu	this week
raishuu	next week
saraishuu	the week after next
shuumatsu	weekend

Activity 6

Discuss your future activities. Ask a classmate

1. if he/she will come to school tomorrow.
2. if he/she will go to a library tomorrow.
3. if he/she will study Japanese this weekend.
4. if he/she will go shopping this weekend.
5. if he/she will see friends this weekend.
6. if he/she will exercise this weekend.

	Su	M	T	W	Th	F	Sa
konshuu				kyoo	ashita	asatte	
raishuu							
saraishuu							

Talking About Likes and Dislikes

Dialogue 4: Expressing One's Likes and Dislikes 

John Kawamura and Hitomi Machida are talking in a cafeteria.

KAWAMURA: Machida-san wa sakana ga suki desu ka.
MACHIDA: Ee, toku ni osashimi ga suki desu.
KAWAMURA: Watashi wa osashimi ga kirai desu.
MACHIDA: Hontoo desu ka!

Dialogue 3 KAWAMURA: Ms. Machida, what are you going to do this weekend? MACHIDA: I will go shopping with my friends. How about you, Mr. Kawamura? KAWAMURA: Of course, I am going to study Japanese. MACHIDA: You sure are diligent, Mr. Kawamura.

Dialogue 4 KAWAMURA: Do you like fish, Ms. Machida? MACHIDA: Yes. I especially like raw fish. KAWAMURA: I dislike raw fish. MACHIDA: Really! (lit., *Is that true?*)

言語ノート

Language Note: Talking About Likes and Dislikes

Use the following sentence structures to express likes and dislikes.

> ___ ga suki desu.
> *I (you, he, she, we, they) like ___.*
> ___ ga kirai desu.
> *I (you, etc.) dislike ___.*
> ___ ga suki ja arimasen.
> *I (you, etc.) don't like ___.*

To ask if someone likes something, say

> ___ ga suki desu ka.
> *Do (you, etc.) like ___?*

✷ Activity 7

Ask a classmate whether he or she likes the following things.

Examples:

> Nihongo no kurasu ga suki desu ka. → Hai, suki desu.
> Paatii ga suki desu ka. → Iie, suki ja arimasen.

1. yasai (*vegetable*[*s*]), niku (*meat*), sakana, burokkorii, piza, aisu kuriimu
2. Nihon ryoori (*Japanese food*), Itaria ryoori, Huransu ryoori, Mekishiko ryoori
3. koohii (*coffee*), aisutii, koora, juusu
4. biiru, wain, kakuteru, uisukii
5. huttobooru, sakkaa, tenisu, supootsu
6. bokushingu, sukii, suiee (*swimming*)
7. eega (*movies*), sanpo (*strolling*), benkyoo, paatii
8. jazu, rokku, kurashikku (*classical music*), rappu
9. Madonna, Julia Roberts, Michael Jackson, Tom Cruise

Dialogue 5: Saying What Foods One Especially Likes 

Hitomi Machida and Linda Brown are talking about the foods they like.

MACHIDA: Buraun-san wa donna tabemono ga suki desu ka.
BURAUN: Tabemono desu ka. Soo desu nee. Itaria ryoori ga ichiban suki desu ne.
MACHIDA: Soo desu ka.
BURAUN: Ee, toku ni pasuta ga suki desu.

Soo desu nee is a speech filler (see the Part 2 Language Note on speech fillers).

Dialogue 5 MACHIDA: What kind of food do you like, Ms. Brown? BROWN: You mean food? (lit., *Is it food?*) Let's see. I like Italian food best. MACHIDA: Is that so? BROWN: Yes, I especially like pasta.

言語ノート

Language Note: Echo Questions

In Dialogue 5, Machida asks a question and Brown questions back by repeating a part of Machida's question **(Tabemono desu ka).** Brown's question is called an *echo question*, which consists of a noun and **desu ka.** Echo questions are used often in conversation as a strategy to confirm what the other speaker is asking about or to keep communication channels open while thinking of an answer to the question.

Ashita nan-ji ni gakkoo e ikimasu ka.
What time will you go to school tomorrow?

Gakkoo desu ka. 8-ji ni ikimasu.
You mean school? I will go at eight.

or Ashita desu ka. 8-ji ni ikimasu.
You mean tomorrow? I will go at eight.

Kawamura-san, yoku terebi o mimasu ka.
Mr. Kawamura, do you often watch TV?

Watashi desu ka. Ee, yoku mimasu.
You are asking me? Yes, I watch it often.

or Terebi desu ka. Ee, yoku mimasu.
You mean TV? Yes, I watch it often.

These echo questions, like speech fillers, are frequently used in Japanese conversations as a device to keep communication flowing smoothly. Dialogue 5 contains both an echo question and a speech filler.

Activity 8

Working in pairs, ask questions about the likes and dislikes of Henry Curtis and Mei Lin Chin.

Example:

s1: Chin-san wa jazu ga suki desu ka.
s2: Hai, suki desu.

1. Nihon ryoori

2. niku

3. sakana

4. kohii

Activity 9

Following the example, ask your classmates their preferences in the following areas.

Example:

supootsu—huttobooru, sakkaa, tenisu, bareebooru →
s1: Donna supootsu ga suki desu ka.
s2: Tenisu ga ichiban suki desu.

1. ongaku—kurashikku (*classical music*), jazu, rokku, rappu, kantorii ando uesutan, min'yoo (*Japanese folk music*)
2. nomimono—koohii, o-cha (*green tea*), koora, wain, juusu, biiru, mizu (*water*)
3. kurasu—Nihongo no kurasu, Huransugo no kurasu, Supeingo no kurasu (*Your answer is obvious, isn't it?*)
4. tabemono—yasai, niku, sakana
5. gakki (*musical instrument*)—piano, gitaa, huruuto, doramu

The Japanese Writing System (3)

Hiragana (2)

By writing や **ya,** ゆ **yu,** or よ **yo** small after symbols ending in the vowel **i,** you can transcribe the following sounds. Each syllable is composed of a consonant + **y** + **a, u,** or **o.** (In horizontal writing the small symbols are written lower than the regular-size ones; in vertical writing they are written somewhat to the right.) This **y** is sometimes called a glide or semi-vowel.

きゃ kya	きゅ kyu	きょ kyo
しゃ sha	しゅ shu	しょ sho
ちゃ cha	ちゅ chu	ちょ cho
にゃ nya	にゅ nyu	にょ nyo
ひゃ hya	ひゅ hyu	ひょ hyo
みゃ mya	みゅ myu	みょ myo
りゃ rya	りゅ ryu	りょ ryo
ぎゃ gya	ぎゅ gyu	ぎょ gyo
じゃ ja	じゅ ju	じょ jo
びゃ bya	びゅ byu	びょ byo
ぴゃ pya	ぴゅ pyu	ぴょ pyo

Double Vowels

When two of the same vowel occur together, hold the sound twice as long as a single vowel. In writing, these double vowels are transcribed by adding a corresponding single vowel symbol.

obasan	おばさん	*aunt*
obaasan	おばあさん	*grandmother*
ie	いえ	*house*
iie	いいえ	*no*
suugaku	すうがく	*math*

A double vowel sound **ee** is in most cases written by adding い (**i**).

meeshi	めいし	*name card*
Shitsuree.	しつれい。	*Excuse me.*

There are a few exceptions in which え (**e**) is added.

oneesan	おねえさん	*older sister*
ee	ええ	*yes*

A long vowel **oo** is in most cases written by adding う (**u**).

Doomo arigatoo.	どうもありがとう。	*Thank you.*
ryoori	りょうり	*food*

There are several exceptions in which お (**o**) is added.

ooi	おおい	*many*
tooi	とおい	*far*
too	とお	*ten*
ookii	おおきい	*large, big*

Cases where a double vowel sound **ee** can be indicated by え (**e**) or い (**i**) are limited to ええ／えい or ねえ／ねい. Otherwise, only い is used, as in けい, せい, へい, じい.
Cases where a double vowel sound **oo** can be indicated by お (**o**) or う (**u**) are limited to おお／おう or とお／とう. Otherwise, only う is used, as in こう, のう, ほう, ごう.

Double Consonants

Double consonants (**pp, kk,** etc.) are written using a small っ (**tsu**), which doubles the sound it precedes.

kita	きた	*north*
kitta	きった	*(I) cut*
kako	かこ	*past*
kakko	かっこ	*parenthesis*

However, double **nn** is written with ん(**n**). Note that ん must always follow a vowel sound; it can never begin a word.

hone	ほね	*bone*
honne	ほんね	*true intention*

言語ノート

Language Note: Syllables

Syllables that are used in Japanese can be classified as follows:

1. syllables consisting of only one vowel: あ、い、う、え、お
2. syllables consisting of one consonant and one vowel: か、き、く、け、こ、さ、し、etc.
3. syllables consisting of one consonant, glide **y**, and one vowel: きゃ、きゅ、きょ、しゃ、しゅ、etc.
4. special syllables: ん, っ (double consonant), double vowel

In Japanese, the length of a word is usually counted by the number of syllables included in it.

ki	き	*tree*	one-syllable word
ai	あい	*love*	two-syllable word
osa	あさ	*morning*	two-syllable word
gogo	ごご	*P.M.*	two-syllable word
kyoka	きょか	*permission*	two-syllable word
kin	きん	*gold*	two-syllable word
kagami	かがみ	*mirror*	three-syllable word
kooka	こうか	*effect*	three-syllable word
kippu	きっぷ	*ticket*	three-syllable word
kooi	こうい	*behavior*	three-syllable word
sanpo	さんぽ	*walk*	three-syllable word
gohan	ごはん	*rice; meal*	three-syllable word
kyoomi	きょうみ	*interest*	three-syllable word
gakkoo	がっこう	*school*	four-syllable word
ginkoo	ぎんこう	*bank*	four-syllable word

Note the correspondence between the number of **hiragana** letters in each word and the number of syllables.

It is important that each syllable, irrespective of its type (1 through 4), is pronounced in almost the same amount of time. Thus, uttering a four-syllable word basically takes twice as long as uttering a two-syllable word.

Some Notes on the Writing of Functional Words

Japanese uses several particles (small words) to indicate grammatical functions. They are written in **hiragana**, but you must be careful about how to write some of them.

- The topic particle (indicating the topic of a sentence) **wa** is written は.
- The direction particle (indicating the direction of movement) **e** is written へ.
- The direct object particle (indicating the direct object of a verb) **o** is written を.

はやしさんはまいにちカフェテリアへいきます。
Mr. Hayashi goes to the cafeteria every day.

ブラウンさんはまいあさジョギングをします。
Ms. Brown jogs (does jogging) every morning.

Vocabulary

This is a list of words that you have used or heard in Part 3 of this textbook. Before beginning Part 4, make sure that you know the words listed under the categories **Classroom, Time Expressions,** and **Other Useful Words.** These are considered active vocabulary.

For your reading practice this list is rendered in **hiragana** and **katakana.** In authentic writing, **kanji** would be used in many words.

Classroom

suugaku	すうがく	math
tomodachi	ともだち	friend

Time Expressions

ichi-ji	いちじ	one o'clock
ni-ji	にじ	two o'clock
san-ji	さんじ	three o'clock
yo-ji	よじ	four o'clock
go-ji	ごじ	five o'clock
roku-ji	ろくじ	six o'clock
shichi-ji, nana-ji	しちじ、ななじ	seven o'clock
hachi-ji	はちじ	eight o'clock
ku-ji	くじ	nine o'clock
juu-ji	じゅうじ	ten o'clock
juu-ichi-ji	じゅういちじ	eleven o'clock
juu-ni-ji	じゅうにじ	twelve o'clock
go-hun	ごふん	five minutes
jup-pun	じゅっぷん	ten minutes
juu-go-hun	じゅうごふん	fifteen minutes
ni-jup-pun,	にじゅっぷん、	twenty minutes
ni-jip-pun	にじっぷん	
ni-juu-go-hun	にじゅうごふん	twenty-five minutes
. . . han	〜はん	… thirty (*when telling time*)
san-jup-pun,	さんじゅっぷん、	thirty minutes
san-jip-pun	さんじっぷん	
san-juu-go-hun	さんじゅうごふん	thirty-five minutes
yon-jup-pun,	よんじゅっぷん、	forty minutes
yon-jip-pun	よんじっぷん	
yon-juu-go-hun	よんじゅうごふん	forty-five minutes
go-jup-pun,	ごじゅっぷん、	fifty minutes
go-jip-pun	ごじっぷん	
go-juu-go-hun	ごじゅうごふん	fifty-five minutes

konshuu no shuumatsu	こんしゅうのしゅうまつ	this weekend
mainichi	まいにち	every day
tokidoki	ときどき	sometimes
kyoo	きょう	today
ashita	あした	tomorrow
asatte	あさって	the day after tomorrow
konshuu	こんしゅう	this week
raishuu	らいしゅう	next week
saraishuu	さらいしゅう	the week after next
shuumatsu	しゅうまつ	weekend

Verbs

		(I, you, he, she, we, they)...
benkyoo shimasu	べんきょうします	study
deeto (o) shimasu	デート(を)します	have a date
denwa (o) shimasu	でんわ(を)します	make a phone call
hanashimasu	はなします	speak
ikimasu	いきます	go
kaerimasu	かえります	return
kakimasu	かきます	write
kikimasu	ききます	listen
kimasu	きます	come
mimasu	みます	look, watch
nemasu	ねます	sleep
nomimasu	のみます	drink
okimasu	おきます	get up
renshuu shimasu	れんしゅうします	practice
shimasu	します	do
tabemasu	たべます	eat
yomimasu	よみます	read

Foods/Beverages

aisutii	アイスティー	ice tea
biiru	ビール	beer
hanbaagaa	ハンバーガー	hamburger
juusu	ジュース	juice
kakuteru	カクテル	cocktail
koocha	こうちゃ	black tea
koohii	コーヒー	coffee
koora	コーラ	cola
Nihon ryoori	にほんりょうり	Japanese food
niku	にく	meat
nomimono	のみもの	beverage

o-cha	おちゃ	green tea
o-sake	おさけ	alcoholic beverage
o-sashimi	おさしみ	raw fish, sashimi
pasuta	パスタ	pasta
sakana	さかな	fish
tabemono	たべもの	food
uisukii	ウイスキー	whiskey
wain	ワイン	wine
yasai	やさい	vegetable

Other Nouns

bokushingu	ボクシング	boxing
dorama	ドラマ	drama
doramu	ドラム	drum(s)
earobikusu	エアロビクス	aerobics
eega	えいが	movie(s)
gakki	がっき	musical instrument
gakkoo	がっこう	school
gitaa	ギター	guitar
hon	ほん	book
huruuto	フルート	flute
huttobooru	フットボール	football (American)
jogingu	ジョギング	jogging
kantorii ando uesutan	カントリーアンドウエスタン	country and western
kurashikku	クラシック	classical music
nyuusu	ニュース	news
ongaku	おんがく	music
piano	ピアノ	piano
rajio	ラジオ	radio
rappu	ラップ	rap music
rokku	ロック	rock music
sakkaa	サッカー	soccer
shigoto	しごと	work
shiidii	シーディー	CD
shinbun	しんぶん	newspaper
suiee	すいえい	swimming
sukii	スキー	skiing
supootsu	スポーツ	sports
tenisu	テニス	tennis
terebi	テレビ	TV
toshokan	としょかん	library
uchi	うち	house, home
zasshi	ざっし	magazine

Countries/Languages

Huransugo	フランスご	French language
Itaria	イタリア	Italy
Nihongo	にほんご	Japanese language

Other Useful Words

amari	あまり	not very (*in a negative sentence*)
Hontoo desu ka.	ほんとうですか。	Really? (lit., *Is that true?*)
ichiban	いちばん	(the) best (lit., *number one*)
kirai	きらい	to dislike
majime	まじめ	diligent, eager
mo	も	too, either
suki	すき	to like
tokuni	とくに	especially
yoku	よく	often
zenzen	ぜんぜん	(not) at all (*in a negative sentence*)
hima	ひま	free time
kara… made	から… まで	from, beginning at… until

Part Four

Objectives

Talking about activities and events in the past
Inviting someone to do something
Talking about weekly schedules
Talking about the weather
The Japanese writing system (4): **Katakana** (1)

Talking About Activities and Events in the Past

Dialogue 1: Saying What One Ate the Night Before 

Masao Hayashi is seeing his physician, Dr. Miyai.

MIYAI: Kinoo no yoru nani o tabemashita ka.
HAYASHI: Eeto, kinoo no yoru desu ka. Sukiyaki o tabemashita.
MIYAI: Hoka ni wa.
HAYASHI: Eeto, hoka ni wa... Yakitori o tabemashita.

Yakitori is bite-sized marinated pieces of chicken meat cooked like shish kebab on skewers over an open fire.

Vocabulary: Days and Weeks (2) 

kinoo yesterday
ototoi the day before yesterday
senshuu last week
sensenshuu the week before last

	Su	M	T	W	Th	F	Sa
sensenshuu							
senshuu							
konshuu		ototoi	kinoo	kyoo	ashita	asatte	
raishuu							
saraishuu							

Dialogue 1 MIYAI: What did you eat last night? HAYASHI: Well, last night... I ate sukiyaki. MIYAI: Anything else? HAYASHI: Well, anything else... I ate yakitori.

Vocabulary Library 

Question Words

nani, nan	What
nan-ji	what time
itsu	when
dare	who
doko	where
donna	what kind of
dochira	which one (*between two*)
dore	which (*among three or more*)

Activity 1 

First, listen to your teacher or CD while looking at the following schedule, which describes what Linda Brown did yesterday.

LINDA BROWN'S SCHEDULE FOR YESTERDAY

5:00 A.M.	okimashita (*got up*)
5:30 A.M.	sanpo shimashita (*took a walk*)
6:25 A.M.	asagohan o tabemashita (*ate breakfast*)
8:00 A.M.	gakkoo e ikimashita (*went to school*)
11:50 A.M.	kafeteria de hirugohan o tabemashita (*ate lunch at a cafeteria*)
1:00 P.M.	Kawamura-san to hanashimashita (*talked with Mr. Kawamura*)
3:30 P.M.	toshokan e ikimashita (*went to the library*)
5:45 P.M.	uchi e kaerimashita (*returned home*)
6:15 P.M.	bangohan o tabemashita (*ate dinner*)
8:00 P.M.	terebi o mimashita (*watched TV*)
9:20 P.M.	hon o yomimashita (*read a book*)
11:30 P.M.	nemashita (*went to sleep*)

Can you tell the difference between verb forms expressing daily, habitual actions and those expressing past actions?

Now answer the following questions.

Example:

> Buraun-san wa kinoo nan-ji ni okimashita ka. (*What time did Ms. Brown get up yesterday?*) →
> Gozen 5-ji ni okimashita. (*At 5:00 A.M.*)

1. Gozen 5-ji han ni nani o shimashita ka. (*What did she do at 5:30 A.M.?*)
2. Nan-ji ni asagohan o tabemashita ka.
3. Nan-ji ni gakkoo e ikimashita ka.

4. Nan-ji ni hirugohan o tabemashita ka.
5. Gogo 1-ji ni nani o shimashita ka.
6. Nan-ji ni uchi e kaerimashita ka.
7. Nan-ji ni bangohan o tabemashita ka.
8. Gogo 8-ji kara 9-ji nijippun made nani o mimashita ka.
9. Kinoo nan-ji goro nemashita ka.

Can you answer the following questions?

10. Gozen 6-ji 25-hun ni nani o shimashita ka.
11. Gozen 8-ji ni doko e ikimashita ka.
12. Doko de hirugohan o tabemashita ka.
13. Gogo 1-ji ni dare to hanashimashita ka.
14. Gogo 8-ji kara 9-ji nijippun made nani o shimashita ka.
15. Kinoo no yoru nani o yomimashita ka.

Activity 2 

Step 1: Write down your schedule for yesterday in English.
Step 2: Work in pairs. Explain your schedule to your partner in Japanese.

Dialogue 2: Saying What One Drank the Night Before 

Dr. Miyai and Masao Hayashi continue the consultation.

MIYAI: O-sake wa nomimasu ka.
HAYASHI: Ee, chotto.
MIYAI: Kinoo wa?
HAYASHI: Zenzen nomimasen deshita.

Study Hint

Making a Generalization

Up to this point, you have heard many Japanese verb forms and you may have formed some of your own ideas about how Japanese verbs are conjugated. You may have already guessed the meaning of such particles as **ni, to,** and **de** or how to form question sentences using **nani, doko,** and **dare.** Reading a grammar book and memorizing grammar rules is not the only way to learn a new language. Making generalizations or guessing about grammatical rules or the meaning of vocabulary items will shorten the time it takes to acquire a new language. Don't be afraid to take risks. Don't hesitate to guess while listening or reading. Be willing to make generalizations. Risk takers are better language learners.

Dialogue 2 MIYAI: Do you drink sake? HAYASHI: Yes, a little bit. MIYAI: How about yesterday? HAYASHI: I didn't drink at all.

Activity 3

Now let's talk about your life. Answer the following questions.

1. Kinoo nan-ji ni okimashita ka.
2. Kinoo asagohan o tabemashita ka. Tabemasen deshita ka.
3. Kinoo gakkoo e kimashita ka. Kimasen deshita ka.
4. Kinoo koohii o nomimashita ka. Nomimasen deshita ka.
5. Kinoo toshokan e ikimashita ka.
6. Kinoo Nihongo o benkyoo shimashita ka.
7. Senshuu kaimono ni ikimashita ka.
8. Senshuu eega o mimashita ka.

Inviting Someone to Do Something

Dialogue 3: Making Plans with Another Person 

Mei Lin Chin and Masao Hayashi are making plans.

CHIN: Hayashi-san, kyoo no gogo eega ni ikimasen ka.
HAYASHI: Kyoo no gogo desu ka. Kyoo wa nan'yoobi desu ka.
CHIN: Eeto, kin'yoobi desu.
HAYASHI: Jaa, daijoobu desu yo.

An apostrophe (') indicates that the preceding **n** is pronounced ん; it is not part of the following syllable.

言語ノート

Language Note: Invitation

You can invite someone to do something by using the nonpast, negative form of verbs plus **ka,** as the following sentences show.

Issho ni hirugohan o tabemasen ka.
Shall we eat lunch together?
Ashita jogingu shimasen ka.
Shall we jog tomorrow?
Eega o mimasen ka.
Shall we watch a movie?

When you accept an invitation, you can say

Ee, ii desu ne.
Yes, that's good.
Ee, yorokonde.
Yes, with pleasure

Dialogue 3 CHIN: Mr. Hayashi, shall we go to a movie this afternoon (lit., *today's P.M.*)? HAYASHI: This afternoon... What day of the week is it today? CHIN: Well, it's Friday. HAYASHI: Then, it's OK.

When you politely decline an invitation, you can say

> Chotto...
> *I cannot do that.* (lit., *a little bit...*)
> Sumimasen ga, chotto...
> *I'm sorry, but I cannot.* (lit., *I am sorry, but a little...*)
> Ee, demo chotto...
> *Yes, but I cannot do that.* (lit., *Yes, but a little...*)

Activity 4

Listen to your instructor or CD, and write down in English what the speaker is inviting someone else to do. Also, indicate whether or not the other speaker accepted an invitation.

Vocabulary: Days of the Week

nichiyoobi	Sunday
getsuyoobi	Monday
kayoobi	Tuesday
suiyoobi	Wednesday
mokuyoobi	Thursday
kin'yoobi	Friday
doyoobi	Saturday
konshuu no getsuyoobi	this Monday (lit., *Monday of this week*)
senshuu no kayoobi	last Tuesday (lit., *Tuesday of last week*)
raishuu no kin'yoobi	next Friday (lit., *Friday of next week*)
nan'yoobi	what day of the week?

Activity 5

Listen to your instructor or CD. On a separate sheet of paper write down what day of the week the speaker is asking someone else to do something with him or her.

1. ...
2. ...
3. ...
4. ...
5. ...

予定メモ	
1 日 仏滅	
2 月 大安	初午
3 火 赤口	節分 豆まき
4 水 先勝	立春
5 木 友引	
6 金 先負	
7 土 仏滅	
8 日 大安	針供養
9 月 赤口	
10 火 先勝	
11 水 友引	建国記念の日
12 木 先負	
13 金 仏滅	
14 土 大安	バレンタインデー
15 日 赤口	
16 月 先勝	
17 火 友引	「主婦の友」3月号発売日
18 水 先負	
19 木 仏滅	雨水
20 金 大安	
21 土 赤口	
22 日 先勝	
23 月 友引	
24 火 先負	
25 水 仏滅	
26 木 大安	
27 金 赤口	
28 土 友引	

Activity 6

Work in pairs. One of you will ask the other to do the following together. The latter will accept or decline the invitation. Practice by changing roles.

1. have lunch tomorrow
2. go to the library the day after tomorrow
3. watch TV this afternoon
4. have lunch at the cafeteria
5. study Japanese next week

Talking About Weekly Schedules

Dialogue 4: Making Plans for a Dinner 

Masao Hayashi and Mei Lin Chin are making arrangements to have dinner together.

HAYASHI: Chin-san, kin'yoobi issho ni yuugohan o tabemasen ka.
CHIN: Eeto, kin'yoobi desu ka. Kin'yoobi wa chotto…
HAYASHI: Sore wa zannen desu ne.
CHIN: Demo, doyoobi wa daijoobu desu yo.

Activity 7

Step 1: In your notebook, draw a grid and fill it in with your own activities from Sunday of last week through Saturday of next week.
Step 2: Work in pairs. Looking at your partner's grid, ask about his/her activities.

Talking About the Weather

Dialogue 5: Exchanging Greetings 

Linda Brown and her landlord, Kunio Sano, run into each other in front of Linda's apartment.

BURAUN: Ohayoo gozaimasu.
SANO: Ah, Buraun-san, ohayoo gozaimasu.
BURAUN: Ii otenki desu ne.
SANO: Soo desu ne.

Refer to the Language Note: Greetings, on page 8.

Dialogue 4 HAYASHI: Ms. Chin, shall we have dinner together on Friday? CHIN: Well, Friday is not good. (lit., *Is it Friday? A little bit…*) HAYASHI: That's too bad. (lit., *That's regrettable.*) CHIN: But Saturday is OK with me.

Dialogue 5 BROWN: Good morning. SANO: Oh, Ms. Brown. Good morning. BROWN: It's nice weather, isn't it? SANO: Yes, that's right.

Vocabulary: Weather Expressions Often Used as Greetings 

Ii otenki desu ne.	It's good/nice weather, isn't it?
Hidoi otenki desu ne.	It's terrible weather, isn't it?
Hidoi ame desu ne.	It's raining hard, isn't it?
Hidoi yuki desu ne.	It's snowing a lot, isn't it?
Kyoo wa samui desu ne.	It's cold today, isn't it?
Kyoo wa atsui desu ne.	It's hot today, isn't it?
Kyoo wa atatakai desu ne.	It's warm today, isn't it?
Kyoo wa suzushii desu ne.	It's cool today, isn't it?

Activity 8

Work in pairs. Practice greeting each other in the following situations.

1. 

2. 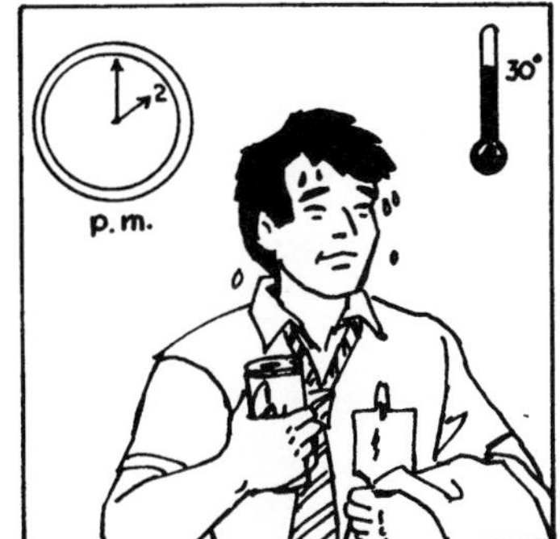

3. 

4. 

5. 

The Japanese Writing System (4)

Katakana (1)

The second syllabary used in writing Japanese is very similar to **hiragana.** The forty-six symbols represent the same sounds and many even resemble their **hiragana** counterparts. The differences are in appearance and in use. **Katakana** is more angular compared to the flowing lines of **hiragana.** Generally speaking, the use of **katakana** is restricted to loanwords, onomatopoeic (sound effect) words, and words the writer wishes to emphasize. Plant and animal names are also often written in **katakana.**

Over the centuries the Japanese language has borrowed many foreign words from Chinese and Western languages, especially English, French, and German. In transcribing Western loanwords, the Japanese usually try to replicate the foreign pronunciation with **katakana.** Thus, *Porsche* becomes **porushe,** ポルシェ. Because foreign loanwords give an impression of sophistication and modernity, you will find them used frequently in fashion magazines and advertisements and among young urbanites, even when a perfectly good native Japanese word exists.

Included in the category of onomatopoeic words written with **katakana** are words expressing natural sounds (*meow, bang,* etc.) and those expressing manner (*twinkle, zigzag,* etc.). There are so many **katakana** words in Japanese that entire dictionaries are devoted just to foreign loanwords and to onomatopoeic words.

Here is the basic **katakana** syllabary.

ア a	イ i	ウ u	エ e	オ o
カ ka	キ ki	ク ku	ケ ke	コ ko
サ sa	シ shi	ス su	セ se	ソ so
タ ta	チ chi	ツ tsu	テ te	ト to
ナ na	ニ ni	ヌ nu	ネ ne	ノ no
ハ ha	ヒ hi	フ hu	ヘ he	ホ ho
マ ma	ミ mi	ム mu	メ me	モ mo
ヤ ya		ユ yu		ヨ yo
ラ ra	リ ri	ル ru	レ re	ロ ro
ワ wa				ヲ o
ン n				

Use the diacritical marks ﾞ and ﾟ, just as you do in **hiragana.**

ガ ga	ギ gi	グ gu	ゲ ge	ゴ go
ザ za	ジ ji	ズ zu	ゼ ze	ゾ zo
ダ da	ヂ ji	ヅ zu	デ de	ド do
バ ba	ビ bi	ブ bu	ベ be	ボ bo
パ pa	ピ pi	プ pu	ペ pe	ポ po

Similarly, add small ヤ **ya,** ユ **yu,** and ヨ **yo** just as in **hiragana.**

キャ kya	キュ kyu	キョ kyo
シャ sha	シュ shu	ショ sho
チャ cha	チュ chu	チョ cho
ニャ nya	ニュ nyu	ニョ nyo
ヒャ hya	ヒュ hyu	ヒョ hyo
ミャ mya	ミュ myu	ミョ myo
リャ rya	リュ ryu	リョ ryo
ギャ gya	ギュ gyu	ギョ gyo
ジャ ja	ジュ ju	ジョ jo
ビャ bya	ビュ byu	ビョ byo
ピャ pya	ピュ pyu	ピョ pyo

Double Vowels

In **katakana,** double vowels are written with the vowel extender ー**(choo-on kigoo).**

aato	アート	*art*
kii	キー	*key*
suutsu	スーツ	*suit*
sukeeto	スケート	*skate, skating*
nooto	ノート	*notebook*

Double Consonants

As in **hiragana,** double consonants are written with a small ッ **tsu** that doubles the following consonant.

katto	カット	*cut*
beddo	ベッド	(*Western-style*) *bed*

Vocabulary

This is a list of words that you have used or heard in Part 4 of this textbook. Before beginning Part 5, make sure that you know the words listed under the categories **Greetings and Polite Expressions, Time Expressions**, and **Other Useful Words.** These are considered active vocabulary.

For your reading practice this list is rendered in **hiragana** and **katakana.** In authentic writing, **kanji** would be used in many words.

Greetings and Polite Expressions

Ohayoo gozaimasu.	おはようございます。	Good morning. (*formal*)
Yorokonde	よろこんで	with pleasure

Time Expressions

kinoo	きのう	yesterday
ototoi	おととい	the day before yesterday
senshuu	せんしゅう	last week
sensenshuu	せんせんしゅう	the week before last
mainichi	まいにち	every day

Days of the Week

nichiyoobi	にちようび	Sunday
getsuyoobi	げつようび	Monday
kayoobi	かようび	Tuesday
suiyoobi	すいようび	Wednesday
mokuyoobi	もくようび	Thursday
kin'yoobi	きんようび	Friday
doyoobi	どようび	Saturday
konshuu no getsuyoobi	こんしゅうのげつようび	this Monday (lit., *Monday of this week*)
senshuu no kayoobi	せんしゅうのかようび	last Tuesday (lit., *Tuesday of last week*)
raishuu no kin'yoobi	らいしゅうのきんようび	next Friday (lit., *Friday of next week*)
nan'yoobi	なんようび	what day of the week?

Question Words

dare	だれ	who
dochira	どちら	which (*among three or more*)
doko	どこ	where
donna	どんな	what kind of
dore	どれ	which one (*between two*)
itsu	いつ	when
nani	なに	what
nan-ji	なんじ	what time

Foods/Beverages

sukiyaki	すきやき	sukiyaki
yakitori	やきとり	yakitori

Other Useful Words

atatakai	あたたかい	warm (weather)
atsui	あつい	hot (weather)
daijoobu	だいじょうぶ	OK (lit., *safe*)
hidoi	ひどい	hard, terrible, a lot
ii otenki	いいおてんき	nice/good weather
issho ni	いっしょに	together
samui	さむい	cold (weather)
suzushii	すずしい	cool (weather)
zannen desu ne	ざんねんですね	that's too bad (lit., *that's regrettable*)
hoka no (ni)	ほかの（に）	other (*in addition*)

Part Five

Objectives

Asking location
Numbers from 21 to 10,000
Asking about existence
Asking about price
Talking more about likes and dislikes
The Japanese writing system (5): **Katakana** (2); Uses of **kanji, hiragana,** and **katakana; Introduction to kanji**

Asking Location

Dialogue 1: Asking Where Something Is Located 

John Kawamura is at a department store.

KAWAMURA: Sumimasen. Kasa wa doko desu ka.
TEN'IN: Hai, kasa wa san-kai desu.
KAWAMURA: A, soo desu ka. Arigatoo gozaimasu.
TEN'IN: (*bows*).

Hai, kasa wa san-kai desu.

Dialogue 1 KAWAMURA: Excuse me. Where are the umbrellas? CLERK: (Yes.) They are on the third floor. KAWAMURA: Oh, I see. (Lit., *Oh, is that right?*) Thank you. CLERK: (*bows*).

One way to ask the location of something is to say

____ wa doko desu ka. *Where is ____?*

To indicate the location of something, say

____ wa (*place*) desu. ____ *is at/on* (*place*).

Use the counter suffix **-kai** to name floors of a building. Add **chika** (*underground*) before the number to indicate a basement level. For example, **chika san-kai** (often written as **B3** in Japan) is three stories underground.

Floors of a Building

B1 chika ik-kai
1 ik-kai
2 ni-kai
3 san-kai
4 yon-kai
5 go-kai
6 rok-kai
7 nana-kai
8 hachi-kai (*or* hak-kai)
9 kyuu-kai
10 juk-kai (*or* jik-kai)
11 juu-ik-kai

An alternate pronunciation for the third floor is **san-gai.**

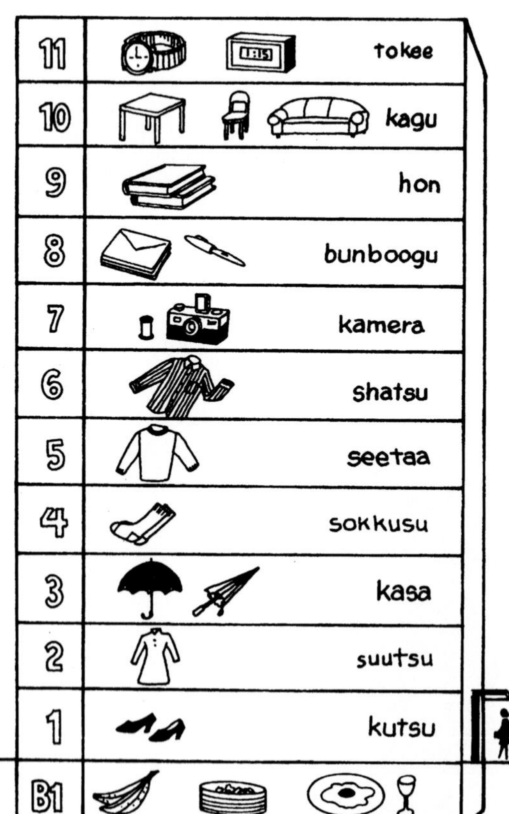

Activity 1

Ask a classmate where the following items are, referring to the store directory and using Dialogue 1 as a model.

1. kamera
2. seetaa
3. sokkusu
4. suutsu
5. kagu
6. tokee
7. shatsu
8. hon
9. kaban
10. teeburu

Dialogue 2: Asking Where Someone's Home Is 

Linda Brown inquires about the location of John Kawamura's home.

BURAUN: Kawamura-san no uchi wa doko desu ka.
KAWAMURA: Setagaya desu.
BURAUN: Chotto tooi desu ne.
KAWAMURA: Ee.

Activity 2

Use the following map to practice Dialogue 2, making substitutions for the names and underlined parts.

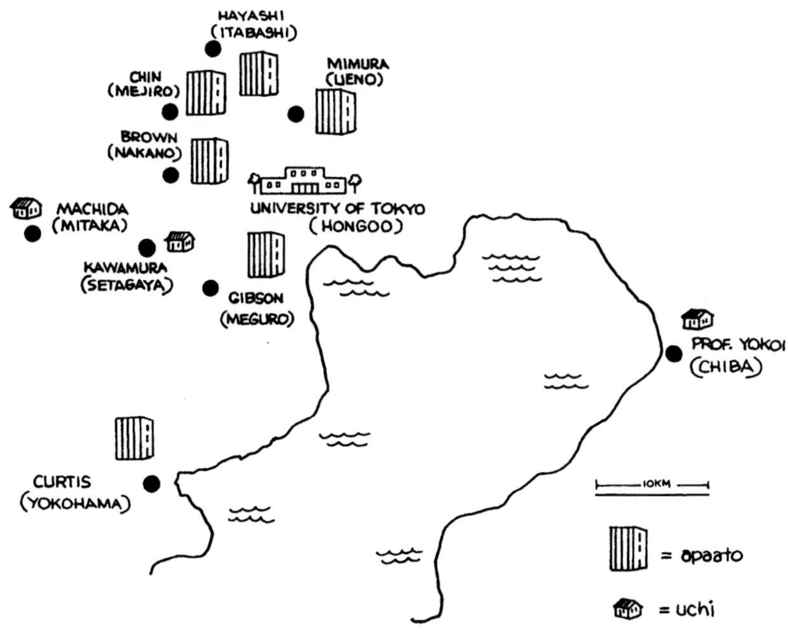

Dialogue 2 BROWN: Where is your house, Mr. Kawamura? KAWAMURA: It's in Setagaya. BROWN: That's a bit far, isn't it? KAWAMURA: Yes.

✷ Activity 3

Now ask a classmate where his or her house or apartment is. Do you think it is close to or far from your school?

Useful words:

uchi	*house, home* (informal)
apaato	*apartment*
ryoo	*dormitory*
daigaku	*university*
(Totemo) chikai desu.	*It's (very) close.*
(Totemo) tooi desu.	*It's (very) far.*

Numbers from 21 to 10,000

Large Numbers

21	ni-juu-ichi	700	nana-hyaku
29	ni-juu-kyuu, ni-juu-ku	800	hap-pyaku
30	san-juu	900	kyuu-hyaku
40	yon-juu	996	kyuu-hyaku-kyuu-juu-roku
50	go-juu	1,000	sen
60	roku-juu	2,000	ni-sen
70	nana-juu, shichi-juu	3,000	san-zen
80	hachi-juu	4,000	yon-sen
90	kyuu-juu	5,000	go-sen
99	kyuu-juu-kyuu, kyuu-juu-ku	6,000	roku-sen
100	hyaku	7,000	nana-sen
101	hyaku-ichi	8,000	has-sen
110	hyaku-juu	9,000	kyuu-sen
153	hyaku-go-juu-san	9,990	kyuu-sen-kyuu-hyaku-kyuu-juu
200	ni-hyaku		
300	san-byaku	9,999	kyuu-sen-kyuu-hyaku-kyuu-juu-ku
400	yon-hyaku		
500	go-hyaku	10,000	ichi-man
600	rop-pyaku		

✷ Activity 4

Read these numbers aloud.

1. 34
2. 66
3. 87
4. 108
5. 196
6. 459
7. 555
8. 803
9. 1,001
10. 1,562
11. 2,073
12. 5,555
13. 8,906
14. 9,713

Asking About Existence

Dialogue 3: Asking What's Available 

John Kawamura is at the student cafeteria of the University of Tokyo.

KAWAMURA: Sumimasen. Supagetti wa arimasu ka.
UEETORESU: Sumimasen ga, chotto...
KAWAMURA: Ja, hanbaagaa wa arimasu ka.
UEETORESU: Hai, arimasu.
KAWAMURA: Ja, hanbaagaa o onegai shimasu.
UEETORESU: Hai, 220-en desu.

Arimasu is a verb meaning *to exist* or *to have.* To ask whether something exists, say

___ wa arimasu ka. *Is there (Do you have) ___?*

言語ノート

Language Note: Saying No (Without Saying No)

Sumimasen ga, chotto... in Dialogue 3 literally means *I am sorry, but a little bit....* In Japan it is considered clumsy and impolite to say no directly. For example, in this case, to say **Iie, arimasen** (*No, we don't have any*) would be grammatically correct but socially inappropriate. There are a number of ways to indicate a negative answer indirectly. **Sumimasen ga, chotto...** or just **Chotto...** said with a trailing intonation is one of these strategies.

Activity 5

Now practice Dialogue 3 with a classmate, using the following menu.

Tookyoo Daigaku Kafeteria menyuu

supagetti	urikire	Nomimono	
piza	urikire	koora	¥100
suteeki	¥1100	juusu	¥180
sushi	urikire	aisu miruku	urikire
omuretsu	¥470	aisutii	¥120
raamen	¥400	koohii	¥150
Hanbaagaa		Saido Oodaa	
hanbaagaa	¥220	hurenchi hurai	¥90
chiizu baagaa	¥330	onion ringu	¥170
daburu baagaa	¥420	suupu	¥150
janbo baagaa	¥510	sarada	¥230
chikin baagaa	urikire		
fisshu baagaa	¥350		

Dialogue 3 KAWAMURA: Excuse me. Do you have spaghetti? WAITRESS: I'm sorry, but... KAWAMURA: Then, do you have hamburgers? WAITRESS: Yes, we do. KAWAMURA: Then, I would like a hamburger. WAITRESS: Certainly (lit., *Yes*). That's 220 yen.

Asking About Price

Dialogue 4: Asking How Much Something Is 

Linda Brown is at the university cafeteria.

BURAUN: Sumimasen. Chiizubaagaa wa arimasu ka.
UEETORESU: Hai, arimasu.
BURAUN: Ikura desu ka.
UEETORESU: 330-en desu.
BURAUN: Jaa, chiizubaagaa to koohii o onegai shimasu.
UEETORESU: Arigatoo gozaimasu. 480-en desu.

To is a particle meaning *and*. It can connect two or more nouns to express such meaning as *A and B* and *A, B, and* C.

言語ノート

Language Note: Asking Price

The most common way to ask how much something costs is to say **Ikura desu ka.**

—Kore wa ikura desu ka.	*How much is this?*
—3,000-en desu.	*It's 3,000 yen.*
—Kono tokee wa ikura desu ka.	*How much is this watch?*
—9,500-en desu.	*It's 9,500 yen.*

Dialogue 4 BROWN: Excuse me. Do you have cheeseburgers? WAITRESS: Yes, we do. BROWN: How much are they? WAITRESS: 330 yen. BROWN: Well then, please give me a cheeseburger and coffee. WAITRESS: Thank you. That will be 480 yen.

Dialogue 5: Ordering a Meal 

Heather Gibson is at the student cafeteria.

GIBUSON: Fisshubaagaa wa arimasu ka.
UEETORESU: Hai, arimasu.
GIBUSON: Ikura desu ka.
UEETORESU: 350-en desu.
GIBUSON: Ja, fisshubaagaa o onegai shimasu.
UEETORESU: O-nomimono wa ikaga desu ka.
GIBUSON: Ie, kekkoo desu.

...wa ikaga desu ka is commonly used to make a suggestion. More informally, **...wa doo desu ka** is used.

言語ノート

Language Note: *Kekkoo desu*

Kekkoo desu can mean *It's fine* or *No, thank you,* depending on the context. In Dialogue 5, **kekkoo desu** means *No, thank you.* In the following exchange, it means *It's fine.*

—Kore de ii desu ka. *Is this OK?*
—Ee, kekkoo desu. *Yes, it's fine.*

Activity 6

Pair up with a classmate and practice ordering at a **kissaten. Kissaten** are coffee shops where people go to talk or rendezvous with friends or business contacts, to relax, to eat, or just to kill time. Order from the coffee shop menu.

Dialogue 6: Ordering Coffee 

Henry Curtis is at a coffee shop.

KAATISU: Koohii wa arimasu ka.
UEETORESU: Hai. Aisu to hotto ga arimasu ga…
KAATISU: Soo desu ne. Aisu o onegai shimasu.
UEETORESU: 550-en desu.

Dialogue 5 GIBSON: Do you have fishburgers? WAITRESS: Yes, we do. GIBSON: How much are they? WAITRESS: 350 yen. GIBSON: Well then, I would like a fishburger. WAITRESS: How about something to drink? GIBSON: No, thank you.

Dialogue 6 CURTIS: Do you have coffee? WAITRESS: Yes. We have ice coffee and hot coffee. CURTIS: Let me see. Ice coffee, please. WAITRESS: 550 yen, please.

DRINKS
お 飲 物

ブレンドコーヒー …………………………… ¥400
YōKōのオリジナルの香りをお楽しみください。

アメリカンコーヒー ………………………… ¥400
一日に何回も飲む人のコーヒーです。

カフェオレ(Hot or Ice) ………………… ¥600
ミルクとコーヒー2つの味の調和をお楽しみください。

カフェウィンナー ………………………… ¥600
生クリームとコーヒーの2つの味を一度に味わってください。

カフェカプチーノ ………………………… ¥650
シナモンの香りをお楽しみください。

エスプレッソコーヒー …………………… ¥600
コクと香りの世界がお楽しみいただけます。

アイリッシュコーヒー …………………… ¥800
アイリッシュウイスキーの入った大人のコーヒーです。

レモンティー ……………………………… ¥400
ダージリン葉を使用した香り高い紅茶です。

ロイヤルティー …………………………… ¥600
本格派の紅茶。

ロシアンティー …………………………… ¥600
ジャムの甘さと紅茶の香りを楽しんでください。

フレーバーティー(アールグレ・アップル
・ストロベリー) …………………………… ¥500
飲むほどに味のある紅茶です。

ミルク(Hot or Ice) ……………………… ¥600

100パーセントFresh Juiceです。

オレンジジュース ………………………… ¥750

グレープフルーツジュース ……………… ¥800

グレープジュース ………………………… ¥800

アップルジュース ………………………… ¥650

レモンジュース …………………………… ¥750
サンキストレモンを絞った生の味です。

FOODS
お 食 事

サンドイッチはイギリスパンです。

ヒレカツサンドイッチ …………………… ¥1,200
カツの厚みとイギリスパンの調和した力作です。

フィンガーサンドイッチ ………………… ¥1,000
女性にやさしい一口タイプのサンドイッチです。

アメリカンクラブハウスサンドイッチ …… ¥1,500
ボリュームタップリのアメリカ風サンドイッチです。

ハンバーグサンドイッチ ………………… ¥1,000
牛肉と玉子だけのYōKō自満のサンドイッチです。

ワッフル …………………………………… ¥1,000
YōKōのオリジナルの味をお楽しみください。

A LA CARTE
アラカルト

フルーツ(季節ごとに変わります) …… ¥1,000
四季のバラエティーに富んだメニューです。

フルーツクリームヨーグルト …………… ¥800
アイスクリームとフルーツを添えたヨーグルトです。

ヨーグルトドリンク ……………………… ¥700
ヘルシー志向の人に最適な飲物です。

ココア ……………………………………… ¥800
ヨーロッパスタイルのやさしい飲物です。

ペリグリーノ ……………………………… ¥500
イタリア産自然炭酸水です。

ビール(小ビン) ………………………… ¥600

Koohii shoppu

Activity 7

Practice Dialogue 6 with your classmates, replacing the underlined parts with the following.

1. aisu kuriimu	banira	chokoreeto
2. juusu	orenji	gureepu
3. piza	peparoni	bejitarian
4. koocha	remon	miruku
5. koohii	moka	kona

Talking More About Likes and Dislikes

Dochira (*which*) is used to ask for a choice between two items. To choose among three or more items, use **dore.** Study these examples that use **dochira** to ask and answer which of two items is preferred.

Nihon ryoori to Itaria ryoori to dochira ga suki desu ka.
Between Japanese food and Italian food, which do you prefer?

Nihon ryoori ga suki desu.
I prefer Japanese food.

Dochira mo suki desu.
I like both.

Dochira mo kirai desu. Huransu ryoori ga suki desu.
I don't like either. I prefer French food.

Saa, wakarimasen ne.
Well, I don't know.

Uun… Muzukashii desu ne.
Um, it's tough.

Activity 8  

Listen to your instructor or the CD, and on a separate piece of paper write down the items that each person likes.

Activity 9

Work in pairs. Ask your partner which of the following he or she likes more.

1. yasai	niku
2. Itarian doresshingu	Hurenchi doresshingu
3. koohii	o-cha
4. tenisu	goruhu
5. jazu	kantorii ando uesutan

The Japanese Writing System (5)

Katakana (2)

In **katakana** you can use a small vowel symbol in combination with other symbols to create foreign sounds introduced into Japanese with loanwords.

イェ	ye	イェメン	yemen	*Yemen*
ウィ	wi	ウィンター	wintaa	*winter*
ウェ	we	ウェーター	weetaa	*waiter*
ウォ	wo	ウォーター	wootaa	*water*
キェ	kye	キェー	kyee	(screaming sound)
ギェ	gye	ギェー	gyee	(screaming sound)
クァ	kwa	クァトロ	kwatoro	*cuatro* (Spanish)
クィ	kwi	クィック	kwikku	*quick*
クェ	kwe	クェート	kweeto	*Kuwait*
クォ	kwo	クォーター	kwootaa	*quarter*
シェ	she	シェイプアップ	sheipuappu	*workout*
ジェ	je	ジェリー	jerii	*Jerry*
チェ	che	チェーン	cheen	*chain*
ツァ	tsa	ツァー	tsaa	*Tsar*
ツェ	tse	ツェッペリン	Zepperin	*(Led) Zeppelin*
ツォ	tso	ツォイス	tsoisu	*Zeus* (German)
ティ	ti	ティー	tii	*tea*
ディ	di	ディーゼル	diizeru	*diesel*
デュ	dyu	プロデューサー	purodyuusaa	*producer*
トゥ	tu	トゥエンティー	tuentii	*twenty*
ドゥ	du	ドゥー	duu	*do (it yourself)*
ヒェ	hye	ヒェー	hyee	(screaming sound)
ファ	fa	ファッション	fasshon	*fashion*
フィ	fi	フィルム	firumu	*film*
フュ	fyu	フュージョン	fyuujon	*fusion*
フェ	fe	フェリー	ferii	*ferryboat*
フォ	fo	フォーム	foomu	*form*
ヴァ	va	ヴァイオリン	vaiorin	*violin*
ヴィ	vi	ヴィオラ	viora	*viola*
ヴ	vu	クリスマス・イヴ	kurisumasu ibu	*Christmas Eve*
ヴェ	ve	ベートーヴェン	Beetooven	*Beethoven*
ヴォ	vo	ヴォリューム	voryuumu	*volume*

Some Japanese transcribe the foreign sound [v] as ヴ, but most simply use バ、ビ、ブ、ベ、or ボ、which represent the more usual Japanese pronunciation. Note that the **katakana** spelling of foreign loanwords may differ from person to person, depending on each speaker's pronunciation.

言語ノート

Language Note: Katakana Kuizu

According to one survey, about 5 percent of the vocabulary listed in a medium-size Japanese dictionary for native speakers are **katakana** loanwords from Western languages. (These **katakana** loanwords are usually called **gairaigo.**) In fact, more and more **gairaigo** are used every day in Japan, reflecting the increasing interaction of Japanese people with foreigners and foreign countries. **Gairaigo** is pervasive in Japan. Let's take a look at one typical young Japanese urbanite, Mr. Kimura. Can you guess what each **katakana** word means? (Answers are in Appendix 4, p. 510.)

Mr. Kimura lives in an **apaato** in the suburbs of Tokyo. He gets up with the noisy sound of an **araamu kurokku.** He shaves with a **sheebaa** and brushes his teeth with a **ha-burashi.** He eats **toosuto** with **bataa** and **jamu** and drinks **koohii** for breakfast. He goes to work in his **ootomachikku (kaa)** with **kaa sutereo, san ruuhu,** and **ea kon.** On the way to his company, he listens to **shiidii** of **pop myuujikku.** He arrives at the **biru** of his company at 8:45 A.M. From underground **paakingu** he goes to his **ofisu** by **erebeetaa.** Between noon and 1 P.M. is his **ranchi taimu.** He eats lunch at a nearby **resutoran.** He likes **karee raisu.** After lunch, he goes to the **koohii shoppu** and has **remon tii.** After work, he has a **deeto** with his **fianse,** who is a **konpyuuta puroguramaa** at the same company. He plans to marry her, so he gave her an **engeeji ringu** last month. After eating **dinaa** at a **Huransu resutoran,** they go for a **doraibu** to the top of a mountain. From there, they can see the beautiful **neon** of the city. After returning home from his **deeto,** Mr. Kimura drinks **uisukii.** He takes a **shawaa.** He sleeps in a **beddo.**

Uses of **Kanji, Hiragana,** and **Katakana**

As you now know, to write modern Japanese you need to use a combination of **kanji** (*Chinese characters*), **hiragana,** and **katakana.** The general rules of each script's use can be summarized as follows.

1. **Kanji** are usually used to represent such content words as nouns, adjective roots, adverbs, and verb roots.
2. **Hiragana** is used to represent, in most cases, such functional words as particles, verb conjugational endings, and so forth.
3. **Katakana** is used to represent loanwords from Western languages and onomatopoeic words.

For instance,

兄	は	フランス	から	帰	りました。
kanji	hiragana	katakana	hiragana	kanji	hiragana

兄	*older brother* (noun)
は	(topic particle [functional word])
フランス	*France* (loanword)
から	*from* (particle)
帰	*to return* (verb stem)
りました	(past, polite form [verb conjugational ending])

By the way, the only exception to writing with all three scripts is children's books (because young children have not studied many **kanji, hiragana** is used phonetically in place of **kanji**).

言語ノート

Language Note: Word Space and Punctuation

In Japanese writing, no space is used between words. An exception is books and other written materials for young children: Because they are written entirely in **hiragana** and **katakana,** they need word spaces to make them readable. The lack of word spacing in written Japanese is due to the influence of Chinese writing, which does not use spaces between words. Moreover, word boundaries are quite clear when **hiragana, katakana,** and **kanji** are intermixed. In fact, in many cases the changes in script in a sentence coincide with word boundaries.

Similarly, the co-use of the three systems makes it possible for readers to easily tell where a clause or sentence ends. For this reason, a punctuation system was not fully developed until about fifty years ago. In modern Japanese, the following punctuation marks are used.

。	**maru**	a period, a question mark
、	**ten**	a comma
「」	**kagikakko**	quotation marks
・	**nakaten**	midpoint
…	**santen riidaa**	ellipsis points

The Japanese period is used to end a sentence, but the usage of the Japanese comma is not clear-cut. It resembles the English comma, but writers vary in how they use it. The quotation marks are used to set off quoted speech, titles of works (books, movies, etc.), and words the writer wishes to emphasize (somewhat as English writers underline words). The midpoint separates the individual words of **katakana** loanwords (e.g., トレーニング・センター), including personal names (the midpoint occurs between the first and last name; e.g., リンダ・ブラウン), or connects two nouns with the meaning *and.* Finally, as in English, Japanese ellipsis points are used to indicate missing words. You will also occasionally see question marks and exclamation points, both borrowed from Western languages.

Introduction to **Kanji**

Japan's Ministry of Education requires Japanese grade schools to teach 1,006 **kanji** from grades one through six. These **kanji** are called **kyooiku kanji** (*educational Chinese characters*). By the time they graduate from high school, Japanese are expected to know a total of 1,945 **kanji.** These 1,945 **kanji** are called **jooyoo kanji** (*Chinese characters for everyday use*). Not only must students learn these **kanji,** but the Ministry of Education also recommends that newspapers and magazines use only **jooyoo kanji** plus about 280 other characters used in people's names (or else provide the pronunciation for the unsanctioned **kanji**). Generally, educated Japanese know more than these required **kanji.**

Kanji represent both sound and meaning. Most characters have more than one sound or reading. Centuries ago, when **kanji** were originally borrowed from Chinese for transcribing spoken Japanese, their Chinese pronunciations came along with them. These Chinese readings are called **on-yomi** (**on**-*readings*). When Chinese characters were used to write Japanese concepts or words, the native Japanese pronunciations were also assigned to the characters. These native Japanese readings are called **kun-yomi** (**kun**-*readings*). For historical reasons, many **kanji** have more than one **on**-reading and more than one **kun**-reading. How do you know which reading applies? The answer is context. For instance, the character 人 meaning *person* is read **hito** in the phrase あの人 (*that person*), but it is read **jin** in the word アメリカ人 (*American*). In 三人 (*three people*), 人 is read **nin. Hito** is the **kun-yomi,** and **jin** and **nin** are the **on-yomi.** The more you practice reading Japanese and the more thoroughly you master spoken language, the more quickly and intuitively you will be able to choose the correct reading.

言語ノート

Language Note: Hurigana

Because one **kanji** may have several different pronunciations (e.g., twenty for the character 生), it can be difficult even for native speakers of Japanese to remember all of them. For rarely occurring pronunciations and for rarely used **kanji** (those not included in the standard 1,945), the remedy is **hurigana.** This tiny **hiragana** or **katakana** written above the character (or to the right in vertical writing) provides the correct reading. You will see much **hurigana** in children's books, books dealing with difficult subjects, and textbooks for Japanese language students. Here is a sample of what it looks like.

佐野(さの)さんの御夫婦(ごふうふ)はわたしのアパートの管理人(かんりにん)です。

山本(やまもと)さんの勤(つと)める喫茶店(きっさてん)は中野(なかの)の住宅街(じゅうたくがい)にあります。

言語ノート

Language Note: Vertical Writing and Horizontal Writing

Japanese can be written both vertically and horizontally. Vertical writing is commonly used in newspapers and magazines. The lines are read from right to left and from top to bottom. Literature books also follow this system. Textbooks, except Japanese language textbooks for native speakers, generally use horizontal writing, in which case you read letters from left to right. Horizontal writing is especially common in books that include many foreign words, mathematical formulas, and so on. When Japanese people write a letter, they use either vertical or horizontal writing depending on their personal preference (formal letters are usually vertically written). Young people seem to prefer using horizontal writing in letters.

再生によって古くなったり傷んだ組織をリフレッシュメントできないか

阿形清和

I. 修理と治療

「古くなったもの・悪くなったものは切って捨て、よいもの・新しいものに交換する。」不況下のリストラのパターンとして定着しつつあるが、最新メカの修理パターンでもある。研究機器が壊れて修理を頼むと、サービスマンが来て何を修理するかと思えば、ただ基板を交換して帰るだけで何万円と修理費を取られることになる。昔は、修理といえば、壊れた部品を取り出してサービスマンが念入りにチェックして修理する姿を思い浮かべたものだったが。最近は修理＝交換というパターンが定着してしまった。

人間の病気を治す場合は、修理とよばずに治療というのだが、移植による治療は上にあげた機械の修理とほぼ精神を同じくしているよう気がする。悪くなった臓器を取り出し、健常な他人の臓器を移植する。この大胆なアイデアを誰が考え、初めて実行したかは知らないが、生き物としての人間を一歩進んでロボットのようなものとして見たこの治療法は、人類史上特筆すべきものであることは間違いない。移植が行われた当初においては、悪魔の治療法だとか何やかやと騒がれたに違いないのだが、今では、脳死判定が話題になっても移植そのものが話題になることはなくなっている。それほど移植が定着し、さらに、時代は人工臓器へと移行しつつある。丸ごと交換の時代なのである。

II. 再生で細胞のリフレッシュメントはできないか

そんな時代に、再生による治療などと時代錯誤的な特集を組んだとお思いの読者も多いかもしれない。

Refreshment of Adult Tissues by Regeneration
AGATA Kiyokazu 姫路工業大学理学部生命科学科

1

コンピュータがある教室

1988年2月某日。

わたしは、大学の池の見える教室にいます。

教室とはいってもこの教室はふつうの教室とはちょっと違っています。教室には、黒板も教卓もありません。16台のパソコンが向い合わせに3列ならんでいるだけです。16台ぜんぶのパソコンの前には学生がひとりずつすわっています。

ときどき、キーボードをたたく音がします。本のページをくる音がします。

「くやしい、これが絶対正解だと思ったのに。」

「ああ、また最初からやりなおし。これで3回目だ。」

こんな声が聞こえてきます。

ここは、神戸学院大学のCAI教育施設、通称761教室です。CAIとは、Computer Assisted（または Aided）Instruction を省略したことばで、コンピュータを使った教育であることはごぞんじですね。

Vocabulary

This is a list of words that you have used or heard in Part 5 of this textbook. Make sure that you know the words listed under the categories **Greetings and Polite Expressions, Classroom, Numbers,** and **Other Useful Words.** These are considered active vocabulary.

For your reading practice this list is rendered in **hiragana** and **katakana.** In authentic writing, **kanji** would be used in many words.

Greetings and Polite Expressions

Chotto.	ちょっと。	Well (no)… (lit., *A little*…)
Ikaga desu ka	いかがですか。	How about…
Kekkoo desu.	けっこうです。	No, thanks.
Onegai shimasu.	おねがいします。	Please (give me)…

Classroom

kaban	かばん	bag
teeburu	テーブル	table

Numbers

san-juu	さんじゅう	thirty
yon-juu	よんじゅう	forty
go-juu	ごじゅう	fifty
roku-juu	ろくじゅう	sixty
nana-juu, shichi-juu	ななじゅう、しちじゅう	seventy
hachi-juu	はちじゅう	eighty
kyuu-juu	きゅうじゅう	ninety
hyaku	ひゃく	one hundred
ni-hyaku	にひゃく	two hundred
san-byaku	さんびゃく	three hundred
yon-hyaku	よんひゃく	four hundred
go-hyaku	ごひゃく	five hundred
rop-pyaku	ろっぴゃく	six hundred
nana-hyaku	ななひゃく	seven hundred
hap-pyaku	はっぴゃく	eight hundred
kyuu-hyaku	きゅうひゃく	nine hundred
sen	せん	one thousand
ni-sen	にせん	two thousand
san-zen	さんぜん	three thousand
yon-sen	よんせん	four thousand
go-sen	ごせん	five thousand
roku-sen	ろくせん	six thousand
nana-sen	ななせん	seven thousand
has-sen	はっせん	eight thousand
kyuu-sen	きゅうせん	nine thousand
ichi-man	いちまん	ten thousand

Foods/Beverages

aisu	アイス	ice coffee/ice
aisukuriimu	アイスクリーム	ice cream
banira	バニラ	vanilla
bejitarian	ベジタリアン	vegetarian
chiizubaagaa	チーズバーガー	cheeseburger
chokoreeto	チョコレート	chocolate
gureepu	グレープ	grape(s)
hanbaagaa	ハンバーガー	hamburger
hotto	ホット	hot coffee
koohii	コーヒー	coffee
orenji	オレンジ	orange
peparoni	ペパロニ	pepperoni
piza	ピザ	pizza
regyuraa	レギュラー	regular (*not decaf*)
supagetti	スパゲッティ	spaghetti
yasai	やさい	vegetable

Nouns

apaato	アパート	apartment
daigaku	だいがく	university
jiinzu	ジーンズ	jeans
kagu	かぐ	furniture
kamera	カメラ	camera
kasa	かさ	umbrella
ryoo	りょう	dormitory
seetaa	セーター	sweater
shatsu	シャツ	shirt
sokkusu	ソックス	socks
suutsu	スーツ	suit
tokee	とけい	watch
uchi	うち	house, home

Other Useful Words

-en	～えん	¥___ (*counter for yen*)
-kai	～かい	___ floor (*counter for floors of a building*)
chotto	ちょっと	a little
ikura	いくら	how much?
kono	この	this ___
tooi	とおい	far
chikai	ちかい	close, nearby

チェックリスト

Use this checklist to confirm that you can now

- □ Greet others and introduce yourself
- □ Talk about your classroom
- □ Use numbers up to 10,000
- □ Ask and tell telephone numbers and time
- □ Ask what something is
- □ Talk about daily activities
- □ Talk about future activities and events
- □ Talk about activities and events in the past
- □ Express what you like and dislike
- □ Invite someone to do something
- □ Talk about weekly schedules
- □ Talk about the weather
- □ Ask about location, existence, and price

Introduction to *Yookoso!*

Now that you have finished **Getting Started,** we can say welcome **(yookoso)** to the heart of your textbook. Here you will begin studying grammar, **kanji** (*Chinese characters*), and other essentials for mastering Japanese. The rest of this book is divided into seven chapters, each of which revolves around a single theme—classmates, daily life, food, shopping, and so on.

When you start a chapter, take a look at the list of objectives to get a good idea of what you will learn and to focus your mind on the reasons for studying the material.

Following that list, each chapter has three parts called ***Vocabulary and Grammar***. They contain two sections: **Vocabulary and Oral Activities** and **Grammar and Practice Activities.**

The **Vocabulary and Oral Activities** section introduces vocabulary relating to the chapter theme and includes one or two (or sometimes more) oral activities that will help you learn and use these new words and expressions.

Grammar and Practice Activities contains one or more grammar points. Each point begins with brief dialogues illustrating the use of the new grammar in context. These dialogues are followed by explanations of the grammar. Oral and written activities allow you to practice the new grammar using vocabulary you already know.

Language Skills is the part of the chapter where you'll put your new knowledge of vocabulary and grammar to work in more real-life situations.

The first section of this part is called **Reading and Writing.** It contains two reading selections with activities and two writing activities. The reading materials relate to the chapter topics, and the writing focuses on the vocabulary and grammatical structures you have just studied, so it will be very useful to review the vocabulary and **kanji** lists at the end of the chapter before doing these activities.

In **Language Functions and Situations,** you will study important functional expressions used to apologize, to ask for directions, to ask someone to repeat, and so on. You'll practice how to communicate in a restaurant or a department store. Dialogues in this section are models for interaction with native speakers in many real-life situations, and activities and role play provide you with opportunities to practice handling those situations.

The conversations and narrations you hear in the **Listening Comprehension** section will be on the now-familiar topics covered in the chapter. These activities will strengthen your ability to understand spoken Japanese.

Each chapter ends with a short section called ***Vocabulary,*** a summary list of words, expressions, and **kanji** that you are responsible for learning and being able to use in the chapter and in future chapters. These are the lists we suggest you review before you do the **Language Skills** part of each chapter.

After the ***Vocabulary*** and **kanji** lists is a checklist that you can use to check your progress on the chapter objectives. This is followed, at the very end of each chapter, by a two-page ***Review*** containing exercises that review the chapter's important vocabulary and grammatical structures one more time before leaving those topics.

Throughout the text you will see many more of the features you have already encountered in **Getting Started.** You will see authentic Japanese print materials that you would encounter in Japan—ads, tickets, and magazine clippings for example. You will also see many brief notes that will help you learn more about Japan and its language and people. Culture notes （文化ノート） offer useful cultural information. Linguistic notes （言語ノート） offer insights into interesting facts about the Japanese language, brief explanations of useful grammar points, and hints for communicating more effectively in Japanese.

So it's time to move ahead. Good luck and have fun.

1

第一章 クラスメート

Classmates

大学(だいがく)のキャンパス

Objectives

In this lesson you are going to

- Talk about nationalities and languages
- Learn to identify things and people
- Learn to express possession
- Learn to exchange personal information
- Talk about your campus
- Learn to use personal pronouns and demonstratives
- Learn to ask questions
- Write to a pen pal
- Learn to introduce friends
- Learn to introduce yourself

YOOKOSO! MULTIMEDIA

Review and practice grammar and vocabulary from this chapter and watch video clips on the *Yookoso!* Interactive CD-ROM. Visit the *Yookoso!* Online Learning Center at **www.mhhe.com/yookosome** for additional exercises and resources.

Vocabulary and Grammar 1A

Vocabulary and Oral Activities

Nationalities and Languages

アクティビティー 1

ダイアログ：この人はだれですか。(*Who is this person?*)

山口さんとカワムラさんが写真を見ています。

山口： この人はだれですか。
カワムラ： その人はブラウンさんです。
山口： 大学のクラスメートですか。
カワムラ： はい、そうです。

Yamaguchi-san to Kawamura-san ga shashin o mite imasu.

YAMAGUCHI: Kono hito wa dare desu ka.
KAWAMURA: Sono hito wa Buraun-san desu.
YAMAGUCHI: Daigaku no kurasumeeto desu ka.
KAWAMURA: Hai, soo desu.

Now ask about the other people in the photograph, modeling your conversation after the dialogue. Replace the underlined words as necessary. An alternate ending to the dialogue follows.

いいえ、違います。______ です。(Iie, chigaimasu. ______ desu.)
(*No, that's not right. He/She is ______.*)

Kawamura is a Japanese family name. Because John Kawamura is an American citizen, however, his name is written in **katakana.**

Mr. Yamaguchi and Mr. Kawamura are looking at a photo. YAMAGUCHI: Who is this person? KAWAMURA: That's Ms. Brown. YAMAGUCHI: Is she (your) classmate at the university? KAWAMURA: Yes, that's right.

Study Hint

This chapter continues to provide romanization, but try to refer to the Japanese writing as much as possible. From the next chapter on, you will be reading Japanese with no romanization as a crutch. Now is the time to start reading Japanese!

Vocabulary: People at School

クラスメート	**kurasumeeto**	classmate
友だち	**tomodachi**	friend
大学生	**daigakusee**	college student

Review: 学生(がくせい)、先生(せんせい)

NATIONALITIES AND LANGUAGES

Country	Nationality	Language
日本(にほん) Japan	日本人(にほんじん)	日本語(にほんご)
アメリカ U.S.	アメリカ人(じん)	英語(えいご)
イギリス England	イギリス人	英語(えいご)
イタリア Italy	イタリア人	イタリア語(ご)
カナダ Canada	カナダ人	英語(えいご)／フランス語(ご)
韓国(かんこく) South Korea	韓国人(かんこくじん)	韓国語(かんこくご)
シンガポール Singapore	シンガポール人	英語(えいご)／中国語(ちゅうごくご)
スペイン Spain	スペイン人	スペイン語(ご)
台湾(たいわん) Taiwan	台湾人(たいわんじん)	中国語(ちゅうごくご)
中国(ちゅうごく) China	中国人(ちゅうごくじん)	中国語(ちゅうごくご)
ドイツ Germany	ドイツ人	ドイツ語(ご)
ブラジル Brazil	ブラジル人	ポルトガル語(ご)
フランス France	フランス人	フランス語(ご)
香港(ほんこん) Hong Kong	香港人(ほんこんじん)	中国語(ちゅうごくご)
メキシコ Mexico	メキシコ人	スペイン語(ご)
ロシア Russia	ロシア人	ロシア語(ご)

言語ノート

Nationalities and Languages

With few exceptions, you can form the word for someone's nationality or language by attaching a suffix to the name of his or her country. Add the suffix 人(じん: *people/person*) for the nationality and 語 (ご: *language*) for the language. To ask someone's nationality or what language(s) he or she speaks, use the following expressions. Remember that since the subject isn't explicitly stated here, context will determine about whom you are talking.

> お国(くに)はどちらですか。—アメリカです。
> *What country are (you) from?—(I) am from America.*
> 何語(なにご)を話(はな)しますか。—英語(えいご)を話(はな)します。
> *What language(s) do (you) speak?—I speak English.*

You can also ask someone's nationality by saying 何人(なにじん)ですか. However, this question sounds very rude when asked of someone directly.

アクティビティー　2

チンさんは中国人(ちゅうごくじん)です。(*Ms. Chin is Chinese.*)

カワムラ：この人(ひと)はチン・メイリンさんです。
山口(やまぐち)：チンさんは中国人(ちゅうごくじん)ですか。
カワムラ：はい、そうです。中国語(ちゅうごくご)を話(はな)します。

KAWAMURA: Kono hito wa Chin Meirin-san desu.
YAMAGUCHI: Chin-san wa Chuugoku-jin desu ka.
KAWAMURA: Hai, soo desu. Chuugoku-go o hanashimasu.

Practice the dialogue based on the following information.

PERSON	COUNTRY
リンダ・ブラウン	アメリカ
ホセ・ロドリゲス	メキシコ
クロード・ミレー	フランス
ハンス・シュミット	ドイツ
アナ・ラポーソ	ブラジル
キム・チョンヒ	韓国(かんこく)

KAWAMURA: This is Ms. Mei-Lin Chin. YAMAGUCHI: Is Ms. Chin Chinese? KAWAMURA: Yes, that's right. She speaks Chinese.

Grammar and Practice Activities

1. Identification: The Copulaです

レストランで

カワムラ：すみません。あれは何(なん)ですか。
ウエーター：あれは「すきやき」です。
カワムラ：じゃ、あれをお願(ねが)いします。

ブラウン：あの人(ひと)は林(はやし)さんではありませんか。
カワムラ：どの人(ひと)ですか。
ブラウン：ほら、あの人(ひと)です。
カワムラ：いいえ、林(はやし)さんじゃありませんよ。

Reminder: 「 and 」 are quotation marks.

1.1 To identify people and things in Japanese, you can use the following grammatical structure, where X and Y are nouns or pronouns.

X	は	Y	です。	X is Y.
これ		ペン		*This is a pen.*
わたし		ブラウン		*I am Brown.*
すきやき	は	日本料理(にほんりょうり)	です。	*Sukiyaki is a Japanese dish.*
町田(まちだ)さん		学生(がくせい)		*Ms. Machida is a student.*
受付(うけつ)け		あそこ		*The reception desk is over there.*

This structure means *X is equivalent to Y*, *X is a member of the group Y*, or *X is described* (or *modified*) *by Y*.

は is usually called a *topic particle*. It indicates that the preceding noun is the topic of the sentence. For instance, in this sentence the speaker would like to talk about Mr. Takada.

高田(たかだ)さんはエンジニアです。
Mr. Takada is an engineer.

Usage of the topic particle will be discussed in more detail later.

At a restaurant KAWAMURA: Excuse me. What is that? WAITER: That's sukiyaki. KAWAMURA: Then, please give me that.

BROWN: Isn't that person Mr. Hayashi? KAWAMURA: Which person? BROWN: Over there. (lit., *Look.*) (I mean) that person. KAWAMURA: No, that's not Mr. Hayashi.

です is called the *copula*. It roughly corresponds to the verb *to be.* Like other Japanese verbs, です does not change form to agree with the subject of the sentence in number or person. In other words, (*I*) *am*, (*you*) *are*, (*he*) *is*, (*they*) *are,* and so on, are all expressed with the same form です. です also marks a certain level of politeness, which will be discussed later.

1.2 The negative form of です is ではありません (contracted to じゃありません in more informal speech).

X	は	Y	ではありません（じゃありません）。	X isn't Y.
これ	は	ペン	ではありません（じゃありません）。	*This is not a pen.*
わたし	は	ブラウン	ではありません（じゃありません）。	*I am not Brown.*
すきやき	は	中国料理（ちゅうごくりょうり）	ではありません（じゃありません）。	*Sukiyaki is not a Chinese dish.*
町田（まちだ）さん	は	先生（せんせい）	ではありません（じゃありません）。	*Ms. Machida is not a teacher.*
受付（うけつ）け	は	ここ	ではありません（じゃありません）。	*The reception desk is not here.*

1.3 Yes/No questions are formed in Japanese simply by adding か (the *interrogative* or *question particle*) to the end of a sentence. You can think of か as a verbal question mark.

あの人（ひと）は町田（まちだ）さんです。
That person is Ms. Machida.
あの人は町田さんですか。
Is that person Ms. Machida?

あの人は町田さんではありません。
That person is not Ms. Machida.
あの人は町田さんではありませんか。
Isn't that person Ms. Machida?
(rising intonation)

With falling intonation, this sentence can mean *Oh, I see. That person isn't Ms. Machida.*

Here are some typical ways to answer a yes/no question.

あの人（ひと）は町田（まちだ）さんですか。
Is that Ms. Machida?

YES

はい、町田（まちだ）さんです。
Yes, it's Ms. Machida.
はい、そうです。
Yes, that's right.

NO

いいえ、町田さんではありません。
（いいえ、町田さんじゃありません。）
No, it's not Ms. Machida.
いいえ、そうではありません。
（いいえ、そうじゃありません。）
No, that's not right.
いいえ、ちがいます。
No, that's wrong (lit., *different*).

OTHER

すみません、わかりません。
I'm sorry, but I don't know.

言語ノート

Alternative Questions

To ask either/or questions, string the two alternate questions together: A ですか。B ですか (*Is it A? Is it B?* or in smoother English, *Is it A or B?*).

あれは日本料理(にほんりょうり)ですか、中国料理(ちゅうごくりょうり)ですか。
Is that Japanese food or Chinese food?
これは万年筆(まんねんひつ)ですか、ボールペンですか。
Is this a fountain pen or a ballpoint pen?

1.4 The particle も means *too*. Substitute も for は in the X は Y です construction—X も Y です—to say that *X is a member of Y, too* (or *X, too, is described by* [or *equivalent to*] *Y*).

わたしはアメリカ人(じん)です。
I am an American.
— 本当(ほんとう)ですか。わたしもアメリカ人(じん)です。
— *Really? I am an American, too.*

アクティビティー 3

何人(なにじん)ですか。何語(なにご)を話(はな)しますか。(*What is his nationality? What language does he speak?*)

Answer these questions for each person listed below.

例(れい) ポール・マッカートニー →
ポール・マッカートニーはイギリス人(じん)です。英語(えいご)を話(はな)します。

例 *example(s)*

1. メル・ギブソン
2. ボリス・エリツィン
3. ジャッキー・チャン
4. ジュリア・ロバーツ
5. フリオ・イグレシアス
6. デイヴィッド・ボイ
7. 三島由紀夫(みしまゆきお)

アクティビティー 4

イギリス人です。(*He's English.*)

Can you describe someone famous or anyone around you with the following traits?

例(れい) イギリス人(じん)、英語(えいご)
→ ヒュー・グラントはイギリス人(じん)です。
英語(えいご)を話(はな)します。

1. オーストラリア人(じん)、英語(えいご)
2. 日本人(にほんじん)、日本語(ご)
3. メキシコ人(じん)、スペイン語(ご)
4. フランス人(じん)、フランス語(ご)
5. ドイツ人(じん)、ドイツ語(ご)

アクティビティー 5

スミスさんは先生です。(*Ms. Smith is a teacher.*)

Connect the appropriate words from the columns on the left and right to make…は …です sentences.

マドンナ	飲(の)み物(もの)
わたし	日本人(にほんじん)
アコード	学生(がくせい)
川端康成(かわばたやすなり)	アメリカ人(じん)
コーラ	コンピュータ
マッキントッシュ	ホンダの車(くるま) (car)

2. Possessive Particle の

2.1 の is a particle used to connect and relate nouns (or pronouns). The result is a noun phrase. X の Y means *Y of X* in a broad sense, and thus carries the meanings *Y belongs to X, Y is a part of X, Y is possessed by X, Y has a characteristic of X*, and so on, depending on the context.

N1	の	N2	
わたし		本(ほん)	*my book*
大学(だいがく)		図書館(としょかん)	*the university library*
町田(まちだ)さん	の	万年筆(まんねんひつ)	*Ms. Machida's fountain pen*
アメリカ		州(しゅう)	*a state in America*
コットン		ジーンズ	*cotton jeans*

Throughout this book, N1 stands for *a noun* and N2 stands for *another noun*, or *Noun 1* and *Noun 2*.

The particle の can connect more than two nouns or pronouns.

わたしの友(とも)だちの大学(だいがく)
my friend's university
三村(みむら)さんのガールフレンドの家(いえ)
the house of Mr. Mimura's girlfriend

2.2 When the item possessed is clear from the context, it can be omitted as shown in the following examples.

これはだれのセーターですか。—ブラウンさんのです。
Whose sweater is this? —It's Ms. Brown's.

あれもブラウンさんのセーターですか。—いいえ、町田(まちだ)さんのです。
Is that also Ms. Brown's sweater? —No, it's Ms. Machida's.

アクティビティー 6

友(とも)だちの名前(なまえ)は...。(*My friend's name is...*)

Complete these sentences with ...です.

[例(れい)] わたしは... →
わたしは東京大学(とうきょうだいがく)の学生(がくせい)です。*or*
わたしは21さいです。(*I'm 21 years old.*) *or*
わたしは10月生(がつう)まれです。(*I was born in October.*)

1. わたしの日本語の先生は. . . 。
2. わたしのクラスメートの＿＿＿さんは. . . 。
3. わたしの先生のなまえは. . . 。
4. マーガレット・サッチャーは. . . 。
5. ジョン・カワムラさんは. . . 。

Vocabulary and Grammar 1B

Vocabulary and Oral Activities

Personal Information

Vocabulary: Personal Information

名前	**namae**	name
出身	**shusshin**	origin; hometown
専攻	**senkoo**	major
学部	**gakubu**	(academic) department
学年	**gakunen**	year in school; school year
一年生	**ichinensee**	freshman
二年生	**ninensee**	sophomore
三年生	**sannensee**	junior
四年生	**yonensee**	senior
大学院生	**daigakuinsee**	graduate student

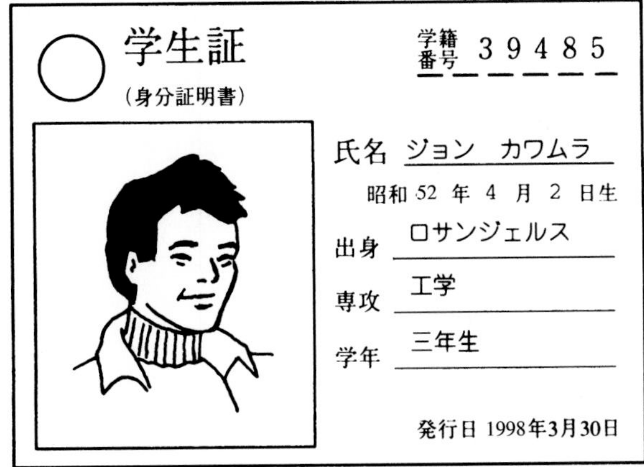
学生証
(身分証明書)
学籍番号 39485
氏名 ジョン カワムラ
昭和 52 年 4 月 2 日生
出身 ロサンジェルス
専攻 工学
学年 三年生
発行日 1998年3月30日

文化ノート

CULTURE NOTE • 出身(しゅっしん) Origins

Japanese often ask the question ご出身はどちらですか。(*Where are you from?*) To this question, a variety of responses is possible. You can give your hometown, the place where you were born, as the answer. For example, ロサンゼルスの出身です。(*I am from Los Angeles.*) If you moved away from your birthplace as a child and you have a stronger attachment to a different place, you can give that place as the answer. To Japanese, 出身 means the place you identify with geographically, mentally, and emotionally, so it has more meanings than *birthplace.* For example, the word is also used to indicate what school you graduated from and what social group you are from. Someone who graduated from the University of Tokyo might say 東京大学(とうきょうだいがく)の出身です。(*I am a graduate of* [lit., *I am from*] *the University of Tokyo.*) Or you might hear 農家(のうか)の出身です。(*I am from a farmer's family.*)

One of the reasons Japanese people ask this question so often is that the notions of in-group and out-group are of central importance in Japanese society. Depending on whether or not someone is a member of your group, your language, behavior, and attitude will differ. Asking this question is a way for Japanese to find out whether someone belongs to their in-group and to discover any common ground. To foreigners, Japanese will often substitute the question どちらのお国(くに)の方(かた)ですか。(*What country are you from?*) as a means to break the ice and identify any common experience.

Vocabulary Library 

Academic Subjects and Majors

人類学	**jinruigaku**	anthropology
美術	**bijutsu**	art
生物学	**seebutsugaku**	biology
化学	**kagaku**	chemistry
コンピュータ・サイエンス	**konpyuuta·saiensu**	computer science
経済学	**keezaigaku**	economics
教育学	**kyooikugaku**	education
工学	**koogaku**	engineering
外国語	**gaikokugo**	foreign languages
歴史学	**rekishigaku**	history
法学	**hoogaku**	law
言語学	**gengogaku**	linguistics
文学	**bungaku**	literature
数学	**suugaku**	mathematics
音楽	**ongaku**	music
哲学	**tetsugaku**	philosophy
物理学	**butsurigaku**	physics
政治学	**seejigaku**	political science
社会学	**shakaigaku**	sociology

If your major is not listed here, ask your instructor. Be aware, however, that some subjects frequently taught at North American universities are not taught at Japanese universities.

文化ノート

CULTURE NOTE • Japanese Universities and Colleges

In order to enter a Japanese university or college, you must take a nationally administered examination and/or an entrance exam specific to the school you wish to enter. These exams are usually held between January and March. (In Japan, the academic year starts in April.) The competition to enter prestigious national and private universities is severe, with medical schools and dental schools being the most difficult to get into. The extraordinarily intense pressure has led some to call this experience "examination hell." Many students who fail the entrance examination for the university of their choice decide to wait a year and retake the exam the following year, studying at a cram school or on their own in the meantime. These students are called 浪人 (ろうにん: *masterless samurai*).

When students apply to universities, they specify which department they wish to enter. During their freshman and sophomore years, however, students study a required core liberal arts curriculum consisting of 教養科目 (きょうようかもく: lit., *general education subjects*). As upperclassmen, they can study 専門科目 (せんもんかもく: *specialized subjects*).

While getting into a university can be extremely difficult, it is almost impossible to flunk out. Many students study little, treating the undergraduate years as a welcome break between the pressures of high school and the responsibilities to come later.

I passed the entrance exam of the University of Tokyo!

言語ノート

Academic Subjects and Departments

Most academic subjects are expressed by adding 学 (がく: [*study*] *of*) to a relevant noun. For example, 経済学 (けいざいがく: *economics*) is a combination of 経済 (けいざい: *economy*) and 学. Academic department names are formed by adding 学部 (がくぶ: *academic department, faculty*) to the same relevant noun. Thus, 経済 plus 学部 becomes *Department of Economics,* or 経済学部 (けいざいがくぶ). Similarly, 美術 (びじゅつ: *fine arts*) plus 学部 (*academic department*) becomes the *Department of Fine Arts,* or 美術学部 (びじゅつがくぶ). Japanese undergraduates typically identify their department as a way of stating their major.

わたしは文学部(ぶんがくぶ)の学生(がくせい)です。 — *I am a student in the Department of Literature.*

カワムラさんは工学部(こうがくぶ)の三年生(さんねんせい)です。 — *Mr. Kawamura is a junior in the Engineering Department.*

アクティビティー 7

ダイアログ：専攻(せんこう)は何(なん)ですか。(*What is his/her major?*)

山口(やまぐち)：ブラウンさんのご出身(しゅっしん)はどこですか。
ブラウン：ボストンの出身(しゅっしん)です。
山口：何年生(なんねんせい)ですか。
ブラウン：三年生(さんねんせい)です。
山口：専攻(せんこう)は何(なん)ですか。
ブラウン：歴史学(れきしがく)です。

YAMAGUCHI: Buraun-san no go-shusshin wa doko desu ka.
BURAUN: Bosuton no shusshin desu.
YAMAGUCHI: Nannensee desu ka.
BURAUN: Sannensee desu.
YAMAGUCHI: Senkoo wa nan desu ka.
BURAUN: Rekishigaku desu.

YAMAGUCHI: Where are you from, Ms. Brown? BROWN: I'm from Boston. YAMAGUCHI: What year student are you? BROWN: I'm a junior. YAMAGUCHI: What is your major? BROWN: It's history.

Now talk about Linda Brown's classmates based on the following table.

NAME 名前(なまえ)	NATIONALITY 国籍(こくせき)	HOMETOWN 出身(しゅっしん)	YEAR 学年(がくねん)	MAJOR 専攻(せんこう)
ジョン・カワムラ	アメリカ	ロサンゼルス	三年生(さんねんせい)	工学(こうがく)
ヘザー・ギブソン	カナダ	エドモントン	二年生(にねんせい)	経済学(けいざいがく)
チン・メイリン	中国(ちゅうごく)	ペキン	二年生(にねんせい)	化学(かがく)
ヘンリー・カーチス	アメリカ	アトランタ	四年生(よねんせい)	コンピュータ・サイエンス
林 正男(はやしまさお)	日本(にほん)	阿蘇(あそ)	二年生(にねんせい)	法学(ほうがく)
町田(まちだ)ひとみ	日本	東京(とうきょう)	三年生(さんねんせい)	フランス文学(ぶんがく)

アクティビティー 8

インタビュー：ご出身(しゅっしん)はどこですか。(*Where are you from?*)

Following the example, ask your classmates questions.

STUDENT 1: ご出身(しゅっしん)はどこですか。
STUDENT 2: シアトルです。
s1: 何年生(なんねんせい)ですか。
s2: 二年生(にねんせい)です。
s1: 専攻(せんこう)は何(なん)ですか。
s2: 生物学(せいぶつがく)です。

s1: Go-shusshin wa doko desu ka.
s2: Shiatoru desu.
s1: Nannensee desu ka.
s2: Ninensee desu.
s1: Senkoo wa nan desu ka.
s2: Seebutsugaku desu.

---

s1: Where are you from? s2: I'm from Seattle. s1: What year are you in? s2: I'm a sophomore.
s2: What is your major? s2: It's biology.

言語ノート

Asking for Personal Information

Here are some common ways of eliciting personal information. Note the use of the honorific prefix **o-** or **go-** when referring to someone else's name, residence, etc.; remember to drop these prefixes when talking to an out-group member about your own name, residence, and so on, or that of a member of your in-group (for example, a sister or a co-worker).

お名前(なまえ)は（何(なん)ですか）。	O-namae wa (nan desu ka).	*(What is) your name?*
ご出身(しゅっしん)は（どちらですか）。	Go-shusshin wa (dochira desu ka).	*Where are you from?*
お国(くに)は（どちらですか）。	O-kuni wa (dochira desu ka).	*What country are you from?*
おすまいは（どちらですか）。	O-sumai wa (dochira desu ka).	*Where do you live?*
お年(とし)は（おいくつですか）。	O-toshi wa (o-ikutsu desu ka).	*How old are you?*
お電話番号(でんわばんごう)は（何番(なんばん)ですか）。	O-denwa bangoo wa (nan-ban desu ka).	*What is your telephone number?*

In all of the above questions, you can omit the words in parentheses. Similarly, when answering these questions, you can say,

名前(なまえ)はジョン・カワムラです。	Namae wa Jon Kawamura desu.	*My name is John Kawamura.*

or simply

ジョン・カワムラです。	Jon Kawamura desu.	*(My name) is John Kawamura.*

Vocabulary: Age 

The counter suffix **-sai** (*years old*) is used with the Sino-Japanese system of numerals to express a person's age. For ages 1 through 10, the Japanese system of numerals — 一つ、二つ、etc.—may also be used. You will study more about these two number systems in **Chapter 2.** *Twenty* has its own special word, 二十（はたち）.

	SINO-JAPANESE SYSTEM	JAPANESE SYSTEM
1 year old	is-sai 一歳	hitotsu 一つ
2 years old	ni-sai 二歳	hutatsu 二つ
3 years old	san-sai 三歳	mittsu 三つ

	SINO-JAPANESE SYSTEM	JAPANESE SYSTEM
4 years old	yon-sai 四歳	yottsu 四つ
5 years old	go-sai 五歳	itsutsu 五つ
6 years old	roku-sai 六歳	muttsu 六つ
7 years old	nana-sai 七歳	nanatsu 七つ
8 years old	has-sai 八歳	yattsu 八つ
9 years old	kyuu-sai 九歳	kokonotsu 九つ
10 years old	jus-sai 十歳	too 十
11 years old	juu-is-sai 十一歳	
12 years old	juu-ni-sai 十二歳	
20 years old	ni-jus-sai 二十歳 ni-jis-sai 二十歳	hatachi 二十
25 years old	ni-juu-go-sai 二十五歳	
46 years old	yon-juu-roku-sai 四十六歳	
99 years old	kyuu-juu-kyuu-sai 九十九歳	
100 years old	hyaku-sai 百歳*	

To ask someone's age, use one of these expressions:

お年(とし)は（おいくつですか）。
How old are (you)?
（山口(やまぐち)さんは）おいくつですか。
How old are (you, Mr. Yamaguchi)?
（カワムラさんは）何歳(なんさい)ですか。
How old are (you, Mr. Kawamura)?
—22歳(さい)です。
—(I am) 22 years old.

The age of a baby under one year old is usually given with the counter ～ヶ月(months), which is read かげつ. (This counter is also written カ月 or か月.)

—7ヶ月(かげつ)です。
— (He or she is) seven months old.

---

* Japanese have the longest average lifespan of the people of any nation in the world: 76.4 years for men and 82.8 years for women (in 1995). (Keizai Koho Senta, *Japan: An International Comparison* [1998].)

Vocabulary: Months

一月	**ichi-gatsu**	January	七月	**shichi-gatsu**	July
二月	**ni-gatsu**	February	八月	**hachi-gatsu**	August
三月	**san-gatsu**	March	九月	**ku-gatsu**	September
四月	**shi-gatsu**	April	十月	**juu-gatsu**	October
五月	**go-gatsu**	May	十一月	**juu-ichi-gatsu**	November
六月	**roku-gatsu**	June	十二月	**juu-ni-gatsu**	December

Examples of how speakers talk about months follow.

今月(こんげつ)は何月(なんがつ)ですか。	Kongetsu wa nan-gatsu desu ka.	*What month is it this month?*
—十月(じゅうがつ)です。	—Juu-gatsu desu.	*—It's October.*
カワムラさんは何月生まれですか。	Kawamura-san wa nan-gatsu umare desu ka.	*What month were you born in, Mr. Kawamura?*
—四月(しがつ)生まれです。	—Shi-gatsu umare desu.	*—I was born in April.*

✸ アクティビティー 9

本当(ほんとう)ですか。違(ちが)いますか。(*True or False?*)

Look at the table. Are the statements below true or false?

NAME	AGE	MONTH OF BIRTH	HOMETOWN	RESIDENCE	TELEPHONE NUMBER
Masao Hayashi	19	May	Aso	Itabashi	03-3682-0961
Hitomi Machida	20	December	Tokyo	Mitaka	0422-45-4986
Kunio Sano	67	March	Yamagata	Nakano	03-3497-1276
Satomi Yamaguchi	22	May	Tokyo	Setagaya	03-5782-0876
Yuriko Yamaguchi	51	February	Hukushima	Setagaya	03-5782-0876

1. 林(はやし)さんのご出身(しゅっしん)は阿蘇(あそ)です。
2. 林(はやし)さんのおすまいは板橋(いたばし)です。
3. 町田(まちだ)さんは二十歳(はたち)です。
4. 町田さんは十一月(じゅういちがつ)生まれです。
5. 佐野(さの)さんは七十六歳(ななじゅうろくさい)です。
6. 佐野さんのご出身(しゅっしん)は中野(なかの)です。
7. 佐野さんのお電話番号(でんわばんごう)は03-3497-1276です。
8. 山口(やまぐち)さとみさんは二十二歳(にじゅうにさい)です。
9. 山口(やまぐち)さとみさんのご出身(しゅっしん)は福島(ふくしま)です。
10. 山口(やまぐち)さとみさんと山口ゆり子(こ)さんのおすまいは世田谷(せたがや)です。
11. 山口(やまぐち)ゆり子(こ)さんは五十一歳(ごじゅういっさい)です。

Remember that the particle と is used to connect two nouns.

文化ノート

CULTURE NOTE • Asking Personal Questions

If Japanese people sometimes seem overly curious about your age, it may be because age is one of the factors that go into determining the appropriate style and politeness level of speech. (Generally, a younger person speaks more politely to an older one.)

Similarly, don't be offended if Japanese ask lots of questions about your family. In Japan, despite weakening traditional values, the family is still the most important social unit and has much bearing on one's happiness and social standing. If your family is solid and supportive, Japanese will be happy for you. Those persistent questions arise from a desire to ascertain that you, too, have a good family you can rely on.

アクティビティー 10

何月(なんがつ)生まれですか。(*What month was he/she born in?*)

Based on the following ID, answer the questions.

1. 町田(まちだ)さんのご出身(しゅっしん)はどこですか。
2. 町田さんはおいくつですか。
3. 町田さんのおすまいは。
4. 町田さんは何月(なんがつ)生まれですか。
5. 町田さんのお電話番号(でんわばんごう)は。
6. 町田さんは何歳(なんさい)ですか。

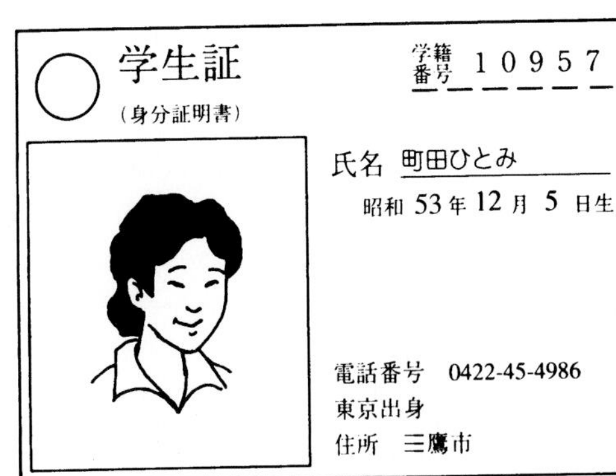
学生証
(身分証明書)
学籍番号 10957
氏名 町田ひとみ
昭和 53 年 12 月 5 日生
電話番号 0422-45-4986
東京出身
住所 三鷹市

アクティビティー 11

ダイアログ：もう一度お願いします。(*Once more, please.*)

大学の事務室で

事務員：お名前は。
ブラウン：リンダ・ブラウンです。
事務員：お電話番号は。
ブラウン：すみません。もう一度お願いします。
事務員：お電話番号は。
ブラウン：03-5871-8952です。
事務員：すみません。ゆっくりお願いします。
ブラウン：03-5871-8952です。

Daigaku no jimushitsu de

JIMUIN: O-namae wa.
BURAUN: Rinda Buraun desu.
JIMUIN: O-denwa bangoo wa.
BURAUN: Sumimasen. Moo ichido onegai-shimasu.
JIMUIN: O-denwa bangoo wa.
BURAUN: 03-5871-8952 desu.
JIMUIN: Sumimasen. Yukkuri onegai-shimasu.
BURAUN: 03-5871-8952 desu.

言語ノート

お願いします。

お願（ねが）いします (lit., *Please do me a favor*) is a polite, infinitely useful phrase that can mean *Please* (*do something for me*) or *Please give me*… For example, when making a purchase or when ordering in a restaurant, you might say これ、お願いします (*I would like this,* or *Please give me this*). In the same situations you could use お願いします to get the clerk's or waiter's attention (*Could you help me, please?*).

In fact, anytime you would like someone to do something for you, you can simply use this expression instead of making a specific request. If you are on the receiving end of such a request, you will have to figure out from context what the speaker is asking you to do. For instance, in the preceding dialogue, もう一度（いちど）お願いします means *Please say it once more.*

At a university office CLERK: May I have your name? BROWN: Linda Brown. CLERK: May I have your phone number? BROWN: Excuse me, would you repeat that? (lit., *Excuse me. Once more, please.*) CLERK: May I have your phone number? BROWN: 03-5871-8952. CLERK: Excuse me, would you say that slowly? BROWN: 03-5871-8952.

✸ アクティビティー 12

お名前(なまえ)は。*(May I have your name?)*

Role-play the situation in **Activity 11** using もう一度(いちど)お願(ねが)いします and ゆっくりお願(ねが)いします as necessary. Student 1 (the office clerk) should write down the information provided by Student 2.

s1: お名前(なまえ)は。
s2: _____です。
s1: ご出身(しゅっしん)は。
s2: _____です。
s1: 何月(なんがつ)生まれですか。
s2: _____ 生まれです。
s1: おすまいは。
s2: _____です。
s1: お電話番号(でんわばんごう)は。
s2: _____です。

Grammar and Practice Activities

3. Personal Pronouns and Demonstratives

ブラウン：	(写真(しゃしん)を指(さ)しながら) この人(ひと)はだれですか。
町田(まちだ)：	どの人(ひと)ですか。
ブラウン：	このセーターの人(ひと)です。
町田：	ああ、これはわたしの友(とも)だちのジョンソンさんです。
ブラウン：	高田(たかだ)さんのオフィスはどこですか。
受付(うけつ)け：	3階(かい)です。
ブラウン：	エレベーターはどこですか。
受付け：	あちらです。

BROWN: (Pointing to someone in a photo) Who is this person? MACHIDA: Which person? BROWN: This person wearing (lit., *of*) a sweater. MACHIDA: Oh, that (lit., *this*) is my friend Mr. Johnson.

BROWN: Where is Mr. Takada's office? RECEPTIONIST: It is on the third floor. BROWN: Where is the elevator? RECEPTIONIST: It's over there.

3.1 Personal pronouns are used to refer to a person without mentioning his or her name. Following are the most common personal pronouns in Japanese. Notice that this is one subject area where a singular/plural distinction is frequently made. Pronouns have varying levels of politeness and some are used only by or in reference to women or men, so you must be careful in selecting which pronoun to use.

SINGULAR		PLURAL	
私(わたし)	I	私(わたし)たち	we
僕(ぼく)	I (*male, informal*)	僕(ぼく)たち	we (*male, informal*)
あたし	I (*female, informal*)	あたしたち	we (*female, informal*)
あなた	you	あなたたち	you
		あなたがた	you
彼(かれ)	he	彼(かれ)ら、彼たち	they (*male*)
彼女(かのじょ)	she	彼女(かのじょ)ら、彼女たち	they (*female*)
あの人(ひと)	he/she	あの人(ひと)たち	they
あの方(かた)	he/she (*polite*)	あの方(かた)たち	they (*polite*)

Pronouns are used mostly for emphasis in Japanese and are usually omitted. In particular, あなた is considered an intimate pronoun—women traditionally call their husbands あなた—so people tend to avoid it except when talking to family members or close friends. (It is sometimes seen in impersonal writing, such as the instructions for using a product.) It is also considered rude to refer to an older person or other social superior as 彼(かれ) or 彼女(かのじょ). In formal situations or when talking to or about strangers or superiors, it is best to use the person's name or title.

> あの人 literally means *that person.*
> 方 is a polite substitute for 人 *person.*

これは佐野(さの)さんのハンドバッグですか。
Is this your handbag, Ms. Sano?

The first-person pronouns (*I, we*) are usually omitted, unless there is no other way to make clear what the subject of the sentence is. If a conversation or paragraph starts with a sentence that lacks a subject, you can usually assume that the underlying subject is *I* or *we*. If the first sentence is a question without a stated subject, the underlying subject is probably *you*.

(わたしは) カワムラです。どうぞよろしく。
I am Kawamura. It's nice to meet you.

(あなたは) ブラウンさんじゃありませんか。
Aren't you Ms. Brown?

> When you talk with your classmates, try to use their real names instead of あなた. When you don't understand what other students say, try to use such phrases as すみません。もう一度(いちど)お願(ねが)いします。ゆっくりお願いします, etc.

3.2 Demonstrative pronouns are used to point out or to indicate a specific person, thing, place, or direction. The following chart shows the primary demonstratives in Japanese.

	THING	PLACE	DIRECTION
こ-series	これ	ここ	こちら
そ-series	それ	そこ	そちら
あ-series	あれ	あそこ	あちら
ど-series	どれ	どこ	どちら

Each column follows the pattern of こ-そ-あ-ど (the first syllable of each word) from top to bottom. For this reason, Japanese demonstratives are often called こそあどことば or **ko-so-a-do** words.

- The こ-series is used to point out whatever is close to the speaker.
- The そ-series is used to point out whatever is close to the hearer.
- The あ-series points out whatever is some distance from both the speaker and the hearer.
- The ど-series are interrogatives used to ask which one, which place, or which direction.

これはブラウンさんの本(ほん)ですか。
Is this Ms. Brown's book?
それをお願(ねが)いします。
I would like that one.
図書館(としょかん)はあそこです。
The library is over there.
カワムラさんのコーヒーはどれですか。
Which one is Mr. Kawamura's coffee?

In most contexts, it is rude to use これ、それ、あれ、どれ to refer to people. Instead, こちら、そちら、あちら、どちら are used.

こちらは東京(とうきょう)大学(だいがく)の横井(よこい)先生(せんせい)です。
This is Professor Yokoi of the University of Tokyo.
ブラウンさんはどちらですか。
Which one of you is Ms. Brown?

Demonstrative adjectives, which modify nouns and come before them, also follow the **ko-so-a-do** pattern.

	DEMONSTRATIVE ADJECTIVES
こ-series	この
そ-series	その
あ-series	あの
ど-series	どの

この本(ほん)はブラウンさんの本(ほん)です。
This book is Ms. Brown's book.
あの映画(えいが)は日本(にほん)の映画(えいが)ですか。
Is that movie a Japanese movie?

どの means *which of three or more alternatives.* Similarly, どれ means *which one of three or more alternatives.*

> ブラウンさんの本はどの本ですか。
> *Which book is yours, Ms. Brown?* (out of three or more books)
> カワムラさんのかばんはどれですか。
> *Which bag is Mr. Kawamura's?* (out of three or more bags)

If the choice is between two alternatives, use どちら.

> 林さんの本はどちらですか。
> *Which one is your book, Mr. Hayashi?* (There are two books.)

言語ノート

どちらへ Where to?

When you are on the way out of the door, friends, neighbors, or colleagues may ask you どちらへ (*Where to?*) or おでかけですか (*Are you going out?*). These are not nosy questions, but rather common formulaic greetings to those who are about to go somewhere. The feeling behind these expressions is that the speaker is happy because you are healthy enough to go out, or perhaps the speaker is concerned that you have to go out so often. Whichever the sentiment, the remark conveys a wish for a safe return.

In replying, you need not be specific about where you are going. The best answer to these questions is ええ、ちょっとそこまで (*Yes, just around the corner* [lit., *Yes, just to over there*]).

アクティビティー 13

これはビールですか。(*Is this beer?*)

Formulate questions, following the example.

[例] ラジカセ (combined radio and tape cassette player) →
これはラジカセですか。

1. ワープロ
2. スーツケース
3. 辞書
4. えんぴつ
5. ワイン

Now answer the questions you made, following the example.

[例] これはラジカセですか。→
いいえ、ラジカセじゃありません。CDプレーヤーです。

1. コンピュータ
2. かばん
3. 教科書
4. ペン
5. ジュース

Make dialogues following the example.

[例(れい)] これはだれのラジカセですか。町田(まちだ)さん →
町田(まちだ)さんのラジカセです。

1. ブラウンさん
2. カーティスさん
3. 横井先生(よこいせんせい)
4. 林(はやし)さん
5. 佐野(さの)さん

アクティビティー 14

友(とも)だちも二十歳(はたち)です。(*My friend is 20, too.*)

Make up appropriate follow-up sentences using も.

[例(れい)] ブラウンさんはアメリカ人(じん)です。→ カワムラさんもアメリカ人(じん)です。

1. わたしの先生(せんせい)は45さいです。
2. わたしは学生(がくせい)です。
3. 「アミーゴ」はスペイン語(ご)です。
4. バナナはくだものです。
5. サッカーはスポーツです。
6. すきやきは日本料理(にほんりょうり)です。
7. パナソニックは日本(にほん)のメーカーです。

Vocabulary and Grammar 1C

Vocabulary and Oral Activities

Around Campus

Vocabulary: Around Campus

事務室(じむしつ)	**jimushitsu**	administration office
ビル	**biru**	building
実験室(じっけんしつ)	**jikkenshitsu**	laboratory
寮(りょう)	**ryoo**	dormitory

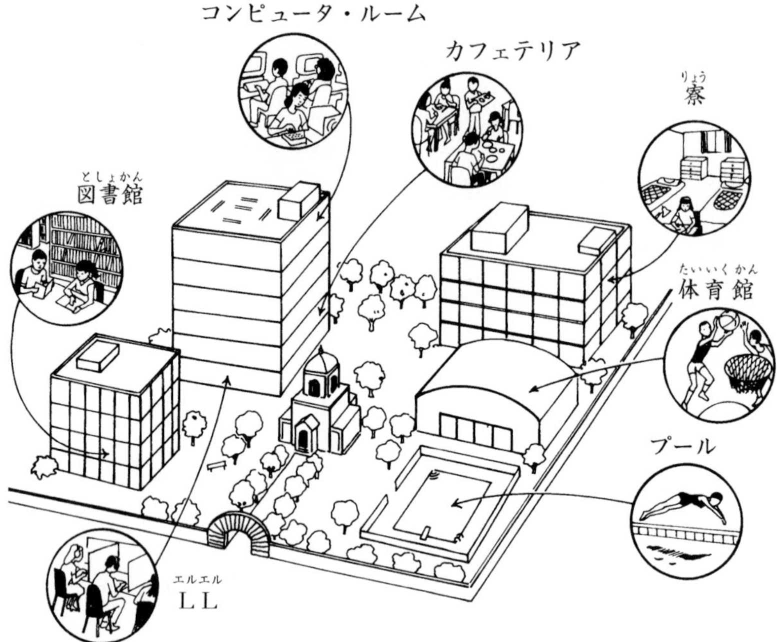

✹ アクティビティー 15

ダイアログ：図書館(としょかん)はどこですか。(*Where is the library?*)

キャンパスで

ブラウン：すみません。図書館(としょかん)はどこですか。
学生(がくせい)：あそこです。
ブラウン：文学部(ぶんがくぶ)はどこですか。
学生：あのビルの３階(かい)です。

Kyanpasu de

BURAUN: Sumimasen. Toshokan wa doko desu ka.
GAKUSEE: Asoko desu.
BURAUN: Bungakubu wa doko desu ka.
GAKUSEE: Ano biru no san-kai desu.

Vocabulary: Days of the Week

日曜日	**nichiyoobi**	Sunday
月曜日	**getsuyoobi**	Monday
火曜日	**kayoobi**	Tuesday

On campus BROWN: Excuse me. Where is the library? STUDENT: It's over there. BROWN: Where is the Literature Department? STUDENT: It's on the third floor of that building.

水曜日	**suiyoobi**	Wednesday
木曜日	**mokuyoobi**	Thursday
金曜日	**kin'yoobi**	Friday
土曜日	**doyoobi**	Saturday
何曜日ですか。	**Nan'yoobi desu ka.**	What day of the week is it?

✸ アクティビティー 16

時間割 (*Class schedules*)

Answer the questions based on the schedules below.

[例] 数学のクラスは何曜日ですか。→ 月曜日です。

John's schedule

M	T	W	Th	F	S
math		German	physics		German
math	Japanese culture		engineering		
		computer science	engineering		
				Japanese	

Linda's schedule

M	T	W	Th	F	S
			history		
anthro-pology	Japanese culture	economics	history	political science	
literature		French		political science	
				Japanese	

1. 日本文化 (*Japanese culture*) のクラスは何曜日ですか。
2. 歴史学のクラスは何曜日ですか。
3. コンピュータのクラスは何曜日ですか。
4. 工学のクラスは何曜日ですか。
5. 人類学のクラスは何曜日ですか。
6. フランス語のクラスは何曜日ですか。
7. 物理学のクラスは何曜日ですか。

Now write down your class schedule and explain it to your classmates.

Grammar and Practice Activities

4. Asking Questions: Interrogatives

ブラウン：あれは何(なん)ですか。
町田(まちだ)：あれは「のり」です。
山口(やまぐち)：あの人(ひと)はだれですか。
カワムラ：クラスメートの林(はやし)さんです。
山口：ご出身(しゅっしん)はどこですか。
カワムラ：九州(きゅうしゅう)です。
山口：あの方(かた)はどなたですか。
カワムラ：あの方(かた)は横井先生(よこいせんせい)です。
山口：何(なん)の先生(せんせい)ですか。
カワムラ：日本文化(にほんぶんか)です。

4.1 Questions starting with *who, why, where, when, what,* or *which* are sometimes called *wh-questions* in English. In Japanese, you can make questions corresponding to wh-questions quite easily.

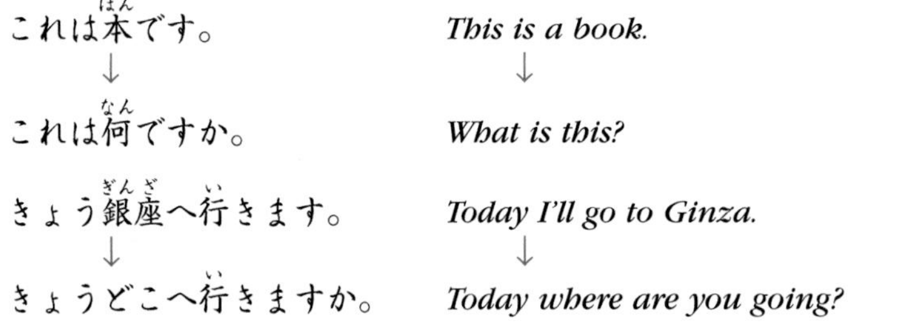

これは本(ほん)です。	*This is a book.*
↓	↓
これは何(なん)ですか。	*What is this?*
きょう銀座(ぎんざ)へ行(い)きます。	*Today I'll go to Ginza.*
↓	↓
きょうどこへ行(い)きますか。	*Today where are you going?*

Likewise, to answer a wh-question, simply replace the question word with the answer and drop the question particle か.

あの人(ひと)はだれですか。	*Who is that person?*
↓	↓
(あの人(ひと)は)ブラウンさんです。	*(That person) is Ms. Brown.*

BROWN: What is that? MACHIDA: That's seaweed.

YAMAGUCHI: Who is he? KAWAMURA: He is Mr. Hayashi, one of my classmates. YAMAGUCHI: Where is he from? KAWAMURA: He's from Kyushu. YAMAGUCHI: Who is that person? KAWAMURA: That's Professor Yokoi. YAMAGUCHI: ...of what is she a professor? KAWAMURA: Japanese culture.

4.2 Three basic interrogatives are introduced in this chapter.

1. 何（なに、なん）= *what*

   When this interrogative is followed by a word starting with [d], [t], [k], or [n], it is pronounced なん. Otherwise, it is なに.

   これは何(なん)ですか。
   What is this?

   これは何(なん)の本(ほん)ですか。
   What (kind of) book is this?

   何(なに)を食(た)べますか。
   What are you going to eat?

   When this interrogative is attached to other words, it is pronounced なに to mean *what* and なん to mean *how many* or *how much.*

   あなたのセーターは何色(なにいろ)ですか。
   What color is your sweater?

   カワムラさんは何歳(なんさい)ですか。
   How old is Mr. Kawamura?

2. だれ、どなた = *who*

   (どなた is more polite than だれ.)

   あの人(ひと)はだれですか。
   Who is that person?

   あの方(かた)はどなたですか。
   Who is that person? (much more polite)

3. どこ = *where*

   どこで昼(ひる)ごはんを食(た)べますか。
   Where are you going to eat lunch?

OTHER INTERROGATIVES

- いつ = *when*

  いつデパートへ行(い)きますか。
  When are you going to the department store?

- どちら、どっち = *which of two; where*
  (どっち is informal.)

  横井先生(よこいせんせい)の研究室(けんきゅうしつ)はどちらですか。
  Where is Professor Yokoi's office?

  ブラウンさんの本(ほん)はどっちですか。
  Which one (of the two) is Ms. Brown's book?

- どれ = *which of three or more*

  どれがギブソンさんの本ですか。

  Which one is Ms. Gibson's book?

- いくつ = *how many, how old*

  いくつりんごを食べますか。

  How many apples are you going to eat?

  カワムラさんはおいくつですか。

  How old is Mr. Kawamura?

- いくら = *how much* (price)

  この雑誌はいくらですか。

  How much is this magazine?

The above interrogatives function like nouns. Connect them to other nouns with の. Remember the pattern X の Y (私 の本).

これは何の教 科書ですか。

What (kind of) textbook is this?

これはだれの本ですか。

Whose book is this?

どちらの本が好きですか。

Which book (of the two) do you like?

MORE INTERROGATIVES

- どんな = *what kind of*

  どんな映画が好きですか。

  What kind of movies do you like?

- どう = *how, how about*

  これはどうですか。

  How about this one?

  日本語のクラスはどうですか。

  How is your Japanese class?

- どうして、なぜ = *why*

  どうして町田さんと話しましたか。

  Why did you talk to Ms. Machida?

  なぜ日本語を勉 強しますか。

  Why are you studying Japanese?

言語ノート

Particles は and が

Here are some general guidelines on when to use は and when to use が in the sentence construction X [は／が] Y です. You will study the difference between these particles in detail later, but for now remember the following.

1. Use が after a question word (who, where, etc.) and in the answer to a question using such a question word.

   どれがカワムラさんの本(ほん)ですか。
   Which one is Mr. Kawamura's book?

   これがカワムラさんの本(ほん)です。
   This is Mr. Kawamura's book.

   どの人(ひと)がブラウンさんですか。
   Which person is Ms. Brown?

   あの人(ひと)がブラウンさんです。
   That person is Ms. Brown.

2. Use は in statements or questions that seek to identify or describe X.

   これは本(ほん)です。
   This is a book.

   あれは本(ほん)ですか。
   Is that a book?

3. Use は in negative statements.

   あの人(ひと)はカワムラさんではありません。
   That person is not Mr. Kawamura.

アクティビティー 17

これは町田(まちだ)さんのペンですか。(*Is this Ms. Machida's pen?*)

Fill in the blanks.

[例(れい)] これは（　　）のペンですか。—それは町田(まちだ)さんのペンです。(だれ)

1. これは（　　）の教科書(きょうかしょ)ですか。—それは日本語(にほんご)の教科書(きょうかしょ)です。
2. あの人(ひと)は（　　）ですか。—わたしの日本語(にほんご)の先生(せんせい)です。

3. ブラウンさんは（　　）のご出身（しゅっしん）ですか。—ボストンの出身（しゅっしん）です。

4. きょうは（　　）曜日（ようび）ですか。—金曜日（きんようび）です。

5. 図書館（としょかん）は（　　）ですか。—あそこです。

6. カワムラさんの本（ほん）は（　　）ですか。—これです。

アクティビティー　18

寮（りょう）はどこですか。(*Where is your dorm?*)

These are answers to questions. What do you think the questions were? Write down possible questions.

[例（れい）]　450円（えん）です。→ この雑誌（ざっし）はいくらですか。

1. 横井先生（よこいせんせい）です。
2. カナダです。
3. あそこです。
4. カフェテリアです。
5. 明日（あした）いきます。
6. はい、そうです。
7. あちらです。
8. 95歳（さい）です。
9. わたしのコンピュータです。
10. 午前（ごぜん）10時（じ）です。

✸ アクティビティー　19

大学（だいがく）のキャンパス (*University campus*)

Bring a map of your campus to class and practice asking a classmate the location of several places. Pointing to the map, use あそこ、そこ、ここ、あちら、etc. in answering.

Ask a classmate where places on campus are.

s1: _____はどこですか。

s2: このビルの_____です。

アクティビティー 20

ダイアログ：これはだれのボールペンですか。(*Whose ballpoint pen is this?*)

林(はやし)：これはだれのボールペンですか。
ギブソン：わたしのです。
林：あれもギブソンさんのボールペンですか。
ギブソン：いいえ、あれは町田(まちだ)さんのです。

HAYASHI: Kore wa dare no boorupen desu ka.
GIBUSON: Watashi no desu.
HAYASHI: Are mo Gibuson-san no boorupen desu ka.
GIBUSON: Iie, are wa Machida-san no desu.

アクティビティー 21

林(はやし)さんのです。(*It's Mr. Hayashi's.*)

s1: これはだれの本(ほん)ですか。
s2: 林(はやし)さんのです。

Based on the following illustration, tell who each item belongs to.

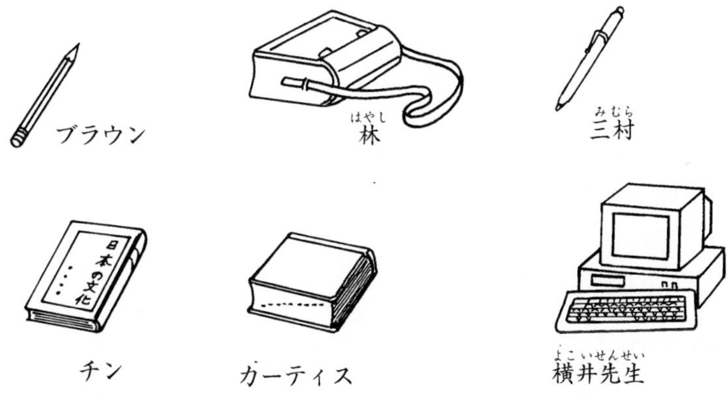

アクティビティー 22

What do you say in the following situations? Answer in Japanese.

[例(れい)] You are looking at the display counter in a store selling folk crafts, and you are curious about an unfamiliar item near the salesperson.
→ それは何(なん)ですか。

HAYASHI: Whose ballpoint pen is this? GIBSON: It's mine. HAYASHI: Is that your ballpoint pen, too? GIBSON: No, it's Ms. Machida's.

1. You are still in the folk craft store. You pick up an interesting object and ask the salesperson what the item in your hand is.
2. You introduce Professor Yokota, who is next to you, to one of your classmates.
3. Your friend has asked to see one of your books. Ask which one (of many books you have) he/she would like to look at.
4. There are two buildings in front of you. Ask which one the library is.
5. Someone who seems to be lost has asked you where the cafeteria (カフェテリア) is. Tell him/her the cafeteria is in that building over there.

Language Skills

Reading and Writing

Reading 1 フランス人(じん)のクラスメート

Before You Read

The following passage describes a foreign student in Japan. Your task is to retrieve the following information.

1. the name of the student
2. the name of his university
3. where he is from
4. his nationality
5. his major
6. what year student he is
7. what classes he is taking

Here are some key words that will help you locate each piece of information.

1. 名前(なまえ) *name*
2. 大学(だいがく) *university*
3. 出身(しゅっしん) *hometown, origin*
4. a word ending in ～人(じん)
5. 専攻(せんこう) *major*, a word ending in 学(がく)
6. a word ending in 年生(ねんせい)
7. words ending in 学(がく); if he is taking a language course, a word ending in 語(ご)

While reading you may want to refer to the Vocabulary Library of academic subjects and majors on page 92.

Now Read It!

Look for the preceding information while reading the passage as quickly as possible.

彼(かれ)の名前(なまえ)はピエール・ノワールです。学生(がくせい)です。彼(かれ)はパリの出身(しゅっしん)です。フランス人です。今(いま)、東京大学(とうきょうだいがく)の三年生(さんねんせい)です。専攻(せんこう)は文学(ぶんがく)です。今(いま)、日本語(にほんご)、日本文学(にほんぶんがく)、社会学(しゃかいがく)、人類学(じんるいがく)のクラスを取(と)っています。

今 *now*

～を取っています *is taking (courses)*

After You Finish Reading

Using the information you retrieved, complete the ID to the right. Don't use **kanji** you haven't learned to write yet. Just use **hiragana** for now.

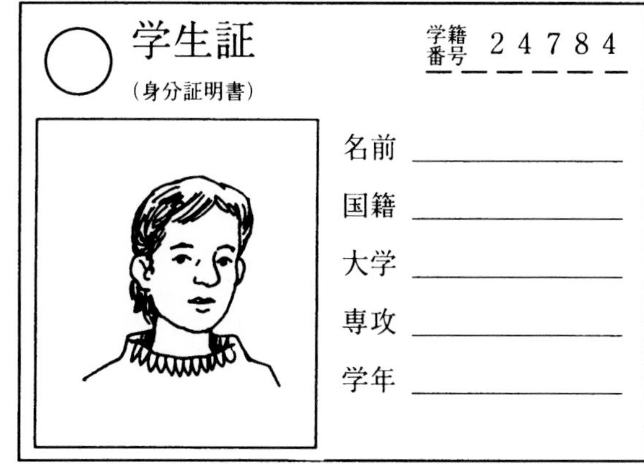

Study Hint

Learning Kanji

The study of **kanji** should be approached systematically if you are to master their complexities. Each **kanji** may have several meanings. It most likely has several **on**-readings and **kun**-readings, and which reading applies depends on where it is used.

Many students make flash cards for each individual **kanji** and try to memorize the characters in that way. However, memorizing the shape of a character is only half the job, because the pronunciation of the **kanji** changes depending on the context. For example, 名 is pronounced な in the word 名まえ (*name*), and 人 is pronounced ひと in the phrase あのひと (*that person*), but 名人, a compound meaning *master, expert,* is pronounced めいじん. This is why it is a good idea to make up flash cards for the compound words as well as the individual **kanji.**

Yookoso! introduces more **kanji** than most textbooks, but it does not introduce unfamiliar compounds without indicating their pronunciations, so keep your spoken vocabulary in mind when you read. For example, if you know that the Japanese word for *Japanese person* is **Nihonjin,** you will not be tempted to pronounce 日本人 as **hi-hon-hito.**

All in all, repetition and constant exposure are the best ways to absorb **kanji.** Read and reread your textbook. Write and rewrite sentences containing the new **kanji.** Try to find familiar **kanji** or compounds in Japanese newspapers and magazines.

Don't get discouraged. Even Japanese people require several years of study to achieve a standard level of literacy in **kanji.** And believe it or not, memorizing **kanji** actually becomes easier after the first five hundred or so!

Writing 1

Write a short profile of yourself, following the format of **Reading 1.** Start with わたしの名前(なまえ)は...

After you finish writing, exchange profiles with a classmate. Is there any similarity in your profiles?

Reading 2 ペンパルをさがしています！

Before You Read

Next you will read a Pen Pal Wanted ad. First, make a list of points you would mention in describing yourself if you were to place such an ad in the paper. Among those points, how many can you express in Japanese?

Now Read It!

Don't worry about the new words and **kanji** you may run across. Just read quickly and find who is looking for a pen pal.

ペンパルをさがしています！

わたしたちはアメリカ人の大学生です。トリシア、デニース、ケートです。ウエスト・コースト大学の四年生です。２２歳です。日本語のクラスのクラスメートです。トリシアとデニースは経済学の専攻です。ケートはコンピューター・サイエンスの専攻です。日本人の大学生のペンパルをさがしています。かならず返事を書きます。日本語でけっこうです。

Tricia Rosen
P.O. Box 1481
West Coast, CA 94156 U.S.A.

After You Finish Reading

Answer the following questions.

1. Who is looking for pen pals?
2. Where and what are they studying?
3. What class are they taking together?
4. What kind of pen pal are they looking for?

Guesswork

1. ペンパルをさがしています appears at the beginning and toward the end of the ad. What do you think さがしています means?
2. At the end of the ad, the word 日本語(にほんご) appears in a short sentence. What do you think that sentence means?

Writing 2

1. First, write down in Japanese five to ten questions to ask your partner. The questions must ask for personal information.
2. Pair up and ask the questions you prepared.
3. Based on your partner's answers, write a brief profile of him or her in Japanese.

Language Functions and Situations

Introducing Friends

クラスで

ブラウン: 横井先生(よこいせんせい)、ご紹介(しょうかい)します。こちらはローラ・ヒルさんです。
ヒルさんはアメリカの大学(だいがく)のクラスメートです。

横井先生(よこいせんせい): ヒルさん、はじめまして。どうぞよろしく。

ヒル: こちらこそ、どうぞよろしく。

Kurasu de

BURAUN: Yokoi-sensee, go-shookai shimasu. Kochira wa Roora Hiru-san desu.
Hiru-san wa Amerika no daigaku no kurasumeeto desu.

YOKOI SENSEE: Hiru-san, hajimemashite. Doozo yoroshiku.

HIRU: Kochira koso. Doozo yoroshiku.

言語ノート

こちらこそ

こちらこそ literally means *It's this side* or *It's my side.* For example, when you meet someone and he or she says はじめまして、どうぞよろしく, you can reply with こちらこそ, meaning *I am the one (who's glad to meet you)*. When someone bumps into you and says どうもすみません (*I am sorry*), you can say こちらこそ (*I'm the one* [*who is to blame*]). Or suppose you borrow a friend's car, notice a

---

In class BROWN: Professor Yokoi. Let me introduce someone to you. This is Ms. Laura Hill. Ms. Hill is my classmate at my American university. PROFESSOR YOKOI: Ms. Hill, it's nice to meet you. HILL: Likewise, it's nice to meet you.

transmission problem, and repair it. When you return the car and thank your friend with どうもありがとうございました, he or she might say いいえ、こちらこそ (*I'm the one [who should say thank you]*).

カフェテリアで

ブラウン：林(はやし)さん、友(とも)だちを紹介(しょうかい)します。
ローラ・ヒルさんです。
アメリカの大学(だいがく)のクラスメートです。
林(はやし)：ヒルさん、はじめまして。林(はやし)です。
ブラウンさんからよく聞(き)いています。
ヒル：はじめまして。ヒルです。

Kafeteria de

BURAUN: Hayashi-san, tomodachi o shookai shimasu. Roora Hiru-san desu. Amerika no daigaku no kurasumeeto desu.
HAYASHI: Hiru-san, hajimemashite. Hayashi desu. Buraun-san kara yoku kiiteimasu.
HIRU: Hajimemashite. Hiru desu.

言語ノート

Introductions

Here are some common expressions used in introductions.

ご紹介(しょうかい)します。
Let me introduce (someone to you).
こちらはギブソンさんです。
This is Ms. Gibson.
はじめまして。
How do you do? (lit., *This is the first time.*)
どうぞよろしく。
It's nice to meet you. (lit., *Please be kind to me.*)

Role Play

Practice the following situations with your classmates.

1. Your friend is visiting your university. Introduce him or her to one of your professors. The professor will ask several questions of the visiting friend.

At a cafeteria BROWN: Mr. Hayashi, let me introduce my friend to you. This is Laura Hill. She is my classmate at my American university. HAYASHI: Ms. Hill, nice to meet you. I am Hayashi. I've heard a lot about you from Ms. Brown. HILL: Nice to meet you. I am Hill.

2. You have brought your friend to a student lounge. Introduce him or her to one of your classmates. Those who have been introduced will ask several questions of each other.

Introducing Yourself

カワムラ：自己紹介させていただきます。東京大学のジョン・カワムラです。ロサンゼルスの出身です。専攻は工学です。三年生です。どうぞよろしく。

KAWAMURA: Jikoshookai sasete itadakimasu. Tookyoo Daigaku no Jon Kawamura desu. Rosanzerusu no shusshin desu. Senkoo wa koogaku desu. Sannensee desu. Doozo yoroshiku.

Now introduce yourself to the class.

言語ノート

Self-Introductions

Self-introductions are a common occurrence at meetings and gatherings in Japan. A typical self-introduction starts this way.

自己紹介させていただきます。
Let me introduce myself.

If you want to be more humble, you can add 失礼ですが (*Excuse me but*...) before this expression. Then mention your name, affiliation, and so on. If you know someone who has a relationship with the person or group you are introducing yourself to, it's a good idea to mention that also.

横井先生の学生です。
I am a student of Professor Yokoi.
ブラウンさんのクラスメートです。
I am a classmate of Ms. Brown.

Conclude your self-introduction with どうぞよろしく and a polite bow.

KAWAMURA: Allow me to introduce myself. I am John Kawamura of the University of Tokyo. I am from Los Angeles. My major is engineering. I am a junior. It's nice to meet you.

Listening Comprehension

Sally MacDonald talks about five classmates in her Japanese culture class. While listening to her descriptions, write down the name, hometown, nationality, major, year, and age of each person. You may wish to make a chart before you begin.

Vocabulary

Personal Information

がくねん	学年	academic year
だいがくせい	大学生	college student
いちねんせい	一年生	first-year student
にねんせい	二年生	sophomore
さんねんせい	三年生	junior
よねんせい	四年生	senior
だいがくいんせい	大学院生	graduate student
がくぶ	学部	academic department
こくせき	国籍	nationality
しゅっしん	出身	hometown; origin
せんこう	専攻	academic major
でんわばんごう	電話番号	telephone number
なまえ	名前	name

People

ともだち	友だち	friend

Loanword: クラスメート

Review: 学生(がくせい)、先生(せんせい)

Places on Campus

けんきゅうしつ	研究室	professor's office
じむしつ	事務室	administration office
たいいくかん	体育館	gym
じっけんしつ	実験室	laboratory

ビル		building
りょう	寮	dormitory

Loanwords: カフェテリア、キャンパス、プール

Review: 教室（きょうしつ）、大学（だいがく）、図書館（としょかん）

Nationalities/Languages

アメリカじん	アメリカ人	American (*person*)
イギリスじん	イギリス人	British (*person*)
イタリアじん／イタリアご	イタリア人／イタリア語	Italian (*person/language*)
えいご	英語	English (*language*)
カナダじん	カナダ人	Canadian (*person*)
かんこくじん／かんこくご	韓国人／韓国語	Korean (*person/language*)
スペインじん／スペインご	スペイン人／スペイン語	Spaniard/Spanish (*language*)
シンガポールじん	シンガポール人	Singaporean
たいわんじん	台湾人	Taiwanese (*person*)
ちゅうごくじん／ちゅうごくご	中国人／中国語	Chinese (*person/language*)
ドイツじん／ドイツご	ドイツ人／ドイツ語	German (*person/language*)
にほんじん／にほんご	日本人／日本語	Japanese (*person/language*)
ブラジルじん	ブラジル人	Brazilian (*person*)
フランスじん／フランスご	フランス人／フランス語	French (*person/language*)
ポルトガルじん／ポルトガルご	ポルトガル人／ポルトガル語	Portuguese (*person/language*)
ほんこんじん	香港人	Hong Kong native
メキシコじん	メキシコ人	Mexican (*person*)
ロシアじん／ロシアご	ロシア人／ロシア語	Russian (*person/language*)
くに	国	country

Review: 話（はな）す

Months

いちがつ	一月	January	はちがつ	八月	August
にがつ	二月	February	くがつ	九月	September
さんがつ	三月	March	じゅうがつ	十月	October
しがつ	四月	April	じゅういちがつ	十一月	November
ごがつ	五月	May	じゅうにがつ	十二月	December
ろくがつ	六月	June	なんがつ	何月	what month
しちがつ	七月	July			

Days of the Week

にちようび	日曜日	Sunday	もくようび	木曜日	Thursday
げつようび	月曜日	Monday	きんようび	金曜日	Friday
かようび	火曜日	Tuesday	どようび	土曜日	Saturday
すいようび	水曜日	Wednesday	なんようび	何曜日	what day of the week

Question Words

だれ	誰	who	なにじん	何人	what nationality
どこ		where	なんがつ	何月	what month
どちら		where (*polite*)	なんさい	何歳	how old
どなた		who (*polite*)	なんねんせい	何年生	what year (in school)
なに、なん	何	what	なんようび	何曜日	what day of the week
なにご	何語	what language			

Other Words

あそこ	that place over there	そちら		that place; there (*polite*)
あちら	that place over there (*polite*)	その		that…
あの	that…over there	それ		that thing
あれ	that thing over there	です		to be
か	(*question marker*)	ではありません		(*negative of* です)
が	(*subject marker*)	どこ		where
ここ	this place; here	どちら		where (*polite*); which (of two)
こちら	this place; here (*polite*)	どの		which… (of more than two)
この	this…	どれ		which thing (of more than two)
これ	this thing	は		(*topic marker*)
じゃありません	(*negative of* です)(*informal*)	も		too
そこ	that place; there	わたし	私	I; me

Study Hint

Learning New Vocabulary

Vocabulary is one of the most important tools for successful communication in a foreign language. What does it mean to know vocabulary? And what is the best way to learn vocabulary?

1. Memorization is only part of the learning process. Using new vocabulary to communicate requires practicing that vocabulary in context. What do you associate with this word? When might you want to use it? Create a context—a place, a situation, a person, or a group of people—for the vocabulary that you want to learn, or use a context from the text. The more associations you make with the word, the easier it will be to remember. Practice useful words and phrases over and over, thinking about their meaning, until you can produce them automatically. You may find it useful to "talk to yourself," saying aloud the words you want to learn.
2. Carefully study the words in vocabulary lists and drawings. If a word is of English origin, be especially aware of its form and

meaning. Sometimes the form and meaning are quite different from the original. For example, デパート came from the English phrase *department store* and has the same meaning as the English. コンセント means *plug outlet*, although it came from the English word *consent*.

3. After studying the list or illustration, cover the English and give the English equivalent of each Japanese word.
4. When you are able to translate the Japanese without hesitation and without error, reverse the procedure; cover the Japanese and give the Japanese equivalent of each English word. Write out the Japanese words in the appropriate script (but use **hiragana** if you haven't studied the appropriate **kanji** yet) once or several times and say them aloud.
5. Vocabulary lists and flash cards can be useful as a review or as a self-test.

Note that the best way to learn vocabulary is to use it as much as possible in conversation and in writing.

Kanji

Learn these **kanji:**

日	年	二	七	先
本	何	三	八	話
学	月	四	九	語
生	人	五	十	大
名	一	六	百	

言語ノート

The Six Types of Kanji

Kanji (*Chinese characters*) originated in China. In China, **kanji** were categorized into one of six basic classifications depending primarily on how the character was formed. The pictograph, the most primitive type of **kanji,** was created as a representation of the physical appearance of an object. In modern Japanese there are relatively few of these characters.

Kanji of the second type represent numbers, positional relations, or abstract concepts.

Kanji in the third group are a combination of two or more of the first two types of **kanji.**

→ → 日
hi (sun)

→ 二 → 二
ni (two)

木 + 木 → 林
hayashi (woods)

The fourth and most important type of **kanji** consists of one part that represents some aspect of its meaning and another part that suggests how it was pronounced in classical Chinese. For example, **aji, mi** (*flavor*) consists of a mouth (the square) and the character for *not yet* with the idea being, "This is a character that has something to do with the mouth and sounds like the word for *not yet*. More than 80 percent of the **kanji** used in modern Japanese fall into this category.

口 + 未 → 味
aji, mi (flavor)

The fifth classification of **kanji** contains characters whose meanings have changed or been extended over the centuries. For example, the character whose original meaning was *to play a musical instrument* now has an additional meaning of *enjoy*.

楽
raku (music → delight)

Finally, there are **kanji** that were borrowed to express new meanings simply because of their sounds, irrespective of their meanings. For example, the Chinese took a **kanji** meaning *two people facing each other* and used it to represent *north,* which was pronounced the same.

北
(hoku/north—originally meant people facing each other)

チェックリスト

Use this checklist to confirm that you can now

- ▫ Talk about nationalities and languages
- ▫ Identify things and people
- ▫ Express possession
- ▫ Exchange personal information
- ▫ Talk about your campus
- ▫ Use personal pronouns and demonstratives
- ▫ Ask questions
- ▫ Write to a pen pal
- ▫ Introduce friends
- ▫ Introduce yourself

Review Chapter 1

アクティビティー　1

学生証（がくせいしょう） (*Student ID*)

What do you think the following words mean? Look for hints on Henry Curtis' student ID.

1. 年齢（ねんれい）
2. 生年月日（せいねんがっぴ）
3. 出身地（しゅっしんち）
4. 専攻（せんこう）
5. 住所（じゅうしょ）
6. 国籍（こくせき）
7. 学部（がくぶ）

学生証
（身分証明書）

学籍番号　1 0 9 5 7

氏名　ヘンリー・カーティス

年齢　22
生年月日　1976.7.14
国籍　アメリカ
出身地　アトランタ市
住所　横浜市西区中央 2-18
学部　工学
専攻　コンピューター・サイエンス

アクティビティー　2

ここにサインしてください。(*Please sign here.*)

Complete the sentences to make yes-no questions. Then ask your classmates these questions. If someone answers yes, ask for his or her signature on a separate piece of paper. Don't ask the same person more than two questions in a row.

[例（れい）]　カワムラさんは(school year) _____ ですか。
s1: 二年生（にねんせい）ですか。
s2: はい、そうです。
s1: ここにサインしてください。

1. (*person's name*) _____ さんは(*nationality*) _____ ですか。
2. (*person's name*) _____ さんは(*language*) _____ を話（はな）しますか。
3. _____ の出身（しゅっしん）ですか。
4. _____ の専攻（せんこう）ですか。

5. ____のクラスを取(と)っていますか。

6. (*person's name*)____さんは____の学生(がくせい)ですか。

7. (*person's name*)____さんは____ですか。

アクティビティー　3

Vocabulary Review

Which of the words listed in parentheses is most closely connected to the first word given?

[例(れい)]　名前(なまえ)（一年生(いちねんせい)、ヘザー・ギブソン、図書館(としょかん)、日本人(にほんじん)）
ヘザー・ギブソンです。

1. 大学(だいがく)（アメリカ、出身(しゅっしん)、学部(がくぶ)、金曜日(きんようび)）
2. 図書館(としょかん)（本、ジュース、カフェテリア、教室(きょうしつ)）
3. 学生(がくせい)（パーティー、勉強(べんきょう)、日曜日(にちようび)、友(とも)だち）
4. 専攻(せんこう)（ＬＬ、月曜日(げつようび)、日本文化(にほんぶんか)、クラスメート）
5. スケジュール（水曜日(すいようび)、学生(がくせい)、友(とも)だち、事務室(じむしつ)）

アクティビティー　4

インタビュー　(*Interview*)

You have studied a variety of ways to elicit information from others. Here is a chance to practice what you've learned. First, with a partner write questions that ask about the listed information. Then, split up and ask the questions of one classmate you have not talked with often. Feel free to ask other questions, too.

1. name
2. age
3. where he or she lives now
4. where he or she is from
5. what year student he or she is
6. academic major
7. nationality
8. what he or she likes
9. what he or she doesn't like
10. whether he or she studies on weekends

2

第二章 わたしの町（まち）

My Town

東京（とうきょう）の町（まち）

Objectives

In this lesson you are going to

- Talk about commuting
- Learn about using adjectives and adverbs
- Talk about places around town
- Learn how to express existence
- Learn how to express location
- Learn to use positional words
- Learn how to count and express numerals and counters
- Learn how to express likes and dislikes
- Talk about your hometown and neighborhood
- Learn to make sure you are communicating

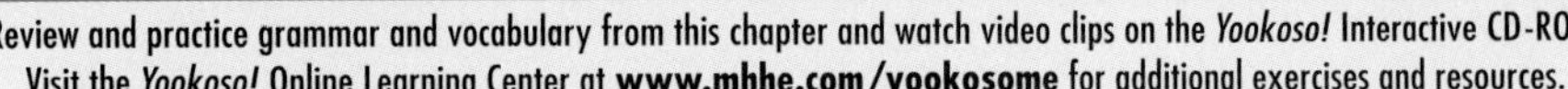

YOOKOSO! MULTIMEDIA

Review and practice grammar and vocabulary from this chapter and watch video clips on the *Yookoso!* Interactive CD-ROM. Visit the *Yookoso!* Online Learning Center at **www.mhhe.com/yookosome** for additional exercises and resources.

Vocabulary and Grammar 2A

Vocabulary and Oral Activities

Commuting

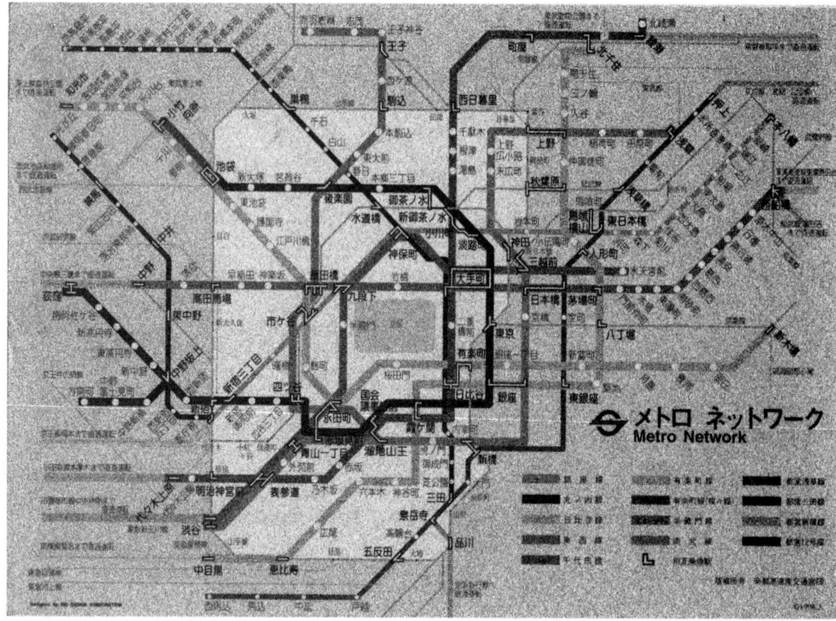

Vocabulary: Commuting 

徒歩(で)	on foot	便利(な)	convenient
…に近いです	is close to…	不便(な)	inconvenient
…から遠いです	is far from…		

便利(不便) cannot be used to mean *suited (not suited)* for one's schedule. Japanese say 3時はつごうがいいです (*Three o'clock is convenient for me*) and 4時はつごうがわるいです (*Four o'clock is inconvenient for me*).

アクティビティー　1

ダイアログ：地下鉄で10分ぐらいです。(*It's about 10 minutes by subway.*)

ブラウンさんと三村さんが話しています。

ブラウン：三村さんのアパートはどこですか。
三村：上野です。
ブラウン：大学に近いですね。
三村：ええ、地下鉄で10分ぐらいです。とても便利ですよ。

X で *via, by means of X;* Y から *from Y;* とても *very;* 上野 *area of Tokyo.*

Vocabulary: Counting Minutes and Hours 

To count minutes use the counter suffix, ～分 (ふん; after some sounds, ぷん) with the Sino-Japanese series of numerals. (See **Grammar 9.1,** p. 156.) The counter suffix for counting hours is 時間(じかん).

一分	いっぷん	one minute
二分	にふん	two minutes
三分	さんぷん	three minutes
四分	よんぷん、よんふん	four minutes
五分	ごふん	five minutes
六分	ろっぷん	six minutes
七分	ななふん、しちふん	seven minutes
八分	はっぷん	eight minutes
九分	きゅうふん	nine minutes
十分	じゅっぷん	ten minutes
一時間	いちじかん	one hour
二時間	にじかん	two hours
一時間半	いちじかんはん	one and a half hours
三時間二十五分	さんじかんにじゅうごふん	three hours twenty-five minutes

Alternatively, the counter suffix ～分間 (～ふんかん、～ぷんかん) may also be used when expressing duration of minutes: 五分話しました or 五分間話しました (*I talked for 5 minutes*). But only ～分 can name a particular minute: 一時五分に行きました (*I went at 1:05*).

Ms. Brown and Mr. Mimura are talking BROWN: Where is your apartment, Mr. Mimura? MIMURA: It's in Ueno. BROWN: It's close to the university, isn't it? MIMURA: Yes. It's about ten minutes by subway. It's very convenient.

✹ アクティビティー 2

どこですか。(*Where is it?*)

Practice the dialogue in アクティビティー **1**, substituting information from the chart below.

Useful Word: ちょっと *a bit*

NAME/TYPE OF RESIDENCE	PLACE	PROXIMITY TO SCHOOL	TRANSPORTATION METHOD/TIME REQUIRED	CONVENIENCE
カワムラさんのうち	世田谷	ちょっと遠い	電車 50分	ちょっと不便
林さんのアパート	板橋	近い	バス 30分	便利
横井先生のうち	千葉	遠い	車 一時間半	不便
チンさんのアパート	目白	とても近い	電車 15分	とても便利
大野先生のうち	横浜	とても遠い	電車 二時間	とても不便

Grammar and Practice Activities

5. Adjectives and Adverbs

林：ブラウンさんの大学は大きいですか。
ブラウン：いいえ、あまり大きくありません。
林：有名ですか。
ブラウン：いいえ、あまり有名じゃありません。

HAYASHI: Is your university large, Ms. Brown? BROWN: No, it's not very large. HAYASHI: Is it famous? BROWN: No, it's not very famous.

カワムラ：あの人(ひと)はだれですか。
チン：町田(まちだ)さんのボーイフレンドです。
カワムラ：ハンサムな人(ひと)ですね。
チン：ええ。

Useful Vocabulary: Basic Adjectives 

大きい／大きな	おおきい／おおきな	big; large
小さい／小さな	ちいさい／ちいさな	small
多い	おおい	many
少ない	すくない	few
新しい	あたらしい	new
古い	ふるい	old
いい／よい		good
よくない		not good; bad
悪い	わるい	bad
静か（な）	しずか（な）	quiet; peaceful
うるさい		noisy; disturbing
きれい（な）		attractive; clean
きたない		dirty
広い	ひろい	spacious; wide
狭い	せまい	small (*in area*); narrow
低い	ひくい	low
高い	たかい	high; expensive
安い	やすい	inexpensive
面白い	おもしろい	interesting
有名（な）	ゆうめい（な）	famous
にぎやか（な）		lively
つまらない		boring
むずかしい		difficult
やさしい		easy; kind
長い	ながい	long
短い	みじかい	short
おいしい		delicious
まずい		bad tasting

In this textbook, adjectives are listed in their dictionary form. Na-adjectives are differentiated by adding (な) to the listed dictionary form.

The i-adjective いい is somewhat irregular. It is the colloquial form of よい and is used more commonly in informal conversation. The negative form of both いい and よい is よくない. (See Conjugating Adjectives, Chapter 4.)

5.1 *Adjectives* are words that modify nouns. In the phrase *a red sweater, red* is an adjective. In Japanese as well, the adjective precedes the noun in such a phrase: 赤(あか)いセーター (*red sweater*). This usage is called *prenominal use,* meaning *before the noun.*

Adjectives do not always precede nouns, however. In English, there are sentences such as *That sweater is red.* Likewise, in the equivalent Japanese

---

KAWAMURA: Who is that (person)? CHIN: That's Ms. Machida's boyfriend. KAWAMURA: He's nice looking. (lit., *He is a nice-looking person.*) CHIN: Yes.

sentence—あのセーターは赤(あか)いです—the adjective 赤(あか)い appears in the latter part of the sentence, which is called the predicate. (The predicate contains the verb and everything that comes after the subject.) We will call this use of an adjective the *predicate use.*

There are two types of adjectives in Japanese. We will call one type *i-adjectives* because their dictionary form (the form listed in dictionaries) always ends in the syllable い. (赤(あか)い is an i-adjective.) Another type of adjective is the *na-adjective,* named for the な that follows them in the prenominal use. These are some examples of these two types of adjectives in their dictionary form.

I-ADJECTIVES		NA-ADJECTIVES	
赤(あか)い	red	元気(げんき)	healthy
あまい	sweet	静(しず)か	quiet
やさしい	gentle	きれい	pretty
暑(あつ)い	hot	ハンサム	handsome
きびしい	strict	有名(ゆうめい)	famous

Note that there are several na-adjectives (like きれい) whose dictionary form ends in い. You'll just have to memorize those.

I-adjectives are of Japanese origin, while most na-adjectives are of foreign origin (from Chinese or Western languages).

5.2 The prenominal and predicate uses of i-adjectives and na-adjectives are summarized in the following chart.

I-ADJECTIVE	
prenominal use	おもしろい本(ほん) (*interesting book*)
predicate use (affirmative)	あの本はおもしろいです。 *That book is interesting.*
predicate use (negative)	あの本はおもしろくありません or あの本はおもしろくないです。 *That book is not interesting.*

NA-ADJECTIVE	
prenominal use	静(しず)かな町(まち) (*quiet town*)
predicate use (affirmative)	あの町は静かです。 *That town is quiet.*
predicate use (negative)	あの町は静かではありません or あの町は静かじゃないです。 *That town is not quiet.*

The affirmative of either type of adjective in the predicate use is formed by adding です to the dictionary form. To form the negative predicate use, you must distinguish between i-adjectives and na-adjectives. In the case of na-adjectives, simply change です to its negative form ではありません (or the colloquial contraction じゃありません or じゃないです). For i-adjectives, however, you must change the ending of the adjective. This process is called *conjugation.* Notice that the dictionary form of all i-adjectives ends in い. This い is actually an ending attached to the root of the adjective. To make a negative, simply replace this final い with く and add ありません or ないです. These two negative forms are identical in meaning and politeness level.

Some adjectives have alternate conjugations in the prenominal use.

1. 大きい (*large*) and 小さい (*small*) may take な prenominally even though they are i-adjectives. In this usage the final い is dropped.

   大きい人　大きな人　*large person*

   小さい人　小さな人　*small person*

2. Some adjectives take the 〜くの form in front of a noun. Change the final い to く and add の.

   近い　*near*　近くの大学　*nearby university*

   遠い　*far*　遠くの大学　*faraway university*

5.3 *Adverbs* modify adjectives, verbs, and other adverbs and are usually positioned before the word they modify.

とてもきれいな女の人
a very pretty woman

わたしは肉をたくさん食べました。
I ate a lot of meat.

その大学はあまり有名ではありません。
That university is not very famous.

Both とても and あまり mean *very, so,* or *extremely.* But あまり is used only in negative sentences. In conversation あんまり, a variant of あまり, is often used instead.

アクティビティー　3

この大学は新しいです。 (*This university is new.*)

Practice the following as shown in the example.

[例]　この大学は古いですか。(新しい)
→いいえ、この大学は古くありません。
新しいです。

Useful Vocabulary: きびしい *strict,* 重(おも)い *heavy,* 軽(かる)い *lightweight,* 長(なが)い *long,* 短(みじか)い *short,* 厚(あつ)い *thick,* うすい *thin,* おいしい *delicious*

1. そのビルは高(たか)いですか。(低(ひく)い)
2. この本(ほん)はおもしろいですか。(つまらない)
3. この肉(にく)はおいしいですか。(まずい)
4. あの先生(せんせい)はきびしいですか。(やさしい)
5. このスーツは高(たか)いですか。(安(やす)い)
6. このテレビは重(おも)いですか。(軽(かる)い)
7. 日本語(にほんご)はむずかしいですか。(やさしい)
8. 山口(やまぐち)さんのスピーチは長(なが)いですか。(短(みじか)い)
9. その本(ほん)は厚(あつ)いですか。(うすい)
10. あなたのうちは広(ひろ)いですか。(せまい)

アクティビティー 4

あのまるいものは何(なん)ですか。(*What is that round thing?*)

Practice, following the example.

[例] 古(ふる)い、ビル → あの古(ふる)いビルは何(なん)ですか。
ハンサム、人(ひと) → あのハンサムな人(ひと)はだれですか。

Useful Vocabulary: きかい *machine,* まじめ(な) *serious,* もの *thing; item,* まるい *round,* 親切(しんせつ)(な) *kind,* 器用(きよう)(な) *skillful,* へん(な) *strange*

1. おもしろい、人(ひと)
2. きれい、女(おんな)の人(ひと)
3. 大(おお)きい、きかい
4. きたない、もの
5. 静(しず)か、人(ひと)
6. 親切(しんせつ)、男(おとこ)の人(ひと)
7. やさしい、男(おとこ)の人(ひと)
8. へん、もの
9. まじめ、男(おとこ)の人(ひと)
10. 便利(べんり)、きかい
11. まるい、もの
12. 器用(きよう)、女(おんな)の人(ひと)

アクティビティー　5

その話はおかしいです。 (*That story is funny!*)

Change affirmative sentences to negative, and negative sentences to affirmative.

[例]　このアパートはとても便利です。→
　　このアパートはあまり便利ではありません。
　　その人はあまりきびしくありません。→
　　その人はとてもきびしいです。

Useful Vocabulary: 若い *young,* 安全(な) *safe,* 話 *tale; story,* 元気(な) *healthy,* おかしい *funny; strange,* 近所 *neighborhood,* 町 *town*

1. この近所はとても静かです。
2. あの男の人はあまり若くありません。
3. その大学はとても古いです。
4. この車はあまり 安全じゃありません。
5. この町はとてもにぎやかです。
6. この話 はとてもおかしいです。
7. カーティスさんはとても元気です。
8. あの人はあまりエレガントではありません。
9. このバナナはあまりおいしくありません。
10. このドレスはあまり安くありません。

アクティビティー　6

その先生は有名な人です。 (*That teacher is a famous person.*)

Rewrite these sentences following the examples.

[例]　あれはつまらない本です。→ あの本はつまらないです。

Useful Word: はで(な) *gaudy; bright-colored*

1. これは安い時計です。
2. あれはとても静かな村です。
3. この町はとても小さいです。
4. これは古いカーテンです。
5. このネクタイははでです。
6. あの町はにぎやかです。
7. あれはとても有名なビルです。

アクティビティー　7

おもしろいですか、つまらないですか。 *(Is it interesting or boring?)*

Choose one adjective that best fits the given noun and make a sentence. Translate the sentence into English.

[例]　日本語(にほんご)のクラスやさしい、おもしろい、むずかしい、つまらない
　　→日本語(にほんご)のクラスはつまらないです。(*Japanese class is boring.*)

1. わたし
   静(しず)か、にぎやか、元気(げんき)、まじめ、ハンサム、きれい
2. わたしの日本語(にほんご)の先生(せんせい)
   きれい、うつくしい (*beautiful*)、ハンサム、やさしい、エレガント、若(わか)い
3. アーノルド・シュワルツネーガー
   タフ、やさしい、若(わか)い、静(しず)か、いそがしい、ハンサム
4. エディー・マーフィー
   元気(げんき)、やさしい、いそがしい、おもしろい、ハンサム
5. わたしの大学(だいがく)
   有名(ゆうめい)、大(おお)きい、むずかしい、やさしい、いい
6. わたしのうち
   大(おお)きい、小(ちい)さい、きれい、ひろい、せまい、きたない
7. わたしのとなりの人(ひと) (*the person next to me*)
   うるさい、きれい、ハンサム、やさしい、へん、静(しず)か
8. この練習(れんしゅう) (*exercise*)
   むずかしい、やさしい、つまらない、長(なが)い

Study Hint

Learning Grammar

Learning a language is similar to learning any other skill; knowing about it is only part of what is involved. Consider swimming, for example. Through books you could become an expert in talking about swimming; but until you actually got into a pool and practiced swimming, you would probably not swim very well. In much the same way, if you memorize all the grammar rules but spend little time practicing them, you will not be able to communicate very well in Japanese.

Since the best way to learn grammar is to use grammatical structures in actual contexts, the first few exercises in each section of the chapter are designed to let you practice the new structures and vocabulary in communicative situations. You may be able to pick up the new structures almost without thinking as you imitate the models in the communicative activities.

Accompanying each set of communicative activities is an explanation of the grammar you have been practicing. First read the explanations, asking your instructor about any parts that you don't understand, and analyze the sample sentences. Then begin to practice. Do the activities that follow the explanation, and then check your answers. When you are certain that your answers are correct, practice doing each exercise several times until you can do them automatically. As you do the exercises, pay attention to spelling and pronunciation and think about how you would use the forms in real life.

Always remember that language learning is cumulative. When you move on to the next chapter, you can't forget or ignore what you learned in this chapter any more than you can forget your arithmetic when you start learning algebra. A few minutes spent each day reviewing "old" topics will increase your confidence and success in communicating in Japanese.

アクティビティー 8

インタビュー：大学(だいがく)に近(ちか)いですか。(*Is it close to the university?*)

Pair up and ask the following questions.

s1: ＿＿＿さんのうちはどこですか。
s2: ＿＿＿です。
s1: 大学(だいがく)に近(ちか)いですか。
s2: はい、近(ちか)いです。＿＿＿で＿＿＿分です。
(いいえ、遠(とお)いです。＿＿＿で＿＿＿分です。)
s1: 便利(べんり)ですね。(不便(ふべん)ですね。)

文化ノート

CULTURE NOTE • Long Commutes

According to one recent survey, the average commuting time of workers living in the greater Tokyo area is one hour thirty-five minutes—each way! What's more, 20 percent of the surveyed workers spend over two hours getting to (or from) work. Because affordable housing is scarce in central Tokyo where many of the jobs are, the majority of workers have to live in outlying suburbs and cities some distance from the city center. Because the train and subway systems are so well-developed in Tokyo—they are extensive networks of punctual, frequent trains—about 50 percent of commuters use trains and/or subways, while only 25 percent use cars.

東京駅：電車で二時間です。遠いですね。

Vocabulary and Grammar 2B

Vocabulary and Oral Activities

Cities and Neighborhoods

Vocabulary: Cities and Towns

近所	きんじょ	neighborhood
区	く	ward of a city
郊外	こうがい	suburbs
市	し	city
人口	じんこう	population
所	ところ	place
町	まち	town
村	むら	village

…町 (lit., *town;* pronounced まち or ちょう) is usually subdivided into numbered districts called …丁目 (ちょうめ).

✸ アクティビティー 9

ダイアログ：どんなところですか。(*What kind of place is it?*)

カワムラ：林(はやし)さんのご出身(しゅっしん)はどこですか。
林(はやし)：九州(きゅうしゅう)の阿蘇(あそ)です。
カワムラ：どんなところですか。
林：小(ち)さい町(まち)です。
カワムラ：きれいな町(まち)ですか。
林：ええ。

Now practice the dialogue replacing the underlined parts with the following words.

1. 大(おお)きい、古(ふる)い
2. きれいな、静(しず)かな
3. 古(ふる)い、小(ち)さい

✸ アクティビティー 10

古山(ふるやま)さんのうちはどこですか。(*Where is Mr. Huruyama's house?*)

Talk about the commute experience and neighborhood of each student listed below. Pair up and use the model dialogue as a guide.

[例] s1: 古山(ふるやま)さんのうちはどこですか。
s2: 横浜(よこはま)の郊外(こうがい)です。
s1: 大学(だいがく)に近(ちか)いですか。
s2: いいえ、電車(でんしゃ)で1時間(じかん)20分(ぷん)です。
s1: どんなところですか。
s2: 静(しず)かなところです。

NAME	RESIDENCE	COMMUTES . . .	NEIGHBORHOOD
Mikawa	house in Koohu	2 hours by train	inconvenient
Hanada	apartment in Choohu	55 minutes by car	beautiful
Kanai	house in Shibuya	30 minutes by subway	convenient
Nomura	apartment in Ueno	5 minutes by bus	lively

KAWAMURA: Where are you from, Mr. Hayashi? HAYASHI: I am from Aso, Kyushu. KAWAMURA: What kind of place is it? HAYASHI: It's a small town. KAWAMURA: Is it an attractive town? HAYASHI: Yes.

s1: Where is Mr. Huruyama's house? s2: It's in the suburbs of Yokohama. s1: Is it close to the university? s2: No, it's an hour and twenty minutes away by train. s1: What kind of place is it? s2: It's a quiet place.

Grammar and Practice Activities

6. Expressing Existence: The Verbs あります and います

レストランで
カワムラ：すみません。ドイツのビールはありますか。
ウエイター：すみません。ありません。でも、オランダのビールはあります。
カワムラ：そうですか。じゃ、オランダのビールをお願(ねが)いします。

ブラウン：すみません。電話(でんわ)はありますか。
林(はやし)：ええ、そこにあります。

ギブソン：林(はやし)さんはいますか。
カワムラ：いいえ。

ブラウン：あっ、林(はやし)さんはカフェテリアにいますよ。
ギブソン：本当(ほんとう)ですか。林(はやし)さんはいつもカフェテリアにいますね。

6.1 To express existence in Japanese, you can use the verbs あります (dictionary form ある) and います (dictionary form いる). あります is used to denote the existence of inanimate objects and abstract concepts (e.g., notebooks, coffee, dead bodies, flowers, air, love, and ideas), while います is used to express the existence of living things (e.g., people, animals, and insects, but not plant life).

ある and いる are the plain forms of あります and います, respectively. (See 言語ノート.)

言語ノート

Polite Form Versus Plain Form

Japanese has two different speech styles, the plain and the polite. The polite form is used when speaking to people outside your own group or to people within your group who rank above you. The plain form is used when speaking to close friends, family members, children, animals, and people who rank below you. The overall politeness of a sentence is determined by the last verb, because certain grammatical structures within the sentence—you will learn them later—require the plain form even when you are speaking politely.

At a restaurant KAWAMURA: Excuse me, do you have German beer? WAITER: I'm sorry, we don't. But we have Dutch beer. KAWAMURA: I see. Then, I would like Dutch beer.

BROWN: Excuse me. Is there a phone (I could use)? HAYASHI: Yes, there's one there.

GIBSON: Is Mr. Hayashi here? KAWAMURA: No. BROWN: Oh, he's in the cafeteria. GIBSON: Really? He's always in the cafeteria.

The beginning of this textbook focuses on the polite forms. These are the forms most commonly used when talking to people you don't know very well, and you will not accidentally offend anyone by using them. Besides, the polite forms are completely regular and easier to memorize than the plain forms!

6.2 This is the simplest way to say *X exists* or *there is/are X.*

EXISTENT	PARTICLE	VERB (AFFIRMATIVE)
N (inanimate)	が	ある (あります)
N (animate)	が	いる (います)

There is ____; *There are* ____.

N stands for *noun.*

6.3 The nonexistence of something is expressed by the negative forms of the same verbs.

EXISTENT	PARTICLE	VERB (NEGATIVE)
N (inanimate)	が	ない (ありません)
N (animate)	が	いない (いません)

There isn't ____; *There aren't* ____.

ない and いない are the plain forms of ありません and いません, respectively.

6.4 The location or position where something or someone exists usually occurs at the beginning of the above sentence structures and is marked with the particle に.

LOCATION	PARTICLE に	EXISTENT	PARTICLE が	VERB
N1	に	N2 (inanimate)	が	ある (あります)
N1	に	N2 (animate)	が	いる (います)

There is/are ____ *at/in* ____.

ここに本(ほん)があります。
There are books here.
ここに辞書(じしょ)はありません。
There are no dictionaries here.
そこにペンはありますか。
Is there a pen over there?
公園(こうえん)に何(なに)がありますか。
What is there in the park?

Note that the particle は is used in negative and yes/no questions instead of が.

うちに犬がいます。
There is a dog at my house.
教室に三村さんはいません。
Mr. Mimura is not in the classroom.
そこにカワムラさんはいますか。
Is Mr. Kawamura there?
今、教室にだれがいますか。
Who is in the classroom now?

6.5 When you would like to say how many or how much of something exists, a phrase denoting quantity comes just before the verb of existence.

LOCATION	PARTICLE に	EXISTENT	PARTICLE が	QUANTITY	VERB
N1	に	N2 (inanimate)	が		ある(あります)
N1	に	N2 (animate)	が		いる(います)

There is one _____ at/in _____.
There are (number) _____s at/in _____.

N1 and N2 stand for two different nouns.

ここにチョコレートがひとつあります。
Here is one piece of chocolate.
あそこに学生が三人います。
There are three students.
ここにアメリカ人は何人いますか。
How many Americans are here?

アクティビティー 11

父は家にいます。(*Father is in the house.*)

Make sentences using あります or います based on the information provided.

1. (in this class) (chalkboard)
2. (in my room) (computer)
3. (in the cafeteria) (classmates)
4. (in Nakano) (Ms. Brown's apartment)
5. (in this class) (students)
6. (at home) (my bicycle)
7. (at the library) (books)

アクティビティー 12

ここに何がありますか。 (*What is there here?*)

Make five existential sentences based on inanimate and living things around you.

Vocabulary and Grammar 2C

Vocabulary and Oral Activities

Buildings and Places Around Town

Vocabulary: Places Around Town

道	みち	street; road
通り	とおり	avenue; street
建物	たてもの	building
家	いえ	house
うち		house; home; family
公園	こうえん	park
学校	がっこう	school
病院	びょういん	hospital
映画館	えいがかん	movie theater
銀行	ぎんこう	bank

さくら町
中町
みなと町
郵便局
レストラン
教会
大学
一丁目
ガソリンスタンド
公園
図書館
交番
食堂
二丁目
ホテル
銀行
スーパー
映画館
喫茶店
病院
三丁目
駐車場
デパート
四丁目
バス停

Both 家 and うち mean *house*, but the nuances are different. 家 usually refers to a private house in contrast to a company building, government office, or store. On the other hand, うち refers to the place where one leads one's life or where a family resides—in other words, a *home*. うち is sometimes used to mean the people who live in one house, or a *family*.

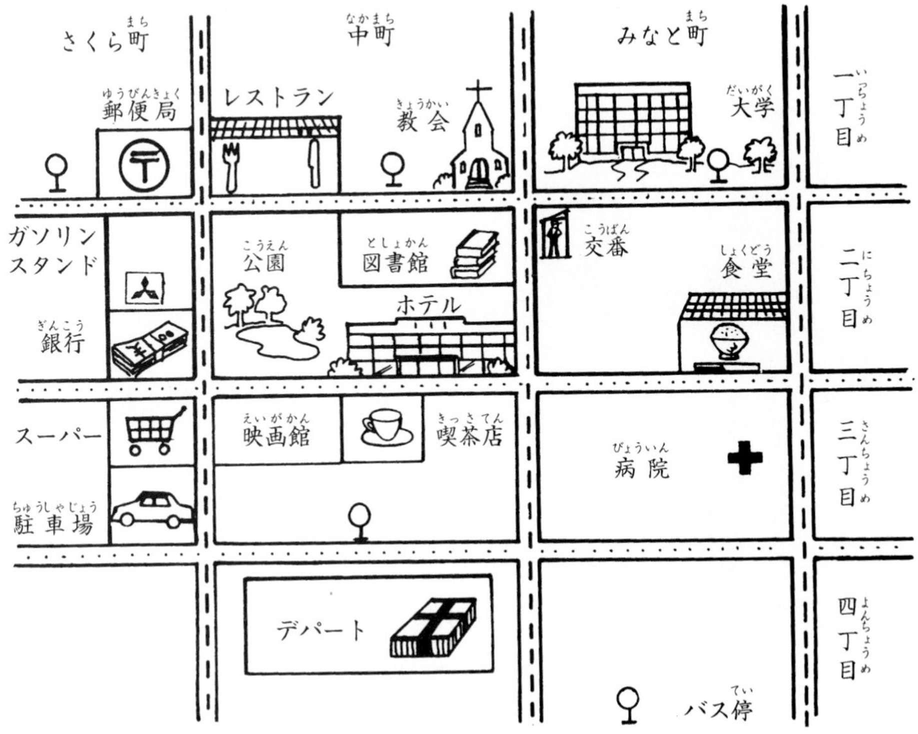

郵便局	ゆうびんきょく	post office
交番	こうばん	police box
喫茶店	きっさてん	coffee (lit., *tea*) shop
ホテル		hotel
(お)寺	(お)てら	Buddhist temple
神社	じんじゃ	Shinto shrine
教会	きょうかい	church
レストラン		restaurant
食堂	しょくどう	dining hall; informal restaurant
スーパー		supermarket
デパート		department store
ガソリン・スタンド		gas station
駐車場	ちゅうしゃじょう	parking lot
バス停	バスてい	bus stop

Review: 大学(だいがく)、図書館(としょかん)、ビル

文化ノート

CULTURE NOTE • 交番(こうばん) *Police Boxes*

In Japan, you will see a *police box* or 交番 in almost every block of a city. The "box" may be a tiny free-standing structure or an office open to the street in a larger building. The policemen (おまわりさん) stationed at each police box patrol the neighborhood (often on bicycles) to help prevent crime, but probably their most frequently performed service is to give directions to people who are lost or don't know how to get to their destination. The boxes are usually open twenty-four hours a day, so citizens always know they can go there for help. It is said that the presence of these police boxes contributes, to a great extent, to the low crime rate in Japan.

プリンスホテルはどこですか。

アクティビティー　13

どこにありますか。(*Where is it?*)

Work in pairs. Look at the preceding map and tell where each place is.

[例]　銀行(ぎんこう)はどこにありますか。
　　さくら町(まち)2丁目(ちょうめ)にあります。

文化ノート

CULTURE NOTE • Japanese Addresses

Japanese addresses are structured very differently from addresses in most parts of the world. Only the main streets in the cities have names, and individual buildings may not have numbers. Large cities such as Tokyo and Osaka are divided into 区 (く) or wards; the 区 are divided into 町 (ちょう), which are towns or neighborhoods; the 町 are divided into 丁目 (ちょうめ); and the blocks (番地 [ばんち]) within each 丁目 are numbered, as are the individual "lots" within each block.

A typical address is 東京都　中野区　野方 2-1-5 or, Tokyo metropolitan area, Nakano ward, Nagata-choo, second choome, first block, fifth "lot." Note that the address narrows the location down from the largest area to the smallest.

People customarily navigate by landmarks, such as stores or schools, rather than streets or intersections. Stores often include maps in their advertisements, giving directions from the nearest station or bus stop, and Japanese people are accustomed to drawing informal maps to help others get around. When all else fails, there's always the **kooban,** where the police consult their detailed neighborhood maps to guide confused pedestrians and drivers to their destinations.

✹ アクティビティー　14

どこにいますか。(*Where is he/she?*)

The following company message board shows where each employee has gone. Practice asking where each person is with your classmates.

[例]　山田(やまだ)さんは今(いま)どこにいますか。—高田(たかだ)さんのオフィスにいます。

NAME	WENT TO	WILL BE BACK
Yamada	Mr. Takada's office	3 P.M.
Tanaka	restaurant	2 P.M.
Yoshida	New York	tomorrow
Saitoo	library	4:30 P.M.
Sawai	Hiroshima	next Monday

Grammar and Practice Activities

7. Indicating Location

ブラウン：すみません。カフェテリアはどこにありますか。
学生(がくせい)：あのビルの一階(いっかい)にあります。
ブラウン：どうもありがとうございます。
学生(がくせい)：どういたしまして。

カワムラ：町田(まちだ)さんはどこにいますか。
チン：今(いま)、横井先生(よこいせんせい)の研究室(けんきゅうしつ)にいます。
カワムラ：横井先生(よこいせんせい)の研究室(けんきゅうしつ)はどこですか。
チン：このビルの三階(さんかい)です。

7.1 The simplest way to indicate the location of something or someone is to use the sentence structure N1 は N2 です, where N1 is a noun indicating a specific thing or person and N2 is a noun representing a place.

銀行(ぎんこう)はどこですか。—銀行(ぎんこう)はあそこです。
Where is the bank? —The bank is over there.

ブラウンさんはどこですか。—ブラウンさんは図書館(としょかん)です。
Where is Ms. Brown? —Ms. Brown is at the library.

BROWN: Excuse me. Where is the cafeteria? STUDENT: There is one on the first floor of that building.
BROWN: Thank you very much. STUDENT: You're welcome.
KAWAMURA: Where is Ms. Machida? CHIN: Right now she is in Professor Yokoi's office.
KAWAMURA: Where is Professor Yokoi's office? CHIN: It's on the third floor of this building.

7.2 In addition, you can use the following structures.

EXISTENT	PARTICLE は	LOCATION	PARTICLE に	QUANTITY	VERB
N1 (inanimate)	は	N2	に		ある(あります)
N1 (animate)	は	N2	に		いる(います)

(number) _____ *is/are at/in* _____ .

銀行(ぎんこう)はどこにありますか。—銀行(ぎんこう)はあそこにあります。
Where is the bank? —It (the bank) is over there.
カワムラさんはカフェテリアにいますか。
Is Mr. Kawamura in the cafeteria?
学生(がくせい)はここに三人(さんにん)います。
There are three students here.

Note the differences between these structures and those expressing existence that are presented in **Grammar 6.5.** These structures require は instead of が, and the location + に comes immediately before the verb. The structure presented in **Grammar 6.5** is used to state ***whether or not*** *people or things exist at a certain place,* whereas the structures presented here are used to state ***where*** *people or things exist.*

8. Positional Words 

カワムラ：机(つくえ)の下(した)にかばんがありますよ。
ブラウン：だれのカバンですか。
カワムラ：さあ…かばんの中(なか)にペンとノートと財布(さいふ)がありますよ。
ブラウン：財布(さいふ)の中(なか)には何(なに)がありますか。
カワムラ：お金(かね)とクレジット・カードがあります。

カワムラ：ブラウンさんはどこにいますか。
町田(まちだ)：あの部屋(へや)の中(なか)にいます。
カワムラ：あの赤(あか)いドアの部屋(へや)ですか。
町田：ええ、そうです。

KAWAMURA: There is a bag under the desk (you know). BROWN: Whose bag is it? KAWAMURA: I wonder... There are pens, notebooks, and a wallet inside it. BROWN: What's inside the wallet? KAWAMURA: There are money and credit cards.

KAWAMURA: Where is Ms. Brown? MACHIDA: She's in that room. KAWAMURA: You mean that room with the red door? MACHIDA: Yes, that's right.

8.1 Such phrases as *in front of* and *to the left of* are expressed in Japanese with the following structure.

N	POSSESSIVE PARTICLE の	POSITIONAL WORD	
机(つくえ)	の	上(うえ)	*on (top of) the desk*
ブラウンさん	の	右(みぎ)	*to the right of Ms. Brown*
東京大学(とうきょうだいがく)	の	そば	*near the University of Tokyo* (lit., *in the vicinity of the University of Tokyo*)

These locational phrases can modify nouns, in which case they precede the noun and are linked to it with the possessive particle の (*of*).

> 机(つくえ)の上(うえ)の本(ほん)
> *the book on the desk* (lit., *the desk's top's book*)
>
> ギブソンさんの右(みぎ)の人(ひと)
> *the person on Ms. Gibson's right* (lit., *Ms. Gibson's right side's person*)

8.2 When these locational phrases are used as the location with existential verbs, they are followed by the particle に, as discussed in **Grammar 6.4** and **7.2**.

> 机(つくえ)の上(うえ)に何(なに)がありますか。—机(つくえ)の上(うえ)に本(ほん)があります。
> *What is on the desk? —There is a book on the desk.*
>
> ブラウンさんの右(みぎ)にだれがいますか。—ブラウンさんの右(みぎ)にカワムラさんがいます。
> *Who is to the right of Ms. Brown? —Mr. Kawamura is on the right side of Ms. Brown.*

Vocabulary: Positional Words

上	うえ	on; above; up	後ろ	うしろ	back; behind
下	した	under; below; down	間	あいだ	between
左	ひだり	left	向かい	むかい	facing; across from
右	みぎ	right	隣	となり	next to; next door
中	なか	in; inside	そば		nearby
外	そと	outside; out	回り	まわり	around
前	まえ	front	横	よこ	side

For a list of other important positional words, see p. 152 of this chapter.

AとBの間 *between A and B*

アクティビティー 15

どこにありますか。 (***Where is it?***)

Make dialogues following the example.

[例] s1: (レストラン) s2: (映画館のとなり) →
s1: レストランはどこにありますか。
s2: 映画館のとなりにあります。

1. s1: (カーティスさん) s2: (図書館の前)
2. s1: (交番) s2: (銀行とスーパーの間)
3. s1: (駐車場) s2: (公園の後ろ)
4. s1: (林さん) s2: (ギブソンさんの右)
5. s1: (喫茶店) s2: (ホテルの中)

アクティビティー 16

本の上に何がありますか。 (***What is on the book?***)

Answer the following questions, using this illustration.

1. 机の上に何がありますか。
2. 箱の中に何がありますか。
3. 本の上に何がありますか。
4. かばんはどこにありますか。

5. カレンダーはどこにありますか。
6. ブラウンさんの後(うし)ろに何(なに)がありますか。
7. カワムラさんはどこにいますか。
8. ギブソンさんはどこにいますか。

アクティビティー 17

どこにいますか。 (*Where is everybody?*)

Answer the following questions, using the illustration. (Everybody's names are on p. 155.)

Useful Vocabulary: ベンチ *bench,* 鳥(とり) *bird,* 犬(いぬ) *dog,* 木(き) *tree*

1. ギブソンさんはどこにいますか。
2. ギブソンさんの右(みぎ)にだれがいますか。
3. ベンチの下(した)に何(なに)がいますか。
4. ベンチの横(よこ)にだれがいますか。
5. 町田(まちだ)さんはどこにいますか。
6. 木(き)の上(うえ)に何(なに)がいますか。
7. 車(くるま)の中(なか)にだれがいますか。
8. 車(くるま)の後(うし)ろにだれがいますか。

✸ アクティビティー 18

ダイアログ：スーパーはどこにありますか。(*Where is the supermarket?*)

道(みち)で

s1: すみません。このへんに<u>スーパー</u>はありますか。

s2: ええ、<u>駅(えき)の前(まえ)</u>にありますよ。

s1: どんな建物(たてもの)ですか。

s2: <u>白(しろ)い、大(おお)きな建物(たてもの)</u>ですよ。

s1: どうもありがとうございました。

s2: どういたしまして。

白い *white*

As you have seen, すみません can be used in a variety of contexts. You have used it to convey an apology (*I'm sorry*) or your gratitude, especially when someone has gone out of their way for you (*thank you*). In this dialogue, すみません is used to get someone's attention in order to ask for help (*excuse me*).

Practice the dialogue, substituting the following words and expressions for the underlined portions.

1. レストラン
   銀行(ぎんこう)のとなり
   グリーンのビル
2. 郵便局(ゆうびんきょく)
   映画館(えいがかん)と病院(びょういん)の間(あいだ)
   赤(あか)い、小(ちい)さな建物(たてもの)
3. 病院(びょういん)
   公園(こうえん)のそば
   白(しろ)い、きれいな建物(たてもの)
4. 食堂(しょくどう)
   図書館(としょかん)の前(まえ)
   古(ふる)い建物(たてもの)
5. ホテル
   映画館(えいがかん)の右(みぎ)
   グレーのビル

言語ノート

Sentence-Final よ

The sentence-final particle よ is used by a speaker to indicate strong conviction about a statement or to indicate that he or she is giving new information to the listener; that is, information that the speaker thinks he or she, but not the listener, knows.

On the street A: Excuse me. Is there a <u>supermarket</u> around here? B: Yes, there's one <u>in front of the station</u>. A: What kind of building is it? B: It's <u>a large, white building</u>. A: Thank you very much. B: You're welcome.

カフェテリアはどこですか。
Where is the cafeteria?
あそこですよ。
It's over there.

わかりますか。
Do you understand?
ええ、もちろんわかりますよ。
Yes, of course, I understand.

Note that, in general, sentence-final よ is not appropriate when speaking to a superior, because it can sound too direct or abrupt.

Vocabulary Library

More Positional Words

真ん中	まんなか	middle
はじ		edge
北	きた	north
南	みなみ	south
東	ひがし	east
西	にし	west
こちら側	こちらがわ	this side
向こう側	むこうがわ	the other side

アクティビティー 19

ボールは箱(はこ)の上(うえ)にあります。(*The ball is on the box.*)

What relation does the ball(s) have to the box in the following illustrations?

Useful Word: 箱 *box*

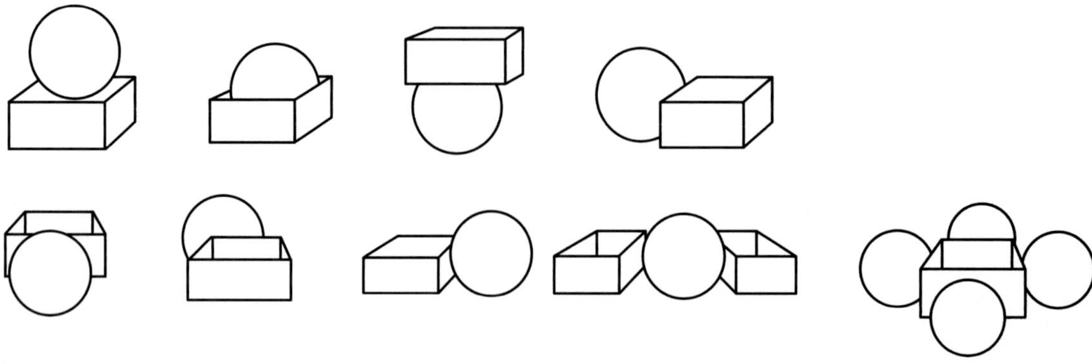

✸ アクティビティー 20

どこにありますか。(*Where is it?*)

Look at the picture and answer the following questions.

1. スーパーはどこにありますか。
2. 郵便局はどこにありますか。
3. レストラン「フラミンゴ」はどこにありますか。
4. 学校はどこにありますか。
5. 駐車場はどこにありますか。
6. デパートはどこにありますか。
7. 地下鉄の駅はどこにありますか。
8. 喫茶店のとなりに何がありますか。

Make your own questions to ask your classmates.

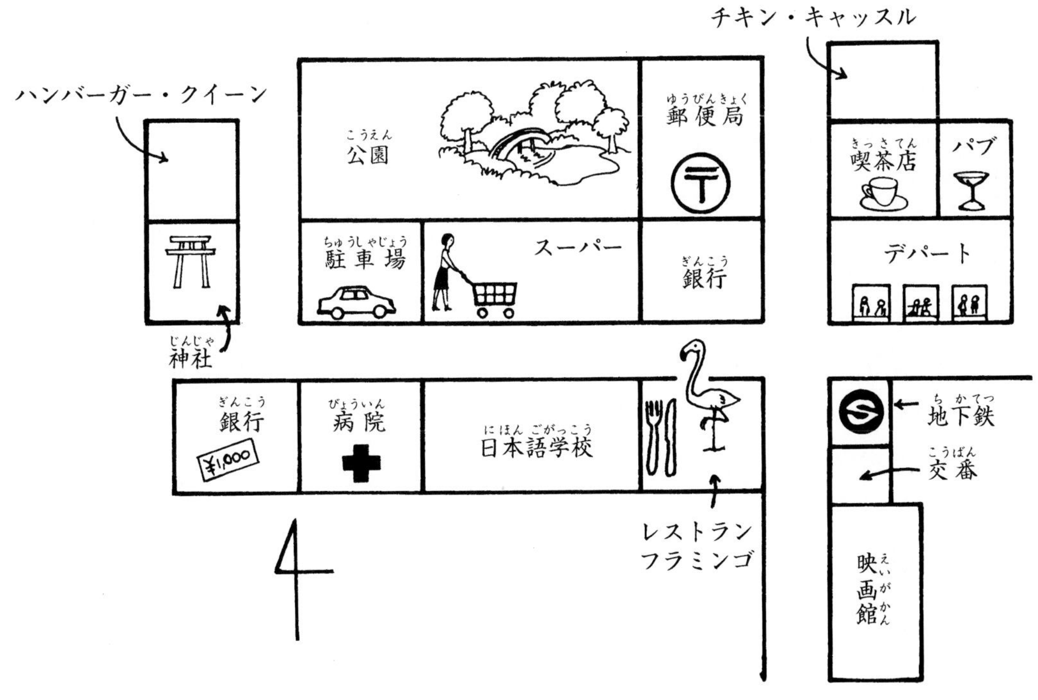

✹ アクティビティー 21

ダイアログ：いいレストランはありますか (*Is there a good restaurant?*)

カワムラさんと町田さんが話しています。

カワムラ：この近所にいいレストランはありますか。
町田：ええ、ありますよ。となりのビルの4階にあります。
カワムラ：名前は。
町田：「ナポレオン」です。

Using the dialogue as a guide, ask your classmates whether each of the following things exists near their house or apartment. If yes, ask specifically where it is (e.g., *Is it next to a shopping mall?*). In addition, ask what it's called.

1. bank
2. good restaurant
3. convenience store (コンビニエンス・ストア)
4. beautiful park
5. movie theater
6. good hotel
7. hospital
8. large supermarket
9. tall building
10. famous school

✹ アクティビティー 22

どこにいますか。(*Where is he?*)

Based on the illustration, answer the following questions.

1. チンさんはどこにいますか。
2. 町田さんはどこにいますか。
3. カーティスさんはどこにいますか。
4. 林さんはどこにいますか。
5. ギブソンさんはどこにいますか。
6. カワムラさんの右にだれがいますか。
7. 横井先生の前にだれがいますか。
8. 横井先生の後ろにだれがいますか。

Mr. Kawamura and Ms. Machida are talking. KAWAMURA: Is there a good restaurant in this neighborhood? MACHIDA: Yes, there is. There is one on the fourth floor of the building next door. KAWAMURA: What's it called? MACHIDA: "Napoleon."

9. Numerals and Counters

カワムラ：すみません。佐藤(さとう)さんのうちはどこでしょうか。
おまわりさん：このへんに佐藤(さとう)さんは三軒(さんけん)あります。
どの佐藤(さとう)さんですか。
カワムラ：佐藤良男(さとうよしお)さんです。
おまわりさん：佐藤良男(さとうよしお)さんも二人(ふたり)います。

ブラウン：この家(いえ)には部屋(へや)がいくつありますか。
不動産屋(ふどうさんや)：五(いつ)つあります。
ブラウン：トイレはいくつありますか。
不動産屋：二つあります。一階(いっかい)に一(ひと)つ、二階(にかい)に一(ひと)つです。

KAWAMURA: Excuse me. Where is Mr. Satoo's residence? POLICEMAN: There are three Satoos in this neighborhood. Which Mr. Satoo do you mean? KAWAMURA: Mr. Yoshio Satoo. POLICEMAN: There are two Yoshio Satoos.

BROWN: How many rooms does this house have? REAL ESTATE AGENT: It has five. BROWN: How many bathrooms does it have? REAL ESTATE AGENT: It has two. There is one on the first floor, and another on the second floor.

9.1 There are two numerical systems in Japanese: the Japanese system and the Sino-Japanese system. In the Japanese system, which covers only from one to ten, つ is the general counter. After 11, there is only one system: the Sino-Japanese system.

Refer to Appendix 3.

Numbers 1 through 10

	JAPANESE SYSTEM	SINO-JAPANESE SYSTEM		JAPANESE SYSTEM	SINO-JAPANESE SYSTEM
1	ひとつ（一つ）	いち（一）	6	むっつ（六つ）	ろく（六）
2	ふたつ（二つ）	に（二）	7	ななつ（七つ）	しち／なな（七）
3	みっつ（三つ）	さん（三）	8	やっつ（八つ）	はち（八）
4	よっつ（四つ）	し／よん（四）	9	ここのつ（九つ）	きゅう／く（九）
5	いつつ（五つ）	ご（五）	10	とお（十）	じゅう（十）

9.2 Large numbers are expressed in units of 10,000（万), 100,000,000 (億; *100 million*), and 1,000,000,000,000 (兆; *1 trillion*).

0 (zero) is read as ゼロ or 零(れい)。

Large Numbers

10	じゅう(十)
100	ひゃく(百)
1,000	(いっ) せん ([一] 千)
10,000	いちまん (一万)
100,000	じゅうまん (十万)
1,000,000	ひゃくまん (百万)
10,000,000	(いっ) せんまん ([一] 千万)
100,000,000	いちおく (一億)

Notice these phonological (sound) changes when 1, 3, 6, 8, and 10 appear before 百、千、or 兆.

1	一千（いっせん)、一兆(いっちょう)
3	三百（さんびゃく)、三千（さんぜん)
6	六百（ろっぴゃく)
8	八百（はっぴゃく)
10	十兆（じゅっちょう *or* じっちょう)

Since the Japanese number system goes from thousands to ten thousands instead of from thousands to millions, English-speakers sometimes have trouble reading large numbers aloud.

A handy way to avoid confusion is to imagine that the number has a comma every four places from the right. The four digits to the left of the comma are read as multiples of 万, and the next four digits beyond that are read as multiples of 億.

22,000 → 2,2000 or 二万二千
600,000 → 60,0000 or 六十万
1,000,000 → 100,0000 or 百万
250,000,000 → 2,5000,0000 or 二億五千万

In real life, of course, Japanese people write large numbers with commas every three places.

9.3 When you count objects, you have to attach counter suffixes (a suffix is an element attached to the end of another element) to numbers. Which counter you use depends on the classification of what you count. Although there are many counters in Japanese (there is a dictionary just of counters), the number of commonly used counters is limited.

Some Important Counters

Bold characters indicate counters already introduced. You should know these.

a. ～人 (にん) people
b. ～ヶ月 (かげつ) number of months
c. ～台 (だい) heavy machinery, vehicles, office equipment, etc.
d. ～番 (ばん) number of order (No. 1, No. 2, etc.)
e. ～度 (ど) ...times (occurrences, repetitions); degrees (temperature)
f. ～時間 (じかん) number of hours
g. ～枚 (まい) thin, flat items (paper, bedsheets, floppy disks, toast, etc.)
h. ～着 (ちゃく) clothes
i. ～課 (か) lessons
j. ～歳 (さい) age
k. ～冊 (さつ) books, notebooks, boundvolumes
l. ～頭 (とう) large animals (elephant, whale, horse, etc.)
m. ～分 (ふん) minutes
n. ～杯 (はい) cupfuls or glassfuls
o. ～本 (ほん) long, thin items (pencil, banana, leg, tree, road, tapes, etc.)
p. ～階 (かい) floors of a building
q. ～足 (そく) shoes, socks, footwear
r. ～匹 (ひき) small animals (dog, cat, etc.)
s. ～羽 (わ) birds
t. ～軒 (けん) houses, buildings
u. ～倍 (ばい) ...times (magnification)
v. ～回 (かい) ...times (occurrences)
w. ～個 (こ) round or square objects (pears, bars of soap, boxes, etc.)

山口さんのうちには車が二台あります。
There are two cars at Mr. Yamaguchi's house.
カウンターの上にブラウスが三枚あります。
There are three blouses on the counter.
テーブルの上にバナナが五本あります。
There are five bananas on the table.

Blouses and sweaters are counted with 〜枚. Pants are counted with 〜本.

Depending on the numbers that come before the counters, some counters show phonological changes. Notice the exception for counting people (人). *One* and *two* use the Japanese system, while the rest use the Sino-Japanese system.

Refer to Appendix 4.

	〜人 (にん)	〜台 (だい)	〜個 (こ)	〜分 (ふん)	〜軒 (けん)
1	ひとり	いちだい	いっこ	いっぷん	いっけん
2	ふたり	にだい	にこ	にふん	にけん
3	さんにん	さんだい	さんこ	さんぷん	さんけん
					さんげん
4	よにん	よんだい	よんこ	よんぷん	よんけん
5	ごにん	ごだい	ごこ	ごふん	ごけん
6	ろくにん	ろくだい	ろっこ	ろっぷん	ろっけん
7	ななにん	ななだい	ななこ	ななふん	ななけん
	しちにん	しちだい	しちこ	しちふん	しちけん
8	はちにん	はちだい	はっこ	はっぷん	はっけん
			はちこ	はちふん	はちけん
9	きゅうにん	きゅうだい	きゅうこ	きゅうふん	きゅうけん
	くにん				
10	じゅうにん	じゅうだい	じゅっこ	じゅっぷん	じゅっけん
			じっこ	じっぷん	じっけん

9.4 When you would like to ask *how many,* attach 何 (なん) before these counters. The interrogative corresponding to the general counter 〜つ is いくつ.

このクラスに学生は何人いますか。
How many students are there in this class?
ここに本が何冊ありますか。
How many books are here?
まどはいくつありますか。
How many windows are there?

After 何, some counters undergo a sound change.

何杯 (なんばい)
何本 (なんぼん)
何匹 (なんびき)

アクティビティー 23

何本(なんぼん)ありますか。 *(How many [long, thin objects] are there?)*

What counter do you think is used to count the following? Refer to the preceding list of counters.

1. socks
2. fingers
3. computers
4. horses
5. jackets
6. envelopes
7. movie theaters
8. streets
9. parks
10. goldfish

アクティビティー 24

車(くるま)が一台(いちだい)あります。*(There's one car.)*

These are answers. What are the questions in Japanese?

1. There are five pencils on the desk.
2. There are three cars at home.
3. There are two windows in the classroom.
4. There is one person to the left of Mr. Yamada.
5. There are ten books in my bag.
6. There are six coffee shops in this town.
7. There are eight books over there.
8. There are three bananas on the table.
9. There are three parks in this neighborhood.

アクティビティー 25

高(たか)いですね。*(It's expensive, isn't it!)*

[例] —The average starting salary in your future career
—三万(さんまん)ドルです。

1. How many dollars (ドル) are each of these?
   a. a year's tuition, room, and board for an on-campus student at your college or university
   b. the price of the car you hope to own some day
   c. the average price of a house in your community
   d. the value of ¥1,000,000 in your country's currency (Check the business section of your local newspaper if you don't know the current exchange rate.)

e. the current jackpot in your state or province's lottery
f. the annual salary of your favorite sports star
g. the price of the computer you hope to own some day

2. As you plan your trip to Japan on a moderate budget, you decide that you can spend $75 per night for a hotel, $25 a day for meals, and $25 a day for incidentals. (Your Japan Rail Pass will take care of most of your transportation needs.) How many yen will you need each day? (Use the exchange rate you looked up earlier.)

アクティビティー 26

銀行は何軒ありますか。(*How many banks are there?*)

カワムラ： 銀行はこの近所に何軒ありますか。
山口： 三軒あります。

Ask a classmate how many gas stations, movie theaters, and other establishments there are in the neighborhood.

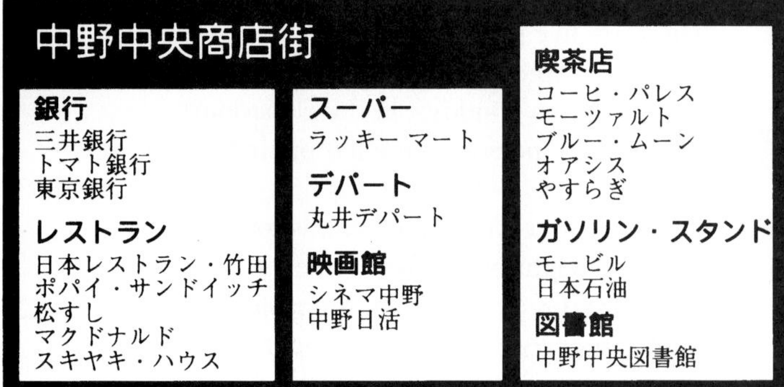

アクティビティー 27

ダイアログ：学生は何人いますか。(*How many students are there?*)
町田さんとブラウンさんが話しています。

町田： ブラウンさんの日本語のクラスに学生は何人いますか。
ブラウン： ええと、全部で15人ぐらいいます。
町田： 全部アメリカ人ですか。
ブラウン： いいえ、中国人が五人とカナダ人が二人います。

KAWAMURA: How many banks are there in this neighborhood? YAMAGUCHI: There are three.

Ms. Machida and Ms. Brown are talking MACHIDA: How many students are in your Japanese class, Ms. Brown? BROWN: Uh…there are a total of fifteen students. MACHIDA: Are they all Americans? BROWN: No, there are five Chinese and two Canadians.

Vocabulary: Counting People 

一人	ひとり	one person
二人	ふたり	two people
三人	さんにん	three people
四人	よにん	four people
五人	ごにん	five people
六人	ろくにん	six people
七人	しちにん ななにん	seven people
八人	はちにん	eight people
九人	きゅうにん、くにん	nine people
十人	じゅうにん	ten people
十一人	じゅういちにん	eleven people
百人	ひゃくにん	one hundred people
何人	なんにん	how many people

アクティビティー 28

何人(なんにん)いますか。(*How many people are there?*)

Answer these questions about your class.

1. このクラスに学生(がくせい)は何人(なんにん)いますか。
2. 先生(せんせい)は何人(なんにん)いますか。
3. 男(おとこ) (*male*) の学生(がくせい)は何人(なんにん)いますか。
4. 女(おんな) (*female*) の学生(がくせい)は何人(なんにん)いますか。
5. 日本人(にほんじん)は何人(なんにん)いますか。
6. アメリカ人(じん)は何人(なんにん)いますか。

10. Expressing Likes and Dislikes: 好き and きらい

町田(まちだ)：ブラウンさんはどんな学科(がっか)が好(す)きですか。
ブラウン：歴史学(れきしがく)が好(す)きです。
町田(まちだ)：きらいな学科(がっか)はありますか。
ブラウン：ええ、数学(すうがく)が大(だい)きらいです。
林(はやし)：ブラウンさんはお酒(さけ)が好(す)きですか。
ブラウン：あまり好(す)きではありません。
林さんは。
林(はやし)：大好(だいす)きです。

MACHIDA: What academic subject do you like, Ms. Brown? BROWN: I like history. MACHIDA: Is there any subject that you don't like? BROWN: Yes, I hate math.

HAYASHI: Do you like sake, (Ms. Brown)? BROWN: I don't like it very much. How about you, (Mr. Hayashi)? HAYASHI: I love it.

Such meanings as *I like* and *I dislike* are expressed by na-adjectives 好(す)き and きらい, respectively. You can use these adjectives both prenominally and predicatively.

> わたしの好(す)きな町(まち)
> *a town I like; a favorite town of mine*
> わたしのきらいなところ
> *a place I dislike*
> 山口(やまぐち)さんはあの喫茶店(きっさてん)が好(す)きです。
> *Mr. Yamaguchi likes that coffee shop.*
> チンさんは大(おお)きい町(まち)がきらいです。
> *Ms. Chin doesn't like large cities.*

Note that the object of liking and disliking (*coffee shops* and *cities* in the above examples) is marked with the particle が.

言語ノート

Different Degrees of Liking and Disliking

野菜(やさい)が好(す)きですか。	*Do you like vegetables?*
—はい、大好(だいす)きです。	*—Yes, I like them very much.*
—はい、好きです。	*—Yes, I like them.*
—まあまあです。	*—They're okay.* (lit., *So-so.*)
—あまり好きではありません。	*—I don't like them very much.*
—いいえ、きらいです。	*—No, I dislike them.*
—いいえ、大(だい)きらいです。	*—No, I hate them.*

アクティビティー 29

好(す)きですか；きらいですか。 (*Do you like or dislike it?*)

What's your Japanese-language and culture interest quotient? Ask a classmate the following questions. What's the score?

(5 points)	(4)	(3)	(2)	(1)	(0)
大好(だいす)き	好(す)き	まあまあ	きらい	大(だい)きらい	わかりません (*I'm unfamiliar with it.*)

1. てんぷらが好きですか。
2. すしが好きですか。
3. ひらがなが好きですか。
4. カタカナが好きですか。
5. 漢字が好きですか。
6. 日本語のクラスが好きですか。
7. 日本語の先生が好きですか。 (Be careful!)
8. 歌舞伎が好きですか。
9. すもうが好きですか。

Total points: ______ 点

点 is a counter for points.

アクティビティー 30

大きい町が好きですか。 (*Do you like large towns?*)

Answer these questions.

1. 大きい町が好きですか、小さい町が好きですか。
2. 静かなところが好きですか、にぎやかなところが好きですか。
3. 新しい町が好きですか、古い町が好きですか。
4. どんな映画が好きですか。

   Useful words: アクション映画、SF映画、コメディー、ロマンス、ドラマ

5. どんな音楽が好きですか。

   Useful words: クラシック、ロック、ラップ、カントリーアンドウエスタン、ゴスペル

6. どんな食べ物が好きですか。
7. どんな食べ物がきらいですか。
8. どんなスポーツが好きですか。
9. どんな学科 (*academic subject*) が好きですか。

アクティビティー 31

大きい町が好きですか、小さい町が好きですか。(*Do you like big towns or little towns?*)

Answer the following questions.

1. 日本料理が好きですか。
2. 勉強が好きですか。

3. どんなスポーツが好きですか。

4. どんな音楽が好きですか。

5. 静かなところが好きですか、にぎやかなところが好きですか。

6. 大きい町が好きですか、小さい町が好きですか。

7. どんな料理が好きですか。

8. どんな食べ物 (*food*) がきらいですか。

✹ アクティビティー　32

この町が好きな人は何人いますか。(*How many people like this town?*)

Choose one question from the following list and ask it of ten classmates. Then report to the class how many people answered yes.

[例]　肉が好きですか。
—はい、好きです。
—いいえ、きらいです。
肉が好きな人は八人いました。
肉がきらいな人は二人いました。

1. 魚が好きですか。
2. サラダが好きですか。
3. 日本料理が好きですか。
4. パーティーが好きですか。
5. この大学が好きですか。
6. この町が好きですか。
7. スポーツが好きですか。
8. お酒 (*sake*) が好きですか。
9. バナナが好きですか。
10. 日本語のクラスが好きですか。

Language Skills

Reading and Writing

Reading 1 ブラウンさんのアパートの近所（きんじょ）

Before You Read

Linda Brown lives in an apartment in Nakano. The following passage describes her apartment and neighborhood. Before reading it, look at the map. Can you remember what the place labels mean? If not, go to the **Vocabulary** section and find them.

Do you remember these words indicating positions?

回り（まわ）	となり	上（うえ）
右（みぎ）	前（まえ）	間（あいだ）
左（ひだり）	向（む）こう側（がわ）	後（うし）ろ

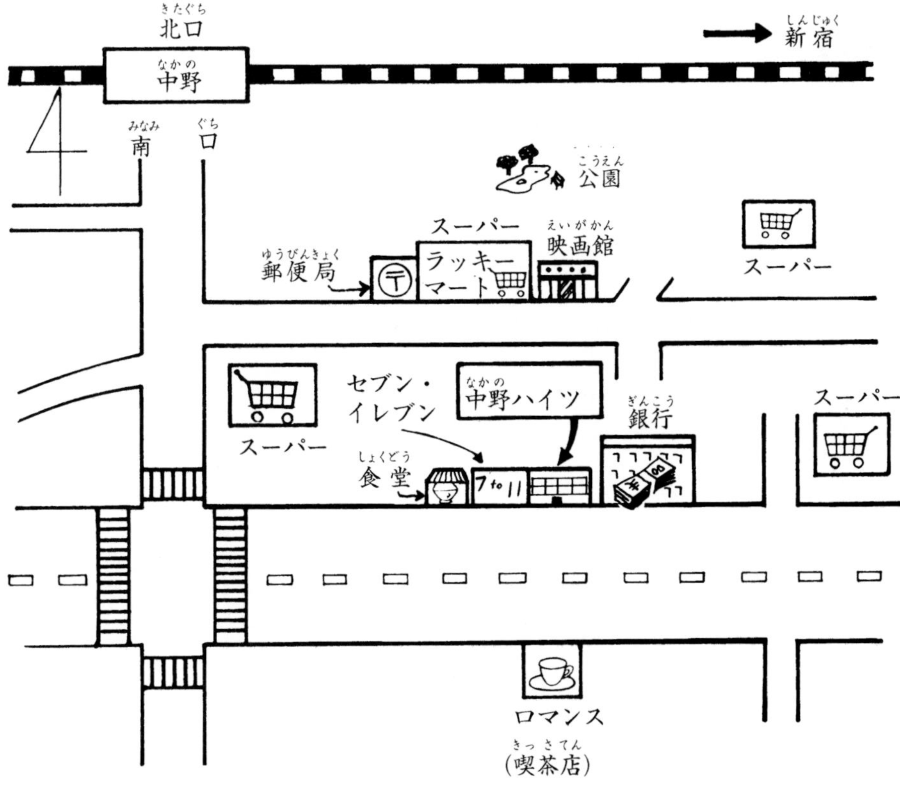

Now Read It!

ブラウンさんのアパートは東京の中野にあります。中野は電車で新宿から10分ぐらいです。ブラウンさんのアパートは駅から徒歩で5分です。東京大学まで地下鉄で30分です。とても便利です。

ブラウンさんのアパートの名前は「中野ハイツ」です。3階建てです。

ブラウンさんのアパートは2階にあります。

アパートの回りにはいろいろなものがあります。アパートの右には銀行があります。アパートの左にはセブンイレブンがあります。セブンイレブンのとなりに食堂があります。とても小さな食堂です。でも、とてもおいしいです。ですから、いつもお客さんがたくさんいます。ブラウンさんはその食堂のカレーライスが大好きです。

アパートの前には広い道があります。道の向こう側に喫茶店があります。名前は「ロマンス」です。「ロマンス」にはウエートレスが3人います。ウエートレスの山本さゆりさんはブラウンさんのいい友だちです。

「ロマンス」の上にパブがあります。

ブラウンさんのアパートの近所にはスーパーが4軒あります。ブラウンさんは「ラッキーマート」が好きです。このスーパーは郵便局と映画館の間にあります。小さなスーパーです。とても安いです。

スーパーの後ろに小さな公園があります。

ブラウンさんは中野が大好きです。

中野 *Nakano (a place in Tokyo)*

から *from*

まで *(up) to*

中野ハイツ *Nakano Heights* (name of an apartment building) / 3 階建て *three-story* (building)

いろいろ(な) *various* / もの *things*

でも *however; but* / おいしい *delicious*

ですから *therefore* / いつも *always* / お客さん *customer*

パブ *pub*

After You Finish Reading

Answer these questions in English.

1. How long does it take to go from Shinjuku to Nakano by electric train?
2. How many minutes does it take to walk from Nakano Station to Linda's apartment?
3. How many floors does Linda's apartment building have?
4. What is to the left of Linda's apartment?
5. What is to the left of that?
6. Why does the small restaurant have many customers?
7. What does Linda like to eat there?
8. What is across the street from the apartment?
9. Where is the pub?
10. How many supermarkets are there in Linda's neighborhood?
11. Where is Lucky Mart?
12. What is behind Lucky Mart?

Fill in the blanks.

1. ブラウンさんのアパートから東京大学まで地下鉄で(　　)ぐらいです。
2. ブラウンさんのアパートは「中野ハイツ」の(　　)にあります。
3. アパートの(　　)にはいろいろなものがあります。
4. アパートの(　　)には銀行があります。
5. セブンイレブンのとなりの小さな食堂はとても(　　)です。
6. アパートの(　　)に広い道があります。
7. 「ロマンス」にはウエートレスが(　　)います。
8. 「ロマンス」の(　　)にパブがあります。
9. 「ラッキーマート」は郵便局と映画館の(　　)にあります。
10. 公園は「ラッキーマート」の(　　)にあります。

Writing 1

Imagine you live in the apartment marked with ● on the map below. Write a paragraph describing your neighborhood. Start with わたしのアパートのとなりにスーパーがあります.

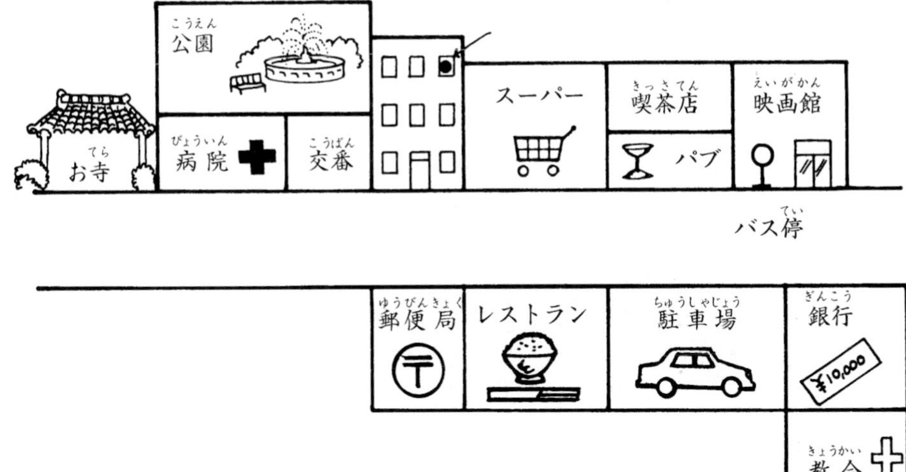

Reading 2 林さんのふるさと

ふるさと *hometown*

Before You Read

Pair up with a classmate. Discuss which of the following you can find in large cities, in very small towns, or in both.

1. 電車(でんしゃ)の駅(えき)
2. 地下鉄(ちかてつ)の駅(えき)
3. 大学(だいがく)
4. バス停(てい)
5. 病院(びょういん)
6. 映画館(えいがかん)
7. ホテル
8. 銀行(ぎんこう)
9. 喫茶店(きっさてん)
10. デパート
11. スーパー
12. レストラン
13. 交番(こうばん)

What is the counter for each of the following?

1. 人(ひと)
2. ベンチ
3. 家(いえ)
4. 犬(いぬ)
5. 道(みち)

Now Read It!

This passage is a description of Mr. Hayashi's hometown village. What things listed in the first prereading activity can be found in his hometown? (Some may not be mentioned.)

カワムラさんのクラスメートの林(はやし)さんは九州(きゅうしゅう)の小(ちい)さい村(むら)の出身(しゅっしん)です。人口(じんこう)は八百人(はっぴゃくにん)ぐらいです。家(いえ)が百五十軒(ひゃくごじゅっけん)あります。病院(びょういん)はありません。ホテルもありません。デパートもありません。レストランもありません。

村(むら)は九州(きゅうしゅう)の真(ま)ん中(なか)にあります。村(むら)の回(まわ)りに高(たか)い山(やま)がたくさんあります。山の向(む)こうに大(おお)きい町(まち)があります。村と町の間(あいだ)には道(みち)が一本(いっぽん)あります。町からバスで一時間(いちじかん)です。電車(でんしゃ)はありません。

村にバス停(てい)が一つ(ひと)あります。バス停は小さいスーパーの前(まえ)にあります。バス停(てい)の横(よこ)に古(ふる)いベンチが一つあります。ベンチの回(まわ)りにいつも村(むら)の人(ひと)がいます。スーパーのとなりに交番(こうばん)があります。交番の向(む)かいに林さんの家(いえ)があります。

九州 *Kyushu* (large island in southern Japan)

山 *mountain*

向こう *over*

バス停 (*bus stop*)

After You Finish Reading

1. What things listed in the first prereading activity exist in Mr. Hayashi's village?
2. Tell whether each of the following is true or false.
   a. Mr. Hayashi's village has a population of about 600.
   b. His village has 150 houses.
   c. His village is in the middle of Kyushu.
   d. His village is surrounded by mountains.

e. There are two roads connecting his village and the next town.
f. It takes two hours to travel by bus from his village to the next town.
g. There is a bus stop in front of a small supermarket.
h. The bench is new.
i. There is a police box next to the supermarket.
j. Mr. Hayashi's house is across the street from the police box.

3. Ask a classmate five questions in Japanese about the passage.

Writing 2

Write a short paragraph describing your neighborhood. Try to use あります and positional words.

Language Functions and Situations

Making Communication Work

Here are some useful techniques for making sure you're communicating effectively.

1. Ask someone to repeat something.

s1: スーパーは銀行(ぎんこう)の前(まえ)にあります。
s2: すみません。もう一度(いちど)ゆっくりお願(ねが)いします。
s1: スーパーは銀行(ぎんこう)の前(まえ)にあります。

2. Check that you have understood.

s1: スーパーは銀行(ぎんこう)の前(まえ)にあります。
s2: 銀行(ぎんこう)の前(まえ)ですね。
s1: はい、そうです。

s1: 学生(がくせい)は26人(にん)います。
s2: 25人(にん)ですか。
s1: いいえ、26人です。

3. Say you have understood.

s1: ギブソンさんは図書館(としょかん)にいます。
s2: はい、わかりました。

4. Say you didn't understand.

s1: スーパーはあの映画館(えいがかん)のとなりにあります。
s2: すみません。わかりません。
s1: じゃ、つれていってあげましょう。(*Then, I'll take you there.*)

5. Show you are listening.

s1: あそこに銀行(ぎんこう)がありますね。
s2: ええ。
s1: そのとなりにレストランがありますね。
s2: はい。
s1: 喫茶店(きっさてん)はあのレストランの上(うえ)にあります。

言語ノート

あいづち (*Yes, I'm following you…*)

One of the first things you notice when talking with Japanese people is that they frequently nod or interject はい, ええ, ああ, そうですか, うんうん, and so on after each phrase you utter. This is not a sign of impatience, boredom, or rudeness. Rather, they are engaging in the participatory style of communication that characterizes spoken Japanese. With these short interjections called あいづち, the listener is letting you know that he or she is still following you: "Yes, I'm following you, so please continue." (Even though はい [*yes*] is one of these **aizuchi**, here it doesn't necessarily mean *yes, I agree.*)

If the listener does *not* show any reaction a Japanese speaker may feel so uneasy that he will stop and ask わかりますか (*Do you understand?*) or start over at the beginning of the conversation, perhaps speaking more deliberately, on the assumption that the listener didn't understand. This happens frequently in telephone conversations; if the listener misses too many あいづち, the speaker will start over with もしもし (*Hello?*). Mastering the correct use of あいづち will go a long way toward enhancing your fluency.

Showing Location on a Map

道(みち)で

s1: すみません。赤坂(あかさか)ホテルはどこですか。
s2: 赤坂(あかさか)ホテルですか。ここに地図(ちず)がありますから、見(み)てください。
s1: どうもすみません。
s2: 今(いま)ここにいます。赤坂(あかさか)ホテルはここです。
となりに映画館(えいがかん)と銀行(ぎんこう)があります。大(おお)きな白(しろ)いビルです。

On the street s1: Excuse me. Where is Akasaka Hotel? s2: Akasaka Hotel? Here is a map, so please take a look. s1: Thank you for taking the trouble. s2: (pointing to a spot on the map) We are here (now). (pointing to a different spot) Akasaka Hotel is here. Next to it are a movie theater and a bank. It is a large, white building.

s1: ここから何分(なんぷん)ぐらいですか。
s2: そうですね。10分(じゅっぷん) ぐらいですね。
s1: どうもありがとうございました。
s2: どういたしまして。

Role-Play

Use the map here to practice showing location or giving directions to a classmate. Assume that you are standing in front of the station. Try to use some of the phrases you learned in **Making Communication Work.** Use your imagination to describe the building and how long it takes to get there.

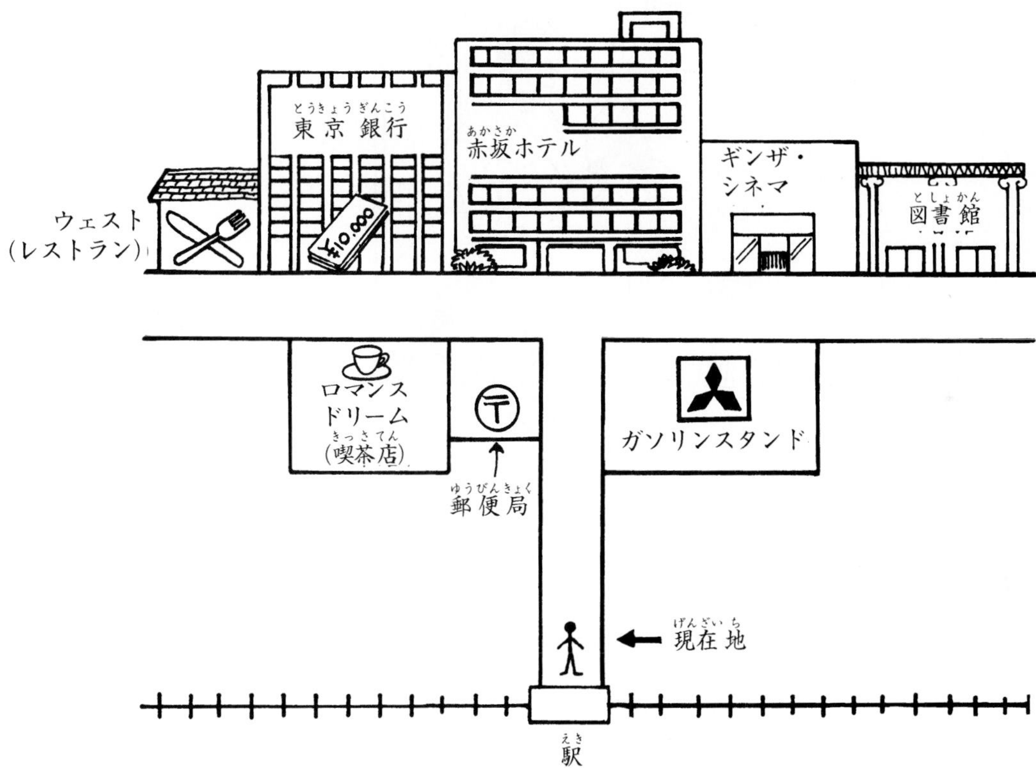

s1: Approximately how many minutes is it from here? s2: Let me see…it's about ten minutes.
s1: Thank you very much. s2: You're welcome.

Listening Comprehension

While listening to your instructor, draw the items mentioned at the appropriate places in the picture.

Vocabulary

Transportation

ジェイアール	JR	JR (Japan Railways)
くるま	車	car
じてんしゃ	自転車	bicycle
ちかてつ	地下鉄	subway
でんしゃ	電車	electric train
とほ	徒歩	walking; on foot

Loanwords: タクシー、バス

Places

いえ	家	house	じんじゃ	神社	(Shinto) shrine
うち		house; (my) home	たてもの	建物	building
えいがかん	映画館	movie theater	ちゅうしゃじょう	駐車場	parking lot
えき	駅	station	とおり	通り	avenue; street
おてら	お寺	(Buddhist) temple	ところ	所	place
きっさてん	喫茶店	coffee (lit., *tea*) shop	としょかん	図書館	library
きょうかい	教会	church	バスてい	バス停	bus stop
ぎんこう	銀行	bank	びょういん	病院	hospital
きんじょ	近所	neighborhood	まち	町	town
こうえん	公園	park	みち	道	street
こうがい	郊外	suburbs	むら	村	village
こうばん	交番	police box	ゆうびんきょく	郵便局	post office
し	市	city			
しょくどう	食堂	dining hall; informal restaurant			

Loanwords: ホテル、レストラン、ガソリンスタンド、スーパー、デパート

Review: 学校(がっこう)、大学(だいがく)、ビル

Nouns

じんこう	人口	population
たべもの	食べ物	food

Adjectives

あかい	赤い	red
あたらしい	新しい	new
あつい	暑い	hot
あつい	厚い	thick
あまい		sweet
いい		good
うすい		thin
うるさい		noisy; annoying
おおい	多い	many; much
おおきい／おおきな	大きい／大きな	large; big
おもい	重い	heavy
おもしろい		interesting, funny
かるい	軽い	light
きたない	汚い	dirty
きびしい		strict
きれい(な)		attractive; pretty; clean
げんき(な)	元気(な)	healthy; energetic

しずか(な)	静か(な)	quiet; peaceful
しろい	白い	white
しんせつ(な)		kind
すくない	少ない	few
せまい	狭い	small in area; narrow
だいきらい(な)	大嫌い(な)	hated
だいすき(な)	大好き(な)	favorite; very well-liked
たかい	高い	high; expensive
ちいさい／ちいさな	小さい／小さな	small
ちかい	近い	near; close
つまらない		boring; dull
とおい	遠い	far
ながい	長い	long
にぎやか(な)		lively
ひくい	低い	low
ひろい	広い	spacious; wide
ふべん(な)	不便(な)	inconvenient
ふるい	古い	old
べんり(な)	便利(な)	convenient
みじかい	短い	short
まずい		bad tasting
まじめ		serious
むずかしい		difficult
やさしい		easy; lenient; nice
やすい	安い	inexpensive; cheap
ゆうめい(な)	有名(な)	famous
わかい	若い	young
わるい	悪い	bad

Loanword: ハンサム(な)、エレガント(な)、タフ(な)

Review: 好(す)き(な)、嫌(きら)い(な)

Adverbs

あ(ん)まり	(+ *negative*) not so much
たくさん	a lot
まあまあ	so-so, passable

Review: とても

Verbs

ある	there is/are (*inanimate things*)
いる	there is/are (*people, animals*)

Counting Time

いっぷん	一分	one minute	はっぷん	八分	eight minutes
にふん	二分	two minutes	きゅうふん	九分	nine minutes
さんぷん	三分	three minutes	じゅっぷん、じっぷん	十分	ten minutes
よんぷん、よんふん	四分	four minutes	いちじかん	一時間	one hour
ごふん	五分	five minutes	いちじかんはん	一時間半	one and a half hours
ろっぷん	六分	six minutes	にじかん	二時間	two hours
ななふん、しちふん	七分	seven minutes			

Counting People

ひとり	一人	one person	しちにん	七人	seven people
ふたり	二人	two people	はちにん	八人	eight people
さんにん	三人	three people	きゅうにん、くにん	九人	nine people
よにん	四人	four people	じゅうにん	十人	ten people
ごにん	五人	five people	じゅういちにん	十一人	eleven people
ろくにん	六人	six people	ひゃくにん	百人	hundred people

Large Numbers

じゅう	十	ten	いっせんまん	一千万	ten million
ひゃく	百	hundred	いちおく	一億	hundred million
せん	千	thousand	じゅうおく	十億	billion
いちまん	一万	ten thousand	ひゃくおく	百億	ten billion
じゅうまん	十万	hundred thousand	いっせんおく	一千億	hundred billion
ひゃくまん	百万	million	いっちょう	一兆	trillion

Counters

かい	〜階	(*counter for floors of a building*)
けん	〜軒	(*counter for houses*)
さい	〜歳	(*counter for age*)
じかん	〜時間	(*counter for hours*)
にん	〜人	(*counter for people*)
ほん	〜本	(*counter for long* [*often cylindrical*] *items*)

Review: 分(ふん)

Positional Words

あいだ	間	between
うえ	上	on; over; up
うしろ	後ろ	behind; back
した	下	below; under; down

そと	外	outside
そば		near
となり	隣	next to
なか	中	inside
ひだり	左	left
まえ	前	front
まわり	回り	around
まんなか		right in the middle
みぎ	右	right
むかい	向かい	across from; facing
よこ	横	side

Kanji

Learn these **kanji:**

間	右	方
半	中	近
上	外	遠
下	前	有
分	後	
小	時	
好	山	
町	口	
田	千	
左	万	

チェックリスト

Use this checklist to confirm that you can now

- □ Talk about commuting
- □ Use adjectives and adverbs
- □ Talk about places around town
- □ Express existence
- □ Express location
- □ Use positional words
- □ Count and express numerals and counters
- □ Express likes and dislikes
- □ Talk about hometown and neighborhood
- □ Make sure you are communicating

Review Chapter 2

アクティビティー　1

この近所(きんじょ)においしいレストランはありませんか。(*Isn't there a good restaurant in this neighborhood?*)

Practice the dialogue several times, using some of the following words in the opening question and substituting other words as appropriate.

Adjectives: おいしい、安(やす)い、便利(べんり)、いい、きれい、有名(ゆうめい)、静(しず)か

Places: 食堂(しょくどう)、喫茶店(きっさてん)、公園(こうえん)、ディスコ、パブ、博物館(はくぶつかん) (*museum*)

s1: この近所(きんじょ)においしいフランス・レストランはありませんか。
s2: ええ、ありますよ。
s1: 名前(なまえ)は。
s2: 「マルセイユ」です。
s1: どこですか。
s2: 住友銀行(すみともぎんこう)のとなりです。
s1: じゃ、大学(だいがく)に近(ちか)いですね。
s2: ええ、車(くるま)で 10 分(ぷん)くらいです。一緒(いっしょ)に行(い)きませんか。
s1: ええ、いいですね。いつがいいですか。
s2: 金曜日(きんようび)の6時(じ)ごろはどうですか。
s1: ええ、いいですよ。どこで会(あ)いましょうか。
s2: 大学(だいがく)の前(まえ)はどうですか。
s1: ええ、いいですよ。
s2: じゃ、金曜日(きんようび)に。
s1: ええ、じゃ、また。

アクティビティー　2

日本語学校はどこにありますか。(*Where is the Japanese Language School?*)

Work in pairs. Student 1 will look at the following map in which six places are not identified (blank spaces). Student 2 will look at the map on p. 151 in Chapter 2, in which the locations of these places are identified. Student 1 will find the location of each place by asking Student 2 questions.

[例]　s1: 日本語学校はどこにありますか。
　　　s2: 日本語学校ですか。_____にあります。

1. ハンバーガー・クイーン　3. 郵便局　5. パブ
2. 日本語学校　4. 駐車場　6. 交番

アクティビティー　3

With a classmate, explore general preferences in at least two of the following three topics by asking and answering questions. Get as much information as you can about each area, and keep track of what you learn from your partner.

Form your questions with expressions like ～が好きですか。～がきらいですか, etc.

1. クラス：　やさしいクラス、むずかしいクラス、大きいクラス、小さいクラス、午前のクラス、午後のクラス、やさしい先生のクラス、きびしい先生のクラス
2. 町：　大きい町、小さい町、静かな町、にぎやかな町、便利な町、きれいな町、山に近い町、海に近い町
3. 飲み物：　コーヒー、お茶、ミルク、コカ・コーラ、ダイエット・コーク、ワイン、ビール、ウイスキー

Then report some of your findings to the class.

3

Everyday Life

第三章　日常生活（にちじょうせいかつ）

今日（きょう）の晩（ばん）ごはんはすきやきです。

Objectives

In this lesson you are going to

- Talk about schedules
- Learn about the basic structure of verbs
- Talk about daily activities
- Learn to use past, polite verb forms
- Learn more about particles showing grammatical relationships
- Talk about weekends and holidays
- Learn a new way to make suggestions
- Practice making phone calls
- Learn how to extend an invitation

YOOKOSO! MULTIMEDIA

Review and practice grammar and vocabulary from this chapter and watch video clips on the *Yookoso!* Interactive CD-ROM. Visit the *Yookoso!* Online Learning Center at **www.mhhe.com/yookosome** for additional exercises and resources.

Vocabulary and Grammar 3A

Vocabulary and Oral Activities

Schedules

Vocabulary: Days and Times of Day

今日	きょう	today
明日	あした	tomorrow
昨日	きのう	yesterday
あさって		the day after tomorrow
おととい		the day before yesterday
今朝	けさ	this morning
今日の午後	きょうのごご	this afternoon
今晩	こんばん	tonight

Review: 午前(ごぜん)、午後(ごご)、朝(あさ)、昼(ひる)、夕方(ゆうがた)、夜(よる)

アクティビティー 1

ダイアログ：いつも忙(いそが)しいですね。(*You are always busy, aren't you!*)

ブラウン：三村(みむら)さん、明日(あした)の午後(ごご)はひまですか。
三村(みむら)：残念(ざんねん)ですが、アルバイトがあります。
ブラウン：じゃあ、あさっての午後(ごご)はどうですか。
三村：ううん。あさってはクラブのミーティングがあります。
ブラウン：三村(みむら)さんはいつも忙(いそが)しいですね。

Now practice the dialogue substituting different times and activities.

BROWN: Mr. Mimura, are you free tomorrow afternoon? MIMURA: I'm sorry, but I have a part-time job. BROWN: Then, how about the afternoon of the day after tomorrow? MIMURA: Well, I have a club meeting the day after tomorrow. BROWN: You are always busy, aren't you!

言語ノート

Asking If Someone Has Free Time

These are common ways to ask if someone has free time and some ways to respond to the questions.

明日(あした)、ひまですか。
Are you free tomorrow?
ええ、ひまですが…
Yes, I'm free, but… (*what do you have in mind?*)
ちょっと用事(ようじ)があります。
I have some things to attend to.

明日(あした)、時間(じかん)がありますか。
Do you have any (*free*) *time tomorrow?*
はい、ありますよ。
Yes, I do.
ちょっと忙(いそが)しいです。
I'm (a bit) busy.

明日(あした)、忙(いそが)しいですか。
Are you busy tomorrow?
ええ、ちょっと…
Yes, (sorry, but I'm) a bit (busy).
いいえ、ひまですよ。
No, I have no plans. (lit., *I'm free.*)

文化ノート

CULTURE NOTE • Part-Time Jobs for College Students

In Japanese, part-time jobs are commonly called アルバイト, or バイト for short, from the German word *arbeit* meaning *work*. Part-time workers are called アルバイター, or recently パートタイマー (from English *part-timer*). Many Japanese college students have part-time jobs, most commonly as tutors (家庭教師 [かていきょうし]) for elementary and secondary school children. Others work as waiters, waitresses, delivery workers, or shop clerks. The student affairs office of any university has a bulletin board posting job opportunities, but the most popular sources of information are the daily and weekly magazines devoted to part-time job listings, such as とらばーゆ and 求人(きゅうじん)パートバイト情報(じょうほう).

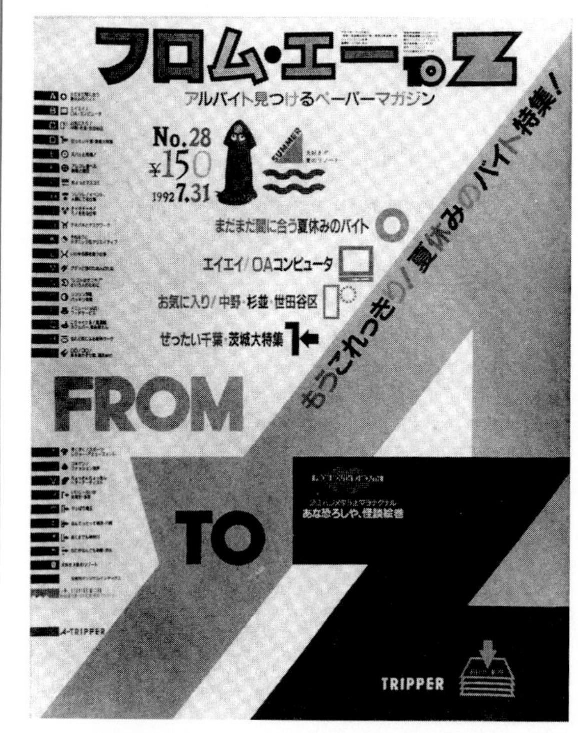

アルバイト・マガジン：いいアルバイトはありませんか。

Vocabulary: Days of the Month

一日	ついたち	the first	十二日	じゅうににち	the twelfth
二日	ふつか	the second	十三日	じゅうさんにち	the thirteenth
三日	みっか	the third	十四日	じゅうよっか	the fourteenth
四日	よっか	the fourth	十五日	じゅうごにち	the fifteenth
五日	いつか	the fifth	十六日	じゅうろくにち	the sixteenth
六日	むいか	the sixth	十七日	じゅうしちにち	the seventeenth
七日	なのか	the seventh	十八日	じゅうはちにち	the eighteenth
八日	ようか	the eighth	十九日	じゅうくにち	the nineteenth
九日	ここのか	the ninth	二十日	はつか	the twentieth
十日	とおか	the tenth	二十四日	にじゅうよっか	the twenty-fourth
十一日	じゅういちにち	the eleventh			

Note that from the second through the tenth, Japanese numbers are used and that the first, fourteenth, twentieth, and twenty-fourth are irregular.

アクティビティー　2

ダイアログ：何日ですか。(*What is the date?*)

林：ギブソンさん、来週の金曜日はひまですか。
ギブソン：来週の金曜日…何日ですか。
林：ええと、14日です。
ギブソン：残念ですが、試験があります。

Practice this dialogue based on the following schedule.

January

S	M	T	W	Th	F	S
						1
ski club 2	3	4	today 5	part-time job 6	7	8
9	10	11	12	part-time job 13	exam 14	party 15
ski club 16	17	exam 18	19	part-time job 20	21	22
23	24	25	exam 26	part-time job 27	28	29
30	31					

Vocabulary: Weeks, Months, and Years

今週	こんしゅう	this week
来週	らいしゅう	next week
先週	せんしゅう	last week
今月	こんげつ	this month
来月	らいげつ	next month
先月	せんげつ	last month
今年	ことし	this year
来年	らいねん	next year
去年	きょねん	last year
昨年	さくねん	last year
何日	なんにち	what day
何月	なんがつ	what month
何年	なんねん	what year
何曜日	なんようび	what day of the week
何年何月何日ですか。		What is the date (lit., *year, month, and day*)?

去年 sounds more informal than 昨年.

HAYASHI: Ms. Gibson, are you free next Friday? GIBSON: Next Friday… What is the date?
HAYASHI: Uh… it is the fourteenth. GIBSON: I'm sorry, but I have an exam.

文化ノート

Culture Note • 年号(ねんごう)

The Western system of counting years (1999, 2000, etc.) is commonly used in Japan, but the traditional Japanese system, based on the reigns of emperors, is still a part of everyday life. In the past, the reign of a single emperor might encompass several eras, but since 1868, the accession of each new emperor has marked the beginning of a new era. Within each era the years are numbered starting with one. The emperor chooses an auspicious name, or 年号(ねんごう), for his era, and after he dies he is known by that name. For example, the emperor who reigned from 1868 to 1912 chose the name 明治(めいじ) or "bright rule" for his era, and he has been known posthumously as 明治天皇(めいじてんのう), or Emperor Meiji. The subsequent 年号 are: 大正(たいしょう) "great righteousness" (1912–late 1926); 昭和(しょうわ) "shining peace" (late 1926–early 1989); 平成(へいせい) "peace growing" (1989–).

The first year of the 年号 is called 元年(がんねん), and the subsequent ones are simply numbered: 二年, 三年, etc. If you ever live in Japan you will need to know this system, because many forms and documents require you to state dates in that way. A good way to become familiar with the system is to determine what your birth year is and then work forward or backward to figure out other years. For example, if you were born in 1980, you would put down 昭和 55 年 as the year of your birth.

昭和49年生(う)まれです。
I was born in ***Showa*** *(year) 55.*
昭和55年5月8日生まれです。
I was born on May 8, ***Showa*** *(year) 55.*
今日(きょう)は平成11年7月5日です。
Today is July 5, 1999.

Note that dates are expressed in the order year-month-day whether the Western or Japanese system is used.

アクティビティー 3

来週(らいしゅう)の水曜日(すいようび)は何日(なんにち)ですか。(*What day is next Wednesday?*)

Review the words for months and days of the week.

Ask your partner the following questions.

1. 来週(らいしゅう)の水曜日(すいようび)は何日(なんにち)ですか。
2. 来週(らいしゅう)の月曜日(げつようび)は何日(なんにち)ですか。
3. 来月(らいげつ)の三日(みっか)は何曜日(なんようび)ですか。
4. 来月(らいげつ)は何月(なんがつ)ですか。
5. 来月(らいげつ)の十四日(じゅうよっか)は何曜日(なんようび)ですか。
6. 来週(らいしゅう)の金曜日(きんようび)は何月(なんがつ)何日(なんにち)ですか。
7. 誕生日(たんじょうび)(*birthday*)は何月(なんがつ)何日(なんにち)ですか。
8. 何年生(なんねんう)まれですか。(*What year were you born?*)

アクティビティー 4

誕生日(たんじょうび)は何月(なんがつ)何日(なんにち)ですか。(*What day is your birthday?*)

Walk around the classroom and ask your classmates when their birthdays are. For each month, have one person write his or her birth date and signature on your paper. Can you collect twelve signatures, one for each month? Do any two people in your class have the same birthday?

[例] s1: 誕生日(たんじょうび)は何月(なんがつ)何日(なんにち)ですか。
s2: 四月(しがつ)一日(ついたち)です。
s1: ここにサインしてください。

Grammar and Practice Activities

11. The Basic Structure of Japanese Verbs

11.1 In Chapter 2, you learned how to conjugate (change the form of) adjectives to form the negative (e.g., 大きい→大きくない). Japanese verbs also change form, or conjugate, to express a variety of meanings.

You have already studied several Japanese verbs, including 洗(あら)います [*I*] *wash,* 聞(き)きます [*I*] *listen,* 話(はな)します [*I*] *speak,* 立(た)ちます [*I*] *stand up,* 読(よ)みます [*I*] *read,* あります [*there*] *exists,* 泳(およ)ぎます [*I*] *swim,* 食(た)べます [*I*] *eat,* 寝(ね)ます [*I*] *go to bed* and 見(み)ます [*I*] *see, watch.* The verbs all end in ます because these are the ます forms of these verbs. In order to look up any of these verbs in a Japanese dictionary, you need to know the verb's dictionary form, which is listed in the following chart. Each dictionary form consists of two parts, a root and an ending.

DICTIONARY FORM	MEANING	ROOT	ENDING
Class 1 Verbs			
洗(あら)う	to wash	洗	う
聞(き)く	to listen	聞	く
話(はな)す	to speak	話	す
立(た)つ	to stand up	立	つ
読(よ)む	to read	読	む
ある	to exist	あ	る
泳(およ)ぐ	to swim	泳	ぐ

Class 2 Verbs			
食(た)べる	to eat	食べ	る
寝(ね)る	to go to sleep	寝	る
見(み)る	to see	見	る
着(き)る	to wear	着	る

Notice the different endings between the two groupings of verbs. The ending of the first group is variable, while that of the second group is always る. In this textbook, the first group of verbs are called *Class 1* verbs, while the second group of verbs are called *Class 2* verbs. The simple (but not foolproof) rule for distinguishing between these two classes is this: if the dictionary form of a verb ends with a syllable from the i-column (い、き、し、ち、etc.) or the e-column (え、け、せ、て、etc.) of the **hiragana** syllabary + る, it is a Class 2 verb. Otherwise it is a Class 1 verb.

CLASS 2 VERBS

	-a	-i	-u	-e	-o	
食(た)				べ		+ る
				寝(ね)		+ る
		見(み)				+ る
		着(き)				+ る

The dictionary form of all Class 1 verbs ends in one of the syllables in the u-column of the **hiragana** syllabary. (Note that ある ends in る, but its root does not end in a syllable from the i-column or the e-column, so it is not a Class 2 verb.)

CLASS 1 VERBS

	-a	-i	-u	-e	-o	
洗(あら)			う			(あ row)
書(か)			く			(か row)
話(はな)			す			(さ row)
立(た)			つ			(た row)
読(よ)			む			(み row)
あ			る			(ら row)
泳(およ)			ぐ			(が row)

Class 1 and Class 2 verbs conjugate in different but regular ways.

In addition, there are two irregular verbs in Japanese: 来(く)る (*to come*) and する (*to do*). In this textbook these irregular verbs are called *Class 3* verbs. You will have to memorize the conjugation of these verbs individually. All compound verbs with する belong to Class 3: 勉強(べんきょう)する (*to study*), 運動(うんどう)する (*to exercise*), 電話(でんわ)する (*to call*), and so on.

Here are how some common verbs are classified.

You will learn more about these compound verbs with する (called nominal verbs) later on.

CLASS 1 VERBS		CLASS 2 VERBS		CLASS 3 VERBS	
洗(あら)う	to wash	食(た)べる	to eat	する	to do
行(い)く	to go	起(お)きる	to get up	来(く)る	to come
聞(き)く	to listen	出(で)かける	to go out		
話(はな)す	to speak	出(で)る	to leave		
飲(の)む	to drink	変(か)える	to change		
働(はたら)く	to work	見(み)る	to see; watch		
休(やす)む	to take a rest	着(き)る	to wear; put on		
乗(の)る	to ride				

11.2 The three primary meanings expressed in every Japanese verb form are tense, politeness, and affirmation/negation.

There are two basic tenses in Japanese: *past* and *nonpast*. The past tense is used to express past actions and events (*I played baseball, he remained in the hospital,* etc.). The nonpast tense is used to express present, habitual, and future actions and events (*I get up at 6:00 every morning, I will go to school later, I'm going to study tomorrow,* etc.).

Japanese verbs do not conjugate in terms of the person and number of the subject.

Japanese verbs also take different forms depending on the degree of politeness the speaker or writer wishes to show the listener or reader. As you learned in Chapter 2, the *plain form* is used when speakers address very familiar people on the same social level, such as close friends. It is also used in diaries and in newspaper articles. And as you will see later, verbs in certain positions in a sentence must be in the plain form. On the other hand, the *polite form* is used, for instance, to address people with whom one is not well acquainted or to speak impersonally with in-group people (such as one's superior). In addition, it is used to address most out-group people, in personal letters, TV news, and most public speeches. The polite form is the appropriate speech register among adult speakers who are getting to know each other.

In Japanese, verbs take different endings depending on whether they are *affirmative* or *negative*.

In addition, different grammatical elements are added to the end of verb forms to express such meanings as ability and probability. The resultant forms consisting of verbs and grammatical elements also conjugate in terms of the three primary meanings.

11.3 The dictionary form of Japanese verbs is actually the *nonpast, plain, affirmative form;* for example, 書(か)く (*to write*) and 食(た)べる (*to eat*). When you look up a verb in the dictionary, this is the form you will find. The plain form can be considered a basis for conjugating the polite form.

The nonpast, plain, negative form is made as follows.

CLASS 1 VERBS

Root + the a-column **hiragana** corresponding to the dictionary form ending + ない

DICTIONARY FORM ROOT + ENDING	NONPAST, PLAIN, NEGATIVE FORM
書(か) + く	書(か) + か + ない
話(はな) + す	話(はな) + さ + ない
立(た) + つ	立(た) + た + ない
読(よ) + む	読(よ) + ま + ない
泳(およ) + ぐ	泳(およ) + が + ない

u-column	→	a-column
く	→	か
す	→	さ
つ	→	た
む	→	ま
ぐ	→	が

When the dictionary form ending of a Class 1 verb is う—for example, 洗(あら)う (*to wash*), 買(か)う (*to buy*) — わ is inserted between the root and ない to form the nonpast, plain, negative.

DICTIONARY FORM ROOT + ENDING	NONPAST, PLAIN, NEGATIVE FORM
洗(あら) + う	洗(あら) + わ + ない
買(か) + う	買(か) + わ + ない

Although such verbs as 切(き)る (*to cut*), 知(し)る (*to know*), 帰(かえ)る (*to go back*), 走(はし)る (*to run*), and 入(はい)る (*to enter*) look like Class 2 verbs and satisfy the (not foolproof) rule for identifying Class 2 verbs, they belong to Class 1 and conjugate as such. Thus, their nonpast, plain, negative form is made following the same rule presented above.

DICTIONARY FORM ROOT + ENDING	NONPAST, PLAIN, NEGATIVE FORM
切(き) + る	切(き) + ら + ない
知(し) + る	知(し) + ら + ない
帰(かえ) + る	帰(かえ) + ら + ない
走(はし) + る	走(はし) + ら + ない
入(はい) + る	入(はい) + ら + ない

Note that the nonpast, plain, negative form of ある (*to exist*) (see **Grammar 6,** Chapter 2) is simply ない. ない is an i-adjective representing negativity.

CLASS 2 VERBS

Root + ない

DICTIONARY FORM ROOT + ENDING	NONPAST, PLAIN, NEGATIVE FORM
食(た)べ + る	食(た)べ + ない
見(み) + る	見(み) + ない
着(き) + る	着(き) + ない

CLASS 3 VERBS

DICTIONARY FORM	NONPAST, PLAIN, NEGATIVE FORM
する	し + ない
来(く)る	来(こ) + ない

アクティビティー 5

よく見(み)てください。(*Please look carefully.*)

Are these verbs Class 1, Class 2, or Class 3? Each is cited in its dictionary form.

ある *to exist*
いる *to exist*
できる *to be able to do*
使(つか)う *to use*
作(つく)る *to make*
笑(わら)う *to laugh*

歩(ある)く *to walk*
走(はし)る *to run*
踊(おど)る *to dance*
歌(うた)う *to sing*
泳(およ)ぐ *to swim*
待(ま)つ *to wait*
泣(な)く *to cry*
教(おし)える *to teach*
見(み)せる *to show*

休(やす)む *to take a rest*
料理(りょうり)する *to cook*
飛(と)ぶ *to fly*
考(かんが)える *to think*
会(あ)う *to meet*
住(す)む *to live*
わかる *to understand*
やめる *to quit*

アクティビティー 6

林(はやし)さんは起(お)きない。(*Hayashi-san won't get up.*)

Write the nonpast, plain, negative form of these verbs. Use **hiragana** for **kanji** you have not yet studied.

起(お)きる *to get up*
食(た)べる *to eat*
みがく *to brush (teeth)*
洗(あら)う *to wash*
出(で)かける *to go out*
行(い)く *to go*
飲(の)む *to drink*
勉強(べんきょう)する *to study*
見(み)る *to see*
寝(ね)る *to go to bed*
着(き)る *to put on (clothes)*
浴(あ)びる *to take (a shower)*
入(はい)る *to enter*
言(い)う *to say*

歌(うた)う *to sing*
いる *to exist*
使(つか)う *to use*
話(はな)す *to speak*
乗(の)る *to ride*
働(はたら)く *to work*
休(やす)む *to rest*
眠(ねむ)る *to sleep*
会(あ)う *to meet*
洗濯(せんたく)する *to do laundry*
死(し)ぬ *to die*
とかす *to comb*

Vocabulary and Grammar 3B

Vocabulary and Oral Activities

Daily Activities

Vocabulary: Everyday Activities 1

夕ごはんを食べる	ゆうごはんをたべる	to eat dinner, supper
出かける	でかける	to step out; to leave for
買い物に出かける	かいものにでかける	to go out shopping

Review: 朝ごはん(昼ごはん、晩ごはん)を食べる、テレビを見る、コーヒーを飲む、仕事をする

晩ごはん, which you studied in **Getting Started,** and 夕ごはん are identical in meaning.

1. 起きる

2. 寝る

3. 新聞を読む

4. 昼ごはんを食べる

5. お茶を飲む

6. 勉強する

アクティビティー　7

ダイアログ：毎日何時に起きますか。(*What time do you get up every day?*)

カワムラさんと町田さんが話しています。

カワムラ：町田さんは、毎日何時に起きますか。
町田：5時です。
カワムラ：わあ、はやいですね。
町田：ええ、5時半から6時までジョギングをします。

With a classmate, practice the dialogue, substituting various activities from the vocabulary and the six illustrations above. Choose new times suitable for each activity.

Grammar and Practice Activities

12. The Nonpast, Polite Form of Verbs

ブラウン：三村さんは毎日何時に起きますか。
三村：六時半に起きます。
ブラウン：毎日朝ごはんを食べますか。
三村：いいえ、朝ごはんは食べません。
ブラウン：なぜですか。
三村：朝は時間がありませんから…

チン：明日のパーティーに行きますか。
町田：いいえ、行きません。
チン：なぜですか。
町田：夜、友だちが来ますから…

The nonpast, polite, affirmative and negative form of Class 1 and Class 2 verbs are made as follows.

Mr. Kawamura and Ms. Machida are talking. KAWAMURA: What time do you get up every day, (Ms. Machida)? MACHIDA: I get up at 5:00. KAWAMURA: Wow, that's early! MACHIDA: Yes, I go jogging from 5:30 to 6:00.

BROWN: What time do you get up every day? MIMURA: I get up at 6:30. BROWN: Do you eat breakfast every day? MIMURA: No, I don't eat breakfast. BROWN: Why not? MIMURA: Because I don't have time in the morning.

CHIN: Are you going to tomorrow's party? MACHIDA: No, I'm not going. CHIN: Why not? MACHIDA: Because I have friends coming over (lit., *Because friends are coming*) in the evening.

CLASS 1 VERBS

Take the last hiragana of the dictionary form and change it to its corresponding -i syllable. This gives you the conjunctive form. Then add ます for the affirmative or ません for the negative.

EXAMPLE:

わかる *understand*
Change the る to り: わかり
Add ます: わかります
ません: わかりません

Other Class 1 verbs follow the same pattern.

DICTIONARY FORM ROOT + ENDING	AFFIRMATIVE FORM	NEGATIVE FORM
洗(あら) + う	洗 + い + ます	洗 + い + ません
書(か) + く	書 + き + ます	書 + き + ません
話(はな) + す	話 + し + ます	話 + し + ません
立(た) + つ	立 + ち + ます	立 + ち + ません
読(よ) + む	読 + み + ます	読 + み + ません
あ + る	あ + り + ます	あ + り + ません
泳(およ) + ぐ	泳 + ぎ + ます	泳 + ぎ + ません

u-column	→	i-column
く	→	き
す	→	し
つ	→	ち
む	→	み
る	→	り
ぐ	→	ぎ

CLASS 2 VERBS

Take the る off the plain form. This gives you the conjunctive form. Then add ます for the affirmative or ません for the negative.

DICTIONARY FORM ROOT + ENDING	AFFIRMATIVE FORM	NEGATIVE FORM
食(た)べ + る	食べ + ます	食べ +ません
見(み) + る	見 + ます	見 + ません
着(き) + る	着 + ます	着 + ません

CLASS 3 VERBS

DICTIONARY FORM	AFFIRMATIVE FORM	NEGATIVE FORM
する	し + ます	し + ません
来(く)る	来(き) + ます	来(き) + ません

To summarize, the nonpast, polite, affirmative and negative forms of verbs are formed by adding ます and ません to the conjunctive form.

言語ノート

送り仮名(おくりがな)

Most verbs and adjectives are written in a combination of **kanji** and **hiragana.** Usually the **kanji** in a word represents the root, and the **hiragana** represent the grammatical endings, although there may be some overlap, especially in Class 2 verbs. The **hiragana** used to write the endings are called **okurigana** ("send-off" kana).

Here are some examples of verbs and adjectives with **okurigana.**

大(おお)きい	大きくないです
食(た)べます	食べません

Always memorize the **kun** reading of a **kanji** with the **okurigana** of its dictionary form. If you memorize 見 simply as み, you risk getting it mixed up with all the other **kanji** that are pronounced that way.

アクティビティー　8

わかります、わかりません　(*understand, don't understand*)

Write the nonpast, formal, affirmative and negative forms of these verbs.

1. 起(お)きる　*to get up*
2. 洗(あら)う　*to wash*
3. みがく　*to brush (teeth)*
4. 走(はし)る　*to run*
5. 食(た)べる　*to eat*
6. 飲(の)む　*to drink*
7. 出(で)かける　*to go out*
8. 待(ま)つ　*to wait*
9. 行(い)く　*to go*
10. 乗(の)る　*to ride*
11. 着(つ)く　*to arrive*
12. 会(あ)う　*to meet*
13. 見(み)る　*to see*
14. 泳(およ)ぐ　*to swim*
15. する　*to do*
16. 帰(かえ)る　*to return*
17. 休(やす)む　*to rest*
18. 入(はい)る　*to enter*
19. 読(よ)む　*to read*
20. 寝(ね)る　*to sleep*
21. 来(く)る　*to come*
22. 話(はな)す　*to speak*

アクティビティー 9

スミスさんは来ません。(*Mr. Smith isn't coming.*)

Transform plain verbs into polite verbs and vice versa.

[例] チンさんは毎日6時に起きる。→
チンさんは毎日6時に起きます。

1. ビールを飲みます。
2. 明日、ロサンゼルスへ行く。
3. 今日の午後、山田さんに会います。
4. ブラウンさんは来週、アメリカから帰る。
5. 毎日、運動します。
6. あなたは何を食べるか。
7. パーティーへ来るか。
8. わたしはテレビを見ない。
9. 町田さんを待ちますか。
10. シュミットさんは日本語を話さない。

アクティビティー 10

まりこさんは大学へ行きます。(*Mariko is going to the university.*)

Make sentences using the words provided. (Change the verbs to their polite forms.)

[例] (6時) (毎日) (起きる) → わたしは毎日6時に起きます。

1. (7時) (いつも) (朝ごはんを食べる)
2. (7時半) (毎朝) (大学へ行く)
3. (8時) (毎日) (クラスが始まる)
4. (12時) (毎日) (昼ごはんを食べる)
5. (3時) (いつも) (クラスが終わる)
6. (4時) (毎日) (図書館へ行く)
7. (5時) (いつも) (大学から帰る)
8. (6時) (毎日) (夕ごはんを食べる)
9. (7時) (いつも) (テレビを見る)

10. (9時) (毎日) (日本語を勉強する)
11. (11時) (毎晩) (寝る)

アクティビティー 11

いいえ、食べません。(*No, we won't eat.*)

Make dialogues following the example.

[例] (明日) (大学へ行く) (いいえ) →
—明日大学へ行きますか。
—いいえ、行きません。

1. (毎朝) (運動する) (いいえ)
2. (いつも) (コーヒーを飲む) (はい)
3. (よく) (町田さんに会う) (はい)
4. (毎日) (テレビを見る) (いいえ)
5. (毎晩) (レストランで食べる) (いいえ)

アクティビティー 12

毎晩早く寝ます。(*I go to sleep early every night.*)

Complete the following sentences. Your sentences must include the polite form of a verb.

[例] 毎朝6時に… → 毎朝6時にシャワーを浴びます。

1. 日曜日の朝…
2. 毎日午前8時に…
3. わたしは毎日…
4. 日本語のクラスは…
5. わたしとガールフレンドはいつも…
6. わたしは来週の月曜日…
7. 土曜日の午後…
8. わたしは来年…

アクティビティー 13

今日はクラスに行きません。(*I'm not going to class today.*)

Rewrite the following paragraph, substituting polite verb forms.

Useful Vocabulary: 始まる *to start,* 終わる *to finish*

わたしは毎日午前五時に起きる。それから、家の回りを散歩する。午前六時にコーヒーを飲む。朝ごはんは食べない。午前七時に家を出る。午前七時のバスに乗る。午前八時に大学のクラスが始まる。十二時にカフェテリアで昼ごはんを食べる。午後一時にクラスへ行く。クラスは午後三時に終わる。わたしの友だちは図書館へ行く。でも、わたしは行かない。午後四時に家に帰る。それから、六時まで勉強する。六時に夕ごはんを食べる。そのあと、テレビを見る。午後十時にいつも寝る。

言語ノート

Expressions of Surprise

Here are some common ways to express surprise.

わあ。	*Wow!*
本当(ですか)。	*Really?* (lit., *Is that true?*)
うそ。	*You're kidding.* (lit., *That's a lie.*) (frequently used by young women; very colloquial)
まさか。	*Impossible! That can't be! No way!*
何ですって。	*What!* (lit., *What did you say?*)
信じられない。	*Incredible!* (lit., *I can't believe it.*)

アクティビティー 14

カワムラさんのスケジュール (*Mr. Kawamura's schedule*)

Use the table to answer the questions that follow it.

JOHN KAWAMURA'S DAILY SCHEDULE

6:00	get up
6:30	breakfast
8:30	Japanese class

12:00	lunch
1:30	study at the library
3:00	coffee break
4:00	return home
until 6:00	read (books)
6:15	dinner
7:00	watch TV
9:00	study Japanese
11:45	go to bed

1. カワムラさんは午前何時(ごぜんなんじ)に起(お)きますか。
2. 午前(ごぜん)6時半(じはん)に何(なん)をしますか。
3. 何時(なんじ)に昼(ひる)ごはんを食(た)べますか。
4. 午後(ごご)1時半(じはん)に何(なに)をしますか。
5. 何時(なんじ)にコーヒーを飲(の)みますか。
6. 何時(なんじ)に家(いえ)へ帰(かえ)りますか。
7. 何時(なんじ)に夕(ゆう)ごはんを食(た)べますか。
8. 午後(ごご)7時(じ)から9時まで何(なに)をしますか。
9. 午後(ごご)9時(じ)から何(なに)を勉強(べんきょう)しますか。
10. カワムラさんは何時(なんじ)に寝(ね)ますか。、
11. カワムラさんは何時間(なんじかん) (*how many hours*) ぐらい寝(ね)ますか。

アクティビティー 15

ダイアログ：そのあとは。(*What about after that?*)

林(はやし)さんとギブソンさんが話しています。

林(はやし)：ギブソンさん、今日(きょう)の午後(ごご)は忙(いそが)しいですか。
ギブソン：ええ、とても。1時(じ)に日本語(にほんご)のクラスがあります。
それから、図書館(としょかん)で勉強(べんきょう)します。
林：じゃあ、そのあとは。
ギブソン：そのあと、友(とも)だちに会(あ)います。
林：そうですか。

The verb 会う *to meet with, see* (a person) takes the particle に or と to indicate the person met.

Mr. Hayashi and Ms. Gibson are talking HAYASHI: Ms. Gibson, are you busy this afternoon? GIBSON: Yes, very. I have a Japanese class at one o'clock. And then I'm going to study at the library. HAYASHI: Well, how about after that? GIBSON: After that, I'm meeting a friend. HAYASHI: I see.

Describe Mr. Kawamura's schedule from アクティビティー 14 using the conjunctions presented in the following **Language Note.**

言語ノート

Connecting Sequential Actions

Here are some conjunctions commonly used to connect sentences expressing sequential actions or events.

それから
and then… (lit., *from that*)
そして
and (*then*)… (lit., *so doing*)
そのあと
after that…

7時(じ)に朝(あさ)ごはんを食(た)べます。それから、新聞(しんぶん)を読(よ)みます。
I eat breakfast at 7:00. And then I read the newspaper.

図書館(としょかん)に行(い)きました。そして、本を読(よ)みました。
I went to the library. And (then) I read some books.

レストランで夕(ゆう)ごはんを食べます。そのあと、映画(えいが)を見(み)ます。それから、ディスコへ行きます。
I'll eat dinner at a restaurant. After that, I'll see a movie. And then, I'll go to a disco.

アクティビティー 16

あなたのスケジュールは。(*What about your schedule?*)

Working in pairs, ask your partner questions about his or her daily schedule. Use the answers you get to write a schedule.

[例] s1: 何時(なんじ)に起(お)きますか。
s2: _____時(じ)に起(お)きます。
s1: それから、何(なに)をしますか。
s2: _____。

Vocabulary: Everyday Activities 2

シャワーを浴びる	シャワーをあびる	to take a shower
うちを出る	うちをでる	to leave home

(お)風呂に入る	(お)ふろにはいる	to take (lit., *enter*) a bath
歯を磨く	はをみがく	to brush one's teeth
顔を洗う	かおをあらう	to wash one's face
服を着る	ふくをきる	to put on clothes
～に乗る	～にのる	to ride or get on… (*a vehicle—train, bus, car, etc.*)
働く	はたらく	to work
休む	やすむ	to take a rest; to take time off

Review: 電話(でんわ)(を)する、買い物(かいもの)(を)する

寝坊(ねぼう)する

料理(りょうり)する

音楽(おんがく)を聞(き)く

運動(うんどう)する

アクティビティー 17

ダイアログ：寝坊(ねぼう)しました。(*I overslept.*)

ブラウンさんと林(はやし)さんが話(はな)しています。

ブラウン：今日(きょう)は日本(にほん)文化(ぶんか)のクラスへ行(い)きましたか。
林(はやし)：ええ。ブラウンさん、クラスに来(き)ませんでしたね。
ブラウン：ええ、今朝(けさ)、寝坊(ねぼう)しました。
林：そうですか。

Ms. Brown and Mr. Hayashi are talking BROWN: Did you go to Japanese culture class today? HAYASHI: Yes. You weren't in class, were you? BROWN: No. I overslept this morning. HAYASHI: I see.

13. The Past, Polite Form of Verbs

林：	昨日は何時に家に帰りましたか。
ブラウン：	午後6時ごろです。
林：	夕ごはんに何を食べましたか。
ブラウン：	ステーキを食べました。
ブラウン：	今何時ですか。
チン：	10時15分です。
ブラウン：	もうカワムラさんに電話をしましたか。
チン：	いいえ、まだです。10時半にかけます。

The past, polite forms of verbs are formed as follows.

Affirmative　the conjunctive form + ました
Negative　the conjunctive form + ませんでした

DICTIONARY FORM	CONJUNCTIVE FORM	PAST, POLITE, AFFIRMATIVE FORM	PAST, POLITE, NEGATIVE FORM
Class 1 Verbs			
洗う	洗い	洗いました	洗いませんでした
立つ	立ち	立ちました	立ちませんでした
Class 2 Verbs			
食べる	食べ	食べました	食べませんでした
見る	見	見ました	見ませんでした
Class 3 Verbs			
する	し	しました	しませんでした
来る	来	来ました	来ませんでした

HAYASHI: What time did you return home yesterday? BROWN: About 6.00 P.M. HAYASHI: What did you eat for dinner? BROWN: I ate steak.

BROWN: What time is it now? CHIN: It's 10:15. BROWN: Have you already called Mr. Kawamura? CHIN: No, not yet. I'll call him at 10:30.

アクティビティー 18

たくさん書きました。(*I wrote a lot.*)

Write the affirmative and negative past, polite forms of the verbs listed in アクティビティー 8.

アクティビティー 19

ビールを飲みましたか。(*Did you drink beer?*)

Give affirmative and negative answers to the following questions.

[例] 昨日、ビールを飲みましたか。→
はい、飲みました。
いいえ、飲みませんでした。

1. 先週、映画を見ましたか。
2. 昨日、日本語を勉強しましたか。
3. おととい、本を読みましたか。
4. 昨日はうちにいましたか。
5. 今日、朝ごはんを食べましたか。
6. 昨日、日本語のクラスがありましたか。
7. 去年、高田さんはアメリカへ行きましたか。
8. 昨日、たくさんテレビを見ましたか。
9. おととい、スポーツをしましたか。
10. 昨日、お風呂に入りましたか。

アクティビティー 20

何時に学校から帰りましたか。(*What time did you come home from the university?*)

Make dialogues following the example. Use the past, polite form of verbs.

[例] (起きる) → —(*partner's name*) は昨日何時に起きましたか。
—6時に起きました。

Useful words: お茶 *tea,* 手紙 *letter*

1. (朝ごはんを食べる)
2. (学校へ行く)
3. (お茶を飲む)
4. (図書館で勉強する)
5. (散歩をする)
6. (電話をかける)
7. (音楽を聞く)
8. (友だちと話す)
9. (手紙を書く)
10. (寝る)

アクティビティー 21

4時半にコーヒーを飲みました。(*I drank coffee at* 4:30.)

Make up dialogues based on the example below.

[例] get up, 5:30 →—昨日何時に起きましたか。
—5時半に起きました。

1. get up, 5:30
2. go jogging, 6:00
3. eat breakfast, 6:30
4. leave home, 7:00
5. board a train, 7:15
6. go to class, 8:00
7. eat lunch, 12:20
8. drink coffee, 1:00
9. go to the library, 1:20
10. exercise, 3:40
11. go home, 5:30
12. watch TV, 6:00
13. eat dinner, 7:15
14. study Japanese, 8:45
15. listen to music, 10:40
16. go to bed, 11:30

アクティビティー 22

昨日は何をしましたか。(*What did you do yesterday?*)

Complete these sentences. Use the past, polite form of verbs.

1. わたしは去年…
2. 田中さんは昨日の夜…
3. わたしと山口さんは先週、…
4. 昨日は…

5. 今日(きょう)の朝(あさ)、…
6. 先週(せんしゅう)の土曜日(どようび)、…
7. いつもうちで…
8. 昨日(きのう)、6時(じ)から10時(じ)まで…
9. うちの前(まえ)に…
10. 大学(だいがく)からうちまで…

アクティビティー 23

林(はやし)さんのスケジュール (*Mr. Hayashi's schedule*)

Here is what Mr. Hayashi did yesterday. Describe his day in Japanese, or ask your classmates about his schedule.

Useful word: 法学(ほうがく) *(study of) law*

6:00	got up	1:00	studied at the library
6:15	took a shower	3:00	exercised
6:30	drank coffee	5:00	returned home
6:35	read the newspaper	6:00	cooked dinner
6:45	ate breakfast	7:30	ate dinner
7:15	watched TV	8:30	called a friend
8:00	left home	9:00	listened to the stereo
9:00	went to his Japanese culture class	9:30	studied law
10:30	went to his law class	10:30	took a bath
12:00	ate lunch with classmates	11:00	went to bed

アクティビティー 24

昨日(きのう)_____しましたか。(*Did you do _____ yesterday?*)

Ask a classmate if he or she did the following yesterday. If the answer is yes, ask related questions such as *What time did you do that?*

1. oversleep
2. take a shower
3. drink tea
4. exercise
5. read the newspaper
6. call a friend
7. listen to music
8. take a bath
9. go to a library
10. watch TV

Vocabulary: Expressions of Frequency 

～回	～かい	…times (*counter for occurrences*)
AにB回	AにBかい	B times per A
一日に何回	いちにちになんかい	how many times a day
一週間に二回	いっしゅうかんににかい	two times a week
一ヶ月に四回	いっかげつによんかい	four times a month

…週間 and …ヶ月 are counters for the duration of weeks and months, respectively.

毎日	まいにち	every day
毎週	まいしゅう	every week
毎月	まいつき	every month
毎朝	まいあさ	every morning
毎晩	まいばん	every night
いつも		all the time
よく		often, a lot
時々	ときどき	sometimes
たまに		once in a while
あまり		(*with negative*) not very much; not very often
ほとんど		(*with negative*) hardly; almost never
全然	ぜんぜん	(*with negative*) not at all

The kanji 々 is used to repeat the preceding kanji.

アクティビティー 25

ダイアログ：一日(いちにち)に三回(さんかい)歯(は)を磨(みが)きます。(*I brush my teeth three times a day.*)

林(はやし)さんとブラウンさんが話(はな)しています。

林(はやし)：ブラウンさんは歯(は)がきれいですね。
ブラウン：一日(いちにち)に三回(さんかい)磨(みが)きます。林(はやし)さんは。
林：あまり磨(みが)きません。
ブラウン：一日(いちにち)に一回(いっかい)ですか。
林：いいえ、一週間(いっしゅうかん)に一回(いっかい)です。
ブラウン：うそ！

言語ノート

Adverbs Used in Negative Sentences

Some adverbs are used primarily in negative sentences. Two examples are あまり (*not very much, not very often*) and 全然(ぜんぜん) (*not at all*).

わたしはあまり映画(えいが)へ行きません。
I don't go to the movies very often.
わたしの父(ちち)は全然(ぜんぜん)テレビを見ません。
My father doesn't watch TV at all.

Mr. Hayashi and Ms. Brown are talking. HAYASHI: Ms. Brown, you have such nice teeth (lit., *your teeth are pretty, aren't they*). BROWN: I brush them three times a day. How about you? HAYASHI: I don't brush them much. BROWN: Do you mean (lit., *is it*) once a day? HAYASHI: No, once a week. BROWN: You're kidding!

ほとんど can be used in affirmative or negative sentences, but its meaning changes in these different contexts. In the affirmative it means *almost,* while in the negative it means *almost never* or *hardly ever.*

> 山田さんはほとんど毎日シャワーを浴びます。
> *Mr. Yamada takes a shower almost every day.*
> 山田さんはほとんどお風呂に入りません。
> *Mr. Yamada hardly ever takes a bath.*

Vocabulary Library 

Everyday Activities 3

髪をとかす	かみをとかす	to comb one's hair
ひげをそる		to shave one's facial hair (lit., *beard*)
服を脱ぐ	ふくをぬぐ	to take off clothes
服を着替える	ふくをきがえる	to change clothes
運転(を)する	うんてん(を)する	to drive (*vehicles*)
散歩(を)する	さんぽ(を)する	to take a walk, stroll
洗濯(を)する	せんたく(を)する	to do laundry
掃除(を)する	そうじ(を)する	to clean (*house, a room, etc.*)
眠る	ねむる	to fall asleep

✹ アクティビティー 26

よくしますか。(*Do you do that often?*)

Tell how often you do the following, selecting from the following degrees of frequency (ordered from most frequent to least frequent).

1 = 毎日	3 = よく	5 = あまりしない
2 = ほとんど毎日	4 = 時々	6 = 全然しない

a. 歯を磨く
b. シャワーを浴びる
c. お風呂に入る
d. 朝ごはんを食べる
e. コーヒーを飲む
f. 部屋 (*room*) を掃除する

g. 料理(りょうり)をする
h. 買(か)い物(もの)をする
i. 新聞(しんぶん)を読(よ)む
j. 映画(えいが)を見(み)る
k. ラジオを聞(き)く
l. テレビを見(み)る
m. お酒(さけ)を飲(の)む
n. 運動(うんどう)する
o. デートをする
p. 勉強(べんきょう)する
q. 電話(でんわ)する

14. Particles Showing Grammatical Relationships

In Japanese, the grammatical roles of some words in a sentence—subject, direct object, and so on—are identified by particles, also known as postpositions. These short words indicate the grammatical function of the word or phrase preceding them. Particles are a key element of Japanese grammar. The following explanation provides an overview of various particles. It is not a complete explanation by any means, but it should give you a good idea of why you have been using certain particles in particular situations, and prepare you for new usages you will encounter from now on.

14.1 が and は were explained briefly in Chapter 1. が is a *subject particle.* It marks a word or phrase that is the subject of a sentence. は (pronounced **wa**) is called the *topic particle* because it is often used to mark a word or phrase that tells what the sentence is about.

Because topics and subjects are sometimes hard to distinguish, in many cases either は or が would be grammatically acceptable, though not interchangeable. For example

1. わたしはアメリカ人です。　　*I am American.*
2. わたしがアメリカ人です。　　*I am American.*

Both sentences are grammatically correct. However, if someone asks だれがアメリカ人ですか (*Who is American?*) sentence 2 is the only appropriate answer. On the other hand, if you were introducing yourself, sentence 1 is the only appropriate answer. You will learn the use of and differences between は and が as you progress through this textbook. For now, it may help to think of は as being used to introduce a general topic (as in 1.) or to refer to a topic already in discussion, whereas が shifts emphasis to the subject it follows (***I** am American*).

14.2 The particle を has several uses.

1. を marks (follows) a direct object. (A direct object is something or someone directly affected by the action of a verb.) The direct objects are underlined in the following examples.

   わたしは朝(あさ)ごはんを食(た)べます。
   I will eat breakfast.

昨日(きのう)スーパーでコーラを買(か)いました。
I bought cola at the supermarket yesterday.

何(なに)を着(き)ますか。
What are you going to wear?

Caution: Just because a word is a direct object in an English sentence doesn't mean its counterpart in the Japanese equivalent is also a direct object. Many Japanese verbs require に (*to*) where you might expect を. Here are some constructions to watch out for.

バスに乗(の)りました。
I rode a bus. (lit., *I got onto a bus.*)

ブラウンさんは高田(たかだ)さんに会(あ)いました。
Ms. Brown met Mr. Takada.

日本が好(す)きです。
I like Japan.

パーティーに出(で)ました。
I attended the party.

2. を is also used to indicate a place or object from which something or someone leaves. In this usage, it carries the sense of *from* or *out of.*

   午前(ごぜん)8時(じ)に家(いえ)を出(で)ます。
   I leave home at 8:00 A.M.

3. を is further used to indicate a place that something moves over, along, or through.

   橋(はし)を渡(わた)りました。
   I crossed the bridge.

   道(みち)を歩(ある)きます。
   I walk down the street.

14.3 に is one of the most versatile particles. Here are some of its many uses.

1. Point in time (*at, on, in*)

   カワムラさんは7時(じ)に朝(あさ)ごはんを食(た)べます。
   Mr. Kawamura eats breakfast at seven o'clock.

   月曜日(げつようび)にロサンゼルスへ行(い)きました。
   I went to Los Angeles on Monday.

   1975年(ねん)に生(う)まれました。
   I was born in 1975.

   Only time words with a specific name or number (Tuesday, October 31, six o'clock, etc.) take に. Words indicating relative time (today, tomorrow, next year) and those indicating duration (thirty minutes, five days) do not take に.

ギブソンさんは今日、東京へ来ます。
Ms. Gibson will come to Tokyo today.

来週忙しいです。
I will be busy next week.

毎日、ジョギングします。
I jog every day.

2. Location or existence

そこに銀行があります。
There is a bank there (lit., *in that place*).

高田さんはどこにいますか。
Where is Mr. Takada?

3. Purpose (*for, in order to*) when the verb is 行く or 来る.

昨日デパートへ買い物に行きました。
Yesterday I went shopping at the department store. (lit., *Yesterday I went to the department store for shopping.*)

4. Direction of an action

山口さんは毎日 お風呂に入ります。
Mr. Yamaguchi takes a bath every day. (lit., *Mr. Yamaguchi enters a bath every day.*)

林さんは8時の電車に乗りました。
Mr. Hayashi got on the eight o'clock train.

14.4 The particle へ also marks the direction toward which an action moves. While に marks movement toward a specific place, へ indicates motion in a general direction. However, the difference is unimportant in many cases, and the two particles are often interchangeable.

明日京都へ行きます。 *I will go to Kyoto tomorrow.*

チンさんはここへ来ますか。 *Is Ms. Chin coming here?*

いつ家へ帰りますか。 *When will you return home?*

14.5 で has three major uses. で marks the location where an action takes place.

カーティスさんはいつもここで昼ごはんを食べます。
Mr. Curtis always eats lunch here.

図書館で勉強します。
I will study at the library.

It also marks the instrument used to carry out an action.

ナイフでりんごを切(き)りました。 *I cut the apple with a knife.*

電車(でんしゃ)で学校(がっこう)へ来(き)ます。 *I come to school by train.*

The particle で also marks the reason or cause of an action. This usage corresponds to the English *because of* or *for.* You will use it later on.

昨日(きのう)、病気(びょうき)で学校(がっこう)を休(やす)みました。
Yesterday I was absent from school because of illness.

今(いま)、ビジネスでロサンゼルスにいます。
I am in Los Angeles now for business.

14.6 The particle から (*from*) is used to express the starting point in space or time of an action, and the particle まで ([*up*] *to, until*) is used to represent its ending point.

東京(とうきょう)から京都(きょうと)まで新幹線(しんかんせん)で行(い)きます。
I will go from Tokyo to Kyoto via Shinkansen (the bullet train).

わたしは1時(じ)から3時(じ)まで図書館(としょかん)にいます。
I will be at the library from 1:00 to 3:00.

14.7 In Chapter 1, you learned that the particle も means *too* or *as much as.* When placed after a regular noun or pronoun, it usually means *too.* Be careful where you place も, because you can change the meaning of the sentence. In Chapter 5 we will see how it is used to mean *as much (many) as* and *both.*

わたしもアイスクリームが好(す)きです。
I also like ice cream (in addition to someone else).

わたしはアイスクリームも好(す)きです。
I also like ice cream (in addition to something else).

去年(きょねん)、ローマへも行(い)きました。
Last year, I went to Rome too (in addition to some other place).

アメリカからも学生が来(き)ました。
Students came from the United States, too.

When this particle is used in the subject or direct object position, it replaces は, が, or を. But it follows other particles, resulting in such combinations as にも, からも, までも, でも, and へも.

その本(ほん)は図書館(としょかん)にあります。 *That book is at the library.*

その本(ほん)はわたしのうちにもあります。 *That book is at my home too.*

デパートへ行(い)きます。 *I will go to a department store.*

スーパーへも行(い)きます。 *I will go to a supermarket too.*

Here is a summary of these combinations and replacements of particles.

が → も は → も を → も に → にも へ → へも で → でも

14.8 The particle と means *together with.*

ブラウンさんと映画(えいが)へ行(い)きました。
I went to the movies with Ms. Brown.
三村(みむら)さんと会(あ)いましたか。
Did you meet with Mr. Mimura?

As you have already studied, this particle is also used to connect two or more nouns or pronouns in the sense of *and.*

アイスクリームとチョコレートが好(す)きです。
I like ice cream and chocolate.

Remember: You cannot use と to connect adjectives, adverbs, verbs, or sentences.

14.9 Japanese is sometimes called a "word order-free" language because its word order is not so strictly fixed as in English. A verb or a predicate comes in the sentence-final position, but other elements can be ordered more freely. This is possible because particles indicate the grammatical function of a word or a phrase. Therefore, even if you move a word or a phrase around, as long as it is followed by a particle you can tell its grammatical function. In English, however, the grammatical function of a word or phrase is often determined by word order.

Nevertheless, a natural word order does exist in Japanese, as shown here.

N は／が (time) (place) (indirect object) (direct object) **V**

わたしは明日(あした)ロサンゼルスから東京(とうきょう)へ発(た)ちます。
I will leave Los Angeles for Tokyo tomorrow.
わたしの妹(いもうと)は明日(あす)、デパートでくつを買(か)います。
My sister will buy shoes at a department store tomorrow.

アクティビティー 27

机の上に何がありますか。(*What's on the desk?*)

Fill in the blanks.

[例] 7時(に)起きます。

1. 机 (　　) 上 (　　) 本があります。
2. テレビ (　　) 見ます。
3. 毎晩、8時 (　　) 家 (　　) 帰ります。
4. 時々、ラジオ (　　) 音楽(*music*) (　　) 聞きます。
5. 来週東京 (　　) 行きます。東京 (　　) ブラウンさん (　　) 会います。
   来月東京 (　　) 帰ります。
6. そのアメリカ人はフォーク (　　) てんぷらを食べました。
7. わたしはうち (　　) 大学 (　　) 電車で行きます。
8. 昨日カーティスさんはだれ (　　) 話しましたか。
9. デパートへ買い物 (　　) 行きました。
10. どんな本 (　　) 好きですか。

アクティビティー 28

何時にどこへ行きましたか。(*Where did you go; what time?*)

Fill in the blanks.

今日の朝、わたしは6時半 (　　) 起きました。そして、顔 (　　) 洗いました。7時 (　　) 7時半 (　　) 公園 (　　) 散歩しました。8時 (　　) 大学 (　　) 行きました。9時 (　　) 12時 (　　) クラス (　　) ありました。昼ごはんはカフェテリア (　　) ハンバーガー (　　) 食べました。ミルク (　　) 飲みました。3時 (　　) 町田さん (　　) としょかん (　　) 行きました。5時 (　　) 家 (　　) 帰りました。6時 (　　) 夕ごはん (　　) 食べました。それから、ラジオ (　　) 音楽 (　　) 聞きました。十時 (　　)、友だち (　　) 電話しました。11時 (　　) シャワー (　　) 浴びました。11時半 (　　) 寝ました。

アクティビティー 29

いつも家で夕ごはんを食べます。(*I always eat supper at home.*)

Make a dialogue using the words given in parentheses. Use the correct particles.

[例] s1: 町田さんは先週デパートへ行きましたか。
s2: (はい) → はい、行きました。

s1: (いつ買い物に行く)
s2: (先週の土曜日)
s1: (だれと)
s2: (山口さん)
s1: (何) (買う)
s2: (ブラウス) (買う)
s1: 町田さんはよくレストランへ行きますか。
s2: (あまり)
s1: いつも家で夕ごはんを食べますか。
s2: (いつも)
s1: (昨日) (何) (食べる)
s2: (ステーキ) (食べる)
s1: (どんな) (食べ物) (好きです)
s2: (ほとんど) (何でも *everything*)

Vocabulary and Grammar 3C

Vocabulary and Oral Activities

Weekends and Holidays

Vocabulary: Holidays and Vacations

平日	へいじつ	weekday
週末	しゅうまつ	weekend
休みの日	やすみのひ	day off; holiday

休む	やすむ	to take time off; take a rest
祝日	しゅくじつ	national holiday
夏休み	なつやすみ	summer vacation
冬休み	ふゆやすみ	winter vacation
休暇	きゅうか	vacation
休暇を取る	きゅうかをとる	to take a vacation

アクティビティー 30

週末はひまです。(*I am free on weekends.*)

How do you spend your weekends? Did you do any of these activities last weekend?

1. 部屋を掃除する

2. 遅くまでテレビを見る

3. デートをする

4. 働く

5. 10時まで寝る
6. 勉強する
7. 映画を見る
8. 図書館に行く
9. 散歩する
10. スポーツをする
11. 洗濯する (*do laundry*)
12. 何もしない (*not do anything*)

アクティビティー　31

ウィークデーと週末(*Weekdays and weekends*)

Here are the weekday and weekend schedules of Mr. Takada, Linda Brown's next-door neighbor. Answer the questions below.

Useful Vocabulary: ブランチ *brunch,* 会社 *company,* ウィークデー *weekday,* 週末 *weekend*

月曜日～金曜日＝ウィークデー		土曜日～日曜日＝週末	
6:00	get up	9:00	get up
6:05	take a shower	9:30	drink coffee
6:15	eat breakfast	9:45	read the newspaper
6:45	leave home	10:15	watch TV
7:00	get on the bus	11:00	eat brunch
8:00	start work	12:00	clean the apartment
9:00	attend a meeting	1:00	go shopping
10:30	drink coffee	2:30	do laundry
12:00	eat lunch	5:00	go to a restaurant
1:00	drink coffee	7:00	listen to the stereo
2:00	meet with clients	8:00	read a book
4:45	leave the company	9:30	eat a snack
6:00	arrive home	11:00	watch TV
6:30	cook dinner	12:30	go to bed
7:30	eat dinner		
8:00	watch TV		
10:00	take a bath		
11:00	go to bed		

1. 高田さんは、ウィークデー、何時に起きますか。週末、何時に起きますか。
2. 高田さんは、週末、会社へ行きますか。
3. 高田さんは、ウィークデー、何時と何時にコーヒーを飲みますか。高田さんは、週末、何時にコーヒーを飲みますか。
4. 高田さんは、ウィークデー、洗濯をしますか。
5. 高田さんは、週末、朝ごはんを食べますか。
6. 高田さんは、ウィークデーも週末もテレビを見ますか。
7. 高田さんは、ウィークデーも週末も夕ごはんを作りますか。(作る*make, cook*)

Make your own questions to ask your classmates.

There are two terms that mean *weekday,* ウィークデー and 平日 (へいじつ). The first is customarily used in ordinary conversation, while 平日 is used on more formal occasions, such as an interview, and in writing.

言語ノート

Connecting Disjunctive Sentences

Disjunctive conjunctions are words used to link two sentences that express contrasting ideas. A disjunctive conjunction frequently used in conversation is でも (*but, even so*). This conjunction begins the second sentence of the contrasting pair.

ウィークデー、午前6時に起きます。でも、週末、午前10時に起きます。

I get up at 6:00 A.M. on weekdays. But I get up at 10:00 A.M. on weekends.

In written discourse, the conjunction しかし (*however*) is often used.

平日は会社へ行く。しかし、週末は行かない。

I go to the office (lit., *company*) *on weekdays. However, I don't go there on weekends.*

A disjunctive conjunction is also a word joining two contrasting independent clauses (that is, complete sentences) into a single compound sentence. One used very frequently in conversation is が (*but*). Unlike the English position of *but* at the beginning of the second clause, が attaches to the end of the first clause; the pause in speech and the comma in writing fall *after* が.

ウィークデーは午前6時に起きますが、週末は午前10時に起きます。

I get up at 6:00 A.M. on weekdays, but I get up at 10:00 A.M. on weekends.

Japanese often end sentences with this が and a trailing intonation, expecting the listener to know what the rest of the compound sentence would be from context.

すみませんが…

I'm sorry, but… (we don't have any; I can't do it this time; etc.)

Excuse me, but… (could you help me?; I have a question; etc.)

アクティビティー 32

ウィークデーは早く起きます。(*On weekdays I get up early.*)

Add a contrasting clause to complete the following sentences comparing weekday and weekend schedules.

Useful word: 遅く *late* (adverb)

1. ウィークデーの朝はシャワーを浴びます。でも、_____
2. 週末はテニスをしますが、_____
3. 先週のウィークデーは毎日勉強しました。でも、_____
4. ウィークデーは毎日図書館へ行きます。でも、_____
5. ウィークデーはカフェテリアで昼ごはんを食べますが、_____
6. ウィークデーは夜新聞を読みます。でも、_____
7. ウィークデーは早く(*early*)寝ますが、_____

文化ノート

CULTURE NOTE • 国民の祝日 *National Holidays*

The following are national holidays in Japan.

1月1日	元日	*New Year's Day*
1月 第2月曜 (*variable*)	成人の日	*Coming-of-Age Day*
2月11日	建国記念の日	*National Foundation Day*
3月21日 (*variable*)	春分の日	*Vernal Equinox Day*
4月29日	緑の日	*Greenery Day*
5月3日	憲法記念日	*Constitution Day*
5月5日	子供の日	*Children's Day*
7月20日	海の日	*Marine Day*
9月15日	敬老の日	*Respect-for-the-Aged Day*
9月23日 (*variable*)	秋分の日	*Autumnal Equinox Day*
10月10日	体育の日	*Health-Sports Day*
11月3日	文化の日	*Culture Day*
11月23日	勤労感謝の日	*Labor Thanksgiving Day*
12月23日	天皇誕生日	*Emperor's Birthday*

成人の日—on this holiday, the Japanese celebrate those who turned 20 years old in the preceding year. You are considered an adult in Japan when you reach 20 years of age. (That is also the age of legal majority, when you can begin voting and drinking alcohol.)

憲法記念日 is the day commemorating the promulgation of the Constitution that was drafted after World War II.

文化の日 is the day celebrating the development of culture and the proclamation of the new Constitution. On this day, those who have contributed to the enhancement of culture, technology, and community are awarded medals.

成人(せいじん)の日(ひ)：わたしたちは二十歳(はたち)です。

Grammar and Practice Activities

15. Making Suggestions: 〜ましょう

カワムラ：林(はやし)さん、おそいですね。
ブラウン：ええ、どうしましょうか。
カワムラ：もう少(すこ)し待(ま)ちましょう。
ブラウン：でも、もう9時(じ)ですよ。出(で)かけましょうか。
カワムラ：ええ、そうしましょう。

林(はやし)：チンさんがいませんね。
カワムラ：ええ。
林：チンさん、病気(びょうき)ですか。
カワムラ：さあ。
林：ぼくが家(いえ)に電話(でんわ)しましょうか。

KAWAMURA: Mr. Hayashi is late, isn't he? BROWN: Yes. What shall we do? KAWAMURA: Let's wait for him a little longer. BROWN: But it's already nine o'clock. Shall we leave (now)? KAWAMURA: Yes, let's do that.

HAYASHI: Ms. Chin isn't here, is she? KAWAMURA: That's right. (lit., *Yes.*) HAYASHI: Is she sick? KAWAMURA: I don't know. HAYASHI: Shall I call her at home?

15.1 The ましょう form, or the polite, volitional form of a verb, is made by adding ましょう to the conjunctive form. Here are some examples.

DICTIONARY FORM	CONJUNCTIVE FORM	ましょう FORM
Class 1 Verbs		
洗(あら)う	洗(あら)い	洗(あら)いましょう
立(た)つ	立(た)ち	立(た)ちましょう
Class 2 Verbs		
食(た)べる	食(た)べ	食(た)べましょう
見(み)る	見(み)	見(み)ましょう
Class 3 Verbs		
する	し	しましょう
来(く)る	来(き)	来(き)ましょう

15.2 The ましょう form is used to suggest, propose, or invite (*Let's*… or *Shall we*…*?*).

> 一緒(いっしょ)に勉強(べんきょう)しましょうか。
> ***Shall we study together?***
> 昼(ひる)ごはんを食(た)べましょう。
> ***Let's eat lunch.***
> 電車(でんしゃ)で行(い)きましょうか。タクシーで行(い)きましょうか。
> ***Shall we go by train or taxi?***

Because the ましょう form expresses the speaker's volition, without consideration to the hearer's preferences, it tends to sound somewhat pushy and forceful. It is politer to use the nonpast, polite, negative form of a verb + か when inviting someone to do something together or when making a suggestion.

> 一緒(いっしょ)に夕(ゆう)ごはんを食(た)べませんか。
> ***Shall we eat dinner together?***
> ***Would you like to eat dinner together?*** (lit., ***Won't you eat dinner together*** [***with me***]***?***)
> 来週(らいしゅう)、デパートへ行(い)きませんか。
> ***Shall we go to a department store next week?***
> ***Would you like to go to a department store next week?*** (lit., ***Won't you go to a department store next week?***)

When you already know that the hearer is willing to do something together, the use of the ましょう form does not sound pushy. For example,

レストランへ行きませんか。
Shall we go to a restaurant?
ええ、いいですね。
Yes, that sounds nice.
どこへ行きましょうか。
Where shall we go?

or

のどがかわきましたね。
I am thirsty, aren't you?
ええ、とても。
Yes, very much.
ジュースを飲みましょうか。
Shall we drink juice?

15.3 The ましょう form is also used when offering to do something for someone or when expressing one's own volition.

わたしがブラウンさんに話しましょう。
I will talk to Ms. Brown.

わたしがワインを買いましょうか。
Shall I buy wine?

When the first person subject is expressed explicitly as in the preceding examples, it implies that "I but not anyone else" will do something. When the first person subject is not expressed, it simply expresses the speaker's volition without such an implication.

さあ、勉強しましょう。
Well, I guess I will start studying.
Well, I'm going to study now.

言語ノート

Accepting and Declining Offers

To accept an offer, say

はい、お願いします。
Yes, please.
どうもありがとうございます。
Thank you very much.
どうもすみません。
Thank you for your trouble. (lit., *I'm sorry for your trouble.*)

To turn down an offer, say

いいえ、けっこうです。
No, thank you.
(lit., *No, I'm fine.*)

アクティビティー 33

さあ、泳ぎましょう。(*Let's go swimming now.*)

Rewrite each sentence using the ましょう form.

[例] コーラを飲(の)む → コーラを飲みましょう。

1. 映画(えいが)を見(み)る
2. コンサートへ行(い)く
3. ケーキを食(た)べる
4. ジョギングする
5. 本を読(よ)む
6. 買物(かいもの)に出(で)かける
7. プールで泳(およ)ぐ
8. 日本語で話す

アクティビティー 34

あとで話(はな)しましょうか。(*Let's talk later.*)

Complete the following dialogues using the ましょう form.

[例] (ブラウンさんに電話(でんわ)する) (*accept*) →
—わたしがブラウンさんに電話しましょうか。
—ええ、お願(ねが)いします。
(掃除(そうじ)する) (*decline*) →
—わたしが掃除しましょうか。
—いいえ、けっこうです。

1. (山口(やまぐち)さんに聞(き)く) (*accept*)
2. (洗濯(せんたく)をする) (*decline*)
3. (横井先生(よこいせんせい)の研究室(けんきゅうしつ)に行(い)く) (*accept*)
4. (その本を読(よ)む) (*accept*)
5. (料理(りょうり)する) (*decline*)

アクティビティー 35

ダイアログ：何(なに)を見(み)ましょうか。(*What shall we see?*)

林(はやし)さんとギブソンさんが話(はな)しています。

林(はやし)：ギブソンさん、今週(こんしゅう)の土曜日(どようび)、一緒(いっしょ)に映画(えいが)を見(み)ませんか。
ギブソン：ええ。何(なに)を見ましょうか。
林：カラテ・キッドはどうですか。
ギブソン：いいですね。

Practice the preceding dialogue, substituting the following activities for the first and second underlined phrases. (Use the appropriate form.) Make up your own substitution for the third underlined phrase.

Useful word: プール *swimming pool*

1. 買(か)い物(もの)に行(い)く、どこへ行く
2. ジョギングをする、どこでする
3. 夕(ゆう)ごはんを食(た)べる、どこで食べる
4. ドライブする (*to go on a drive*)、どこへ行(い)く
5. 泳(およ)ぐ (*to swim*)、どこで泳ぐ

言語ノート

Making a Suggestion

In the preceding dialogue, the phrase …はどうですか is used to make a suggestion.

東急(とうきゅう)デパートはどうですか。
How about Tookyuu Department Store? (e.g., as a possible place to do shopping)

大学のプールはどうですか。
How about the college swimming pool? (e.g., as a possible place to swim)

The phrase …はいかがですか is a more formal equivalent of …はどうですか. A shop clerk at a department store might say the following while showing a pen to a customer.

このペンはいかがですか。
How about this pen? (as the one to buy)

Mr. Hayashi and Ms. Gibson are talking. HAYASHI: Ms. Gibson, would you like to (lit., *won't you*) see a movie together this Saturday? GIBSON: Yes, what shall we see? HAYASHI: How about Karate Kid? GIBSON: That sounds good. (lit., *That's good.*)

アクティビティー 36

休みましょうか。(*Shall we take a break?*)

Following the example, complete these conversations using 〜ましょう.

[例] 疲れましたね。(*I'm tired, aren't you?*) →
ええ、休みましょうか。(*Yes, shall we take a break?*)

Useful Vocabulary: 食べる、飲む、家に帰る、図書館で勉強する、先生に聞く

1. おなかがすきましたね。(*I am hungry, aren't you?*)
2. のどがかわきましたね。(*I am thirsty, aren't you?*)
3. もう6時ですね。
4. ここはうるさいですね。(*It is noisy here, isn't it?*)
5. この問題、むずかしいですね。(*This problem is difficult, isn't it?*)

アクティビティー 37

ダイアログ：ぼくが電話しましょう。(*I will make the phone call.*)

カワムラさんと林さんが話しています。

カワムラ：今、何時ですか。
林：ええと、2時半です。ブラウンさん、おそいですね。
カワムラ：ええ。ブラウンさんに電話しませんか。
林：ええ、ぼくが電話しましょう。
カワムラ：お願いします。

Mr. Kawamura and Mr. Hayashi are talking KAWAMURA: What time is it now? HAYASHI: Uh, it's 2:30. Ms. Brown is late, isn't she? KAWAMURA: Yes, shouldn't we call her (lit., *Ms. Brown*)? HAYASHI: Yes. I will make the call. KAWAMURA: Thank you. (lit., *Please do it for me.*)

16. Conjoining Nouns: と and や

カワムラ：横井先生(よこいせんせい)の研究室(けんきゅうしつ)にだれがいますか。
町田(まちだ)：横井先生(よこいせんせい)とブラウンさんがいます。
カワムラ：チンさんは。
町田：研究室(けんきゅうしつ)の外(そと)にいます。

ブラウン：事務室(じむしつ)にだれがいますか。
町田(まちだ)：カワムラさんや林(はやし)さんがいます。
ブラウン：カーティスさんは。
町田：ええ、カーティスさんもいます。

You can join nouns together with と or や. と (*and*) is used to enumerate *all* objects that exist in a certain place or *all* objects that belong to a certain category, while や (*and things like that*) is used to list only representative objects. Thus, と is exhaustive, and や is not. You may conjoin as many nouns as you like with these particles. Remember: you cannot use these particles to connect adjectives, verbs, or sentences.

アクティビティー 38

だれが来(き)ましたか。(*Who came?*)

Answer each question two ways, first using と and then や.

1. 昨日(きのう)、だれが来(き)ましたか。 (*Hayashi, Chin, and Gibson*)
2. 夕(ゆう)ごはんに何(なに)を食(た)べましたか。(*steak, salad, and fruit*)
3. そこにだれがいますか。(*Brown, Kawamura, Curtis, and Chin*)
4. どんなコンピュータがありますか。(*IBM, Apple, NEC, and Toshiba*)
5. どんなスポーツが好(す)きですか。(*basketball, football, and tennis*)

KAWAMURA: Who is in Professor Yokoi's office? MACHIDA: Professor Yokoi and Ms. Brown.
KAWAMURA: How about Ms. Chin? MACHIDA: She is outside the office.

BROWN: Who is in the administrative office? MACHIDA: Mr. Kawamura, Mr. Hayashi, and others.
BROWN: How about Mr. Curtis? MACHIDA: Yes, he's there, too.

Language Skills

Reading and Writing

Reading 1 ブラウンさんの日常生活(にちじょうせいかつ)

Before You Read

The following passage describes Linda Brown's daily life. Before reading it, work with a partner to arrange the following activities in the order you think average students perform them.

_____ 夕(ゆう)ごはんを食(た)べる	_____ 家(いえ)に帰(かえ)る
_____ 大学(だいがく)へ行(い)く	_____ クラスに出(で)る
_____ 起(お)きる	_____ 昼(ひる)ごはんを食(た)べる
_____ 朝(あさ)ごはんを食べる	_____ 寝(ね)る

Work in pairs. Which of the following activities do both you and your partner do every morning? Which do neither of you do?

_____ 歯(は)を磨(みが)く	_____ パジャマを脱(ぬ)ぐ
_____ ラジオを聞(き)く	_____ 髪(かみ)をとかす
_____ シャワーを浴(あ)びる	_____ 服(ふく)を着(き)る
_____ 朝(あさ)ごはんを食(た)べる	_____ 電車(でんしゃ)に乗(の)る
_____ コーヒーを飲(の)む	_____ 新聞(しんぶん)を読(よ)む
_____ テレビを見(み)る	_____ ジョギングをする
_____ 顔(かお)を洗(あら)う	

Now Read It!

わたしは毎朝(まいあさ)6時に起きます。まず、顔(かお)を洗(あら)います。そして、歯を磨(みが)きます。それから、ジョギングをします。7時(じ)ごろ朝(あさ)ごはんを食(た)べます。7時半(はん)にうちを出(で)ます。わたしのアパートは中野駅(なかのえき)のそばにあります。アパートから駅(えき)まで五分(ふん)歩(ある)きます。そして、地下鉄(ちかてつ)で大学(だいがく)へ行(い)きます。アパートから大学まで30分(ぷん)ぐらいかかります。

まず *first of all*

駅 *station*／歩く *to walk*

かかる *to take*

クラスは8時に始まります。わたしの専攻は日本文化です。毎日、日本文化、日本語のクラスに出ます。午前のクラスは12時に終わります。いつも大学のカフェテリアで昼ごはんを食べます。午後のクラスは1時から始まります。そして、4時に終わります。クラスの後、時々、図書館へ行きます。月曜日と水曜日と金曜日は友だちとエアロビクスのレッスンに行きます。

いつもアパートに5時か6時に帰ります。夕ごはんは7時半ごろ食べます。時々、アパートのそばの食堂へ行きます。

夜は日本語の勉強します。本もよく読みます。ミステリーが好きです。テレビはあまり見ません。カセットやCDで音楽をよく聞きます。毎日、12時ごろ寝ます。

始まる *to start*

終わる *to finish*

…の後 *after…*

五時か六時 *five o'clock or six o'clock*

言語ノート

Approximate Numbers

These words, when appended to quantities or points in time, make the numerical entities approximate.

1. ごろ (*around*) is used to express an approximate point in time, such as a day, month, or hour.

   毎日5時ごろ起きます。
   I get up around 5:00 every day.

2. ぐらい or くらい (*about*) is used to express an approximate quantity. くらい and ぐらい are interchangeable.

   日本語のクラスには三十人ぐらいの学生がいます。
   There are about thirty students in the Japanese language class.

   東京から京都まで3時間ぐらいかかります。
   It takes about three hours from Tokyo to Kyoto.

   その本は二千円くらいです。
   That book costs (lit., *is*) *about 2,000 yen.*

3. ほど (*about*) is also used to express approximate quantity. ほど is used in the sense of *as much as* with all but small numbers.

   レタスを二つほどください。
   Let me have two heads of lettuce.

   ここから15分ほどかかります。
   It takes (as much as) about fifteen minutes from here.

After You Finish Reading

1. Based on information provided in the passage, write up a detailed daily schedule for Linda Brown, indicating her activities from 6:00 A.M. to midnight. Indicate A.M. and P.M. with 午前 and 午後.
2. Now look at the second paragraph carefully. Identify all the particles in the paragraph and explain how each is used.

Writing 1

Write a short paragraph about your daily life. Use this beginning.

わたしは毎朝(まいあさ) _____ 時(じ)に起(お)きます。それから...

Reading 2 ブラウンさんの週末(しゅうまつ)

Before You Read

The following passage describes what Linda Brown did last weekend. Which of the following do you usually do on weekdays and which do you usually do on weekends?

_____ 寝坊(ねぼう)する	_____ 映画(えいが)を見(み)る
_____ 勉強(べんきょう)する	_____ 友(とも)だちと電話(でんわ)で話(はな)す
_____ 買(か)い物(もの)をする	_____ 大学(だいがく)へ行く
_____ 掃除(そうじ)をする	_____ レコードを聞(き)く
_____ 洗濯(せんたく)をする	_____ レストランへ行く
_____ 図書館(としょかん)へ行(い)く	

Match items in the first column to related items in the second column.

1. 誕生日(たんじょうび)	a. 日曜日(にちようび)
2. コインランドリー	b. ギフト
3. パーティー	c. デパート
4. 週末(しゅうまつ)	d. ワイン
5. 買(か)い物(もの)	e. 洗濯(せんたく)

Now Read It!

土曜日(どようび)と日曜日(にちようび)は大学が休(やす)みです。土曜日(どようび)は午前(ごぜん)9時(じ)ごろ起(お)きます。土曜日の朝(あさ)はいつもアパートの前(まえ)の喫茶店(きっさてん)に行きます。この喫茶店(きっさてん)のコーヒーはとてもおいしいです。お昼まで喫茶店でコーヒーを飲みます。土曜日の午後はアパートの掃除をします。夜はクラスメートと外に出かけます。先週の土曜日はカワムラさんと映画を見ました。今週の土曜日は町田さんと買い物に行きます。土曜日はいつも午後11時か12時ごろアパートに帰ります。日曜日はいつも、お昼ごろ起きます。午後は近くのコイン・ランドリーで洗濯をします。夜、ちょっと勉強します。来週の日曜日はカワムラさんの誕生日です。カワムラさんは二十一歳になります。町田さんの家でパーティーがあります。来週の日曜日は朝早く起きます。町田さんの家で、パーティーの準備を手伝います。町田さんと一緒にケーキやごちそうを作ります。

昨日、カワムラさんのバースデー・プレゼントを買いました。カワムラさんはコンピュータが好きです。それで、コンピュータのソフトウェアを買いました。

おいしい *delicious* / お昼 *noontime*

コイン・ランドリー *laundromat*

...になる *to become*

準備 *preparation* / 手伝う *to help; to assist* / 一緒に *together* / ごちそう *delicious food*

作る *to make; to cook*

それで *therefore*

After You Finish Reading

1. Tell whether each of the following is true or false.
   a. Linda drinks coffee at a coffee shop until noon on Saturdays.
   b. Linda went out with Hitomi Machida last Saturday.
   c. Linda goes to bed at 11:00 P.M. or 12:00 midnight on Saturdays.
   d. Linda cleans her apartment and does her laundry on Sundays.
   e. Next Sunday is John Kawamura's twenty-first birthday.
   f. Hitomi Machida will come to Linda's apartment next Sunday to help Linda prepare for the party.
   g. Linda will buy computer software for John Kawamura.
2. Arrange the following activities in the order Linda Brown does them on Saturday. Create a narrative using appropriate conjunctions.

   ____ アパートに帰る
   ____ 喫茶店へ行く
   ____ 掃除をする
   ____ コーヒーを飲む
   ____ 午前9時ごろ起きる
   ____ 友だちと出かける

Writing 2

Drawing from the journal notations on the following page, write a short paragraph about what John Kawamura did last weekend.

DIARY	
Sat	Sun
10:00 got up read paper 11:00 watched TV 12:00 ate lunch 1:00 did laundry 2:00 cleaned house 4:00 went to movie 7:00 ate at a tempura restaurant 10:00 went to pub 12:00 returned home and went to bed	9:30 got up 10:00 took shower 11:00 listened to music 12:00 called Linda Brown 2:00 went shopping with Linda 5:00 went to McDonald's 7:00 came home 8:00 studied Japanese 10:30 went to bed

Language Functions and Situations

Making a Phone Call

山口（やまぐち）：もしもし、山口（やまぐち）です。
ブラウン：もしもし、ブラウンです。カワムラさんをお願（ねが）いします。
山口：ちょっとお待（ま）ちください。
カワムラ：もしもし、カワムラです。
ブラウン：ブラウンです。

田中（たなか）：もしもし。
ブラウン：もしもし、山口（やまぐち）さんですか。
田中：いいえ、違（ちが）います。
ブラウン：3567-3981ですか。
田中：いいえ、3567-3891です。
ブラウン：あっ、どうもすみません。間違（まちが）えました。
田中：いいえ。

YAMAGUCHI: Hello. This is Yamaguchi speaking. BROWN: Hello. This is Brown. May I speak to Mr. Kawamura? (lit., *Please give me Mr. Kawamura.*) YAMAGUCHI: Wait a moment, please. KAWAMURA: Hello. This is Kawamura speaking. BROWN: This is Brown.

TANAKA: Hello. BROWN: Hello. Is this Mr. Yamaguchi? TANAKA: No, it isn't. (lit., *No, it's different.*) BROWN: Is this 3567-3981? TANAKA: No, this is 3567-3891. BROWN: Oh, I'm very sorry. I must have made an error. (lit., *I made a mistake.*) TANAKA: That's OK. (lit., *Not at all.*)

山口：もしもし、山口です。
ブラウン：もしもし、ブラウンです。カワムラさんをお願いします。
山口：カワムラさんは大学へ行きましたよ。
ブラウン：そうですか。では、また電話します。じゃ、失礼します。
山口：失礼します。

山口：もしもし、山口です。
ブラウン：もしもし、カワムラさんはいますか。
山口：今、いませんよ。
ブラウン：そうですか。ブラウンですが、電話をお願いします。
山口：電話番号をお願いします。
ブラウン：3965-9133です。

言語ノート

Talking on the Telephone

もしもし。
Hello.
林です。
This is Hayashi speaking./This is the Hayashi residence. (lit., *This is Hayashi.*)
チンさんをお願いします。
May I speak to Ms. Chin? (lit., *Please give me Ms. Chin.*)
間違い電話です。
You've dialed the wrong number. (lit., *This is the wrong number.*)
間違えました。
I made a mistake.
また電話します。
I will call back.
伝言をお願いします。
May I leave a message?

YAMAGUCHI: Hello. This is the Yamaguchi residence. BROWN: Hello. This is Brown. May I speak to Mr. Kawamura? YAMAGUCHI: Mr. Kawamura went to the university. BROWN: I see. Then, I will call him back. Goodbye. YAMAGUCHI: Goodbye.

YAMAGUCHI: Hello. This is the Yamaguchi residence. BROWN: Hello. Is Mr. Kawamura there? YAMAGUCHI: Mr. Kawamura is not here now. BROWN: I see. This is Brown. Can you ask him to call me? YAMAGUCHI: May I have (lit., *Please give me*) your phone number? BROWN: 3965-9113.

Role Play

Working with a partner, practice the following situations.

1. Call the Yamamoto residence and ask for Ms. Moore, who is boarding there.
2. You have received a call, but it is the wrong number.
3. Call the Muranaka residence. You learn that Mr. Muranaka is not there and say that you will call back later.
4. Call the Sano residence. Ms. Sano is not there. Say that you would like her to call you back.

Extending an Invitation

大学で

林：ギブソンさん、今日の午後、ひまですか。
ギブソン：ええ。
林：一緒に夕ごはんを食べませんか。
ギブソン：ええ、もちろん。どこがいいですか。
林：「さくらレストラン」はどうですか。
ギブソン：ええ、それはいいですね。

大学で

チン：今日は何時にクラスが終わりますか。
カーティス：3時です。
チン：映画に行きませんか。
カーティス：ええ、いいですね。
チン：どの映画がいいですか。
カーティス：「ニンジャ」はどうですか。
チン：ええ、いいですね。
カーティス：どこで会いましょうか。
チン：図書館の前はどうですか。
カーティス：ええ、いいですよ。

At the university HAYASHI: Ms. Gibson, are you free this afternoon? GIBSON: Yes. HAYASHI: Shall we have dinner together? GIBSON: Yes, certainly (lit., *of course*). Where shall we go? (lit., *Where is good?*) HAYASHI: How about the Sakura Restaurant? GIBSON: Yes, that sounds good.

At the university CHIN: What time is your class over today? CURTIS: At three o'clock. CHIN: Shall we go to the movies? CURTIS: Yes, that would be good. CHIN: Which movie shall we see? (lit., *Which movie is good?*) CURTIS: How about *Ninja*? CHIN: Yes, that would be good. CURTIS: Where shall we meet? CHIN: How about in front of the library? CURTIS: (Yes) That would be fine.

三村（みむら）： ギブソンさん、明日（あした）コンサートに行（い）きませんか。
ギブソン： すみません。明日（あした）はちょっと仕事（しごと）があります。
三村： そうですか。残念（ざんねん）ですね。

言語ノート

Let's Do Something Together

The ましょう form or the nonpast, negative form of a verb is commonly used to suggest doing something together. (See **Grammar 15** for more about the ましょう form.)

一緒（いっしょ）に夕（ゆう）ごはんを食（た）べましょう。
Let's have dinner together.

一緒に夕ごはんを食べませんか。
Would you like to have dinner together?
(lit., *Won't you have dinner together* [*with me*]*?*)

To agree, say

ええ、いいですね。
Yes, that sounds good.

To decline, say

すみません。またこの次（つぎ）。
I'm sorry, but (let's do it) next time.

いいですね。でも、また今度（こんど）。
That would be nice, but (let's make it) next time.

どうもありがとうございます。でも、今はちょっと...。
Thank you very much. But I am afraid now is a bit...
(*inconvenient*).

林さんへ

来週の土曜日、わたしのアパートに来ませんか。
アメリカのビデオを見ます。
カーティスさんも来ます。

ブラウン

2月24日

Role Play

Practice the following situations with your classmates.

1. Ask one of your classmates when his or her classes are over today, and issue an invitation to do the following.
   a. jog with you after class
   b. drink beer with you after class

MIMURA: Ms. Gibson, would you like to go to a concert tomorrow? GIBSON: I'm sorry. I have (lit., *a little*) work tomorrow. MIMURA: I see. That's too bad.

c. eat pizza with you after class
d. go shopping with you after class

2. Invite a classmate to have lunch with you next Monday. Suggest eating at your favorite restaurant near the university. If your classmate is busy next Monday, ask when he or she is free. Remember that it is rude to say no directly in Japanese; if you are busy next Monday use one of the responses you learned in the previous Language Note, **Let's Do Something Together.**
3. Call one of your classmates and invite him or her to your home this Saturday. Give simple directions and use descriptions of your house and neighborhood.

Listening Comprehension

1. Mr. Kunio Hasegawa, one of the richest Japanese who ever lived, was murdered in the British-style garden of his large mansion in Kamakura last night. You are a police chief in Kamakura. One of your detectives, Nobuo Maruyama, interviewed six suspects about their activities last night. Listen to his report. Then list what each suspect did throughout the evening and at what time. The six suspects are Mr. Hasegawa's wife, Tamako; his daughter, Sawako; his son, Muneo; his mistress, Junko Suzuki; his chauffeur, Kazuo Morimoto; and his brother-in-law, Haruki Kameda.
2. Listen to the results of a survey on the lifestyle of Japanese people. Complete the following table by filling in the appropriate numbers.

Japanese who get up before 6:30 A.M.	%
Japanese who eat breakfast	%
Japanese who start work before 8:30 A.M.	%
Japanese who eat lunch between noon and 1:00 P.M.	%
Japanese workers who return home before 7:00 P.M.	%
Japanese workers who go drinking after work	%
Japanese who watch TV every night	%
Japanese who go to bed before 11:00 P.M.	%

Vocabulary

Time Expressions

あさって		the day after tomorrow	こんばん	今晩	tonight
あした	明日	tomorrow	せんげつ	先月	last month
おととい		the day before yesterday	せんしゅう	先週	last week
きのう	昨日	yesterday	なんじかん	何時間	how many hours
きょう	今日	today	なんにち	何日	what day
きょねん	去年	last year	なんねん	何年	what year
けさ	今朝	this morning	らいげつ	来月	next month
ことし	今年	this year	らいしゅう	来週	next week
こんげつ	今月	this month	らいねん	来年	next year
こんしゅう	今週	this week			

Review: 朝、午前、午後、時間、何月、何曜日、昼、夕方、夜、夕辺

Everyday Activities

いえをでる	家を出る	to leave home
うんどうする	運動する	to exercise
おふろにはいる	お風呂に入る	to take a bath
かおをあらう	顔を洗う	to wash one's face
シャワーをあびる	シャワーを浴びる	to take a shower
しょくじ(を)する	食事(を)する	to have a meal
つかれる	疲れる	to become tired
でかける	出かける	to go out
でんわ(を)する	電話(を)する	to make a telephone call
ねぼうする	寝坊する	to oversleep
のる	乗る	to ride (a vehicle)
はたらく	働く	to work
はをみがく	歯を磨く	to brush one's teeth
ふくをきる	服を着る	to put on clothes
やすむ	休む	to take a rest; to take time off
ゆうごはんをたべる	夕ごはんを食べる	to have dinner; to have supper
りょうり(を)する	料理(を)する	to cook

Review: 朝ごはん、行く、起きる、買い物(を)する、帰る、聞く、仕事をする、食べる、寝る、飲む、話す、晩ごはん、昼ごはん、勉強する、見る、読む

Days of the Month

ついたち	一日	the first	じゅうににち	十二日	the twelfth
ふつか	二日	the second	じゅうさんにち	十三日	the thirteenth
みっか	三日	the third	じゅうよっか	十四日	the fourteenth
よっか	四日	the fourth	じゅうごにち	十五日	the fifteenth
いつか	五日	the fifth	じゅうろくにち	十六日	the sixteenth
むいか	六日	the sixth	じゅうしちにち	十七日	the seventeenth
なのか	七日	the seventh	じゅうはちにち	十八日	the eighteenth
ようか	八日	the eighth	じゅうくにち	十九日	the nineteenth
ここのか	九日	the ninth	はつか	二十日	the twentieth
とおか	十日	the tenth	にじゅうよっか	二十四日	the twenty-fourth
じゅういちにち	十一日	the eleventh			

Frequency

あまり		(*with negative*) not very much	まいあさ	毎朝	every morning
いつも		always	まいしゅう	毎週	every week
～かい	~回	...times (*counter for occurrences*)	まいつき	毎月	every month
ぜんぜん	全然	(*with negative*) not at all	まいにち	毎日	every day
たまに		once in a while	まいばん	毎晩	every night
ときどき	時々	sometimes	よく		often
ほとんど		almost			
ほとんど～		(*with negative*) almost never; hardly			

Conjunctions

そして	and then
そのあと	after that
それから	and then

Particles

が	(*subject particle*)	は	(*topic particle*)
から	from	へ	(*direction particle*)
で	at; by means of	まで	up to; until
と	with	も	too
に	(*indirect object particle*)	を	(*direct object particle*)

Nouns

ウィークデー		weekday	なつやすみ	夏休み	summer vacation
へいじつ	平日	weekday	ふゆやすみ	冬休み	winter vacation
しゅうまつ	週末	weekend			
やすみのひ	休みの日	day off; holiday			

Adjectives

いそがしい	忙しい	busy
ひま(な)	暇(な)	free (*not busy*)

Verb Endings

～ましょう	let's…	～ました	(*past, polite, affirmative*)
～ます	(*nonpast, polite, affirmative*)	～ませんでした	(*past, polite, negative*)
～ません	(*nonpast, polite, negative*)		

Kanji

Learn these **kanji:**

朝	飲	見
明	入	起
午	休	読
昼	夕	火
来	今	水
行	週	木
聞	曜	金
食	毎	土
出	回	会

チェックリスト

Use this checklist to confirm that you can now

- ☐ Talk about schedules
- ☐ Understand the basic structure of verbs
- ☐ Talk about daily activities
- ☐ Use past, polite verb forms
- ☐ Use particles showing grammatical relationships
- ☐ Talk about weekends and holidays
- ☐ Make suggestions in a new way
- ☐ Make phone calls
- ☐ Extend an invitation

Review Chapter 3

アクティビティー　1

Vocabulary review

Which of the words listed in parentheses is most closely connected to the first word given?

[例]　朝ごはん（ステーキ、ピザ、シリアル、ビール、本）→
シリアルです。朝ごはんにいつも食べます。

1. 朝の六時（寝る、勉強する、起きる、電話する、話す）
2. クラス（起きる、寝る、勉強する、食べる、飲む）
3. 図書館（昼ごはん、寝る、ビールを飲む、本を読む）
4. 見る（ステレオ、夕ごはん、テレビ、新聞、トイレ）
5. 読む（新聞、朝ごはん、寝る、シャワー、お風呂）
6. 運動（朝ごはん、エアロビクス、図書館、本、勉強、寝る）
7. 顔（磨く、飲む、出かける、洗う、浴びる）
8. お風呂（磨く、浴びる、入る、起きる、寝る）
9. 週末（木曜日、金曜日、土曜日、月曜日、火曜日）
10. 着る（ラジオ、ステレオ、ベッド、服、図書館）

アクティビティー　2

月間スケジュール (*Monthly schedule*)

Using the following calendar page, discuss Heather Gibson's activities. Assume that today is March 15th.

[例]　昨日、パーティーに行きました。

S	M	T	W	Th	F	S
			March			
	shopping 1	cleaning 2 judo	see prof. 3	4	part-time job 5	free 6
free 7	study 8	library 9 judo	study 10	exam 11	part-time job 12	see Hayashi 13
party 14	**today** 15	study 16 judo	exam 17	movie 18	part-time job 19	shopping 20
see Hayashi 21	22	library 23 judo	study 24	exam 25	part-time job 26	party 27
laundry cleaning 28	see Brown 29	concert 30 judo	movie 31			

アクティビティー　3

週末(しゅうまつ)はいつも忙がしいです。(*I'm always busy on the weekend.*)

What do you do on the weekend? Decide whether each of the following statements is true or false in your case.

1. 早(はや)く起(お)きません。
2. 顔(かお)を洗(あら)いません。
3. 家(いえ)にいません。
4. 勉強(べんきょう)しません。
5. 運動(うんどう)します。
6. 部屋(へや)を掃除(そうじ)します。
7. 洗濯(せんたく)をします。
8. テレビを見(み)ます。
9. 映画(えいが)を見ます。

アクティビティー　4

In Chapter 3 you have learned many expressions and grammatical structures necessary to talk about everyday and weekend activities. To review them, make up several questions on one of the following topics and interview at least five classmates to see if they share any particular habits (e.g., they tend to go to bed late, to study at a library, not to eat breakfast, and so on.)

1. 勉強(べんきょう)
2. 運動(うんどう)
3. 朝(あさ)
4. 夜(よる)
5. 食事(しょくじ)

4

第四章 天気・気候

Weather and Climate

今日は雨です。

Objectives

In this lesson you are going to

- Talk about weather reports
- Talk about the four seasons
- Talk about forecasting
- Learn how to conjugate adjectives
- Learn to use comparatives and superlatives
- Learn how to express plain, nonpast negative and plain past
- Learn how to explain a reason using ～ので
- Study the -te form of adjectives and verbs
- Learn how to express possibility
- Learn how to ask questions about the Japanese language

YOOKOSO! MULTIMEDIA

Review and practice grammar and vocabulary from this chapter and watch video clips on the *Yookoso!* Interactive CD-ROM. Visit the *Yookoso!* Online Learning Center at **www.mhhe.com/yookosome** for additional exercises and resources.

Vocabulary and Grammar 4A

Vocabulary and Oral Activities

Weather Reports

今日(きょう)のお天気(てんき)

暑(あつ)いです

寒(さむ)いです

雨(あめ)です

晴(は)れです

くもりです

雪(ゆき)です

風(かぜ)が強(つよ)いです

言語ノート

Talking About the Weather

Discussing the weather is a ritual of daily conversation in many cultures, and Japan is no exception. In Japanese, a reference to the weather—いいお天気(てんき)ですね (*It's fine weather, isn't it?*)—can serve as a greeting, a substitute for *Hello, how are you?* This is partly because in former times Japan's economy was based on agriculture, especially rice cultivation; many people were concerned about the weather because it affected their livelihoods. In Japan today the weather is a neutral, impersonal topic for everyday conversations with new or old acquaintances. As you will see in **Reading 1** of this chapter, a reference to the weather or season is also a standard opening line for a personal letter.

Vocabulary: Weather and Climate 

(お)天気	(お)てんき	weather
気候	きこう	climate
天気予報	てんきよほう	weather forecast
天気図	てんきず	weather map
いい天気	いいてんき	good weather
悪い天気	わるいてんき	bad weather
晴れる	はれる	to clear up
くもる		to become cloudy; to be cloudy
雨が降る	あめがふる	to rain (lit., *rain falls*)
雪が降る	ゆきがふる	to snow (lit., *snow falls*)
気温	きおん	(air) temperature
…度	…ど	…degrees (*counter*)
暖かい	あたたかい	warm
涼しい	すずしい	cool
むし暑い	むしあつい	sultry; hot and humid
風が吹く	かぜがふく	The wind blows.
風が弱い	かぜがよわい	There is a slight breeze. (lit., *The wind is weak.*)
台風	たいふう	typhoon
零下…	れいか…	…below zero

Review: 高い、低い

寒い and 冷たい both translate as *cold* in English. 寒い is used to refer to seasons, climates, atmosphere, while 冷たい refers to a cold object that a person can touch or sense directly. Therefore, 寒い気候 *cold climate*, but 冷たい飲み物 *a cold drink*, 冷たい風 *a cold wind*, and 冷たい人 *a cold (-hearted) person.* The parallel terms for *hot* are both pronounced あつい. The difference is apparent only when writing: 暑い refers to seasons, climates, etc. while 熱い refers to other things, such as 熱いコーヒー *hot coffee.*

✹ アクティビティー 1

ダイアログ：今日はどんなお天気ですか。(*What is the weather like today?*)

電話で

ブラウン：長野は今日、どんなお天気ですか。
友だち：晴れですよ。
ブラウン：気温は何度ぐらいですか。
友だち：10度ぐらいです。とても涼しいです。
ブラウン：風はありますか。
友だち：いいえ、ありません。

Practice this dialogue, drawing on information in the following table.

(Temperatures are in degrees Celsius. See the **Culture Note** following the table.)

On the phone BROWN: What is the weather like in Nagano today? FRIEND: It's sunny and clear. BROWN: (About) what is the temperature? FRIEND: It's about 10 degrees. It's quite cool. BROWN: Is there a breeze (lit., *wind*)? FRIEND: No, there isn't.

PLACE	WEATHER	TEMPERATURE	WIND
Nara	Rainy	18 degrees, warm	Weak wind
Kumamoto	Cloudy	25 degrees, warm	Weak wind
Yamagata	Snow	0 degrees, cold	Strong wind
Kanazawa	Cloudy	5 degrees, cool	No wind
Naha	Clear	30 degrees, hot	Weak wind

文化ノート

CULTURE NOTE • °C

When Japanese say 20度 (*20 degrees*), they mean *20 degrees Celsius*. In Japan only the Celsius (centigrade) system is used to measure temperature. To specify which system you are using, you can say 摂氏20度 (*20°C*) or 華氏68度 (*68°F*), but don't expect Japanese to know the Fahrenheit (華氏) system. If you are good at calculating in your head, the formula for converting °C to °F is (°C × 9/5) + 32. Otherwise, you might want to start learning the system by remembering a few benchmark equivalents: the Celsius freezing point is 0 degrees, the boiling point is 100 degrees, and so on (see the scale below for more guideposts). One way or another, you will have to get used to the metric system in order to function freely in Japan.

Celsius	−20	−10	0	10	20	30	40
Fahrenheit	−4	14	32	50	68	86	104

アクティビティー 2

雨がよく降りますか。(*Does it rain often?*)

Ask your partner what the weather is like in January where he or she grew up. Complete the table following the example of Tokyo.

For words expressing frequency, review Chapter 3.

	東京	YOUR HOMETOWN	YOUR PARTNER'S HOMETOWN
晴れる	よく晴れます。		
くもる	時々くもります。		
雨	時々 降ります。		
雪	ほとんど降りません。		
気温	5度ぐらいです。		
風	時々 強い風が吹きます。		

Grammar and Practice Activities

17. Conjugating Adjectives

ブラウン：昨日(きのう)寒(さむ)かったですね。
林(はやし)：ええ、本当(ほんとう)に。
ブラウン：わたしのアパートには、ストーブがまだありませんから、
こまりました。
林：それはたいへんでしたね。

町田(まちだ)：プールはどうでしたか。
チン：人がとても多(おお)かったです。
町田：水(みず)はきれいでしたか。
チン：いいえ、あまりきれいではありませんでした。
町田：それはよくありませんでしたね。

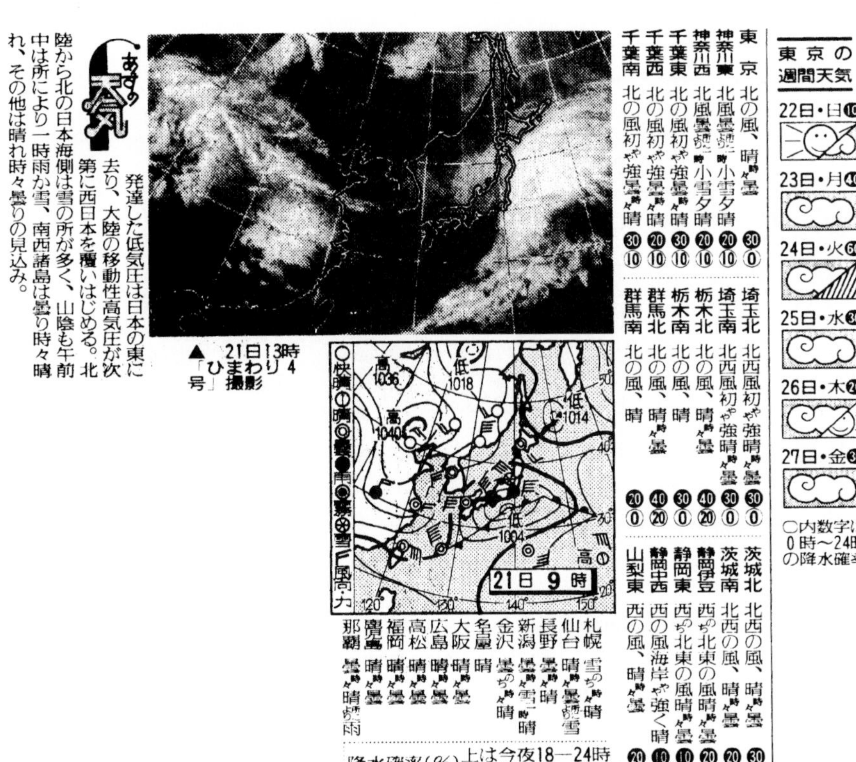

BROWN: It was cold yesterday, wasn't it? HAYASHI: Yes, really. BROWN: I had a hard time, because there isn't a heater in my apartment yet. HAYASHI: That must have been awful! (lit., *That was awful, wasn't it?*)

MACHIDA: How was the swimming pool? CHIN: There were a lot of people. MACHIDA: Was the water clean? CHIN: No, it wasn't very clean. MACHIDA: That's not good. (lit., *That wasn't good.*)

17.1 You have already studied the two types of Japanese adjectives, i-adjectives and na-adjectives. Both types of adjectives, like verbs, conjugate in terms of tense, politeness, and affirmation/negation and have at least eight basic conjugated forms when used as predicates (that is, when not in prenominal position).

17.2 You encountered the nonpast forms of i- and na-adjectives in Chapter 2, **Adjectives and Adverbs.** They are formed as follows.

I-ADJECTIVES: 寒(さむ)い (*COLD*)

Nonpast	Plain	Polite
Affirmative	Root + い (i.e., dictionary form) = 寒(さむ)い	Dictionary form + です = 寒(さむ)いです
Negative	Root + く + ない = 寒(さむ)くない	Root + く + ない + です = 寒(さむ)くないです or Root + く + ありません = 寒(さむ)くありません

ないです expresses a stronger level of negation than ありません.

NA-ADJECTIVES: 静(しず)か (*QUIET*)

Nonpast	Plain	Polite
Affirmative	Dictionary form + だ = 静(しず)かだ	Dictionary form + です = 静(しず)かです
Negative	Dictionary form + ではない or じゃない = 静(しず)かではない or 静(しず)かじゃない	Dictionary form + ではありません or じゃありません = 静(しず)かではありません or 静(しず)かじゃありません

だ is the plain, nonpast, affirmative form of the copula です.

じゃ is a contraction of では and is somewhat less formal and more colloquial than では.

Notice that na-adjectives themselves do not conjugate. Rather, the conjugated forms of the copula です (see **Grammar 1**) are appended to the dictionary form of a na-adjective.

17.3 The past forms of i-adjectives are formed as follows.

I-ADJECTIVES: 寒い (*COLD*)

Past	Plain	Polite
Affirmative	Root ＋ かった ＝ 寒(さむ)かった	Plain, past ＋ です ＝ 寒(さむ)かったです
Negative	Root ＋く＋ なかった ＝ 寒(さむ)くなかった	Root ＋く＋ なかったです ＝ 寒(さむ)くなかったです or Root ＋く＋ ありませんでした ＝ 寒(さむ)くありませんでした

大野先生(おおのせんせい)はとてもきびしかったです。
Professor Oono was very strict.
その問題(もんだい)はあまりむずかしくありませんでした。
That problem wasn't very difficult.
その映画(えいが)はぜんぜんおもしろくなかった。
That movie wasn't at all interesting.

The past forms of na-adjectives are formed by adding the conjugated forms of the copula です to their dictionary form.

NA-ADJECTIVES: 静か (*QUIET*)

Past	Plain	Polite
Affirmative	静(しず)かだった	静(しず)かでした
Negative	静(しず)かではなかった or 静(しず)かじゃなかった	静(しず)かではあり ませんでした or 静(しず)かじゃあり ませんでした

その公園(こうえん)は静(しず)かでした。
That park was quiet.
チンさんはあまり元気(げんき)ではありませんでした。
Ms. Chin wasn't feeling very well (lit., *wasn't very healthy*).
空(そら)がとてもきれいだった。
The sky was quite lovely.
あの人(ひと)はあまり親切(しんせつ)じゃなかった。
That person was not very kind.

17.4 よい (or いい) meaning *good* shows some irregularity, although it is an i-adjective.

Nonpast	Plain	Polite
Affirmative	よい or いい	いいです
Negative	よくない	よくありません or よくないです

Past	Plain	Polite
Affirmative	よかった	よかったです
Negative	よくなかった	よくありませんでした or よくなかったです

いい and いいです are colloquial forms of よい and よいです. These colloquial forms are more commonly used than よい（です） in informal conversations.

あの辞書はよくなかった。
That dictionary wasn't good.

アクティビティー　3

忙しかったですか。(*Was he busy?*)

Disagree with these statements, using the model as a guide.

[例]　ボストンは寒かったですか。(暑い) →
いいえ、寒くなかったです (寒くありませんでした)。暑かったです。

1. お天気は悪かったですか。(いい)
2. 東京は涼しかったですか。(暖かい)
3. その本はおもしろかったですか。(つまらない)
4. そこはきれいでしたか。(きたない)
5. そのレストランは静かでしたか。(うるさい)
6. 東京の冬は長かったですか。(短い)
7. まゆみさんは忙しかったですか。(ひま)

8. その先生はきびしかったですか。(やさしい)
9. その山(やま) (*mountain*) は高(たか)かったですか。(低(ひく)い)
10. その学生(がくせい)はまじめ (*serious*) でしたか。(ふまじめ *lazy, not serious*)

アクティビティー　4

映画(えいが)はおもしろくなかった。(*The movie wasn't good.*)
Change these sentences to the past tense, preserving the politeness level, as shown in the example.

[例]　あの映画(えいが)はおもしろくない。→ あの映画(えいが)はおもしろくなかった。

1. アラスカはいつも寒(さむ)いです。
2. 日本の夏(なつ)はむし暑(あつ)い。
3. 4月は毎日(まいにち) 暖(あたた)かい。
4. 今年(ことし)の夏(なつ)は涼(すず)しい。
5. ブラウンさんは元気(げんき)じゃありません。
6. あの本はよくない。
7. 天気(てんき)がいつも悪(わる)い。
8. カワムラさんはハンサムだ。
9. ギブソンさんはエレガントです。
10. この大学は有名(ゆうめい)ではない。

アクティビティー　5

先生は昨日(きのう)は元気(げんき)でしたが... (*The teacher was fine yesterday, but...*)

Complete the following sentences by filling in each blank with the past form of an adjective.

[例]　あの人は昨日(きのう)は (　　) が、今日(きょう)は病気(びょうき)です。→
　　あの人は昨日(きのう)は元気(げんき)でしたが、今日(きょう)は病気(びょうき)です。

1. わたしは昨日(きのう)は (　　) が、今日(きょう)はひまです。
2. 昨日(きのう)は (　　) が、今日(きょう)は暑(あつ)いです。
3. 東京(とうきょう)は昨日(きのう)は気温(きおん)が (　　) が、今日(きょう)は低(ひく)い。
4. そのショッピングセンターは昨日(きのう)は人が (　　) が、今日(きょう)は少(すく)ない。
5. 図書館(としょかん)は昨日(きのう)は (　　) が、今日(きょう)はうるさい。

The plain form + が is common in writing but in speech is usually used by male speakers. Females tend to use the plain form + けれども (けど).

6. 昨日は風が（　　）が、今日は弱いです。
7. 昨日は天気が（　　）が、今日は悪い。
8. 「ジョーズI」は（　　）が、「ジョーズIV」はつまらないです。

アクティビティー　6

昨日は月曜日でした。(*Yesterday was Monday.*)

Substituting 昨日 for 今日, change each predicate in the following passage to the corresponding past form.

今日は1月23日です。朝からとても寒いです。でも、お天気はとてもいいです。空がとてもきれいです。風がありますが、あまり強くありません。今日は土曜日ですから、クラスがありません。宿 題 (*homework*) もありません。だから (*because of that*)、わたしはひまです。今日は部屋 (*room*) を掃除します。わたしの部屋はとてもきたないです。それから、洗濯もします。わたしのルームメートは 病 気です。部屋にいます。

✹ アクティビティー　7

昨日はどんなお天気でしたか。(*What was the weather like yesterday?*)

Use this summary of yesterday's weather in five Japanese cities to answer the questions that follow.

PLACE	WEATHER	TEMPERATURE	WIND
Sapporo	Snow	−5 degrees, cold	Strong wind
Sendai	Cloudy	7 degrees, cool	No wind
Maebashi	Rain	9 degrees, cool	Strong wind
Hiroshima	Clear	15 degrees, warm	No wind
Kagoshima	Clear	27 degrees, hot	Weak wind

1. 昨日、札幌はどんなお天気でしたか。寒かったですか。暑かったですか。風はありましたか。
2. 仙台はどんなお天気でしたか。気温は何度でしたか。風はありましたか。

3. 前橋はどんなお天気でしたか。涼しかったですか。暖かかったですか。風は強かったですか。弱かったですか。
4. 広島のお天気はよかったですか。涼しかったですか。暖かかったですか。
5. 鹿児島のお天気はよかったですか、悪かったですか。寒かったですか。暑かったですか。気温は何度でしたか。

Now talk about yesterday's weather in your town with your classmates.

18. Comparatives and Superlatives

林：ロサンゼルスはマイアミより暑いですか。
カワムラ：いいえ、マイアミのほうが暑いです。
林：では、ロサンゼルスとマイアミとどちらのほうがたくさん雨が降りますか。
カワムラ：マイアミのほうがたくさん降ります。

チン：札幌と仙台と東 京の中でどこが一番寒いですか。
町田：札幌です。
チン：その三の中でどこが一番北にありますか。
町田：札幌が一番北にあります。
チン：なるほど。

ブラウン：仙台と山形とどちらのほうが寒いですか。
三村：山形のほうが寒いです。
ブラウン：じゃ、どちらのほうが雪がたくさん降りますか。
三村：やはり、山形のほうですね。1メートル†ぐらい降ります。

18.1 A sentence that compares *two* quantities or qualities, such as *John is taller than Mary* or *John ate more than Mary,* is called a *comparative sentence.* A Japanese comparative sentence takes one of two forms, as follows. Y より means *more than Y* or *compared to Y.*

Note that unlike English, adjectives in Japanese do not have comparative or superlative forms.

HAYASHI: Is it hotter in Los Angeles than in Miami? KAWAMURA: No, it's hotter in Miami. HAYASHI: Well, which has more rain—Los Angeles or Miami? KAWAMURA: It rains more in Miami.

CHIN: Which is coldest—Sapporo, Sendai, or Tokyo? MACHIDA: Sapporo. CHIN: Among them, which is furthest north? MACHIDA: Sapporo is furthest north. CHIN: I see.

BROWN: Which is colder, Sendai or Yamagata? MIMURA: Yamagata is colder. BROWN: Then, which has more snow? MIMURA: As you might expect, Yamagata. It snows about one meter.

†One meter is about 3.3 feet. Some people say メーター instead of メートル.

X	は	Y	より	adjective

X is more…than Y. (lit., *More than Y, X is…*)

東京(とうきょう)は大阪(おおさか)より大きい。
Tokyo is larger than Osaka. (lit., *More than Osaka, Tokyo is large.*)
林(はやし)さんは三村(みむら)さんよりまじめですか。
Is Mr. Hayashi more serious than Mr. Mimura? (lit., *More than Mr. Mimura, is Mr. Hayashi serious?*)

X	は	Y	より	adverb + verb

X does…more (…) *than Y.* (lit., *More than Y, X does…*)

今年(ことし)の冬(ふゆ)は去年(きょねん)の冬より雨(あめ)がたくさん降(ふ)りました。
It rained more this winter than last winter.
ブラウンさんはギブソンさんより早(はや)く起(お)きました。
Ms. Brown got up earlier than Ms. Gibson.

18.2 To ask a comparative question, use the following construction, which means *Of X and Y, which (alternative) is/does (more)…*

X	と	Y	と	どちら（のほう）が	adjective or adverb + verb	か

Which (alternative) is more…—X or Y?
Which (alternative) does…more (…) —X or Y?

The answer to this question takes the following form, meaning *The (alternative of) X is (more)…*

X	（のほう）が	adjective or adverb + verb

X is more…
X does (something) more…

横井(よこい)先生と大野(おおの)先生とどちら（のほう）がきびしいですか。

Who is stricter—Professor Yokoi or Professor Oono? (lit., *Of Professor Yokoi and Professor Oono, which* [*alternative*] *is strict?*)

大野(おおの)先生のほうがきびしいです。

Professor Oono is stricter. (lit., *The alternative of Professor Oono is strict.*)

ブラウンさんとギブソンさんとどちら（のほう）が早(はや)く起(お)きますか。

Who gets up earlier—Ms. Brown or Ms. Gibson? (lit., *Of Ms. Brown and Ms. Gibson, which* [*alternative*] *gets up early?*)

ブラウンさんのほうが早(はや)く起(お)きます。

Ms. Brown gets up earlier. (lit., *The alternative of Ms. Brown gets up early.*)

Notice that when はやい is used in its temporal meaning of *early*, the character 早い is used. When はやい means fast or quick, use the character 速い.

言語ノート

Adverbs Used with Comparatives

The following adverbs expressing degree are often used in comparative sentences.

ずっと	*by far*
もっと	*more*
少(すこ)し or ちょっと	*a little*

この大学はあの大学よりずっと大きい。

This university is far bigger than that university.

アンカレッジはバンクーバーよりもっと寒(さむ)いです。

Anchorage is colder (lit., *more cold*) *than Vancouver.*

山口(やまぐち)さんは高田(たかだ)さんより少(すこ)し（ちょっと）若(わか)い。

Mr. Yamaguchi is a bit younger than Mr. Takada.

The counter …倍(ばい) (*times,* as in magnification) or a specific number (plus the appropriate counter, if necessary) specifies the extent of the difference in comparisons. These expressions come before adjectives or adverbs.

この電車(でんしゃ)はあの電車(でんしゃ)より3倍(ばい)速(はや)い。

This train is three times faster than that train.

カプチーノはカフェオレより200円(えん)高(たか)いです。

Cappuccino costs 200 yen more than cafe au lait.

18.3 A *superlative sentence* is one that compares the quality or quantity of *three or more* entities and specifies which entity has most of that quality or quantity. For instance, *Who is the most popular actress in the United States—Julia Roberts, Vanna White, or Pia Zadora?*

A Japanese superlative sentence takes one of the following forms. (一番 [lit., *number one*] means *most*.)

XとYとZ	の中で or のうちで	Xが (or other particle)	一番	adjective or adverb + verb

X is the most... among X, Y, and Z.
X does... the most (...) among X, Y, and Z.

ロンドンとパリとモスクワの中で、モスクワが一番寒い。
Among London, Paris, and Moscow, Moscow is the coldest.

あの四人のうちで、ギブソンさんが一番速く走ります。
Among those four people, Ms. Gibson runs fastest.

ビール、ジュース、コーラの中でコーラを一番よく飲みます。
Among beer, juice, and cola, I drink cola most often.

18.4 An *equative sentence* is one that equates two entities. For example, *He is as tall as I am.* Equative sentences in Japanese are expressed as follows.

X	は	Y	と	同じぐらい	adjective or adverb + verb

As you remember, 同じ means *same* and ぐらい means *about*. The phrase 同じぐらい means *to (about) the same extent* or *to (about) the same degree.* This sentence means *X is about the same as Y with regard to...*

広島の三月は鹿児島の三月と同じぐらい暖かいです。
March in Hiroshima is about as warm as March in Kagoshima.

町田さんは林さんと同じぐらいよくここに来ます。
Ms. Machida comes here about as often as Mr. Hayashi.

A negative equative sentence such as *A is not as... as B* is expressed with this structure. (ほど means *as much as.*)

X	は	Y	ほど	negative form of adjective or adverb + negative form of verb

X is/does not…as much as Y.

春の夜は秋の夜ほど寒くない。
Spring evenings aren't as cold as fall evenings.

あの人はチンさんほど速く話しません。
That person doesn't talk as fast as Ms. Chin.

アクティビティー　8

この大学のほうが大きいです。 (*This university is bigger.*)

Make dialogues, following the pattern of the example.

[例]　(この大学) (あの大学) (大きい) →
—この大学とあの大学とどちらが大きいですか。
—この大学のほうが大きいです or この大学です。

1. (この町) (フローレンス) (きれい)
2. (ペプシ) (コーク) (おいしい)
3. (日本の車) (アメリカの車) (安い)
4. (フロリダ) (ネバダ) (雨がたくさん降る)
5. (去年の夏) (今年の夏) (暑い)
6. (トロント) (エドモントン) (雪が多い)
7. (昨日) (今日) (涼しい)
8. (南日本) (北日本) (台風がたくさん来る)

アクティビティー　9

あなたはわたしより速いです。(*You are quicker than I am.*)

Fill in the blanks to complete the sentences.

[例]　このセーターはあのセーターより (高いです)。

1. 東京はニューヨークより (　　)。
2. アメリカは日本より人口が (　　)。

3. アメリカ人は日本人より（　　）。
4. 日本はメキシコより（　　）。
5. わたしはカワムラさんより（　　）。
6. わたしの日本語の先生は横井(よこい)先生より（　　）。
7. 日本語はラテン語より（　　）。
8. この本はあの本より（　　）。

アクティビティー 10

わたしはあなたほど速(はや)くありません。(*I'm not as quick as you.*)

Change the following into negative sentences.

[例]　この大学(だいがく)はあの大学より大きいです。→
　　あの大学(だいがく)はこの大学ほど大きくありません。

1. 林(はやし)さんはカワムラさんよりたくさん食(た)べます。
2. 京都(きょうと)は東京(とうきょう)より古(ふる)いです。
3. 昨日(きのう)は今日(きょう)よりむし暑(あつ)かった。
4. 林(はやし)さんは三村(みむら)さんよりお酒(さけ)が好(す)きだ。
5. チンさんはシュミットさんより日本語をじょうずに (*skillfully, well*) 話す。
6. 札幌(さっぽろ)は秋田(あきた)より雪(ゆき)が多(おお)く(*a lot*) 降(ふ)ります。
7. 町田(まちだ)さんは本田(ほんだ)さんよりキュートです。
8. この映画(えいが)はあの映画(えいが)よりおもしろかった。

アクティビティー 11

誰(だれ)が一番(いちばん)速(はや)いですか。 (*Who is the quickest?*)

Using the words provided, make dialogues as shown in the example.

[例]　（ヘミングウェー）（ホーソン）（クラベル）（有名(ゆうめい)）→
　　—ヘミングウェーとホーソンとクラベルの中で誰(だれ)が一番(いちばん)有名ですか。
　　—ヘミングウェーが一番(いちばん)有名(ゆうめい)です。

Use the interrogative だれ (*who*) when asking about people, どれ (*which one*) when asking about things, concepts, and events, and どこ (*where*) when asking about places.

1. (日本語) (ロシア語) (アラビア語) (むずかしい)
2. (プレリュード) (ミヤタ) (アクラ・レジェンド) (高(たか)い)
3. (シカゴ) (ロサンジェルス) (ダラス) (風(かぜ)が強(つよ)い)
4. (ミシガン) (フロリダ) (アイダホ) (暖(あたた)かい)
5. (バス) (車(くるま)) (電車(でんしゃ)) (便利(べんり))
6. (スーパー) (デパート) (セブン・イレブン) (安(やす)い)
7. (ビール) (お茶(ちゃ)) (コーヒー) (よく飲(の)む)

アクティビティー　12

どの名前(なまえ)が一番(いちばん)好(す)きですか。 (*What name do you like best?*)

Answer the following questions in Japanese.

1. アメリカで一番(いちばん)大きい都市(とし) (*city*) はどこですか。
2. アメリカで一番(いちばん)古(ふる)い都市(とし)はどこですか。
3. 世界(せかい) (*world*) で一番(いちばん)高(たか)い建物(たてもの)は何ですか。
4. アメリカで一番(いちばん)きれいな都市(とし)はどこですか。
5. アメリカで一番(いちばん)有名(ゆうめい)な日本人はだれですか。
6. 日本の食(た)べ物(もの)の中で何(なに)が一番(いちばん)好(す)きですか。
7. 一年中(いちねんじゅう)で何月(なんがつ)が一番(いちばん)暑(あつ)いですか。
8. 一年中(いちねんじゅう)で何月(なんがつ)が一番(いちばん)寒(さむ)いですか。
9. 一年中(いちねんじゅう)で何月(なんがつ)が一番(いちばん)忙(いそが)しいですか。
10. スポーツの中で何(なに)が一番(いちばん)おもしろいですか。
11. 日本語の中でどのことば (*word*) が一番(いちばん)好(す)きですか。

アクティビティー　13

どちらのほうが暖(あたた)かいですか。(*Which place is warmer?*)

Look at the following table of Japanese cities (arranged in order of northernmost to southernmost) while your instructor describes the weather for tomorrow.

TOMORROW'S WEATHER

City	Weather	Temperature	Wind	Notes
Sapporo	Snow (30 cm)	−15°C	North, 20 km/h	Heavy snowfall
Aomori	Clear	−12°C	West, 5 km/h	Foggy
Niigata	Snow (10 cm)	−11°C	North, 30 km/h	Snowstorm
Tokyo	Cloudy	5°C	No wind	Rain in the afternoon
Shizuoka	Cloudy	14°C	South, 5 km/h	Storm at night
Nagoya	Rain (5 mm)	18°C	No wind	Cloudy in the afternoon
Osaka	Clear	9°C	East, 5 km/h	Clear until Saturday
Hiroshima	Rain (15 mm)	17°C	South, 5 km/h	Cloudy in the afternoon
Kagoshima	Rain (40 mm)	21°C	West, 50 km/h	Typhoon No. 2 Thursday
Naha	Clear	30°C	No wind	Sultry

Now look at the preceding table and describe the weather in several cities to a classmate.

[例] s1: 東京は、どんなお天気ですか。
s2: くもりです。午後は雨です。気温は5度ぐらいです。風はありません。

Answer the following questions.

1. 札幌と青森とどちらのほうが寒いですか。
2. 札幌と新潟とどちらのほうが雪がたくさん降りますか。
3. 青森と札幌と新潟の中でどこが一番寒いですか。
4. 静岡と大阪とどちらのほうが暖かいですか。
5. 大阪と那覇とどちらのほうが暑いですか。
6. 広島と名古屋と鹿児島の中でどこが一番雨が降りますか。
7. 新潟と札幌とどちらのほうが風が強いですか。
8. どこが一番風が強いですか。
9. どこが一番寒いですか。
10. どこが一番暑いですか。

km = kilometer (5/8 of a mile) ...km/h is read 時速/... キロ(メートル)

Typhoons are identified by number, starting with 1 each year. The counter ...号 [*number*] is used with typhoons.

Vocabulary Library

Precipitation and Other Weather Terms

湿度	しつど	humidity
気圧	きあつ	air pressure
小雨	こさめ	light rain
にわか雨	にわかあめ	shower
どしゃぶり		downpour (*of rain*)
梅雨	つゆ	rainy season (*in June and July*)
降水量	こうすいりょう	precipitation
嵐	あらし	storm
あられ		hail

文化ノート

CULTURE NOTE • Types of Rain

Rain has exerted a strong influence on Japanese life and culture since ancient times. For centuries the majority of Japanese people made their living in agriculture, for which rainfall is crucial. The amount and type of rain determined success or failure for a farmer's crop. Over the years, the Japanese coined many words to distinguish different types of rain. Among them are さみだれ (*early summer rain*), しぐれ (*drizzle*), にわかあめ (*shower*), はるさめ (*spring rain*), あきさめ (*autumn rain*), and むらさめ

今日は雨がシトシト降ります。

(*passing rain*). There are also numerous ways to describe the manner of the rain's fall with onomatopoeia. (The Japanese language includes so many onomatopoeia that entire dictionaries are devoted to them.)

> 雨がザーザー降ります。
> *It rains cats and dogs.* (lit., *It rains "zaa zaa."*)
> 雨がシトシト降ります。
> *It drizzles.* (lit., *It rains "shito shito."*)
> 雨がポツポツ降ります。
> *It rains in big scattered drops.* (lit., *It rains "potsu potsu."*)

Although a greater volume of rain falls in the autumn, Japan has a rainy season—called 梅雨 (つゆ)—that consists of more or less constant drizzle for a month or so starting in mid-June. While the rainy season is uncomfortably cold and damp or hot and humid, it is, as the Japanese frequently remind themselves, good for the farmers.

✷ アクティビティー 14

何月が一番寒いですか。 (*Which month is coldest?*)

Using this table* of actual average temperatures and rainfall in Tokyo, answer the questions that follow.

東京

Month	1	2	3	4	5	6	7	8	9	10	11	12
Temp. (°C)	5	6	8	14	18	22	25	27	23	17	12	7
Precip. (mm)	54	63	102	128	148	181	125	137	193	181	93	56

1. 東京は7月と8月とどちらが暑いですか。
2. 何月が一番寒いですか。
3. 4月と5月とどちらのほうがたくさん雨が降りますか。
4. 1月と2月と3月の中で何月が一番雨が多いですか。
5. 何月が一番雨が多いですか。

Now, look at these statistics about the climate in five international cities and answer the questions. (Temperature is in degrees centigrade, and precipitation is in millimeters.)

Month	1	2	3	4	5	6	7	8	9	10	11	12
LONDON												
Temperature	4	4	7	9	12	16	18	17	15	11	7	5
Precipitation	53	40	37	38	46	46	56	59	50	57	64	48

*Source: *Science Almanac 1991.* Figures are the average for the period 1951 to 1980.

Month	1	2	3	4	5	6	7	8	9	10	11	12
PARIS												
Temperature	3	4	7	10	14	17	19	18	16	11	7	4
Precipitation	54	43	32	38	52	50	55	62	51	49	50	49
SYDNEY												
Temperature	22	22	21	18	16	13	12	13	15	18	19	21
Precipitation	104	125	129	101	115	141	94	83	72	80	77	86
MOSCOW												
Temperature	−10	−9	−4	5	12	17	19	17	11	4	−2	−7
Precipitation	31	28	33	35	52	67	74	74	58	51	36	36
BUENOS AIRES												
Temperature	24	23	20	17	13	11	10	11	14	16	20	22
Precipitation	92	84	122	87	78	55	42	58	88	100	79	90

1. ロンドンでは何月が一番気温が高いですか。何月が一番気温が低いですか。
2. ロンドンでは何月が一番降水量（*precipitation*）が多いですか。何月が一番降水量が少ないですか。
3. シドニーとブエノスアイレスとどちらが1月の気温が高いですか。
4. シドニーとブエノスアイレスとどちらが7月の降水量が多いですか。
5. ロンドンとパリとモスクワの中でどこが8月の気温が一番高いですか。

Make up similar questions about the table to ask your classmates.

19. The Past, Plain Forms of Verbs

さとみ：昨日、映画に行ったの。
大助：うん。
さとみ：何を見たの。
大助：「ニンジャ」。おもしろかったよ。

Note that plain forms of verbs and adjectives are used in these conversations between family members (between brother and sister in the first dialogue and between

SATOMI: Did you go to the movies yesterday? DAISUKE: Yeah. SATOMI: What did you see? DAISUKE: *Ninja.* It was good. (lit., *It was interesting.*)

ゆり子(こ)：さとみ、昼(ひる)ごはんを食(た)べたの。
さとみ：ええ、カワムラさんと「ユアーズ」で食(た)べたわ。
ゆり子：「ユアーズ」…どこにあるの。
さとみ：先月(せんげつ)、駅(えき)の前(まえ)にできたのよ。
知(し)らないの？

mother and daughter in the second). As discussed in **Grammar 11,** Chapter 3, plain forms are common in conversations among members of the same in-group.

19.1 You have studied the past, polite forms of the three classes of verbs. The formation of the past, plain forms of Class 2 verbs is very simple.

For the definition of *past, plain,* and the three classes of verbs, review **Grammar 11** in Chapter 3. For the sake of explanation, we will start with Class 2 verbs here.

Affirmative: Root + た	Negative: Root + なかった

DICTIONARY FORM	ROOT	PAST, PLAIN, AFFIRMATIVE	PAST, PLAIN, NEGATIVE
食(た)べる *to eat*	食(た)べ	食(た)べた	食(た)べなかった
見(み)る *to see*	見(み)	見(み)た	見(み)なかった
着(き)る *to wear*	着(き)	着(き)た	着(き)なかった
変(か)える *to change*	変(か)え	変(か)えた	変(か)えなかった

19.2 The past, plain forms of Class 3 verbs (the irregular verbs する and くる) are as follows.

DICTIONARY FORM	PAST, PLAIN, AFFIRMATIVE	PAST, PLAIN, NEGATIVE
する *to do*	した	しなかった
来(く)る *to come*	来(き)た	来(こ)なかった

19.3 The past, plain, negative form of Class 1 verbs is formed on the same stem as the plain, nonpast negative, but the ending is なかった instead of ない。

YURIKO: Satomi, did you eat lunch? SATOMI: Yes, I ate with Mr. Kawamura at Yours. YURIKO: Yours? Where is it? SATOMI: It opened in front of the station last month. Don't you know (about it)?

DICTIONARY FORM ROOT + ENDING	NONPAST, PLAIN, NEGATIVE FORM	PAST, PLAIN, NEGATIVE FORM
書(か) + く	書(か) + か + ない	書(か) + か + なかった
話(はな) + す	話(はな) + さ + ない	話(はな) + さ + なかった
立(た) + つ	立(た) + た + ない	立(た) + た + なかった
死(し) + ぬ	死(し) + な + ない	死(し) + な + なかった
読(よ) + む	読(よ) + ま + ない	読(よ) + ま + なかった
乗(の) + る	乗(の) + ら + ない	乗(の) + ら + なかった
泳(およ) + ぐ	泳(およ) + が + ない	泳(およ) + が + なかった
洗(あら) + う	洗(あら) + わ + ない	洗(あら) + わ + なかった

u-column	→	a-column
く	→	か
す	→	さ
つ	→	た
ぬ	→	な
む	→	ま
る	→	ら
ぐ	→	が

The past, plain, negative form of ある *to exist* is simply なかった.

Remember that this rule applies to the formation of the nonpast, plain, negative form of these verbs: 洗わない, 言わない.

The past, plain, affirmative form of Class 1 verbs depends on the dictionary form ending.

1. When the dictionary ending is く

   Rule: Change it to いた.

   書(か)く → 書(か)いた (*wrote*)

   There is only one exception to this rule: 行く(*to go*).

   行(い)く → 行(い)った (*went*)

2. When the dictionary ending is ぐ

   Rule: Change it to いだ.

   泳(およ)ぐ → 泳(およ)いだ (*swam*)

3. When the dictionary ending is う, つ, or る

   Rule: Change it to った.

   買(か)う → 買(か)った (*bought*)

   立(た)つ → 立(た)った (*stood*)

   乗(の)る → 乗(の)った (*rode*)

4. When the dictionary ending is ぬ, む, or ぶ

   Rule: Change it to んだ.

   死(し)ぬ → 死(し)んだ (*died*)

As mentioned in **Grammar 11,** Chapter 3, ない in 書(か)かない, 食(た)べない, しない, etc. (the nonpast, plain, negative form) is an adjective expressing negativity. It is an i-adjective and conjugates as such. In this chapter, you have already studied how to form the past, plain forms of i-adjectives. In the past, plain, negative forms 書かなかった, 食べなかった, しなかった, etc., なかった is the past, plain form of ない.

読む → 読んだ (*read* [*past*])

呼ぶ → 呼んだ (*called*)

5. When the word ending is す

   Rule: Change it to した.

   話す → 話した (*spoke*)

Note that the past, plain, affirmative forms of 読む and 呼ぶ happen to have the same sound sequence: よんだ. Their accent patterns, however, are different.

The conjugations of the past, plain, affirmative form of Class 1 verbs are summarized in the following table.

DICTIONARY ENDING	PAST, PLAIN, AFFIRMATIVE ENDING	EXAMPLES
く	→いた	書く→書いた exception 行く→行った
ぐ	→いだ	泳ぐ→泳いだ
う、つ、る	→った	買う→買った 立つ→立った 乗る→乗った
ぬ、む、ぶ	→んだ	死ぬ→死んだ 読む→読んだ 呼ぶ→呼んだ
す	→した	話す→話した

Here are some sample sentences using the past, plain form of verbs.

昨日の夜、雨がたくさん降った。
It rained a lot last night.

強い風が一日 中 吹いた。
A strong wind blew all day.

山田さんはアメリカへ行ったけど、わたしは行かなかった。
Mr. Yamada went to America, but I didn't.

昨日は8時から10時までテレビを見た。その後、ラジオを聞いた。
I watched TV from 8:00 to 10:00 yesterday. After that, I listened to the radio.

かれは夕ごはんをぜんぜん食べなかった。
He didn't eat any dinner at all.

The past, plain, affirmative form of a verb is used to express a past action or event in an informal context. It is also used as a component of several other grammatical structures you will study later on. These other significant grammatical structures require the ability to conjugate this verb form, so it is important that you master this form now.

In most cases, the past, plain, affirmative form of a verb ends in **-ta,** so we will refer to this form as the ta-form.

The past, plain, affirmative form of an adjective is also called the ta-form of an adjective.

アクティビティー 15

8時に出(で)かけました。(*I went out at 8:00.*)

Put these sentences into the past tense, maintaining the plain form of the verb.

[例] チンさんは中国語(ちゅうごくご)で話す。→ チンさんは中国語で話した。

1. ブラウンさんは5時半に起(お)きる。
2. 歯(は)を一日に3回(かい)磨(みが)く。
3. 毎日(まいにち)10キロ走(はし)る。
4. オレンジ・ジュースを飲(の)む。
5. 高田(たかだ)さんは7時に出(で)かける。
6. デパートの前でギブソンさんを待(ま)つ (*wait*)。
7. 毎日(まいにち)クラスへ行(い)く。
8. 家(いえ)から大学までバスに乗(の)る。
9. 図書館(としょかん)でチンさんに会(あ)う。
10. テレビでニュースを見(み)る。
11. 午後(ごご)プールで泳(およ)ぐ。
12. フランス語を勉強(べんきょう)する。
13. 土曜日(どようび)は家(いえ)で休(やす)む。
14. お風呂(ふろ)に入(はい)る。
15. 12時に寝(ね)る。
16. いつもパーティーに来(く)る。

アクティビティー 16

チンさんは出(で)かけた。(*Ms. Chin went out.*)

Rewrite the following sentences changing the verb form from polite to plain.

[例] 昨日(きのう)東京(とうきょう)へ来(き)ました。→ 昨日東京へ来た。

1. 先週(せんしゅう)は雨(あめ)がたくさん降(ふ)りました。
2. デパートでプレゼントを買(か)いました。
3. パーティーでは山田(やまだ)さんに会(あ)いませんでした。
4. 高田(たかだ)さんは昨日(きのう)、ワシントンから帰(かえ)りました。
5. わたしはぜんぜん勉強(べんきょう)しませんでした。
6. 昨日(きのう)、ブラウンさんと話しませんでした。
7. かれのおじいさん (*grandfather*) は去年(きょねん)死(し)にました。
(死ぬ: *to die*)
8. 今朝(けさ)、歯(は)を磨(みが)きませんでした。
9. 昨日(きのう)はお酒(さけ)を飲(の)みましたか。
10. 昨日(きのう)、顔(かお)を洗(あら)いませんでした。
11. もうテレビのニュースは見(み)ましたか。
12. ここに何時(なんじ)に着(つ)きました (*arrived*) か。
13. 昨晩(さくばん)はあまり寝(ね)ませんでした。
14. ディズニーランドでコーヒーカップに乗(の)りました (*rode*)。
15. 林(はやし)さんはもう出(で)かけましたか。
16. 高田(たかだ)さんはスーパーへ行(い)きました。
17. 一週間(いっしゅうかん)お風呂(ふろ)に入(はい)りませんでした。
18. シャワーは浴(あ)びましたか。

20. Explaining a Reason: …のだ

林(はやし)：昨日(きのう)はクラスに来(き)ませんでしたね。
三村(みむら)：ええ、アルバイトがあったんです。
林：今日(きょう)はクラスに出(で)るんですか。
三村：ええ、雨(あめ)が降(ふ)ったから、テニスの練習(れんしゅう)がないです。

HAYASHI: You didn't come to class yesterday, did you? MIMURA: No (lit., *Yes*), because I had a part-time job. HAYASHI: Are you going to attend class today? MIMURA: Yes. Because it rained, I don't have (lit., *there isn't*) tennis practice.

ブラウン：林(はやし)さんは何を笑(わら)っているのですか。
町田(まちだ)：さあ、わかりません。
ブラウン：林(はやし)さん、何(なに)がおかしいんですか。
林(はやし)：今(いま)、漫画(まんが)を読(よ)んでいるんです。ハハハ…

カーティス：ストーブはどこですか。
チン：寒(さむ)いんですか。
カーティス：風邪(かぜ)をひいたんです。
チン：いつからですか。
カーティス：昨日(きのう)からです。

林(はやし)：北海道(ほっかいどう)は寒(さむ)かったんじゃありませんか。
ギブソン：はい、とても寒(さむ)かったです。
林：雪(ゆき)はたくさんありましたか。
ギブソン：いいえ、ぜんぜんなかったんです。
林：ぜんぜんなかったんですか。
ギブソン：はい、ぜんぜん。

Sentences ending in のだ (polite form のです) explain the reason for some event or information known to both speaker and hearer. In colloquial speech んだ (polite form んです) commonly replaces のだ (のです).

Consider these two sentences, for example.

寒(さむ)いですか。
寒(さむ)いんですか。

In the first sentence, the speaker has no idea whether or not the person addressed feels cold. Therefore, it is simply a straightforward question: *Are you cold?* In the second, the speaker assumes that the person addressed feels cold because, say, he is shivering or wearing a thick sweater. The second sentence, then, asks for an explanation: *Is it that you're cold?*

Similarly, if you see a friend getting ready to do something, it would be odd to say

何(なに)をしますか。
What are you going to do?

BROWN: What is Mr. Hayashi laughing at? MACHIDA: I don't know. BROWN: Mr. Hayashi, what is funny? HAYASHI: I'm reading a comic book (now). Ha, ha, ha…

CURTIS: Where is the heater? CHIN: Are you cold? CURTIS: (It's that) I caught a cold. CHIN: Since when? CURTIS: Since yesterday.

HAYASHI: Wasn't it cold in Hokkaido? GIBSON: Yes, it was very cold. HAYASHI: Was there a lot of snow? GIBSON: No, there wasn't any at all. HAYASHI: There wasn't any at all? GIBSON: That's right, (lit., *Yes*) none at all.

because you have actually seen his or her preparations and know that he or she is about to do something. This information is shared between the two of you, so it's more appropriate to say

> 何をするんですか。
> *What are you going to do?* (lit., *What is it that you are going to do?*)

Verbs, adjectives, and nouns may precede のです(んです). In the case of verbs, the plain form is used.

> チンさんにもう言ったんですか。
> *Did you already tell Ms. Chin?* (lit., *Is it that you already told Ms. Chin?*)
> 林さんに電話しないのですか。
> *Aren't you going to call Mr. Hayashi?*

The plain form of i-adjectives may also precede のです.

> なぜ顔が赤いんですか。
> *Why is your face red?*
> 夏でしたが、あまり暑くなかったんです。
> *It was summer, but it wasn't very hot.*

When the nonpast, affirmative form of na-adjectives or nouns is used, な precedes のです(んです).

> 三村さんはどうして有名なんですか。
> *Why is Mr. Mimura famous?*
> 林さんは学生ではないんですか。
> *Isn't Mr. Hayashi a student?*
> チンさんは元気だったんですか。
> *Was Ms. Chin well?*

言語ノート

Answering Negative Questions

In English, you answer in the same way whether you are asked a question affirmatively or negatively. Thus, whether you are asked, "Will you attend today's class?" or "Won't you attend today's class?" you would say "Yes, I will attend" or "No, I won't attend."

In Japanese, the way you answer a negative question depends on the addressee's presupposition or previous knowledge. In the dialogue on p. 265, Hayashi asks 北海道は寒かったんじゃありませんか

(*Wasn't it cold in Hokkaido?*), assuming that it must have been cold in Hokkaido around that time. In this case, you would answer

はい、寒(さむ)かったです。
Yes, it was cold.
いいえ、寒(さむ)くありませんでした。
No, it wasn't cold.

On the other hand, when he asks the question ぜんぜんなかったんですか (*Wasn't there snow at all?*), Hayashi already knows that there was no snow at all. In this case, you would answer

はい、ぜんぜんありませんでした。
lit., *Yes, there wasn't any at all.*
いいえ、たくさんありました。
lit., *No, there was a lot.*

Let's consider another example. Someone asks you クラスへ行(い)かないんですか. (*Aren't you going to class?*) If you think the questioner assumes you won't go to class, you would respond

はい、行きません。
lit., *Yes, I won't go.*
いいえ、行きます。
lit., *No, I will go.*

If you think the questioner assumes you *will* go to class, you would respond

はい、行きます。
Yes, I will go.
いいえ、行きません。
No, I won't go.

You have to decide how to answer based on your guess about the questioner's knowledge, his or her facial expression, and other contextual factors. In addition, the intonation pattern of the question differs depending on the assumption. For example,

クラスへ行かないんですか。 assumes that you will go
クラスへ行かないんですか。 assumes that you won't go

✷ アクティビティー 17

くつを買うんです。 (*Yes, I'm going to buy shoes.*)

Complete these dialogues using the cue in parentheses and んです.

[例] デパートへ行くんですか。(ブラウスを買います。) →
はい、ブラウスを買うんです。

1. 林さん、たくさん飲みますね。(お酒が好きです。)
2. 映画に行かないんですか。(明日、試験 [*exam*]です。)
3. スキーへ行くんですか。(雪がたくさん降りました。)
4. セーターを買ったんですか。(とても寒いです。)
5. この問題はわかりませんか。(先週、休みました。)
6. 昨日学校へ来ませんでしたね。(アルバイトがありました。)
7. 明日家にいないんですか。(スケートに行きます。)
8. アパートは便利なんですか。(駅にとても近いです。)
9. 学校へ行かないんですか。(今、休みです。)

✷ アクティビティー 18

なぜですか。(*Why?*)

Make up dialogues, using the model as an example.

[例] パーティーに行かない →
s1: パーティーに行かなかったんですか。
s2: ええ、病気 (*sick*) だったんです。

Useful Vocabulary (reasons): 雪が降る、ひま(な)、天気がいい、週末、暑い、時間がある、雨が降る、寒い、きたない、誕生日、病気、仕事がある

1. スキーに行く
2. 家にいた
3. レストランで夕ごはんを食べる
4. 映画を見る
5. クラスに行かない
6. 掃除する
7. 10時に起きる
8. プールで泳ぐ
9. 12時まで勉強する

言語ノート

Asking and Answering *Why?*

Two interrogative pronouns are used to ask why: なぜ and どうして. In very informal speech, either can be used alone to mean *Why?* Otherwise follow the examples of usage below.

なぜですか。
Why (is that)?
どうしてですか。
Why (is that)?
なぜピクニックに行きませんでしたか。
Why didn't you come to the picnic?
どうしてクラスを休みましたか。
Why did you miss class?

To answer why or to give a reason, use the conjunction から (*because*) or ので (*because; it being that…*).

雨が降ったから、行きませんでした。
Because it rained, I didn't go.
病気だったので、休みました。
Because I was sick, I took the day off.

Or you can simply say

雨が降ったからです。
(It's) Because it rained.
病気だったのです or 病気だったんです。
It's that I was sick.

アクティビティー 19

暑いから、海へ行きましょう。(*Because it's hot, let's go to the ocean.*)

Complete the following sentences. How many different sentences can you make?

[例] 暑いから、… →
暑いから、海へ行きましょう。
暑いから、アイスクリームを食べます。
暑いから、クーラーを買います。

1. 昨日はとても寒かったので、
2. 台風が来たので、
3. 今日は暖かいから、
4. 風がとても強いので、
5. 天気がいいから、
6. 雪がたくさん降ったから、

Vocabulary and Grammar 4B

Vocabulary and Oral Activities

Enjoying the Four Seasons

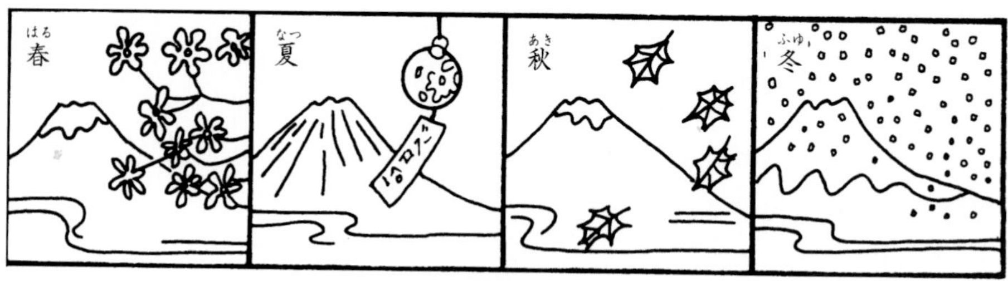

Vocabulary: Seasons and Seasonal Activities

季節	きせつ	season
四季	しき	four seasons
カレンダー		calendar
泳ぐ	およぐ	to swim
スキーをする		to ski
スケートをする		to skate
山登りをする	やまのぼりをする	to climb mountains
釣りをする	つりをする	to fish
キャンプ（に行く）	キャンプ（にいく）	(to go) camping
ハイキング（に行く）	ハイキング（にいく）	(to go) hiking
花見（に行く）	はなみ（にいく）	(to go) cherry blossom viewing

アクティビティー 20

どの季節が一番好きですか。(*Which season do you like best?*)

Answer the following questions.

1. 春は何月から何月までですか。
2. 夏は何月から何月までですか。
3. 秋は何月から何月までですか。

4. 冬は何月から何月までですか。
5. シドニーの8月はどんな季節ですか。
6. ニューヨークの8月はどんな季節ですか。
7. シドニーの1月はどんな季節ですか。
8. ニューヨークの1月はどんな季節ですか。
9. どの季節が一番暑いですか。
10. どの季節が一番寒いですか。
11. どの季節が一番雨が降りますか。
12. どの季節が一番好きですか。

クラスメートと花見に来ました。

アクティビティー 21

どの季節にしますか。 (*In what season do you do that?*)

In what season(s) do you do these activities? Ask your partner, following the example.

[例] スキーをする →
s1: どの季節にスキーをしますか。
s2: 冬です。

Do You Remember? The interrogative どの asks which one of three or more alternatives. To ask which one of two, use どちら. Review **Grammar 4,** Chapter 1.

1. 海で泳ぐ
2. ピクニックに行く
3. スケートをする
4. 山登りをする
5. キャンプに行く
6. 釣りをする
7. ゴルフをする
8. 花見に行く

What activities do you do in each of the four seasons? Discuss in class. Are there any activities you can do only in a specific season?

アクティビティー 22

今年の夏は暖かいですけれども… (*This summer is warm but…*)

Complete the sentences, using the model as an example.

[例] 今年の夏は暖かいですけれども、去年の夏は… →
今年の夏は暖かいですけれども、去年の夏は涼しかったです。

1. 今年の夏は雨が多いですが、去年の夏は…
2. 夏は雨がたくさん降りますが、冬は…
3. 今年の冬は暖かいですけれども、去年の冬は…
4. おととしの冬は雪がたくさん降りましたが、去年の冬は…
5. 夏は台風がたくさん来ますが、冬は…
6. 今週は暑いですけれども、先週は…
7. 今年は雨が多いですけれども、去年は…
8. 今日は風が弱いですが、昨日は…
9. 今月は気温が高いですけれども、先月は…

言語ノート

Linking Disjunctive Clauses with けれども

You've already learned several ways to link disjunctive or contrasting ideas, including が (*but*), でも (*but*), and しかし (*however*). Another common connector is けれども. Unlike those you have studied so far, けれども can be used either as a conjunction (i.e., to join two independent clauses into one sentence) or as a transitional phrase at the beginning of the second of two contrasting sentences. It is roughly equivalent to *although* or *however*.

ここは冬は寒いですけれども、雪はあまり降りません。
Although winters are cold here, it doesn't snow much.

ここは冬は寒いです。けれども、雪はあまり降りません。
Winters are cold here. Nevertheless, it doesn't snow much.

Of the linking words mentioned in this note, が is most common and expresses the least contrast. でも is common in informal conversation, while しかし tends to sound bookish or formal. けれども may be shortened to けども in informal conversation, and も is often dropped (yielding けれど or けど) to express a lesser degree of contrast.

As shown in the preceding examples, the particle は often marks items being compared or contrasted, regardless of which conjunction or transition is used.

You should also be aware that in general ～ですけれども is limited to conversation. In writing, you will find that ～ですが or ～です。けれども～ are more commonly used.

Grammar and Practice Activities

21. The Te-Form of Adjectives and the Copula

カワムラ：町田(まちだ)さんの家(いえ)のそばにスーパーはありますか。
町田(まちだ)：ええ。
カワムラ：どんなスーパーですか。
町田：大きくて、安(やす)いスーパーです。
カワムラ：町田(まちだ)さんはいつもそのスーパーで買(か)い物(もの)するんですか。
町田：ええ、近(ちか)くて、便利(べんり)ですから。

チン：山田(やまだ)さんのガールフレンドはどんな人ですか。
林(はやし)：とてもきれいで、やさしい人ですよ。
チン：本当(ほんとう)ですか。山田(やまだ)さんはけちで、いじわるでしょう。
なぜ、そんないいガールフレンドがいるんですか。
林：さあ、わかりませんね。

KAWAMURA: Is there a supermarket near your house Mr. Machida? MACHIDA: Yes. KAWAMURA: What kind of supermarket is it? MACHIDA: It is a big and inexpensive supermarket. KAWAMURA: Do you always shop there? MACHIDA: Yes, because it is nearby and convenient.

CHIN: What kind of person is Mr. Yamada's girlfriend? HAYASHI: Yes, she's a very pretty, sweet person. CHIN: Really? Mr. Yamada is miserly and mean. Why does he have such a nice girlfriend? HAYASHI: Hmm, I don't know.

21.1 An important conjugated form of adjectives and verbs is what we shall call the *te-form.* In **Grammar 21** and **22,** you will study the te-form of adjectives, the copula, and verbs.

21.2 The te-form of adjectives may be used to link together adjectives or whole clauses in a sentence, as *and* is used in English. The te-form can be used only when adjectives are in a nonfinal position in a sentence.

Create the te-form of i-adjectives by adding くて to the root.

DICTIONARY FORM	ROOT	TE-FORM
赤(あか)い *red*	赤(あか)	赤(あか)くて
おいしい *tasty*	おいし	おいしくて
寒(さむ)い *cold*	寒(さむ)	寒(さむ)くて
いい (よい) *good*	よ	よくて (irregular)

21.3 The te-form of na-adjectives is formed by adding で to the dictionary form.

DICTIONARY FORM	TE-FORM
きれい *pretty*	きれいで
静(しず)か *quiet*	静(しず)かで
便利(べんり) *convenient*	便利(べんり)で
ハンサム *handsome*	ハンサムで

21.4 Study these sample sentences.

彼女(かのじょ)は若(わか)くて、きれいだ。
She is young and pretty.
静(しず)かで、便利(べんり)なところが好(す)きです。
I like quiet, convenient places.

In the following examples, the clause ending in the te-form adjective indicates a reason or cause for the following clause.

この辞書(じしょ)は重(おも)くて、不便(ふべん)です。
This dictionary is heavy and (therefore it's) inconvenient.
父(ちち)はお酒(さけ)が大好(だいす)きで、いつもたくさん飲(の)みます。
My father loves sake and always drinks a lot.

日本語のクラスが好きで、日本語をたくさん勉強する。
I like my Japanese class, and (that's why) I study Japanese a lot.

When you conjoin two or more adjectives this way, they must be all favorable or all unfavorable in meaning. For instance, the following sentence sounds unnatural.

あのスーパーはきれいで、高いです。
That supermarket is clean and expensive.

In such a case, you must use a conjunction for joining contrasting or contradictory statements.

あのスーパーはきれいですが、高いです。
あのスーパーはきれいだけど、高いです。
That supermarket is clean, but it's expensive.

You can use either the plain or polite form in front of けど.

21.5 The te-form of the copula です (plain form だ) is で. It is used to conjoin nouns.

町田さんは日本人で、東京の出身です。
Ms. Machida is a Japanese national and is from Tokyo.
カワムラさんは東京大学の学生で、専攻は工学です。
Mr. Kawamura is a student at the University of Tokyo, and his major is engineering.

A clause ending in a noun ＋で can explain a reason or cause for what follows.

病気で、クラスを休みました。
I was sick and (so I) missed class.

アクティビティー 23

高くて、まずいです。(It's expensive and not good.)
Make sentences by combining the words and phrases provided.

[例] (あのレストラン) (高い) (まずい) →
あのレストランは高くて、まずいです。もう行きません！

1. (あの人のスピーチ) (長い) (つまらない)
2. (日本語の先生) (やさしい) (親切 [*kind*])
3. (このケーキ) (あまい) (おいしい)
4. (このラップトップ・コンピュータ) (重い) (不便)
5. (カナダの冬) (寒い) (長い)
6. (わたしの大学) (大きい) (有名)

7. (山口さん) (エレガント) (きれい)

8. (カワムラさん) (ハンサム) (やさしい)

9. (高田(たかだ)さん) (26歳(さい)) (サラリーマン)

10. (チンさん) (中国人(ちゅうごくじん)) (ペキンの出身(しゅっしん))

アクティビティー 24

うるさくて、きたないところです。(*It's a noisy, dirty place.*)

Answer the following questions using two adjectives.

[例] あの町(まち)は静(しず)かですか。→
ええ、静(しず)かで、いいところです。(*or* いいえ、車(くるま)が多(おお)くて、うるさい [*noisy*]です。)

Useful Vocabulary: うるさい *noisy,* 遠(とお)い *far,* たいへん *terrible, awful*

1. あなたの近所(きんじょ)は便利(べんり)ですか。
2. 12月は雪(ゆき)が多(おお)いですか。
3. 日本の夏(なつ)は暑(あつ)いですか。
4. あなたのアパートは駅(えき)から近(ちか)いですか。
5. ボーイフレンドはハンサムですか。
6. 大野(おおの)先生のクラスは好(す)きですか。

アクティビティー 25

日本語のクラスはむずかしくて、つまらない。(*Japanese class is hard and boring.*)

Make sentences about each topic, combining as many appropriate adjectives as possible from those listed.

[例] 日本語のクラス
(やさしい、おもしろい、むずかしい、つまらない) →
日本語のクラスはやさしくて、おもしろいです。(*or* 日本語のクラスはやさしいですが、つまらないです。)

1. わたし
(静(しず)か、にぎやか、元気(げんき)、いんき [*gloomy*]、ようき [*cheerful*])
2. ジュリア・ロバーツ
(エレガント、若(わか)い [*young*]、きれい、ほそい [*slim*]、元気(げんき)、やさしい、ようき、いんき)

3. アーノルド・シュワルツネーガー
(タフ、やさしい、元気、若い、いんき、静か、強い)

4. エディー・マーフィー
(元気、いんき、きびしい、若い、やさしい、忙しい、おもしろい)

5. わたしの学校
(大きい、むずかしい、やさしい、いい、静か、有名)

6. わたしの家
(大きい、小さい、きれい、広い [*spacious*]、せまい [*small in area*]、きたない)

7. わたしのとなりの人 (***the person next to me***)
(うるさい、きれい、ハンサム、いんき、ようき、若い、やさしい、へん [*strange*]、まじめ)

8. この練習 (***exercise***)
(むずかしい、やさしい、つまらない、長い、短かい、おもしろい)

22. The Te-Form of Verbs

林：新しいビデオがあるんですよ。うちに来て、見ませんか。
ギブソン：ええ、ぜひ。
林：じゃ、明日5時ごろにうちに来てください。
ギブソン：はい、じゃあ、明日。

高田：明日は何をするんですか。
ギブソン：部屋を掃除して、洗濯をします。高田さんは。
高田：会社へ行って、仕事をします。
ギブソン：明日は日曜日ですよ！

HAYASHI: I have a new video. Won't you come over (lit., *to my home*) and watch it? GIBSON: Yes, by all means. HAYASHI: Then please come over (lit., *to my home*) around 5:00 tomorrow. GIBSON: Yes. See you tomorrow.

TAKADA: What are you going to do tomorrow? GIBSON: I'll clean my room and do some laundry. How about you? TAKADA: I'll go to my company and work. GIBSON: Tomorrow is Sunday, you know!

22.1 If you have mastered formation of the past, plain, affirmative form of verbs (that is, the ta-form), you can master the te-form very easily. Observe the following examples.

	TA-FORM	TE-FORM
Class 1		
書く	書いた	書いて
行く	行った	行って
泳ぐ	泳いだ	泳いで
買う	買った	買って
呼ぶ	呼んだ	呼んで
Class 2		
食べる	食べた	食べて
見る	見た	見て
Class 3		
する	した	して
来る	来た	来て

As you can see, the te-form of verbs is formed by changing the た to て or だ to で.

22.2 The te-form of verbs is usually combined with other components to form grammatical constructions. For instance, the te-form of a verb + ください (*please give me*) is used to ask someone to do something for you. It literally means *Please give me your doing of* (*something*), in other words, *Please do*…

> ここに名前を書いてください。
> *Please write your name here.*
> 日本語で話してください。
> *Please speak in Japanese.*

This is a fairly direct way to make a request and should therefore be used with caution, especially when speaking with superiors or strangers.

どうぞ (*Please, go ahead*) is often added to the beginning of these request sentences to make your request sound politer.

> どうぞたくさん食べてください。
> *Please eat as much as you want.* (lit., *Please eat a lot.*)

22.3 You can express a succession of actions or events simply by connecting clauses that end in the te-form of a verb. For example,

スーパーに行って、アイスクリームを買う。

I will go to the supermarket and buy ice cream.

わたしは六時に起きて、歯を磨いて、顔を洗いました。

I got up at 6:00, brushed my teeth, and washed my face.

There is no grammatical limit on the number of verb clauses you can string together with this construction. The actions or events must usually take place within a short period of time and be related to one another in some sense. In most cases, they also should be listed in the same order in which the events occurred.

The tense and the speaker's attitude are expressed in the sentence-final verb—in the examples above, 買（か）う and 洗（あら）いました. All the preceding te-forms of verbs assume the same tense and other attributes of the sentence-final verb. Therefore, since 洗いました is past tense, you know that the first two actions—getting up and brushing teeth—also took place in the past. Because of the politeness level of 洗いました, you can tell that the speaker is speaking politely. In the first example, by the plain form of the final verb you can tell that the speaker is conveying information informally.

To summarize, you cannot know the tense and the speaker's attitude or emotion until you hear the last verb.

言語ノート

Conjoining Sequential Actions

You already studied how to express sequential actions and events using the transitions そして、それから、and そのあと (Chapter 3). In addition to these transitions and the te-form of verbs, you can also link sequential actions with a te-form of a verb + から. This pattern adds a temporal emphasis: A から, B (after A, B).

夕ごはんを食べて新聞を読んでから、日本語を勉強しました。

After eating dinner and reading the newspaper, I studied Japanese.

ブラウンさんに会ってから、話しましょう。

Let's talk about it after we meet Ms. Brown.

22.4 The te-form of verbs can be used to express a cause-and-effect relationship where the first clause explains a reason for the second. You will have to determine from context whether a causal connection is intended. For example,

寝坊して、学校におくれた。
I overslept and (so) I was late for school.
古いケーキを食べて、病気になりました。
I ate some old cake, and (because of that) I got sick.

アクティビティー 26

少し休んでください。(*Please take a short break.*)

Change each verb to its te-form + ください.

[例] ギブソンさんと話す → ギブソンさんと話してください。

1. 早く起きる
2. 車を洗う
3. 夕ごはんを食べる
4. くすり (*medicine*) を飲む
5. 大学の前で待つ
6. スーパーへ行く
7. タクシーに乗る
8. ブラウンさんに会う
9. このかばんを見る
10. 今日の新聞を読む
11. 中に入る (*to enter*)
12. 4時にここに来る

アクティビティー 27

少し休んで、テレビを見ました。(I *took a rest and watched TV.*)

Using te-forms, combine the sentences provided into one past tense sentence.

[例] (朝起きる) (コーヒーを飲む) → 朝起きて、コーヒーを飲んだ。

1. (お風呂から出る) (ビールを飲む)
2. (バスに乗る) (デパートへ行く) (セーターを買う)
3. (シャワーを浴びる) (ひげをそる)
4. (ドレスを着る) (デートに出かける)
5. (夕ごはんを食べる) (日本語を勉強する)
6. (カワムラさんの家へ行く) (話す)

7. (家に帰る)(寝る)
8. (ワープロを使う [*to use a word processor*])(手紙 [*letter*] を書く)

アクティビティー 28

毎日のこと (*Everyday things*)

Complete the following sentences based on your own experience.

[例] 朝起きて、→ 朝起きて、トイレに行きます。

Useful word: はく *to wear (shoes, socks, etc.)*

1. 日本語のクラスへ行って、
2. カフェテリアへ行って、
3. 昼ごはんを食べて、
4. バスに乗って、
5. スニーカーをはいて、
6. セーターを着て、
7. 本を読んで、
8. うちに帰って、

アクティビティー 29

夏、何をしましたか。(*What did he do in the summer?*)

Using the information provided, tell what the person did in each sentence.

[例] —カワムラさんは夏、何をしましたか。
—アメリカに帰って、友だちに会いました。

1. winter, go to the mountains, ski
2. spring, go to a park, view cherry blossoms
3. fall, go to Nagano, hike
4. summer, go to the ocean, swim

Vocabulary and Grammar 4C

Vocabulary and Oral Activities

Forecasting

Vocabulary: Forecasting

空	そら	sky
霧	きり	fog
洪水	こうずい	flood
日照り	ひでり	drought

Rain and Other Precipitation

夕立	ゆうだち	evening shower
大雨	おおあめ	heavy rain
雷	かみなり	thunder
稲妻	いなずま	lightning
吹雪	ふぶき	snowstorm
大雪	おおゆき	heavy snow
みぞれ		sleet
霜	しも	frost
露	つゆ	dew

アクティビティー 30

ダイアログ：冬(ふゆ)はどんな気候(きこう)ですか。 (*What is the climate like in winter?*)

林(はやし)：エドモントンの冬(ふゆ)はどんな気候(きこう)ですか。
ギブソン：雪(ゆき)がたくさん降(ふ)って、とても寒(さむ)いです。
林(はやし)：夏(なつ)はどうですか。
ギブソン：夏は涼(すず)しくて、おだやかな気候(きこう)です。

HAYASHI: What is the climate like in Edmonton in winter? GIBSON: It snows a lot, and it's very cold.
HAYASHI: What about summer? GIBSON: Summers are cool, and the weather is mild.

Practice the dialogue, using the following pattern and information.

—(place) の (season) はどんな気候(きこう)ですか。
—________。

1. —New York, winter
   —rainy and cold
2. —Seattle, fall
   —clear and warm
3. —Sapporo, spring
   —cloudy and cool
4. —Tokyo, summer
   —clear and sultry

アクティビティー 31

Odd Man Out

In each of the following groups of words, one word does not belong to the same category as the others. Identify it and tell why it is different.

1. 暑(あつ)い、いい、寒(さむ)い、涼(すず)しい、暖(あたた)かい
2. 晴(は)れ、くもり、雨(あめ)、高(たか)い、雪(ゆき)
3. 北(きた)、南(みなみ)、風(かぜ)、東(ひがし)、西(にし)
4. 春(はる)、冬(ふゆ)、夏(なつ)、海(うみ)、秋(あき)
5. 雨(あめ)、雪(ゆき)、雲(くも)、くもり、晴(は)れ
6. 吹雪(ふぶき)、霜(しも)、みぞれ、小雨(こさめ)
7. 洪水(こうずい)、晴(は)れ、日照(ひで)り、台風(たいふう)
8. 露(つゆ)、霧(きり)、空(そら)、にわか雨(あめ)

Grammar and Practice Activities

23. Expressing Probability and Conjecture

ブラウン：林(はやし)さんは来(く)るでしょうか。
町田(まちだ)：さあ、どうでしょうか。
ブラウン：来(こ)ないかもしれませんね。
町田：さあ、わかりませんね。

BROWN: Do you suppose Mr. Hayashi will come? MACHIDA: Hmm, I wonder. BROWN: He may not come, isn't that right? MACHIDA: Hmm, I don't know.

ブラウン：昨日(きのう)のパーティーはどうでしたか。おもしろかったでしょう。*
町田(まちだ)：ええ、とてもおもしろかったです。
ブラウン：ギブソンさんはパーティーにいましたか。
町田：ええと、いたかもしれません。いや、いなかったかもしれません。

23.1 There are a variety of ways to express conjecture or uncertainty in Japanese. Two of the most commonly used expressions are でしょう (plain form だろう) meaning *probably* and かもしれません (plain form かもしれない) meaning *may* or *maybe*. The major difference between these two expressions is that かもしれません expresses a greater degree of uncertainty.

When making a conjecture relating to yourself, かもしれない—not だろう—is used.

ジョンソンさんは日本語がわかるでしょう。
Ms. Johnson probably understands Japanese.
ジョンソンさんは日本語がわかるかもしれません。
Ms. Johnson may understand Japanese.

Nouns, adjectives, and verbs precede these expressions. When the speaker is guessing what will happen in the present or future, the following forms are used.

noun i-adjective (nonpast, plain) na-adjective (dictionary form) verb (nonpast, plain form)	+	でしょう (だろう) *or* かもしれません (かもしれない)

When the preceding nouns, adjectives, and verbs are negative, they take the following forms.

noun + で(は)ない i-adjective (nonpast, plain, negative) na-adjective (dictionary form + で[は]ない) verb (nonpast, plain, negative form)	+	でしょう (だろう) *or* かもしれません (かもしれない)

BROWN: How was the party yesterday? It must have been fun, huh? MACHIDA: Yes, it was great fun. BROWN: Was Ms. Gibson there? MACHIDA: Uhh, she may have been. No, maybe she wasn't.

* In the second dialogue, おもしろかったでしょう。ends in a rising intonation.

明日(あした)は雨(あめ)でしょう。
It probably will rain tomorrow.
あの人は学生ではないでしょう。
That person probably is not a student.
明日(あした)は暑(あつ)いでしょう。
It probably will be hot tomorrow.
明日(あした)は寒(さむ)くないでしょう。
It probably won't be cold tomorrow.
あの人はまじめかもしれません。
That person may be serious.
明日(あした)は雪(ゆき)が降(ふ)るかもしれません。
It might snow tomorrow.
明日(あした)はここに来(こ)ないかもしれません。
I might not come here tomorrow.

To express a conjecture or to guess about what happened in the past, use these forms.

noun だった i-adjective (past, plain) na-adjective (past, plain) verb (past, plain)	+	でしょう (だろう) *or* かもしれません (かもしれない)

When the elements that precede a conjecture about the past are negative, the following forms are used.

noun ではなかった (じゃなかった) i-adjective (past, plain, negative) na-adjective (past, plain, negative) verb (past, plain, negative)	+	でしょう (だろう) *or* かもしれません (かもしれない)

昨日(きのう)東京(とうきょう)は雨(あめ)だったでしょう。
It probably rained in Tokyo yesterday.
あの人は先生ではなかったでしょう。
That person probably wasn't a teacher.
昨日(きのう)東京は寒(さむ)かったでしょう。
It probably was cold in Tokyo yesterday.
昨日(きのう)大阪(おおさか)は暑(あつ)くなかったでしょう。
It probably wasn't hot in Osaka yesterday.

あの学生はまじめだったかもしれません。
That student may have been serious.
Maybe that student was serious.

あの町はきれいではなかったかもしれません。
That town may not have been clean.

ブラウンさんはあそこに行ったかもしれません。
Ms. Brown may have gone there.

高田さんはあそこに行かなかったかもしれません。
Mr. Takada may not have gone there.

23.2 でしょう is often accompanied by adverbs expressing degrees of certainty, such as the following (listed in order of increasing certainty).

多分	*probably*
おそらく	*possibly, in all likelihood*
きっと	*certainly, surely*

Because of the strong probability expressed by きっと, it cannot be used with かもしれません.

かれは多分来るでしょう。
He will probably come.

かれはおそらく山下さんに電話をかけるでしょう。
Most likely he will call Mr. Yamashita.

あの学生はきっと日本語を勉強しているでしょう。
That student surely must be studying Japanese.

でしょう is often used to ask an indirect question, in which case the question particle か is pronounced with a falling intonation. As you might have guessed, this is a somewhat more formal way to ask a question.

かれはもう起きましたか。
Did he get up already?

かれはもう起きたでしょうか。
Do you suppose he already got up?
I wonder if he already got up.

でしょう pronounced with a rising intonation asks for the hearer's confirmation—*isn't it? aren't you? don't you agree?*

あなたも来るでしょう。↑
You're coming too, aren't you?

その映画はおもしろかったでしょう。↑
That movie was interesting, don't you think?

アクティビティー 32

これがわかるでしょう。(*You probably understand this.*)

Respond to the following questions using でしょう or かもしれません.

1. あの人はどこの国の人ですか。
2. あの人は何歳ですか。
3. 明日はどんなお天気でしょうか。
4. あの人は昨日どこへ行きましたか。
5. あのセーターは安いですか。高いですか。
6. 今、東京は暑いですか。
7. あの人はどんな人ですか。
8. 12月はニューヨークとワシントンとどちらが寒いですか。
9. ここから一番近い駅まで何分かかりますか。
10. あの人は昨日何をしましたか。

アクティビティー 33

あなたはどう思いますか。(*What do you think?*)

What can you guess about each of these pictures? State your conjectures.

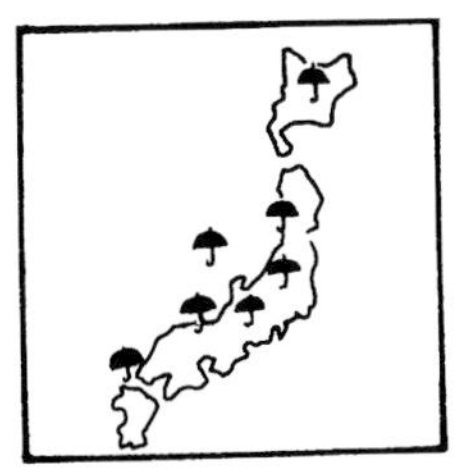

1. 明日はどんなお天気ですか。

2. 林さんは大丈夫ですか。

3. あのレストランはおいしいですか。

4. ジョンソンさんは日本語がわかりますか。

5. 台風は来ますか。

アクティビティー 34

ダイアログ：雨が降るかもしれません。(*It might rain.*)

ブラウン：いやなお天気ですね。
林：ええ、空が暗いですね。
ブラウン：午後は雨が降るでしょうか。
林：ええ、嵐が来るかもしれません。

アクティビティー 35

明日はどんなお天気でしょうか。(*What will the weather be like tomorrow?*)

While looking at the following table, listen to your instructor forecast tomorrow's weather.

[例] 函館は雪が降るでしょう。

Useful Vocabulary: 東 *east,* 西 *west,* 南 *south,* 北 *north*

CITY	WEATHER	TEMPERATURE	WIND
Hakodate	Cloudy, P.M. snow	−3, cold	North, strong
Hukushima	Clear, occasionally cloudy	−1, cold	West, weak
Gihu	Rain	8, cool	East, weak
Kobe	Cloudy, occasionally clear	17, warm	South, weak
Kochi	Rain	27, hot	No wind
Yakushima	Clear	30, hot	South, weak

アクティビティー 36

明日は雨が降るでしょう。(*It will rain tomorrow.*)

You are a TV meteorologist. Using the following data, give a weather forecast. Don't forget to use でしょう or かもしれません.

BROWN: The weather is unpleasant, isn't it? HAYASHI: Yes. The sky is dark (isn't it?). BROWN: I wonder if it will rain this afternoon. HAYASHI: Yes. It just might storm. (lit., *A storm might come.*)

Kushiro	cloudy, occasional snow, very cold −15 degrees, very strong north wind
Okayama	sunny, very good weather 20 degrees, warm, no wind
Nara	cloudy in the morning, rain in the afternoon a little cold, 5 degrees, light westerly breeze
Miyazaki	cloudy, occasional rain in the morning foggy in the morning, warm, 22 degrees, no wind

✸ アクティビティー 37

明日(あした)のお天気(てんき)は？ (*What about tomorrow's weather?*)

Working with a partner, draw a map of your town or region. One of you will play a TV meteorologist predicting tomorrow's weather. As you make your predictions, draw appropriate weather symbols and temperatures on the map. The second person will play a TV anchor asking the meteorologist questions about the weather. Be creative.

Language Skills

Reading and Writing

Reading 1 ブラウンさんへの手紙(てがみ)

Before You Read

You are writing a letter in English to a friend, telling her about your ski vacation. How do you start your letter? What are the standard elements of an English personal letter (e.g., date, your name, etc.)? Where do you place them in a letter?

Japanese letters usually start with 拝啓(はいけい), which roughly corresponds to *Dear Sir* or *Dear Madam.* This introductory greeting is generally followed by a reference to the weather or season. In what season do you think each of the following phrases would be used in a Japanese letter?

1. 毎日(まいにち)暑(あつ)いです。
2. 最近(さいきん)雪(ゆき)が多(おお)くて、たいへんです。
3. そちらは梅雨(つゆ)の季節(きせつ)でしょうか。ここは毎日雨(あめ)が降(ふ)ります。
4. さくら (*cherry blossoms*) がとてもきれいです。
5. 北風(きたかぜ)が吹いて、寒(さむ)いです。
6. 台風(たいふう)の季節(きせつ)に入(はい)りました。
7. 南風(みなみかぜ)が吹(ふ)いて、とても暖(あたた)かいです。

Now Read It!

Yooichi Takada wrote this letter to Linda Brown from Hokkaido, where he has been vacationing.

拝啓

ブラウンさん、お元気ですか。私は元気です。こちらは寒くて、たいへんですが、東京はどうですか。

さて、私は先週の土曜日に北海道に着きました。日曜日に雪がたくさん降りました。私の家の近くに山があります。月曜日に友だちとその山へ行って、スキーをしました。月曜日はいいお天気で、朝から夕方までスキーをしました。

火曜日は私の誕生日でした。家のそばの喫茶店でバースデー・パーティーがありました。友だちがたくさん来ました。

あさって、東京に帰ります。おみやげを買って、帰りますので、楽しみにしてください。

今日はこれで失礼します。寒いですから、お体に気をつけてください。

敬具

二月十五日

高田洋一

リンダ・ブラウン様

After You Finish Reading

1. Find the following information in the letter.

Date	Inquiry about addressee's health
Sender's name	Reference to sender's health
Addressee's name	Closing remarks
Reference to weather or season	Closing (e.g., Sincerely)

2. In English, discuss in class the differences between English letters and Japanese letters.
3. How many details did you understand? Answer the following to test yourself.
   a. What is the weather like in Hokkaido?
   b. When did Mr. Takada go to Hokkaido?
   c. When did it snow?
   d. When did Mr. Takada go skiing?
   e. What was the weather like the day he went skiing?
   f. When was Mr. Takada's birthday?
   g. What did he do on his birthday?
   h. When is Mr. Takada returning to Tokyo?
   i. When did Mr. Takada write this letter?

文化ノート

CULTURE NOTE • How to Write a Letter in Japanese

Here is the standard format of a Japanese personal letter.

1. opening word or phrase, such as 拝啓(はいけい)
2. preliminary remarks: reference to the weather or season, inquiry about the addressee's health (often followed by reference to the writer's health), etc.
3. main body
4. concluding remarks: best wishes for the addressee's health, regards to the addressee's family, etc.
5. closing word or phrase such as 敬具(けいぐ)
6. date
7. sender's full name
8. addressee's full name (with the title 様(さま), not さん), is usually used in personal letters
9. postscript: anything sender forgot to include in the main body

When writing a letter, you generally use politer language than when talking directly to the addressee.

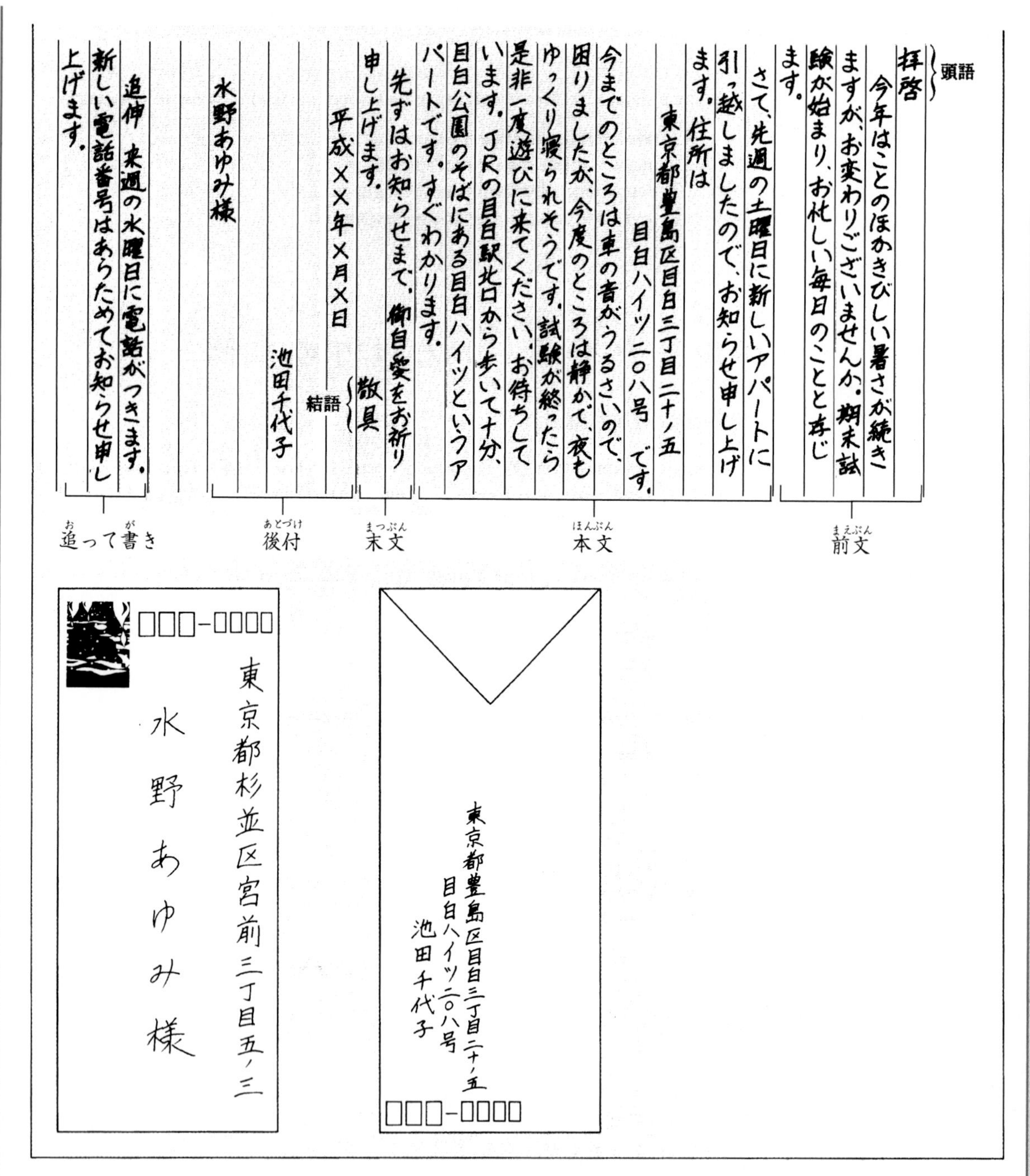
拝啓　頭語

今年はことのほかきびしい暑さが続きますが、お変わりございませんか。期末試験が始まり、お忙しい毎日のことと存じます。

さて、先週の土曜日に新しいアパートに引っ越しましたので、お知らせ申し上げます。住所は

東京都豊島区目白三丁目二十ノ五

目白ハイツ二〇八号　です。

今までのところは車の音がうるさいので、困りましたが、今度のところは静かで、夜もゆっくり寝られそうです。試験が終ったら是非一度遊びに来てください。お待ちしています。JRの目白駅北口から歩いて十分、目白公園のそばにある目白ハイツというアパートです。すぐわかります。

先ずはお知らせまで。御自愛をお祈り申し上げます。

敬具　結語

平成××年×月×日

池田千代子

水野あゆみ様

追伸　来週の水曜日に電話がつきます。新しい電話番号はあらためてお知らせ申し上げます。

Writing 1

Write a short letter to a friend in Japanese. Include the following in your letter.

1. reference to the season or weather
2. inquiry about your friend's health
3. description of your Japanese language study
4. invitation to visit your house next month

Reading 2: トラベル・ガイド：いろは町(まち)の気候(きこう)

Before You Read

You are planning to make a short trip during a school break. You have decided to visit Iroha, a small town near Kyoto. You would like to know the climate there and what clothes you should take, so you consult a travel guidebook. It includes many words you haven't learned, but you can read enough to get the information you need. Before reading the following page from the guidebook, list words relating to each of these topics.

季節(きせつ)　雨(あめ)　雪(ゆき)
気温(きおん)　風(かぜ)

Describe in Japanese the kind of weather you associate with these items.

1. オーバー
2. レインコート
3. ショートパンツ
4. セーター
5. 傘(かさ) (*umbrella*)
6. T-シャツ
7. ノースリーブス

Now Read It!

いろは町(まち)の気候(きこう)

春(はる)は昼間(ひるま)は暖(あたた)かいが、朝夕(あさゆう)はまだ寒(さむ)い。セーターがいる。雨(あめ)はほとんど降(ふ)らない。4月は桜(さくら)がきれいだ。山(やま)も美(うつく)しくて、多(おお)くの人がハイキングを楽(たの)しむ。

6月から7月の梅雨(つゆ)の季節(きせつ)は、雨(あめ)が多(おお)い。ちょっと寒(さむ)い日(ひ)が多(おお)い。傘(かさ)やレインコートがいる。この季節(きせつ)は、お寺(てら)の庭(にわ)がとても美しい。いろは町(まち)の夏(なつ)はむし暑(あつ)い。夏の平均気温(へいきんきおん)は28度(ど)、平均湿度(へいきんしつど)は90%だ。カジュアルな服(ふく)がいい。夕方雨(ゆうがたあめ)がよく降(ふ)る。傘(かさ)がいる。

昼間 *daytime* / まだ *still* / …がいる *one needs…*

桜 *cherry blossoms* / 山 *mountain* / 美しい *beautiful*

楽しむ *to enjoy*

庭 *garden*

平均 *average* / 湿度 *humidity* / カジュアル *casual, informal*

秋は毎日いい天気が続く。山がとても美しい。秋は一年中で一番美しい季節だ。昼間は15度ぐらいだ。秋夕は涼しいので、セーターやコートがいる。

11月から、寒い北風が吹いて、気温も下がる。いろは町の冬はきびしい。京都より気温が2〜3度低い。12月から2月まで雪が降る。お寺の庭にも雪が降って、本当に美しい。お寺や神社には暖房がないので、お寺や神社の中でもオーバーがいる。

下がる *to go down*

暖房 *heater*

After You Finish Reading

Tell what the weather is like in each season in Iroha.

In what season should these people visit Iroha?

1. ギブソン　雪が好きです。
2. 町田　ハイキングが好きです。
3. 横井先生　雨の季節のお寺はきれいで、いいですね。
4. 林　暑い季節が好きです。

京都の夏祭 (*summer festival*)：祇園祭

Writing 2

Write a short description in Japanese of the weather and the four seasons for some place in your home country.

Language Functions and Situations

Asking Questions About the Japanese Language

Japanese native speakers are a good source of information about the language. Here are some simple ways to ask someone for help when studying Japanese.

1. Asking about pronunciation

   すみません。これはどう発音しますか。—「とうざいなんぼく」です。

   Excuse me. How do you pronounce this? —**Too-zai-nan-boku.** (*East-west-south-north.*)

   東西南北

> **A**lternative expression:
> これを発音してくださいますか。*Would you pronounce this for me?*

2. Asking how to read **kanji**

   すみません。この漢字はどう読みますか。—「あさゆう」です。

   Excuse me. How do you read these **kanji***?* —**Asayuu.** (*Morning and evening.*)

   朝夕

> **A**lternative expression:
> この漢字を読んでくださいますか。*Would you read this (these) kanji for me?*

3. Asking about writing

   すみません。「あつい」は漢字でどう書きますか。—こう書きます。

   Excuse me. How do you write ***hot*** *in* **kanji***?* —*You write it like this.* (said while writing)

   暑い

> **A**lternative expression:
> 「あつい」という漢字を書いてくださいますか。*Would you write the kanji for* ***"atsui"*** *for me?*

4. Asking about meaning

   すみません。「湿度」はどういう意味ですか。—空気の中の水分のことです。英語で *humidity* といいます。

   Excuse me. What does **shitsudo** *mean? —It means* ***the moisture in the air****. In English, you say* ***humidity****.*

> **A**lternative expression:
> 「湿度」の意味を教えてくださいますか。*Would you please tell me the meaning of* ***"shitsudo"****?*

Asking for Assistance with **Kanji**

ギブソン：林さん、ちょっとすみません。日本語を教えてください。
林：ええ、いいですよ。何ですか。
ギブソン：「ゆき」は漢字でどう書きますか。
林：雨の下にカタカナの「ヨ」です。
ギブソン：ちょっと書いてください。

GIBSON: Mr. Hayashi, excuse me. Can you teach me some Japanese? HAYASHI: Yes, sure. What can I do for you? (lit., *What is it?*) GIBSON: How do you write *snow* in **kanji?** HAYASHI: Write a **katakana yo** under the character for *rain.* (lit., ***It is a katakana yo under rain.***) GIBSON: Please write it for me.

林：こう書きます。
ギブソン：ありがとうございます。

ブラウン：横井先生、質問があるんですが、...
横井：ええ、何ですか。
ブラウン：この漢字は何と読みますか。
横井：「しつど」と読みます。*humidity* のことです。
ブラウン：「温度」とは違いますか。
横井：ええ、違います。
ブラウン：「温度」を書いていただけますか。
横井：こう書きます。
ブラウン：ありがとうございます。

言語ノート

Making Polite Requests

The most common way to make a request is to use the te-form of a verb + ください (*please give me the doing of...*).

名前を書いてください。
Please write down your name.

As discussed earlier, どうぞ makes your request more polite.

どうぞ教えてください。
Please tell me. or *Please teach me.*

More polite forms of request include the following, in increasing order of politeness.

te-form of verb + { くださいますか / くださいませんか / いただけますか / いただけませんか }

明日電話してくださいますか。
Would you call me tomorrow?
ブラウンさんと話していただけませんか。
Would you please talk with Ms. Brown?

HAYASHI: You write it like this. GIBSON: Thank you.

BROWN: Professor Yokoi, I have a question but... (could you help me?) YOKOI: Yes, what is it? BROWN: How do you read this **kanji?** YOKOI: You read it **shitsudo.** It means *humidity*. BROWN: Is it different from **ondo?** YOKOI: Yes, it's different. BROWN: Would you please write **ondo** for me? YOKOI: You write it like this. BROWN: Thank you very much.

アクティビティー 38

日本人に聞(き)いてください。(*Ask a Japanese.*)

Find a native speaker of Japanese on your campus and ask for the following information.

1. Pronunciation and meaning of these characters
   a. 南西　　b. 夕立　　c. 日中
2. How to write these phrases in **kanji**
   a. こうてい *high and low*
   b. こうてん *good weather*
   c. だんじょ *man and woman*

Don't forget to use polite requests when you ask these questions.

Listening Comprehension

As you listen to the forecast for tomorrow, jot down what the weather will be for each of the following cities: Sapporo, Sendai, Hukushima, Utsunomiya, Tokyo, Nagoya, Wakayama, Hiroshima, Hukuoka, and Miyazaki.

Vocabulary

Weather

あたたかい	暖かい	warm
あめ	雨	rain
かぜ	風	wind
きあつ	気圧	air pressure
きおん	気温	temperature
きこう	気候	climate
くも	雲	cloud
くもり		cloudy
さむい	寒い	cold
すずしい	涼しい	cool
たいふう	台風	typhoon
たいよう	太陽	sun
てんき	天気	weather
てんきず	天気図	weather map
てんきよほう	天気予報	weather forecast
…ど	…度	…degrees (*counter*)
はれ	晴れ	clear weather; sunny and clear
ふく	吹く	to blow (*used with wind*)
ふる	降る	to fall (*used with rain, snow, etc.*)
むしあつい	むし暑い	sultry; hot and humid
ゆき	雪	snow

Review: 暑(あつ)い

Seasons

あき	秋	fall; autumn	なつ	夏	summer
きせつ	季節	season	はる	春	spring
しき	四季	four seasons	ふゆ	冬	winter

Loanword: カレンダー

Adjectives

あかるい	明るい	bright (vs. *dark*)
あだやか(な)		calm (*ocean, personality*); gentle (*breeze*)
おもい	重い	heavy
おもしろい	面白い	interesting; fun
くらい	暗い	dark
スマート(な)		slender (*person*)
たいへん(な)	大変(な)	terrible; awful
つまらない		boring
つよい	強い	strong
ながい	長い	long
にぎやか(な)		lively
はやい	早い; 速い	early; quick; fast
ふまじめ(な)	不まじめ(な)	not serious; lazy (*person*)
へん(な)	変(な)	strange
まじめ(な)		serious (*person*)
みじかい	短い	short
むずかしい		difficult
ゆうめい(な)	有名(な)	famous
よわい	弱い	weak
わかい	若い	young

Loanwords: エレガント(な)、キュート(な)、タフ(な)、ハンサム(な)

Review: 新(あたら)しい、いい、忙(いそが)しい、うるさい、(...が) 多(おお)い、きたない、きびしい、きれい(な)、元気(げんき)(な)、静(しず)か(な)、親切(しんせつ)(な)、(...が) 少(すく)ない、せまい、高(たか)い、低(ひく)い、暇(ひま)(な)、広(ひろ)い、不便(ふべん)(な)、古(ふる)い、便利(べんり)(な)、やさしい、安(やす)い、悪(わる)い

Nouns

いなずま	稲妻	lightning	かみなり	雷	thunder
うみ	海	ocean; sea	きた	北	north
おおあめ	大雨	heavy rain	きり	霧	fog
おおゆき	大雪	heavy snow	こうずい	洪水	flood
かさ	傘	umbrella	そら	空	sky

しも	霜	frost
つり	釣り	fishing
つゆ	露	dew
てがみ	手紙	letter
にし	西	west
はなみ	花見	(cherry) blossom viewing
ひがし	東	east
ひでり	日照り	drought
びょうき	病気	sick
ふぶき	吹雪	snowstorm
みぞれ		sleet
みなみ	南	south
やま	山	mountain
やまのぼり	山登り	mountain climbing
ゆうだち	夕立	evening shower
ワープロ		word processor

Loanwords: キャンプ、コート、スキー、スケート、ハイキング

Verbs

およぐ	泳ぐ	to swim
しぬ	死ぬ	to die
つかう	使う	to use

Other Words

おなじ	同じ	same
ぐらい、くらい		about; approximately
はやく	早く; 速く	early; quickly (*adverb*)

Review: たくさん、よく

Grammar

…でしょう	probably (*conjecture, polite*)
…だろう	probably (*conjecture, plain*)
…かもしれません	may; might (*conjecture, polite*)
…かもしれない	may; might (*conjecture, plain*)
…が、	but (*conjunction*)
…から、	because (*conjunction*)
～てください	please do…
…けれども	but (*conjunction*)

Kanji

Learn these characters:

天	東	台	少
気	西	番	強
雨	南	春	弱
雪	北	夏	昨
度	高	秋	暑
風	多	冬	寒
			空

チェックリスト

Use this checklist to confirm that you can now

- ☐ Talk about weather reports
- ☐ Talk about the four seasons
- ☐ Talk about forecasting
- ☐ Conjugate adjectives
- ☐ Use comparatives and superlatives
- ☐ Express plain, nonpast negative and plain past
- ☐ Explain a reason using ～ので
- ☐ Use the -te form of adjectives and verbs
- ☐ Express possibility
- ☐ Ask questions about the Japanese language

Review Chapter 4

アクティビティー　1

どうしますか。 (*What are you going to do?*)

What do you associate with the following weather situations? Make an association, and then compare your answer with that of your classmates. Any similarities?

1. とても暑いです。
2. とても寒いです。
3. 雨です。
4. 雪です。
5. 涼しいです。

a. 家の中にいます。
b. 散歩します。
c. 泳ぎます。
d. スキーをします。
e. 映画に行きます。
f. アイスクリームを食べます。
g. ジョギングをします。
h. ホット・ココアを飲みます。
i. 家で勉強します。
j. 公園で昼ごはんを食べます。

アクティビティー　2

天気予報 (*Weather forecast*)

The following are from weather forecasts in Japan. Tell the season in which each forecast was made.

1. 明日は朝から晴れるでしょう。気温は25度から30度。むし暑いでしょう。夕方、夕立が降るかもしれません。
2. 明日は晴れ、時々くもりでしょう。気温は13度くらい。ちょっと涼しいでしょう。ところで、北海道では昨日、今年初めての雪が降りました。
3. 明日は一日中くもりでしょう。気温は1度。あさってもくもり。夕方から雪が降るかもしれません。
4. 明日は午前中くもり、午後から雨でしょう。気温は15度くらいでしょう。お花見にはあまりいいお天気ではありません。

アクティビティー 3

Trip to Niigata

You would like to go from Tokyo to Niigata by car. Your car is very old, it doesn't have windshield wipers, and it doesn't have a good radiator. Simply speaking, your car doesn't run well in bad weather. Also, it cannot climb steep hills. After listening to a weather report and highway information read by your instructor, decide what route you have to take to make it all the way to Niigata from Tokyo.

Useful expression: 工事中 *under construction*

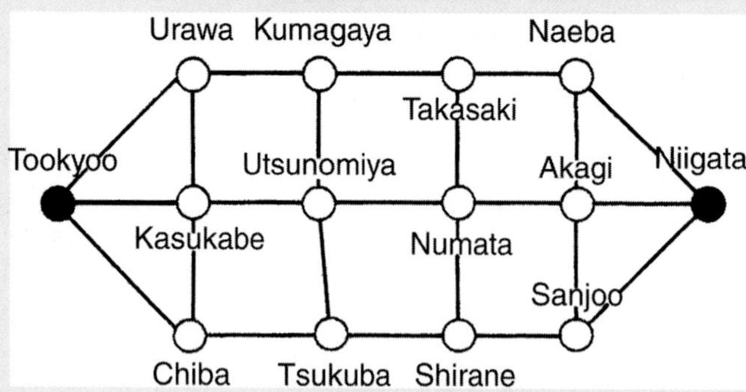

アクティビティー 4

どちらが大きいですか。 (*Which one is bigger?*)

Compare the following items with regard to a quality or quantity given. Follow the example.

[例] (高い) シアーズタワー、エンパイアー・ステート・ビル
シアーズタワーとエンパイアー・ステート・ビルとどちらが高いですか。
→ シアーズタワーのほうが高いです。
(寒い) 夏、春、冬
夏と春と冬の中で、いつが一番寒いですか。
→ 冬が一番寒いです。

1. (むずかしい) 数学、文学
2. (大きい) アメリカ、カナダ
3. (好き) カントリー・アンド・ウエスタン、ジャズ、ロックンロール
4. (安い) ホンダ・アコード、キャデラック
5. (面白い) バスケット・ボール、サッカー、アイス・ホッケー

5

第五章

趣味(しゅみ)・余暇(よか)

Hobbies and Leisure Activities

趣味(しゅみ)は何(なん)ですか。

Objectives

In this lesson you are going to

- Talk about hobbies and pastimes
- Talk about sports
- Talk about family
- Learn how to express *some, every, none,* and *any*
- Learn how to describe abilities
- Practice using nominalizers こと and の
- Study more uses of the particle も
- Learn how to use the potential form of verbs
- Study the **-te** form of verbs ＋います
- Learn about relative clauses
- Learn how to describe a change in state
- Learn how to respond to compliments
- Learn about introducing family members

YOOKOSO! MULTIMEDIA

Review and practice grammar and vocabulary from this chapter and watch video clips on the *Yookoso!* Interactive CD-ROM. Visit the *Yookoso!* Online Learning Center at **www.mhhe.com/yookosome** for additional exercises and resources.

Vocabulary and Grammar 5A

Vocabulary and Oral Activities

Hobbies and Pastimes

Vocabulary: Hobbies and Leisure Activities 

余暇	よか	free time; leisure
趣味	しゅみ	hobby
遊ぶ	あそぶ	to play
楽しむ	たのしむ	to enjoy
特技	とくぎ	special talent; skill
切手集め	きってあつめ	stamp collecting
写真	しゃしん	photography; photograph
園芸	えんげい	gardening
手芸	しゅげい	handicrafts
読書	どくしょ	reading books
絵画	かいが	painting
音楽鑑賞	おんがくかんしょう	music appreciation; listening to music
歌	うた	song
楽器	がっき	musical instrument
茶道	さどう	tea ceremony
コンサート		concert
旅行	りょこう	travel
カルチャーセンター		culture education center; adult school
クラブ		club
レジャー		leisure

Review: 映画(えいが)、音楽(おんがく)、スポーツ、釣(つ)り(に行く)、暇(ひま)(な)

アクティビティー　1

ゴルフはたのしいです。(*Golf is fun.*)

Associate words in the first column with appropriate words in the second column.

1. 写真(しゃしん)	a. ピアノ
2. 読書(どくしょ)	b. 電車(でんしゃ)
3. 映画(えいが)	c. コンサート
4. 園芸(えんげい)	d. 楽(たの)しむ
5. 旅行(りょこう)	e. フィルム
6. 手芸(しゅげい)	f. 図書館(としょかん)
7. 茶道(さどう)	g. クラーク・ゲーブル
8. 趣味(しゅみ)	h. 針(はり)と糸(いと) (*needle and thread*)
9. 切手集(きってあつ)め	i. チューリップ
10. 音楽鑑賞(おんがくかんしょう)	j. 古(ふる)い手紙(てがみ)
11. ボーリング	k. 飲(の)み物(もの)
12. 歌(うた)	l. ボール

Grammar and Practice Activities

24. Interrogative + か／も／でも

町田(まちだ)さんと林(はやし)さんが話していますす。

林(はやし)：町田(まちだ)さんは何(なに)か趣味(しゅみ)がありますか。
町田：そうですね、音楽鑑賞(おんがくかんしょう)ですね。
林：スポーツは何(なに)かしますか。
町田：テニスやバレーボールをします。
　　　林(はやし)さんの趣味(しゅみ)は何(なん)ですか。
林：いやあ、何(なに)もないんですよ。

When asking a social superior about his or her hobbies, use the polite alternate 御趣味(ごしゅみ). See Language Note on p. 336.

Ms. Machida and Mr. Hayashi are talking HAYASHI: Do you (lit., *Ms. Machida*) have any hobbies? MACHIDA: Let me see. My hobby is listening to music. HAYASHI: Do you play any sports? MACHIDA: I play tennis, volleyball, and the like. What is your hobby, Mr. Hayashi? HAYASHI: Well, I don't have any.

24.1 By appending the particles か, も, or でも to an interrogative (question word), you can express a whole range of new meanings.

1. An interrogative followed by か yields a word meaning *some*…
2. An interrogative followed by も means *every*… in affirmative sentences; it means *no*… in negative sentences.
3. An interrogative followed by でも means *any*.

These meanings are summarized in the following table. Note the two exceptions where other terms are used instead of the interrogative + も.

INTERROGATIVE	+ か	+ も **In Affirmative Sentences**	+ も **In Negative Sentences**	+ でも
何(なに)	何(なに)か *something*	みんな、みな 全(すべ)て、全部(ぜんぶ) *everything*	何(なに)も *nothing*	何(なん)でも *anything* (and *everything*), *whatever*
だれ (どなた)	だれか (どなたか) *someone*	みんな、みな (みなさん) *everyone*	だれも (どなたも) *no one*	だれでも (どなたでも) *anyone, whoever*
いつ	いつか *sometime*	いつも *always, all the time*	いつも *never*	いつでも *anytime, whenever*
どこ	どこか *somewhere*	どこも *everywhere*	どこも *nowhere*	どこでも *anywhere, wherever*
どれ	どれか *one of them*	どれも *every one, everything, all of them*	どれも *none of them*	どれでも *any of them, whichever one*
どちら	どちらか *either of two*	どちらも *both of them*	どちらも *neither of them*	どちらでも *either of them, whichever of the two*

何(なに)か食べますか。—ええ、何(なん)でもけっこうです。
Will you eat something? —Yes, anything is fine.
昨日(きのう)は何(なに)か食べましたか。—いいえ、何(なに)も食べませんでした。
Did you eat something yesterday?—No, I ate nothing (*or No, I didn't eat anything*).

> **R**eminder: どれ is used when talking about three or more things. どちら is used when discussing two things.

だれか来ますか。—いいえ、だれも来ません。
Is someone coming? —No, no one is coming.

いつかそこへ行きましょうか。—ええ、いつでもいいですよ。
Shall we go there someday? —Yes, any time is OK.

三村さんはいつもいませんね。—アルバイトで忙しいんですよ。
Mr. Mimura is never present. —He's busy with his part-time jobs, you know.

この三つの中からどれか選んでください。—じゃ、これをください。
Please choose one of these three. —Well then, please give me this one.

どれがいいでしょうか。—どれでも同じです。
Which one is good? —All of them are the same.

どちらか選んでください。—わたしはどちらでもいいですよ。
Please choose one of these (two). —Either is fine with me.

24.2 When the particles に, へ, から, and まで are part of a sentence containing the interrogative + か／も／でも construction, they fall between the interrogative and も or でも.

みんなに会いますか。—いいえ、だれにも会いませんよ。
Will you see everyone? —No, I won't see anyone.

どこかへ行きましたか。—いいえ、どこへも行きませんでした。
Did you go somewhere? —No, I didn't go anywhere.

The particle を is dropped whenever these interrogative-particle combinations are used.

何を見ますか。—何でも見ますよ。
What will you see? —I'm going to see everything.

24.3 Here are some useful expressions formed by combining interrogatives with か.

なぜか *somehow* (*for some reason*)
なぜか村山さんが好きではありません。
Somehow I don't like Ms. Murayama.

どうか *somehow* (often used in requests)
どうか教えてください。
Please (*find a way to*) *instruct me.*

いくつか *some* (*number of*), *several*
日本語のことばをいくつか習いました。
I learned some Japanese words.

アクティビティー 2

何(なん)でも好(す)きです。(*I like everything.*)

Fill in each blank with the appropriate interrogative + particle(s) and complete the dialogues.

1. s1: (　　)飲(の)みますか。
   s2: ええ、コーラはありますか。
2. s1: (　　)へ行きましょうか。
   s2: そうですね。デパートはどうですか。
3. s1: そこに(　　)いますか。
   s2: ええ、林(はやし)さんがいます。
4. s1: この映画(えいが)の中で(　　)を見ましたか。
   s2: いいえ、どれも見ていません。
5. s1: この三冊(さつ)の本の中のどれがいいですか。
   s2: (　　)いいですよ。
6. s1: 今年の夏(なつ)はどこへ旅行(りょこう)しましょうか。
   s2: わたしは(　　)いいですよ。
7. s1: この問題(もんだい)はやさしいですね。
   s2: ええ、(　　)簡単(かんたん)に(*easily*)できますね。
8. s1: 土曜日(どようび)がいいですか、日曜日(にちようび)がいいですか。
   s2: (　　)いいですよ。
9. s1: あそこにだれがいましたか。
   s2: (　　)いませんでした。
10. s1: (　　)へ行きましょうか。
    s2: いいえ、家(いえ)にいましょう。今日は(　　)こんでいます(こんでいる *to be crowded*)。

冊 is a counter for books.

アクティビティー 3

いつもやさしいです。(*She's always kind.*)

Answer these questions. Use interrogatives + か, も, or でも as appropriate.

1. 先週(せんしゅう)の日曜日(にちようび)、どこかへ行きましたか。
2. 何(なに)を食べますか。
3. いつか映画(えいが)を見ませんか。
4. このコンピュータはどれも同(おな)じですか。

5. コーラとジュースとビールのどれがいいですか。

6. 今日の午後、何もしないんですか。

7. あの先生はいつもやさしいですか。

8. だれもこの練習ができないんですか。

アクティビティー　4

この週末何をしますか。(*What are they going to do this weekend?*)

Using the following table, discuss what hobby each person has and what he or she is going to do this weekend.

[例]　s1: 町田さんは何か趣味がありますか。
　　s2: クラシック音楽です。
　　s1: 週末は何かしますか。
　　s2: 日曜日、コンサートへ行きます。

名前	趣味	土曜日	日曜日
ジョン・カワムラ (21歳、大学生)	映画	映画を見る	ジョギングをする
町田ひとみ (20歳、大学生)	クラシック音楽	ステレオを聞く	コンサートへ行く
林 正男 (19歳、大学生)	ない	一日中寝る	テレビを見る
山本さゆり (18歳、ウエートレス)	買い物	デパートへ行く	ブティックへ行く
高田洋一 (26歳、会社員)	ない	仕事をする	仕事一をする
山口健次 (54歳、会社員)	釣り	仕事をする	釣りに行く
ヘザー・ギブソン (20歳、大学生)	スポーツ	エアロビクスをする	スキーに行く

会社員 *company employee*

Vocabulary Library 

More Hobbies

ART

絵をかく	えをかく	to draw a picture
墨絵	すみえ	sumi ink painting
生花	いけばな	flower arranging
書道	しょどう	brush calligraphy

MUSIC AND PERFORMING ARTS

バイオリン		violin
琴	こと	koto (*Japanese zither*)
三味線	しゃみせん	samisen (*Japanese banjo-like instrument*)
日本舞踊	にほんぶよう	Japanese traditional dancing
弾く	ひく	to play (*string instruments*)
吹く	ふく	to play (*wind instruments*)
歌(を歌う)	うた(をうたう)	(to sing) a song
演奏する	えんそうする	to play; to perform on (*a musical instrument*)
クラシック音楽	クラシックおんがく	classical music
演劇	えんげき	(*theatrical*) play

Loanwords: オペラ、ギター、ジャズ、ダンス、ピアノ、ミュージカル、ラップ、ロック

GAMES

テレビゲーム		video game
トランプ(をする)		(to play) cards
碁	ご	go (*a board game*)
将棋	しょうぎ	shogi (*a board game*)
マージャン		mah-jongg
パチンコ		pachinko (*Japanese pinball*)

Loanwords: コンピュータゲーム、チェス

PHOTOGRAPHY

写真(を撮る)	しゃしん(をとる)	(to take) a photo
白黒写真	しろくろしゃしん	black-and-white photo(graphy)
カラー写真	カラーしゃしん	color photo(graphy)

Loanwords: アルバム、カメラ、ビデオカメラ、フィルム

OTHER HOBBIES

骨董品	こっとうひん	antiques
刺繍	ししゅう	embroidery
編物	あみもの	knitting; crochet
手品	てじな	sleight-of-hand; magic
盆栽	ぼんさい	bonsai
ペット(を飼う)	ペット(をかう)	(to keep; to raise) a pet
犬	いぬ	dog
猫	ねこ	cat
鳥	とり	bird
金魚	きんぎょ	goldfish

Loanwords: コンピュータ、ハンティング、ヨガ

文化ノート

CULTURE NOTE • 碁、将棋、マージャン、パチンコ

Four popular Japanese games are **go, shogi, mah-jongg,** and **pachinko.** The first two, **go** and **shogi,** both originally from China, are portable board games, but **pachinko** must be played in a **pachinko** parlor equipped with **pachinko** machines. **Mah-jongg** may be played either at home or at a **mah-jongg** parlor where refreshments are served and high-tech devices "shuffle" and deal the game pieces for you.

Go is a two-player game of sophisticated strategy. Each player in turn places a black or white stone on one of the 361 intersections of a 19 × 19 grid board with the aim of surrounding and capturing territories and the opponent's stones.

チーン、ジャラジャラ！パチンコ屋の中はいつもにぎやかです。

Shogi is a two-player board game similar to chess. Each player manipulates twenty pieces headed by a king. More than 500 Japanese make their living as professional **go** and **shogi** players, and the results of their competitions are reported regularly in the newspapers.

Mah-jongg is played by four people using 136 tiles (resembling dominoes) to make strategic combinations. This game is extremely popular among college students, especially male students who may stay up all night playing, often at **mah-jongg** parlors in commercial districts near their universities.

Pachinko is a Japanese version of pinball that began its rise to phenomenal popularity in the late 1940s. With a knob, the player sends small steel balls into the vertically oriented pinball machine, aiming at specific holes. Depending on which hole a ball enters, varying quantities of steel balls are discharged at the bottom of the machine as the player's winnings. These balls can be reinserted into the machine for extended play or exchanged for merchandise such as cigarettes and candy. Minors are not allowed to play **pachinko.**

言語ノート

Nominal Verbs

Countless new verbs can be formed by appending the verb する (*to do*) to certain foreign loanwords and compound nouns (those composed of two or more characters) of Chinese origin. These are called *nominal verbs*. Add する to 旅行(りょこう) (*travel*) and you get 旅行する (*to travel*). Here are some more nominal verbs you already know.

勉強(べんきょう)する、運動(うんどう)する、料理(りょうり)する
ドライブする、ジョギングする、スポーツする

You cannot make verbs this way out of all loanwords and Chinese-origin compound nouns. For instance, you cannot say 銀行(ぎんこう)する (*to bank*); a completely different verb is required. Nor can you say 会議(かいぎ)する; you have to say 会議(かいぎ)をする (*to have a meeting*). Most (but not all) nouns that can be turned into nominal verbs can also be used as the direct object of する.

勉強(べんきょう)をする、運動(うんどう)をする、料理(りょうり)をする
ドライブをする、ジョギングをする、スポーツをする

アクティビティー　5

レジャーをどのように過ごしますか。(*How do you spend your leisure time?*)

Here is how Japanese spend their free time. The activities are listed in decreasing order of popularity. Answer the questions that follow the table.

順位	女性	%*	男性	%
1	ショッピングをする	46.0	テレビを見る	49.0
2	旅行をする	45.9	寝る	34.8
3	手芸・編物をする	45.9	音楽を聞く	34.7
4	テレビを見る	41.1	旅行をする	32.7
5	読書をする	33.4	スポーツをする	30.3
6	友だちと話す	33.2	読書をする	27.8
7	音楽を聞く	30.8	釣りをする	24.8
8	映画を見る	30.2	映画を見る	24.3
9	レストランへ行く	23.4	マージャンをする	23.5
10	スポーツをする	20.6	パチンコをする	21.7

1. 女性に一番人気がある(*popular*) ことは何ですか。
2. 男性に一番人気があることは何ですか。
3. 女性と男性とどちらがスポーツをするのが好きですか。
4. 女性が7番目に好きなことは何ですか。
5. 男性が7番目に好きなことは何ですか。
6. 男性がして、女性がしないことは何ですか。
7. 女性がして、男性がしないことは何ですか。
8. アメリカ人があまりしないことは何ですか。

Make your own questions to ask your classmates.

順位 *rank* 女性 *women* 男性 *men* ～番目 is a counter for ordinal numbers (first, second, third, etc.)

に of 女性に means *among* in this context.

**Decimal point* is 点 in Japanese. Thus, 45.9% is read 四十五点九パーセント. 49.0 % is read 四十九点ゼロ (or 零) パーセント.

Vocabulary and Grammar 5B

Vocabulary and Oral Activities

Sports

Vocabulary: Sports

スポーツ		sports
試合	しあい	game
ジョギング		jogging
マラソン		marathon; long-distance running
野球	やきゅう	baseball
バスケットボール		basketball
バレーボール		volleyball
テニス		tennis
ゴルフ		golf
フットボール		football
サッカー		soccer
水泳	すいえい	swimming
ダイビング		diving
プール		(*swimming*) pool
ヨット		yacht
キャンピング		camping
エアロビクス		aerobics
サイクリング		bicycling

Review: 泳(およ)ぐ、ハイキング、山登(のぼ)り

アクティビティー 6

私(わたし)の好(す)きなスポーツ (*Sports I like*)

Describe your favorite sports to a classmate in Japanese. Substitute different sports and facilities or equipment for the underlined portions.

> 私(わたし)はテニスをするのが好(す)きです。テニスは小さいボールとラケットを使(つか)います。私(わたし)は野球(やきゅう)を見るのが好(す)きです。週末(しゅうまつ)はテレビで野球(やきゅう)を見ます。

Vocabulary: Skills

上手(な)	じょうず(な)	good at; skillful at
下手(な)	へた(な)	bad at; unskillful at
だめ(な)		no good
得意(な)	とくい(な)	good at and fond of something
苦手(な)	にがて(な)	bad at and dislike something
できる		to be able to do
できない		cannot do

アクティビティー 7

一人(ひとり)でしますか。(*Do you do it alone?*)

Tell what sports satisfy each of the following conditions.

1. 一人(ひとり)でします。
2. 二人(ふたり)でします。
3. 三人以上(いじょう)でします。
4. ボールを使(つか)います。
5. 外(そと) (*outdoors*) でします。
6. 海(うみ)でします。
7. オリンピックの種目(しゅもく) (*event*)です。
8. 冬(ふゆ)のスポーツです。
9. 危険(きけん)な (*dangerous*) スポーツです。

…人で *as…person/people*

…以上(いじょう) means …*or more.* Thus, 三人以上 means *three people or more.*
…以下(いか) means *less than*… 三人以下 means *three people or less* (that is, zero, one, two, or three people).

Grammar and Practice Activities

25. Describing Abilities

カワムラ：町田(まちだ)さんはピンポンが上手(じょうず)ですね。
町田(まちだ)：いいえ、そんなに上手じゃありませんが、大好きです。
カワムラ：一度一緒(いちどいっしょ)にしませんか。
町田：ええ、いいですね。

林(はやし)：町田(まちだ)さんは何か外国語(がいこくご)ができますか。
町田：ええ、フランス語(ご)がちょっとできます。
林：それはすごいですね。
町田：林(はやし)さんは。
林：わたしは外国語(がいこくご)がぜんぜんダメです。

Note the similarity between these expressions and those for stating likes and dislikes (**Grammar 10,** Chapter 2).

25.1 Here is how to express skills and abilities in Japanese.

A + は + B + が	上手(じょうず)	*A is good at B*
(person) (noun)	下手(へた)	*A is poor at B*
	得意(とくい) です（だ）	*A is good at and likes B*
	苦手(にがて)	*A is poor at and dislikes B*
	できます（できる）	*A can do B*

ブラウンさんはダンスが上手(じょうず)ですね。
Ms. Brown, you are good at dancing, aren't you?
歌(うた)が下手(へた)で、いつもこまる。
I am poor at singing, and that always gives me trouble.
ギブソンさんはスケートが得意(とくい)だ。
Ms. Gibson is quite a skater (lit., *is good at and likes skating*).
わたしはフランス語(ご)が苦手(にがて)だ。
I am poor at French (lit., *and dislike it*).

KAWAMURA: You are good at playing table tennis! MACHIDA: No, I'm not that good at it, but I love it. KAWAMURA: How about playing together sometime (lit., *once*)? MACHIDA: Yes, that would be good.

HAYASHI: Can you speak any foreign languages? MACHIDA: Yes, I can speak French a little bit. HAYASHI: That's great. MACHIDA: How about you? HAYASHI: I am totally bad at foreign languages.

チンさんは水泳(すいえい)ができますか。
Ms. Chin, can you swim (lit., *can you do swimming*)?

25.2 上手(じょうず) and 下手(へた) are na-adjectives. 得意(とくい) and 苦手(にがて) are na-adjectives that may also be used as nouns. When used as a noun 得意 means *special skill* or *specialty* and 苦手 means *weakness* or *weak point.*

得意(とくい)な外国語(がいこくご)はスペイン語(ご)です。
My best foreign language is Spanish. (lit., *The foreign language I'm good at and like is Spanish.*)

歌(うた)が上手(じょうず)な人はだれですか。
Who is (*a person who is*) *good at singing?*

料理(りょうり)が下手(へた)な人はたくさんいます。
There are many people who are bad cooks (lit., *poor at cooking*).

私(わたし)の得意(とくい)はオムレツです。(得意 used as noun)
My special dish is omelettes.

苦手(にがて)な課目(かもく)は数学(すうがく)です。
The class I am poor at (*and don't like*) *is math.*

魚料理(さかなりょうり)は苦手(にがて)です。(苦手 used as noun)
Cooking fish is my weak point.

25.3 できます (dictionary form できる) is a Class 2 verb meaning *can do, is possible* and conjugates as such.

兄(あに)は楽器(がっき)ができません。
My older brother cannot play (lit., *do*) *musical instruments.*

雨(あめ)が降(ふ)って、ハイキングができなかった。
It rained, and (*so*) *we couldn't go hiking.*

25.4 In these expressions notice that the direct object (B in the **Grammar 25.1** chart) is marked with the particle が, not を. This is an exception to the rule that direct object nouns and pronouns are marked with the particle を. You already studied two similar exceptions: the na-adjectives 好(す)き and 嫌(きら)い. In addition to the na-adjectives and verb (できます) in the chart, this rule also applies to the verb わかります (*to understand;* dictionary form わかる).

兄(あに)はドイツ語(ご)がわかります。
My older brother understands German.

その答(こた)え (*answer*) がわからなかった。
I didn't understand that answer.

アクティビティー 8

日本語が上手ですか。(*Are you good at Japanese?*)

Following the example, make complete sentences.

[例] (山口さん)(ダンス)(得意)→ 山口さんはダンスが得意です。

1. (山口さんの奥さん)(ボーリング)(上手)
2. (林さん)(バスケットボール)(下手)
3. (シュミットさん)(日本語)(上手ではない)
4. (佐野さん)(あみもの)(得意)
5. (カワムラさん)(フランス語)(苦手)
6. (ギブソンさん)(スキー)(得意)
7. (私)(料理)(できない)
8. (村山さん)(イタリア語)(わかる)

アクティビティー 9

ダンスはできません。(*I can't dance.*)

Make dialogues, following the example.

[例] (バレー／できる)(できない)→
—_____さんはバレーができますか。
—いいえ、できません。

1. (スポーツ／得意)(苦手)
2. (ロシア語／上手)(下手)
3. (バイオリン／上手)(まあまあ)
4. (ピンポン／できる)(できる)
5. (タガログ語／わかる)(わからない)

アクティビティー 10

バスの運転が上手ですか。(*Are you good at driving a bus?*)

Answer these questions truthfully.

1. 車(くるま)の運転(うんてん) (*driving*) が上手(じょうず)ですか。
2. どんな料理(りょうり)が一番得意(ばんとくい)ですか。
3. 日本語(ご)が上手(じょうず)ですか。
4. ご家族(かぞく) (*family*) は日本語(ご)ができますか。
5. どんなスポーツが上手(じょうず)ですか。
6. どんな楽器(がっき)が上手(じょうず)ですか。
7. 食べ物(もの)の中で何(なに)が一番(ばん)きらいですか。
8. 苦手(にがて)な食(た)べ物(もの)は何(なに)ですか。
9. どんな外国語(がいこくご)ができますか。
10. ショッピングが上手(じょうず)ですか。

アクティビティー 11

ダイアログ：野球(やきゅう)が上手(じょうず)ですね。 (*You are good at baseball.*)

カワムラ： 三村(みむら)さんは野球(やきゅう)が上手(じょうず)ですね。
三村(みむら)： いいえ、野球(やきゅう)は好(す)きですが、下手(へた)です。
カワムラ： そんなことありませんよ。
三村： いいえ、ぜんぜんダメですよ。

Selecting from the following sports, answer the questions.

Sports: バスケットボール、バレーボール、空手(からて)、テニス、ピンポン、ゴルフ、スキー、野球(やきゅう)、ソフトボール、サッカー

1. どのスポーツが好(す)きですか。
   (Choose as many as you like and rank them in order of preference.)
2. どのスポーツができますか。
   (Rank the sports you can play in order of your skill level.)

Now compare your answers with your classmates'.

1. みんな、どのスポーツが好(す)きですか。
2. みんなが上手(じょうず)なスポーツは何(なん)ですか。

KAWAMURA: You (lit., *Mr. Mimura*) sure are good at baseball. MIMURA: No, I like baseball, but I'm no good at it. KAWAMURA: That's not true. (lit., *No, there isn't such a case.*) MIMURA: Yes it is. (lit., *No, I am no good at all.*)

後楽園ドーム：野球は日本で一番人気(*popularity*)があります。

文化ノート

CULTURE NOTE • When You Are Praised

It is usually difficult for Japanese to say no, but there are a few situations where Japanese say no immediately. One of those situations is receiving praise. When praised, whether for one's skills, a possession, a family member, or another in-group person, a Japanese first denies the praise or mentions something negative. *No, I'm still learning, No, it's a cheap item, No, my son is not talented.* It is considered rude and unsophisticated to accept praise right away or to boast about one's own skills or talent (or that of an in-group member), even if that skill is self-evident. Predictably, the person making the compliment offers further praise, which is again denied. After two or three exchanges of this kind, the person being praised finally accepts the praise somewhat reluctantly. See **Language Functions and Situations** in this chapter for more examples of how to respond to compliments.

Vocabulary Library

More Sports Terms

投げる	なげる	to throw
受ける	うける	to catch (a ball)
打つ	うつ	to hit
ピンポン、卓球	たっきゅう	table tennis; Ping-Pong
プロ		professional
アマ		amateur
体操	たいそう	gymnastics
乗馬	じょうば	horseback riding
射撃	しゃげき	shooting
空手	からて	karate
柔道	じゅうどう	judo
剣道	けんどう	kendo (*Japanese fencing*)
相撲	すもう	sumo wrestling
陸上競技	りくじょうきょうぎ	track and field
選手	せんしゅ	athlete

Loanwords: ウエイト・リフティング、ジム、バドミントン、ボート、ボーリング、ボクシング、ラケット、ラグビー、ランニング、ロッククライミング、レスリング

文化ノート

CULTURE NOTE • 日本のスポーツ: Japanese Sports

Sumo, a form of wrestling, is considered the Japanese national sport. It started some 2,000 years ago as a religious ritual and is still surrounded in ceremony today. Two sumo wrestlers compete in a dirt ring 4.55 meters in diameter. The object is to force one's opponent out of the ring or to force any part of his body but the soles of his feet to touch the ground. Professional sumo tournaments, each lasting fifteen days, are held six times a year and are televised nationwide. Top-ranked sumo wrestlers attain hero status, including a few non-Japanese who have excelled as professional sumo wrestlers over the years.

Most Japanese train in at least one martial art, most commonly judo or kendo, during their secondary schooling. Judo is now practiced worldwide and is an Olympic event.

Karate originated in China and was further developed in Okinawa. It has become popular in many countries. While judo focuses on balance, karate relies on kicks, thrusts, and strikes to best one's opponent.

Kendo, swordfighting with bamboo staffs, developed from the swordmanship of samurai. Of the various martial arts, judo and kendo in particular place emphasis on moral and spiritual training as well as physical training.

Although interest in soccer and football has been growing, the most popular team sport by far is baseball. Japanese professional baseball consists of

すもうは日本の国技(こくぎ) (*national sport*) です。武蔵丸(むさしまる)（右）はハワイの出身(しゅっしん)です。

twelve teams divided into two leagues, the Pacific League and the Central League. Since the teams are owned by corporations, they sport such names as the Nippon Ham Fighters, Chunichi Dragons, Yakult Swallows, and Yomiuri Giants. Baseball is popular as an amateur sport, too, and the annual nationwide competition among high school baseball teams commands the nation's attention for several days when the playoffs are televised.

Japanese participate in and avidly follow many other sports as well, including golf, tennis, marathon running, rugby, and skiing.

26. Nominalizers: こと and の

高田(たかだ)：日本語(ご)は得意(とくい)ですか。
カワムラ：話(はな)すのは下手(へた)ですが、好(す)きです。
高田：書(か)くのはどうですか。
カワムラ：むずかしいです。でも、漢字(かんじ)を書(か)くのはおもしろいです。

TAKADA: Are you good at Japanese? KAWAMURA: I am poor at speaking it, but I like it. TAKADA: How about writing it? KAWAMURA: It's difficult, but it's fun to write Chinese characters.

A：高田(たかだ)さんはいますか。
B：ええ。でも、高田(たかだ)さんと今(いま)話(はな)すことは無理(むり)です。
A：無理(むり)なことはわかりますが、どうか…
B：ダメです。高田(たかだ)さんは今(いま)忙(いそが)しいんです。

Nominalizers are grammatical elements that change verbs, adjectives, etc., into nouns or noun phrases. In English, for instance, by adding *-ing* to the end of a verb, you form the gerund or noun form. (For example: *see* → *seeing* in *Seeing is believing.*) Thus, *-ing* can be considered a nominalizer in English.

26.1 Generally speaking, only nouns, pronouns, noun phrases, and noun-like elements can be in the subject and object positions of a sentence. When you would like to use verbs and adjectives in those positions, you must change them into noun phrases. In Japanese, こと and の are used to nominalize verbs and adjectives (change them into noun phrases). These two elements are called *nominalizers.* Add one of them to the *plain* form of a verb or adjective to form a noun phrase.

> *plain* form of verb, i-adjective, or na-adjective ＋ こと or の

Here are some examples of each.

1. Plain form of verb ＋ nominalizer

読むこと	読むの
読まないこと	読まないの
読んだこと	読んだの

2. Plain form of i-adjective ＋ nominalizer

大きいこと	大きいの
大きくなかったこと	大きくなかったの

3. Plain form of na-adjective ＋ nominalizer

きれいなこと	きれいなの
きれいではないこと	きれいではないの
(きれいじゃないこと)	(きれいじゃないの)
きれいだったこと	きれいだったの
きれいではなかったこと	きれいではなかったの
(きれいじゃなかったこと)	(きれいじゃなかったの)

A: Is Mr. Takada in? B: Yes, but it's impossible for you to talk to him now. A: I know it's impossible, but please… (let me see him). B: No way. Mr. Takada is busy now.

You can use these noun phrases in the subject or object position of a sentence.

日本語を読むのはやさしいです。
Reading Japanese is easy.

SFを読むことが好きです。
I like reading science fiction.

SF（エスエフ）*science fiction*

その町がきれいなことは有名です。

その町がきれいなのは有名です。
It's well known that that town is pretty. (lit., *The fact that that town is pretty is famous.*)

Note that the plain, nonpast of a na-adjective takes its na-form before こと and の, just as it does before any other noun.

26.2 Although both こと and の can be used to nominalize verbs, adjectives, and sentences, there is some difference in nuance between the two. の is used in sentences that express something subjective (i.e., something directly related to the speaker or something perceived or experienced by the speaker). こと is used when talking more generally or objectively. For example,

日本語を話すのはやさしいです。

日本語を話すことはやさしいです。
Speaking Japanese is easy.

The implication of the first sentence is that the speaker is basing the observation on personal experience. The second sentence does not imply a personal opinion, but rather simply makes a generally known observation that Japanese is easy to speak (compared, say, to writing it). For this reason, こと sometimes sounds a bit formal or bookish. Note the difference in meaning between these two sentences.

ブラウンさんが日本語で話すのを聞いた。
I heard Ms. Brown speak in Japanese.

ブラウンさんがいつも日本語で話すことを聞いて、感心した。
I heard that Ms. Brown always speaks in Japanese, and I was impressed.

In many contexts, you can use either こと or の with little difference in meaning other than the implication just explained. In some contexts, however, only こと or の can be used. For instance

わたしは父がお酒を飲むのを見ていた。
I was watching my father drink sake.

In this sentence, の must be used, because the statement involves the speaker's direct perception.

見ることは信じることだ。
Seeing is believing.

This sentence expresses a general fact, so only こと can be used.

アクティビティー 12

この練習(れんしゅう)をするのはやさしいです。(*It's easy to do this exercise.*)

Complete each sentence, choosing an appropriate phrase from the right-hand column. (More than one alternative is possible.)

1. 日本語(ご)を話(はな)すのは
2. 料理(りょうり)をすることは
3. テニスをすることは
4. 音楽(おんがく)を聞(き)くことは
5. 山田(やまだ)さんが来(き)たのは

a. おもしろい
b. やさしい
c. むずかしい
d. おかしい (*strange*)
e. 体(からだ)にいい (*good for one's health*)

アクティビティー 13

テニスをするのはたのしいです。(*Playing tennis is fun.*)

Following the example, complete each sentence.

[例] (ブラウンさん) (料理(りょうり)を作(つく)ります) (好(す)き)
→ ブラウンさんは料理(りょうり)を作(つく)るのが好(す)きです。

1. (カワムラさん) (バスケットボールをします) (好(す)き)
2. (林(はやし)さん) (運動(うんどう)をします) (きらい)
3. (ギブソンさん) (日本語(ご)を話(はな)します) (上手(じょうず))
4. (チンさん) (歌(うた)を歌(うた)います) (きらい)
5. (町田(まちだ)さん) (ピアノをひきます) (得意(とくい))
6. (三村(みむら)さん) (英語(えいご)を書(か)きます) (苦手(にがて))

アクティビティー 14

わたしはゴルフをするのがきらいです。(*I dislike playing golf.*)

Complete the following sentences using こと or の.

1. わたしは…が好(す)きです。
2. …はむずかしいです。
3. …はやさしいです。
4. …はおもしろいです。
5. わたしは…が得意(とくい)です。
6. わたしは…が苦手(にがて)です。
7. わたしの日本語(ご)の先生は…が上手(じょうず)です。
8. わたしは…が下手(へた)です。
9. …はつまらないです。
10. わたしは…がきらいです。

27. More Uses of the Particle も

ブラウン：山本(やまもと)さん、週末(しゅうまつ)はどうでしたか。
山本(やまもと)：土曜日(どようび)も日曜日(にちようび)も仕事(しごと)がありました。
ブラウン：それはたいへんでしたね。こんどの休(やす)みはいつですか。
山本：今週(こんしゅう)も来週(らいしゅう)も休(やす)みはありません。
ブラウン：本当(ほんとう)ですか。2週間(しゅうかん)も休(やす)みがないんですか。

カワムラ：山口(やまぐち)さんの趣味(しゅみ)は何(なん)ですか。
山口(やまぐち)：写真(しゃしん)を撮(と)ることです。
カワムラ：カメラは何台(なんだい)ありますか。
山口：今(いま)は5台(だい)です。
カワムラ：へえ、5台(だい)もあるんですか。

台 is a counter for cameras

27.1 A も B も means *both A and B* or *A as well as B* in affirmative sentences, and *(n)either A (n)or B* in negative sentences.

カワムラさんもブラウンさんもアメリカ人です。
Both Mr. Kawamura and Ms. Brown are American.
クラシック音楽(おんがく)もロックもあまり好(す)きじゃありません。
I don't like either classical music or rock music very much.
I like neither classical music nor rock music very much.
ここは春(はる)も夏(なつ)も秋(あき)も雨(あめ)がたくさん降(ふ)る。
Here it rains a lot in spring, summer, and fall as well.

27.2 Numeral + counter + も means *as much as* or *as many as* the stated quantity; in other words, the number is higher than the speaker expected or more than usual. When this form is used in negative sentences, the implication is the opposite: the number is smaller than expected, *not even the stated quantity.*

うちから駅(えき)まで2時間(じかん)もかかりました。
It took as much as two hours to get from home to the station.
先週(せんしゅう)のパーティーには300人も来(き)た。
As many as 300 people came to last week's party.

BROWN: Ms. Yamamoto, how was your weekend? YAMAMOTO: I had to work on both Saturday and Sunday. BROWN: That must have been awful. When is your next day off? YAMAMOTO: I don't have a day off this week or next week. BROWN: Really? You don't have a day off for two whole weeks?

KAWAMURA: What is your (lit., *Mr. Yamaguchi's*) hobby? YAMAGUCHI: My hobby is taking photos. KAWAMURA: How many cameras do you have? YAMAGUCHI: Now I have five. KAWAMURA: Wow, you have *five*?

今日のクラスは学生が5人もいない。

There aren't even five students in today's class.

わたしは学校(がっこう)を1日も休(やす)みませんでした。

I didn't miss even one day of school.

アクティビティー　15

わたしはスキーもテニスも好(す)きです。(*I like both skiing and tennis.*)

Following the example, complete these sentences using …も…も.

[例]　カワムラさんはビールが好(す)きです。
　　カワムラさんはワインが好(す)きです。→
　　カワムラさんはビールもワインも好(す)きです。

1. チンさんはパーティーに来(き)ました。
   林(はやし)さんはパーティーに来(き)ました。
2. 机(つくえ)の上にペンがあります。
   机(つくえ)の上にえんぴつがあります。
3. 林(はやし)さんはブロッコリーがきらいです。
   林(はやし)さんはアスパラガスがきらいです。
4. 17日、雨(あめ)が降(ふ)りました。
   18日、雨(あめ)が降(ふ)りました。
5. 三村(みむら)さんはテニスが上手(じょうず)です。
   三村(みむら)さんはピンポンが上手(じょうず)です。

✸ アクティビティー　16

どのぐらいしましたか。(*How long did he do it?*)

Following the example, make a dialogue for each exercise item.

[例]　日本語(ご)を勉強(べんきょう)する／5年 →
　　—日本語(ご)を何(なん)年勉強(べんきょう)したんですか。
　　—5年です。
　　—5年も勉強(べんきょう)したんですか。

1. 寝(ね)る／12時間(じかん)
2. 旅行(りょこう)する／3週間(しゅうかん)
3. ハンバーガーを食(た)べる／6つ
4. 本を読(よ)む／3冊(さつ)
5. ワインを飲(の)む／グラスで7杯(はい)
6. ボーイフレンドがいる／3人

Review counters in Chapter 2. 冊 is a *counter for books,* 杯 is a *counter for glassfuls.*

✸ アクティビティー 17

ダイアログ：見るのは好(す)きです。(*I like watching it.*)

カワムラ：林(はやし)さんはフットボールが好(す)きですか。
林(はやし)：見るのは好(す)きですが、するのはちょっと…
カワムラさんは。
カワムラ：わたしは見るのも、するのも大好(だいす)きです。
林：上手(じょうず)ですか。
カワムラ：まあまあです。

28. Potential Form of Verbs

ブラウン：林(はやし)さん、明日(あした)、学校へ早(はや)く来(く)ることができますか。
林：何時ですか。
ブラウン：6時です。
林：すみませんが、そんなに*早(はや)く起(お)きることはできません。

カワムラ：町田(まちだ)さんはフランス語ができますか。
町田(まちだ)：話(はな)せませんが、ちょっと読めます。
カワムラ：書(か)けますか。
町田：ええ、やさしい文(ぶん)は書けます。

ブラウン：町田(まちだ)さんは、一人で着物(きもの)を着(き)られますか。
町田(まちだ)：いいえ、着物(きもの)を着(き)るのはたいへんです。一人ではちょっと…
ブラウン：じゃあ、どうするんですか。
町田：近(ちか)くの美容院(びよういん)に行きます。

KAWAMURA: Do you (lit., *Mr. Hayashi*) like football? HAYASHI: I like watching it, but I don't like playing it. (lit., *I like watching it, but playing it is a bit…*) How about you? KAWAMURA: I like both watching and playing it very much. HAYASHI: Are you good at it? KAWAMURA: I'm so-so.

BROWN: Mr. Hayashi, can you come to school early tomorrow? HAYASHI: At what time? BROWN: Six o'clock. HAYASHI: I am sorry, but I cannot get up that early.

KAWAMURA: Do you know French? (lit., *Can you, Ms. Machida, do French?*) MACHIDA: I can't speak it, but I can read a little. KAWAMURA: Can you write it? MACHIDA: Yes, I can write easy sentences.

BROWN: Ms. Machida, can you put on a kimono by yourself? MACHIDA: No. It's difficult to put on a kimono. To do that myself is… (impossible). BROWN: Then, what do you do? MACHIDA: I go to a nearby beauty salon.

*そんな, one of the **ko-so-a-do** words, means *that kind of*. そんなに means *like that, that much.*

Grammatical constructions expressing abilities, such as *I can swim* and *he is able to come tomorrow* are called *potential expressions* or *potentials.*

28.1 In Japanese, there are two different ways to express abilities or potential. Both correspond to the English auxiliary verb *can.*

28.2 The first potential structure is a combination of the dictionary form (nonpast, plain, affirmative form) of a verb and ことができる.

dictionary form of verb + ことができる

Note that in this sentence structure you cannot use の in place of こと.

できる is a Class 2 verb, used here to mean *can* or *is able to do.* The entire structure literally means *the doing of (verb) is possible.*

山口(やまぐち)さんは2キロ泳(およ)ぐことができる。
Mr. Yamaguchi can swim two kilometers.
明日(あした)、6時に来(く)ることができますか。
Can you come at 6:00 tomorrow?
昨日(きのう)、ブラウンさんに会(あ)うことができましたか。
Were you able to see Ms. Brown yesterday?

As you can see from these examples, tense, negativity, and formality are expressed in the conjugation of できる; the dictionary form of the preceding verb remains unchanged.

28.3 You can also express abilities and possibilities by conjugating a verb. The conjugated verb forms expressing abilities and possibilities are called the potential forms of a verb and are formed in the following way.

	CLASS 1	CLASS 2	CLASS 3
Rules	root + e-column **hiragana** corresponding to the dictionary ending + る	root + られる	irregular
Examples	書(か)く→書(か)ける 読(よ)む→読(よ)める 会(あ)う→会(あ)える 話(はな)す→話(はな)せる 待(ま)つ→待(ま)てる	食(た)べる→食(た)べられる 見(み)る →見(み)られる 着(き)る →着(き)られる	来(く)る→来(こ)られる する→できる

These potential forms all end in ～る (the ending of the dictionary form of Class 2 verbs), and indeed, they conjugate like Class 2 verbs, whether they are derived from Class 1, 2, or 3 verbs. For example,

CLASS 1	CLASS 2	CLASS 3	CLASS 3
書(か)ける	食(た)べられる	できる	来(こ)られる
書けない	食べられない	できない	来られない
書けた	食べられた	できた	来られた
書けます	食べられます	できます	来られます

u-column	→ e-column
く	→ け
む	→ め
う	→ え
す	→ せ
つ	→ て

漢字(かんじ)が上手(じょうず)に書(か)けます。
*I can write **kanji** well.*
父(ちち)はすしが食べられない。
My father cannot eat sushi.
わたしの子(こ)どもはまだ話(はな)せません。
My child still cannot speak.
ピンポンができますか。
Can you play table tennis?
山口さんは昨日(きのう)来(こ)られなかった。
Mr. Yamaguchi couldn't come yesterday.

In these potential sentences, direct objects are marked with が. In sentences that use the potential form of verbs, the direct object can be marked with either が or を. Therefore

わたしは漢字(かんじ)が上手(じょうず)に書けます。
わたしは漢字を上手に書けます。

are both grammatically correct. Although the meaning is equivalent whether you use が or を, Japanese speakers tend to prefer が in most contexts.

Although some grammarians consider the root ＋られる to be the only correct potential form of Class 2 verbs, many Japanese speakers use a shortened form: the root ＋れる. In fact, nowadays the shortened form is more widely used than the longer form, especially among the younger generation, in informal conversation and writing. For now, learn to produce the traditionally "correct" form and to understand the shortened form.

	-られる FORM (LONG FORM)	-れる FORM (SHORT FORM)
食(た)べる	食(た)べられる	食(た)べれる
見(み)る	見(み)られる	見(み)れる
着(き)る	着(き)られる	着(き)れる

For speakers who use these shortened forms, there is no difference other than accent pattern between the potential forms of 切る (*to cut*; Class 1 verb) and 着る (*to wear*; Class 2 verb).

アクティビティー　18

ダイアログ：泳げますか。(*Can you swim?*)

カワムラ：チンさんの特技は何ですか。
チン：水泳です。
カワムラ：どれぐらい泳げますか。
チン：そうですね。10キロぐらい泳げます。
カワムラ：本当ですか。それはすごいですね。

Answer these questions.

1. 将棋か碁ができますか。
2. マージャンをすることができますか。
3. 上手に写真が撮れますか。
4. 手芸ができますか。
5. 絵が上手に描けますか。
6. 編物ができますか。
7. 何か楽器が弾けますか。
8. 日本料理が作れますか。
9. 日本語が上手に話せますか。
10. 漢字が上手に書けますか。

See the Language Note on p. 333 for an explanation of this use of particle か.

アクティビティー　19

ここで手紙を出すことができます。(*You can mail letters here.*)

Following the example, complete each sentence using ことができます。

[例]　(土曜日に来られます) → 土曜日に来ることができます。

1. 午後図書館へ行けます。
2. 今日の午後、林さんに会えます。
3. 10キロ走れます。
4. 駅まで歩けます。
5. ここで泳げますか。
6. 今、ブラウンさんと話せます。
7. 母に電話できます。

KAWAMURA: What is your special talent?　CHIN: It's swimming.　KAWAMURA: How far can you swim? CHIN: Let me see. I can swim about ten kilometers.　KAWAMURA: Really? That's terrific!

✷ アクティビティー 20

今日来られません。(*He can't come today.*)

Make dialogues using the potential form of each verb.

Useful word: 走る *to run*

[例] (play the guitar) →

—チンさんはギターが弾けますか。

—はい、弾けます。(いいえ、弾けません。)

1. (play tennis)
2. (sing Japanese songs)
3. (run fast)
4. (draw pictures well)
5. (go to a concert with me)
6. (ski)
7. (watch TV with me this afternoon)
8. (read books together with me)
9. (swim in the ocean)
10. (come to my home)

アクティビティー 21

わたしはスペイン語を話せます。(*I can speak Spanish.*)

Answer the following questions.

1. あなたはピアノが弾けますか。
2. あなたは上手に写真が撮れますか。
3. あなたは自転車 (*bicycle*) に乗れますか。
4. あなたはバレーボールができますか。
5. あなたはフランス語で歌えますか。
6. あなたは1キロ泳げますか。
7. あなたは10キロ走れますか。
8. あなたの家族は日本語が話せますか。
9. 明日、映画へ行けますか。
10. 土曜日、大学へ来られますか。

✷ アクティビティー 22

インタビュー：できますか。(*Can you do it?*)

Ask one of the following questions of ten students in your class. Then report to the class how many students responded yes and how many said no.

1. 日本語(ご)の歌(うた)が 歌(うた)えますか。
2. 100メートル泳(およ)げますか。
3. スケートができますか。
4. 刺繍(ししゅう) (*embroidery*) ができますか。
5. スペイン語が話(はな)せますか。
6. 自転車(じてんしゃ) (*bicycle*) に乗(の)れますか。
7. テニスができますか。
8. 柔道(じゅうどう)か 空手(からて)ができますか。

言語ノート

か *or*

The particle か, used between two nouns, means *or.*

将棋(しょうぎ)か碁(ご)ができますか。
Can you play ***shogi*** *or* ***go?***
ジュースかコーラを飲みませんか。
Would you like some (lit., *won't you drink*) *juice or cola?*
ブラウンさんかカワムラさんが行きます。
Ms. Brown or Mr. Kawamura will go.

You may add another か after the second noun with no change in meaning.

ブラウンさんかカワムラさんかが行きます。
柔道(じゅうどう)か空手(からて)ができますか。
Can you do judo or karate?
はい、柔道(じゅうどう)ができます。
Yes, I can do judo.
はい、両方(りょうほう)できます。
Yes, I can do both.
はい、どちらもできます。
Yes, I can do both.
いいえ、どちらもできません。
No, I can't do either.

Both 両方(りょうほう) and どちらも mean *both* (or *either*) of *two.*

Vocabulary and Grammar 5C

Vocabulary and Oral Activities

Family

Vocabulary: Family

家族	かぞく	family
両親	りょうしん	parents
父	ちち	father
母	はは	mother
子供	こども	child; children
息子	むすこ	son
娘	むすめ	daughter
兄弟	きょうだい	siblings
兄	あに	older brother
姉	あね	older sister
弟	おとうと	younger brother
妹	いもうと	younger sister
祖父	そふ	grandfather
祖母	そぼ	grandmother
孫	まご	grandchild; grandchildren
夫婦	ふうふ	husband and wife
夫	おっと	husband
主人*	しゅじん	husband
妻	つま	wife
家内*	かない	wife
おじ		uncle
おば		aunt
親戚	しんせき	relative

Important note: These words are used to refer only to your own family members and relatives. You will study another set of family terms for referring to other people's family members and relatives later in this chapter.

*Although in common use, these words are spurned by some Japanese for their sexist implications. 主人 literally means *master* and 家内, *one inside the home.*

アクティビティー 23

ダイアログ：父です。(*This is my father.*)

町田さんとブラウンさんが写真を見ています。

ブラウン：これは私の家族の写真です。

町田：ブラウンさんの右の男の方はどなたですか。

ブラウン：父です。

町田：この女の子はだれですか。

ブラウン：妹です。

Note the use of the polite 方 and どなた to refer to an older person in contrast to the neutral 子 and だれ for a child.

Practice the dialogue, substituting the following for the underlined parts.

1. ブラウンさんの左の女の方　　母
   水玉 (*polka-dot*) のブラウスの女の方　　姉
2. ブラウンさんの後ろの男の方　　兄
   ストライプ (*stripes*) のシャツの男の子　　弟
3. 白いブラウスの女の方　　祖母
   サングラスの男の方　　祖父

Ms. Machida and Ms. Brown are looking at a photo BROWN: This is a photograph of my family. MACHIDA: Who is the man on your (lit., *Ms. Brown's*) right? BROWN: My father. MACHIDA: Who is this girl? BROWN: My younger sister.

Vocabulary: People

男	おとこ	male
女	おんな	female
人	ひと	person
方	かた	person (*polite*)
子*	こ	child
男の子	おとこのこ	boy
女の子	おんなのこ	girl

Note: While grammatically correct, referring to people as その男(おとこ) or その女(おんな) is rude. You should say その男(おとこ)の人、あの女(おんな)の人 or, more politely, その男(おとこ)の方(かた)、あの女(おんな)の方(かた)、女性(じょせい)、and 男性(だんせい) are also increasingly common, although they are somewhat more formal.

言語ノート

Words Expressing Respect and Politeness

Japanese has a wide range of expressions and structures to convey different levels of speakers' or writers' feeling of respect and politeness. (These expressions and structures are generally called honorifics (敬語(けいご)), which will be introduced gradually, beginning here. Let's take, for example, words meaning *person, people.* In a neutral situation, 人(ひと) is used. To show respect, 方(かた) is used.

The prefixes お or 御(ご) are often added to a word to express respect or politeness. For instance, お年寄(としより) is the honorific counterpart of 年寄 (*old person*). 御趣味(ごしゅみ) is the honorific counterpart of 趣味 (*hobbies*), and it is used to refer to the hobbies of socially superior people. However, you cannot arbitrarily attach お and 御 to any Japanese word. You need to learn the customary usages for each word.

アクティビティー 24

私(わたし)は林(はやし)正男(まさお)です。(*I am Masao Hayashi.*)

Masao Hayashi is describing his family. Are his statements accurate? Correct any that are wrong.

---

*子(こ) and 子供(こども) both mean *child* or *children*. 子(こ) must be used with modifiers—for example, その子(こ)、うちの子(こ)、男(おとこ)の子(こ)—but 子供 can be used alone as well as with modifiers.

1. 林(はやし) 俊男(としお)は 私(わたし)の父(ちち)です。
2. 林(はやし) やすとは 私(わたし)の 弟(おとうと)です。
3. 林(はやし) すみ子は 私(わたし)の姉(あね)です。
4. 林(はやし) くみ子(こ)は 私(わたし)の母(はは)です。
5. 林太郎(はやしたろう)は 私(わたし)の祖母(そぼ)です。
6. 林(はやし) よし子は 私(わたし)のおばです。
7. 林(はやし) はなは 私(わたし)のおじです。

Now look at Masao Hayashi's family from another perspective, as your own family.

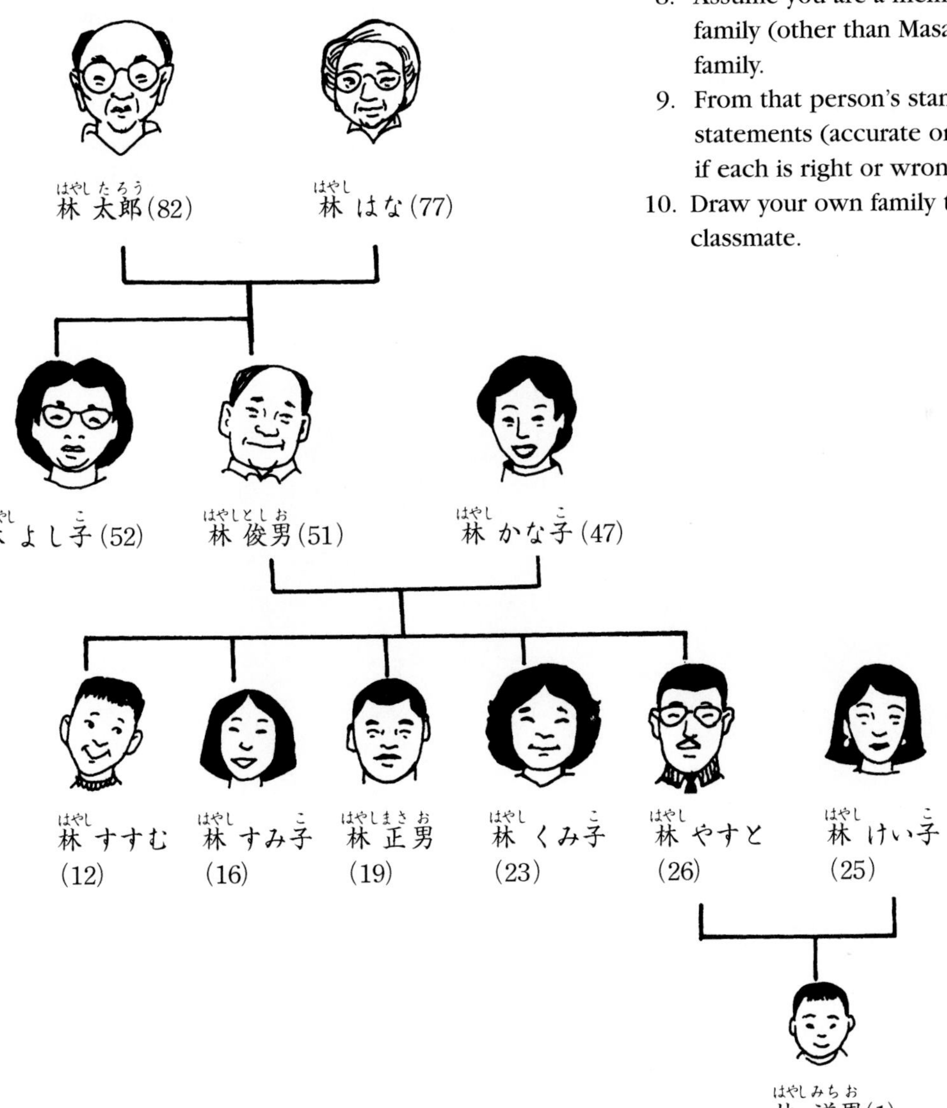

8. Assume you are a member of the Hayashi family (other than Masao). Describe your family.
9. From that person's standpoint, make five statements (accurate or not). Ask a classmate if each is right or wrong.
10. Draw your own family tree. Explain it to a classmate.

CULTURE NOTE • The Japanese Family

Unlike the prewar years, when families were large and several generations lived under one roof, the average Japanese household today consists of a single nuclear family—two parents with one or two children. There is strong social pressure to marry by age thirty if not earlier. The typical couple has their first child within one to three years of marriage, whereupon the wife is expected to quit her job to take care of the child (unless she already quit her job to get married).

Women are also in charge of running the home—managing the family budget, the children's education, and the family's social schedule—while husbands are occupied with their jobs, often long commutes, and after-hours business socializing. As more and more women enter the workforce, these gender-based social roles have begun to change, especially among the younger generation. But married women, even those who have part-time or full-time jobs, still bear the greatest responsibility for managing the household, even after the children have left the nest.

As women have gained more economic independence through increased job opportunities, the divorce rate has risen. The number of single-parent families is also increasing.

Family life in Japan usually revolves around the children, and their education is the central focus of their parents. Even if the father is transferred to a different city or country, the rest of the family may stay behind, for years, so the children can complete their education without disruption. While some Japanese lament the dissolution of the extended and even nuclear family in Japan, blaming it on Western influence, others welcome the options offered by more than one socially acceptable lifestyle. Despite the changes, the family (not the individual) is still seen as the vital social unit in modern Japan.

家族(かぞく)みんなでお茶(ちゃ)の時間(じかん)です。

Vocabulary: Other People's Families 

御家族	ごかぞく	family
御両親	ごりょうしん	parents
お父さん	おとうさん	father
お母さん	おかあさん	mother
お子さん	おこさん	child; children
息子さん	むすこさん	son
娘さん	むすめさん	daughter
お嬢さん	おじょうさん	daughter
御兄弟	ごきょうだい	siblings
お兄さん	おにいさん	older brother
お姉さん	おねえさん	older sister
弟さん	おとうとさん	younger brother
妹さん	いもうとさん	younger sister
おじいさん		grandfather
おばあさん		grandmother
お孫さん	おまごさん	grandchild; grandchildren
御夫婦	ごふうふ	husband and wife
御主人	ごしゅじん	husband
奥さん	おくさん	wife
おじさん		uncle
おばさん		aunt
御親戚	ごしんせき	relative

Important note: These terms are used when referring to someone else's family members or relatives. These words are respectful in contrast to the humble terms for your own family; be careful not to confuse the two sets of terms.

言語ノート

My Father, Your Father

In Japanese, there are at least two words for identifying each family member or relative, one word for identifying your own family member or relative and another for identifying someone else's. For exmple, 父(ちち) refers to the speaker's own father, and お父(とう)さん refers to someone else's father. (You will study some exceptions later.) The former is humble, while the latter is respectful. (Did you recognize the honorific prefix お and honorific suffix さん?) You would never call someone else's father 父(ちち), so it is redundant to say わたしの父 (*my father*). Similarly, when asking someone about his or her father, just use お父さん; in that context it would mean *your father*. These two sets of terms for family members reflect the careful distinction between in-group and out-group in Japanese language and society.

✸ アクティビティー 25

ギブソンさんのお父さんは51歳です。(*Ms. Gibson's father is 51 years old.*)

Now Masao Hayashi is describing Heather Gibson's family. Are the following statements true or false?

1. ギブソンさんのお父さんは49歳です。
2. ギブソンさんのお母さんの名前はマリアンです。
3. ギブソンさんのお兄さんは28歳です。
4. ギブソンさんのお姉さんはコンピュータ・プログラマーです。
5. ギブソンさんのおじいさんは70歳です。
6. ギブソンさんのおばあさんの名前はジュリーです。
7. ギブソンさんの妹さんは20歳です。

モーリス(72)

キャサリン(70)

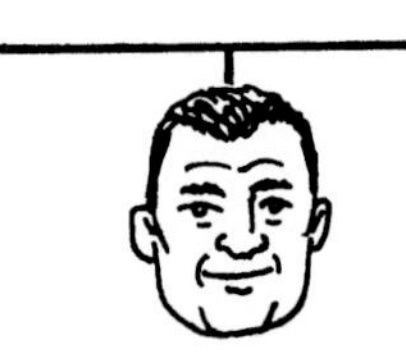

ジョン(51)
エンジニア

マリアン(49)
インテリア・デザイナー

ジュリー
(18)
学生

ヘザー
(20)
学生

ジーン
(28)
コンピュータ・プログラマー

ロジャー
(30)
メカニック

Now try some other family descriptions.

1. Describe the Gibson family, using a family member other than Heather as a point of comparison.

[例] ジョン・ギブソンさんの奥さんの名前はマリアンです。
ジョン・ギブソンさんにはお子さんが四人います。

2. Now assume you are that person and from that person's standpoint, make five statements (accurate or not) about your family. Ask a classmate if each statement is true or false.

Vocabulary Library

More Family Terms

義理の(母)*	ぎりの(はは)	(mother)-in-law
養子	ようし	adopted child
独身	どくしん	single (*not married*) person

HUMBLE FORM		RESPECTFUL FORM		
長男	ちょうなん	御長男	ごちょうなん	oldest son
長女	ちょうじょ	御長女	ごちょうじょ	oldest daughter
甥	おい	おいごさん		nephew
姪	めい	めいごさん		niece
いとこ		おいとこさん		cousin

アクティビティー 26

お姉さんの趣味は何ですか。(*What are your older sister's hobbies?*)

This chart summarizes your family's hobbies and interests. Work with a partner, and answer your classmate's questions about each family member.

[例] —お姉さんの趣味は何ですか。
—姉の趣味は音楽です。ピアノが得意です。

家族	趣味	注 (*Note*)
父	仕事	土曜日、日曜日も働く
母	生花	園芸が好き
兄	音楽を聞く	クラシック音楽が大好き
姉	音楽	ピアノが得意
わたし	読書	いつもフランス語の本を読む
弟	テレビを見る	12時までテレビを見る
妹	スポーツ	空手が好き

*Replace the parenthetical family term with its respectful alternate to refer respectfully to someone else's in-law. Thus, 義理のお母さん (*your/his*) *mother-in-law.*

Grammar and Practice Activities

29. The Te-Form of Verbs + います

A：すみません。高田さんはいますか。
B：ええ、でも、電話をしています。
A：そうですか。じゃ、ここで待ちます。
B：ブラウンさんも高田さんを待っていますよ。

A：あの人はいつもすてきな服を着ていますね。
B：今日はデザイナーズ・ブランドを着ていますよ。
A：ええ。いいドレスですよね。
B：あのドレスは駅の前のブティックで売っていましたよ。

29.1 The te-form of a verb + the auxiliary verb います (いる) can be used to express these two meanings.

1. A continuing action at a certain point in time (like the English progressive tense: *I am reading, He was jogging, They will be eating,* etc.)
2. A state or condition that was created by a previous action or event and that is still maintained at a certain point in time.

Whether this construction has the first or second meaning depends on the nature of the verb being used.

29.2 If the verb indicates an action that can continue once started, such as 食べる or 話す, it has the first meaning. Thus, 食べている = *I am eating*. Other verbs of this kind are 飲む, 歩く, 走る, 歌う, 泳ぐ, 書く, 見る, 使う, 作る, 休む, 勉強する, 会う. Typically, they are actions that could theoretically be continued indefinitely.

山口さんはうちでビールを飲んでいた。
Mr. Yamaguchi was drinking beer at home.

Auxiliary verbs are used with main verbs to express a variety of meanings, such as tense. The following verbs cannot be used with the auxiliary verb います: ある *to exist,* いる *to exist,* いる *to need,* できる *can.* While the *can do* meaning of できる does not allow ～ている, the combination できている does occur with the meaning of *is finished.*

A: Excuse me. Is Mr. Takada in? B: Yes, but he is on the phone. A: I see. Then, I will wait here. B: Ms. Brown is also waiting for him, you know.

A: She always wears nice clothes. B: She's wearing a designer brand today. A: Yes. It's really a fine dress. B: They sell that dress at the boutique in front of the station, you know.

学生が先生と話している。
A student is speaking with the teacher.
母は今、テニスをしています。
My mother is playing tennis now.

29.3 When the verb indicates an action that is noncontinuous, such as 知る (*to come to know*) or 晴れる (*to clear up*), it has the second meaning. Thus, 知っている = I know (that is, *I came to know and I am still in that state*). Other verbs of this type include 死ぬ, 忘れる, 立つ, 座る, 起きる, 言う, 乗る, 着く, 寝る.

あの人を知っていますか。
Do you know that person?
クラスは始まっています。
The class has already started. or *The class is in progress. (That is, the class started and is still in that state.)*
母は起きていた。
My mother was up. (That is, she got up and was still up.)
今日、空は晴れています。
The sky's clear today. (That is, the sky cleared up, and it's still in that state.)

The affirmative answer to this question is はい、知っています *Yes, I know him.* The negative answer is いいえ、知りません *No, I don't know him.*

When such movement verbs as 行く (*to go*), 来る (*to come*), 帰る (*to return*), 入る (*to enter*), and 出る (*to go out*) appear in this construction, the second meaning is expressed.

～ています is often shortened to ～てます in conversations. (That is, い is dropped.)

ギブソンさんが来ています。
Ms. Gibson is here (she came and is still here now).
父はトイレに入っている。
My father is in the bathroom (he entered the bathroom and is still there).

29.4 In some cases, either meaning (1) or (2) is possible, as shown in the following two examples. Verbs in this category include 着る, 取る, and おぼえる.

カーティスさんはセーターを着ています。
Mr. Curtis is putting on a sweater. (1)
Mr. Curtis is wearing a sweater. (That is, he put it on, and it's still on.) (2)
その学生は日本語のたんごをおぼえています。
Those students are memorizing Japanese words (now). (1)
Those students know Japanese words. (That is, they memorized them and still remember them.) (2)

CAUTION: The いる of the te-いる construction and the いる you learned meaning *to exist* are identical in form, but grammatically they are completely different. In the te-form verb + いる construction, *only* いる is used whether or not the subject is animate.

29.5 Sometimes, this construction is used to express a habitual action, one that takes place repeatedly.

わたしは毎朝ジョギングをしています。
I jog every morning.
山口さんは田中さんと毎日デートをしています。
Ms. Yamaguchi has a date with Mr. Tanaka every day.

The difference between these sentences and regular nonpast sentences is that these emphasize the habitual nature of the actions more than do regular nonpast sentences. For example

カワムラさんは毎日ジョギングをします。
カワムラさんは毎日ジョギングをしています。
Mr. Kawamura jogs every day.

The first example simply states the fact that John Kawamura jogs every day. The second example, on the other hand, points out that he makes jogging part of his daily activities.

言語ノート

Have You Already Eaten?

When you are asked whether you have finished doing something and you have not done so, you will answer using the te-いる form. For example,

昼ごはんをもう食べましたか。
Have you already eaten lunch?
—いいえ、まだ食べていません。
—No, I haven't eaten yet.
—いいえ、まだです。
—No, not yet.

When you have already eaten, you answer using the regular past tense form.

—はい、もう食べました。
—Yes, I already ate.

言語ノート

Some Time Expressions

Here are several expressions for indicating how long or since when an action or event has been taking place.

1. Point in time + から = since…

   先週(せんしゅう)からカルチャーセンターへ行っています。

   Since last week, I have been going to (study at) a cultural center.

   去年(きょねん)からスペイン語を勉強(べんきょう)している。

   Since last year, I have been studying Spanish.

2. Time expression + 前(まえ)から = since … ago

   五日前(いつかまえ)から電車(でんしゃ)で学校(がっこう)へ行っています。

   I have been commuting to school by train since five days ago.

   三年前(まえ)から山口さんを知(し)っています。

   I have known Mr. Yamaguchi since three years ago.

   二時間前(まえ)からここにいます。

   I have been here since two hours ago.

You can reword the last sentence as follows.

二時間ここにいます。

I have been here for two hours.

アクティビティー 27

ダイアログ：何(なに)をしていますか。(*What is he doing?*)

電話(でんわ)で

山口(やまぐち)：もしもし、山口(やまぐち)です。
ブラウン：もしもし、ブラウンです。カワムラさんはいますか。
山口：ええ、今(いま)、テレビを見ています。
ブラウン：ちょっとお願(ねが)いします。

On the phone YAMAGUCHI: Hello. This is Yamaguchi speaking. BROWN: Hello. This is Brown. Is Mr. Kawamura there? YAMAGUCHI: Yes, he is watching TV now. BROWN: May I talk to him?

Practice the dialogue, substituting the following activities for the underlined phrase.

1. 料理をする
2. ステレオで音楽を聞く
3. コンピュータ・ゲームをする
4. 写真を撮る
5. 犬と遊ぶ

✷ アクティビティー 28

誰が何をしていますか。(*Who is doing what?*)

Using the following illustration, make dialogues.

[例] —ギブソンさんは今何をしていますか。
—新聞を読んでいます。

アクティビティー　29

いつからしていますか。(*Since when has she been doing it?*)

Rewrite these sentences using the model as an example.

[例]　山口さんは11時に寝ました。→ 山口さんは11時から寝ています。

1. わたしはブラウンさんを2年前に知りました。
2. カワムラさんは30分前にお風呂に入りました。
3. 山口さんの奥さんは3時にデパートに行きました。
4. カーティスさんは去年、日本に来ました。
5. さとみさんは先週、キャンプに出かけました。

Reminder: The particle に following a time expression means *at* (*a certain point in time*). In the same position, the particle から means *from* or *since* (*a certain point in time*).

アクティビティー　30

どんなクラスを取っていますか。(*What classes are you taking?*)

Answer the following questions.

1. 今クラスをいくつ取っていますか。どんなクラスを取っていますか。
   (取る *to take*)
2. いつから日本語を勉強していますか。
3. 毎日、日本語を勉強していますか。
4. 漢字をいくつ知っていますか。
5. 日本語の辞書を持っていますか。
6. あなたはだれか日本人を知っていますか。
7. 今雨が降っていますか。
8. あなたは今ボールペンを使っていますか。
   えんぴつを使っていますか。
9. あなたは今何を着ていますか。
10. あなたは今、立っていますか。すわっていますか。
11. あなたはどこに住んでいますか。(住む *to live*)

30. Relative Clauses

横井：明日のハイキングに行く人はいますか。
ブラウン：はい、カワムラさんと私です。
横井：ハイキングに行く人のミーティングが1時にあります。
来てください。
ブラウン：わかりました。

カワムラ：山口さんの趣味は何ですか。
山口：テニスです。
カワムラ：よくしますか。
山口：いいえ、まわりにテニスができる人があまりいないんです。

30.1 You have already learned that adjectives modifying nouns precede the noun.

おもしろいクラス	*interesting class;fun class*
きれいな部屋	*clean room*

In the examples above, a word modifies another word. When a whole clause modifies a noun, the clause usually takes the form of a relative clause. In English, the relative clause follows the noun it modifies.

the person who came here yesterday
the person whom I saw yesterday
the hamburger that I ate three days ago
a house where I lived for ten years

In English a relative clause (sometimes also called sentential modifiers) is introduced with a relative pronoun or adverb such as *who, whom, which, and where.*

30.2 Japanese relative clauses, like their English counterparts, modify nouns. However, there are some striking differences between the two languages.

1. Relative clauses in Japanese *precede* nouns that they modify.
2. There are no relative pronouns or adverbs required in Japanese. Relative clauses *directly* precede the nouns they modify.

YOKOI: Is anyone here going on tomorrow's hike? BROWN: Yes. Mr. Kawamura and I will go.
YOKOI: There's a meeting at one o'clock for those who are going hiking. Please come.
BROWN: OK. (lit., *I understand.*)

KAWAMURA: What is your hobby? YAMAGUCHI: It's tennis. KAWAMURA: Do you play often?
YAMAGUCHI: No. There aren't many people I know (lit., *around*) who can play.

わたしが昨日(きのう)食べた	ピザ
I ate yesterday	*pizza → the pizza I ate yesterday*
あなたが会(あ)った	人
you met	*person → the person you met*
山田(やまだ)さんと話している	男(おとこ)の人
is talking with Yamada	*man → the man who is talking with Mr. Yamada*
わたしが勉強(べんきょう)した	ところ
I studied	*place → the place where I studied*

As you see from the examples, to form a relative clause in Japanese you simply position a clause before a noun.

30.3 Note that verb forms used in relative clauses must be plain forms.

カワムラさんがいつも勉強(べんきょう)する時間(じかん)
the time when Mr. Kawamura always studies

カワムラさんが見ないテレビの番組(ばんぐみ)
the TV programs Mr. Kawamura doesn't watch

父(ちち)が買(か)ったステレオ
the stereo my father bought

その話を聞(き)かなかった学生
the students who didn't listen to that story

Polite forms are not used in relative clauses. A noun modified by a relative clause (double-underlined) is a noun clause (single-underlined), and may be used in a sentence anywhere a noun can be used.

昨日(きのう)食べたピザはおいしかったですか。
Was the pizza you ate yesterday delicious?

父(ちち)が買(か)ったステレオを見ますか。
Do you want to (lit., *will you*) *look at the stereo my father bought?*

30.4 The possessive marker の is often substituted for the subject particle が in relative clauses and other noun-modifying clauses.

父(ちち)の買(か)ったステレオ
the stereo that my father bought

母(はは)の好(す)きだった本
the book that my mother liked

The topic particle は is not used within relative clauses.

アクティビティー 31

プログラマーはプログラミングをする人です。(*A programmer is someone who does programming.*)

Complete these sentences using a phrase chosen from the list following the exercise items.

[例] (　　　)はゴルフをする人です。→
(ゴルファー)はゴルフをする人です。(*A golfer is a person who golfs.*)

1. (　　　)はギャンブルをする人です。
2. (　　　)はレスリングをする人です。
3. (　　　)は勉強(べんきょう)するところです。
4. (　　　)は本がたくさんあるところです。
5. (　　　)は写真(しゃしん)をとる機械(きかい) (*machine*) です。
6. (　　　)はひまな時間(じかん)です。
7. (　　　)は日本人が話(はな)す言葉(ことば) (*language*) です。
8. (　　　)は映画(えいが)を見るところです。
9. (　　　)は水泳(すいえい)をするところです。

学校(がっこう)、図書館(としょかん)、プール、カメラ、ギャンブラー、レスラー、日本語(ご)、余暇(よか)、映画館(えいがかん)

アクティビティー 32

わたしが先週(せんしゅう)見た映画(えいが)はスピルバーグのです。(*The movie I saw last week was a Spielberg movie.*)

Combine these sentences by using a relative clause. In this practice, use the second sentence as the main clause of the resultant sentence. In other words, make sentences in which the predicate of the second sentence comes at the end.

Note that while わたし is marked with が in the resultant sentence, わたし is the topic of the relative clause, not of the sentence. The topic of the first example is 公園 and is marked with は. The が can be replaced by の as explained in **Grammar 30.4.**

[例] わたしは昨日公園(きのうこうえん)へ行きました。
その公園(こうえん)はきれいでした。→ わたしが昨日(きのう)行った公園はきれいでした。
わたしは先週映画(せんしゅうえいが)を見ました。
その映画(えいが)はアメリカのです。→ わたしが先週(せんしゅう)見た映画はアメリカのです。

1. 父(ちち)は昨日(きのう)カメラを買(か)いました。
   そのカメラは高(たか)かったです。

2. わたしは毎日(まいにち)プールで泳(およ)ぎます。

そのプールはうちのそばにあります。

3. 昨晩(さくばん)レコードを聞きました。

そのレコードは町田(まちだ)さんのレコードです。

4. カルチャーセンターで先生がヨガを教(おし)えています。(教(おし)える *to teach*)

その先生はインドから来(き)ました。

5. わたしはいつも近(ちか)くのレストランへ行きます。

そのレストランは安(やす)くて、おいしいです。

6. ブラウンさんは中野(なかの)に住(す)んでいます。

中野(なかの)は静(しず)かで、便利(べんり)です。

アクティビティー 33

忙(いそが)しい人たち (*Busy people*)

Using the illustration from アクティビティー **28,** make sentences containing a relative clause.

[例] 新聞(しんぶん)を読んでいる女(おんな)の人はギブソンさんです。

アクティビティー 34

生花(いけばな)を教(おし)えている先生 (*The teacher who teaches flower arranging*)

Complete the sentences using relative clauses.

[例] あの方(かた)は(　　)先生ですか。→ あの方(かた)は(日本語(ご)を教(おし)えている)先生ですか。

1. (　　)パーティーはどうでしたか。
2. あなたは(　　)本を読みましたか。
3. (　　)写真(しゃしん)はあまりよくありません。
4. (　　)レストランは大学の北(きた)にあります。
5. これは(　　)CDです。
6. これは(　　)学生の部屋(へや)です。
7. (　　)女(おんな)の人は中国人です。
8. (　　)人をマラソン・ランナーといいます。

アクティビティー 35

教えてください。(*Please tell us.*)

Answer these questions.

1. 日本語を上手に話せる外国人を知っていますか。
2. あなたの家のそばにボーリングができるところがありますか。
3. あなたの家のそばに24時間あいているスーパーはありますか。(あく：*to become open*)
4. あなたの学校に安く昼ごはんを食べられるところがたくさんありますか。
5. あなたの学校の中にはコンサートができるところがありますか。
6. あなたの町のそばにスキーができるところがありますか。
7. あなたはマージャンができる人を知っていますか。
8. あなたはいいステレオを持っている人を知っていますか。
9. あなたは趣味を楽しむ時間がありますか。
10. あなたがいつも飲んでいる飲み物は何ですか。

✸ アクティビティー 36

テレビゲームをしている男の人はだれですか。(*Who is the man who is playing video games?*)

Using the accompanying illustrations, answer these questions.

1. ブラウンさんと話している女の人はだれですか。
2. テレビゲームをしている男の人はだれですか。
3. 手紙を書いている男の人はだれですか。
4. エアロビクスをしている女の人はだれですか。
5. カーティスさんが読んでいる本は何ですか。
6. Tシャツを着ている男の人はだれですか。
7. 三村さんが飲んでいるもの (*thing*) は何ですか。

Now describe each illustration.

アクティビティー 37

フランス語が話せる人はだれですか。(*Who is the person who can speak French?*)

Walk around the classroom interviewing your classmates to find out who satisfies which of the following conditions. Report your results to the class.

1. 空手のできる人
2. カメラを持っている人
3. ピアノが弾ける人
4. 歌が上手に歌える人
5. 昨日ジョギングをした人
6. 先週、映画を見た人
7. 暇がない人
8. 泳げない人

アクティビティー 38

たくさんお金のかかる趣味 (*Hobbies requiring a lot of money*)

List hobbies, games, and sports that satisfy each of the following conditions. Later, compare your list with your classmates' lists.

1. たくさんお金のかかる趣味
2. あまりお金のかからない趣味
3. 4人でするゲーム
4. カードを使うゲーム
5. とても疲れる趣味、スポーツ (*hobbies and sports that tire you*)
6. 家の中でできる趣味
7. アメリカ人がよくするスポーツ
8. 冬、よくするスポーツ

31. Describing a Change in State: なる

カワムラ：林さんのアパートは便利ですか。
林：前は不便でした。でも、近くにスーパーができたので、便利になりました。
カワムラ：それはよかったですね。
林：それに、最近、地下鉄の駅ができたので、もっと便利になりました。

高田：山田さんの娘さんはおいくつですか。
山田：先月６歳になりました。
高田：もうそんなに大きくなったんですか。
山田：ええ、いつの間にか。

できる here means *to be constructed, to be completed.*

The verb なる (Class 1) means *to become, to turn into.*

noun + に
na-adjective + に
root of i-adjective + く
} + なります（なる）

来年、大学生になります。
I will be (lit., *become*) *a college student next year.*
夜になって、静かになりました。
After night fell, it became quiet. (lit., *It became night, and it became quiet.*)
お酒を飲んだので、顔が赤くなった。
Because I drank sake, my face turned red.

KAWAMURA: Is your apartment convenient? HAYASHI: It was inconvenient before, but since a supermarket opened nearby it has become convenient. KAWAMURA: That was lucky (lit., *good*). HAYASHI: In addition, a subway station was built (nearby) recently, so it has become more convenient.
TAKADA: How old is your daughter, Mr. Yamada? YAMADA: She turned six last month. TAKADA: She's already gotten that old (lit., *big*)? YAMADA: Yes, before you know it… (these things happen).

アクティビティー 39

えらんでください。(*Please choose.*)

Fill in the blanks with appropriate adjectives from the list that follows.

Adjectives: 少ない、多い、長い、ひま(な)、上手(な)、赤い、安い、大きい、暖かい、便利(な)、好き(な)、きれい(な)、白い (*white*)

1. 息子は8歳になって、体 (*body*) も (　　) なりました。
2. 床屋 (*barber shop*) へ行かなかったので、髪が (　　) なった。
3. となりに銀行ができて、とても (　　) なりました。
4. 夏になって、仕事は (　　) なった。
5. ピアノを毎日練習しているので、(　　) なった。
6. 秋になって、葉 (*leaves*) が (　　) なりました。
7. セールなので、なんでも (　　) なりました。
8. 春になって、(　　) なった。
9. 6月に入って、雨の日が (　　) なった。
10. 年をとって (*getting older*)、髪が (　　) なった。
11. 掃除をしたので、部屋が (　　) なった。
12. 最近 (*recently*)、すしが (　　) なりました。

アクティビティー 40

わたしは下手なので… (*Because I'm not so good at it…*)

Using the model as an example, complete the sentences.

[例] (ピアノが上手だ) (ピアニスト) →
ピアノが上手なので、ピアニストになりました。

1. (エアロビクスが好きだ) (エアロビクスのインストラクター)
2. (英語が話せる) (英語の先生)
3. (車が好きだ) (カー・レーサー)
4. (プログラミングができる) (プログラマー)
5. (体が大きくて、強い) (ボディーガード)

アクティビティー 41

好(す)きになりました。(*I've come to like it.*)

Following the example, explain how each person has changed.

[例] ゴルフがきらいでした。でも、今(いま)は好(す)きです。→
ゴルフが好きになりました。

1. ピアノが下手(へた)でした。でも、今(いま)は上手(じょうず)です。
2. ブロッコリーがきらいでした。でも、今(いま)は好(す)きです。
3. 読書(どくしょ)が好(す)きでした。でも、今(いま)はきらいです。
4. 中国語(ちゅうごくご)が苦手(にがて)でした。でも、今(いま)は得意(とくい)です。
5. スピーチが苦手(にがて)でした。でも、今(いま)は得意(とくい)です。
6. ドイツ語が上手(じょうず)でした。でも、今(いま)は下手(へた)です。
7. 料理(りょうり)が得意(とくい)でした。でも、今(いま)は苦手(にがて)です。

Language Skills

Reading and Writing

Reading 1 サンライズ・カルチャーセンターのお知(し)らせ

Before You Read

Suppose you have decided to take a class at a local culture center. What information would you like to know about the class? Here are headings from the class schedule for a culture center in Tokyo. Does it include all the information you would need?

クラスの名前(なまえ)　先生　曜日(ようび)　時間　クラス　授業料(じゅぎょうりょう)

What do you think 授業料(じゅぎょうりょう) means?

Association: What words from the list below are related to each of the following: 外国語, 手紙 (*letter*), 料理, and ワイン? You may use the same word more than once.

書く、飲む、食べる、フランス語、紙 (*paper*)、ペン、エプロン、コルク、キッチン、話す、練習、作る、夕ごはん、スペイン語、ランゲージ・ラボ、読む、ことば (*word*)、朝ごはん、グラス、辞書、郵便局、シェフ

Now Read It!

サンライズ・カルチャーセンター

春学期のクラスのお知らせ

サンライズ・カルチャーセンターの春学期のクラスは4月1日から始まります。春学期のクラスをいくつか紹介しましょう。

学期 *semester, quarter* / お知らせ *notice, announcement*

始まる *to start* / いくつか *some, several* / 紹介する *to introduce*

- 英文レター入門

  英文 *English writing* / …入門 *introduction to…*

  「英語は話せるが、書くのは苦手だ。」

  「英語で手紙を書くのはむずかしい。」

  「英語で手紙が書けない。」

  このクラスでは、英語で手紙を書くことを練習します。先生は東京外国語大学の吉田京子先生です。クラスは毎週火曜日、木曜日午後6時から8時までです。授業料は3万5千円です。クラスは東ビル1304号室。

  練習する *to practice*

  授業料 *tuition* / …号室 *room number.*

- ワイン・テイスティング

  ワインが大好きな方！ワイン・テイスティングを楽しみましょう。このクラスでは、フランス、ドイツ、イタリア、スペイン、ポルトガル、アメリカのカリフォルニアの赤ワイン、白ワインを楽しみます。先生はオーシャン・ホテルの川口はじめさんです。クラスは毎週金曜日午後7時から9時までです。授業料は4万6千円です。クラスは南ビル2415号室。学生は20歳以上の方に限ります。

  …以上 *more than* (*compare* …以下 *less than*) / 限る *to be limited to*

- 中国語入門

  中国語は世界で一番多くの人が話していることばです。あなたも中国語を勉強しませんか。春学期のおわりには、簡単な会話をすることができます。

  世界 *world* / ことば *language*

  おわり *end* / 簡単(な) *simple* / 会話 *conversation*

  先生は日本で20年中国語を教えているリン・ホンミン先生です。クラスは毎週月曜日、水曜日、金曜日5時から7時までです。授業料は4万円です。クラスは月曜日と水曜日は北ビル320号室です。金曜日は南ビル140号室のランゲージ・ラボです。

■ 男性のためのクッキング・クラス

食べるのは好きだが、料理をするのは苦手な男性はいませんか。このクラスでは男性でもできる簡単な料理を習います。先生はテレビやラジオでも有名な土井森男先生です。クラスは毎週土曜日午前9時半から12時までです。昼ごはんにはクラスで作ったものをみんなで食べます。授業料は2万8千5百円です。クラスは西ビル654号室です。エプロンを忘れないで下さい。

他に、スペイン語、フランス語、モダン・ダンス、イラスト、生花、ヨガ、書道、ピアノ、フルート、ゴルフ、ピンポンなどのクラスがあります。

男性 *male* / …のため *for (the sake of)…*
作る *to make*
忘れないでください *please don't forget* (*from* 忘れる *to forget*)
他に *in addition*
など *etc.*

After You Finish Reading

The preceding passage describes four classes offered by the Sunrise Culture Center during this coming spring semester. List the name, instructor, dates, times, and tuition for each class in English.

Check your answers with a classmate by using the following dialogue.

s1: すみません。_____のクラスは何曜日の何時からですか。
s2: _____です。
s1: 先生はどなたですか。
s2: _____ 先生です。
s1: 授業料はいくらですか。
s2: _____ 円です。

Which class would you recommend to each of the following people?

1. わたしは来年ペキンとシャンハイへ行きます。
2. わたしは商社 (*trading company*) で働いています。アメリカの会社 (*company*) によく手紙を書きますが、英語はちょっと…
3. 去年20歳になって、はじめてお酒を飲みました。お酒の中ではワインが一番好きです。
4. ぼくは、中野のアパートに一人で住んでいます。夕ごはんはいつもレストランか食堂で食べますが、高くてこまります (*have difficulty*)。

Now study the reading more closely for the following exercises.

1. Find the nominalizers (の and こと) in the description of the English letter-writing class.
2. Find the relative clauses used in the descriptions of the Chinese language and cooking classes.

Writing 1

1. You have decided to enroll in one of the courses offered by the Sunrise Culture Center. Complete the application form (申込書) on p. 360 in Japanese.

コミュニティプラザ・新百合 新規開講サークル

知性と教養とヘルシーな明日のための42講座。

〈8月10日(金)より受付スタート〉

	サークル名	開催週	時間	受講料
月	指圧でリラックス	1・3	10:30～12:00	9,300円 (3ヵ月)
	辰巳流日本舞踊	2・4	10:15～12:00	9,300円 (3ヵ月)
	ヨーロピアンフォークアート	2・4	10:30～12:30	9,300円 (3ヵ月)
	フィットネスフラダンス	毎週	12:30～13:30	12,400円 (2ヵ月)
	作詞入門	1・3	13:00～14:30	12,400円 (3ヵ月)
	シャンソンを楽しく	2・4	15:30～17:00	12,400円 (3ヵ月)
	真向法	毎週	15:30～16:30	12,400円 (2ヵ月)
火	郷土の日本史探訪	2	10:30～12:30	12,400円 (6ヵ月)
	彫金	1・3	10:30～12:30	9,300円 (3ヵ月)
	デンマークラグメーキング	2・4	10:30～12:30	9,300円 (3ヵ月)
	手まり手芸	1・3	13:00～15:00	9,300円 (3ヵ月)
	"書"を学ぶ	1・3	13:00～15:00	9,300円 (3ヵ月)
	暮らしに生かすインテリア	2・4	13:00～14:30	12,400円 (3ヵ月)
	短歌に親しむ	2・4	15:30～17:30	9,300円 (3ヵ月)
水	パッチワークキルト(初級)	2・4	10:30～12:30	9,300円 (3ヵ月)
	ペン習字	毎週	10:30～12:30	12,400円 (2ヵ月)
	話し方と朗読	1・3	13:00～14:30	9,300円 (3ヵ月)
	スウェーデン刺繍	1・3	13:00～15:00	9,300円 (3ヵ月)
	日本画入門	2・4	13:00～15:00	9,300円 (3ヵ月)
	万葉集を読む	1・3	15:30～17:00	9,300円 (3ヵ月)
	エッセイの書き方(入門)	2・4	15:30～17:30	9,300円 (3ヵ月)
木	キーボードを楽しむ	1・3	10:30～12:00	9,300円 (3ヵ月)
	美容気功	毎週	11:00～12:00	12,400円 (2ヵ月)
	木版画を楽しむ	1・3	13:00～15:00	12,400円 (3ヵ月)
	俳画	2	13:00～15:00	9,300円 (6ヵ月)
	三味線の手ほどき	毎週	13:00～15:00	12,400円 (2ヵ月)
	エッグクラフト	2・4	13:00～15:00	9,300円 (3ヵ月)
	般若心経を読む	2・4	15:30～17:30	9,300円 (3ヵ月)
金	日本の庭園とその歴史	1・3	10:30～12:00	12,400円 (3ヵ月)
	レザー工芸	1・3	10:30～12:30	9,300円 (3ヵ月)
	童話を書く	2・4	10:30～12:00	9,300円 (3ヵ月)
	ブラッシュアップ英会話	毎週	10:30～12:00	12,400円 (2ヵ月)
	茶道の歴史と日本文化	2	13:00～15:00	12,400円 (6ヵ月)
	インテリジェンス・チェス	2・4	13:00～15:00	9,300円 (3ヵ月)
	英会話(初級)	毎週	13:00～15:00	12,400円 (2ヵ月)
	御家流 香道	4	15:00～16:00	13,500円 (3ヵ月) (材料費込)
	フォトレッスン	1・3	15:30～17:30	9,300円 (3ヵ月)
	コミュニケーション手話	2・4	15:30～17:30	9,300円 (3ヵ月)
土	40'sピクス	毎週	11:00～12:15	12,400円 (2ヵ月)
	中国語入門	毎週	13:00～14:30	12,400円 (2ヵ月)
	リフレッシュ体操	毎週	13:30～15:00	12,400円 (2ヵ月)
	カードマジック	4	15:30～17:30	9,300円 (6ヵ月)

Class schedule from a culture center in Tokyo

サンライズ・カルチャーセンター
クラス受講申込書

名前

男・女

電話番号

クラスの名前

学期　　春・夏・秋・冬

曜日・時間

場所

授業料

領収書

平成　　年　　月　　日　　＿＿＿＿＿＿＿＿様

¥

但し　　クラスの授業料として

サンライズ・カルチャー・センター校長

山中一男　　印

クラス受講申込書（じゅこうもうしこみしょ）*class attendance application form*

領収書（りょうしゅうしょ）*receipt*

平成 *Heisei (era)*

但し *conditions* / …として *as…*

校長 *school principal*

印 *seal*

2. You have been hired by the Sunrise Culture Center to teach a class. What special skill do you have that you could teach? Write your own course description in Japanese. What days of the week will your class meet? At what time? How much will you charge for tuition?

Reading 2 学生とサラリーマンの余暇調査（よかちょうさ）

Before You Read

If you had some free time, how would you most like to spend it? Rank the following activities in order of preference.

ゴロゴロする (*to loaf around*)

コンサートへ行く
テレビを見る
スポーツをする
友だちと話す
旅行する

Compare your ranking with those of your classmates.

Which of the following do you think are worthwhile activities? Rank them in order of most to least worthwhile.

映画を見る
旅行する
ステレオで音楽を聞く
読書をする
友だちとレストランへ行く
スポーツをする

Compare your ranking with those of your classmates.

Now Read It!

学生とサラリーマンの余暇調査

日本の学生は余暇に何をしているのか。学生500人にこの質問をした。テレビを見ている学生が一番多かった。2位は「家でゴロゴロする」、3位は「スポーツをする」、4位は「喫茶店へ行く」、5位は「友だちとレストランへ行く」だった。テレビを見ている時間は女子学生よりも男子学生のほうが長い。

では、サラリーマンはどうだろうか。同じ質問をサラリーマン500人にした。旅行をするサラリーマンが一番多い。2位は「スポーツをする」、3位は「映画を見る」、4位は「読書をする」、5位は「コンサートへ行く」だった。この調査から、サラリーマンは映画、読書、コンサートなど、教養を深める活動をしていることがわかる。一方、学生は余暇をあまり有効に使っていないことがわかる。

サラリーマン *company worker* / 調査 *survey*
質問 *question*
…位 *number…* (*rank*)
女子 *female* 男子 *male*
教養 *knowledge*
深める *to deepen, increase*
活動 *activity* / 一方 *on the other hand* / 有効に *profitably*

After You Finish Reading

Using the information from the preceding passage, list, in English, the favorite activities of both students and company workers in order.

Do you agree with the claim that company workers spend their free time more productively than students?

List all the relative clauses used in the passage.

Writing 2

Conduct a survey in your class on what your classmates do during their free time. Using your survey results, write a short report in Japanese. Follow the format used in the reading.

Useful expression: 余暇(よか)に何(なに)をしていますか。*What do you usually do during your free time?*

言語ノート

Sound Words

Japanese has a vast number of words that represent sounds. One category of such words, called 擬声語(ぎせいご) (*onomatopoeia*) includes those that imitate natural sounds: for example, the sound of a cat's cry is *meow* in English, ニャー in Japanese. A second category, called 擬態語(ぎたいご), is composed of sound words that represent the manner of an action, a situation, or an image, as if the sound expressed those states. *Zigzag* is one of the few such words found in English. Japanese contains an enormous number of these 擬態語. Some examples are ゴロゴロ ([*the "sound" of someone*] *rattling around—i.e., being idle*), シーン ([*the "sound" of*] *dead silence*), and キラキラ ([*the "sound" of*] *shining*). Note that these sound words are written in **katakana.** Entire dictionaries are devoted to these sound words in Japanese. You will learn more of them as you proceed through this textbook.

Language Functions and Situations

Responding to Compliments

カワムラ：これは山口(やまぐち)さんがかいた絵(え)ですか。
山口(やまぐち)：ええ、そうです。
カワムラ：山口さんは絵(え)が上手(じょうず)ですね。
山口：いやあ、まったくダメなんですよ。
カワムラ：いいえ、そんなことありませんよ。
山口：そうですか。

In written Japanese, emphasis may be added to a word by writing it in **katakana,** even if the word is not a foreign loanword or a sound word. だめ is written in **katakana** here for this reason.

KAWAMURA: Is this the picture you drew, Ms. Yamaguchi? YAMAGUCHI: Yes, that's right. KAWAMURA: You are skilled at drawing, aren't you? YAMAGUCHI: Oh, no. I am no good at all. KAWAMURA: No, that's not true. YAMAGUCHI: Do you think so?

ギブソン：町田(まちだ)さん、きれいなブラウスですね。高(たか)かったでしょう。
町田(まちだ)：いいえ、安(やす)かったんですよ。
ギブソン：え、本当(ほんとう)ですか。よく似合(にあ)いますよ。
町田：そうですか。

How would you respond to the following compliments?

1. スペイン語を話すのが上手(じょうず)ですね。
2. ファッションのセンスがいいですね。
3. わあ、新(あたら)しい車(くるま)ですか。カッコイイですね。(*It looks great.*)
4. ハンサムなボーイフレンドですね。
5. テニスが上手(じょうず)ですね。

Role Play

Work in pairs. One person praises the other for the following. The person complimented responds using the patterns in the dialogues.

Useful word: ヘアースタイル *hairstyle*

1. being good at speaking Japanese
2. being good at cooking
3. his or her **kanji** writing is good
4. his or her hairstyle is nice
5. his or her younger sister is pretty

Introducing a Family Member

山口(やまぐち)：ああ、ブラウンさん、おひさしぶりですね。
ブラウン：ああ、山口(やまぐち)さん。お元気(げんき)ですか。
山口：ええ、まあ、何(なん)とか。あっ、紹介(しょうかい)します。兄(あに)の大助(だいすけ)です。
大助(だいすけ)：山口大助(やまぐちだいすけ)です。妹(いもうと)がいつもお世話になっております。
どうぞよろしく。
ブラウン：妹(いもうと)さんにはいつもお世話(せわ)になっております。どうぞよろしく。

GIBSON: Ms. Machida, that's a pretty blouse. It must have been expensive. MACHIDA: No, it was cheap. GIBSON: Was it really? It suits you well. MACHIDA: Do you think so?

YAMAGUCHI: Oh, Ms. Brown. I haven't seen you for a long time. BROWN: Oh, Ms. Yamaguchi. How are you? YAMAGUCHI: Oh, I'm getting along. (lit., *Yes, well, somehow*...) Let me introduce someone to you. This is my older brother, Daisuke. DAISUKE: I am Daisuke Yamaguchi. Thank you very much for taking care of my younger sister all the time. Nice meeting you. BROWN: I am always taken care of by your younger sister. Nice meeting you.

言語ノート

お世話(せわ)になっております。

When you are introduced by an acquaintance (Mr. X) to one of his family members or colleagues or someone else from his in-group, you may say to the person introduced, X さんにいつもお世話になっております (*I am always taken care of by Mr. X* or *I am always indebted to Mr. X*). This expression indicates that you and Mr. X are very close and have a good relationship. Also, the compliment makes Mr. X feel good in front of his in-group member. The other party may say, いいえ、X がいつもお世話になっております (*No, X is always taken care of by **you*** or *No, X is always indebted to **you***) or X からいつもうかがっております (*I always hear about you from X*). Either statement now makes you feel good. The latter statement indicates that you are such an important person in X's life that he always talks about you. Alternatively, the other party may say, X がいつもご迷惑(めいわく)をおかけしています (*X is always giving you trouble*). This means *Thank you very much for tolerating X's behavior and forgiving him for it.* These expressions are commonly used in such introductions, whether or not your acquaintance really is taking care of you, and whether or not he really gives you much trouble. Think of them as formalities. The point here is that the distinction between in-group and out-group plays a crucial role in the language behavior of Japanese people.

町田(まちだ)：お母(かあ)さん、こちらは大学のカワムラさん。
母(はは)：まあ、ようこそ、カワムラさん。娘(むすめ)からいつもうかがっております。
カワムラ：ジョン・カワムラです。はじめまして。ひとみさんにはいつもお世話(せわ)になっております。
母：いいえ、娘(むすめ)がいつもご迷惑(めいわく)をおかけしております。

MACHIDA: Mother, this is Mr. Kawamura from school (lit., *the university*). MOTHER: Oh, welcome, Mr. Kawamura. I often hear about you from my daughter. KAWAMURA: I'm John Kawamura. How do you do. Hitomi is always a great help to me. MOTHER: Oh, no. My daughter is always troubling you.

言語ノート

How to Address Family Members

Japanese family members may address one another by their first names, but they also use terms that define their relationships.

Naturally enough, Japanese children address their father as お父さん (*father*) and their mother as お母さん (*mother*). パパ *papa* and ママ *mama* are terms of address commonly used by young children. (Other variations also exist.) A husband addresses his wife by her first name (without さん) or おまえ *you* (vulgar) or calls her with おい *hey*. A wife calls her husband by his first name (with さん) or as あなた *you*. おまえ and あなた are the closest everyday Japanese comes to *dear* or *honey*. When a couple has a child, they may call each other by the same terms their child would use: お父さん／パパ and お母さん／ママ. Parents call their child by his or her first name (without any title)—for example, 太郎 (*a boy*) or 裕子 (*a girl*)—or they may append the diminutive title suffix ～ちゃん to a young child's name—太郎ちゃん, 裕子ちゃん. Adding ～ちゃん to a name is like making Tommy out of Thomas or Tom. To boys' names ～君 (a familiar title suffix appended to male names of equals or inferiors) may be added; thus, 太郎君. When a family has more than one child, the terms of address are determined by the youngest child. That child is called by his or her first name. An older brother or sister is called お兄ちゃん *older brother* or お姉ちゃん *older sister* (affectionate forms of お兄さん and お姉さん) by other family members. This helps the youngest member of the family understand his or her relationship to the other family members.

Role Play

Practice the following situations with your classmates.

1. You are at home, and a good friend stops by for a few minutes. Introduce him or her to your family. Tell something about him or her. The friend greets the family members and talks about what you are doing at school.
2. You are shopping with your father or mother at a department store. You happen to run into a classmate from school. Introduce your parents and your classmate.

Listening Comprehension

1. You will hear descriptions of the pastimes of four people: Sasaki, Motoyoshi, Kuramoto, and Tamamura. Jot down their hobbies in English and write a brief account of what each person will do this weekend.
2. You will hear an advertisement for a culture center. Write a brief summary in English of the courses offered, the teachers, class times and places, and any other information, such as tuition charged.

Vocabulary

Hobbies and Pastimes

あそぶ	遊ぶ	to play
あつめる	集める	to collect
いけばな	生花	flower arranging
え	絵	picture
えんげい	園芸	gardening
えんそうする	演奏する	to play (*a musical instrument*)
かいが	絵画	painting
かく		to draw (*a picture*)
がっき	楽器	musical instrument
カルチャーセンター		culture center
きって	切手	stamp
きってあつめ	切手集め	stamp collecting
さどう	茶道	tea ceremony
しゃしん	写真	photography; photograph
しゅげい	手芸	handicrafts
しゅみ	趣味	hobby
たのしむ	楽しむ	to enjoy
とくぎ	特技	special talent
どくしょ	読書	reading (*books*)
とる	取る、撮る	to take (*a class*); to take (*a photo*)

よか	余暇	free time
りょうり	料理	cooking
りょこう	旅行	travel

Loanwords: クラブ、コンサート、ダンス、ドライブ、ヨガ、レジャー

Review: 映画(えいが)、音楽(おんがく)、スポーツ、釣(つ)り、暇(ひま)(な)、練習(れんしゅう)する

Sports

しあい	試合	game
すいえい	水泳	swimming
たっきゅう	卓球	table tennis; Ping-Pong
やきゅう	野球	baseball

Loanwords: エアロビクス、キャンピング、ゴルフ、サイクリング、サッカー、ジョギング、ダイビング、テニス、ハイキング、バスケットボール、バドミントン、バレーボール、ピンポン、プール、フットボール、ボート、ボーリング、マラソン、ヨット、ラグビー、ランニング

Review: 運動(うんどう)、泳(およ)ぐ、スキー、スケート、スポーツ、山登(やまのぼ)り

Family Terms

かぞく	家族	family
あに	兄	older brother
あね	姉	older sister
いもうと	妹	younger sister
いもうとさん	妹さん	younger sister (*respectful*)
おかあさん	お母さん	mother (*respectful*)
おくさん	奥さん	wife (*respectful*)
おこさん	お子さん	child (*respectful*)
おじ		uncle
おじいさん		grandfather (*respectful*)
おじさん		uncle (*respectful*)
おじょうさん	お嬢さん	daughter (*respectful*)
おっと	夫	husband
おとうさん	お父さん	father (*respectful*)
おとうと	弟	younger brother
おとうとさん	弟さん	younger brother (*respectful*)
おにいさん	お兄さん	older brother (*respectful*)
おねえさん	お姉さん	older sister (*respectful*)
おば		aunt
おばあさん		grandmother (*respectful*)
おばさん		aunt (*respectful*)

おまごさん	お孫さん	grandchild (*respectful*)
かない	家内	wife
きょうだい	兄弟	siblings; brothers
ごかぞく	御家族	family (*respectful*)
ごきょうだい	御兄弟	siblings; brothers (*respectful*)
ごしゅじん	御主人	husband (*respectful*)
ごしんせき	御親戚	relative (*respectful*)
こども	子供	child
ごふうふ	御夫婦	married couple (*respectful*)
ごりょうしん	御両親	parents (*respectful*)
しゅじん	主人	husband
しんせき	親戚	relative
そふ	祖父	grandfather
そぼ	祖母	grandmother
ちち	父	father
つま	妻	wife
はは	母	mother
ふうふ	夫婦	married couple
まご	孫	grandchild
むすこ	息子	son
むすこさん	息子さん	son (*respectful*)
むすめ	娘	daughter
むすめさん	娘さん	daughter (*respectful*)
りょうしん	両親	parents

Nouns

おとこ	男	male; man
おとこのこ	男の子	boy
おとこのひと	男の人	man
おんな	女	female; woman
おんなのこ	女の子	girl
おんなのひと	女の人	woman
かた	方	person (*polite*)
こ	子	child
ひと	人	person
みな		all; everyone
みんな		all; everyone
もんだい	問題	question; issue; problem

Na-Adjectives

じょうず(な)	上手(な)	good at; skilled at
とくい(な)	得意(な)	good at and like; forte
にがて(な)	苦手(な)	bad at and dislike; weak point
へた(な)	下手(な)	poor at

Adverbs

いっしょに	一緒に	together
とくに	特に	especially
まったく	全く	totally

Verbs and Verb Forms

できる	to be able to do	～れる	(*shorten form of potential*)
なる	to become; to turn into	～ている	(*progressive*)
わかる	to understand; to be clear	～られる	(*potential*)

Words Formed From Interrogatives

いつか		sometime; someday	どちらか		either
いくつか		some; several	どちらでも		whichever
いつでも		anytime	どちらも		both; neither
いつも		always	どなたか		someone (*polite*)
すべて	全て	all	どなたでも		anyone (*polite*)
ぜんぶ	全部	all	どなたも		everyone (*polite*)
だれか		someone	どれか		one of them
だれでも		anyone	どれでも		any of them
だれも		everyone; no one	どれも		all of them; none of them
どうか		somehow	なぜか		somehow; for some reason
どこか		somewhere	なにか	何か	something
どこでも		anywhere	なにも	何も	everything; nothing
どこも		everywhere; nowhere	なんでも	何でも	anything

Kanji

Learn these characters:

手	勉
家	道
族	書
男	使
女	国
子	作
父	音
母	楽
兄	全
姉	部
弟	運
妹	動

チェックリスト

Use this checklist to confirm that you can now

- □ Talk about hobbies and pastimes
- □ Talk about sports
- □ Talk about family
- □ Express *some, every, none,* and *any*
- □ Describe abilities
- □ Use nominalizers こと and の
- □ Use the particle も in a new way
- □ Use the potential form of verbs
- □ Use the **-te** form of verbs + います
- □ Make relative clauses
- □ Describe a change in state
- □ Respond to compliments
- □ Introduce family members

Review Chapter 5

アクティビティー　1

趣味は何ですか。(*What are their hobbies?*)

Various people made these statements. Identify their hobbies.

1. 「マダム・バタフライ」が好きです。
2. 昨日、ジャイアンツの試合を見ました。
3. カメラをいつも持っています。
4. シチューを作るのが上手です。
5. 去年、中国とメキシコとフランスとエジプトへ行きました。

アクティビティー　2

どんな趣味・スポーツをすすめますか。(*What hobby or sport do you recommend?*)

Your partner is a hobby critic. Ask him or her what hobby or sport he or she recommends for the following people. The critic must give one or two reasons why he or she thinks a particular hobby or sport is most appropriate.

1. 話すのが好きな人
2. 花が好きな人
3. 音楽が好きな人
4. 日本文化について知りたい人
5. 海のそばに住んでいる人
6. お金がたくさんある人
7. 時間があまりない人

アクティビティー　3

家族の一人 (*One family member*)

Work in pairs. Select one member of your partner's family and talk about him or her.

1. 誕生日はいつですか。何歳ですか。
2. 結婚していますか。独身ですか。(*Is he/she married? or single?*)

3. 結婚(けっこん)している人: 結婚して、何年(なんねん)になりますか。(*How many years has he/she been married?*) 奥(おく)さん(御主人(ごしゅじん))はどんな方(かた)ですか。
独身(どくしん)の人: 恋人(こいびと) (*boyfriend/girlfriend*) はいますか。
4. どこに住(す)んでいますか。(*Where does he/she live?*)
5. どんな仕事(しごと)をしていますか。
6. どんな学校を卒業(そつぎょう)していますか。(卒業する *to graduate* [*from*])
7. 趣味(しゅみ)は何(なん)ですか。

アクティビティー　4

町田さんの家族(かぞく) (*Ms. Machida's family*)

Here is a scene at Hitomi Machida's home. Answer these questions.

1. 町田(まちだ)さんのお父(とう)さんは何(なに)をしていますか。
2. 町田(まちだ)さんのおばあさんはどんな人ですか。
3. 本を読んでいる人はだれですか。
4. 町田(まちだ)さんのお父(とう)さんの趣味(しゅみ)は何(なん)だと思(おも)いますか。
5. 町田(まちだ)さんの家族(かぞく)はどんな家族ですか。

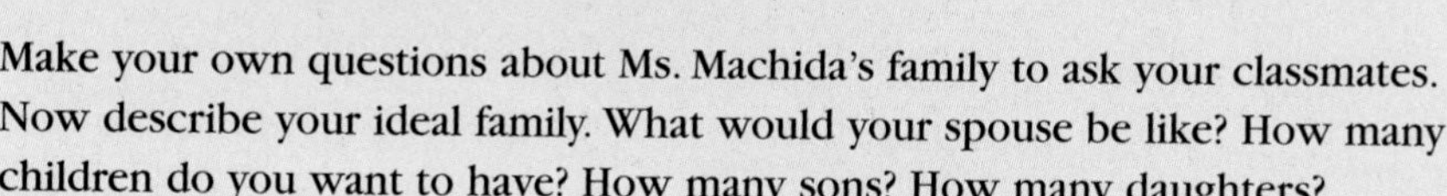

Make your own questions about Ms. Machida's family to ask your classmates. Now describe your ideal family. What would your spouse be like? How many children do you want to have? How many sons? How many daughters?

アクティビティー　5

こんな人はいますか。(*Is there anyone like this here?*)

Walk around in the classroom and find the following people. Do not forget to write down their names.

1. ギターが弾(ひ)ける人
2. 両親(りょうしん)と一緒(いっしょ)に住(す)んでいる人
3. ゴルフをするのが好(す)きな人
4. 歌(うた)が上手(じょうず)な人
5. 趣味(しゅみ)がない人
6. フランス語が話(はな)せる人
7. 先週(せんしゅう)映画(えいが)を見た人
8. 空手(からて)ができる人

6 Food

第六章　食(た)べ物(もの)

ファミリーレストランで昼(ひる)ごはんです。

Objectives

In this lesson you are going to

- Talk about foods and beverages
- Talk about meals and restaurants
- Talk about cooking, flavors, and seasonings
- Learn how to express experiences
- Learn how to express desire
- Learn how to express an opinion
- Practice using 〜すぎる
- Learn about indirect quotation …という
- Learn how to express intention
- Practice using the -te form of verbs + みる, しまう, いく, and くる
- Learn how to convey simultaneous action 〜ながら

YOOKOSO! MULTIMEDIA

Review and practice grammar and vocabulary from this chapter and watch video clips on the *Yookoso!* Interactive CD-ROM. Visit the *Yookoso!* Online Learning Center at **www.mhhe.com/yookosome** for additional exercises and resources.

Vocabulary and Grammar 6A

Vocabulary and Oral Activities

Foods and Beverages

Vocabulary: Foods and Beverages

飲み物	のみもの	drinks; beverages
食料品	しょくりょうひん	foodstuffs
おなかがすく		to get hungry
のどがかわく		to get thirsty

Meat

肉	にく	meat
牛肉	ぎゅうにく	beef
豚肉	ぶたにく	pork
鳥肉	とりにく	chicken
ラム		lamb
ミンチ		ground meat
ひき肉	ひきにく	ground meat

Fish

魚	さかな	fish
貝	かい	shellfish
まぐろ		tuna
さけ		salmon
いか		cuttlefish
たこ		octopus

Vegetables

野菜	やさい	vegetable
レタス		lettuce
にんじん		carrot
豆	まめ	bean; pea
じゃがいも		potato
きゅうり		cucumber
玉ねぎ	たまねぎ	onion
トマト		tomato
ピーマン		green pepper

Fruit

果物	くだもの	fruit
バナナ		banana
みかん		mandarin orange
りんご		apple
なし		pear
ぶどう		grape
レモン		lemon
パイナップル		pineapple
メロン		melon
いちご		strawberry

Beverages

(お)茶	(お)ちゃ	tea (*in general*); Japanese tea
紅茶	こうちゃ	black tea
コーヒー		coffee
牛乳、ミルク	ぎゅうにゅう	milk
ジュース		juice
(お)酒	(お)さけ	sake; alcoholic beverage
ワイン		wine
ビール		beer
カクテル		cocktail
ウイスキー		whiskey
水	みず	water (*unheated*)
(お)湯	(お)ゆ	hot water; boiling water

アクティビティー　1

何が一番好きですか。(*What do you like best?*)

Answer each question. Then rank the items in the order of your preference.

1. どの肉が一番好きですか。牛肉、豚肉、鳥肉
2. どの野菜が一番好きですか。レタス、にんじん、ピーマン
3. どの果物が一番好きですか。バナナ、りんご、ぶどう
4. どの飲み物が一番好きですか。お茶、コーヒー、コーラ
5. どのジュースが一番好きですか。りんご、みかん、ぶどう
6. どのアイスクリームが一番好きですか。バニラ、チョコレート、ストロベリー

Culture Note • お茶(おちゃ)

When you go to a restaurant in America, a waiter or waitress first brings a glass of water. In Japan, when you go to a traditional restaurant, the first thing you are served is green tea. When you visit a residence or a company, generally a cup of green tea is served soon after your arrival. Sometimes, however, visitors are served black tea—紅茶(こうちゃ) literally, *crimson tea* or coffee rather than 緑茶(りょくちゃ) (*green tea*). Many people enjoy 茶道(さどう) (*tea ceremony* [lit., *the way of tea*]), which teaches the practitioner the art of hospitality through ritualized preparation and serving of tea to guests. Young women often study it as part of their preparation for marriage. When you want to chat with someone or take him or her out, you might say お茶でも飲みませんか (*Shall we have some tea?*). In short, tea plays an important role in Japanese life. Most neighborhoods have a specialty tea store that sells many different kinds of tea. These are some of the common offerings.

煎茶(せんちゃ)	sencha (*good-quality green tea*)
番茶(ばんちゃ)	bancha (*an everyday, coarser green tea*)
麦茶(むぎちゃ)	*barley tea* (*served chilled in summer*)
げんまい茶(ちゃ)	*brown-rice tea* (*contains popcorn-like bits of puffed rice*)
抹茶(まっちゃ)	*powdered tea* (*used in the tea ceremony; a popular ice cream flavor*)
ウーロン茶(ちゃ)	*oolong tea* (*chilled in summer*)
昆布茶(こんぶちゃ)	*seaweed "tea"* (*actually, powdered seaweed*)

茶道(さどう)：抹茶(まっちゃ)の味(あじ)はいかがでしょうか。

アクティビティー　2

何ですか。(*What is it?*)

Identify the foods and beverages described in the following sentences.

1. ぶどうから作(つく)るお酒(さけ)です。
2. チキンバーガーに使(つか)う (*use*) 肉(にく)です。
3. オレンジ色(いろ)の果物(くだもの)です。
4. アメリカでバーベキューによく使(つか)う肉(にく)です。日本ではすきやきに使(つか)います。
5. 日本や中国(ちゅうごく)でよく飲(の)む飲み物(もの)です。
6. 赤(あか) (*red*) やみどり (*green*) の果物(くだもの)です。コンピュータの会社(かいしゃ) (*company*) の名前(なまえ)です。
7. 黄色(きいろ) (*yellow*) の果物(くだもの)です。
8. フレンチフライを作(つく)る野菜(やさい)です。
9. ごはん (*cooked rice*) の上にこれをのせて (*put on*)、すしを作(つく)ります。
10. 果物(くだもの)から作(つく)る飲(の)み物(もの)です。

Vocabulary: Meals and Restaurants

Meals

食事	しょくじ	meal
ごはん		meal; cooked rice
おやつ、スナック		snack
夜食	やしょく	evening snack

Places to Eat

レストラン		restaurant
台所	だいどころ	kitchen
キッチン		kitchen

Types of Food

ファーストフード		fast food
デザート		dessert
和食	わしょく	Japanese cuisine
洋食	ようしょく	Western cuisine
中華料理	ちゅうかりょうり	Chinese cuisine

Review: 料理(りょうり)(を)する

言語ノート

米(こめ)、ライス、ごはん

Rice is a staple food in Japan. Many Japanese eat rice more than once a day, often three times a day, and don't feel as if they have eaten a meal unless they've had rice. Waiters at Western-style restaurants in Japan usually ask if you would like to have bread or rice along with your entree. Reflecting the importance of rice in Japanese life, the language has several words referring to rice. A *rice plant* is called 稲(いね). *Uncooked rice* is 米(こめ) or お米. *Cooked rice served in a bowl* is ごはん, while *cooked rice served on a plate* is ライス. ごはん also means *meals* in general. Although the consumption of bread relative to rice has risen over the past decades, rice retains an important place in the diet and in the Japanese people's collective identity as a nation of rice eaters.

アクティビティー 3

朝(あさ)ごはんに何(なに)を食べましたか。(*What did you eat for breakfast?*)

Discuss in class.

1. いつも昼(ひる)ごはんを食べますか。昨日(きのう)昼(ひる)ごはんを食べましたか。何(なに)を食べましたか。
2. 昨日(きのう)夕(ゆう)ごはんを食べましたか。何時(なんじ)に食べましたか。何(なに)を食べましたか。
3. 朝(あさ)ごはんの時(とき)、何(なに)か飲(の)みましたか。何(なに)を飲(の)みましたか。
4. いつも朝(あさ)ごはんを食べますか。今日(きょう)朝(あさ)ごはんを食べましたか。
5. どんな食べ物(もの)が一番(ばん)好(す)きですか。
6. どんな飲み物(もの)が一番(ばん)好(す)きですか。
7. レストランによく行きますか。どんなレストランに行きますか。
8. ファーストフード・レストランへよく行きますか。何(なに)を食べますか。
9. どんなデザートが好(す)きですか。
10. 料理(りょうり)は得意(とくい)ですか。よく料理(りょうり)をしますか。

Culture Note • What Do Japanese Eat?

Thanks to increasing interaction with the people and cultures of other countries, Japanese are eating a wider variety of foods than ever before. While some prefer the traditional breakfast—rice, miso soup, seaweed, raw egg (cracked in a bowl, mixed with soy sauce, and poured on the rice), and fish—others choose a Western breakfast of buttered toast, an egg (usually hard-boiled or fried), coffee, and perhaps a small portion of green salad or small sausages.

For lunch, most Japanese workers and students eat at the company or university cafeteria or at small restaurants in the neighborhood. The most popular fare is simple dishes like noodles (cold or hot, in broth or for dipping, made of buckwheat or wheat), rice with something on top (a pork cutlet, say, or curry sauce), or the special set menu of the day (soup, rice, green salad, and a main dish such as tempura). Some people take their lunch to work in a reusable rectangular container wrapped in a square cloth. Shops also sell such boxed lunches, or 弁当 (べんとう), which are freshly made each day.

Suppers cooked at home range from fried chicken, spaghetti, or stew, to sushi, sukiyaki, and tempura. Chinese, Korean, and French are the most widespread foreign cuisines. As the number of working women has grown in Japan, take-out food (テークアウト) and dining out (外食 (がいしょく)) have become more popular. The overwhelming success of chains such as McDonald's, KFC (Kentucky Fried Chicken), and Baskin Robbins in Japan reflects a changing palate that relishes new flavors.

Whatever and wherever Japanese eat, they usually say いただきます (lit., *I receive this*) before they begin and ごちそうさまでした (lit., *It was a feast*) after they finish. Both are expressions of gratitude directed toward the people and things that made the meal possible—that is, the farmers, the fishermen, the people who prepared the meal, the rain that enabled the crops to grow, and so on.

レストランの前 (まえ) で: 何を食べますか。

Grammar and Practice Activities

32. Expressing Experience: The Ta-Form of Verbs + ことがある

林(はやし)：ブラウンさんは東急(とうきゅう)デパートの食堂(しょくどう)へ行ったことがありますか。
ブラウン：いいえ、まだありません。
林：じゃ、今度(こんど)一緒(いっしょ)に行きませんか。
ブラウン：林さんもまだなんですか。
林：ええ。

カワムラ：レストラン「九州(きゅうしゅう)」を知(し)っていますか。
山口：ええ、新聞(しんぶん)で読んだことがあります。
カワムラ：行ったことはないんですか。
山口：はい、ないんです。

32.1 The following construction is used to express past experiences, with a meaning of *to have (done something) before, to have (done something) once* or literally, *to have the experience of having (done something)*.

> こと in this construction is a nominalizer (see, **Grammar 26,** Chapter 5).

Ta-form of a verb + ことがある (ことがあります)

タイ料理(りょうり)を食べたことがありますか。
Have you ever eaten Thai food?
はい、あります。
Yes, I have.
いいえ、ありません。
No, I haven't.
父(ちち)も料理(りょうり)をしたことがあります。
My father has cooked, too. (lit., *My father also has the experience of having cooked.*)

> The ta-form of a verb is equivalent to the plain, past form of verbs.

HAYASHI: Have you ever been (lit., *gone*) to the dining hall at Tokyu Department Store? BROWN: No, I haven't yet. HAYASHI: Then, shall we go there together sometime (lit., *next time*)? BROWN: You haven't gone yet, either? HAYASHI: No. (lit., *Yes* [*that's right*].)

KAWAMURA: Do you know of the restaurant Kyushu? YAMAGUCHI: Yes. I've read (about it) in the newspaper. KAWAMURA: Haven't you been (lit., *gone*) there? YAMAGUCHI: No (lit., *Yes*), I haven't.

Notice the difference between this construction and the simple past tense.

三年前(ねんまえ)にダイエットしました。

三年前(ねんまえ)にダイエットしたことがあります。

I was on a diet three years ago.

The first sentence (simple past) describes the speaker's diet simply as a past event—I was on a diet three years ago. The second sentence (experience) describes the diet as an experience the speaker had at some time in his life—I have been on a diet before; it was three years ago.

Remember that ない, the plain, negative form of ある, is an adjective and conjugates as such.

32.2 You can express a lack of experience by using the negative forms of ある.

こんなにおいしいすしは食べたことがない。

I have never eaten such delicious sushi.

32.3 Here are several adverbs that are commonly used with this construction.

The に in these and similar expressions is often dropped, without changing the meaning.

1. …年前(ねんまえ)に *…years ago*

   五年前(ねんまえ)にブラウンさんに会ったことがあります。

   I've met Ms. Brown before—five years ago.

2. これまでに、今(いま)までに up to now

   これまでに(今(いま)までに)外国語(がいこく)を勉強(べんきょう)したことがありますか。

   Have you ever studied a foreign language? (lit., *Up to now, have you had the experience of studying a foreign language?*)

3. 一度(ど) *once,* 一度(ど)も *never, not once,* 何度(なんど)も *many times*

   メキシコ料理(りょうり)を食べたことがありますか。

   Have you ever eaten Mexican food?

   はい、一度(ど)あります。

   Yes, once.

   いいえ、一度(ど)もありません。

   No, not ever.

度(ど) is a counter meaning *times* as well as *degrees* (*temperature*). 一度(ど) literally means *one time.* 一度(ど)も is used in negative sentences.

4. まだ + negative *not yet*

   インスタント・ラーメンはまだ食べたことがありません。

   I haven't eaten instant noodles yet. (that is, *I have never eaten them.*)

   この本を読んだことがありますか。—いいえ、まだ読んだことはありません。

   Have you ever read this book?—No, not yet.

Note: You cannot use words indicating the recent past with this construction.

昨日(きのう)テレビを見たことがある。(ungrammatical)

I have watched TV yesterday. (ungrammatical)

アクティビティー　4

東京(とうきょう)へ行ったことがありますか。(*Have you ever been to Tokyo?*)

Make a question using the ta-form of the verb ＋ ことがある, and answer the question according to your own experience.

[例]　お酒(さけ)を飲む →
　　—お酒(さけ)を飲んだことがありますか。
　　—はい、あります。(or いいえ、ありません。)

1. 料理(りょうり)をする
2. 日本へ行く
3. ゴルフをする
4. 日本の音楽(おんがく)を聞く
5. すきやきを食べる
6. お金(かね) (*money*) をおとす (*lose*)
7. お金(かね)をひろう (*find*)

✹ アクティビティー　5

行ったことがありません。(*I've never been there.*)

Make dialogues as shown in the example, using the ta-form of the verb ＋ことがある. Choose a negative or positive answer depending on the second phrase provided.

[例]　(てんぷらを食べる) (一度(ど)も) →
　　—てんぷらを食べたことがありますか。
　　—いいえ、一度(ど)も食べたことがありません。

1. (あのレストランへ行く) (三度(ど))
2. (コーラを飲む) (何度(なんど)も)
3. (ロシア語を勉強(べんきょう)する) (一度(ど))
4. (スピルバーグの映画(えいが)を見る) (五年前(まえ))
5. (日本の食べ物(もの)を買(か)う) (二回(かい)ぐらい)
6. (コンピュータを使(つか)う) (一度(ど))
7. (町田(まちだ)さんに会(あ)う) (三年前(まえ)に一度(ど))
8. (あのプールで泳(およ)ぐ) (一度(ど)も)
9. (この町(まち)に雪(ゆき)が降(ふ)る) (一度(ど)も)
10. (ウェートレスをする) (五年前(まえ))

Review **Grammar 9,** Chapter 2 for the use of ～回(かい).

アクティビティー　6

てんぷらを食べたことがありますか。(*Have you ever eaten tempura?*)

Ask a friend if he or she has had the following experiences.

Useful Expressions: パーティーをする *to have a party,* Dを取(と)る *to receive a D,* 部屋(へや)を掃除(そうじ)する *to clean a room*

1. been to Japan
2. studied French
3. eaten sushi
4. had a party at home
5. received a D at school
6. cleaned his or her room

アクティビティー　7

ダイアログ：イタリアン・レストランへ行ったことがありますか。(*Have you ever been to an Italian restaurant?*)

ブラウンさんとチンさんが話しています。

ブラウン：イタリアン・レストランへ行ったことがありますか。
チン：ええ、ありますよ。
ブラウン：どのレストランですか。
チン：いつも「ナポリ」へ行きます。
ブラウン：ああ、そうですか。あそこのラザーニャを食べたことがありますか。
チン：ええ。とてもおいしいです。

Now answer these questions

1. イタリアン・レストランへ行ったことがありますか。何(なに)を食べましたか。
2. スペイン料理(りょうり)の店(みせ)へ行ったことがありますか。何(なに)を食べましたか。
3. ベトナム料理(りょうり)の店(みせ)へ行ったことがありますか。何(なに)を食べましたか。
4. インド料理(りょうり)の店(みせ)へ行ったことがありますか。何(なに)を食べましたか。
5. メキシコ料理(りょうり)の店(みせ)へ行ったことがありますか。何(なに)を食べましたか。
6. どんな料理(りょうり)を作(つく)ったことがありますか。おいしかったですか。

Ms. Brown and Ms. Chin are talking. BROWN: Have you ever been to an Italian restaurant? CHIN: Yes, I have. BROWN: Which restaurant? CHIN: I always go to Napoli. BROWN: Is that so? Have you ever eaten their lasagna? CHIN: Yes. It's really delicious.

Vocabulary Library 

More Food Words

缶詰	かんづめ	canned food
冷凍食品	れいとうしょくひん	frozen food
前菜	ぜんさい	appetizer
お菓子	おかし	sweets (cakes and confections)
卵	たまご	egg
パン		bread
ラーメン		**ramen** (*Chinese-style wheat noodles*)

Japanese Food

うどん		**udon** (*thick, flat wheat noodles*)
そば		**soba** (*buckwheat noodles*)
てんぷら		tempura (*dipped in batter and fried vegetables and fish*)
すきやき		sukiyaki
漬物	つけもの	pickled vegetable
しいたけ		shiitake mushroom
海苔	のり	a kind of seaweed
みりん		sweet cooking sake
とうふ		tofu; bean curd

Meals

朝食	ちょうしょく	breakfast
昼食	ちゅうしょく	lunch
夕食	ゆうしょく	dinner; supper
軽食	けいしょく	light meal; snack

Loanwords: インスタント・フード、オレンジ、クッキングオイル、ケーキ、サンドイッチ、スパゲッティ、ソーセージ、チーズ、チョコレート、トースト、ハム、バター、マーガリン、ヨーグルト

アクティビティー 8

日本料理(りょうり)の通(つう)ですか。(*Are you a connoisseur of Japanese cuisine?*)

Answer these questions by choosing **a** or **b**.

1. あなたは日本レストランへ行ったことがありますか。
   a. はい、あります。　　b. いいえ、ありません。
2. てんぷらを食べたことがありますか。
   a. はい、あります。　　b. いいえ、ありません。

3. すしを食べたことがありますか。
   a. はい、あります。　　b. いいえ、ありません。

4. はし (*chopsticks*) が上手に使えますか。
   a. はい、使えます。　　b. いいえ、使えません。

5. 日本語のメニューが読めますか。
   a. はい、読めます。　　b. いいえ、読めません。

6. 日本料理を作ったことがありますか。
   a. はい、あります。　　b. いいえ、ありません。

7. 日本料理を作るのが得意ですか。
   a. はい、得意です。　　b. いいえ、得意じゃありません。

8. 日本料理が好きですか。
   a. はい、好きです。　　b. いいえ、きらいです。

9. 昨日日本料理を食べましたか。
   a. はい、食べました。　　b. いいえ、食べませんでした。

10. 明日日本料理を食べますか。
   a. はい、食べます。　　b. いいえ、食べません。

Now rate yourself. How many times did you answer *a*?

7 or more:	You are a true connoisseur of Japanese cuisine.
4-6:	You can appreciate Japanese food but can't shake that craving for hamburgers.
2-3:	You need more practice with chopsticks!
0-1:	Are you in the right class?

33. Expressing a Desire: ほしい, ほしがる, 〜たい, and 〜たがる

町田：カワムラさんは今、何が一番ほしいですか。
カワムラ：そうですね。いい日本語の辞書がほしいですね。
町田：大学の前の本屋にいい辞書がありますよ。
カワムラ：本当ですか。すぐに買いたいですね。

MACHIDA: What do you want most now? KAWAMURA: Let me see... I want a good Japanese dictionary.
MACHIDA: There are good dictionaries at the bookstore in front of the university, you know.
KAWAMURA: Really? I'd like to buy one right now.

林：明日(あした)はギブソンさんの誕生日(たんじょうび)ですね。
ブラウン：そうですね。バースデー・プレゼントは何(なに)にしましょうか。
林：ギブソンさんは何(なに)をほしがっていますか。
ブラウン：さあ、よくわかりません。でも、いつもすしを食べたがっていますよ。
林：そうですか。じゃあ、一緒(いっしょ)にすし屋(や)へ行きましょうか。

言語ノート

食(た)べ物屋(ものや) Eateries

You can make words representing specialized restaurants by adding 屋(や) to the names of foods. For instance

すし → すし屋(や)	**sushi** *restaurant*
そば → そば屋(や)	**soba** *restaurant*
ラーメン → ラーメン屋(や)	**ramen** *restaurant*
中華料理(ちゅうかりょうり) → 中華料理屋(や)	*Chinese restaurant*

Some speakers may use the sentence-final particle な(あ) to express the speaker's emotion directly, to try to convince others, to confirm another's opinion, to express a wish, and so forth.

33.1 In Japanese, there is no single verb meaning *to want* as in *I want a new car*. Instead you must choose between two constructions, depending on who is doing the wanting.

(a)	Xは	+	Yが	+	ほしい
(b)	Xは	+	Yを	+	ほしがる

X want(s) Y

Construction (a) is used when expressing one's own desire or when directly asking another person about his or her desire. ほしい is an i-adjective and conjugates as such.

HAYASHI: Tomorrow is Ms. Gibson's birthday, isn't it? BROWN: That's right. What shall we give her for a birthday gift? (lit., *As for a birthday gift, what shall we decide on?*) HAYASHI: What does she want? (lit., *What is Ms. Gibson wanting?*) BROWN: Hmm, I don't really know. But she wants (lit., *is always wanting*) to eat sushi. HAYASHI: Is that right? Well then, let's go to a sushi restaurant together.

わたしは新(あたら)しい車(くるま)がほしいです。
I want a new car.
いいカメラがほしかった。
I wanted a good camera.
今(いま)、コーヒーはほしくありません。
I don't want coffee now.

As you've studied before, in negative sentences the particle が is often replaced with は.

Construction (b) is used when discussing a third person's desire. ほしがる is a Class 1 verb. The te-form of ほしがる + いる (ほしがっている) is used when expressing a current desire, whereas the nonpast form (ほしがる) expresses a longer term desire.

林さんはもっと本をほしがっています。
Mr. Hayashi wants more books.
妹(いもうと)はあまりお金(かね)をほしがらない。
My younger sister doesn't want money very much.

Notice that the object of desire is marked with が in sentences using the predicate ほしい and with を in those using ほしがる.

わたしは新(あたら)しい車(くるま)がほしい。
I want a new car.
妻(つま)は新(あたら)しい車(くるま)をほしがっている。
My wife wants a new car.

言語ノート

～がる

In Japanese, different grammatical constructions are needed when describing your own emotional state as opposed to that of others. You know your own emotional state, but you can only guess about that of other people from their appearance, behavior, or statements. To describe someone else's emotional state, you can attach ～がる to the root of an adjective to mean *has the appearance of* or *appears to (be)*. Thus, when *you* are lonely, you say

さびしいです。
I am lonely.

But when someone else is lonely, you say

さびしがっています。
He is lonely. (lit., *He appears to be lonely.*)

33.2 Similar to the ほしい／ほしがる pair is the pair of patterns used to express *to want to (do something)*, as in *I want to eat sushi.*

(a)	Xは	+	Yが／を	+	conjunctive form of verb +	たい
(b)	Xは	+	Yを	+	conjunctive form of verb +	たがる

As with ほしい and ほしがる, (a) is used when the speaker expresses a desire or asks about the hearer's desire. (b) is used to describe a third person's desire. The ending 〜たい is an i-adjective and conjugates as such, whereas 〜たがる is a Class 1 verb.

In sentences using 〜たい, the direct object of the verb can be marked with either が or を. However, in sentences using 〜たがる, the direct object is marked only with を.

ヨーグルトが食べたい。
ヨーグルトを食べたい。
I want to eat yogurt.
林さんはヨーグルトを食べたがっている。
Mr. Hayashi wants to eat yogurt.

Here are some more examples.

ステーキが食べたい。
I want to eat steak.

わたしは今朝(けさ)、ごはんは食べたくありません。
I don't want to eat rice this morning.

明日(あした)どこへ行きたいですか。
Where do you want to go tomorrow?

わたしはお酒(さけ)が飲みたかった。
I wanted to drink sake.

The 〜たい form is often used to ask for permission. For instance

このコンピュータを使(つか)いたいのですが、...
I want to use this computer, but... (is it OK?)

中に入(はい)りたいんですが、よろしいですか。
I would like to go inside, but is that all right?

Like the contrast between ほしがる and ほしがっている discussed on the previous page, the te-form of たがる + いる (たがっている) expresses a current desire, whereas the nonpast expresses a longer term desire.

山口(やまぐち)さんはアメリカに来(き)たがっている。
Mr. Yamaguchi wants to come to the United States.

チンさんは家(いえ)に帰(かえ)りたがりません。
Ms. Chin doesn't want to go back home.

言語ノート

Asking What Someone Wants

In Japanese, it is often considered rude to ask someone what he or she desires directly. This is especially true regarding the desires of socially superior people. For instance, it is very rude to ask someone

すきやきが食べたいですか。
Do you want to eat sukiyaki?
どの映画(えいが)を見たいですか。
Which movie do you want to see?

Rather, Japanese speakers tend to ask

すきやきを食べませんか。
Won't you eat sukiyaki?
すきやきはいかがですか。
How about some sukiyaki?
映画(えいが)を見ませんか。
Shall we see a movie?

アクティビティー 9

ダイアログ：どこかへ行きませんか。(*Shall we go somewhere?*)

町田(まちだ)さんとブラウンさんが話しています。

町田(まちだ)：土曜日(どようび)、どこかへ行きませんか。
ブラウン：ええ。町田さんはどこへ行きたいですか。
町田：そうですね。いいレストランへ行きたいですね。
ブラウン：それはいいですね。何(なに)かおいしいものを食べたいですね。

Practice the dialogue, substituting the following for the underlined sentences.

1. イタリア・レストランへ行く
   スパゲッティを食べる
2. 映画館(えいがかん)へ行く
   おもしろい映画(えいが)を見る
3. ショッピングセンターへ行く
   買(か)い物(もの)をする
4. ゲームセンターへ行く
   テレビゲームで遊(あそ)ぶ
5. 林さんのアパートへ行く
   林さんと話す

Ms. Machida and Ms. Brown are talking. MACHIDA: Shall we go somewhere on Saturday? BROWN: Yes. Where do you want to go? MACHIDA: Let me see. I would like to go to a good restaurant, wouldn't you? BROWN: That's a good idea. (lit., *That's good.*) I would like to eat some good food. (lit., *I want to eat something delicious, don't you?*)

アクティビティー 10

遊びたいです。(*I want to play.*)

Change these sentences as shown in the examples.

[例] 昼ごはんを食べる → 昼ごはんが食べたいです。
ビールを飲まない → ビールは飲みたくないです。
ジュースが飲みたいです。

1. ちょっと休む
2. 朝早く起きない
3. フランス語の辞書を買う
4. スーパーへ行かない
5. 働かない
6. 町田さんに会う
7. 映画を見る
8. 林さんと話す
9. 日本語を練習する
10. 今日、宿題をしない

アクティビティー 11

ブラウンさんはステレオを買いたがっています。(*Ms. Brown wants to buy a stereo.*)

Rewrite the sentences you made in アクティビティー**10** starting each new sentence withブラウンさんは.

[例] ブラウンさんは昼ごはんを食べたがっています。
ブラウンさんはビールを飲みたがっていません。

アクティビティー 12

どこへ行きたがっていますか。(*Where does she want to go?*)

Using the information in the pictures, answer these questions.

1. 町田さんは今年の夏、どこへ行きたがっていますか。
2. 今夜、何を食べたがっていますか。
3. だれに会いたがっていますか。
4. 明日、何をしたがっていますか。
5. 何を飲みたがっていますか。
6. 何をしたがっていますか。
7. どんなレコードを聞きたがっていますか。
8. どのビデオを見たがっていますか。

1.

2.

3.

4.

5.

6.

7.

8.

アクティビティー 13

セーターがほしいです。(*I want a sweater.*)

Complete the following sentences.

[例] とても寒いので、(　　)がほしいです。→ とても寒いので、(セーター)がほしいです。

1. 日本語の勉強のために (*for studying Japanese*)、(　　) がほしいです。
2. 今日はいいお天気だから、(　　) たいです。
3. つかれた (*I'm tired*) から、(　　) たいです。

4. おなかがすいた (*I'm hungry*) から、(　　) たいです。
5. 町田さんは昼ごはんに (　　) たがっています。
6. 音楽の好きな山本さんは (　　) をほしがっています。

アクティビティー 14

誰に一番会いたいですか。(*Who do you most want to see?*)

Answer these questions.

1. 今、何が一番食べたいですか。
2. 今、何が一番買いたいですか。
3. 今週の土曜日、何をしたいですか。
4. 今、何がほしいですか。
5. 今、どこへ一番行きたいですか。
6. 今、誰に一番会いたいですか。
7. あなたが一番勉強したい外国語は何ですか。
8. あなたが一番したくないことは何ですか。

アクティビティー 15

何が食べたいですか。(*What do you want to eat?*)

Answer these questions.

1. 今、午前6時半です。何が食べたいですか。
2. 今、午後6時です。とてもおなかがすいています。
   何が食べたいですか。
3. 今日はデートです。どんなレストランへ行きたいですか。
4. 今、午後10時です。日本語を勉強しています。とてもおなかがすきました。何が食べたいですか。
5. 今、日本レストランにいます。何が食べたいですか。
6. 今日の夕ごはんは何が食べたいですか。
7. テニスをしました。のどがかわきました。何が飲みたいですか。

Now pair up. Find out what your partner wants to do on the following occasions. Take notes and save them for アクティビティー **16.**

8. 今、何が一番食べたいですか。
9. デートの時、どんなレストランへ一番行きたいですか。
10. 今、何が一番買いたいですか。
11. この週末、何がしたいですか。
12. 今、だれに一番会いたいですか。
13. 今、どの映画が見たいですか。
14. 次の (*next*) 夏休みにどこへ行きたいですか。
15. 次の冬休みにどこへ行きたいですか。

アクティビティー 16

ダイアログ：ロブスターを食べたがっています。(*She wants to eat lobster.*)

ブラウンさんと林さんが話しています。

ブラウン：林さん、お出かけですか。
林：ええ、ギブソンさんとシーフード・レストランへ行くんです。
ブラウン：それはいいですね。
林：ええ、ギブソンさんがロブスターを食べたがっているんです。

Practice the dialogue, substituting the following expressions for the underlined phrases.

1. ショッピング・センターへ行く　新しいドレスを買う
2. コンサートへ行く　クラシック音楽を聞く
3. プールへ行く　泳ぐ

Now report the results of the interview you conducted in アクティビティー **15** to the class. Use ～たがっています.

[例]　ジョンソンさんは今すしを一番食べたがっています。
キムさんはメキシコ料理の店へ一番行きたがっています。

Ms. Brown and Mr. Hayashi are talking. BROWN: Mr. Hayashi, are you going out? HAYASHI: Yes, I'm going to a seafood restaurant with Ms. Gibson. BROWN: That should be nice. (lit., *That's good, isn't it?*) HAYASHI: Yes. We are going because Ms. Gibson wants to eat lobster. (lit., *It's that Ms. Gibson wants to eat lobster.*)

Vocabulary and Grammar 6B

Vocabulary and Oral Activities

Flavors and Tastes

Vocabulary: Flavors, Tastes, and Seasonings 

Flavors and Tastes

味	あじ	flavor; taste
味がいい	あじがいい	to taste good
味がない	あじがない	to have no taste
味見する	あじみする	to taste a sample
おいしい		tasty; delicious
まずい		not tasty; tastes bad
甘い	あまい	sweet
苦い	にがい	bitter
辛い	からい	spicy; hot (*spicy*); salty
塩辛い	しおからい	salty
酸っぱい	すっぱい	sour
渋い	しぶい	astringent

Seasonings

調味料	ちょうみりょう	seasoning
塩	しお	salt
砂糖	さとう	sugar
胡椒	こしょう	pepper
醤油	しょうゆ	soy sauce
味噌	みそ	miso (*fermented soybean paste*)
酢	す	vinegar
ソース		*a prepared sauce somewhat like steak sauce*

アクティビティー 17

Odd man out

In each of the following groups of words, one word does not belong in the same category as the others. Identify it and tell why it doesn't belong.

[例] ロンドン、東京(とうきょう)、ニューヨーク、モスクワ、パリ
→ 東京(とうきょう)です。日本にあります。(外国(がいこく)の町(まち)ではありません。
カタカナではありません。)

1. ステーキ、ソース、ビーフシチュー、フライドチキン、ポークソテー
2. 高い、甘(あま)い、辛(から)い、塩辛(しおから)い、にがい
3. ワイン、ビール、ウイスキー、カクテル、酢(す)
4. いか、たこ、まぐろ、じゃがいも、さけ
5. トマト、玉(たま)ねぎ、ピーマン、にんじん、こしょう
6. みかん、砂糖(さとう)、なし、りんご、レモン
7. まずい、味(あじ)がない、そば、味(あじ)がいい、渋(しぶ)い
8. みそ、しょうゆ、とうふ、ピザ、そば

Grammar and Practice Activities

34. Expressing an Opinion …と思(おも)う

カーティス：チンさん、明日(あした)、ハイキングに行きますか。
チン：ええ、行けると思(おも)いますが、カーティスさんは？
カーティス：明日(あした)はアルバイトがあるんです。それに、
明日(あした)は雨(あめ)が降(ふ)ると思(おも)いますよ。
チン：そう思(おも)いますか。

CURTIS: Ms. Chin, are you going hiking tomorrow? CHIN: Yes, I think I can go. How about you?
CURTIS: I have a part-time job tomorrow. Also, I think it will rain (tomorrow). CHIN: Do you think so?

ブラウンさんと町田(まちだ)さんが写真(しゃしん)を見ています。

ブラウン：町田(まちだ)さん、この男(おとこ)の人、知(し)ってますか。

町田(まちだ)：ええ、どこかで見たことがありますね。

ブラウン：わたしもそう思(おも)ったんです。

町田：そうそう、思(おも)い出(だ)しました。この人は先週(せんしゅう)のパーティーに来(き)ていたと思(おも)いますよ。

言語ノート

そう

そう is one of the following list of **ko-so-a-do** words used to express manner. (See **Grammar 3,** Chapter 1, for more on **ko-so-a-do** words.)

こう	*like this*	ああ	*like that*
そう	*like that*	どう	*how, in what manner*

そう is used in many common expressions.

はい、そうです。	*Yes, that's right.* (lit., *Yes, it's like that.*)
そうですね。	*Well…* (or, *Let me see…*) or *That's right.* (depending on intonation)
はい、そうします。	*Yes, I will do so.*
そうしましょう。	*Let's do that.*
はい、そう思(おも)います。	*Yes, I think so.*

An opinion can be expressed with the following construction in Japanese, which means *to think* (*that*)… 思(おも)う is a Class 1 verb meaning *to think.*

Plain form of verb, adjective, or copula	+	と思(おも)う(思(おも)います)

ギブソンさんはタクシーで来(く)ると思(おも)います。
I think that Ms. Gibson will come by cab.
山本(やまもと)さんは今日(きょう)は働(はたら)いていないと思(おも)う。
I think that Ms. Yamamoto is not working today.

Ms. Brown and Ms. Machida are looking at a photograph. BROWN: Ms. Machida, do you know this man? MACHIDA: Yes, I have seen him somewhere. BROWN: I thought so, too. MACHIDA: That's right! I just remembered. I think that he was at last week's party.

明日(あした)は寒(さむ)いと思(おも)いますか。
Do you think that it will be cold tomorrow?

What one believes or recalls is also expressed by this construction.

その日はレストランで食事(しょくじ)をしたと思(おも)います。
I think I ate at a restaurant on that day.

あの人は高田(たかだ)さんのお父(とう)さんだと思(おも)う。
I think that person is Mr. Takada's father.

アクティビティー 18

いないと思(おも)います。(*I don't think he's there.*)

Following the example, rewrite each sentence using と思(おも)います。

[例] 今夜(こんや) (*tonight*)、山口(やまぐち)さんはいません。→
今夜(こんや)、山口(やまぐち)さんはいないと思(おも)います。

1. 林さんと話しませんでした。
2. その日、そのレストランは休(やす)みでした。
3. その人に会(あ)ったことがあります。
4. 山口(やまぐち)さんの家(いえ)の台所(だいどころ)はとてもきれいです。
5. ブラウンさんの作(つく)ったケーキはとてもおいしかったです。
6. あの男(おとこ)の人はコック(*cook*)です。
7. さとみさんは料理(りょうり)をしています。

アクティビティー 19

Look at the illustrations, and answer the following questions.

1. 

2. 

3. 

4. 

5. 

6. 

7. 

1. カワムラさんはよく勉強(べんきょう)すると思(おも)いますか。
2. ブラウンさんは日本語が上手(じょうず)に話せると思(おも)いますか。
3. この近所(きんじょ)は静(しず)かだと思(おも)いますか。
4. ギブソンさんは料理(りょうり)が上手(じょうず)だと思(おも)いますか。
5. 林さんはたくさん食べると思(おも)いますか。
6. 町田さんは何(なに)をほしがっていると思(おも)いますか。
7. チンさんはどこへ行ったと思(おも)いますか。

35. 〜すぎる

町田：大野(おおの)先生のクラスはどうですか。
ブラウン：宿題(しゅくだい)が多(おお)くて、たいへんです。
町田：そうですか。大野(おおの)先生はちょっときびしすぎますよね。
ブラウン：ええ、本当(ほんとう)に。

カワムラ：林さん、大丈夫(だいじょうぶ)ですか。
林：ええ、ちょっと飲みすぎましたね。
カワムラ：一人で帰(かえ)れますか。
林：ええ、何(なん)とか。

To add the meaning *too much* or *excessively* to a verb or adjective, add the verb すぎる to the appropriate form, as shown. すぎる is a Class 2 verb meaning *to exceed.*

VERBS	I-ADJECTIVES	NA-ADJECTIVES
Conjunctive Form	**Root** + すぎる	**Root (Dictionary Form)**
飲む → 飲み 食べる → 食べ する → し 来(く)る → 来(き)	むずかしい → むずかし 大(おお)きい → 大き	静(しず)か（な）→ 静(しず)か はで（な）→ はで

MACHIDA: How is Professor Ono's class? BROWN: There is lots of homework, so it's tough. MACHIDA: Is that right? Professor Ono is a little too strict, isn't he? BROWN: Yes, really.

KAWAMURA: Mr. Hayashi, are you all right? HAYASHI: Yes, I have drunk a little too much. KAWAMURA: Can you get home yourself? HAYASHI: Yes, I can manage. (lit., *Yes, somehow.*)

あの人はちょっと話しすぎますね。
That person talks a little too much.

この部屋(へや)はちょっと暑(あつ)すぎませんか。
Isn't this room a little too hot?

このケーキは甘(あま)すぎて、食べられない。
This cake is too sweet to eat. (lit., *This cake is too sweet, so I can't eat it.*)

この問題(もんだい)は私(わたし)にはむずかしすぎる。
This question is too difficult for me.

アクティビティー 20

むずかしすぎます。(*It's too difficult.*)

Fill in the blanks with the appropriate forms of the words listed here.

長(なが)い、あつい、飲む、広(ひろ)い、辛(から)い、食べる、高(たか)い、にぎやか、静(しず)か

1. このコーヒーは(　　)すぎて、飲めません。
2. 昨日(きのう)はすきやきを(　　)すぎました。
3. 父(ちち)はちょっとお酒(さけ)を(　　)すぎます。
4. あのダイヤはちょっと(　　)すぎて、買(か)えません。
5. この家(いえ)は部屋(へや)が8つもあって、(　　)すぎます。
6. あのレストランのカレーは(　　)すぎる。
7. あの映画(えいが)は4時間(じかん)で、ちょっと(　　)すぎる。

アクティビティー 21

むずかしくありません。やさしすぎます。(*It's not difficult. It's too easy.*)

What do you say in these situations? Answer using 〜すぎる。

[例] when a cake is too sweet → このケーキは甘(あま)すぎます。

1. when an exam is very difficult
2. when there are many difficult **kanji** in a reading passage
3. when someone is working too much
4. when the room is too cold
5. when someone is playing music too loudly
6. when an exam is very easy
7. when a sweater is too big for you

アクティビティー 22

どう思(おも)いますか。(*What do you think?*)

林(はやし)さんとギブソンさんが台所(だいどころ)で話しています。

ギブソン：これ、ちょっと味見(あじみ)してください。
林：ああ、いいにおいですね。
ギブソン：どう思いますか。
林：ウーン、<u>ちょっと甘(あま)すぎる</u>と思(おも)います。

Practice the dialogue, substituting the underlined part with the following.

1. とてもおいしい
2. ちょっと酸(す)っぱい
3. おもしろい味(あじ)だ
4. ちょっと辛(から)すぎる
5. ぜんぜん味(あじ)がない

アクティビティー 23

どのレストランがいいと思(おも)いますか。(*Which restaurant do you think is good?*)

Answer the following questions according to the table. Use ～と思(おも)います。

値段 *price* / おすすめ品 *recommended dish* / 休み *day(s) closed*

名前(なまえ)	タイプ	値段(ねだん)	味(あじ)	おすすめ品(ひん)	休(やす)み
ふじ	日本	¥	★★★	すきやき	月
アミーゴ	メキシコ	¥¥	★	タコス	日
マキシム	フランス	¥¥¥	★★★	エスカルゴ	火
モナリザ	イタリア	¥¥¥	★	ピザ	月
ホンコン	中国(ちゅうごく)	¥¥	★★	全部(ぜんぶ)	日
バーガー・クイーン	ファーストフード	¥	★	ハンバーガー	24時間オープン

[例] —「ふじ」はどんなレストランですか。
—安(やす)くて、おいしいレストランだと思(おも)います。

Mr. Hayashi and Ms. Gibson are talking in the kitchen. GIBSON: Please taste this for me. HAYASHI: Mmm, it smells good. (lit., *Mmm, it's a good smell, isn't it?*) GIBSON: What do you think? HAYASHI: Hmm, I think <u>it is a little too sweet</u>.

1. 「ふじ」は何(なに)がおいしいですか。
2. 「アミーゴ」は何曜日(なんようび)が休(やす)みですか。
3. 「マキシム」は高(たか)いですか。安(やす)いですか。
4. 「モナリザ」はおいしいですか。まずいですか。
5. 「ホンコン」は何(なに)がおいしいですか。
6. 「バーガー・クイーン」は休(やす)みがありますか。
7. 今日(きょう)はデートです。どのレストランがいいですか。
8. 今日(きょう)はお金(かね)があまりありません。どのレストランがいいですか。

言語ノート

Asking For and Expressing Opinions

To ask for someone's opinion, say

…(を)どう思(おも)いますか。
What do you think about…?

For example

あのレストランの料理(りょうり)をどう思(おも)いますか。
What do you think of that restaurant's food?

とてもおいしいと思(おも)います。
I think they are very delicious.

When you don't have an opinion, or wish to avoid expressing an opinion, you can say

さあ、わかりません。
Hmm, I don't know.

When soliciting agreement with your view, you can say

…と思(おも)いませんか。
Don't you think (that)…?

For instance

あのレストランは、高(たか)すぎると思(おも)いませんか。
Don't you think that restaurant is too expensive?

In addition, you can use this phrase to try to change someone's opinion.

でも、サービスがいいと思(おも)いませんか。
But don't you think that their service is good?

✸ アクティビティー 24

ダイアログ：「ふじ」というレストランへ行ったことがありますか。
(*Have you ever been to the restaurant Huji?*)

カーティス：「ふじ」というレストランへ行ったことがありますか。
　　チン：ええ。よく行きますよ。
カーティス：どんなレストランですか。
　　チン：安(やす)くて、おいしいレストランだと思(おも)います。

Practice the dialogue, substituting information from the table in アクティビティー **23** for the underlined phrases.

36. Quoting Speech: ...という

カワムラ：すみません。*Plug outlet* はどこですか。
　　町田：プラグアウトレット？ああ、日本語ではコンセントといいます。
カワムラ：日本語では *plug outlet* をコンセントというんですか。
　　町田：ええ、おかしいですか。

ギブソン：あの角(かど)の新(あたら)しいレストランへ行きましたか。
　　チン：「ハングリーベアー」というレストランですか。
ギブソン：ええ、そうです。
　　チン：昨日(きのう)行きました。ブラウンさんも行ったと言っていましたよ。

36.1 The verb 言(い)う means *to say, to tell,* or *to be called.* This verb is used in the following construction to say what something or someone is called or named. In this usage, the verb is not written in **kanji.**

(Aは)　+　Xを　+　Yと　+　言(い)う (言(い)います)

A calls X Y

CURTIS: Have you ever been to the restaurant Huji?　CHIN: Yes, I go there often.　CURTIS: What kind of restaurant is it?　CHIN: I think the food's good, and it's inexpensive. (lit., *I think it is an inexpensive, delicious restaurant.*)

KAWAMURA: Excuse me. Where is the plug outlet?　MACHIDA: Plug outlet? Oh, it's called **konsento** in Japanese.　KAWAMURA: You call a plug outlet **konsento** (*consent*)?　MACHIDA: Yes, is it funny?

GIBSON: Did you go to the new restaurant at that corner?　CHIN: Do you mean the restaurant called Hungry Bear?　GIBSON: Yes, that's right.　CHIN: I went yesterday. Ms. Brown also said that she had been there.

日本人はこれを何といいますか。
What do Japanese call this?
日本人はこれをたこといいます。
Japanese call this ***tako*** *(octopus).*

When the topic (Aは) is omitted (when A is unknown or understood from context), X is usually marked with the topic marker は instead of を.

これはいかといいます。
This is called ***ika*** *(cuttlefish).*

> In colloquial speech, …という（いいます）very often changes to …っていう（いいます）, as in これはいかっています。

36.2 Use the same verb to make a noun phrase meaning *X called* (or *named*) *Y.*

Y + という + X

ジョン・カワムラという学生
a student named John Kawamura
東京大学という大学
a university called the University of Tokyo
島根という県はどこにありますか。
Where is the prefecture Shimane?
これは何という料理ですか。
What is this dish called? (lit., *As for this, it is a dish called what*)?

> In colloquial speech, …っていう is often used rather than …という. For example, 東京大学っていう大学

言語ノート

Quote Marker と

The particle と in という is called a *quote marker* and is used to mark the end of a quotation. In addition, it indicates the content of thinking (…と思う), writing (…と書(か)く), and hearing (…と聞く).

あの人は先生だろうと思った。
I thought that that person was probably a teacher.
今日は寒かったと日記に書いた。
I wrote in my diary that it was cold today.
林さんは九州に帰ると聞きました。
I heard that Mr. Hayashi will return to Kyushu.

36.3 There are two ways to quote someone's words—*direct quotation* and *indirect quotation.* Direct quotation is the quoting of someone's words verbatim, exactly as they were spoken. In English, direct quotations are set off with quotation marks. For example

He said, "I am hungry."

Indirect quotation, on the other hand, may be a paraphrasing of someone else's words; the object is to convey the basic content of the utterance, not the specific words. For example

He said that he was hungry.

In Japanese, direct quotations usually take the following structure.

「　　」, と言う (or some other communication verb)

「　　」, called かぎ括弧 (かぎかっこ), are equivalent to quotation marks. The information contained within the quotation marks is as it was spoken, so you can use either polite or plain forms of predicates.

「早く起きてください。」と山口さんは言いました。
Mr. Yamaguchi said, "Please get up early."
高田さんは、「明日来ますか。」とわたしに聞きました。
Mr. Takada asked me, "Are you coming tomorrow?"

Indirect quotations take the following structure.

Clause ending in a plain form of verb, adjective, or copula	+	と言う (言います) (or other verb of communication)

No quotation marks are used, and only the plain form of a verb, adjective, or the copula can be used in front of と in this case.

三村さんは明日来ると言いました。
Mr. Mimura said he will come tomorrow.
そこに行かなかったとカーティスさんは言った。
Mr. Curtis said that he didn't go there.
そのりんごは甘いとブラウンさんは言っています。
Ms. Brown says (lit., *is saying*) *those apples are sweet.*

Some communication verbs often used in these constructions are 言う *to say, to tell,* 伝える *to convey,* 述べる *to state,* 聞く *to hear, to ask,* and 話す *to speak.*

かれのお父さんは有名だったと聞きました。
I heard that his father had been famous.

When the subject of the clause preceding と言う is in the third person, and the tense of 言う is nonpast, it is better to use 言っている.

アクティビティー　25

ダイアログ：何(なん)と言(い)ったんですか。(*What did he say?*)

カワムラ：町田(まちだ)さん、泣(な)いているんですか。
町田(まちだ)：ええ、林(はやし)さんがひどいことを言(い)ったんですよ。
カワムラ：何(なん)と言(い)ったんですか。
町田：<u>私(わたし)の作(つく)ったケーキがまずい</u>と言(い)ったんですよ。
カワムラ：それはひどいですね。

Practice the dialogue, substituting the following insensitive comments for the underlined phrase. Remember to change each to the appropriate quoted form.

1. 「町田(まちだ)さんは料理(りょうり)がへたですね。」
2. 「町田(まちだ)さんのヘアースタイルは面白(おもしろ)いですね。」
3. 「町田(まちだ)さんの作(つく)ったクッキーは味(あじ)がぜんぜんありませんね。」
4. 「町田(まちだ)さんのファッション・センスは最低(さいてい) (*the worst*) ですね。」
5. 「町田(まちだ)さんのボーイフレンドがきれいな女(おんな)の人と歩(ある)いていましたよ。」

アクティビティー　26

何(なん)と言(い)いますか。(*How do you say it?*)

Answer these questions.

1. 日本語で *breakfast* を何(なん)と言いますか。
2. 日本語で *vegetable* を何(なん)と言いますか。
3. この教科書(きょうかしょ)は何(なん)と言いますか。
4. あなたの学校(がっこう)は何(なん)と言いますか。
5. 英語(えいご)で「料理(りょうり)」を何(なん)と言いますか。
6. 日本語で電話(でんわ)をかけます。何(なん)と言(い)いますか。
7. これからごはんを食べます。何(なん)と言(い)いますか。
8. ごはんが終(お)わりました。何(なん)と言(い)いますか。

KAWAMURA: Ms. Machida, are you crying? MACHIDA: Yes, Mr. Hayashi said a terrible thing (to me). KAWAMURA: What did he say? MACHIDA: He said that <u>the cake I made tastes bad</u>. KAWAMURA: Yes, that's terrible (*what he said*).

✸ アクティビティー 27

「ようこそ」という本です。(*It's the book called* Yookoso.)

Following the example, make dialogues.

[例] (これ)(飲み物)(カルピス)→
—これは何という飲み物ですか。
—カルピスという飲み物です。

1. (あれ)(映画館)(テアトロシアター)
2. (あれ)(果物)(キィウィ)
3. (ここ)(町)(中野)
4. (これ)(車)(セリカ)
5. (あそこ)(レストラン)(セブンシーズ)
6. (これ)(教科書)(ようこそ)

カルピス, or **Calpis** (sold in America as *Calpico*), is a sweet, fermented milk drink popular in the summertime.

✸ アクティビティー 28

ボストンという町を知っていますか。(*Do you know the city Boston?*)

Make a dialogue, following the example.

[例] ブラウンさんはカワムラさんのクラスメートです。→
—ブラウンさんという人を知っていますか。
—ええ、カワムラさんのクラスメートです。

1. アコードは日本の車です。
2. 東京大学はブラウンさんの大学です。
3. ラッキーマートはブラウンさんの近所のスーパーです。
4. おでんは日本の食べ物です。
5. しょうゆは日本の調味料です。

おでん is a Japanese stew of vegetables, fish rolls, tofu, and hard-boiled eggs.

アクティビティー 29

早くすると言いました。(*She said she'd do it quickly.*)

Rewrite these direct quotation sentences into their indirect quotation equivalents.

[例] かれは「そのメロンが好きです。」と言いました。→
かれはそのメロンが好きだと言いました。

1. 町田さんは「レストランへ行きました。」と言った。
2. チンさんはわたしに「中国語を教えています。」と言いました。
3. カワムラさんは「ハンバーガーが好きですか。」と聞きました。
4. テレビのレポーターは「ハワイはとても暑いですよ。」と言っています。
5. 林さんは「英語が話せません。」と言った。
6. 山口さんは「毎日料理しました。」と言いました。
7. 山本さんは「新聞を読んでいません。」と言いました。
8. カーティスさんは「昼ごはんを食べましたか。」と聞いた。
9. ギブソンさんは「二十日は土曜日です。」と言いました。
10. ブラウンさんは「雨の日が好きではありません。」といつも言っています。

アクティビティー 30

有名人にインタビューしました。(*I interviewed famous people!*)

Using the model as an example, tell who made each statement. Choose from the famous people listed here.

フアン・バルデス、コロネル・サンダース、ジュリア・チャイルド、
サラ・リー、ジェニー・クレイグ

[例] 「エアロビクスが好きです。」→
ジェーン・フォンダがエアロビクスが好きだと言いました。

1. 「料理の本 (*cookbook*) をたくさん書きました。」
2. 「コロンビアでコーヒーを作っています。」
3. 「私の作ったケーキはおいしいですよ。」
4. 「みんなが私のダイエットをしています。」
5. 「KFC (ケンタッキー・フライド・チキン) は、私が始めました (*began*)。」

What do you think the following people said?

ビル・クリントン、マイケル・ジョーダン、マドンナ、
ボー・ジャクソン

Vocabulary and Grammar 6C

Vocabulary and Oral Activities

Cooking

Vocabulary: Cooking Terms 

Food Preparation

料理の本	りょうりのほん	cookbook
材料	ざいりょう	ingredient(s)
生	なま	raw
切る	きる	to cut
煮る	にる	to boil (*to cook in liquid*)
焼く	やく	to broil; to grill; to bake
いためる		to stir-fry
あげる		to deep-fry
蒸す	むす	to steam
ゆでる		to cook in boiling water

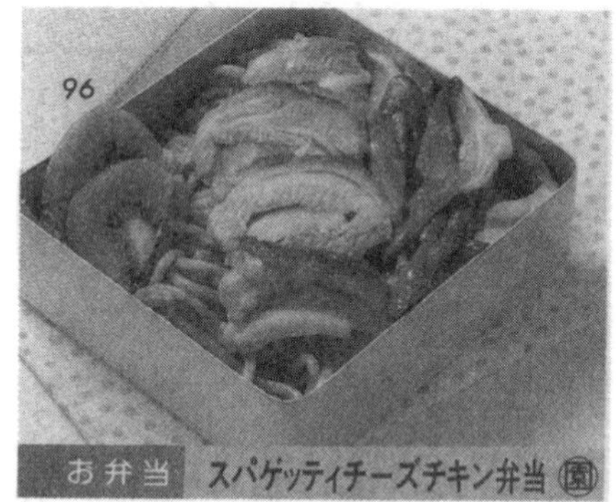

酒蒸しにした鶏肉小¼枚は厚みに切り込みを入れてチーズをはさみ、両面を油焼きにする。ゆでたスパゲッティは炒めて塩、胡椒、ケチャップで調味する。スパゲッティの上にチキンをのせ、グリーンアスパラと生椎茸のソテー、キーウィを添える。

鶏レバー400gは塩水で血抜きして一口大に切り、葱の葉先などを加えて下ゆでする。鍋にレバー、葱のぶつ切り、生姜の薄切り各少少、小玉葱10個を入れ、醤油¼カップ、みりんまたは砂糖少々、シナモン大さじ½を加えて汁けがなくなるまで煮る。

バター70g、粉砂糖50g、卵黄1個分、おろしレモン皮1個分、小麦粉120gで生地を作り、小さな型に敷いて焼き上げ、ケースに。卵黄2個分、大さじで砂糖2、小麦粉1、牛乳150ccでカスタードを作ってケースにつめ、フルーツとホイップクリームで飾る。

Utensils and Appliances

包丁	ほうちょう	cleaver; big cutting knife
鍋	なべ	pan; pot
かんきり		can opener
せんぬき		bottle opener
皿	さら	plate; dish
コップ		glass
茶碗	ちゃわん	rice bowl or teacup
(お)椀	(お)わん	soup bowl
箸	はし	chopsticks
冷蔵庫	れいぞうこ	refrigerator

Loanwords: オーブン、クッキング・スクール、グラス、スプーン、ナイフ、ナプキン、フォーク、フライパン、レシピー、レンジ

アクティビティー 31

連想 (*Association*)

Provide short answers to each of the following items.

1. What process do you use to prepare each of the following foods?
   a. ゆで卵
   b. ケーキ
   c. きゅうり
   d. じゃがいも
   e. ひき肉
   f. すきやき
   g. てんぷら
2. What do you do with the following utensils?
   a. 箸
   b. せんぬき
   c. 鍋
   d. 包丁
   e. かんきり

アクティビティー 32

何がいりますか。(*What do you need?*)

Work in pairs. Ask your partner what ingredient you need to prepare the following dishes.

Useful expression: …がいります。*You need…*

[例] s1: サンドイッチを作ります。何がいりますか。
s2: パンとハムとレタスとチーズがいります。

1. すきやき
2. フルーツ・サラダ
3. 野菜サラダ
4. すし
5. てんぷら

Now change partners. Report your first partner's answers as done in the example.

[例] パンとハムとレタスとチーズがいると言いました。

Grammar and Practice Activities

37. Expressing Intention: つもり and the Volitional Form of Verbs

ブラウン：	町田さん、昼ごはんはどうするつもりですか。
町田：	ええと、カフェテリアで食べるつもりです。ブラウンさんは。
ブラウン：	学校の外で食べようと思います。カフェテリアにはあきましたから…
町田：	そうですね。私も学校の外で食べようかなあ…

37.1 One way to express one's intention is with this construction. (つもり is a noun meaning *plan, intention.*)

Dictionary form of verb + つもりだ (つもりです)

to intend to… or *to plan to…*

毎日野菜を食べるつもりです。
I intend to eat vegetables every day.
チンさんの誕生日にすしを作るつもりです。
I plan to make sushi for Ms. Chin's birthday.

37.2 Another way to express one's intention is with the following construction. Here the intention is weaker and more tentative.

BROWN: Ms. Machida, what are you planning to do about lunch? MACHIDA: Uh…I'm planning to eat at the cafeteria. What about you? BROWN: I'm thinking of eating off campus (lit., *outside school*). I'm tired of the cafeteria. MACHIDA: You're right. Maybe I should eat off campus, too…

Plain, volitional form of verbs + と思う(と思います)

to think one will (do)... or *to think of (doing)...*

The plain, volitional form of verbs is formed in the following way.

CLASS 1 VERBS	CLASS 2 VERBS	CLASS 3 VERBS
Root + the o-column **hiragana** corresponding to the dictionary ending + う	Root + よう	Irregular
買う → 買おう 書く → 書こう 話す → 話そう 立つ → 立とう 死ぬ → 死のう 読む → 読もう 乗る → 乗ろう 泳ぐ → 泳ごう	食べる → 食べよう 見る → 見よう 着る → 着よう	する → しよう 来る → 来よう

u-column	→	o-column
う	→	お
く	→	こ
す	→	そ
つ	→	と
ぬ	→	の
む	→	も
る	→	ろ
ぐ	→	ご

The polite, volitional form of verbs is what you know as the ましょう form of verbs (see **Grammar 15,** Chapter 3).

The ましょう form of verbs, as you will remember, is used to ask someone to do something with you or to offer to do something for someone.

PLAIN VOLITIONAL FORM	POLITE VOLITIONAL FORM (ましょう FORM)
一緒に昼ごはんを食べよう。	一緒に昼ごはんを食べましょう。
Let's eat lunch together.	
わたしがその肉を買おう。	わたしがその肉を買いましょう。
I will buy that meat.	

牛 肉が安いので、すきやきを作ろうと思います。
Since beef is cheap, I think I'll make sukiyaki.

そのレストラン・ガイドを読もうと思う。
I think I'll read that restaurant guide.

When you have had an intention for some time, use the volitional form of a verb + と思っています (と思っている) rather than と思います(と思う).

今度のデートにはあのレストランへ行こうと思っています。
I have been thinking of going to that restaurant on our next date.

37.3 To say you don't intend to do something, use either of the following constructions. The second is the stronger of the two.

nai form of verb + つもりだ(つもりです)

to intend not to (do)...

The nai form of a verb is the plain, nonpast, negative form of a verb.

Dictionary form of verb + つもりはない(つもりはありません)

to have no intention of (doing)...

あの辞書(じしょ)を買(か)わないつもりです。
I intend not to buy that dictionary.
あの辞書(じしょ)を買(か)うつもりはありません。
I have no intention of buying that dictionary.

37.4 As discussed before, the nonpast form of verbs can also express intention or will.

明日(あした)、カワムラさんと一緒(いっしょ)に宿題(しゅくだい)をします。
Tomorrow I will do homework together with Mr. Kawamura.
Tomorrow I am going to do homework together with Mr. Kawamura.

This sentence implies that it has been decided to do homework together with Mr. Kawamura, and I will do so. On the other hand,

明日(あした)、カワムラさんと一緒(いっしょ)に宿題(しゅくだい)をするつもりです。
simply means: *I plan to do homework together with Mr. Kawamura tomorrow.*

言語ノート

Talking About Plans

You can ask about someone's plans with the following expressions.

明日何(あしたなに)かするつもりですか。
Are you planning to do something tomorrow?
明日何(あしたなに)をする予定(よてい)ですか。
What are you planning to do tomorrow? (lit., *Tomorrow, your schedule is to do what?*)

You can state your own plans using 〜つもりです, as discussed above.

> 映画(えいが)に行くつもりです。
> *I am planning to go to the movies.*

When you don't have any plans, you can say

> 予定(よてい)はありません。
> *I don't have any plans.*
>
> 別(べつ)に何(なに)もしません。
> *I won't do anything in particular.*

When you don't know what you are going to do or you would like to avoid answering specifically, just say

> わかりません。
> *I don't know.*

✸ アクティビティー 33

ダイアログ：パーティーをするつもりです。(*I'm planning to have a party.*)

カワムラ：土曜日(どようび)はチンさんの誕生日(たんじょうび)ですね。
町田(まちだ)：ええ、それで、うちでパーティーをするつもりです。
カワムラ：それはいい考(かんが)えですね。
町田：<u>バースデー・ケーキを作(つく)ろう</u>と思(おも)っています。

Now practice the dialogue, substituting the following phrases for the underlined phrase.

1. バースデー・ケーキを買(か)う
2. チンさんのボーイフレンドも呼(よ)ぶ (*invite*)
3. みんなでゲームをする
4. たくさん写真(しゃしん)をとる

アクティビティー 34

休(やす)もうと思(おも)います。(*I think I'll take a break.*)

Rewrite the following using the volitional form of the verb + と思います。

KAWAMURA: This Saturday is Ms. Chin's birthday, isn't it? MACHIDA: Yes, so I'm planning to have a party at my home. KAWAMURA: That's a good idea. MACHIDA: I'm thinking of <u>making a birthday cake</u>.

1. 朝早く起きる
2. 毎朝ジョギングをする
3. 朝ごはんを毎日食べる
4. コーヒーを飲むのをやめる (*stop, quit*)
5. スーパーで夕ごはんの材料 (*ingredients*) を買う

アクティビティー 35

どこへ行くつもりですか。(*Where are you planning to go?*)

Answer these questions.

1. 今晩何を食べるつもりですか。
2. 明日何をするつもりですか。
3. 今週の週末は何をしようと思いますか。
4. 今年の夏はどこかへ行くつもりですか。
5. 今年の冬休みは何をしようと思いますか。

Note that it is rude to ask your superior's intention using ...つもりですか。You should use ...おつもりですか, as in 何をするおつもりですか。

アクティビティー 36

ゴルフをするつもりでしたが雨が降りました。(*I planned to play golf, but it rained.*)

Make sentences based on the following table.

[例] 学校へ行くつもりでしたが、病気で家にいました。(*I planned to go to school, but I stayed home because of illness.*)

ORIGINAL INTENTION	ACTUAL RESULTS
go to school	stayed home because of illness
make sukiyaki	couldn't make it because there was no meat
buy pork	couldn't buy any because I didn't have the money
call Ms. Brown	forgot
go hiking	couldn't go because of rain

Study Hint

How to Remember Verb Conjugations

The verb conjugation system of Japanese is simple compared with, say, Latin or Greek. Basically, only two Class 3 verbs, する and 来る, are irregular verbs whose conjugation you have to memorize. For Class 2 verbs, auxiliary verb endings and other expressions are attached to the root (i.e., the dictionary form minus る: 食べ for 食べる、見 for 見る). The conjugation of Class 1 verbs may seem somewhat complicated, but there is some regularity. Look at the following chart of Class 1 verb conjugations.

	書く	話す	立つ	読む	乗る	泳ぐ
PLAIN, NEGATIVE, NONPAST	書かない	話さない	立たない	読まない	乗らない	泳がない
POLITE, AFFIRMATIVE, NONPAST	書きます	話します	立ちます	読みます	乗ります	泳ぎます
DICTIONARY FORM	書く	話す	立つ	読む	乗る	泳ぐ
IMPERATIVE FORM	書け	話せ	立て	読め	乗れ	泳げ
VOLITIONAL FORM	書こう	話そう	立とう	読もう	乗ろう	泳ごう

Notice that the sequence of sounds following the root of each verb follows the same sequence of the Japanese syllabary: *a, i, u, e, o*. It's easy to learn these conjugated forms of Class 1 verbs by studying what vowel comes after the root for each form. (You will study the imperative form later.)

アクティビティー 37

こんな時、どうしますか。(*What are you going to do at a time like this?*)

For each phrase in the first column, choose an appropriate phrase from the second column and connect them in a logical sentence.

[例] とても暑い　　アイスティーを飲む →
とても暑いので、アイスティーを飲もうと思います。

1. 今日は、ピザが食べたい。　　卵をたくさん買う
2. 料理が上手になりたい　　夕ごはんはすきやきにする
3. 今日は牛肉が安かった　　サラダを作る
4. ギブソンさんは肉を食べない　　イタリア・レストランで食べる
5. オムレツを作りたい　　クッキング・スクールへ行く

38. The Te-Form of Verbs + Verbs みる, しまう, いく, and くる

カワムラ：今日、あのレストランはあいているでしょうか。
山口(やまぐち)：さあ、わかりませんね。
カワムラ：電話(でんわ)をして、聞いてみましょう。
山口：ぼくが電話(でんわ)をしてみます。

カーティス：夕(ゆう)ごはんは食べましたか。
林：ええ、もう食べてしまいました。
カーティス：そうですか。それはざんねんですね。ピザを買(か)ってきたんですが、...
林：まだ、食べられますよ。お皿(さら)を持(も)ってきます。

ギブソン：コンサートは何時(なんじ)からですか。
林：7時(じ)からです。
ギブソン：じゃあ、夕(ゆう)ごはんを食べていきましょう。
林：うん、そうしましょう。

38.1 The te-form of a verb is combined with other verbs to express several important meanings in Japanese. In this section, you will study four of these combinations. The te-form of a verb + みる means *to do (something) in order to see what happens or what it's like*. Sometimes this translates as *to try* in the sense of *to sample (something)* or *to give (something) a try.*

> Note: When used with the te-form of verbs, these four verbs are written in **hiragana,** not **kanji.**

一度(ど)すしを食べてみました。
I ate some sushi to see what it's like.
I tried sushi once.
そこへ行ってみましょう。
Let's go there and see what it's like.
そのお酒(さけ)を飲んでみたが、味(あじ)は悪(わる)かった。
I tried some of that liquor, and (lit., *but*) *it tasted bad.*

KAWAMURA: Is that restaurant open today do you think? YAMAGUCHI: Hmm, I don't know. KAWAMURA: Let's call and ask. YAMAGUCHI: I'll call and see.

CURTIS: Have you eaten dinner? HAYASHI: Yes, I already ate. CURTIS: Oh really? That's too bad. I went and bought a pizza but… (I guess you don't want any). HAYASHI: I still have room, you know. (lit., *I still can eat.*) I'll bring a plate.

GIBSON: What time does the concert start? (lit., *From what time is the concert?*) HAYASHI: It starts at seven o'clock. (lit., *It's from seven o'clock.*) GIBSON: Well then, let's eat dinner and then go. HAYASHI: Yeah, let's do that.

38.2 The te-form of a verb + しまう literally means *to finish doing* (*something*). In other words, it is used to express the completion of an action or an event. This construction focuses on the completed state of an action or an event.

わたしはもう宿題(しゅくだい)をしてしまいました。
I already finished doing my homework.

そのアイスクリームは全部(ぜんぶ)食べてしまった。
I ate all of that ice cream.

Another way to say *to finish doing* is the conjunctive form of a verb + 終(お)わる: 食べ終わる (*to finish eating*). By the way, the meaning *to start doing* is expressed by the conjunctive form of a verb + 始(はじ)める: 飲み始める (*to start drinking*).

言語ノート

もう and まだ

When the adverb もう is used in affirmative sentences, it means *already, yet.*

もう5時になりましたか。
Is it five o'clock yet? (lit., *Did it already become five o'clock?*)
ええ、もう5時15分です。
Yes, it's already 5:15.

When used in negative sentences, もう means *anymore.*

もうあのレストランへは行きません。サービスが本当(ほんとう)に悪(わる)いんですから。
I won't go to that restaurant anymore. Because the service is really bad.

The adverb まだ, on the other hand, means *still* in affirmative sentences.

まだ時間がありますか。
Is there still time?

林さんはまだ寝(ね)ていますよ。多分(たぶん)疲(つか)れているんでしょう。
Mr. Hayashi is still sleeping. Maybe he is tired.

まだ means (*not*) *yet* in negative sentences.

三村(みむら)さんはまだ来(き)ていません。寝坊(ねぼう)したんでしょう。
Mr. Mimura has not come in yet. He probably overslept.
日本へはまだ行ったことがありません。
I haven't been to Japan yet.

The usages of もう and まだ are summarized in the following table.

	AFFIRMATIVE	NEGATIVE
もう	already, yet	(not) anymore, any longer
まだ	still	not yet

しまう itself is a Class 1 verb and conjugates as such.

This construction sometimes implies that something happened that should not have happened or someone did something that should not have been done. In these cases, this construction implies the speaker's or the agent's regret.

わたしは妹(いもうと)のデザートを食べてしまった。
I ate my sister's dessert (by mistake).

10時まで寝(ね)てしまいました。
I slept until ten o'clock.

It depends on the context which of the two meanings しまう expresses.

38.3 The te-form of a verb + いく has the following meanings.

1. To do something and then leave that place
   山田(やまだ)さんは父(ちち)と話していきました。
   Ms. Yamada talked with my father and then left.

2. To do something in a direction moving away from the speaker's or subject's current location (or away from the speaker's or subject's location before the action began)
   わたしは学校(がっこう)へ走(はし)っていきました。
   I ran to school (said when at home).

3. Some currently ongoing action or state will keep changing into the future
   この映画(えいが)はこれから面白(おもしろ)くなっていきますよ。
   This movie will get interesting from this point on.

38.4 The te-form of a verb + くる can mean the following.

1. To do something and then come toward the speaker
   母(はは)は学校(がっこう)でわたしの先生と話してきました。
   My mother talked with my teacher at school and then came here.
   スーパーへ行って、リンゴを買(か)ってきてください。
   Please go to a supermarket and buy apples (and then, come back here).

2. To do something in a direction moving toward the speaker's current location
   わたしは学校(がっこう)へ歩(ある)いてきました。
   I walked to school (said when at school).

3. Some action or event begins or is in progress
   わたしは少(すこ)し日本語がわかってきました。
   I have started understanding Japanese a little. (or, *I have come to understand a little Japanese.*)
   雨(あめ)が降(ふ)ってきた。
   It has started raining.

Both te-form + いく and te-form + くる express ongoing actions or events, as illustrated in the third definition of each form. In deciding which to use, take into consideration these nuances: くる is more subjective and personal, whereas いく is more objective and impersonal. In other words, くる indicates more physical or psychological involvement on the part of the speaker.

言語ノート

行くと来(く)る

行く and 来(く)る do not necessarily correspond to English *to go* and *to come*. For example, when called in English, you might respond *I'm coming*. In Japanese, however, you would respond すぐ行きます (*I'll go right away*). 行く is used when the speaker, or someone or something else, moves away from the speaker's current position. On the other hand, 来る is used when the speaker, or someone or something else, moves to the speaker's current position.

アクティビティー 38

ちょっと食べてみます。(*I'll try eating it.*)

Make dialogues using the te-form of the verb in parentheses + みる. Be creative!

[例] そのステーキはおいしいですか。(食べる) →
—そのステーキはおいしいですか。
—食べてみてください。 *or* ちょっと食べてみます。

1. この問題(もんだい) (*question*) がわかりますか。(聞く)
2. ペプシとコークとどちらがおいしいですか。(飲む)
3. 明日(あした)、山田(やまだ)さんが来(き)ます。(会(あ)う)
4. これが料理(りょうり)の本です。(作(つく)る)
5. これはとても面白(おもしろ)い本ですよ。(読む)
6. あのレストランはおいしいですよ。(行く)

アクティビティー 39

あっ!食べてしまいました。(*Oh! I ate it all up.*)

Make a dialogue by using the te-form of the verb +しまう.

[例] (あの本)(読む)
—あの本はどうしましたか。(*What happened to that book?*)
—もう読んでしまいました。

1. (カワムラさん)(帰る)
2. (昨日買ったアイスクリーム)(食べる)
3. (手紙)(書く)
4. (ビデオ)(見る)
5. (ウイスキー)(飲む)
6. (宿題 [*homework*])(する)
7. (ナイフとフォーク)(洗う)
8. (チンさんのバースデー・ケーキ)(買う)

アクティビティー 40

走っていきましょう。(*Let's run.*)

Make dialogues using the te-form of the verb + いく.

[例] コンサートまでまだ時間がありますよ。(ショーウインドーを見る) →
—コンサートまでまだ時間がありますよ。
—じゃあ、ショーウインドーをちょっと見ていきましょう。

1. 安いりんごがありますよ。(買う)
2. 今日は寒いですよ。(セーターを着る)
3. もう12時ですね。(昼ごはんを食べる)
4. もう1時ですよ。ミーティングは1時15分からですよ。(走る)
5. カーティスさんがいますよ。(話す)
6. つかれましたね。(*I'm tired, aren't you?*) (休む)
7. 新しいCDがありますよ。(聞く)
8. ビールがたくさんあります。どうぞ。(*Please*… [*have some*].) (飲む)

アクティビティー 41

ちょっと行ってきます。(*I'll be right back.*)

Make dialogues using the te-form of the verb + くる.

[例] ペンはありますか。(買う)→
—ペンはありますか。
—ええ、買ってきました。

1. 一緒(いっしょ)に夕(ゆう)ごはんを食べませんか。(食べる)
2. 山田(やまだ)さんと話しましたか。(話す)
3. 予習(よしゅう)しましたか。(教科書(きょうかしょ)を読む)
4. 肉(にく)はありますか。(買(か)う)
5. 早(はや)かったですね。(*You are early, aren't you?*)(走(はし)る)
6. 顔(かお)(*face*)が赤(あか)いですね。(お酒(さけ)を飲む)
7. 山下(やました)さんは家(いえ)にいますか。(3時(じ)に帰(かえ)る)
8. なぜわらっているんですか。(*Why are you laughing?*)
(おもしろい映画(えいが)を見る)

アクティビティー 42

どこで聞きましたか。だれが言(い)いましたか。(***Where did you hear that? Who said that?***)

Where do you think the following statements were made? Choose from the places listed here.

台所(だいどころ)、図書館(としょかん)、デパート、スーパー、レストラン

1. ちょっと甘(あま)すぎます(*too sweet*)ね。
2. このブラウスを着(き)て(*try on*)みてください。
3. この本を読んでみよう。
4. このステーキをたのんで(*order*)みましょう。
5. この新(あたら)しいステーキ・ソースを買(か)ってみましょう。

Who do you think made the following statements? Choose from the people listed here.

日本のサラリーマン、日本語の学生、ジョン・グレン、コック(*cook*)、スチュワーデス

6. パリとロンドンとローマに行ってきました。
7. 料理(りょうり)をたくさん作(つく)ってきました。
8. 夜(よる)十時まで働(はたら)いてきました。
9. 漢字(かんじ)をたくさん勉強(べんきょう)してきました。
10. また宇宙(うちゅう)(*outer space*)へ行ってきました。

39. Expressing Simultaneous Actions: 〜ながら

カワムラ：おなかがすきましたね。お昼(ひる)ごはんにしましょうか。
町田：ええ、そうしましょう。ここにすわりましょう。
カワムラ：外(そと)のけしきを見ながら、食べられますね。
町田：そうですね。

To express two actions taking place simultaneously, use 〜ながら (*while*) in this construction.

Clause 1: conjunctive form of a verb + ながら, Clause 2

The agent of the two actions must be identical. Thus, although you can use this construction to say *While studying, I ate,* you cannot use it to say *While my wife was talking on the phone, I was cooking dinner.* Notice that in English the clause beginning with while (the subordinate action) usually comes last.

コーヒーを飲みながら、ブラウンさんと話した。
I talked with Ms. Brown while drinking coffee.

レコードを聞きながら、朝(あさ)ごはんを食べましょう。
Let's eat breakfast while listening to a record.

✸ アクティビティー 43

ダイアログ：勉強(べんきょう)しながら、食べます。(*I will eat while studying.*)

山口(やまぐち)：カワムラさん、ごはんですよ。
カワムラ：今(いま)、勉強(べんきょう)で忙(いそが)しいんです。
山口：じゃ、あとにしますか。
カワムラ：いいえ、勉強(べんきょう)しながら、食べます。

KAWAMURA: I'm hungry, aren't you? Shall we have lunch? (lit., *Shall we make it lunch?*) MACHIDA: Yes, let's do that. Let's sit here. KAWAMURA: We can eat while looking at the scenery outdoors, can't we? MACHIDA: Yes.

YAMAGUCHI: Mr. Kawamura, dinner is ready (lit., *it's dinner*)! KAWAMURA: I'm busy studying now. (lit., *I'm busy with studying now.*) YAMAGUCHI: Then, will you eat (lit., *decide on*) later? KAWAMURA: No, I will eat while studying.

Practice the dialogue, substituting the following for line 2. Use the 〜しながら form in line 4.

1. 今(いま)、テレビを見ています
2. 今(いま)、ステレオを聞いています
3. 今(いま)、お酒(さけ)を飲んでいます

アクティビティー 44

TVを見ながら、電話(でんわ)で話しました。(*She talked on the phone while watching TV.*)

Join the clauses into a complete sentence using 〜ながら.

[例] (ポップコーンを食べた)(本を読む)→
ポップコーンを食べながら、本を読んだ。

1. (ワインを飲む)(ステーキを食べた)
2. (町(まち)を歩(ある)く)(写真(しゃしん)をたくさん取(と)りました)
3. (テレビを見る)(勉強(べんきょう)しました)
4. (メモ [*notes*]を取(と)る)(三村(みむら)さんの話を聞く)
5. (昼(ひる)はアルバイトをする)(夜(よる)は学校(がっこう)へ行っています)

✸ アクティビティー 45

いいと思(おも)いますか。悪(わる)いと思(おも)いますか。(*Do you think it's good or bad?*)

State your opinion about the following.

1. テレビを見ながら、ごはんを食べる。
2. 野菜(やさい)を毎日(まいにち)食べる。
3. 朝(あさ)ごはんを食べない。
4. コーヒーを一日に三杯(さんばい)飲む。
5. 電話(でんわ)で話しながら、食事(しょくじ)をする。
6. 毎日(まいにち)、日本料理(りょうり)を食べる。
7. 毎日(まいにち)、お酒(さけ)をたくさん飲む。
8. 毎日(まいにち)、ファーストフード・レストランへ行く。

Language Skills

Reading and Writing

Reading 1 バイキング料理「むらさき」

Before You Read

Work in pairs. Discuss with your partner what information is included in restaurant guides. Then look at the following words, which are commonly used in Japanese restaurant guides. Can you guess what each means?

営業時間　　駐車場　　値段　　電話番号

Here are a few exercises to prepare you for new words in the reading.

1. As you have already studied, 英語 means *English language* in Japanese. An English-Japanese dictionary is called 英和辞典, while a Japanese-English dictionary is called 和英辞典. Now, what do you think 和食 means?
2. 和室 means *Japanese-style room,* while 洋室 means *Western-style room.* 和風 means *Japanese style,* whereas 洋風 means *Western style.* Now, what do you think 洋食 means?

Now Read It!

レストラン・ガイド

バイキング料理「むらさき」

バイキング料理を食べたことはありますか。バイキング料理のレストランはたくさんあります。しかし、安くて、おいしいレストランを見つけるのは、むずかしいです。東京・上野にある「むらさき」はバイキング料理のレストランですが、ここの料理は安くて、おいしいことで有名です。昼ごはん、夕ごはんは、いつも満員です。

メニューはサラダ、スープ、和食、洋食、デザート、フルーツ、パン、ごはん、飲み物など、全部で150種類以上あります。サラダは、野菜サラダ、フルーツサラダ、ツナサラダ、エッグサラダなど。ドレッシングはフレンチ、イタリアン、和風、など。スープは野菜、オニオン、コーン、

バイキング料理 *all-you-can-eat dining* (lit., *Viking food*)

上野 *Ueno (district in Tokyo)*

満員 *full capacity*

など *et cetera* / 種類 *kinds, varieties* / ～以上 *more than…*

クラムチャウダー、コンソメなど。和食はてんぷら、すきやき、さしみ、すしなど20種類。洋食はステーキ、とんかつ、ハンバーグなど25種類。デザートはチーズケーキ、キャロットケーキ、プリン、アップルパイ、チョコレートケーキ、アイスクリームなどがあります。果物の好きな人はみかん、りんご、バナナ、パイナップル、パパイアなども食べられます。

値段は大人が4500円で、子供は1500円です。お酒は飲み放題で2000円です。日本酒、ウイスキー、赤ワイン、白ワイン、カクテル、ビールなどがあります。

日曜日午前9時から午後2時まではシャンペンを無料でサービスしています。場所は、上野デパートのとなり、上野駅から歩いて、10分で、とても便利です。駐車場は上野デパートの地下にあります。営業時間は火曜日から土曜日は午前11時から午後10時まで。日曜日は午前9時から午後9時まで。月曜日はお休みです。予約は(03)3781-3945まで。

とんかつ *pork cutlet*
プリン *custard*
値段 *price, charge* / 大人 *adult* / 飲み放題 *all you can drink*
日本酒 *sake* (lit., *Japanese liquor*)
無料 *free of charge* / サービスする *to offer for free*
場所 *place, location*
駐車場 *parking lot* / 地下 *underground* / 営業時間 *business hours* (*hours open to business*)
予約 *reservation*

After You Finish Reading

1. Lately, the number of foreign customers has been increasing at Murasaki restaurant. The owner has decided to produce a simple brochure about his restaurant in English. Help him compose the brochure by filling in the missing information in English.

RESTAURANT MURASAKI

All You Can Eat!

Price: Adults ¥ _____
(all you can drink, additional ¥ _____)
Children ¥ _____

MENU

Salad: _____
Soup: _____
Main dishes: Japanese varieties _____ Western varieties _____
Dessert: _____
Fruit: _____
Alcoholic Beverages: _____

Business Hours: Tue-Sat from _____ to _____
Sun from _____ to _____
(free champagne from _____ to _____)
Closed Monday

Location: _____ next to _____
Parking: _____

2. You work for Murasaki. One of your jobs is to answer questions telephoned in by potential customers. How do you respond to these questions?

   a. 場所はどこですか。
   b. 営業時間は何時から何時までですか。
   c. バイキングの値段はいくらですか。
   d. 和食はどんなものがありますか。
   e. 洋食は何種類ありますか。
   f. サラダはどんなものがありますか。
   g. お酒は無料ですか。
   h. 日曜日はあいています (*open*) か。
   i. 駐車場はありますか。
   j. 休みは何曜日ですか。

Writing 1

Using the following brochure, write down a short description of this restaurant.

ホテル東京レストラン・やまと

昼食食べ放題（ビュッフェ・スタイル）

日曜日午前9時から午後3時まで

大人1500円（シャンペン無料）

子供800円

メニュー

フルーツ：オレンジ、バナナ、パイナップル、メロン
サラダ：シェフ・サラダ
スープ：オニオン、コーン、野菜、チキン・ヌードル
スペーシャル：パン、卵料理、ベーコン、ソーセージ、フライド・ポテト
デザート：チーズケーキ、アイスクリーム、プリン、パイ

Reading 2 あなたの食事チェック

Before You Read

Work in pairs and discuss the following with your partner.

1. **What time do people generally eat the following meals or snacks?**
   a. 朝ごはん
   b. 昼ごはん
   c. おやつ
   d. 夕ごはん
   e. 夜食
2. **What do you usually eat for each of the above meals? Are your meals well balanced?**

Now Read It!

A Japanese women's weekly magazine runs a column called "Check Your Diet," in which a dietitian analyzes the diet of a chosen reader. Last month, Hitomi Machida was interviewed for this section.

町田ひとみ（20）学生

今週の「あなたの食事チェック」は東京大学でフランス文学を専攻している町田ひとみさんです。町田さんは東京の三鷹にご両親と住んでいます。趣味は料理で、一週間に3回ぐらい夕ごはんを作ります。

朝ごはん	6:45 a.m. 家で パン、牛乳、ジュース、バナナ
昼ごはん	12:00 大学のカフェテリアで ポークソテー、サラダ、ヨーグルト、コンソメ・スープ、パン
おやつ	3:00 p.m. 喫茶店で コーヒー、チーズケーキ
夕ごはん	7:00 p.m. 家で ごはん、みそ汁、漬物、サラダ、クリーム・シチュー、みかん
夜のおやつ	ポップコーン、コーヒー
カロリー	2865 Kcal

「町田さんの話」最近、太ってきたので、食事の量を少なくしています。でも、2月24日は、とてもおなかがすいていたので、ちょっと食べ過ぎたと思います。前は、一日3回ごはんを食べていましたが、今は一回で、朝ごはんと昼ごはんはパンを食べています。和食より洋食のほうが好きなので、昼ごはんも夕ごはんも洋食が多いです。母も働いているので、インスタント食品、冷凍食品、テークアウト、外食も増えてきました。一日にコーヒーを4杯飲むので、少なくしたいと思っています。

「栄養士・金井さと子先生の話」町田さんの食事はバランスがとてもいいと思います。昼ごはんも肉を食べていますが、サラダを食べているので、問題はありません。コーヒーの飲みすぎはよくありませんね。

After You Finish Reading

You interviewed Hitomi Machida for the magazine column. Answer Ms. Kanai's questions about Ms. Machida, following the example.

[例] どこに住んでいますか。→
—どこに住んでいますか。
—三鷹に住んでいると言いました。

1. 趣味は何ですか。
2. 一週間に何回ぐらい夕ごはんを作りますか。
3. 2月24日の朝ごはんに何を食べましたか。
4. 昼ごはんはどこで食べましたか。
5. 2月24日は食べすぎたと思いますか。
6. ごはんは一日何回食べていますか。
7. 和食と洋食、どちらが好きですか。
8. インスタント食品をよく食べますか。
9. コーヒーを一日何杯 (*glassfuls*) 飲みますか。

Work in pairs. Ask your partner what he or she ate yesterday. Do you think your partner's meals are well balanced?

Writing 2

Write a short paragraph about your eating habits, meals, and so on. Cover at least the following points.

1. what you usually eat
2. your favorite foods
3. foods you don't like
4. whether you drink coffee a lot
5. whether you eat instant foods or frozen foods a lot

Language Functions and Situations

Asking and Expressing Opinions

台所(だいどころ)で

カワムラ：この肉(にく)、どう思(おも)いますか。

町田(まちだ)：新(あたら)しくて、いい肉(にく)だと思(おも)います。いくらでしたか。

カワムラ：ええと、100g千円(せんえん)でした。

町田：ええ！ちょっと高(たか)すぎると思(おも)いませんか。

カワムラ：そうですか。

ギブソン：林さんをどう思(おも)いますか。

町田：そうですね。とてもやさしい人だと思(おも)います。

ギブソン：ハンサムだと思(おも)いますか。

町田：さあ…

Role Play

Work with a partner. One of you is a reporter and the other is a restaurant critic. The reporter asks for the critic's opinion of a certain local restaurant. The reporter must ask about price, what dishes are served, whether the service is good, whether alcoholic beverages are available, and so on. The reporter should take notes.

At a Restaurant

ウェイター：いらっしゃいませ。メニューをどうぞ。

カワムラ：どうも。

ウェイター：ご注文(ちゅうもん)は。

カワムラ：サラダとステーキをお願(ねが)いします。

ウェイター：はい。お飲み物(もの)は。

カワムラ：赤(あか)ワインをお願(ねが)いします。

In the kitchen KAWAMURA: What do you think of this meat? MACHIDA: I think it tastes good and fresh. (lit., *I think it's fresh, good meat.*) How much was it? KAWAMURA: Uh, it was 1,000 yen per 100 grams. MACHIDA: What? Don't you think that's a bit too expensive? KAWAMURA: Do you think so? (lit., *Is that so?*)

GIBSON: What do you think of Mr. Hayashi? MACHIDA: Hmm. I think he's very sweet. GIBSON: Do you think he's handsome? MACHIDA: Hmm…

WAITER: Welcome. Here is a menu. KAWAMURA: Thank you. WAITER: May I have your order? KAWAMURA: I would like a salad and steak. WAITER: Yes. How about a drink? KAWAMURA: I would like red wine.

ウェイター：デザートは。
カワムラ：いいえ、けっこうです。
ウェイター：かしこまりました。
ウェイター：お待(ま)たせ致(いた)しました。ステーキです。どうぞ。
カワムラ：お勘定(かんじょう)をお願(ねが)いします。

言語ノート

Useful Expressions When Dining Out

Here are some expressions that are useful in restaurants.

6時に予約(よやく)があります。
I have a reservation for six o'clock.
四人ですが、テーブルはありますか。
I'd like a table for four. (lit., *We're four, but do you have a table [to accommodate us]?*)
どんな飲み物(もの)がありますか。
What kinds of drinks do you have?
注文(ちゅうもん)したいんですが、…。
Can I order now? (lit., *I want to order but…*)
今日(きょう)は何(なに)がおいしいですか。
What is good today?
サラダはけっこうです。
No salad, thank you.
初(はじ)めに、スープをお願(ねが)いします。
I'd like to start with soup.
お水(みず)をお願(ねが)いします。
May I have some water?
すきやきにします。
I'll have sukiyaki.
デザートは後(あと)でお願(ねが)いします。
I'd like dessert later.
メニューを見せてください。
Would you bring me a menu? (lit., *Please show me a menu.*)

Role Play

You are at a restaurant with several classmates. One of you is the waiter or waitress and the others are customers. Use the menu below to order your meal.

WAITER: How about dessert? KAWAMURA: No, thank you. WAITER: As you wish, (lit., *Certainly.*)… WAITER: Here is your steak… KAWAMURA: I would like the bill, please.

イタリア料理の店　ミラノ

メニュー

サラダ

アンティパスタ（コンビネーション、二人前）	1600
シーザーサラダ	760
シーフードサラダ（いか、たこ、えび、貝）	850
パイナップルとアーモンドのサラダ	670

スープ

ミネストローネスープ	350
ポタージュ	400

パスタ

シーフードスパゲッティ	780
ミートボールスパゲッティ	760
カルボナーダ	690
ラザーニャ	800
トルテリーニ（ペストソース付き）	730
ラビオリ	780

ピザ

ミラノオリジナルピザ	760
ペパローニピザ	710
ハワイアンピザ	820
シーフードピザ	840
ベジタリアンピザ	650

ピラフ

シーフードピラフ	680
ドリア（ライスグラタン）	660

ディナーセット

（ディナーセットにはサラダかスープ、ライスかパン、アイスクリーム、コーヒーが付きます。）

Aセット（イタリア風ステーキ）	4500
Bセット（えびのクリームソース煮）	3800
Cセット（ポテトグラタン）	3200

デザート

ティラミス	390
ナポリタンアイスクリーム	290
ビスコーティ（3種類のクッキー）	330
エクレア	390
ナポリオン	360
アマレートチーズケーキ	400

飲み物

（ブレンドコーヒーとアメリカンコーヒーは、おかわり自由です。）

ブレンドコーヒー	350
アメリカンコーヒー	370
紅茶（レモン・ミルク）	350
カプチーノ	450
エスプレッソ	450
カフェオーレ	400
ウインナーコーヒー	430
オレンジスカッシュ	450
レモンスカッシュ	470
ミルク（アイス・ホット）	350
ミネラルウオーター	500
ビール　中	680
大	900
ワイン（赤・ロゼ・白）	700
アマレート	600
キアンティ	700

Listening Comprehension

Ms. Yamamoto and Ms. Okada are talking about the eating habits of Japanese while looking at the results of a recent survey. While listening to their conversation, fill in the following table. Their conversation won't provide exhaustive information, so you won't be able to fill in all the blanks.

	RANK AND PERCENTAGE				
	1 (%)	2 (%)	3 (%)	4 (%)	5 (%)
What kind of cuisine do Japanese like most?					
What kind of food do Japanese cook most?					
What food do Japanese children like most?					
What foods don't Japanese children like?					
What beverages do Japanese children drink most?					

Vocabulary

Meals

おやつ		snack
ごはん		meal; cooked rice
しょくじ	食事	meal
だいどころ	台所	kitchen
ちゅうかりょうり	中華料理	Chinese cuisine
のみもの	飲み物	beverage
やしょく	夜食	evening snack
ようしょく	洋食	Western cuisine
わしょく	和食	Japanese cuisine

Loanwords: キッチン、コック、スナック、デザート、ファーストフード、レストラン

Review: 朝(あさ)ごはん、喫茶店(きっさてん)、食堂(しょくどう)、食べる、飲む、昼(ひる)ごはん、夕(ゆう)ごはん、料理(りょうり)する

Foods

いか		cuttlefish	かい	貝	shellfish
いちご		strawberry	かんづめ	缶詰	canned food
おかし	お菓子	sweets	ぎゅうにく	牛肉	beef

きゅうり		cucumber	ピーマン		green pepper
くだもの	果物	fruit	ひきにく	ひき肉	ground meat
こめ	米	rice (*uncooked*)	ぶたにく	豚肉	pork
さけ		salmon	ぶどう		grape
じゃがいも		potato	まぐろ		tuna
しょくりょうひん	食料品	foodstuffs	まめ	豆	bean; pea
たこ		octopus	みかん		mandarin orange
たまご	卵	egg	やさい	野菜	vegetable
たまねぎ	玉ねぎ	onion	りんご		apple
とりにく	鳥肉	chicken	れいとうしょくひん	冷凍食品	frozen food
なし		pear			
にく	肉	meat			
にんじん		carrot			

Loanwords: スープ、トマト、パイナップル、バナナ、メロン、ラム、レタス、レモン、ミンチ、パン、ラーメン

Review: 魚(さかな)

Beverages

(お)さけ	(お)酒	liquor; sake	(お)みず	(お)水	water
(お)ちゃ	(お)茶	tea	ぎゅうにゅう	牛乳	milk
(お)ゆ	(お)湯	hot water; boiling water	こうちゃ	紅茶	black tea
			コーヒー		coffee

Loanwords: ウイスキー、カクテル、ジュース、ビール、ミルク、ワイン

Taste and Flavors

あじ	味	taste, flavor	ちょうみりょう	調味料	seasoning
あじがいい	味がいい	to taste good	にがい		bitter
あじがない	味がない	to have no taste	まずい		not tasty
あじみする	味見する	to taste a sample	みそ	味噌	miso
あまい	甘い	sweet			
おいしい		delicious; tasty			
からい	辛い	spicy; hot (*spicy*); salty			
クッキングオイル		cooking oil			
こしょう	胡椒	pepper			
さとう	砂糖	sugar			
しお	塩	salt			
しおからい	塩辛い	salty			
しぶい	渋い	astringent			
しょうゆ	醤油	soy sauce			
す	酢	vinegar			
すっぱい	酸っぱい	sour			
ソース		a prepared sauce (*somewhat like steak sauce*)			

Food Preparation

あげる		to deep-fry
いためる		to stir-fry
きる	切る	to cut
ざいりょう	材料	ingredient(s)
なま	生	raw
にる	煮る	to boil (*to cook in liquid*)
むす	蒸す	to steam
やく	焼く	to broil; to grill; to bake
ゆでる		to cook in boiling water
りょうりのほん	料理の本	cookbook

Utensils and Appliances

(お)わん	(お)椀	soup bowl
かんきり		can opener
コップ		glass
さら	皿	plate; dish
せんぬき		bottle opener
ちゃわん	茶碗	rice bowl or teacup
なべ	鍋	pan; pot
はし	箸	chopsticks
ほうちょう	包丁	cleaver; big cutting knife
れいぞうこ	冷蔵庫	refrigerator

Other Words

ああ		like that
いう	言う	to say
おなかがすく		to be hungry
おもう	思う	to think
おわる	終わる	to finish
こう		like this
...ことがある		to have done...; to have experience doing...
〜すぎる		to do... too much; to be excessively...
そう		like that
〜たい		to want to (do)
〜たがる		to want to (do)
たべる	食べる	to eat
つかう	使う	to use
...つもりだ		to intend to...
〜ていく		to do and leave
〜てくる		to do and come
〜てしまう		to complete
〜てみる		to try to

と		(*quote marker*)
...という	と言う	to say that...; called/named...
どう		how
...とおもう	と思う	to think that...
～ながら		while
...にする		to decide on
のどがかわく		to be thirsty
のむ	飲む	to drink
はじめる	始める	to start
ほしい		to want
ほしがる		to want
まだ		not yet
もう		already; yet
～ようとおもう	ようと思う	to think of (doing)...
よてい	予定	plan

Kanji

Learn these **kanji:**

思	茶	魚	品
終	酒	味	和
始	牛	悪	洋
物	鳥	料	夜
肉	湯	理	言
事	野	米	貝

チェックリスト

Use this checklist to confirm that you can now

- □ Talk about foods and beverages
- □ Talk about meals and restaurants
- □ Talk about cooking, flavors, and seasonings
- □ Express experiences
- □ Express desire
- □ Express an opinion
- □ Use ～すぎる
- □ Express indirect quotation...と言(い)う
- □ Express intention
- □ Use the -te form of verbs + みる, しまう, いく, and くる
- □ Convey simultaneous action ～ながら

Review Chapter 6

アクティビティー　1

連想 (*Association*)

What or who do you think of when you see these words?

1. たくさん食べる
2. 和食
3. 朝ごはん
4. 生のもの
5. 味
6. 辛い
7. 機内食 (*in-flight meal*)
8. まずい
9. 冷蔵庫 (*refrigerator*)
10. ファーストフード・レストラン

アクティビティー　2

家族と食事 (*My family and food*)

What eating habits have you noticed in your family? First, answer these questions, and then compare your answers with those of your classmates. Are some of them similar? How are they different?

1. 一日に何回食事をしますか。何時に食べますか。
2. 食事は家族一緒にしますか。
3. だれが食事を作りますか。
4. 食事をしながら、話をしますか。誰が一番話しますか。誰が一番静かですか。
5. 食事をしながら、テレビを見ますか。食事をしながら、音楽を聞きますか。
6. 食事をしながら、何を飲みますか。
7. 食卓 (*dinner table*) のマナーはいいですか。悪いですか。普通 (*average*) ですか。
8. 一週間に何回外食します (*dine out*) か。
9. どんな食べ物が好きですか。きらいですか。

アクティビティー　3

何を食べますか。(*What are you going to eat?*)

What should you eat on the following occasions?

1. 食欲 (*appetite*) がありません。何か軽いものを食べたいです。
2. おなかがとてもすきました。何を食べたいですか。
3. ちょっとのどがかわきました。食事の前に何か飲みたいです。
4. とてもいいレストランにいます。メインディッシュの前に何を食べますか。メインディッシュの後に何を食べますか。(*I will pay for you, so order anything you like.*)
5. ダイエットをしています。何を食べますか。
6. 菜食主義 (*vegetarian*) です。レストランで何を食べますか。
7. 来週、ボストンに行くつもりです。何を食べたいですか。
8. 今日は病気です。何を食べますか。
9. 明日は試験です。今夜は勉強します。何を飲みますか。
10. 明日朝早く起きたいです。今夜は早く寝たいです。何を飲みますか。

アクティビティー　4

どう思いますか。(*What do you think?*)

Describe the picture below. Using the following questions as a guide, invent necessary details. As you describe the scene, express your own opinions and conjectures.

1. 何時ですか。
2. ここはどこですか。
3. 男の人はだれですか。
4. 女の人はだれですか。
5. 男の人は何と言っていますか。
6. 女の人は何と言っていますか。
7. 二人はどこへ行くつもりですか。

7

第七章 買い物

Shopping

今日は新宿にショッピングに来ました。

Objectives

In this chapter you are going to

- Talk about shops and stores
- Talk about shopping
- Talk about clothes
- Learn to express when something happens
- Practice using the indefinite pronoun の
- Learn to use the 〜たら conditional
- Learn how to express purpose using the particle に
- Practice reporting hearsay: …そうだ
- Learn to express whether…or not: …かどうか
- Practice giving reasons using …し、…し

YOOKOSO! MULTIMEDIA

Review and practice grammar and vocabulary from this chapter and watch video clips on the *Yookoso!* Interactive CD-ROM. Visit the *Yookoso!* Online Learning Center at **www.mhhe.com/yookosome** for additional exercises and resources.

Vocabulary and Grammar 7A

Vocabulary and Oral Activities

Shops and Stores

Vocabulary: Shops and Stores

ショッピング		shopping
売る	うる	to sell
買う	かう	to buy
商店街	しょうてんがい	shopping district; shopping street
店	みせ	store; shop
市場	いちば	market; marketplace
肉屋	にくや	butcher shop
魚屋	さかなや	fish store
八百屋	やおや	vegetable store; greengrocer's
果物屋	くだものや	fruit store

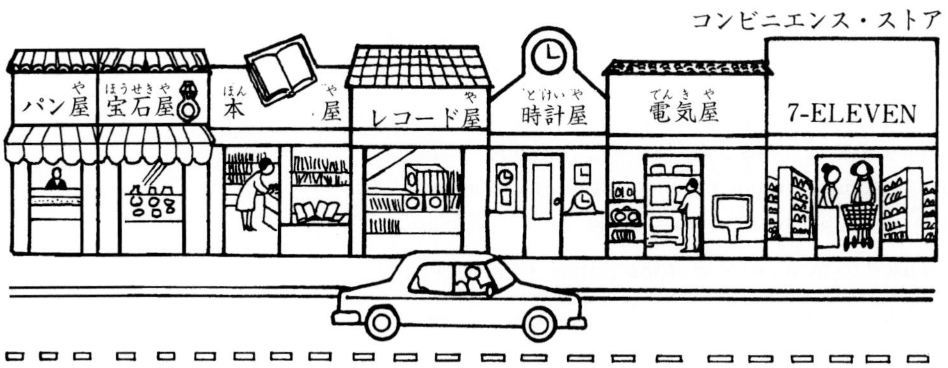

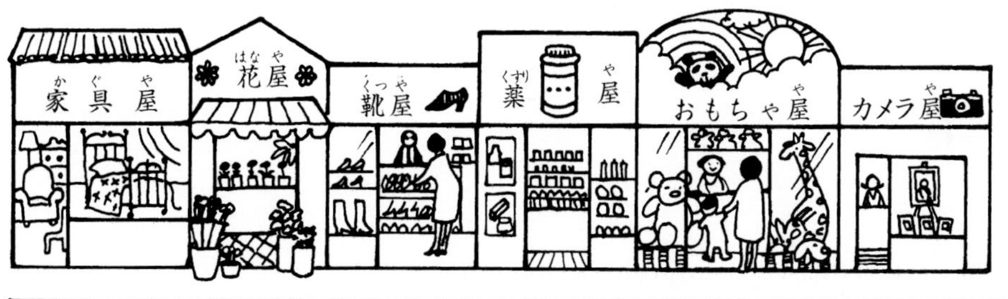

パン屋	パンや	bakery
宝石屋	ほうせきや	jeweler's
ケーキ屋	ケーキや	pastry shop
酒屋	さかや	liquor store
本屋	ほんや	bookstore
文房具屋	ぶんぼうぐや	stationery store
レコード屋	レコードや	record store; music store
時計屋	とけいや	watch shop
電気屋	でんきや	electric appliance store
家具屋	かぐや	furniture shop
花屋	はなや	flower shop; florist
靴屋	くつや	shoe store
薬屋、薬局	くすりや、やっきょく	drugstore; pharmacy
眼鏡屋	めがねや	eyeglasses store; optician's
クリーニング屋	クリーニングや	dry cleaner's
カメラ屋	カメラや	camera shop

Review: 買(か)い物(もの)、スーパー、デパート

言語ノート

屋(や)と店(てん)

Shop names ending in 屋(や), a slightly older usage, are also used to refer to the shop owners or salespeople working at the shops. For example, the owner of a 時計屋(とけいや) (*watch store*) may be called 時計屋 or 時計屋さん. Use the politer さん to those in the watch vendor's in-group (including him). As in English, in Japanese you can say 肉屋(にくや)に行った (*I went to the butcher shop*) or 肉屋さんに行った (*I went to the butcher's*) with no change in meaning. In many cases, 店 (*shop*) is used instead of the 屋 of a store name. For example, レコード屋 and レコード店(てん) are both used to mean *record store.* Unlike 屋, however, shop names ending in 店(てん) cannot be used to refer to a person at the shop.

アクティビティー　1

どこにいますか。(*Where are you?*)

Where are you when you say this? Match the statement with the appropriate store.

1. このバッファリンはいくらですか。
2. このスカート、ドライ・クリーニングお願(ねが)いします。
3. このスニーカのサイズは何センチですか。
4. 日本語の教科書(きょうかしょ)はありますか。
5. このサングラス、ちょっと大きすぎますね。
6. 明日は「母(はは)の日」ですから、カーネションを買(か)いましょう。
7. 今日はバナナが安(やす)いですね。
8. そのチーズケーキ二つとアップルパイ三つください。
9. U2の新(あたら)しいCDはありますか。
10. 鉛筆(えんぴつ)10本ください。

a. 文房具屋(ぶんぼうぐや)
b. 果物屋(くだものや)
c. 本屋(ほんや)
d. ケーキ屋(や)
e. レコード屋(や)
f. 花屋(はなや)
g. 薬屋(くすりや)
h. 眼鏡屋(めがねや)
i. クリーニング屋(や)
j. 靴屋(くつや)

For ～すぎる, refer to **Grammar 35,** Chapter 6.

アクティビティー　2

どこで買(か)えますか。どこで売(う)っていますか。(*Where can you buy them? Where do they sell them?*)

Tell where you can buy these things. Which item in each group is not available there?

Review the potential form of verbs (**Grammar 28,** Chapter 5) and the te-form + います construction (**Grammar 29,** Chapter 5).

1. りんご、みかん、バナナ、トースター、パイナップル
2. レタス、キャベツ、いす、じゃがいも、にんじん
3. 牛肉(ぎゅうにく)、マトン、鳥肉(とりにく)、豚肉(ぶたにく)、ケーキ
4. アスピリン、バンドエイド、ハンマー、ワセリン、ビタミン
5. ベーグル、クロワッサン、フランスパン、ブーツ、サンドイッチ
6. ウイスキー、酒(さけ)、コーヒー、ビール、ワイン
7. テレビ、ドレス、ラジオ、テープ・レコーダー、ステレオ
8. 辞書(じしょ)、雑誌(ざっし)、まんが (*comic books*)、本、時計(とけい)

Grammar and Practice Activities

40. When Something Happens: Temporal Clauses Ending in 時(とき)

ブラウン：きれいなブラウスですね。
町田：このあいだ、デパートでセールがあった時、買(か)ったんです。
ブラウン：町田さんはよく買(か)い物(もの)に行くんですか。
町田：ええ、今度(こんど)行く時(とき)、ブラウンさんもさそいましょう。

カワムラ：山口(やまぐち)さんは外国語(がいこくご)を勉強(べんきょう)したことがありますか。
山口(やまぐち)：ええ、学生の時、ドイツ語を勉強(べんきょう)しました。
カワムラ：ドイツ語はお上手(じょうず)ですか。
山口：若(わか)い時(とき)は、ちょっと話せましたが、今はすっかり忘(わす)れました。

40.1 The noun 時(とき) (*time*), modified by nouns, adjectives, and verbs, forms a clause equivalent to English *when*…

PART OF SPEECH	時 CLAUSE FORMATION	EXAMPLE
Nouns	Noun ＋ の ＋ 時(とき)	子供(こども)の時(とき)、ディズニーランドに 行ったことがあります。 *When I was a child, I went to Disneyland.*
I-adjectives	Dictionary form ＋ 時(とき)	今度(こんど)肉(にく)が安(やす)い時(とき)、すきやきを作(つく)りましょう。 *Let's make sukiyaki some other* (lit., *next*) *time when meat is inexpensive.*
Na-adjectives	Adjective ＋ な ＋ 時(とき)	暇(ひま)な時(とき)、また来(き)ます。 *When I am free, I will come here again.*
Verbs	Dictionary form (nonpast, plain) ＋ 時(とき)	テニスをする時(とき)は、教(おし)えてください。 *Please let me know when you are going to play tennis.*
	Ta-form (past, plain) ＋ 時(とき)	京都(きょうと)へ行った時(とき)、この絵(え)を買(か)いました。 *I bought this picture when I went to Kyoto.*

BROWN: That's a pretty blouse. MACHIDA: I bought it the other day when there was a sale at the department store. BROWN: Do you go shopping often? MACHIDA: Yes, I'll invite you along next time I go.

KAWAMURA: Have you ever studied a foreign language? YAMAGUCHI: Yes, when I was a student, I studied German. KAWAMURA: Are you good at German? YAMAGUCHI: When I was young, I could speak a little, but I've forgotten it all now.

40.2 As you see, both the nonpast form and the past form of verbs are used in this temporal clause.

The nonpast form is used for an action or event that has not been completed when the action or event expressed by the following, main clause of the sentence takes place. For example

> 東京(とうきょう)へ行く時(とき)、教(おし)えてください。
> *When you go to Tokyo, please let me know.* (*That is, when you decide you will go to Tokyo, please let me know you are going.*)
>
> 東京(とうきょう)へ行く時(とき)、新幹線(しんかんせん)に乗(の)りました。
> *On the way to Tokyo, I rode the bullet train.* (lit., *When going to Tokyo, I rode the bullet train.*)

Although we have been using **kanji** for the word とき, it is actually often written in **hiragana** whenever it means *when, in the case that.* The **hiragana** form is perfectly acceptable, and quite common, in such cases.

The nonpast is used here because the action of going to Tokyo was not completely over while you were riding the train.

In addition, the nonpast may mean *whenever.*

> 買(か)い物(もの)をする時(とき)、クレジットカードを使(つか)います。
> *Whenever I shop, I use a credit card.*

On the other hand, the past form is used for an action or event that is completed when the action or event expressed in the main clause takes place.

> 東京(とうきょう)へ行った時(とき)、地下鉄(ちかてつ)に乗(の)りました。
> *When I went to Tokyo, I rode the subway.*
>
> 東京(とうきょう)へ行った時(とき)、ブラウンさんに会(あ)うつもりです。
> *When I am in Tokyo* (lit., *When I have gone to* [*and am still in*] *Tokyo*), *I plan to see Ms. Brown.*

The reason the past form 行った is used here is that the action of going to Tokyo must be completed before the speaker is able to see Ms. Brown. The choice between nonpast and past is determined by the temporal relationship between the action in the first clause and the action in the second clause. The use of a past verb does not necessarily mean the action has already occurred. The action expressed by 行った is sometimes completed (thus, in the past) and sometimes not yet completed in the real world.

40.3 Because the 時 clause indicates a specific time, the particle に, used to specify a time, may follow this clause.

> 先週(せんしゅう)デパートに行った時(とき)に、この靴下(くつした)を買(か)いました。
> *When* (lit., *At the time when*) *I went to the department store last week, I bought this pair of socks.*

40.4 時 is a noun, so it can be modified by such demonstrative adjectives as この, そんな, and どんな.

A variety of particles can be attached to 時.

> その時(とき)、何をしていましたか。
> *What were you doing at that time?*

こんな時は、電気屋さんを呼びましょう。
Let's call an electrician at times like this.

どんな時、クレジットカードを使いますか。
On what occasions (lit., *At what sorts of times*) *do you use your credit card?*

言語ノート

Asking *When*

The interrogative いつ (*when*) is used to elicit the specific time when something happens or occurs.

いつこのソファーを買いましたか。
—去年の11月に買いました。
When did you buy this couch?
—We bought it last November.

The phrases どんな時 and どのような時 (lit., *what kind of time*) are used to ask *when* less specifically.

どんな時、クレジットカードを使いますか。
—値段の高いものを買う時に使います。
When do you use a credit card?
—I use it when I buy something expensive.

どのような時、そのドレスを着ますか。
—フォーマルなパーティーに行く時に着ます。
On what occasions do you wear that dress?
—I wear it when I go to formal parties.

アクティビティー 3

ダイアログ：ケーキ屋さんに行った時、金井さんに会いました。(*When I went to the pastry shop, I saw Mr. Kanai.*)

カワムラ：昨日、ケーキ屋さんに行った時、金井さんに会いました。
山口：そうですか。
カワムラ：バースデー・ケーキを買っていましたよ。
山口：だれかの誕生日だったんでしょう。

KAWAMURA: When I went to the pastry shop yesterday, I saw Mr. Kanai. YAMAGUCHI: Is that right? KAWAMURA: He was buying a birthday cake. YAMAGUCHI: It was probably someone's birthday.

Practice the dialogue, substituting the following words for the first and second underlined portions. Change the third underlined portion on your own.

1. カメラ屋　　フィルム
2. おもちゃ屋　　プラモデル (*plastic model*)
3. 本屋　　ガイドブック
4. レコード屋　　クラシック音楽のレコード
5. 文房具屋　　ノート

アクティビティー　4

どんな時、アイスコーヒーを飲みますか。(*On what occasions do you drink iced coffee?*)

Using the model as an example, make dialogues.

[例]　(アイスコーヒーを飲む)(暑い)→

s1: どんな時、アイスコーヒーを飲みますか。

s2: 暑い時、アイスコーヒーを飲みます。

1. (買い物に行きます)(暇)
2. (本を読む)(時間がある)
3. (コートを着る)(寒い)
4. (図書館へ行く)(勉強する)
5. (ネクタイをしめる)(仕事へ行く)
6. (日本語を話す)(日本人の友だちと話す)

アクティビティー　5

日本に行った時… (*When I went to Japan…*)

Join the following clauses into sentences using 時.

[例]　(デパートへ行きます)(タクシーを使いました)→

デパートへ行く時、タクシーを使いました。

(デパートへ行きます)(ブラウスを買いました)→

デパートへ行った時、ブラウスを買いました。

1. (買い物に行きます)(いつも友だちと行きます)
2. (静かです)(本を読みます)
3. (コンサートへ行きます)(プログラムを買います)
4. (日本語を話します)(ゆっくり[*slowly*]話してください)
5. (仕事がありません)(昼ごろ起きる)

6. (暇(ひま)です)(ウインドーショッピングをします)
7. (学生)(デパートでアルバイトをしました)
8. (日本にいました)(このワープロを買(か)った)

アクティビティー 6

食事(しょくじ)の時(とき)、はしを使(つか)いますか。(*Do you use chopsticks at meals?*)

Answer these questions.

1. 暑(あつ)い時(とき)、何を飲みますか。
2. 高校生(こうこうせい) (*high school student*) の時(とき)、どんなスポーツをしましたか。
3. 今日、日本語のクラスへ行った(来(き)た)時(とき)、何人(なんにん)の学生がいましたか。
4. 日本のレストランへ行った時(とき)、はし (*chopsticks*) を使(つか)いますか、フォークを使(つか)いますか。
5. 写真(しゃしん)をとる時(とき)、オートマチック・カメラを使(つか)いますか。
6. ジョギングをする時(とき)は何を着(き)ますか。
7. どんな時、お酒(さけ)を飲みますか。
8. 暇(ひま)な時(とき)、何をしますか。
9. 映画館(えいがかん)へ行った時(とき)、前にすわりますか、後ろにすわりますか。
10. どんな時(とき)、レストランへ行きますか。

Vocabulary Library 

More Stores

米屋	こめや	rice dealer
食料品店	しょくりょうひんてん	grocery store
金物屋	かなものや	hardware store
洋品店	ようひんてん	Western clothing store
婦人服店	ふじんふくてん	women's wear store
ふとん屋	ふとんや	futon store
呉服屋	ごふくや	kimono store
化粧品店	けしょうひんてん	cosmetics store
床屋	とこや	barbershop (*colloquial*)
理髪店	りはつてん	barbershop
美容院	びよういん	beauty parlor
お菓子屋	おかしや	confectionery shop
おもちゃ屋	おもちゃや	toy store

Loanwords: コンビニエンス・ストア、ブティック

アクティビティー　7

こんな時(とき)、どこへ行きますか。(*Where do you go on this occasion?*)

On these occasions, what store do you go to?

[例]　おなかがすきました。ポテトチップがほしいです。→
　　ポテトチップがほしい時(とき)は、スーパーに行きます。

Useful word: 持(も)っていく *to take*

1. 今夜(こんや)はすきやきが食べたいんですが…
2. うちの時計(とけい)がこわれました (*is broken*)。
3. 頭(あたま)がいたいんですが… (*my head hurts…*)
4. 野菜(やさい)ジュースを作(つく)りたいんですが…
5. 夏だから、髪(かみ) (*hair*) を短(みじ)かく切(き)りたい (*want to cut*) んですが…
6. 今夜(こんや)はすしを作(つく)りましょう。
7. 明日(あした)、パーティーをします。
8. デザイナーズ・ブランドのドレスがほしいんですが…
9. ペンのインクがもうありません。
10. このスカート、きたないですね。

Vocabulary: Colors

色	いろ	color
白、白い	しろ、しろい	white
黒、黒い	くろ、くろい	black
赤、赤い	あか、あかい	red
青、青い	あお、あおい	blue
黄色、黄色い	きいろ、きいろい	yellow
緑	みどり	green
茶色、茶色い	ちゃいろ、ちゃいろい	brown (lit., *tea color*)
灰色	はいいろ	gray
水色	みずいろ	light blue (lit., *water color*)
派手(な)	はで(な)	bright; gaudy
地味(な)	じみ(な)	subdued (*in color*)
暗い	くらい	dark
明るい	あかるい	light; bright
薄い	うすい	light (*in color*); pale
濃い	こい	dark (*in color*); deep

Note: Where two words are given for a color, the first is a noun, and the second is an i-adjective.

アクティビティー 8

(*Association*)

What color(s) do you associate with the following?

1. お金(かね)
2. アメリカ
3. 冬(ふゆ)
4. 夏(なつ)
5. 秋(あき)
6. 日本
7. りんご
8. レモン
9. 夢(ゆめ) (*dream*)
10. 愛(あい) (*love*)
11. 情熱(じょうねつ) (*passion*)
12. 嫉妬(しっと) (*envy*)
13. 結婚(けっこん) (*marriage*)

文化ノート

CULTURE NOTE • 色(いろ): Colors

Learning a foreign language means learning to see the world in a new way. The color spectrum provides a good example of this. In Japanese the color 青(あお) encompasses both blue and green. This color is used in such set phrases as 青空(あおぞら: *blue sky*) and 青信号(あおしんごう: *green light, in a traffic signal*). Nowadays, distinction is often made between green and blue with 緑(みどり) or グリーン used to indicate green and 青 meaning blue. 緑 is the same word used to name the national holiday 緑の日(みどりのひ: *Greenery Day*) and symbolizes greenery, nature, and the environment. Other color symbolism includes the combination of red and white to represent festivity or congratulations. Black and white combined are used in decorations for funerals.

In another shift of the color spectrum, blue movies are known as ピンク映画(ピンクえいが) in Japan. A number of colors derive their names from the environment. 茶色(ちゃいろ: *brown*) literally means tea color, 灰色(はいいろ: *gray*) literally translates as ash color, 桃色(ももいろ: *pink*) is peach color, and so on. Notice that in traditional kimono as well as Western fashions, bright colors are considered suitable for wear by children and young women, but in general the older one gets, the more subdued colors one is expected to wear, with the elderly wearing muted tones of brown, gray, and navy.

アクティビティー 9

どんな色(いろ)が好きですか。(*What color do you like?*)

Answer these questions.

1. あなたはどんな色(いろ)が好きですか。
2. きらいな色(いろ)はありますか。
3. あなたの車(くるま)はどんな色(いろ)ですか。

4. 教室の壁 (*wall*) はどんな色ですか。
5. 派手な色はどんな色ですか。
6. 地味な色はどんな色ですか。
7. 暗い色はどんな色ですか。
8. 明るい色はどんな色ですか。
9. クラスの中に赤いもの (*thing*) はありますか。
10. クラスの中に青いものはありますか。

Vocabulary Library 

More Colors

藍色	あいいろ	indigo blue	金色	きんいろ	gold
クリーム色	クリームいろ	cream-colored	銀色	ぎんいろ	silver
オレンジ色	オレンジいろ	orange	透明(な)	とうめい(な)	transparent
紫	むらさき	purple			

Loanwords: ブルー、ダークブルー、ライトブルー、グリーン、ピンク、グレー

41. Indefinite Pronoun の

ブラウン：その青いブラウスを見せてください。
店員：はい、どうぞ。
ブラウン：白いのはありませんか。
店員：申し訳ありませんが、このデザインで、白はないんです。
こちらの黄色やピンクのはいかがですか。
ブラウン：もっと地味なのはありませんか。
店員：派手なのはおきらいですか。

おきらい is a polite form of きらい.

41.1 The indefinite pronoun の, which must be used after adjectives or relative clauses, means *one* or *ones*. In other words, it replaces a noun or refers to a person, thing, concept, etc., that is clear from the context.

BROWN: Please show me that blue blouse. CLERK: Here you are. (lit., *Yes, here it is.*) BROWN: Do (lit., *Don't*) you have a white one? CLERK: I'm sorry, but we don't have white in this design. How about these yellow and pink ones? BROWN: Don't you have one in a plainer color? CLERK: You don't like brightly colored ones?

I-adjectives	Plain forms	+ の
Na-adjectives	Dictionary form ＋な／だった	
Verbs	Plain forms	
Copula	(だ→)な or だった	

わたしはその赤いのが好きです。
I like that red one.

どれでも好きなのを取ってください。
Please take anything you like (lit., *whichever ones you like*).

明日来るのはカワムラさんと林さんです。
The ones who will come tomorrow are Mr. Kawamura and Mr. Hayashi.

今日、デパートで買ったのは何ですか。—今日デパートで買ったのはシャツです。
What is it that you bought at the department store today? —What I bought at the department store today is a shirt.

クラスの中で、アメリカ人なのは私だけです。
I am the only American in my class. (lit., *Of* [*my*] class, the one who is American is me only.)

Note that when a verb falls in front of the indefinite pronoun の, the resulting clause functions as a relative clause in the sense that it modifies の.

言語ノート

だけ

だけ is a particle meaning *only, just, alone*. As seen in the following examples, it modifies the preceding noun (or pronoun).

薬局ではアスピリンだけ(を)買った。
I bought only aspirin at the drugstore.

ブラウンさんだけ(が)来ました。
Only Ms. Brown came.

Note that these sentences including だけ can be rewritten by using しか + negative.

薬局ではアスピリンしか買わなかった。

ブラウンさんしか来ませんでした。

だけ also can modify a clause or a sentence. For example

聞いただけです。
I just asked. (i.e., *All I did was ask.*)

チーズケーキを買っただけです。
I just bought cheesecake. (i.e., *All I did was buy cheesecake.*)

41.2 Note that the indefinite pronoun の is different from the possessive particle の (**Grammar 2**, Chapter 1) and the nominalizer の (**Grammar 26**, Chapter 5).

POSSESSIVE PARTICLE

ブラウンさんの ネックレスはきれいですね。
Your (lit., *Ms. Brown's*) *necklace is pretty, isn't it?*
ブラウンさんの はきれいですね。
Yours (lit., *Ms. Brown's*) *is pretty, isn't it?* (omission of ネックレス)

INDEFINITE PRONOUN

黒(くろ)い靴(くつ)がほしいです。
I want black shoes.
黒(くろ)いの がほしいです。
I want black ones. (の refers to shoes.)

NOMINALIZER

ギブソンさんが帽子(ぼうし)を買(か)ったのを知(し)っていますか。
Do you know that Ms. Gibson bought a hat?

INDEFINITE PRONOUNS

ギブソンさんが買(か)ったのは何ですか。
What is it (lit., *the one*) *that Ms. Gibson bought?*

アクティビティー 10

ダイアログ：この赤(あか)いのはどうですか。(*How about this red one?*)

ブラウン：この白(しろ)いブラウスはいくらですか。
店員(てんいん)：9500 円でございます。
ブラウン：もう少(すこ)し安(やす)いのはありますか。
店員：では、この赤(あか)いのはどうでしょうか。7600 円でございます。

でございます is a very polite form of です. Note that the shop clerk is using a very polite level of speech with the customer.

Practice the dialogue, substituting the following for the underlined portions.

1. 派手(はで)な　　このピンク
2. 小さい　　あの青(あお)い
3. フォーマルな　　あのケースの中にある
4. カジュアルな　　その白(しろ)いブラウスの右にある

BROWN: How much is this white blouse? CLERK: It's 9,500 yen. BROWN: Do you have a cheaper one? CLERK: Well, how about this red one? It's 7,600 yen.

アクティビティー 11

甘(あま)いのをお願(ねが)いします。(*The sweet one, please.*)

Using the model as an example, make dialogues.

[例] ケーキ、甘(あま)い、甘くない →
s1: すみません。ケーキをください。
s2: 甘(あま)いのがいいですか。甘(あま)くないのがいいですか。
s1: 甘(あま)いのをお願(ねが)いします。

1. スカート、長(なが)い、短(みじか)い
2. テープレコーダー、大きい、小さい
3. アイロン、重(おも)い (*heavy*)、軽(かる)い (*lightweight*)
4. ネクタイ、派手(はで)、地味(じみ)
5. リボン、黒(くろ)い、赤(あか)い

アクティビティー 12

小さいのがいいです。(*The small one is better.*)

Rewrite the second sentence of each question using the indefinite pronoun の.

[例] 小さい車(くるま)がいいです。→ 小さいのがいいです。

1. その赤(あか)いセーターはいいですね。でも、この黒(くろ)いセーターはわたしには似合(にあ)いません (*doesn't suit*) ね。
2. この紙(かみ)はちょっとうすい (*thin*) ですね。あつい (*thick*) 紙(かみ)はありますか。
3. このアパートは不便(ふべん)です。もっと便利(べんり)なアパートを探(さが)しましょう。(探(さが)す *to look for*)
4. こんなブランドは聞いたことがありません。有名(ゆうめい)なブランドはありますか。
5. このカレーは辛(から)すぎます。からくないカレーがあちらにありますから、それを食べましょう。

アクティビティー 13

わたしが行ったのは宝石店(ほうせきてん)です。(*Where I went was the jewelry shop.*)

Using the model as an example, change these sentences using the indefinite pronoun の.

[例] 昨日(きのう)、私(わたし)がスーパーへ行きました。→
昨日(きのう)、私(わたし)が行ったのはスーパーです。

山口さんは、私の右にいます。→
わたしの右にいるのは山口さんです。

1. 先週ブラウスを買いました。
2. あの店でおいしいケーキを売っています。
3. 私がブラウンさんに電話しました。
4. 昨日、林さんはステーキを食べました。
5. この本はたいへん有名です。
6. 東京の電車はとても便利です。

Vocabulary and Grammar 7B

Vocabulary and Oral Activities

Shopping

Vocabulary: Shopping

バーゲンセール		bargain sale
(お)客(さん)	(お)きゃく(さん)	customer

主人	しゅじん	store owner	領収書	りょうしゅうしょ	receipt (*usually handwritten*)
店員	てんいん	store clerk			
値段	ねだん	price	レシート		receipt (*usually printed by cash registers*)
おつり		change			
お金	おかね	money	レジ		cash register; cashier
払う	はらう	to pay			

Review: 安(やす)い、高(たか)い

アクティビティー 14

いくらですか。(*How much is it?*)

Look at the illustration and answer the following questions.

1. 大きいアルバムはいくらですか。小さいのはいくらですか。
2. 日本製(せい)の万年筆(まんねんひつ)(*fountain pen*)はいくらですか。ドイツ製(せい)のはいくらですか。

(country name) 製(せい)(の) means *made in*... For example, フランス製(せい) means *made in France*.

3. 日本製の万年筆の下にあるかばんはいくらですか。カウンターの後ろにあるのはいくらですか。

4. ショーケースの上にあるボールペンはいくらですか。ブラウンさんが持っているのはいくらですか。

5. ショーケースの中にあるワープロはいくらですか。カワムラさんが見ているのはいくらですか。

文化ノート

CULTURE NOTE • Handling Japanese Money

The denominations of coins currently circulated in Japan are 1 yen, 5 yen, 10 yen, 50 yen, 100 yen, and 500 yen. 5-yen and 50-yen coins have a hole in the middle. The denominations of Japanese bills are 1,000 yen, 2,000 yen, 5,000 yen, and 10,000 yen. The images on these bills are of Soseki Natsume, a writer in the Meiji era (1868–1912), for the 1,000-yen bill, Shureimon gate in Okinawa, commemorating the 2000 G8 Summit, for the 2,000-yen bill, Inazo Nitobe, a diplomat in the Meiji era, for the 5,000-yen bill, and Yukichi Hukuzawa, an educator in the same era, for the 10,000-yen bill.

Traditionally, Japanese people have considered it improper to talk about or show money in public, so when they give or return money, it is likely to be in an envelope. If they don't have an envelope, they might say はだかで申し訳ありません (*Sorry about the naked money*). When Japanese count out change, they use subtraction rather than addition. Thus, when you pay 5,000 yen for a 4,300-yen item, the shop clerk gives you 700 yen after subtracting 4,300 yen from 5,000 yen. The shop clerk says something like

> 4,300円です。5,000円頂戴(ちょうだい)いたします。700円のおつりでございます。
>
> *That's 4,300 yen.* (Then, on receiving the customer's money) *I have received 5,000 yen. Here is your change, 700 yen.*

In most stores and shops the clerks use a tray to return change to you.

日本のお金

Vocabulary Library

More on Shopping

商品	しょうひん	goods; merchandise

Customer Service

セール		sale
売り出し	うりだし	bargain sale
見本	みほん	sample items
包み紙	つつみがみ	wrapping paper
包む	つつむ	to wrap
サービス		something given for free (lit., *service*)
広告	こうこく	advertisement
注文(する)	ちゅうもん(する)	order (*n.*) to order
配達(する)	はいたつ(する)	delivery (to deliver)
返品(する)	へんぴん(する)	returned merchandise (to return merchandise)

Loanwords: カタログ、ショーウインドー、メールオーダー

Paying

価格	かかく	price
値切る	ねぎる	to haggle over price
請求書	せいきゅうしょ	bill
現金	げんきん	cash
分割払い	ぶんかつばらい	installment purchase
クレジットばらい		credit purchase
割引(する)	わりびき(する)	discount (*n.*) (to discount)

Loanwords: クレジットカード、ローン

アクティビティー 15

ショッピングが好きですか。(*Do you like shopping?*)

Discuss in class.

1. ショッピングが好きですか。
2. バーゲンセールによく行きますか。
3. バーゲンセールでは何%の割引(わりびき) (*discount*) がありますか。
4. 現金(げんきん) (*cash*) で買(か)い物(もの)をしますか。クレジットカードで買(か)い物(もの)をしますか。
5. クレジットカードを何枚(まい)持(も)っています (*have*) か。どんなカードを持(も)っていますか。

6. 買ったものを返品した (*returned*) ことがありますか。
7. どんなものを分割払い (*on installment*) で買いますか。
8. どんなものをメールオーダーで買いますか。

Grammar and Practice Activities

42. Making If-Then Statements: The たら Conditional

カワムラ：ブラウンさんはまだ来ませんか。
林：ええ、まだです。おそいですね。
カワムラ：タクシーだったら、10分もかからないんですがね…
林：おかしいですね。
カワムラ：とにかく、来たら、すぐ教えてください。

カワムラ：あの車、いいですね。
チン：ええ、お金があったら、買うんですが…
カワムラ：もう少し安かったら、ぼくも買いたいんですがね…
チン：カワムラさん、そんなにお金があるんですか。

カワムラ：三村さんのアパートは駅に近くて便利ですね。
三村：ええ。でも、もう少し新しかったら、いいんですが…
カワムラ：そんなに古くないでしょう。
三村：それに、となりの人が静かだったら、もっといいんですが…

42.1 *If it rains, I will stay at home* is called a conditional sentence. In such a sentence, the clause introduced by *if* expresses the condition under which the second clause will occur. The first *if* clause is usually called the conditional clause, and the other is called the resultant clause. There are several types of conditionals

---

KAWAMURA: Hasn't Ms. Brown arrived yet? HAYASHI: No, not yet. She's late, isn't she? KAWAMURA: If she used a taxi, it wouldn't take even ten minutes… HAYASHI: Something's not right. (lit., *It's strange, isn't it?*) KAWAMURA: Anyway, when she comes, please let me know immediately.

KAWAMURA: That's a great car, isn't it! CHIN: Yes, if I had the money, I'd buy it but… KAWAMURA: If it were a little cheaper, I would like to buy it, too. CHIN: Mr. Kawamura, do you have that much money?

KAWAMURA: Your apartment is conveniently close to the station, isn't it? MIMURA: Yes. But I wish it were a little newer. (lit., *But if it were a little newer, it would be good, but…*) KAWAMURA: It's not that old, is it? MIMURA: Besides, I wish the neighbors were quiet. (lit., *If the people next door were quiet, it would be nicer.*)

in Japanese; you will study them gradually. The one presented here, the たら conditional, is used to express a simple relationship between a conditional clause and the resultant clause.

CONDITIONAL CLAUSE			
	Affirmative	**Negative**	
Verb I-adjective Na-adjective Copula	the past, plain form + ら	the past, plain, negative form + ら	+ resultant clause

The conditional clause is often preceded by もしも or, more commonly, もし (*if, supposing*), both of which emphasize the suppositional nature of the clause.

> 雨が降ったら、ハイキングには行きません。
> *If it rains, I won't go hiking.*
>
> もしそこにブラウンさんがいなかったら、お金を払えませんでした。
> *If Ms. Brown had not been there, I would not have been able to pay* (lit., *the money*).
>
> もし暑かったら、窓を開けてください。
> *If you are hot, please open the window.*
>
> そんなに寒くなかったら、外で食べましょう。
> *If it is not that cold, let's eat outside.*
>
> もっと元気だったら、みんなと山へ行くんですが...
> *If I were healthier, I would go to the mountains with everyone.*

42.2 This conditional is typically used when the resultant clause expresses a request, suggestion, permission, volition, or prohibition.

> 買い物から帰ったら、勉強しましょう。
> *Let's study after we return from shopping.*
>
> 新しい靴を買ったら、見せてください。
> *If you buy a new pair of shoes, please show them to me.*
>
> 土曜日、いいお天気だったら、ピクニックに行きませんか。
> *If the weather is good on Saturday, would you like to go on a picnic?*

42.3 This conditional may be used to express a hypothetical situation.

> お金があったら、いいコンピューターを買いたい。
> *If I had money, I would like to buy a good computer.*

林(はやし)さんがもっとハンサムだったら、デートするんですが…
If Mr. Hayashi were more handsome, I would date him.

42.4 This conditional may be used to indicate actual (i.e., not hypothetical) sequences of actions or events. The resultant clause is commonly in the past tense. When used in this sense, ～たら is similar to *when.*

林さんのアパートへ行ったら、ギブソンさんがいた。
When I went to Mr. Hayashi's apartment, Ms. Gibson was there.

42.5 The expression ～たらいい can be used to express a wish, regret, suggestion, etc.

明日(あした)晴(は)れたらいいですね。
I hope the weather will be good tomorrow. (lit., *It would be nice if it's clear tomorrow, wouldn't it?*)

アクティビティー 16

ダイアログ：安(やす)かったら買(か)うんですが。(*If it were cheaper, I would buy it.*)

ブティックで

町田：あのセーターいいですね。
ブラウン：ええ、きれいな色(いろ)ですね。買(か)わないんですか。
町田：ええ、もう少(すこ)し安(やす)かったら、買(か)うんですが…
ブラウン：そうですね。2万円(えん)はちょっと高(たか)すぎますね。

Practice the dialogue, substituting the following words in Machida's role. Make up appropriate substitutions for the underlined portions of Brown's role.

1. 冷蔵庫(れいぞうこ)、もう少(すこ)し小さい
2. スカート、サイズが大きい
3. ステレオ、CDプレーヤーがついている (*a CD player is attached*)
4. コンピュータ、もう少(すこ)しメモリーが大きい
5. ワープロ、日本語が使(つか)える
6. バッグ、違(ちが)う色(いろ)
7. スポーツ・カー、お金(かね)がある

At a boutique MACHIDA: That sweater is nice, isn't it! BROWN: Yes, it's a pretty color, isn't it? Aren't you going to buy it? MACHIDA: No. If it were a little cheaper, I would buy it… BROWN: That's true. Twenty thousand yen is a bit expensive, isn't it!

アクティビティー 17

安(やす)かったら、買(か)いましょう。(*If it's cheap, let's buy it.*)

Fill in the blanks with the たら form.

[例]　(　　)、買(か)いましょう。(安(やす)い) → 安かったら、買(か)いましょう。

1. パーティーに(　　)、ブラウンさんに会(あ)った。(行く)
2. カーティスさんに(　　)、わかりますよ。(聞く)
3. (　　)、家にいます。(寒(さむ)い)
4. あなたがステレオを(　　)、わたしも買(か)います。(買(か)う)
5. ライトを(　　)、暗(くら)くなった。(消(け)す[*to turn off*])
6. その部屋(へや)が(　　)、そこで話しましょう。(静(しず)か)
7. 今、そこに家を(　　)、とても高(たか)いですよ。(建(た)てる[*to build*])
8. チンさんが(　　)、教(おし)えてください。(来る)
9. その本が(　　)、貸(か)して(*lend*)ください。(面白(おもしろ)い)

アクティビティー 18

もし下手(へた)でなかったら… (*If I weren't so bad at it…*)

Using the model as an example, make hypothetical conditional sentences. Make up an appropriate final clause.

[例]　わたしは病気(びょうき)です。→ もし病気(びょうき)でなかったら、学校へ行くでしょう。

1. 明日、試験(しけん)があります。
2. わたしは日本語が上手(じょうず)ではありません。
3. わたしはお金(かね)があまりありません。
4. わたしはステレオを持(も)っていません。
5. 雨(あめ)が降(ふ)っています。

アクティビティー 19

これが終(お)わったら、どうしますか。(*What will you do when you finish this?*)

Make conditional sentences, using the model as an example.

[例]　おなかがすく→おなかがすいたら、何か食べます。

1. マドンナが来(く)る。
2. 6時になる。
3. 1万(まん)ドルある。
4. マイケル・ジャクソンから電話(でんわ)が来(く)る。
5. そのコートが安(やす)い。
6. フランス語が上手(じょうず)だ。
7. 春(はる)が来(く)る。
8. 車(くるま)がある。
9. 日本へ行く。

アクティビティー　20

えり好(ごの)みするお客(きゃく)さん(*Picky shoppers*)

Look at the following illustrations. Under what circumstances would you buy each item?

[例]　1万円(まんえん)だったら、買(か)います。

1.

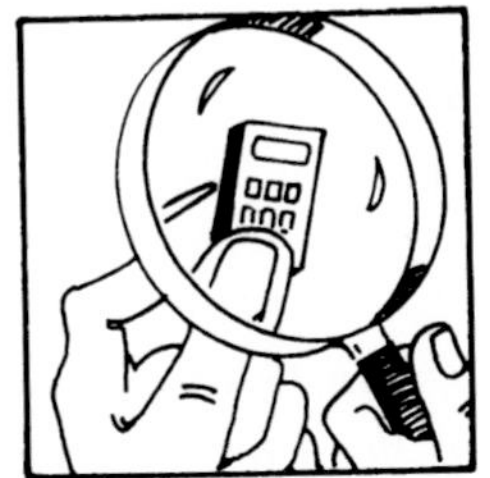

2.

3.

4.

5.

6.

Vocabulary and Grammar 7C

Vocabulary and Oral Activities

Clothes

Vocabulary: Clothes 

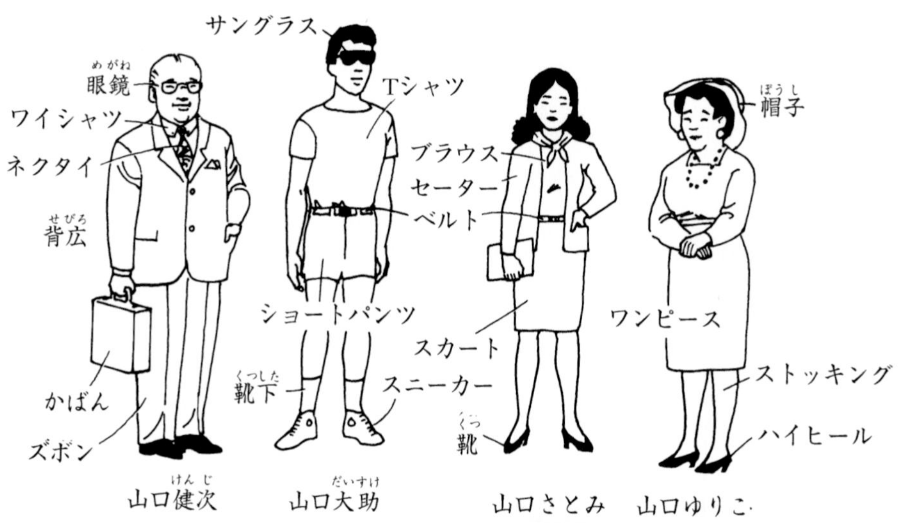

着る	きる	to wear; to put on
はく		to wear; to put on (*over your legs or feet: pants, shoes, skirts etc.*)
かぶる		to wear; to put on (*your head: hats, helmets, etc.*)
つける		to wear; to put on (*things that need attaching: earrings, bras, etc.*)
脱ぐ	ぬぐ	to take off
洋服	ようふく	Western-style clothes
和服	わふく	Japanese-style clothes
着物	きもの	kimono
背広	せびろ	suit
ワイシャツ		(men's) dress shirt (lit., *white shirt*)
ネクタイ		necktie
ドレス		dress
ワンピース		dress (lit., *one piece*)
セーター		sweater
ブラウス		blouse
マフラー		scarf

ハンカチ		handkerchief
眼鏡	めがね	glasses
サングラス	サングラス	sunglasses
ズボン		trousers
スカート		skirt
コート		coat
下着	したぎ	underwear
シャツ		shirt
パンツ		briefs (lit., *pants*)
パンティー		panties
ブラジャー		bra (lit., *brassiere*)
パジャマ		pajamas
ネグリジェ		negligee
水着	みずぎ	bathing suit
靴	くつ	shoe
ブーツ		boot
靴下	くつした	sock
ストッキング		stockings (*especially women's*)
帽子	ぼうし	hat; cap
ベルト		belt
スポーツウェア		sportswear
Tシャツ		T-shirt
ジーンズ、ジーパン		jeans
ショートパンツ		shorts

アクティビティー 21

どんなお天気(てんき)ですか。(*What is the weather like?*)

What is the weather like in each city, if the following are descriptions of appropriate dress?

Review vocabulary relating to weather and climate (p. 240).

1. 東京(とうきょう)：道子(みちこ)さんはレインコートを着(き)ています。傘(かさ)もさしています。(*She is using an umbrella, too.*) いいお天気(てんき)ですか。お天気が悪(わる)いですか。
2. 札幌(さっぽろ)：吉田(よしだ)さんはあついコートを着(き)ています。スノーブーツもはいています。帽子(ぼうし)もかぶっています。夏(なつ)ですか。冬(ふゆ)ですか。何が降(ふ)っていますか。
3. 熊本(くまもと)：金井(かない)さんはショートパンツをはいています。半袖(はんそで) (*short sleeves*) のシャツを着(き)ています。サンダルをはいています。夏(なつ)ですか。冬(ふゆ)ですか。暑(あつ)いですか。寒(さむ)いですか。

4. 岡山：友子さんはブラウスを着ています。ジャケットもコートも着ていません。どんな季節ですか。寒いですか。

5. 金沢：山下さんはセーターを着ています。そして、その上に、ジャケットを着ています。暑いですか。寒いですか。

Vocabulary Library

More on Clothes

Clothing

衣服	いふく	clothes
長袖(の)	ながそで(の)	long sleeves (*n.*); (long-sleeved)
半袖(の)	はんそで(の)	short sleeves (*n.*); (short-sleeved)
上着	うわぎ	jacket; suit coat
制服	せいふく	uniform
手袋	てぶくろ	gloves
着替える	きがえる	to change clothes

Loanwords: サンダル、スリッパ、ポケット

Accessories

指輪	ゆびわ	ring

Loanwords: イヤリング、ネックレス、ピアス (*pierced earring*)、ブレスレット、ブローチ (*brooch*)

Fashion

Loanwords: ファッション、ファッション・ショー、モデル、デザイン、デザイナー

Sewing

縫う	ぬう	to sew
繕う	つくろう	to mend
編む	あむ	to knit
ミシンをかける		to use a sewing machine
はさみ		scissors
糸	いと	thread
針	はり	needle
アイロンをかける		to iron
ファスナー		zipper
ボタン		button

シャツにアイロンをかける *to iron a shirt*

Fabric and Fiber

絹	きぬ	silk
綿	めん	cotton
毛皮	けがわ	fur
無地	むじ	plain (*no pattern*); solid color
縞	しま	stripe
模様	もよう	pattern
厚い	あつい	thick
薄い	うすい	thin

Loanwords: ウール、ストライプ、チェック、ナイロン、プリント、ポリエステル

アクティビティー　22

何を着(き)ますか。(*What are you going to wear?*)

Tell what you will wear on the following days.

1. 今は五月です。春(はる)です。いいお天気(てんき)です。暖(あたた)かいです。
2. 今は十二月です。今はスキーへ行きます。
3. 今は八月です。夏(なつ)です。とてもむし暑(あつ)いです。わたしは日本の会社(かいしゃ) (*company*) のサラリーマンです。
4. 今は八月です。今日(きょう)もむし暑(あつ)いです。今日(きょう)は休(やす)みです。海(うみ)へ行きます。
5. 今は六月です。梅雨(つゆ)の季節(きせつ)です。毎日雨(あめ)が降(ふ)ります。デパートへ買(か)い物(もの)に行きます。
6. 今は十月です。秋(あき)です。昼(ひる)は暖(あたた)かいですが、夜(よる)はちょっと寒(さむ)いです。
7. 今は三月です。まだ、寒いです。雨(あめ)も時々(ときどき)降(ふ)ります。

言語ノート

着る、はく、かぶる

Japanese use different verbs meaning *to put on* or *wear,* depending on which part of the body the clothing is worn or how the item is attached. Study the chart that follows. 着(き)る is a general term that includes items worn on the torso or upper torso, such as dresses or shirts. はく covers items worn on the legs or feet, such as slacks or socks. Headgear requires the verb かぶる. Items for the hand, such as gloves or rings, call for はめる.

ITEMS	TO PUT ON OR WEAR	TO TAKE OFF
	on torso	
背広(せびろ) ワンピース セーター 上着(うわぎ) シャツ コート 着物(きもの)	着(き)る	脱(ぬ)ぐ

ITEMS	TO PUT ON OR WEAR	TO TAKE OFF
	on legs or feet	
ズボン スカート ジーンズ 靴（くつ） 靴下（くつした）	はく	脱（ぬ）ぐ
	on head	
帽子（ぼうし） ヘルメット	かぶる	脱（ぬ）ぐ、取（と）る
ネクタイ	しめる（する）	
	accessories; things that need "attaching"	
ベルト ブラジャー 時計（とけい） イヤリング	する	取る、はずす
	on hands or fingers	
指輪（ゆびわ）	はめる	
眼鏡（めがね）	かける (lit., *to hang on*)	

アクティビティー 23

ダイアログ：はいてみますか。(*Will you try them on?*)

ブラウン：どの<u>靴</u>（くつ）がいいでしょうか。
店員（てんいん）：これはいかがでしょうか。
ブラウン：そうですね。
店員：ちょっと<u>はいて</u>みますか。
ブラウン：ええ。

Practice the dialogue, substituting the following items. Change the underlined verb (*put on*) as appropriate.

BROWN: Which <u>shoes</u> do you recommend (lit., *are good*)? CLERK: How about these? BROWN: Hmm. . . CLERK: Will you <u>try</u> them <u>on</u>? BROWN: Yes.

1. ワンピース
2. スカート
3. 指輪(ゆびわ)
4. 眼鏡(めがね)
5. セーター
6. ブーツ
7. 帽子(ぼうし)

アクティビティー 24

ファッション・ショー! (*Fashion show!*)

Work in pairs. You will describe what your partner is wearing today. But first, ask several questions about your partner's clothing.

[例] 町田さんは今日(きょう)はピンクと白(しろ)のブラウスを着(き)ています。このブラウスは去年(きょねん)の誕生日(たんじょうび)のプレゼントでした。町田さんが今日(きょう)はいているスカートは今年(ことし)の三月に伊勢丹(いせたん)デパートで買(か)いました。町田さんがはいている赤(あか)のハイヒールはイタリア製(せい)です。町田さんがしているイヤリングとネックレスはパールです。

Grammar and Practice Activities

43. Going Somewhere with a Purpose: Using the Particle に to Express Purpose

カワムラ： 林(はやし)さんはどこに行ったんですか。
ブラウン： 花(はな)を買(か)いに行きました。
カワムラ： そうですか。チンさんは？
ブラウン： 服(ふく)を着替(きが)えに、アパートに帰(かえ)りました。

山口(やまぐち)： シンさんは何をしに来(き)たのですか。
カワムラ： 本を借(か)りに来たんです。
山口： そうですか。あの人も学生ですか。
カワムラ： ええ、日本文化(ぶんか)を勉強(べんきょう)しに来(き)ているんです。

KAWAMURA: Where did Mr. Hayashi go? BROWN: He went to buy flowers. KAWAMURA: I see. What about Ms. Chin? BROWN: She returned to her apartment to change clothes.

YAMAGUCHI: Why did Mr. Shin come here? (lit., *What did Mr. Shin come to do?*) KAWAMURA: He came to borrow some books. YAMAGUCHI: I see. Is he a student, too? KAWAMURA: Yes, he came here to study Japanese culture.

In the following construction, the particle に expresses purpose. Here に corresponds to *to* or *in order to* in English.

Conjunctive form of a verb + the particle に +	(motion verb) 行く *to go* 来る *to come* 帰る *to return home* もどる *to return* 出かける *to go out* 出る *to leave*

to go (come, etc.) in order to (do)…

テニスをしに行きませんか。
Shall we go play tennis? (lit., *Won't you go to play tennis?*)

ブラウンさんが本を返しに来ました。
Ms. Brown came to return some books.

父は友人に会いに出かけました。
Father went out to see his friend.

高田さんは昼ごはんを食べに出ました。
Mr. Takada left to eat lunch.

アクティビティー 25

ダイアログ：ワープロを見に行くんです。(*I will go look at word processors.*)
アパートの前で

高田：ブラウンさんもお出かけですか。
ブラウン：ええ、本屋へ雑誌を買いに行ってきます。高田さんは。
高田：ぼくは電気屋にワープロを見にいくんです。
ブラウン：同じ方向ですね。一緒に行きましょうか。
高田：ええ、そうしましょう。

Practice the dialogue substituting the following stores or places for 本屋 and 電気屋. Change the rest of the underlined phrases appropriately.

Useful expressions: 本を借りる／返す *to borrow / return a book,* お金をおろす *to withdraw money,* 貯金をする *to deposit money,* 手紙を出す *to mail a letter*

In front of the apartment TAKADA: Are you also going out? BROWN: Yes, I am going to the bookstore to buy a magazine. What about you? TAKADA: I am going to an electric appliance shop to look at word processors. BROWN: We're going in the same direction, aren't we? (lit., *It's the same direction, isn't it?*) Shall we go together? TAKADA: Yes, let's do that.

1. パン屋(や)　家具屋(かぐや)
2. 肉屋(にくや)　レストラン
3. 図書館(としょかん)　銀行(ぎんこう)
4. 郵便局(ゆうびんきょく)　映画館(えいがかん)
5. スーパー　コンビニエンス・ストア (or コンビニ)

アクティビティー 26

トマトを買(か)いに行きました。(*She went to buy some tomatoes.*)

Using the model as an example, combine two sentences into one.

[例] 山本(やまもと)さんは出かけました。カワムラさんに会(あ)います。→
山本さんはカワムラさんに会(あ)いに出かけました。

1. 三村(みむら)さんは行きました。電話(でんわ)をかけます。
2. ブラウンさんは出(で)かける。スキーをします。
3. チンさんは来(き)ました。カーティスさんと話します。
4. 山口(やまぐち)さんとカワムラさんは行きました。映画(えいが)を見ます。
5. 山口(やまぐち)さんは帰(かえ)りました。昼(ひる)ごはんを食べます。
6. 町田さんはもどりました。服(ふく)を着替(きが)えます。

アクティビティー 27

何をしに行きましたか。(*What did he go to do?*)

Look at the picture and make a dialogue starting with 何をしに行きましたか.

[例] —何をしに行きましたか。
—コーヒーを飲みに行きました。

1.

2.

3.

4.

5.

44. Reporting Hearsay: …そうだ

林(はやし)：ブラウンさんのアパートはとてもいいそうですね。
ブラウン：ええ、新(あたら)しいし、いいアパートですよ。
林：駅(えき)に近(ちか)くて、便利(べんり)だそうですね。
ブラウン：ええ、駅から歩(ある)いて5分です。

ブラウン：伊勢丹(いせたん)デパートでセールがあるそうですよ。
ギブソン：本当(ほんとう)ですか。
ブラウン：ええ、セーターやコートが40%引(び)きだそうです。
ギブソン：わあ、今日(きょう)の午後行ってみませんか。

チン：ねえ、ねえ、聞いて下(くだ)さい。
三村(みむら)：何ですか。
チン：ギブソンさんが林(はやし)さんにプロポーズしたそうです。
三村：冗談(じょうだん)でしょう。信(しん)じられない。

44.1 Here is one way to report hearsay, that is, information you have heard secondhand.

I-adjectives	Plain forms	+ そうだ (そうです)
Na-adjectives	Dictionary form + だ／だった	
Verbs	Plain forms	
Copula	Plain forms	

I hear(d) that, they say that, it is said that…

あの魚屋(さかなや)はとても安(やす)いそうです。
I hear that that fish store is very inexpensive.

HAYASHI: I hear that your apartment is very nice. BROWN: Yes, it's new, and (thus) it's a good apartment. HAYASHI: I hear that it is conveniently close to the station. BROWN: Yes, it's five minutes from the station on foot.

BROWN: I hear there's a sale at Isetan Department Store. GIBSON: Really? BROWN: Yes, I heard that sweaters, coats, and some other items are 40 percent off. GIBSON: Wow. Shall we go there this afternoon (and see what we find)?

CHIN: Say, listen to this. MIMURA: What (is it)? CHIN: I heard that Ms. Gibson proposed to Mr. Hayashi. MIMURA: You must be kidding. (lit., *It must be a joke.*) I cannot believe it.

東京の地下鉄は便利だそうだ。
It is said that subways in Tokyo are convenient.

カワムラさんはクリーニング屋に行くそうです。
I heard that Mr. Kawamura is going to the dry cleaner's.

林さんはレコード屋でチンさんに会ったそうです。
I heard that Mr. Hayashi met Ms. Chin in a record store.

44.2 To clarify the source, preface your statement with (*source*) によると or (*person's name*) の話では, both of which mean *According to…*

新聞によると、今野菜がとても高いそうです。
According to the newspaper, vegetables are very expensive now.

チンさんによると、その人は眼鏡をかけているそうです。
According to Ms. Chin, that person wears glasses.

ギブソンさんの話では、エドモントンにとても大きい商店街があるそうです。
According to Ms. Gibson, there is a very large shopping mall in Edmonton.

言語ノート

Another Way to Report Hearsay

In informal speech, hearsay is often reported in the following manner:

…(ん)ですって (female speakers only), …(ん)だって (informal), …って (informal) (*Someone*) said that …(って, here, is a variant of quote marker と.)

ブラウンさんの話だと、デパートでバーゲンセールがあるんだって。
Ms. Brown was saying that there is a sale at the department store.

林さんの話によると、明日試験がないって。
I heard from Mr. Hayashi that there won't be an exam tomorrow.

カワムラさんが新しいステレオを買ったんですって。
I heard that Mr. Kawamura bought a new stereo. (female speaker)

アクティビティー 28

あの店（みせ）はサービスがいいそうです。(*They say the service is good at that shop.*)

Using the model as an example, make sentences.

[例]　ブラウン：あの店（みせ）はサービスがいいですよ。→
　　ブラウンさんの話（はなし）では、あの店（みせ）はサービスがいいそうです。

1. 林：ギブソンさんはカナダの出身（しゅっしん）です。
2. チン：このケーキはあそこのお菓子屋（かしや）で買（か）いました。
3. カワムラ：そのビールは酒屋（さかや）で売（う）っています。
4. カーティス：あのワープロは高（たか）かったですよ。
5. 山口：主人（しゅじん）は若（わか）い時（とき）、ハンサムでした。
6. 山本（やまもと）：高田さんのネクタイはちょっと派手（はで）でした。
7. 高田（たかだ）：フィルムはデパートでも買（か）えますよ。

アクティビティー 29

四国（しこく）の出身（しゅっしん）だそうです。(*Apparently she's from Shikoku.*)

Using the model as an example, make sentences.

[例]　カワムラ：林さんはどこの出身（しゅっしん）ですか。
　　　　　林：九州（きゅうしゅう）です。→
　　林さんは九州（きゅうしゅう）の出身（しゅっしん）だそうです。

1. ブラウン：高田（たかだ）さんの車（くるま）は新（あたら）しいんですか。
　　高田（たかだ）：いいえ、古（ふる）いです。
2. 町田：チンさんのアパートは便利（べんり）ですか。
　　チン：あまり便利（べんり）じゃありません。
3. カワムラ：北海道（ほっかいどう）はどうでしたか。
　　山口（やまぐち）：雪（ゆき）が降（ふ）って、とても寒（さむ）かったです。
4. 山本（やまもと）：ブラウンさん、しばらくですね。
　　ブラウン：ええ、京都（きょうと）へ行っていたんです。
5. 町田：夏休（なつやす）みはどうしますか。
　　ブラウン：近所（きんじょ）の洋品店（ようひんてん）でアルバイトをします。

45. Saying Whether or Not Something Is True: …かどうか

チン：本を探(さが)しているんですが…
本屋(ほんや)さん：どのような本ですか。
チン：漢字(かんじ)の書き順(じゅん)についての本なんです。
本屋(ほんや)さん：あるかどうか、見てみましょう。

ブラウン：そば、おそいですね。
町田：ええ、もう出(で)たかどうか、電話(でんわ)してみます。
ブラウン：お願(ねが)いします。

ブラウン：これ、町田さんが作(つく)ったんですか。
町田：ブラウンさんが好きかどうかわからなかったけど、作(つく)ってみたんです。
ブラウン：わたし、天(てん)ぷらが大好きなんですよ。
町田：おいしいかどうかわかりませんが、食べてみてください。
ブラウン：ウーン、おいしい。

けど is a colloquial form of けれども.

X かどうか means *whether or not X.* X may be a noun, adjective, or predicate.

Noun	Noun or noun + だった	+ かどうか
I-adjective	Plain form	
Na-adjective	Root or root + だった	
Verb	Plain form	

このペンが林(はやし)さんのかどうかわかりません。
I don't know whether or not this pen is Mr. Hayashi's.
その人が日本人だったかどうかおぼえていません。
I don't remember whether or not that person is (lit., *was*) *Japanese.*
そのレストランがおいしいかどうかだれかに聞いてみましょう。
Let's ask someone whether or not that restaurant is good.

CHIN: I am looking for a book but… (can you help me?) BOOKSTORE OWNER: What kind of book? CHIN: A book about **kanji** stroke order. BOOKSTORE OWNER: Let me check if we have it. (lit., *I'll look and see whether or not we have it.*)

BROWN: The **soba** noodles have not arrived yet. (lit., *The **soba** is late, isn't it?*) MACHIDA: Yes, I'll call and see whether or not they already left. BROWN: Thank you. (lit., *I make a request of you.*)

BROWN: Did you make this? MACHIDA: I didn't know whether or not you would like it, but (yes) I made it. BROWN: I love tempura. MACHIDA: I don't know whether or not it tastes good, but please try it (lit., *eat it and see*). BROWN: Mm, this is delicious.

このセーター が高(たか)かったかどうかおぼえていない。
I cannot remember whether or not this sweater was expensive.

その車(くるま)を買(か)うかどうかまだわからない。
I still don't know whether or not I will buy that car.

カワムラさんが買(か)い物(もの)から帰(かえ)ってきたかどうか見てきます。
I will go see whether or not Mr. Kawamura has come back from shopping.

アクティビティー 30

行くかどうかわかりません。(*I don't know if we'll go or not.*)

Answer these questions, using the model as an example.

[例] そのセーターはデパートで買(か)えますか。(母(はは)に聞く) →
買(か)えるかどうかわからないから、母(はは)に聞いてみます。

1. カワムラさんはパーティーに来(き)ましたか。(ブラウンさんに聞く)
2. 明日雨(あめ)が降(ふ)りますか。(テレビの天気予報(てんきよほう)を見る)
3. カナダはロシアより大きいですか。(図書館(としょかん)で調(しら)べる[*check at the library*])
4. ギブソンさんはカナダ人ですか。(ギブソンさんに聞く)
5. カワムラさんは部屋(へや)で勉強(べんきょう)していますか。(見る)
6. カーティスさんはコンサートに行きますか。(電話(でんわ)で聞く)
7. この肉(にく)はすきやき用(よう)(*for use in sukiyaki*)ですか。(肉屋(にくや)さんに聞く)

アクティビティー 31

ダイアログ：とても安(やす)かったそうです。(*I heard that it was very inexpensive.*)

町田：ギブソンさんのあのセーター、とてもいいデザインですね。
ブラウン：ええ、昨日、近所(きんじょ)のブティックで買(か)ったそうです。
町田：高(たか)かったでしょうね。
ブラウン：いいえ、バーゲンセールで、とても安かったそうです。

MACHIDA: That sweater of Ms. Gibson's has a very good design, doesn't it? BROWN: Yes, I heard that she bought it at a boutique in her neighborhood yesterday. MACHIDA: It must have been expensive. (lit., *It probably was expensive, don't you think?*) BROWN: No, I heard that, due to a sale, it was very inexpensive.

町田：本当(ほんとう)ですか。わたしもほしいわ。
ブラウン：じゃ、まだバーゲンセールをしているかどうか聞(き)いてみましょう。

言語ノート

Sentence-Final Particles

You have already studied that some important meanings such as interrogatives and speaker's emotions and attitudes are expressed by sentence-final particles. In the preceding dialogue, わ in わたしもほしいわ is the particle used by female speakers to express their admiration, desire, or surprise; to try to convince the hearer of their claim or judgment; or to confirm their judgment. In this context, male speakers would say ぼくもほしいな(あ). な(あ) is a sentence-final particle expressing exclamation, desire, or wish and can be used by both male and female speakers. These sentence-final particles are more often used in colloquial speech than in formal speech.

As students in Professor Yokoi's class get acquainted with each other and come to feel closer to each other, their speech style will change to more informal, colloquial speech, and diversified sentence-final particles will be used. You will learn them gradually in Book 2 of *Yookoso*.

アクティビティー 32

家計簿(かけいぼ) (*Household accounts log*)

Work in a group of three. Following is Mrs. Yamaguchi's log where she keeps track of household expenses. First, Student 1 asks Student 2 the following questions, as in the first part of the example. Then, Student 3 asks Student 1 the same questions, as in the second part of the example.

[例]

s1: りんごは100gいくらでしたか。
s2: 100g 230円(えん)でした。
s3: りんごは100gいくらでしたか。
s1: 100g 230円だったそうです。

1. 肉屋(にくや)で何を買(か)いましたか。
2. 花屋(はなや)で何を買(か)いましたか。
3. 八百屋(やおや)で何を買(か)いましたか。

MACHIDA: Really? I want (to get) one, too. BROWN: Then, let's ask (Ms. Gibson) whether or not the sale is still going on (and see what she says).

4. 酒屋(さかや)でビールを何本買(か)いましたか。一本いくらでしたか。

5. バンドエイドはいくらでしたか。

6. 明日何を買(か)うつもりですか。

7. サミットストアのセールはいつからいつまでですか。

8月 August	15日(土) 日( ) 旧暦6月21日 自由日付欄		16日(日) 日( ) 旧暦6月22日		17日(月) 日( ) 旧暦6月23日	
	品目	金額	品目	金額	品目	金額
収入		千 百 十		千 百 十		千 百 十
レシート添付欄						
肉・魚 乳製品類	牛肉 100g 560円× 400g	2240				
野菜類	レタス1つ150円 ×2つ トマト100g60円 ×400g	300 240				
調味料 その他の食品	りんご100g230円 ×300g	690				
副食計		3470				
主食						
外食						
嗜好品	ビール1本560円 ×6本	3360				
食費合計		6830				
住居・備品						
光熱・水道						
衣服						
医療・衛生	バンドエイド	480				
教育						
教養・娯楽	本2冊	1950				
交際						
交通・通信	切手	560				
花	ダリア	420				
貯蓄・保険						
支出合計						
現在高						
クレジット使用控え						
★印の料理は、巻頭に写真と作り方つき	スパゲッティ ★夏野菜のスープ煮 卵サラダ（レタス・胡瓜）		冷凍いかとセロリの中国風うま煮 辛子あえ（げそ・胡瓜） 高野豆腐の煮物		かき玉汁 鶏ささ身とえびのくず打ち なすとピーマンの醤油炒め	
日記欄	明日から18日までサミットストアでセール。明日，バナナ，スイートコーン，パン牛乳を買う。		カワムラさん，夜出かける。さとみ，20日まで長野でキャンプ。		南さんと銀座でショッピング。	

文化ノート

CULTURE NOTE • Metric System

Japanese use the metric system of measurement. Instead of pounds and ounces, grams (g) and kilograms (kg) are used to quantify weight. Liquids (milk, gasoline, rainwater, etc.) are measured in cubic centimeters (cc) and liters (l). When measuring linear distance, Japanese use centimeters (cm), meters (m), and kilometers (km). Here is a conversion table for figuring metric measurements from those used in the United States.

インチ (*inch*) × 2.54 = センチ（メートル）(cm)
フィート (*feet*) × 0.31 = メートル (m)
マイル (*mile*) × 1.61 = キロ（メートル）(km)
オンス (*ounce*) × 28 = グラム (g)
ポンド (*pound*) × 0.45 = キロ（グラム）(kg)

Now answer these questions.

あなたは何キログラムありますか。

あなたの家から大学まで何キロメートルありますか。

あなたの身長 (*height*) は何センチメートルですか。

アクティビティー 33

インタビュー (*Interview*)

Work in pairs. Follow these instructions, and report the results to class later.

1. 買い物が好きかどうか聞いてください。
2. 昨日、買い物に行ったかどうか聞いてください。
3. クレジットカードをよく使うかどうか聞いてください。
4. 今、クレジットカードを持っている (*is carrying*) かどうか聞いてください。
5. 今、現金を持っているかどうか聞いてください。
6. 今日か明日、買い物に行くつもりかどうか聞いてください。
7. バーゲンセールの時によく買い物をするかどうか聞いてください。
8. 洋服にたくさんお金をかける (*to spend*) かどうか聞いてください。
9. 1万ドル以上のものを買ったことがあるかどうか聞いてください。

～以上 *equal to or more than…*

46. Giving Reasons with …し、…し

町田：ギブソンさんはこのスーパーでいつも買い物するんですか。
ギブソン：ええ、アパートに近いし、大きいし、店員さんも親切です。
町田：そうですか。新しいし、きれいだし、いいスーパーですね。

三村：カワムラさん、お酒を飲んでいきませんか。
カワムラ：もうおそいし、…
三村：一杯だけ、どうですか。
カワムラ：明日、試験もあるし、…

46.1 し, coming after adjectives, verbs, and the copula, is used to enumerate mutually compatible facts or conditions in an emphatic way. Often the enumerated factors lead up to a conclusion or result that may be stated or understood from context.

あのレストランは安いし、おいしい。
That restaurant is cheap, and what's more, the food is delicious. (lit., *That restaurant is cheap* ***and*** *delicious.*)

The wording of the preceding example is more emphatic than あのレストランは安くて、おいしい。Some more examples follow.

カーティスさんはハンサムだし、やさしいし、とてもいい人です。
Mr. Curtis is handsome and sweet—he is a very nice person.
明日は会議もあるし、忙しいです。
I have a meeting tomorrow, among other things (lit., *too*), *so I will be busy.*
お昼ごはんも食べたし、出かけようか。
We've eaten lunch (and gotten ready in other ways)—(so) shall we leave?
寒かったし、雨が降っていたから、外に出たくなかった。
It was cold and it was raining (among other similar reasons), so I didn't want to go out.

MACHIDA: Do you always shop at this supermarket? GIBSON: Yes, it's close to my apartment, it's large, and the clerks are nice. MACHIDA: I see. It's new and clean—it's a good supermarket, isn't it?

MIMURA: Mr. Kawamura, do you want a drink before going back home? KAWAMURA: It's already late, so… MIMURA: How about just one drink (lit., *one glassful*)? KAWAMURA: I have an exam tomorrow, so…

The following forms of predicate precede し.

I-adjective	Plain form	+ し
Na-adjectives	Dictionary form + だ／だった	
Verbs	Plain form	
Copula	Plain form	

46.2 This construction can be used to avoid saying no. By ending the sentence after し, the listener has to fill in the unstated negative conclusion.

もう少(すこ)しいかがですか。—ええ、でも、もうたくさん食べたし、...
How about a little bit more? —Well (lit., *yes*)*, but I already ate a lot... (so no, thank you).*

言語ノート

Saying No Politely

Japanese tend to avoid saying no directly. It is one way to avoid confrontation and preserve harmony, at least on the surface. For this purpose, Japanese employ a variety of ways to say no indirectly, that is, politely. Here are several of these tactics.

1. First agree and then give a reason that you must say no. (*Yes, but...*)

   もう少(すこ)しいかがですか。ええ、でも、もうおなかがいっぱいですから。
   How about a little more? —Yes, but since I'm already full... (no, thank you).

   Sometimes, this is shortened to simply

   ええ、でも、...
   Yes, however...

2. Give an ambiguous answer, one that can be taken as positive or negative.

   明日(あした)、デパートへ行きませんか。—多分(たぶん)。
   Would you like to go to the department store tomorrow? —Maybe.

3. Say you will consult with someone before answering.

   これ買(か)いませんか。—妻(つま)に聞いてみます。
   Won't you buy this? —I will ask my wife (and see what she says).

4. Try to delay your answer.

来週(らいしゅう)、一緒(いっしょ)に東京(とうきょう)へ行きませんか。—明日(あした)、お答(こた)えします。

Would you like to go to Tokyo with me next week? —I'll give you my answer tomorrow.

5. Simply apologize.

これ買(か)いませんか。—すみません。ちょっと…

Won't you buy this? —I'm sorry. It's just…

アクティビティー 34

ダイアログ：軽(かる)いし、はきやすいし… (*They are light and easy to wear…*)

店員(てんいん)：この靴(くつ)はいかがでしょうか。
三村(みむら)：ううん、なかなかいいですね。
店員：ええ、軽(かる)いし、はきやすいし、申(もう)し分(ぶん)ありません。
三村：じゃあ、これをください。

Practice the dialogue, substituting the following.

1. ジャケット　　デザインもいいし、着(き)やすいし
2. カメラ　　オートマチックだし、小さいし
3. エアコン (*air conditioner*)　　音(おと) (*sound*) が静(しず)かだし、リモコン (*remote control*) だし
4. ワープロ　　ポータブルだし、使(つか)いやすい (*easy to use*) し
5. 帽子(ぼうし)　　色(いろ)もきれいだし、デザインもいいし

言語ノート

～やすい、～にくい

やすい and にくい are i-adjectives meaning *easy* and *hard*, respectively. They are used in the following construction.

Conjunctive form of verb + やすい (*easy to…*) or にくい (*difficult, hard to…*)

このペンは書きやすいです。
This pen is easy to write with.

CLERK: How about these shoes? MIMURA: Hmm. They are quite nice. CLERK: Yes. They are lightweight and easy to wear… They are perfect. (lit., *There is nothing to say against them.*) MIMURA: Then, I will take them.

山下さんは話しにくい。
Mr. Yamashita is hard to talk to.
このサンドイッチは食べにくいです。
This sandwich is hard to eat.
これは使(つか)いやすいアイロンですね。
This is an easy-to-use iron.
あれは持(も)ちにくいバッグですね。
This is a hard-to-carry bag.
このシャツは着(き)やすい。
This shirt is easy to wear (i.e., *comfortable*).
この靴(くつ)ははきにくい。
These shoes are hard to put on.

アクティビティー 35

つかれたし、おなかがすいたし、大変(たいへん)です。(*I'm tired, I'm hungry—it's awful!*)

Using the model as an example, complete the sentences.

[例] (広(ひろ)いです)(明(あか)るいです)(いい部屋(へや)ですね) →
広(ひろ)いし、明(あか)るいし、いい部屋(へや)ですね。

1. (きれいな色(いろ)です)(よく似合(にあ)います)(いいセーターですね。)
2. (おいしいです)(安(やす)いです)(いいレストランですね。)
3. (やさしいです)(親切(しんせつ)です)(いい人ですね。)
4. (速(はや)いです)(便利(べんり)です)(東京(とうきょう)のタクシーはいいですね。)
5. (わたしの家(いえ)に近(ちか)いです)(静(しず)かです)(この公園(こうえん)によく来(き)ます。)

アクティビティー 36

安(やす)いし、速(はや)いし、いいバイクです。、(*It's cheap and fast, a good motorbike.*)

Complete the sentences, using the model as an example.

[例] あのレストランは安(やす)いし、…→
あのレストランは安(やす)いし、サービスもいいし、申(もう)し分(ぶん)ありません (*it's faultless*)。

1. わたしのアパートはせまい (*small*) し、
2. 町田さんは頭(あたま)がいい (*smart*) し、

3. この町(まち)は車(くるま)が多(おお)いし、

4. このハンドバッグは軽(かる)いし、

5. この計算機(けいさんき)(*calculator*)は小さいし、

6. カーティスさんはハンサムだし、

7. 今日(きょう)はたくさん食べたし、

Language Skills

Reading and Writing

Reading 1 「サン・ロード」グランド・オープニング・セール

Before You Read

Look at today's (or a recent) newspaper and check out the sale ads. What are the most typical discounts offered?

Match the stores in the first column with the merchandise sold there.

1. 靴屋(くつや)	a. 辞書(じしょ)
2. 宝石屋(ほうせきや)	b. フィルム
3. 花屋(はなや)	c. 野菜(やさい)
4. 呉服屋(ごふくや)	d. クロワッサン
5. パン屋(や)	e. ソファー
6. 肉屋(にくや)	f. ダイヤモンド
7. 魚屋(さかなや)	g. チューリップ
8. 八百屋(やおや)	h. テレビ
9. 本屋(ほんや)	i. 着物(きもの)
10. カメラ屋(や)	j. スニーカー
11. 家具屋(かぐや)	k. まぐろ
12. 電気屋(でんきや)	l. ハム

Guess the meaning of the given term.

1. If 全部(ぜんぶ) means *all,* and 商品(しょうひん) means *merchandise,* what do you think 全品(ぜんぴん) means?
2. If 半分(はんぶん) means *half* and 金額(きんがく) means *amount of money,* what do you think 半額(はんがく) means?
3. 部分(ぶぶん) means *part*. What do you think 一部(いちぶ) means?
4. 五割(ごわり) means *50 percent*. What do you think 二割(にわり) means?

Now Read It!

Linda Brown received an announcement about the grand opening sale at a shopping mall that will open soon near her apartment. Read the announcement. What stores and shops are in the mall? Look at Linda's shopping list following the announcement. What items on her list are on sale? Concentrate on retrieving this information; you need not understand every word in the passage.

ごあいさつ

今月１４日、中野駅南口駅ビルに新しく「サン・ロード」がグランド・オープニングします。１４日は午前１０時から、「サン・ロード」前でオープニング・セレモニーを行います。
オープンを記念して、１４日から２１日まで「サン・ロード」全店が、大売り出しを行います。皆様のお出でを、お待ちしています。
「サン・ロード」のお店と大売り出しの一部をご紹介します。

靴のアイザワ	アディダス、ナイキ２５％引
井上宝石店	ダイヤモンド・リング３０％引
上田呉服店	着物３～４割引
エノモト・ベーカリー	全品半額
薬の小川	化粧品２０％引
香川肉店	スキヤキ用牛肉２割引
八百松	全野菜２０％引
魚定	おさしみ２０～４０％引
高松クリーニング	背広・ドレスクリーニング２５％引
山本金物店	全品半額
ケーキのコトブキ	チーズ・ケーキ１００円
	アップル・パイ２００円
佐藤ブックス	辞書２０％引
ビューティー・コンドー	パーマ４５００円
	カット１６００円
サン・ロードフラワー	ブーケ１５％引
山口カメラ	３５mmカラー・フィルム２４枚撮り
	３００円、DPE ３０％引
カメイ電気	カラー・テレビ、ステレオ１０％引
本田家具	ソファー、ベッド３５％引
ブティック・サン	高級ドレス半額
キッチン・ウエスト	ハンバーガー２１０円

「サン・ロード」の営業時間は

月～金	10:00 A.M.—8:00 P.M.
土	10:00 A.M.—10:00 P.M.
日	12:00 P.M.—8:00 P.M.

This is Linda Brown's shopping list. Check the items or services that are on sale during the grand opening sale at Sun Road shopping mall.

買い物リスト
・ドレス
・机
・ラジカセ
・フランスパン
・日本語の辞書
・イヤリング
・ブーツ
・マスカラ
・レタス
・にんじん
・フィルム
・スカートのクリーニング

After You Finish Reading

Answer these questions.

1. On what side of Nakano Station is Sun Road?
2. When will Sun Road mall open?
3. How long is the opening sale?
4. What time does Sun Road mall open on Saturdays and Sundays?
5. The **kanji** 引 is used repeatedly in the advertisement. What do you think it means in this context?

Writing Practice 1

Write an advertisement based on the following information.

Shopping Center Mercado (メルカード)
Opening: July 14
Opening sale: From July 14 through July 20

Shoe store Okada: all shoes 30% off
Furniture store Murai: sofas 50,000 yen–100,000 yen
Stationery store Yamamoto: all notebooks and pens 50% off
Electric appliance store Electric Land: television sets, stereos 15% off
Hunai Bakery: all bread half price

Business hours: M–Sat 10 A.M.–6 P.M.
Sun 12 noon–9 P.M.

Reading 2 マイ・ファッション

Before You Read

Among the verbs in the second column, which would you use to mean *wear* for each item in the first column?

1. ストッキング
2. 背広(せびろ)
3. ワンピース
4. ブーツ
5. スカート
6. ジーンズ
7. ネックレス
8. ハイヒール

a. 着(き)る
b. はく
c. つける
d. する

What kind of clothes do you associate with the following words?

1. インフォーマル
2. シンプル
3. カジュアル

言語ノート

Shortened *Katakana* Words

When a Western word enters the Japanese language, it may become quite long because each **katakana** character is a syllable, most of which combine a consonant and a vowel. For example, the one-syllable English word *dress* becomes ドレス, a three-syllable word, in Japanese. Many long **katakana** words are shortened or abbreviated in Japanese by cutting off the latter part of the word or, in the case of a two-word loanword, the latter part of both words. The resulting term's meaning may not be readily apparent to a speaker of the source language, but with practice you will get better at guessing what such shortened **katakana** words mean. Here are some examples. デパート (*department store*); テレビ (*television*); マスコミ (*mass communication*); ハンスト (*hunger strike*); ワープロ (*word processor*); パソコン (*personal computer*); ラジカセ (*radio cassette player*); コンビニ (*convenience store*); and パンスト (*panty hose* [*stockings*]).

Now Read It!

Linda Brown and John Kawamura were featured in the *My Fashion* section of a monthly magazine widely read among college students.

マイ・ファッション

今月は東京大学のアメリカ人留学生のリンダ・ブラウンさんとジョン・カワムラさんです。二人は去年の九月に日本文化を勉強しに来日しました。最初は日本語の勉強で大変でしたが、今は日本語もだんだんわかってきて、勉強にレジャーに忙しい毎日を送っています。

リンダ・ブラウン

わたしが今着ているブルーグリーンのワンピースは、ロサンゼルスでおととし買いました。500ドルくらいでした。サマンサー・リーのデザインです。彼女のデザインはシンプルで大好きです。日本では彼女の服が買えないのが、残念です。日本でも買えたら本当にいいですね。今度アメリカに帰ったら、ワンピースかジャケットを買うつもりです。
フォーマルなパーティーにも着ていけます。その時には、同じ色のハイヒール、黒のストッキング、ゴールド・ネックレスと組み合わせます。
黒い靴もいいですね。
時々学校へ着ています。その時には、上に白いジャケットを着ます。
絹100%で、とても着やすいので、わたしの大好きな服です。

ジョン・カワムラ

ぼくはかたくるしい服装は大嫌いです。背広は着たことがありません。いつもジーンズをはいています。靴もスニーカーしかはきません。今ぼくがはいているのはウオッシュアウトしたブルージーンズです。新宿のジーンズ専門店で今年買いました。12,000円くらいでした。ジーンズはたくさん持っています。ストレートが多いですね。黒や白のジーンズも持っています。

このワインレッドのトレーナーは東京大学のです。安いし、着やすいし、トレーナーはたくさん持っています。赤いのや青いのやたくさんあります。一枚 2,000円ぐらいでした。夏はTシャツを着ます。寒い時には、この上にセーターを着たり、ジャンパーを着たりします。
このスニーカーはアメリカで買いました。とても歩きやすいので大好きです。
フォーマルなパーティーには、ブルーのブレザーを着て、ネクタイをしていきます。もちろん、下はジーンズとスニーカーです。ジーンズとスニーカーがだめだったら、パーティーには出ません。ジーンズとスニーカーがウエストコースト出身のぼくのファッションのトレードマークです。

留学生 *foreign student*

来日しました *came to Japan*

最初 *first*

送っています *are spending*

残念(な) *regrettable, too bad*

組み合わせる *to combine*

絹 *silk*

かたくるしい *overly restrained, formal* / 服装 *clothes*

新宿 *Shinjuku (area of Tokyo)*

専門店 *specialty shop*

持っています *owns, has*

トレーナー *sweatshirts*

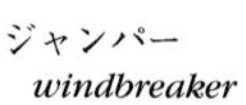

ジャンパー *windbreaker*

After You Finish Reading

1. Unfortunately, Linda's and John's pictures were black-and-white. What color clothes are they wearing in the photos according to the article?
2. Answer these questions.

   Useful expression: 持(も)っている *to own, have*

   a. Where did Linda buy her favorite dress? How much was it?
   b. Who designed the dress?
   c. Can you buy that designer's garments in Japan?
   d. What is Linda planning to buy when she returns to the United States?
   e. What kind of shoes does Linda wear with her favorite dress when she goes to a formal party?
   f. What kind of shoes does Linda wear with it when she goes to school?
   g. Why does Linda like this dress?
   h. What kind of clothes does John Kawamura dislike?
   i. Has he ever worn a suit?
   j. What kind of jeans does he have?
   k. What color sweatshirts (トレーナー) does he have?
   l. What does he wear in summer? What does he wear when it is cold?
   m. What does he wear when he goes to a formal party?

Writing Practice 2

Write a description of the clothes you are wearing or of a favorite outfit. Model your description after **Reading 2.**

Language Functions and Situations

Shopping

店員(てんいん)：いらっしゃいませ。
カワムラ：チーズ・ケーキはありますか。
店員：はい、一つ250円(えん)です。
カワムラ：じゃあ、三つください。チーズ・ケーキのとなりのケーキは何ですか。
店員：レモン・ケーキです。
カワムラ：いくらですか。

CLERK: Welcome. KAWAMURA: Do you carry cheesecake? CLERK: Yes, it's 250 yen a piece. KAWAMURA: Then please give me three pieces. What is the cake next to the cheesecake? CLERK: That's lemon cake. KAWAMURA: How much is it?

店員：一つ230円です。

カワムラ：それも三つください。

店員：ほかには。

カワムラ：それでけっこうです。

店員(てんいん)：いらっしゃいませ。

林(はやし)：シェーバーがほしいんですが、いいのはありますか。

店員：これはいかがでしょうか。

林：いくらですか。

店員：14,500円です。

林：ちょっと、大きすぎて、使(つか)いにくいんじゃないですか。
それに、ちょっと高いですね。もう少(すこ)し安(やす)くて、小さいのはありませんか。

店員：それでは、これはいかがでしょうか。9,800円です。
とても使(つか)いやすいですよ。

林：いいデザインですね。じゃ、これをください。

店員：ありがとうございます。

店員(てんいん)：いらっしゃいませ。

ブラウン：ブラウスを探(さが)しているんですが、...

店員：ブラウスはこちらですが、どんなものがよろしいでしょうか。

ブラウン：ピンクのブラウスはありますか。

店員：サイズは。

ブラウン：11です。

店員：では、これはいかがでしょうか。

ブラウン：ううん、ちょっと派手(はで)すぎますね。もっと地味(じみ)なのはありますか。

店員：では、こんなのはいかがですか。

ブラウン：きれいな色(いろ)ですね。絹(きぬ)ですか。

店員：はい、絹(きぬ)100%です。

ブラウン：ちょっと、着(き)てみて(*try it on*)もいいですか。

店員：ええ、試着室(しちゃくしつ)はあちらです。

CLERK: It's 230 yen a piece. KAWAMURA: Please give me three of them, too. CLERK: Anything else? KAWAMURA: This will be fine.

CLERK: Welcome. HAYASHI: I'm looking for an electric shaver. (lit., *I want to buy an electric shaver, but*...) Do you have a good one? CLERK: How about this one? HAYASHI: How much is it? CLERK: It's 14,500 yen. HAYASHI: It's a bit too large and hard to use, isn't it? Besides, it's a bit expensive. Don't you have a small one that's a bit cheaper? CLERK: Then how about this one? It's 9,800 yen. It is very easy to use. HAYASHI: It's a nice design, isn't it? I will take this one. CLERK: Thank you very much.

CLERK: Welcome. BROWN: I am looking for a blouse. CLERK: Blouses are over here. What kind would you like? (lit., *What kind is good?*) BROWN: Do you have a pink blouse? CLERK: What size? BROWN: Eleven. CLERK: Then how about this one? BROWN: Hmm. It's too bright. Do you have a more subdued one? CLERK: Well, how about this one? BROWN: It's a pretty color, isn't it? Is this silk? CLERK: Yes, it's 100 percent silk. BROWN: May I try it on? CLERK: Yes. The fitting room is over there...

ブラウン：なかなかいいですね。
店員：たいへんよくお似合(にあ)いです。とても着(き)やすいでしょう。
ブラウン：ここがちょっときついんですが。
店員：いいえ、よくフィットしています。
ブラウン：そうですか。これ、いくらですか。
店員：33,000円(えん)です。
ブラウン：ちょっと高(たか)いですね。
店員：フランス製(せい)ですので、…
ブラウン：ううん、でもデザインもいいから、…じゃ、これをいただきます。
店員：ありがとうございます。

言語ノート

Useful Expressions for Shopping

1. Saying what you are looking for

文房具売場(ぶんぼうぐうりば)はどこですか。
Where is the stationery section?
ワイシャツがほしいんですが、…
I would like a dress shirt (lit., *I want a dress shirt but…* [*do you have any?*])
ドライバーはありますか。
Do you have any screwdrivers?
スーツを見せてください。
Please show me some suits.

2. Asking prices

これ、いくらですか。
How much is this?
これはおいくらですか。
How much is this? (*politer*)
全部(ぜんぶ)でいくらですか。
How much is it in total?
一ついくらですか。
How much is one of them?

BROWN: It's quite nice. CLERK: It looks very good on you. It's very comfortable (lit., *easy to wear*), don't you think? BROWN: It is too tight here. CLERK: No, it fits very well. BROWN: Do you think so? How much is this? CLERK: It's 33,000 yen. BROWN: It's a bit expensive. CLERK: It is made in France, so… BROWN: Hmm. But the design is good, too, so…I will get it (lit., *I will receive this one*). CLERK: Thank you very much.

3. Asking to be shown something else

ほかのを見せてください。
Please show me a different one.

もっと軽(かる)いのはありませんか。
Don't you have a lighter (i.e., *more lightweight*) *one?*

もう少(すこ)し大きいのがいいんですが、…
I prefer a somewhat larger one… (lit., *a somewhat larger one would be good, but… [do you have one?]*)

4. Asking whether you can try something on

着(き)てみてもいいですか。
May I try it on?

試(ため)してみてもいいですか。
May I try it out?

試食(ししょく)できますか。
Can I taste a sample?

5. Saying you have decided to buy something

これをいただきます。
I will take this. (lit., *I'll receive this.*)

これをください。
Please give me this.

これにします。
I have decided on this one.

これでけっこうです。
This will be fine.

6. Saying you have decided not to make a purchase

今日(きょう)はやめておきます。
I'll refrain from buying today.

また、この次(つぎ)にします。
I will buy (lit., *do*) *it next time.*

今日(きょう)はけっこうです。
I won't buy it today. (lit., *Today, I'm fine.*)

7. Paying

はい、3,000円です。
Here's 3,000 yen.

クレジットカードでお願(ねが)いします。
I would like to pay with a credit card.

クレジットカードでお願(ねが)いします。

8. Expressions used by shop clerks

いらっしゃいませ。
Welcome (to our store).

何をお探(さが)しでしょうか。
What are you looking for?

何をさしあげましょうか。
What can (lit., *shall*) *I show you?*

こちらはいかがですか。
How about this one?

かしこまりました。
Certainly. (i.e., *I understand. I will do that.*) (responding to a customer's request)

セーターはこちらにございます。
Sweaters are over here.

申(もう)し訳(わけ)ありませんが、品切(しなぎ)れです。
I am sorry, but it's out of stock.

領収書(りょうしゅうしょ)をどうぞ。
Here is your receipt.

どうもありがとうございました。またお越(こ)し下(くだ)さい。
Thank you very much. Please come again.

Role-Play

Using the following shopping lists and receipts, practice buying a variety of things. Pair up with a classmate; one of you is the store clerk, the other the shopper. Make sure you buy an item that's just the right size, color, etc.

Useful Vocabulary: きつい *tight,* ゆるい *loose,* 消費税（しょうひぜい） *consumption tax*

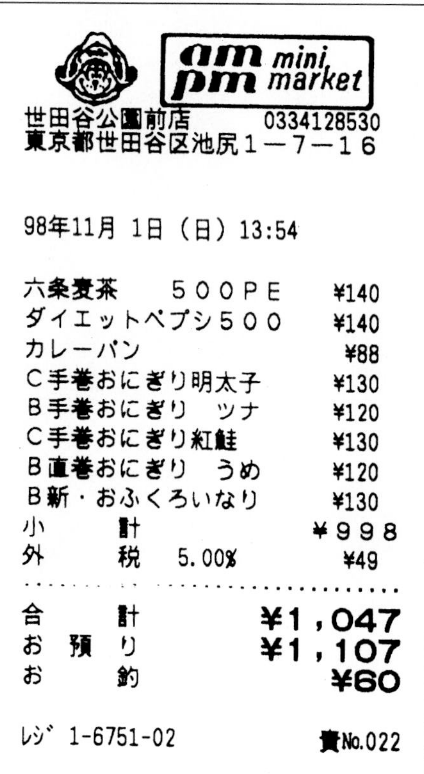

am pm mini market

世田谷公園前店 0334128530
東京都世田谷区池尻１－７－１６

98年11月 1日（日）13:54

六条麦茶	５００ＰＥ	¥140
ダイエットペプシ５００		¥140
カレーパン		¥88
Ｃ手巻おにぎり明太子		¥130
Ｂ手巻おにぎり ツナ		¥120
Ｃ手巻おにぎり紅鮭		¥130
Ｂ直巻おにぎり うめ		¥120
Ｂ新・おふくろいなり		¥130
小 計		¥９９８
外 税	5.00%	¥49
合 計		¥1,047
お 預 り		¥1,107
お 釣		¥60

ﾚｼﾞ 1-6751-02 責No.022

領収書 **Isemaru**

新宿店 03(3352)1111

99/09/10 10 0047 08895 99999

0310 011	セーター	1	12,000
0345 011	ソックス	5	2,500
0551 034	ベルト	1	4,600
小計			19,100
消費税			955
計			20,055
預り			21,000
釣銭			945

買い物リスト

りんご	300g
バナナ	400g
レタス	2つ
じゃがいも	1Kg
たまねぎ	5つ
トマト	3つ
にんじん	4本

ショッピング・リスト

ビデオテープ（VHS） 5本
カセットテープ（120分） 10本
M.C.ハマーのCD
「ホームアローン」のビデオ

Saying Whether Two Things Are the Same or Different

Compare these two pictures. How are they identical? How are they different?

言語ノート

Same or Different?

1. Saying two items are the same

   AはBと同(おな)じです。
   A is the same as B.

   AはBとCが同(おな)じです。
   A is the same as B with regard to C.

   このセーターはあのセーターとサイズが同(おな)じです。
   This sweater is the same as that sweater with regard to the size.

2. Saying two items are different

   AはBと違(ちが)います。
   A is different from B.

   AはBとCが違(ちが)います。
   A is different in C from B.

   わたしのブーツは町田さんのブーツと色(いろ)が違(ちが)います。
   My boots are different in color from Ms. Machida's.

3. Asking whether two items are the same or different

   AとBは同(おな)じですか、違(ちが)いますか。
   Are A and B the same or different?

   このネクタイとあのネクタイは同(おな)じですか、違(ちが)いますか。
   Are this necktie and that necktie the same or different?

Listening Comprehension

1. Five people are talking about what they bought over the weekend. Listen and fill in the blanks.

NAME	STORES	ITEMS/PRICE

2. You will hear a description of what the following four people were wearing last night. Listen and fill in the blanks.

NAME	CLOTHES
Nakamura	
Hara	
Saeki	
Nonoyama	

3. There was a robbery at a convenience store last night. The above four people are questioned by the police because they were seen walking near the store around the time of the robbery. The store owner will describe to the police what the robber was wearing. Who do you think the robber is?

Vocabulary

Stores

いちば	市場	market
かぐや	家具屋	furniture store
カメラや	カメラ屋	camera shop
くすりや	薬屋	drugstore; pharmacy

くだものや	果物屋	fruit store
くつや	靴屋	shoe store
クリーニングや	クリーニング屋	dry cleaner's
ケーキや	ケーキ屋	pastry store
さかなや	魚屋	fish store; fishmonger's
さかや	酒屋	liquor store
しょうてんがい	商店街	shopping mall; shopping street
でんきや	電気屋	electric appliance store
とけいや	時計屋	watch shop
にくや	肉屋	butcher shop
はなや	花屋	flower shop; florist's
パンや	パン屋	bakery
ぶんぼうぐや	文房具屋	stationery store
ほうせきや	宝石屋	jewelry shop
ほんや	本屋	bookstore
みせ	店	shop; store
めがねてん	眼鏡店	eyeglasses store; optician's
やおや	八百屋	vegetable store; green grocer's
やっきょく	薬局	drugstore; pharmacy
レコードや	レコード屋	record store; music store

Loanword: ブティック

Shopping

うりだし	売り出し	sale	てんいん	店員	shop clerk
うる	売る	to sell	ねだん	値段	price
(お)かね	(お)金	money	はらう	払う	to pay
(お)つり		change	～びき	～引き	reduced by …%
きゃく	客	customer	りょうしゅうしょ	領収書	receipt
しゅじん	主人	shop owner	レジ		cash register; cashier

Loanwords: クレジットカード、ショーウインドー、ショッピング、セール、バーゲンセール、レシート

Review: 買(か)い物(もの)、買(か)う

Color

あお	青	blue; green	こい	濃い	dark (*in color*)
あおい	青い	blue; green	じみ(な)	地味(な)	quiet (*in color*); plain
あか	赤	red	しろ	白	white
いろ	色	color	ちゃいろ	茶色	brown
うすい	薄い	light (*in color*); pale	ちゃいろい	茶色い	brown
きいろ	黄色	yellow	はいいろ	灰色	gray
きいろい	黄色い	yellow	はで(な)	派手(な)	bright; gaudy
くろ	黒	black	みどり	緑	green
くろい	黒い	black			

Loanwords: グリーン、グレー、ダークブルー、ピンク、ブルー、ライトブルー

Review: 赤(あか)い、明(あか)るい、暗(くら)い、白(しろ)い

Clothes

かぶる		to wear; to put on (*the head*)
きもの	着物	kimono
きる	着る	to wear; to put on (*the torso*)
くつ	靴	shoe
くつした	靴下	sock
したぎ	下着	underwear
ショートパンツ		shorts
ズボン		trousers
セーター		sweater
せびろ	背広	business suit
つける	付ける	to wear; to put on (*something that "attaches"*)
ぬぐ	脱ぐ	to take off
はく		to wear; to put on (*the feet or legs*)
ハンカチ		handkerchief
パンツ		briefs
ふく	服	clothes
ブラジャー		bra (lit., *brassiere*)
ぼうし	帽子	cap; hat
みずぎ	水着	bathing suit; swimwear
めがね	眼鏡	eyeglasses
ようふく	洋服	Western-style clothes
ワイシャツ		(men's) dress shirt (lit., *white shirt*)
わふく	和服	Japanese-style clothes
ワンピース		dress (lit., *one piece*)

Loanwords: コート、サングラス、ジーンズ、シャツ、スカート、ストッキング、スポーツウェア、Tシャツ、ドレス、ネクタイ、ネグリジェ、パジャマ、パンティー、ブーツ、ブラウス、ブリーフ、ベルト、マフラー

Nouns

あたま	頭	head	きって	切手	stamp
かさ	傘	umbrella	ちょきん(する)	貯金	deposit (*of money*); (to deposit)
かみ	髪	hair	てがみ	手紙	letter

Loanwords: アスピリン、アルバム、サイズ

Verbs

(おかねを)おろす	お金をおろす	to withdraw (money)
かえす	返す	to return
かりる	借りる	to borrow
こわれる		to be broken
だす	出す	to send out; to mail
でございます		(*very polite form of* です)
ねぎる	値切る	to bargain

Adjectives

いたい painful

Loanwords: カジュアル(な)、フォーマル(な)

Other Words

…かどうか	whether	…とき	…時	when…
…し、	and (*emphatic*)	〜にくい		difficult to…
…そうだ	they say	の		one; ones (*pronoun*)
だけ	only	〜やすい		easy to…
〜たら	if			

Kanji

Learn these **kanji:**

同	売	安	青
長	買	店	赤
市	着	員	黄
場	切	色	服
主	円	黒	返
電	引	白	花
			屋
			暗

チェックリスト

Use this checklist to confirm that you can now

- ☐ Talk about shops and stores
- ☐ Talk about shopping
- ☐ Talk about clothes
- ☐ Express when something happens
- ☐ Use the indefinite pronoun の
- ☐ Use the 〜たら conditional
- ☐ Express purpose using the particle に
- ☐ Report hearsay: …そうだ
- ☐ Express whether… or not: …かどうか
- ☐ Give reasons using …し、…し

Review Chapter 7

アクティビティー　1

贈り物 (*Gift*)

You would like to buy something useful for the following people. As in the example, specify a gift item and where to buy it. By the way, the department store near your house is closed for renovation now.

[例]　山田さん: 写真を撮るのが好きです。

→ カメラ屋でフィルムを買います。

1. 吉井さん：子供がたくさんいます。
2. 川口さん：最近結婚しました。(*She recently married.*)
3. 村上さん：甘いものが大好きだそうです。
4. 加納くん：小学生です。
5. 丸山さん：クラシック音楽が大好きです。
6. 酒井さん：風邪で寝ているそうです。
7. 森本さん：夏アメリカに旅行するつもりだそうです。
8. 小林さん：趣味はジョギングだそうです。

アクティビティー　2

Who's who?

Work in pairs. Student 1 covers the answer key* in the footnote and asks who is who in the picture. Student 2 answers by describing what each person is wearing, based on the answer key. Follow the example.

[例]　s1: 山田さんはどの人ですか。

s2: ドレスを着ている人です。

s1: 山田さんはXですか。

s2: はい、そうです。／いいえ、違います。

---

*Activity 2 answers: 1 = b　2 = h　3 = a　4 = f　5 = c　6 = e　7 = g　8 = d

1. 木村さん
2. 本間さん
3. 鈴木さん
4. 佐藤さん
5. 丸山さん
6. 今野さん
7. 星さん
8. 野村さん

アクティビティー　3

買い物が好きですか。(*Do you like shopping?*)

Work in pairs. Discuss the following situations. Determine if they apply to you or your partner.

1. 買い物の時はいつもクレジットカードを使う。
2. バーゲンセールの時に買い物をする。
3. ほしいものは、値段が高いものでも買う。
4. 色がきらいでも、バーゲンでとても安くなっていたら、買う。
5. 何かを買う前に、いろいろな店に行って、値段を調べる (*find out*)。
6. 新聞の広告を見て、買うものを決める (*decide*)。
7. 高いものは分割払い (*installment payments*) で買う。
8. メールオーダーでものをよく買う。
9. インターネットで買い物をよくする。
10. 毎週ショッピングへ行く。
11. お金がたくさんあったら、何を買いますか。
12. どんな時にいいレストランへ行って、食事をしますか。
13. サービスが良かったら、チップはいくらくらい払いますか。

Appendices

APPENDIX 1: Verb Conjugation

	CLASS 1						
Dictionary Form	会う	書く	話す	立つ	死ぬ*	読む	乗る
Root	会(わ)	書	話	立	死	読	乗
Plain, Nonpast, Negative	会わない	書かない	話さない	立たない	死なない	読まない	乗らない
Polite, Nonpast, Affirmative	会います	書きます	話します	立ちます	死にます	読みます	乗ります
ましょう **Form (Polite Volitional)**	会いましょう	書きましょう	話しましょう	立ちましょう	死にましょう	読みましょう	乗りましょう
たい **Form**	会いたい	書きたい	話したい	立ちたい	死にたい	読みたい	乗りたい
Polite Command	会いなさい	書きなさい	話しなさい	立ちなさい	死になさい	読みなさい	乗りなさい

* 死ぬ is the only verb whose dictionary form ends in ぬ.

	CLASS 1		CLASS 2		CLASS 3	
Dictionary Form	泳(およ)ぐ	呼(よ)ぶ	How to create forms	食(た)べる	する	来(く)る
Root	泳	呼	Drop る ending	食べ	Irregular	Irregular
Plain, Nonpast, Negative	泳がない	呼ばない	Root + ない	食べない	しない	来(こ)ない
Polite, Nonpast, Affirmative	泳ぎます	呼びます	Root + ます	食べます	します	来(き)ます
ましょう **Form (Polite Volitional)**	泳ぎましょう	呼びましょう	Root + ましょう	食べましょう	しましょう	来(き)ましょう
たい **Form**	泳ぎたい	呼びたい	Root + たい	食べたい	したい	来(き)たい
Polite Command	泳ぎなさい	呼びなさい	Root + なさい	食べなさい	しなさい	来(き)なさい

	CLASS 1						
Dictionary Form	会(あ)う	書(か)く	話(はな)す	立(た)つ	死(し)ぬ	読(よ)む	乗(の)る
Potential	会える	書ける	話せる	立てる	死ねる	読める	乗れる
Imperative	会え	書け	話せ	立て	死ね	読め	乗れ
ば Conditional	会えば	書けば	話せば	立てば	死ねば	読めば	乗れば
Volitional	会おう	書こう	話そう	立とう	死のう	読もう	乗ろう
Ta-Form	会った	書いた	話した	立った	死んだ	読んだ	乗った
Te-Form	会って	書いて	話して	立って	死んで	読んで	乗って
Other Verbs	洗(あら)う 使(つか)う 歌(うた)う 買(か)う 手伝(てつだ)う 笑(わら)う 言(い)う 習(なら)う	聞(き)く 行(い)く* 磨(みが)く 働(はたら)く はく 歩(ある)く	探(さが)す 直(なお)す	持(も)つ 勝(か)つ 待(ま)つ		飲(の)む 休(やす)む 住(す)む 楽(たの)しむ	帰(かえ)る 入(はい)る 知(し)る 降(お)りる 走(はし)る 泊(と)まる 止(と)まる 取(と)る 切(き)る 終(お)わる 始(はじ)まる

*The ta-form and te-form of 行く are 行った and 行って, respectively.

	CLASS 1		CLASS 2		CLASS 3	
Dictionary Form	泳ぐ	呼ぶ		食べる	する	来る
Potential	泳げる	呼べる	Root + られる	食べられる	できる	来られる
Imperative	泳げ	呼べ	Root + ろ	食べろ	しろ	来い
ば Conditional	泳げば	呼べば	Root + れば	食べれば	すれば	来れば
Volitional	泳ごう	呼ぼう	Root + よう	食べよう	しよう	来よう
Ta-Form	泳いだ	呼んだ	Root + た	食べた	した	来た
Te-Form	泳いで	呼んで	Root + て	食べて	して	来て
Other Verbs	脱ぐ 急ぐ	飛ぶ 遊ぶ		見る 起きる 寝る 出かける 出る 着る 教える All potential verb forms	Nominal verbs (勉強する、洗濯する)	連れてくる 持ってくる

APPENDIX 2: Adjective and Copula Conjugation

Adjectives

	DICTIONARY FORM	PRENOMINAL	PREDICATE			
			Plain			
			Non-past		Past	
			Affirmative	**Negative**	**Affirmative**	**Negative**
I-Adjectives	赤(あか)い	赤い	赤い	赤くない	赤かった	赤くなかった
	いい	いい	いい	よくない	よかった	よくなかった
Na-Adjectives	静(しず)か	静かな	静かだ	静かではない／ 静かじゃない	静かだった	静かではなかった／ 静かじゃなかった

Copula

DICTIONARY FORM	PRENOMINAL	PREDICATE			
		Plain			
		Non-past		Past	
		Affirmative	**Negative**	**Affirmative**	**Negative**
だ	の／である	だ／ である	ではない／ じゃない	だった	ではなかった／ じゃなかった

	PREDICATE						ADVERBIAL
	Polite				Te-Form	Conditional	
	Non-past		Past				
	Affirmative	Negative	Affirmative	Negative			
I-Adjectives	赤いです	赤くありません／ 赤くないです	赤かった です	赤くありません でした／ 赤くなかった です	赤くて	赤ければ	赤く
	いいです	よくありません／ よくないです	よかった です	よくありません でした／ よくなかった です	よくて	よければ	よく
Na-Adjectives	静かです	静かではありません／ 静かじゃ ありません	静かでした	静かではありません でした／ 静かじゃ ありません でした	静かで	静かならば／ 静かであれば	静かに

PREDICATE						ADVERBIAL
Polite				Te-Form	Conditional	
Non-past		Past				
Affirmative	Negative	Affirmative	Negative			
です	ではありません／ じゃありません	でした	ではありません でした／ じゃありません でした	で	なら(ば)／ であれば	N/A

APPENDIX 3: Numbers

NATIVE JAPANESE SYSTEM	SINO-JAPANESE SYSTEM				
1 ひと 一つ	1 いち 一	11 じゅう いち 十一			
2 ふた 二つ	2 に 二	12 じゅう に 十二		200 に ひゃく 二百	2,000 に せん 二千
3 みっ 三つ	3 さん 三	13 じゅうさん 十三	30 さんじゅう 三十	300 さんびゃく 三百	3,000 さん ぜん 三千
4 よっ 四つ	4 し、よん 四	14 じゅうし、じゅうよん 十四	40 よんじゅう 四十	400 よんひゃく 四百	4,000 よん せん 四千
5 いつ 五つ	5 ご 五	15 じゅう ご 十五	50 ごじゅう 五十	500 ごひゃく 五百	5,000 ご せん 五千
6 むっ 六つ	6 ろく 六	16 じゅうろく 十六	60 ろくじゅう 六十	600 ろっ ぴゃく 六百	6,000 ろく せん 六千
7 なな 七つ	7 しち、なな 七	17 じゅうしち、じゅうなな 十七	70 ななじゅう、しちじゅう 七十	700 ななひゃく 七百	7,000 なな せん 七千
8 やっ 八つ	8 はち 八	18 じゅう はち 十八	80 はちじゅう 八十	800 はっ ぴゃく 八百	8,000 はっ せん 八千
9 ここの 九つ	9 く、きゅう 九	19 じゅうく、じゅうきゅう 十九	90 きゅうじゅう 九十	900 きゅう ひゃく 九百	9,000 きゅう せん 九千
10 とお 十	10 じゅう 十	20 にじゅう 二十	100 ひゃく 百	1,000 (いっ)せん (一)千	10,000 いちまん 一万

LARGE NUMBERS

100,000	十万 (じゅうまん)
(*one million*) 1,000,000	百万 (ひゃくまん)
10,000,000	(一)千万 ((いっ)せんまん)
100,000,000	一億 (いちおく)
(*one billion*) 1,000,000,000	十億 (じゅうおく)
10,000,000,000	百億 (ひゃくおく)
100,000,000,000	(一)千億 ((いっ)せんおく)
(*one trillion*) 1,000,000,000,000	一兆 (いっちょう)

NOTES

1. Zero is 零 (れい) or ゼロ.
2. 0.314 is read 零点三一四 (れいてんさんいちよん). 2.236 is read 二点二三六 (にてんにさんろく). (点 (てん) = point)
3. The native Japanese system exists for 1 through 10 only. After 11, only the Sino-Japanese system can be used.
4. Some people read 1,000, 10,000,000, and 100,000,000,000 as 一千 (いっせん)、一千万 (いっせんまん)、and 一千億 (いっせんおく), respectively.

APPENDIX 4: Counters

The following chart lists common counters (suffixes appended to numbers for counting or naming things), most of which are introduced in this book. Notice the phonological changes that occur when some numbers and counters are joined. The first column (～番) represents the simplest case: the Sino-Japanese number is followed by the counter with no phonological changes. In other columns, phonological changes occur in some cases. Such variations are marked with an asterisk (*). Where two pronunciations are provided, either may be used, although a particular pronunciation may predominate in a given situation. (For example, *seven o'clock* is usually pronounced しちじ, except over train station public address systems where ななじ is often used to prevent confusion with *one o'clock* いちじ.) Counters that name something are so indicated; all others are used to count. Each chart groups together counters that vary in similar ways. For more on counters, see **Grammar 9**, Chapter 2.

COUNTERS	ばん ～番	じ ～時	がつ ～月	かい ～回
WHAT IS BEING COUNTED OR NAMED	**Serial Numbers (*Number...*)**	**Hours of the Day (Name) (*...o'clock*)**	**Months (Name)**	**Occurrences (*...times*)**
1	いちばん 一番	いちじ 一時	いちがつ 一月	いっかい 一回*
2	にばん 二番	にじ 二時	にがつ 二月	にかい 二回
3	さんばん 三番	さんじ 三時	さんがつ 三月	さんかい 三回
4	よんばん 四番	よじ 四時*	しがつ 四月*	よんかい 四回
5	ごばん 五番	ごじ 五時	ごがつ 五月	ごかい 五回
6	ろくばん 六番	ろくじ 六時	ろくがつ 六月	ろっかい 六回*
7	ななばん、しちばん 七番	しちじ、ななじ 七時	しちがつ 七月*	ななかい、しちかい 七回
8	はちばん 八番	はちじ 八時	はちがつ 八月	はっかい 八回*
9	きゅうばん 九番	くじ 九時*	くがつ 九月*	きゅうかい 九回
10	じゅうばん 十番	じゅうじ 十時	じゅうがつ 十月	じっかい、じゅっかい* 十回
OTHER COUNTERS WITH SAME PATTERN OF VARIATION	まい ～枚 thin, flat. objects ど ～度 ...degrees (temperature) ...times (occurrences) ばい ～倍 ...times (magnifications)	じかん ～時間 hours, ねん ～年 years (number and name)		こ ～個 pieces かげつ ～ケ月, months か ～課 lessons

COUNTERS	～階 (かい)	～本 (ほん、ぽん、ぼん)	～分 (ふん)	～冊 (さつ)
WHAT IS BEING COUNTED OR NAMED	**Floors (of a Building) (Number and Name)**	**Long, Cylindrical Objects**	**Minutes (Number and Name)**	**Books, Bound Volumes**
1	一階* (いっかい)	一本* (いっぽん)	一分* (いっぷん)	一冊* (いっさつ)
2	二階 (にかい)	二本 (にほん)	二分 (にふん)	二冊 (にさつ)
3	三階 (さんかい、さんがい*)	三本* (さんぼん)	三分* (さんぷん)	三冊 (さんさつ)
4	四階 (よんかい)	四本 (よんほん)	四分 (よんふん)	四冊 (よんさつ)
5	五階 (ごかい)	五本 (ごほん)	五分 (ごふん)	五冊 (ごさつ)
6	六階* (ろっかい)	六本* (ろっぽん)	六分* (ろっぷん)	六冊 (ろくさつ)
7	七階 (ななかい、しちかい)	七本 (ななほん、しちほん)	七分 (ななふん、しちふん)	七冊 (ななさつ、しちさつ)
8	八階* (はっかい)	八本* (はっぽん)	八分* (はっぷん)	八冊* (はっさつ)
9	九階 (きゅうかい)	九本 (きゅうほん)	九分 (きゅうふん)	九冊 (きゅうさつ)
10	十階 (じっかい、じゅっかい*)	十本 (じっぽん、じゅっぽん*)	十分 (じっぷん、じゅっぷん*)	十冊 (じっさつ、じゅっさつ*)
OTHER COUNTERS WITH SAME PATTERN OF VARIATION		～杯 (はい) glass(ful)s cup(ful)s ～匹 (ひき) small animals	～泊 (はく) overnight stays	～章 (しょう) chapters

COUNTERS	～足(そく)	～ページ	～頭(とう)	～人(にん)
WHAT IS BEING COUNTED OR NAMED	**Pairs of Footwear (Shoes, Socks, etc.)**	**Pages (Number and Name)**	**Large Animals**	**People**
1	一足(いっそく)*	一(いっ)ページ*	一頭(いっとう)*	一人(ひとり)*
2	二足(にそく)	二(に)ページ	二頭(にとう)	二人(ふたり)*
3	三足(さんぞく)*	三(さん)ページ	三頭(さんとう)	三人(さんにん)
4	四足(よんそく)	四(よん)ページ	四頭(よんとう)	四人(よにん)*
5	五足(ごそく)	五(ご)ページ	五頭(ごとう)	五人(ごにん)
6	六足(ろくそく)	六(ろっ)ページ*	六頭(ろくとう)	六人(ろくにん)
7	七足(ななそく、しちそく)	七(なな、しち)ページ	七頭(ななとう、しちとう)	七人(しちにん、ななにん)
8	八足(はっそく)*	八(はっ)ページ*	八頭(はっとう)	八人(はちにん)
9	九足(きゅうそく)	九(きゅう)ページ	九頭(きゅうとう)*	九人(きゅうにん、くにん)
10	十足(じっそく、じゅっそく*)	十(じっ、じゅっ)ページ*	十頭(じっとう、じゅっとう*)	十人(じゅうにん)
OTHERS COUNTERS WITH SAME PATTERN OF VARIATION		～ポンド pounds	～通(つう) letters (i.e., pieces of correspondence) ～トン tons ～点(てん) points (e.g., in games, grades) ～滴(てき) drops of liquid	

COUNTERS	～日	～日 (にち)	～晩 (ばん)	～歳 (さい)
WHAT IS BEING COUNTED OR NAMED	**Days of the Month (Name)**	**Days (Number)**	**Nights**	**Age (*...years old*)**
1	一日* (ついたち)	一日 (いちにち)	一晩* (ひとばん)	一歳 (いっさい)、一つ* (ひと)
2	二日* (ふつか)	二日* (ふつか)	二晩* (ふたばん)	二歳 (にさい)、二つ* (ふた)
3	三日* (みっか)	三日* (みっか)	三晩* (みばん)	三歳 (さんさい)、三つ* (みっ)
4	四日* (よっか)	四日* (よっか)	四晩* (よばん)	四歳 (よんさい)、四つ* (よっ)
5	五日* (いつか)	五日 (ごにち、いつか*)	五晩 (ごばん)	五歳 (ごさい)、五つ* (いつ)
6	六日* (むいか)	六日 (ろくにち、むいか*)	六晩 (ろくばん)	六歳 (ろくさい)、六つ* (むっ)
7	七日* (なのか)	七日 (しちにち、なのか*)	七晩 (ななばん)	七歳 (ななさい)、七つ* (なな)
8	八日* (ようか)	八日 (はちにち、ようか*)	八晩 (はちばん)	八歳 (はっさい)、八つ* (やっ)
9	九日* (ここのか)	九日 (くにち、ここのか*)	九晩 (きゅうばん)	九歳 (きゅうさい)、九つ* (ここの)
10	十日* (とおか)	十日 (とおか)	十晩 (じゅうばん)	十歳 (じっさい、じゅっさい)、十* (とお)
OTHER IRREGULAR PRONUNCIATIONS OF NUMBERS AND COUNTERS	十四日* (じゅうよっか) 二十日* (はつか) 二十四日* (にじゅうよっか)	十四日* (じゅうよっか) 二十日* (はつか) 二十四日* (にじゅうよっか)		二十歳* (はたち)

SUFFIXES FOR ORDINAL NUMBERS	〜目(め) (Used with Japanese Numbers) (*the first, the second,* etc.)	〜番目(ばんめ) (Used with Sino-Japanese Numbers)
1	一つ目(ひとつめ)	一番目(いちばんめ)
2	二つ目(ふたつめ)	二番目(にばんめ)
3	三つ目(みっつめ)	三番目(さんばんめ)
4	四つ目(よっつめ)	四番目(よんばんめ)
5	五つ目(いつつめ)	五番目(ごばんめ)
6	六つ目(むっつめ)	六番目(ろくばんめ)
7	七つ目(ななつめ)	七番目(ななばんめ、しちばんめ)
8	八つ目(やっつめ)	八番目(はちばんめ)
9	九つ目(ここのつめ)	九番目(きゅうばんめ、くばんめ)
10	—	十番目(じゅうばんめ)

How to Form Ordinal Numbers

Note: Another way to make ordinal numbers is to add the prefix 第(だい)... (Number...) to the Sino-Japanese numbers (第一(だいいち)、第二(だいに)、第三(だいさん)、第四(だいよん)、第五(だいご)、第六(だいろく)、第七(だいなな)、第八(だいはち)、第九(だいきゅう)、第十(だいじゅう)、and so on). This prefix may be used in combination with some counter suffixes to name ordered things. Examples are 第三章(だいさんしょう) (*Chapter Three*) and 第五課(だいごか) (*Lesson Five*). The suffix 〜目(め) is commonly used in combination with counters to indicate *the ...th.* For example, 九回目(きゅうかいめ) (*the ninth time*), 三日目(みっかめ) (*the third day*), 五足目(ごそくめ) (*the fifth pair of footwear*), 二人目(ふたりめ) (*the second person*), and so on.

When indicating items having no assigned counter or when you are unsure of the counter, you can usually use the general terms above for *the first* (*one*), *the second* (*one*), and so on.

APPENDIX 5: Time, Days, Months, and Years

TELLING TIME

	A.M.	P.M.
	ごぜん 午前	ごご 午後

1:00 いちじ 一時	2:00 にじ 二時	3:00 さんじ 三時	4:00 よじ 四時	5:00 ごじ 五時	6:00 ろくじ 六時
7:00 しちじ、ななじ 七時	8:00 はちじ 八時	9:00 くじ 九時	10:00 じゅうじ 十時	11:00 じゅういちじ 十一時	12:00 じゅうにじ 十二時

いっぷん 一分	にふん 二分	さんぷん 三分	よんふん 四分	ごふん 五分	ろっぷん 六分	ななふん、しちふん 七分	はっぷん 八分	きゅうふん 九分	じっぷん、じゅっぷん 十分

(and so on through 59 minutes)

[例] ごぜんごじにじゅうろっぷん 午前五時二十六分 5:26 A.M. ごごはちじよんじゅうななふん 午後八時四十七分 8:47 P.M.

DAYS OF THE WEEK

しゅうまつ 週末 **Weekend**	へいじつ 平日 **Weekday**					しゅうまつ 週末 **Weekend**
にちようび 日曜日 *Sunday*	げつようび 月曜日 *Monday*	かようび 火曜日 *Tuesday*	すいようび 水曜日 *Wednesday*	もくようび 木曜日 *Thursday*	きんようび 金曜日 *Friday*	どようび 土曜日 *Saturday*

DAYS OF THE MONTH

1 ついたち 一日	2 ふつか 二日	3 みっか 三日	4 よっか 四日	5 いつか 五日	6 むいか 六日	7 なのか 七日
8 ようか 八日	9 ここのか 九日	10 とおか 十日	11 じゅういちにち 十一日	12 じゅうににち 十二日	13 じゅうさんにち 十三日	14 じゅうよっか 十四日
15 じゅうごにち 十五日	16 じゅうろくにち 十六日	17 じゅうしちにち 十七日	18 じゅうはちにち 十八日	19 じゅうくにち 十九日	20 はつか 二十日	21 にじゅういちにち 二十一日
22 にじゅうににち 二十二日	23 にじゅうさんにち 二十三日	24 にじゅうよっか 二十四日	25 にじゅうごにち 二十五日	26 にじゅうろくにち 二十六日	27 にじゅうしちにち 二十七日	28 にじゅうはちにち 二十八日
29 にじゅうくにち 二十九日	30 さんじゅうにち 三十日	31 さんじゅういちにち 三十一日				

MONTHS

いちがつ 一月 *January*	にがつ 二月 *February*	さんがつ 三月 *March*	しがつ 四月 *April*	ごがつ 五月 *May*	ろくがつ 六月 *June*
しちがつ 七月	はちがつ 八月	くがつ 九月	じゅうがつ 十月	じゅういちがつ 十一月	じゅうにがつ 十二月
July	*August*	*September*	*October*	*November*	*December*

YEARS

Western year	ねん 1988年	1989年	1990年	. . .	1998年	1999年	2000年	2001年
Era	しょうわ 昭和*	へいせい 平成						
Japanese year	六十三年	一年 がんねん *or* 元年	二年	. . .	十年	十一年	十二年	十三年

*The **Showa** era began in 1926 and ended when the **Heisei** era began on January 8, 1989. Technically, the first days of 1989 fall in the **Showa** era, so events that occurred within those days (such as someone's birth) are often dated **Showa 64.**

RELATIVE TIME EXPRESSIONS

Days	おととい *the day before yesterday*	きのう (さくじつ) 昨日 *yesterday*	きょう 今日 *today*	あした (あす) 明日 *tomorrow*	あさって *the day after tomorrow*
Weeks	せんせんしゅう 先々週 *the week before last*	せんしゅう 先週 *last week*	こんしゅう 今週 *this week*	らいしゅう 来週 *next week*	さらいしゅう 再来週 *the week after next*
Months	せんせんげつ 先々月 *the month before last*	せんげつ 先月 *last month*	こんげつ 今月 *this month*	らいげつ 来月 *next month*	さらいげつ 再来月 *the month after next*
Years	いっさくねん 一昨年 *the year before last*	きょねん さくねん 去年 or 昨年 *last year*	ことし 今年 *this year*	らいねん 来年 *next year*	さらいねん 再来年 *the year after next*

TIME DURATIONS

	なんぷん かん 何分(間) ***minutes***	なんじかん 何時間 ***hours***	なんにち かん 何日(間) ***days***	なんしゅうかん 何週間 ***weeks***	なんかげつ 何ヶ月 ***months***	なんねん かん 何年(間) ***years***
1	いっぷん かん 一分(間)	いちじかん 一時間	いちにち かん 一日(間)	いっしゅうかん 一週間	いっかげつ 一ヶ月	いちねん かん 一年(間)
2	にふん かん 二分(間)	にじかん 二時間	ふつか かん 二日(間)	にしゅうかん 二週間	にかげつ 二ヶ月	にねん かん 二年(間)
3	さんぷん かん 三分(間)	さんじかん 三時間	みっか かん 三日(間)	さんしゅうかん 三週間	さんかげつ 三ヶ月	さんねん かん 三年(間)
4	よんふん かん 四分(間)	よじかん 四時間	よっか かん 四日(間)	よんしゅうかん 四週間	よんかげつ 四ヶ月	よねん かん 四年(間)
5	ごふん かん 五分(間)	ごじかん 五時間	いつか かん 五日(間)	ごしゅうかん 五週間	ごかげつ 五ヶ月	ごねん かん 五年(間)
6	ろっぷん かん 六分(間)	ろくじかん 六時間	むいか かん 六日(間)	ろくしゅうかん 六週間	ろっかげつ 六ヶ月	ろくねん かん 六年(間)
7	しちふん かん ななふん かん 七分(間)	ななじかん 七時間	なのか かん 七日(間)	ななしゅうかん 七週間	しちかげつ ななかげつ 七ヶ月	しちねん かん ななねん かん 七年(間)
8	はっぷん かん 八分(間)	はちじかん 八時間	ようか かん 八日(間)	はっしゅうかん 八週間	はっかげつ 八ヶ月	はちねん かん 八年(間)
9	きゅうふん かん 九分(間)	くじかん 九時間	ここのか かん 九日(間)	きゅうしゅうかん 九週間	きゅうかげつ 九ヶ月	きゅうねん かん 九年(間)
10	じっぷん かん じゅっぷん かん 十分(間)	じゅうじかん 十時間	とおか かん 十日(間)	じっしゅう かん じゅっしゅうかん 十週間	じっかげつ じゅっかげつ 十ヶ月	じゅうねん かん 十年(間)
14	じゅうよんふん かん 十四分(間)	じゅうよじかん 十四時間	じゅうよっか かん 十四日(間)	じゅうよんしゅうかん 十四週間	じゅうよんかげつ 十四ヶ月	じゅうよねん かん 十四年(間)
20	にじっぷん かん にじゅっぷん かん 二十分(間)	にじゅうじかん 二十時間	はつか かん 二十日(間)	にじっしゅうかん にじゅっしゅうかん 二十週間	にじっかげつ にじゅっかげつ 二十ヶ月	にじゅうねん かん 二十年(間)
24	にじゅうよんふん かん 二十四分(間)	にじゅうよじかん 二十四時間	にじゅうよっか かん 二十四日(間)	にじゅうよんしゅうかん 二十四週間	にじゅうよんかげつ 二十四ヶ月	にじゅうよねん かん 二十四年(間)

APPENDIX 6: **Ko-so-a-do** Words

	こ-SERIES (*this*)	そ-SERIES (*that*)	あ-SERIES (*that over there*)	ど-SERIES (*which, what, etc.*)
Demonstrative Pronoun (*this one, that one, that one over there, which one, etc.*)	これ	それ	あれ	どれ
Demonstrative Adjective (*this, that, that over there, which, etc.*)	この	その	あの	どの
Location (*here, there, over there, where*)	ここ	そこ	あそこ	どこ
Direction* (polite) (*this way, that way, yonder, which way*)	こちら	そちら	あちら	どちら
Direction* (informal) (*this way, that way, yonder, which way*)	こっち	そっち	あっち	どっち
Kind or Type (*this kind of, that kind of, that kind of [far away], what kind of*)	こんな	そんな	あんな	どんな
Extent (*to this extent, to that extent, to that [far] extent, to what extent*)	こんなに	そんなに	あんなに	どんなに
Manner ([*in a manner*] *like this/that/that over there, in what manner*)	こう	そう	ああ	どう

*These **ko-so-a-do** words can also be used to refer to people, things, and locations. Here are some examples.

こちらは横井先生です。
This is Professor Yokoi.

あっちのセーターは9千円ですよ。
That sweater over there is 9,000 yen.

カーティスさんはそちらにいますか。
Is Mr. Curtis there (lit., *at that place*)?

APPENDIX 7: Japanese Accent

Basic Rules

1. In standard Japanese speech, a syllable is pronounced with high pitch or low pitch. Pitch is relative; high or low pitch means higher or lower pitch than that of other syllables in a given word or utterance.
2. In standard Japanese, the pitch of the first syllable of a word is always different from that of the second syllable. Thus, if the first syllable has high pitch, the second one has low pitch, and vice versa.
3. Within a single word, once the pitch falls, it doesn't rise again.

Symbols

In many accent dictionaries published in Japan, accent is indicated with two symbols: — and ⌝ . A horizontal bar over a syllable means that this syllable is pronounced with high pitch. A syllable with no bar over it is pronounced with low pitch. A downturn at the end of a bar ⌝ indicates a fall in pitch—that is, the syllable after the downturn is pronounced with low pitch. Here are some examples.

o ma wa ri sa n   inu   ushi

In the word **omawarisan** (*police officer*), the first syllable is pronouced with low pitch, the second and third syllables are pronounced with high pitch, and the last three syllables are pronounced with low pitch. The two words **inu** (*dog*) and **ushi** (*cow*) have the same accent pattern low-high when pronounced independently. However, the difference in notations indicates that the pitch of, for examle, particles (**wa**, **ga**, **o**, etc.) following these words will differ. Note that the particles do not have fixed pitch; rather, their pitch (high or low) is determined by the preceding word.

inu ga   ushi ga

Accent Patterns of Words

The following chart shows the possible accent patterns of one- to four-syllable words in standard Japanese speech. Also shown is the accent of one-syllable particles when they follow words with these accent patterns. ○ represents a syllable in a given word, and ● denotes a particle.

ONE SYLLABLE	TWO SYLLABLES	THREE SYLLABLES	FOUR SYLLABLES
き (木; *tree*)	ねこ (猫; *cat*)	いのち (命; *life*)	こんばん (今晩; *tonight*)
	いぬ (犬; *dog*)	こころ (心; *heart*)	やまやま (山々; *mountains*)
		おんな (女; *female*)	かがりび (かがり火; *bonfire*)
き (気; *spirit*)	うし (牛; *cow*)	さくら (桜; *cherry tree*)	ともだち (友だち; *friend*)

Recently it has become common, especially among young people, to also say

こころ,

keeping the last syllable raised instead of dropping it.

APPENDIX 8: Kanji List

The following are **kanji** presented for active acquisition in *Yookoso!* In **kanji** dictionaries, **kanji** are listed according to their basic components, or radicals. Within each group sharing the same radical, the kanji are further classified in terms of the number of strokes beyond those which make up the radical. For instance, 本, which has five strokes, is listed below the radical 木, which has four strokes. Thus, you can find 本 in the one-stroke section under the radical 木. A more complex example is 楽, which contains nine strokes outside the radical and is therefore found in the nine-stroke section. The following list indicates the number of strokes for each **kanji** and the radical under which it is listed in *most* **kanji** dictionaries. The numbers following the radicals are the number of strokes remaining after subtracting the stroke-count of the radical. Note that some characters, such as 木、日、and 人, are themselves radicals.

KANJI	TOTAL NUMBER OF STROKES	RADICAL	NAME OF RADICAL	NUMBER OF STROKES BEYOND THE RADICAL
Chapter 1				
日	4	日	(ひ)	0
本	5	木	(き)	1
学	8	子	(こ)	5
生	5	生	(うまれる)	0
名	6	口	(くち)	3
年	6	干	(たてかん)	3
何	7	イ	(にんべん)	5
月	4	月	(つき)	0
人	2	人	(ひと)	0
一	1	一	(いち)	0
二	2	二	(に)	0
三	3	一	(いち)	2
四	5	口	(くにがまえ)	2
五	4	二	(に)	2
六	4	八	(はち)	2
七	2	一	(いち)	1
八	2	八	(はち)	0
九	2	乙	(おつ)	1
十	2	十	(じゅう)	0
百	6	白	(しろ)	1
先	6	儿	(にんにょう)	4
話	13	言	(ごんべん)	6
語	14	言	(ごんべん)	7
大	3	大	(だい)	0

KANJI	TOTAL NUMBER OF STROKES	RADICAL	NAME OF RADICAL	NUMBER OF STROKES BEYOND THE RADICAL

Chapter 2

KANJI	TOTAL NUMBER OF STROKES	RADICAL	NAME OF RADICAL	NUMBER OF STROKES BEYOND THE RADICAL
間	12	門	(もん)	4
半	5	十	(じゅう)	3
上	3	一	(いち)	2
下	3	一	(いち)	2
分	4	刀	(かたな)	2
小	3	小	(しょう)	0
好	6	女	(おんな)	3
町	7	田	(た)	2
左	5	工	(え)	2
右	5	ロ	(くち)	2
中	4	亅	(ぼう)	3
外	5	夕	(ゆうべ)	2
前	9	刂	(りっとう)	7
後	9	彳	(ぎょうにんべん)	6
時	10	日	(ひ)	6
山	3	山	(やま)	0
口	3	口	(くち)	0
千	3	十	(じゅう)	1
万	3	一	(いち)	2
方	4	方	(ほう)	0
近	7	辶	(しんにゅう)	4
遠	13	辶	(しんにゅう)	10
有	6	月	(つき)	2

Chapter 3

KANJI	TOTAL NUMBER OF STROKES	RADICAL	NAME OF RADICAL	NUMBER OF STROKES BEYOND THE RADICAL
朝	12	月	(つき)	8
明	8	日	(ひ)	4
午	4	十	(じゅう)	2
昼	9	日	(ひ)	5
来	7	木	(き)	3
行	6	行	(いく)	0
聞	14	耳	(みみ)	8
食	9	食	(しょく)	0
出	5	凵	(うけばこ)	3
飲	12	食	(しょく)	4
入	2	入	(いる)	0
休	6	イ	(にんべん)	4
夕	3	夕	(ゆうべ)	0
今	4	人	(ひとやね)	2
週	11	辶	(しんにゅう)	8
曜	18	日	(ひ)	14
毎	6	毋	(なかれ)	2
回	6	囗	(くにがまえ)	3

KANJI	TOTAL NUMBER OF STROKES	RADICAL	NAME OF RADICAL	NUMBER OF STROKES BEYOND THE RADICAL

Chapter 3 (cont.)

KANJI	TOTAL NUMBER OF STROKES	RADICAL	NAME OF RADICAL	NUMBER OF STROKES BEYOND THE RADICAL
見	7	見	(みる)	0
起	10	走	(はしる)	3
読	14	言	(ごんべん)	7
火	4	火	(ひ)	0
水	4	水	(みず)	0
木	4	木	(き)	0
金	8	金	(かね)	0
土	3	土	(つち)	0
会	6	人	(ひとやね)	4

Chapter 4

KANJI	TOTAL NUMBER OF STROKES	RADICAL	NAME OF RADICAL	NUMBER OF STROKES BEYOND THE RADICAL
天	4	大	(だい)	1
気	6	气	(きがまえ)	2
雨	8	雨	(あめ)	0
雪	11	雨	(あめ)	3
度	9	广	(まだれ)	6
風	9	風	(かぜ)	0
台	5	口	(くち)	2
番	12	田	(た)	7
春	9	日	(ひ)	5
夏	10	夂	(すいにょう)	7
秋	9	禾	(のぎへん)	4
冬	5	冫	(にすい)	3
東	8	木	(き)	4
西	6	西	(にし)	0
南	9	十	(じゅう)	7
北	5	匕	(ひ)	3
高	10	高	(たかい)	0
多	6	夕	(ゆうべ)	3
少	4	小	(しょう)	1
強	11	弓	(ゆみ)	8
弱	10	弓	(ゆみ)	7
昨	9	日	(ひ)	5
暑	12	日	(ひ)	8
寒	12	宀	(うかんむり)	9
空	8	宀	(うかんむり)	5

Chapter 5

KANJI	TOTAL NUMBER OF STROKES	RADICAL	NAME OF RADICAL	NUMBER OF STROKES BEYOND THE RADICAL
手	4	手	(て)	0
家	10	宀	(うかんむり)	7
男	7	田	(た)	2
女	3	女	(おんな)	0
子	3	子	(こ)	0
母	5	母	(はは)	1
父	4	父	(ちち)	0

KANJI	TOTAL NUMBER OF STROKES	RADICAL	NAME OF RADICAL	NUMBER OF STROKES BEYOND THE RADICAL

Chapter 5 (cont.)

KANJI	TOTAL NUMBER OF STROKES	RADICAL	NAME OF RADICAL	NUMBER OF STROKES BEYOND THE RADICAL
兄	5	儿	(にんにょう)	3
弟	7	弓	(ゆみ)	4
姉	8	女	(おんな)	5
妹	8	女	(おんな)	5
作	7	イ	(にんべん)	5
族	11	方	(ほう)	7
勉	10	カ	(ちから)	8
道	12	辶	(しんにゅう)	9
使	8	イ	(にんべん)	6
国	8	囗	(くにがまえ)	5
音	9	音	(おと)	0
楽	13	木	(き)	9
全	6	人	(ひとやね)	4
部	11	阝	(おおざと)	8
運	12	辶	(しんにゅう)	9
動	11	カ	(ちから)	9

Chapter 6

KANJI	TOTAL NUMBER OF STROKES	RADICAL	NAME OF RADICAL	NUMBER OF STROKES BEYOND THE RADICAL
思	9	心	(こころ)	5
終	11	糸	(いと)	5
始	8	女	(おんな)	5
物	8	牛	(うし)	4
肉	6	肉	(にく)	0
事	8	亅	(はねぼう)	7
茶	9	艹	(くさかんむり)	6
酒	10	水	(みず)	7
牛	4	牛	(うし)	0
鳥	11	鳥	(とり)	0
湯	12	水	(みず)	9
野	11	里	(さと)	4
魚	11	魚	(さかな)	0
味	8	口	(くち)	5
悪	11	心	(こころ)	7
料	10	斗	(とます)	6
理	11	玉	(たま)	7
米	6	米	(こめ)	0
品	9	口	(くち)	6
和	8	口	(くち)	5
洋	9	水	(みず)	6
夜	8	夕	(ゆうべ)	5
言	7	言	(ごんべん)	0
貝	7	貝	(かい)	0

KANJI	TOTAL NUMBER OF STROKES	RADICAL	NAME OF RADICAL	NUMBER OF STROKES BEYOND THE RADICAL

Chapter 7

KANJI	TOTAL NUMBER OF STROKES	RADICAL	NAME OF RADICAL	NUMBER OF STROKES BEYOND THE RADICAL
同	6	口	(くち)	3
長	8	長	(ながい)	0
場	12	土	(つち)	9
市	5	巾	(はば)	2
主	5	、	(てん)	4
電	13	雨	(あめ)	5
売	7	士	(さむらい)	4
切	4	刀	(かたな)	2
店	8	广	(まだれ)	5
引	4	弓	(ゆみ)	1
白	5	白	(しろ)	0
屋	9	尸	(しかばね)	6
黒	11	黒	(くろ)	0
色	6	色	(いろ)	0
買	12	貝	(かい)	5
青	8	青	(あお)	0
赤	7	赤	(あか)	0
服	8	月	(つき)	4
返	7	辶	(しんにゅう)	4
花	7	艹	(くさかんむり)	4
黄	11	黄	(き)	0
員	10	口	(くち)	7
暗	13	日	(ひ)	9
円	4	冂	(どうがまえ)	2

Japanese-English Glossary

This glossary lists all Japanese words presented in this book with the exception of lesser known place names, some proper nouns, conjugated forms, compound words, and foreign loanwords that are very similar to the source language word in pronunciation and meaning.

Entries are arranged in a-i-u-e-o Japanese alphabetical order. As in Japanese dictionaries, each word is presented in hiragana or katakana, followed by the kanji transcription, if appropriate.

Verbs and adjectives are cited in their dictionary form except for a few special cases. The classification is provided for each verb: Class 1, 2, or 3.

Nominal verbs are followed by (する). I-adjectives are unmarked, but na-adjectives are followed by (な).

English translations for nouns are given in the singular; plural is an alternate gloss in most cases. Only the most commonly used polite variants are included.

Finally, remember that these translations are not equivalents but reminders of the meanings you have learned in class. Only real-life context and native usage can be relied on to define the full range of meaning and nuance for each word.

The following abbreviations are used:

adv.	word or phrase that functions as an adverb
C1	Class 1 verb
C2	Class 2 verb
C3	Class 3 verb
coll.	colloquial
conj.	conjunction
dem. adj.	demonstrative adjective
dem. pron.	demonstrative pronoun
dem. adv.	demonstrative adverb
f.	female speech (word used primarily by females)
i-adj.	i-adjective
inf.	informal
interj.	interjection
intr.	intransitive verb
m.	male speech (word used primarily by males)
na-adj.	na-adjective
n.v.	noun that can be made into a nominal verb by appending する (both its nominal meaning and verbal meaning are given)
part.	particle
pl.	plural
p.n.	proper noun
pol.	polite
pron.	pronoun
s.	singular
tr.	transitive verb

あ／ア

ああ *interj.* oh, ahh (*exclamation of surprise and pleasure*) (*2*)
ああ *dem. adv.* like that (*6*)
あい（愛）love (*7*)
あいいろ（藍色）dark blue (*7*)
あいさつ(する)（挨拶[する]）*n.v.* greeting; to greet (*3*)
アイス ice (*GS5*)
アイスクリーム ice cream (*GS5*)
アイスティー ice tea (*GS2*)
アイスミルク cold milk (*GS3*)
あいだ（間）between; AとBの間に between A and B (*2*)
アイロン iron; アイロンをかける to iron (*7*)
あう（会う）*C1, intr.* to see, meet (a person) (*GS3*)
あお（青）blue;（青い）*i-adj.* blue (*7*)
あか（赤）red (*7*);（赤い）*i-adj.* red (*2*)
あかるい（明るい）*i-adj.* bright (*vs. dark*), well-lighted; cheerful (*personality*) (*4*)
あかワイン（赤ワイン）red wine (*5*)
あき（秋）fall, autumn; あきさめ（秋雨）autumn rain (*4*)
あきる（飽きる）*C2, intr.* to become bored, get tired of (*6*)
アクションえいが（アクション映画）action movie (*2*)
アクセサリー accessory, jewelry (*7*)
あける（開ける）*C2, tr.* to open (*GS1*)
あげる（揚げる）*C2, tr.* to deep-fry (*6*)
あさ（朝）morning (*GS2*)
あさごはん（朝ごはん）breakfast (*GS2*)
あさって the day after tomorrow (*4*)
あざやか(な)（鮮やか[な]）*na-adj.* vivid (*7*)
あさゆう（朝夕）morning and evening (*4*)
あじ（味）taste, flavor; あじがいい（味がいい）to taste good; あじがない（味がない）to have no taste; あじがわるい（味がわるい）to taste bad; あじみ(する)（味見[する]）*n.v.* tasting of a sample; to taste a sample; あじわう（味わう）*C1, tr.* to taste (*6*)
あした（明日）tomorrow (*3*)
アスパラガス asparagus (*5*)
アスピリン aspirin (*7*)
あそ（阿蘇）*p.n.* Aso (*a place in Kyushu*) (*2*)
あそこ *dem. pron.* over there (*1*)
あそぶ（遊ぶ）*C1, intr.* to play (*5*)
あたし *pron., inf., f.* I; あたしたち *pron., inf., f., pl.* we (*1*)
あたたかい（暖かい）*i-adj.* warm (*GS4*)
あたま（頭）head (*7*)
あたらしい（新しい）*i-adj.* new (*2*)
あちら *dem. pron., pol.* over there (*1*)
あつい（厚い）*i-adj.* thick (*2*)
あつい（暑い）*i-adj.* hot (*temperature*) (*GS4*)
アップルパイ apple pie (*7*)
あつめる（集める）*C2, tr.* to collect, gather (*5*)
あと(で)（後[で]）after…; later (*3*)
あなた *pron., s.* you; あなたたち *pron., pl.* you (*1*)
あに（兄）older brother (*5*)
あね（姉）older sister (*5*)
あの *dem. adj.* that (*1*)
あのう excuse me, well (*1*)
アパート apartment (*GS3*)
あびる（浴びる）*C2, tr.* to bathe (*GS3*)
あぶらえ（油絵）oil painting (*5*)
アフリカ *p.n.* Africa (*6*)
アマ amateur (*5*)
あまい（甘い）*i-adj.* sweet (*2*)
あまり、あんまり *adv.* (*with negative*) not very much (*2*)
あみもの（編み物）knitting, crocheting (*5*)
あむ（編む）*C1, tr.* to knit, crochet (*7*)
あめ（雨）rain (*GS1*)
アメリカ *p.n.* America (*GS1*); アメリカじん（アメリカ人）American (*1*)
あらう（洗う）*C1, tr.* to wash (*3*)
あらし（嵐）storm (*4*)
アラビアご（アラビア語）Arabic language (*4*)
あられ hail (*4*)
ありがとう thank you (*GS1*)
ある *C1, intr.* there is/there are (inanimate things) (*2*)
あるく（歩く）*C1, intr.* to walk (*GS1*)
アルバイト part-time job, side job (*3*)
アルバム photo album (*5*)
あれ *dem. pron.* that thing over there (*GS1*)
あんぜん(な)（安全[な]）*na-adj.* safe (*2*)

い／イ

いい *i-adj.* good (*GS1*)
いいえ no (*GS1*)
いう（言う）*C1, tr.* to say (*GS1*)
いえ（家）house (*1*)
いか（烏賊）cuttlefish (*6*)
いかが how about (*GS5*)
イギリス *p.n.* England; イギリスじん（イギリス人）English person (*1*)
いく（行く）*C1, intr.* to go (*GS3*)
いくつ how much, how old (*1*)
いくつか some, several (*5*)
いくら how much, however much… (*GS3*)
いけばな（生け花）flower arranging (*5*)
〜いじょう（〜以上）more than… (*5*)
いじわる(な)（意地悪[な]）*na-adj.* mean (*4*)
いす（椅子）chair (*GS1*)
いそがしい（忙しい）*i-adj.* busy (*2*)
いたい（痛い）*i-adj.* painful (*7*)
いたす（致す）*C1, tr., pol.* to do (*4*)
いただきます I will eat now (*said before eating*) (*6*)
いただく *C1, tr., pol.* to receive, partake (*humble*) (*4*)
いためる（炒める）*C2, tr.* to stir-fry (*6*)
イタリア *p.n.* Italy; イタリアご（イタリア語）Italian language; イタリアじん（イタリア人）Italian person (*1*)
いち（一）one (*GS2*)
いちがつ（一月）January (*1*)
いちご（苺）strawberry (*6*)
いちど（一度）once, one time (*GS1*); いちども（一度も）never (*6*)
いちにちじゅう（一日中）all day long (*GS3*)
いちば（市場）market (*7*)
いちばん（一番）number one, best, most (*4*)
いちぶ（一部）part (*7*)

いちわり（一割） ten percent (*7*)
いつ when (*GS4*)
いつか *adv.* sometime, someday; いつでも anytime (*5*); いつも always (*2*)
いつのまにか（いつの間にか） without knowing it (*5*)
いつか（五日） fifth day (*3*)
いっしょに（一緒に） *adv.* together (*GS1*)
いつつ（五つ） five (*2*)
いと（糸） thread (*7*)
いとこ cousin (*5*)
いない not to exist, not there (animate things) (*2*)
いなびかり（稲光）; いなずま（稲妻） lightning (*4*)
いぬ（犬） dog (*2*)
いふく（衣服） clothes (*7*)
いま（今） *adv.* now (*GS2*)
いみ（意味） meaning (*4*)
いも（薯） potato (*6*)
いもうと（妹） younger sister; いもうとさん（妹さん） *pol.* younger sister (*5*)
いや(な)（嫌[な]） *na-adj.* disgusting, repelling (*4*)
イヤリング earring (*7*)
いる *C1, intr.* to exist (*animate things*) (*2*)
いる（要る） *C1, tr.* to need, want (*4*)
いれる（入れる） *C2, tr.* to put something in; to turn on (a switch) (*3*)
いろ（色） color (*7*)
いろいろ(な)（色々[な]） *na-adj.* various (*2*)
インキ ink (*7*)
いんき(な)（陰気[な]） *na-adj.* gloomy (*4*)
インスタント・フード instant food (*6*)
インスタント・ラーメン instant ramen (*6*)
インスタントしょくひん（インスタント食品） instant foodstuffs (*6*)
インタビュー(する) *n.v.* interview; to interview (*6*)

う／ウ

ウイスキー whiskey (*GS2*)
ウール wool (*7*)
うえ（上） on, over, up, top (*2*)
ウエート・リフティング weight lifting (*5*)
ウエートレス waitress; ウエーター waiter (*2*)
うえの（上野） *p.n.* Ueno (*a part of Tokyo*) (*2*)
うかがう（伺う） *C1, tr., pol.* to inquire, ask; to visit; to hear (*5*)
うけつけ（受け付け） receptionist; reception (*1*)
うける（受ける） *C2, tr.* to receive (*5*)
うしろ（後ろ） behind, back (*2*)
うすい（薄い） *i-adj.* thin; light (*in color*), pale (*7*)
うそ（嘘） lie (*3*)
うた（歌） song; うたをうたう（歌を歌う） to sing a song (*5*); うたう（歌う） *C1, tr.* to sing (*3*)
うち house, (*my*) home; inside (*GS3*)
うつ（打つ） *C1, tr.* to hit (*5*)
うつくしい（美しい） *i-adj.* beautiful (*4*)
うどん udon (*thick, flat wheat noodles*) (*6*)
うまれる（生まれる） *C2, intr.* to be born (*1*)
うみ（海） ocean, sea (*4*); うみのひ（海の日） Marine Day (*3*)
うりだし（売り出し） sale (*7*)
うる（売る） *C1, tr.* to sell (*7*)
うるさい *i-adj.* noisy, annoying (*2*)
うわぎ（上着） jacket, suit coat (*7*)
うんうん *interj.* I see, I see; yes, yes (*2*)
うんてん(する)（運転[する]） *n.v.* drive; to drive (*3*)
うんどう(する)（運動[する]） *n.v.* exercise; to exercise (*GS2*)

え／エ

え（絵） picture; えをかく（絵を描く） to draw a picture (*5*)
エアロビクス aerobics (*3*)
えいが（映画） movie; えいがかん（映画館） movie theater (*GS2*)
えいぎょうじかん（営業時間） business hours (*6*)
えいご（英語） English language (*1*); えいぶん（英文） English writing (*5*)
えいよう（栄養） nutrition; えいようし（栄養士） dietician (*6*)
ええ *interj.* yes (*GS1*)
えき（駅） station (*2*)
エスエフ science fiction (*5*); エスエフえいが（エスエフ映画） science fiction movie (*2*)
エッグサラダ egg salad (*6*)
えはがき（絵はがき） picture postcard (*7*)
エプロン apron (*5*)
えび shrimp (*6*)
えらぶ（選ぶ） *C1, tr.* to choose (*5*)
エレガント(な) *na-adj.* elegant (*2*)
エレベーター elevator (*1*)
えん（円） yen (*GS3*)
えんげい（園芸） gardening (*5*)
えんげき（演劇） theatrical play (*5*)
エンジニア engineer (*1*)
えんそう(する)（演奏[する]） *n.v.* performing, playing (musical instrument); to perform, play (musical instrument) (*5*)
えんぴつ（鉛筆） pencil (*GS1*)

お／オ

お honorific prefix (*5*)
おい（甥） nephew; おいごさん *pol.* nephew (*5*)
おいしい *i-adj.* delicious, tasty (*3*)
おいとこさん *pol.* cousin (*5*)
おおあめ（大雨） heavy rain (*4*)
おおい（多い） *i-adj.* many, much, a lot (*2*)
おおきい（大きい） *i-adj.* large, big (*2*)
オーストラリア *p.n.* Australia (*GS2*)
オーバー overcoat (*4*)
オーブン oven (*6*)
おおゆき（大雪） heavy snow (*4*)
おかあさん（お母さん） *pol.* mother (*5*)
おかげさまで thanks to you (*GS1*)
おかし（お菓子） sweets (*cake and confections*) (*6*); おかしや（お菓子屋） confectionery shop (*7*)
おかしい *i-adj.* funny, strange (*2*); おかし(な) *na-adj.* funny, strange (*6*)
おかね（お金） money (*2*)
おきゃくさん（お客さん） customer, passenger, guest (*2*)

おきる（起きる） *C2, intr.* to get up, rise, wake up (*GS3*)
おく（億） hundred million (*2*)
おくさん（奥さん） *pol.* wife (*5*)
おくりがな（送り仮名） okurigana (*3*)
おくる（送る） *C1, tr.* to send; to see someone off (*7*)
おくれる（遅れる） *C2, intr.* to be late (*4*)
おこさん（お子さん） *pol.* child (*5*)
おさけ（お酒） liquor, sake (*GS1*)
おじ uncle; おじさん *pol.* uncle (*5*)
おじいさん *pol.* grandfather (*5*)
おしえる（教える） *C2, tr.* to teach (*3*)
おしゃべり(な) *na-adj.* talkative (*4*)
おじょうさん（お嬢さん） *pol.* daughter, girl (*5*)
おすすめひん（おすすめ品） recommended item (*6*)
おそい（遅い） *i-adj.* late, slow (*3*)
おそく（遅く） *adv.* late (*3*)
おそらく *adv.* perhaps, maybe (*4*)
おだやか(な) *na-adj.* calm (ocean, personality); gentle (breeze) (*4*)
おちゃ（お茶） green tea (*GS3*)
おっと（夫） husband (*5*)
おつり（お釣り） change (money) (*7*)
おてら（お寺） (Buddhist) temple (*2*)
おでん oden (*Japanese stew*) (*6*)
おと（音） sound (*7*)
おとうさん（お父さん） *pol.* father (*5*)
おとうと（弟） younger brother; おとうとさん（弟さん） *pol.* younger brother (*5*)
おとこ（男） man (*2*); おとこのかた（男の方） *pol.* man; おとこのこ（男の子） boy; おとこのひと（男の人） man (*5*)
おとす（落す） *C1, tr.* to drop (*6*)
おととい the day before yesterday (*GS4*)
おととし the year before last (*7*)
おとな（大人） adult (*6*)
おどる（踊る） *C1, tr.* to dance (*3*)
おなか stomach (*3*)
おなかがすく to get hungry (*3*)
おなじ（同じ） same (*4*)
おにいさん（お兄さん） *pol.* older brother (*5*)
おねえさん（お姉さん） *pol.* older sister (*5*)
おねがい（お願い） request (*GS5*)
おば aunt; おばさん *pol.* aunt (*5*)
おばあさん *pol.* grandmother (*5*)
おはよう good morning (*GS1*)
オフィス office (*1*)
おふろ（お風呂） bath; おふろにはいる（お風呂に入る） to take a bath (*3*)
オペラ opera (*5*)
おぼえる（憶える） *C2, tr.* to remember, memorize (*7*)
おまごさん（お孫さん） *pol.* grandchild (*5*)
おまわりさん *coll.* police officer (*2*)
おみやげ souvenir (*4*)
オムレツ omelet (*GS3*)
おもい（重い） *i-adj.* heavy (*2*)
おもう（思う） *C1, tr., intr.* to think; おもいだす（思い出す） *C1, tr.* to remember (*6*)
おもしろい（面白い） *i-adj.* interesting, fun (*2*)
おもちゃや（おもちゃ屋） toy store (*7*)
おやすみなさい good night (*GS1*)
おやつ snack (*6*)
おゆ（お湯） hot water, boiling water (*6*)
およぐ（泳ぐ） *C1, intr.* to swim (*3*)
オランダ *p.n.* Holland (*2*)
おりる（降りる） *C2, intr.* to get off, get down (*3*)
オリンピック Olympics (*5*)
オレンジ orange; オレンジいろ（オレンジ色） orange color (*6*); オレンジ・ジュース orange juice (*GS3*)
おろす *C1, tr.* to withdraw (money) (*7*)
おわる（終わる） *C1, intr.* to end, finish (*3*)
おわん（お椀） soup or rice bowl (*6*)
おんがく（音楽） music (*GS3*); おんがくかんしょう（音楽鑑賞） listening to music, music appreciation (*5*)
おんな（女） woman (*2*); おんなのかた（女の方） *pol.* woman; おんなのこ（女の子） girl (*5*); おんなのひと（女の人） woman (*2*)

か／カ

か *part.* question marker; or (*1*)
〜か（〜課） counter for lessons (*2*)
が *part.* subject marker (*1*); *conj.* but (*3*)
カーテン curtain (*GS1*)
カード card (*5*)
カーネーション carnation (*7*)
ガールフレンド girlfriend (*1*)
〜かい（〜階） counter for floors of a building (*1*); （〜回） counter for frequency (*GS3*)
かい（貝） shellfish (*6*)
かいが（絵画） painting (*5*)
かいぎ（会議） meeting, conference; かいぎをする（会議をする） to have a meeting (*5*)
がいこくご（外国語） foreign language(s) (*1*)
かいしゃ（会社） company (*3*); かいしゃいん（会社員） company worker, employee (*5*)
がいしょく(する)（外食[する]） *n.v.* dining out; to dine out (*6*)
ガイドブック guidebook (*7*)
かいもの(する)（買い物[する]） *n.v.* shopping; to shop (*GS2*)
かいわ（会話） conversation (*5*)
かう（買う） *C1, tr.* to buy (*3*)
かう（飼う） *C1, tr.* to keep, raise (a pet) (*5*)
かえす（返す） *C1, tr.* to return, give back (*7*)
かえる（帰る） *C1, intr.* to return, go back (*GS3*)
かえる（変える） *C2, tr.* to change (*3*)
かお（顔） face; かおをあらう（顔を洗う） to wash one's face (*3*)
かかく（価格） price (*7*)
かがく（化学） chemistry (*1*)
かかる *C1, intr.* to take (time, money), cost (*3*)
かぎ（鍵） key, lock; かぎをかける（鍵をかける） to lock (*7*)
かぎる（限る） *C1, tr.* to limit (*5*)
かく（書く） *C1, tr.* to write (*GS1*)
かく（描く） *C1, tr.* to draw (*5*)
かぐや（家具屋） furniture store (*7*)
がくせい（学生） student; がくせいしょう（学生証） student ID (*1*)

カクテル　cocktail　*(GS2)*
がくねん（学年）year in school; school year　*(1)*
がくぶ（学部）academic department　*(1)*
かけいぼ（家計簿）household finances book　*(7)*
〜かげつ（〜ケ月）counter for months　*(1)*
かける（掛ける）*C2, tr.* to multiply　*(GS2)*; to make a phone call　*(3)*; to put on (glasses, etc.)　*(7)*
かさ（傘）umbrella *(GS3)*; かさをさす（傘をさす）to put up an umbrella　*(7)*
かし（華氏）Fahrenheit　*(4)*
かしこまりました　certainly, at your service　*(6)*
カジュアル(な) *na-adj.* casual　*(7)*
かす（貸す）*C1, tr.* to lend; rent out　*(7)*
かぜ（風）wind; かぜがふく（風が吹く）wind blows　*(4)*
かぜ（風邪）cold, flu;（風邪をひく）to catch a cold　*(4)*
かぞく（家族）family　*(5)*
ガソリン・スタンド　gas station　*(2)*
かた（方）*pol.* person　*(1)*
カタカナ　katakana　*(GS2)*
かたくるしい（堅苦しい）*i-adj.* formal, ceremonious, stiff　*(7)*
カタログ　catalogue　*(7)*
がっか（学科）academic subject　*(2)*
がっき（楽器）musical instrument　*(5)*
がっこう（学校）school　*(GS3)*
かっこういい　*i-adj.* good-looking, stylish　*(5)*
かつどう(する)（活動[する]）*n.v.* activity; to engage in activity, be active　*(5)*
かていきょうし（家庭教師）tutor　*(3)*
かど（角）corner　*(6)*
〜かどうか　whether or not　*(7)*
かない（家内）wife　*(5)*
カナダ *p.n.* Canada　*(GS2)*; カナダじん（カナダ人）Canadian　*(1)*
かなものや（金物屋）hardware store　*(7)*
かね（金）money　*(5)*
かのじょ（彼女）*pron.* she; かのじょたち（彼女たち）*pron. pl.* they (female); かのじょら（彼女ら）*pron. pl.* they (female)　*(1)*
かばん（鞄）bag　*(GS1)*
カフェテリア　cafeteria　*(1)*
かぶる　*C1, tr.* to wear; to put on (the head)　*(7)*
かべ（壁）wall　*(GS1)*
かみ（紙）paper　*(GS1)*
かみ（髪）hair　*(3)*
かみなり（雷）thunder　*(4)*
カメラ　camera　*(GS3)*; カメラてん／カメラや（カメラ店／カメラ屋）camera shop　*(7)*
〜かもしれない　it might…; perhaps… *(conjecture)*　*(4)*
かよう（通う）*C1, intr.* to commute, frequent　*(6)*
かようび（火曜日）Tuesday　*(GS4)*
から　*part.* from; because　*(1)*
カラーしゃしん（カラー写真）color photo(graphy)　*(5)*
からい（辛い）*i-adj.* hot, spicy; salty　*(6)*
カラオケ　karaoke (singing to recorded accompaniment)　*(5)*
からだ（体）body　*(4)*
からて（空手）karate　*(5)*
かり（狩り）hunting　*(5)*
かりる（借りる）*C2, tr.* to borrow; to rent　*(7)*
かるい（軽い）*i-adj.* light, not heavy　*(2)*
カルタ　Japanese card game　*(5)*
カルチャーセンター　culture center　*(5)*
かれ（彼）*pron.* he;（彼たち）*pron. pl.* they (male);（彼ら）*pron. pl.* they (male or mixed gender)　*(1)*
カレー　curry　*(6)*; カレーライス　curry and rice　*(2)*
カレンダー　calendar　*(4)*
かわいい　*i-adj.* cute, pretty　*(5)*
かんがえ（考え）thought, idea　*(6)*;（考える）*C2, intr.* to think　*(3)*
かんきり（缶切り）can opener　*(6)*
かんこく（韓国）*p.n.* South Korea; かんこくご（韓国語）Korean language; かんこくじん（韓国人）South Korean person　*(1)*
かんじ（漢字）kanji　*(2)*
がんじつ（元日）New Year's Day　*(3)*
かんじょう(する)（勘定[する]）*n.v.* tally, calculation, check; to tally, count　*(6)*
かんたん(な)（簡単[な]）*na-adj.* simple, easy　*(5)*
かんづめ（缶詰）canned food　*(6)*
カントリーウエスタン　country and western music　*(2)*
がんねん（元年）first year (in era)　*(3)*

き／キ

き（木）tree, wood　*(2)*
きあつ（気圧）air pressure　*(4)*
きいろ（黄色）yellow　*(6)*; きいろい（黄色い）*i-adj.* yellow　*(7)*
きおん（気温）temperature　*(4)*
きかい（機械）machine　*(2)*
きがえる（着替える）*C2, tr.* to change clothes　*(3)*
きく（聞く）*C1, tr.* to listen, hear, ask　*(GS1)*
きけん(な)（危険[な]）*na-adj.* dangerous　*(5)*
きご（季語）seasonal word *(in literature)*　*(4)*
きこう（気候）climate　*(4)*
きこえる（聞こえる）*C2, intr.* can be heard　*(5)*
キス(する) *n.v.* kiss; to kiss　*(5)*
ぎせいご（擬声語）onomatopoeia　*(5)*
きせつ（季節）season　*(4)*
きた（北）north　*(2)*; きたかぜ（北風）north wind　*(4)*
ギター　guitar　*(5)*
ぎたいご（擬態語）onomatopoeia　*(5)*
きたない（汚い）*i-adj.* dirty, filthy　*(2)*
きつい　*i-adj.* tough, tight　*(2)*
きっさてん（喫茶店）coffee shop　*(2)*
キッチン　kitchen　*(6)*
きって（切手）stamp; きってをあつめる（切手を集める）to collect stamps　*(5)*
きっと　*adv.* certainly, surely　*(4)*
きぬ（絹）silk　*(7)*
きねん(する)（記念[する]）*n.v.* commemoration, memory; to commemorate　*(7)*
きのう（昨日）yesterday　*(GS3)*
きびしい（厳しい）*i-adj.* strict　*(2)*
ギフト　gift, present　*(3)*
きもの（着物）kimono　*(7)*
きゃく（客）customer, passenger　*(7)*
キャベツ　cabbage　*(7)*

キャンパス campus (*1*)
キャンプ(する) *n.v.* camping; to go camping (*4*)
ギャンブル(する) *n.v.* gamble; to gamble (*5*)
きゅう (九) nine (*GS2*); きゅうじゅう (九十) ninety (*GS5*)
きゅうか (休暇) day off; vacation; きゅうじつ (休日) day off (*3*)
きゅうしゅう (九州) *p.n.* Kyushu (*1*)
キュート(な) *na-adj.* cute (*2*)
ぎゅうにく (牛肉) beef (*6*)
ぎゅうにゅう (牛乳) milk (*6*)
きゅうり cucumber (*6*)
きょう (今日) today (*3*)
きよう(な) (器用[な]) *na-adj.* skillful (*2*)
きょういくがく (教育学) education (*academic subject*) (*1*)
きょうかい (教会) church (*2*)
きょうかしょ (教科書) textbook (*GS1*)
きょうしつ (教室) classroom (*GS1*)
きょうだい (兄弟) siblings; brothers (*5*)
きょうと (京都) *p.n.* Kyoto (*3*)
きょうよう (教養) education; culture; liberal arts (*5*); きょうようかもく (教養科目) general education subject (*1*)
きょねん (去年) last year (*3*)
きらい(な) (嫌い[な]) *na-adj.* dislike, hate (*GS2*)
きり (霧) fog (*4*)
ぎりの (義理の) in-law (*5*)
きる (着る) *C2, tr.* to wear; to put on (*torso*) (*3*)
きる (切る) *C1, tr.* to cut (*3*)
きれい(な) *na-adj.* attractive, pretty; clean (*2*)
キロ kilometer; kilogram (*5*)
きをつける (気をつける) to be careful (*4*)
きんいろ (金色) gold color (*7*)
ぎんいろ (銀色) silver color (*7*)
きんがく (金額) price; amount of money (*7*)
きんぎょ (金魚) goldfish (*5*)
ぎんこう (銀行) bank (*GS2*)
ぎんざ (銀座) *p.n.* Ginza (*1*)
きんじょ (近所) neighborhood (*2*)
きんようび (金曜日) Friday (*GS4*)
きんろうかんしゃのひ (勤労感謝の日) Labor day (*3*)

く／ク

く (九) nine (*GS2*); くがつ (九月) September (*1*)
く (区) city ward (*2*)
くすりや (薬屋) drugstore, pharmacy (*7*)
～ください please; give me (*GS2*)
くだもの (果物) fruit (*GS1*); くだものや (果物屋) fruit store (*7*)
くつ (靴) shoe(s); くつした (靴下) socks (*GS3*); くつや (靴屋) shoe store (*7*)
クッキング・オイル cooking oil (*6*)
クッキング・スクール cooking school (*6*)
くに (国) country (*1*)
くみあわせる (組み合わせる) *C2, tr.* to combine (*7*)
くも (雲) cloud (*4*)
くもり (曇り) cloudy; くもる (曇る) *C1, intr.* to become cloudy (*4*)
～くらい、～ぐらい about, approximately (*4*)
くらい (暗い) *i-adj.* dark (*4*)
クラシックおんがく (クラシック音楽) classical music (*5*)
クラス class (*GS2*); クラスメート classmate (*1*)
クラブ club (*5*)
クリーニングや (クリーニング屋) dry cleaner (*7*)
クリーム cream, lotion (*6*)
クリームいろ (クリーム色) cream color (*7*)
グリーン green (*7*)
くりかえす (繰り返す) *C1, tr.* to repeat (*GS1*)
くる (来る) *C3, intr.* to come (*3*)
くるま (車) car (*1*)
グレー gray (*7*)
グレープ grape (*GS5*)
クレジット・カード credit card (*2*)
くろ (黒) black; くろい (黒い) *i-adj.* black (*7*)
クロワッサン croissant (*7*)

け／ケ

けいぐ (敬具) sincerely (*used in a letter*) (*4*)
けいざいがく (経済学) economics (*1*)
けいさんき (計算機) calculator (*7*)
けいしょく (軽食) light meal, snack (*6*)
けいろうのひ (敬老の日) Respect-for-the-Aged Day (*3*)
ケーキ cake (*6*); ケーキや (ケーキ屋) cake shop (*7*)
ケース case (*7*)
けがわ (毛皮) fur (*7*)
けさ (今朝) this morning (*2*)
けしき (景色) scenery (*6*)
けしゴム (消しゴム) eraser (*GS1*)
けしょうひん (化粧品) cosmetics; けしょうひんてん (化粧品店) cosmetics store (*7*)
けち(な) *na-adj.* miserly (*4*)
ケチャップ ketchup (*6*)
～げつかん (～月間) counter for duration in months (*3*)
けっこう(な) (結構[な]) *na-adj.* good, satisfactory (*GS5*)
げつようび (月曜日) Monday (*GS4*)
けど *conj. coll.* although, but; けれども *conj.* although, but (*7*)
～けん (～軒) counter for houses, buildings (*2*)
げんき(な) (元気[な]) *na-adj.* healthy, energetic (*4*)
けんきゅうしつ (研究室) professor's office; research office (*1*)
げんきん (現金) cash (*7*)
けんこう(な) (健康[な]) *na-adj.* healthy (*2*)
げんごがく (言語学) linguistics (*1*)
けんこくきねんび (建国記念日) National Foundation Day (*3*)
けんどう (剣道) Japanese swordmanship, fencing (*5*)
けんぽうきねんび (憲法記念日) Constitution Day (*3*)

こ／コ

こ (子) child (*4*)
ご (碁) go (*Japanese board game*) (*5*)

ご（五） five (*GS2*); ごがつ（五月） May (*1*); ごじゅう（五十） fifty (*GS5*)
ご（御） honorific prefix (*5*)
こい（濃い） dark (*in color*) (*7*)
コインランドリー laundromat (*3*)
こう *dem.adv.* like this (*4*)
〜ごう（〜号） number… (*room, apartment*) (*2*)
こうえん（公園） park (*2*)
こうがい（郊外） suburbs (*2*)
こうがく（工学） engineering (*1*)
こうがくぶ（工学部） engineering department (*1*)
こうきゅう(な)（高級[な]） *na-adj.* first-class (*7*)
こうこく（広告） advertisement (*7*)
〜ごうしつ（〜号室） room number… (*5*)
こうずい（洪水） flood (*4*)
こうすいりょう（降水量） precipitation (*4*)
こうちゃ（紅茶） black tea (*6*)
こうばん（交番） police box (*2*)
コート coat (*4*)
コーヒー coffee (*GS2*)
コーヒーメーカー coffeemaker (*6*)
コーラ cola (*GS2*)
ごかぞく（御家族） *pol.* family (*5*)
ごきょうだい（御兄弟） *pol.* siblings; brothers (*5*)
こくせき（国籍） nationality (*1*)
こくばん（黒板） chalkboard (*GS1*); こくばんけし（黒板消し） chalkboard eraser (*GS1*)
こくみん（国民） citizen(s), the people (*3*)
ここ *dem.pron.* here (*1*)
ごご（午後） afternoon, P.M. (*GS2*)
ここのか（九日） ninth day (*3*)
ここのつ（九つ） nine (*2*)
こさめ（小雨） light rain (*4*)
ごしゅじん（御主人） *pol.* husband (*5*)
こしょう（胡椒） pepper (*6*)
ごしんせき（ご親戚） *pol.* relative (*5*)
ゴスペル gospel music (*2*)
ごぜん（午前） morning, A.M. (*GS2*); ごぜんちゅう（午前中） all morning (*3*)
こたえ（答） response, answer (*5*); こたえる（答える） *C2, intr.* to respond (*3*)
ごちそう（御馳走） treat (food) (*3*); ごちそうさまでした（御馳走様でした） *pol.* thank you for the food (*said after meal*) (*6*)
こちら *dem.pron.* here (*1*); こちらがわ（こちら側） this side (*2*)
コック cook, chef (*6*)
こっとうひん（骨董品） antique (*5*)
コットン cotton (*1*)
コップ glass, cup (*6*)
こと（琴） koto (*Japanese lute*) (*5*)
こと thing, matter, fact; nominalizer (*5*)
ことができる to be able to do…, can do… (*5*)
ことし（今年） this year (*3*)
ことば（言葉） word, language (*4*)
こども（子供） child (*5*); こどものひ（子供の日） Children's Day (*3*)
この *dem.pron.* this (*1*)
ごはん（御飯） meal, cooked rice (*3*)
ごふくや（呉服屋） kimono store (*7*)
こまる *C1, intr.* be in difficulty, have trouble (*4*)
こむ（混む） *C1, intr.* to get crowded (*5*)
こめ（米） rice (*uncooked*) (*6*); こめや（米屋） rice dealer (*7*)
コメディ comedy (*2*)
ごらく（娯楽） entertainment; pastime (*5*)
ゴルフ golf (*4*)
これ *dem.pron.* this thing (*GS1*)
これまでに until now, by now (*6*)
ころ、ごろ（頃） around, approximately (*GS3*)
ゴロゴロする *C3, intr.* to loaf, idle one's time away (*5*)
コロンビア *p.n.* Colombia (*6*)
こわれる（壊れる） *C2, intr.* to get broken (*7*)
こんげつ（今月） this month (*1*)
コンサート concert (*5*)
こんしゅう（今週） this week (*3*)
コンセント plug outlet (*6*)
コンソメ consommé (*6*)
こんど（今度） this time (*3*)
こんにちは good afternoon (*GS1*)
こんばん（今晩） tonight (*3*); こんや（今夜） tonight (*7*); こんばんは good evening (*greeting*) (*GS1*)
コンビニエンス・ストア convenience store (*7*)
コンピュータ・サイエンス computer science (*1*); コンピューターゲーム computer game (*5*)

さ／サ

さあ *interj.* Lets's begin; well, I don't know… (*2*)
サークル circle, club, activity group (*5*)
サービス(する) *n.v.* service, something given for free; to give (do) for free (*7*)
サーフィン(する) *n.v.* surfing; to surf (*6*)
〜さい（〜歳） counter for age (*1*)
さいきん（最近） *adv.* recently (*5*)
サイクリング(する) *n.v.* cycling; to cycle (*5*)
さいしょ（最初） *adv.* first (*7*)
サイズ size (*7*)
さいふ（財布） wallet (*2*)
ざいりょう（材料） ingredient (*6*)
サイン(する) *n.v.* signature; to sign (*3*)
さがす（探す） *C1, tr.* to look for (*1*)
さかな（魚） fish (*GS2*); さかなや（魚屋） fish store (*7*); さかなをつる（魚を釣る） to catch fish (*5*)
さかや（酒屋） liquor store (*7*)
さく（咲く） *C1, intr.* to bloom (*4*)
さくねん（昨年） last year (*3*)
さくら（桜） cherry blossom (*4*)
さけ（鮭） salmon (*6*)
さす *C1, tr.* to put up (*umbrella*) (*7*)
さそう（誘う） *C1, tr.* to invite (*7*)
〜さつ（〜冊） counter for books, notes (*2*)
サッカー soccer (*5*)
ざっし（雑誌） magazine (*GS3*)
さて *conj.* by the way; well… (*4*)
さとう（砂糖） sugar (*6*)
さどう（茶道） tea ceremony (*5*)
さびしい（寂しい） *i-adj.* lonely (*7*)
〜さま（〜様） *pol.* Mr., Mrs., Ms., Miss, etc. (*4*)

さみだれ（五月雨） early summer rain *(4)*
さむい（寒い） *i-adj.* cold *(GS4)*
さよ(う)なら good-bye *(GS1)*
さら（皿） plate, dish *(6)*
サラダ salad *(GS3)*; サラダドレッシング salad dressing *(6)*
サラリーマン salaried worker, white-collar worker *(5)*
さわる（触る） *C1, intr.* to touch *(3)*
〜さん Mr., Mrs. Ms., Miss, etc. *(GS1)*
さん（三） three *(GS2)*
さんがつ（三月） March *(1)*
サングラス sunglasses *(7)*
さんじゅう（三十） thirty *(GS5)*
サンダル sandal *(7)*
サンドイッチ sandwich *(6)*
ざんねん(な)（残念[な]） *na-adj.* sorry; too bad *(GS4)*
さんぽ(する)（散歩[する]） *n.v.* walk, stroll; to take a walk/stroll *(GS2)*

し／シ

し（四） four *(GS2)*; しがつ（四月） April *(1)*
し（市） city *(2)*
〜し and (*emphatic*) *(7)*
〜じ（〜時） ...o'clock *(GS2)*
しあい(する)（試合[する]） *n.v.* game, match *(5)*
しいたけ shiitake mushroom *(6)*
シーディー CD (compact disk) *(7)*
ジーパン jeans; ジーンズ jeans *(7)*
シーフード seafood *(6)*
ジェイアール JR (Japan Railways) *(2)*
シェフ chef *(6)*
しお（塩） salt; しおからい（塩辛い） *i-adj.* salty *(6)*
〜しか only (*with negative*) *(7)*
しかし *conj.* but, however *(3)*
じかん（時間） time; counter for hours *(2)*
じかんわり（時間割） timetable *(1)*
しき（四季） four seasons *(4)*
しぐれ（時雨） drizzle *(4)*
しけん(する)（試験[する]） *n.v.* examination; to examine *(3)*
じこしょうかい(する)（自己紹介[する]） *n.v.* self-introduction; to introduce oneself *(1)*
しごと(する)（仕事[する]） *n.v.* job, work; to work *(GS3)*
ししゅう(する)（刺繍[する]） *n.v.* embroidery; to do embroidery *(5)*
じしょ（辞書） dictionary *(GS1)*
しずか(な)（静か[な]） *na-adj.* quiet, peaceful *(2)*
した（下） below, under, down *(2)*
したぎ（下着） underwear *(7)*
しち（七） seven *(GS2)*; しちがつ（七月） July *(1)*; しちじゅう（七十） seventy *(GS5)*
しちゃくしつ（試着室） fitting room *(7)*
シチュー stew *(5)*
じっけんしつ（実験室） laboratory *(1)*
しつど（湿度） humidity *(4)*
しっと(する)（嫉妬[する]） *n.v.* envy, jealousy; to be jealous *(7)*
しつもん(する)（質問[する]） *n.v.* question; to ask a question *(GS1)*
しつれい(する)（失礼[する]） *n.v.* discourtesy; be discourteous excuse oneself *(GS1)*
じてんしゃ（自転車） bicycle *(2)*
シトシト drizzle (*weather*) *(4)*
しなぎれ（品切れ） out of stock, sold out *(7)*
しぬ（死ぬ） *C1, intr.* to die *(4)*
しばらく it's been a long time (*greeting*); *adv.* a little while *(GS1)*
しぶい（渋い） *i-adj.* astringent *(6)*
じぶん（自分） oneself, self; （自分で） by oneself *(6)*
しま（縞） stripe *(7)*
〜しまう *C1, tr.* to finish... *(6)*
じみ(な)（地味[な]） *na-adj.* quiet (*in color*), plain *(7)*
ジム gym *(5)*
じむしつ（事務室） administration office *(1)*
しめる（閉める） *C2, tr.* to close (*door, window, etc.*) *(3)*
しも（霜） frost *(4)*
じゃあ *interj.* well, then... *(GS1)*
シャープペンシル mechanical pencil *(GS1)*
〜じゃありません *coll.* negative of です *(1)*
しゃかいがく（社会学） sociology *(1)*
じゃがいも potato *(6)*
しゃげき(する)（射撃[する]） *n.v.* shooting; to shoot *(5)*
ジャケット jacket *(7)*
しゃしん（写真） photography, photograph *(1)*; しゃしんをとる（写真を撮る） to take a photo *(5)*
ジャズ jazz *(GS2)*
シャツ shirt *(7)*
しゃみせん（三味線） shamisen (*Japanese musical instrument*) *(5)*
シャワー shower; シャワーをあびる（シャワーを浴びる） to take a shower *(3)*
シャンペン champagne *(6)*
じゅう（十） ten *(GS2)*; じゅうがつ（十月） October *(1)*; じゅうまん（十万） hundred thousand *(2)*
じゅういちがつ（十一月） November *(1)*; じゅういちにち（十一日） eleventh day *(3)*
〜しゅうかん（〜週間） counter for weeks *(3)*
じゅうごにち（十五日） fifteenth day *(3)*
じゅうさんにち（十三日） thirteenth day *(3)*
じゅうしょ（住所） address *(1)*
ジュース juice *(GS2)*
じゅうどう（柔道） judo *(5)*
じゅうにがつ（十二月） December *(1)*; じゅうににち（十二日） twelfth day *(3)*
しゅうぶんのひ（秋分の日） Autumnal Equinox Day *(3)*
しゅうまつ（週末） weekend *(3)*
じゅうよっか（十四日） fourteenth day *(3)*
じゅぎょうりょう（授業料） tuition *(5)*
しゅくじつ（祝日） national holiday *(3)*
しゅくだい（宿題） homework *(4)*
しゅげい（手芸） handicrafts *(5)*
しゅじん（主人） husband; shop owner *(5)*
しゅっしん（出身） hometown; origin *(1)*

しゅみ（趣味） hobby (*5*)
しゅもく（種目） event; item (*5*)
しゅるい（種類） kind, type (*6*)
じゅんい（順位） rank, ranking (*5*)
じゅんび（する）（準備［する］） *n.v.* preparation; to prepare (*3*)
しゅんぶんのひ（春分の日） Vernal Equinox Day (*3*)
しょうかい（する）（紹介［する］） *n.v.* introduction; to introduce (*1*)
しょうぎ（将棋） shogi (*Japanese board game*) (*5*)
しょうしゃ（商社） trading company (*5*)
じょうず（な）（上手［な］） *na-adj.* good at, skilled at (*5*); じょうずに（上手に） *adv.* skillfully (*4*)
じょうだん（冗談） joke (*7*)
しょうてんがい（商店街） shopping mall, shopping street (*7*)
じょうねつ（情熱） passion (*7*)
じょうば（乗馬） horseback riding (*5*)
しょうひん（商品） goods, merchandise (*7*)
じょうぶ（な）（丈夫［な］） *na-adj.* robust, strong, tough (*7*)
しょうゆ（醤油） soy sauce (*6*)
しょうわ（昭和） Showa era (*3*)
ショーウインドー show window (*6*)
ショートパンツ shorts (*4*)
ジョギング（する） *n.v.* jogging; to jog (*5*)
しょくじ（する）（食事［する］） *n.v.* meal; to eat a meal (*6*); しょくどう（食堂） dining hall; informal restaurant (*2*); しょくりょうひん（食料品） foodstuffs (*6*); しょくりょうひんてん（食料品店） grocery store (*7*)
じょしがくせい（女子学生） female student (*5*)
じょせい（女性） woman (*5*)
ショッピング（する） *n.v.* shopping; to shop (*7*)
しょどう（書道） brush calligraphy (*5*)
しらせ（知らせ） notice, announcement (*5*)
しる（知る） *C1, tr.* to know (*3*)
しろ（白） white (*7*);（白い） *i-adj.* white (*2*)
しろくろしゃしん（白黒写真） black-and-white photo(graphy) (*5*)
しろワイン（白ワイン） white wine (*5*)
シンガポール *p.n.* Singapore; シンガポールじん（シンガポール人） Singaporean (*1*)
しんかんせん（新幹線） bullet train (*3*)
じんこう（人口） population (*2*)
じんじゃ（神社） Shinto shrine (*2*)
しんじる（信じる） *C2, tr.* to believe, trust (*3*)
しんせき（親戚） relative (*5*)
しんせつ（な）（親切［な］） kind (*2*)
シンプル（な） *na-adj.* simple (*7*)
しんぶん（新聞） newspaper (*GS3*)
じんるいがく（人類学） anthropology (*1*)

す／ス

す（酢） vinegar (*6*)
すいえい（水泳） swimming (*GS2*)
すいさいが（水彩画） watercolor (*5*)
すいようび（水曜日） Wednesday (*GS4*)
すうがく（数学） mathematics (*1*)
スーパー supermarket (*2*)
スープ soup (*GS3*)
スカート skirt (*7*)
すき（な）（好き［な］） *na-adj.* like, favor (*2*)
スキー ski (*GS2*); スキーをする to ski (*4*)
すきやき sukiyaki (*GS1*)
〜すぎる（〜過ぎる） *C2, intr.* to do…excessively (*with conjunctive form of verbs*) (*6*)
すぐ（に） *adv.* immediately (*6*)
すくない（少ない） *i-adj.* few, little (*2*);（少なく） *adv.* few, little (*6*)
スケート skate; スケートをする to skate (*4*)
スケジュール schedule (*3*)
すごい *i-adj.* awesome; terrible; very (*5*)
すこし（少し） *adv.* a little, a bit (*3*)
すごす（過ごす） *C1, tr.* to spend, pass (*time*) (*5*)
すし（寿司） sushi (*GS1*); すしや（寿司屋） sushi restaurant (*6*)
すずしい（涼しい） *i-adj.* cool (*GS4*)
スチュワーデス stewardess (*5*)
すっかり *adv.* totally (*7*)
ずっと *adv.* all the way (*4*)
すっぱい（酸っぱい） *i-adj.* sour (*6*)
ステーキ steak (*GS3*)
ステレオ stereo (*5*)
ストーブ space heater (*4*)
ストッキング stockings (*7*)
ストライプ stripe (*5*)
ストロベリー strawberry (*6*)
スナック snack (*6*)
スニーカー sneaker (*4*)
スノーブーツ snow boots (*7*)
スパゲッティー spaghetti (*6*)
スピーチ speech (*4*)
スプーン spoon (*6*)
スペイン *p.n.* Spain; スペインご（スペイン語） Spanish language; スペインじん（スペイン人） Spaniard (*1*)
すべて（全て） all (*5*)
スポーツ sports (*GS2*); スポーツ・カー sports car; スポーツウエア sportswear (*7*); スポーツせんしゅ athlete (*5*)
ズボン trousers (*7*)
スマート（な） *na-adj.* slender (*person*) (*2*)
すまい（住まい） housing, residence (*1*)
すみえ（墨絵） India ink painting (*5*)
すみません excuse me, I'm sorry (*GS1*)
すむ（住む） *C1, intr.* to reside, live (*3*)
すもう（相撲） sumo wrestling (*5*)
スリッパ slipper (*7*)
する *C3, tr.* to do (*GS3*)

せ／セ

〜せい（〜製） made in… (*7*)
せいきゅうしょ（請求書） bill, invoice (*7*)
せいじがく（政治学） political science (*1*)
せいじんのひ（成人の日） Coming-of-Age Day (*3*)
せいねんがっぴ（生年月日） birth date (*1*)

せいふく（制服） uniform (7)
せいぶつがく（生物学） biology (*1*)
セーター sweater (*GS3*)
セール bargain sale (7)
せっし（摂氏） centigrade (4)
せびろ（背広） suit (7)
セブンイレブン（7-イレブン） *p.n.* 7-Eleven store (2)
せまい（狭い） *i-adj.* narrow, not spacious (2)
ゼロ zero (*GS2*)
せわ(する)（世話[する]） *n.v.* care; to take care of, help (5)
せん（千） thousand (*GS3*)
ぜん〜（全〜） all; ぜんてん（全店） all store(s); ぜんぴん（全品） all items (7); ぜんぶ（全部） all (5); ぜんぶで（全部で） *adv.* in total (2)
せんげつ（先月） last month (3)
せんこう(する)（専攻[する]） *n.v.* academic major; major in (*1*)
ぜんさい（前菜） appetizer (6)
せんしゅう（先週） last week; せんせんしゅう（先々週） the week before last (*GS4*)
せんせい（先生） teacher, professor (*GS1*)
ぜんぜん（全然） not at all (*with negative*) (3)
せんたく(する)（洗濯[する]） *n.v.* laundry; to do laundry (3)
せんぬき（栓抜き） bottle opener (6)
せんもんかもく（専門科目） specialized subject (*1*)
せんもんてん（専門店） specialty store (7)

そ／ソ

そう *dem. adv.* like that; that way (*GS1*)
そうです that's right, that's so (*GS1*)
そうですね well, let me see (*GS2*)
そうじ(する)（掃除[する]） *n.v.* cleaning; to clean (*house, room*) (3)
〜そうだ they say… (*with plain form of verb*) (7)
ソース Worcestershire-type sauce (6)
ソーセージ sausage (6)
〜そく（〜足） counter for shoes, socks (2)
そこ、そちら *dem. pron.* there (*1*)
そして *conj.* and then (3)
そと（外） outside (2)
その *dem. adj.* that thing (*1*)
そのあと（その後） after that (3)
そば near (2)
そば（蕎麦） soba (*buckwheat noodles*); そばや（蕎麦屋） soba restaurant (6)
そふ（祖父） grandfather (5)
ソファー sofa, couch (7)
ソフトウエア software (3)
そぼ（祖母） grandmother (5)
そら（空） sky (4)
そる（剃る） *C1, tr.* to shave (3)
それ *dem. pron* that (*1*)
それから and then (3)
それで therefore; then; and so (3)
そんな *dem. adj.* that kind of … (4)
そんなに *dem. adv.* that much, that many (5)

た／タ

〜だ to be (3)
ダークブルー dark blue (7)
〜たい *i-adj.* to want to do … (*with conjunctive form of verb*) (6)
〜だい（〜台） counter for machines (2)
たいいくかん（体育館） gym (*1*)
たいいくのひ（体育の日） Health-Sports Day (3)
ダイエット diet (6)
だいがく（大学） university; だいがくせい（大学生） university student; だいがくいんせい（大学院生） graduate student (*1*)
だいきらい(な)（大嫌い[な]） *na-adj.* hated, disliked intensely (2)
たいしょう（大正） Taisho era (3)
だいじょうぶ(な)（大丈夫[な]） *na-adj.* OK, good enough (*GS4*)
だいすき(な)（大好き[な]） *na-adj.* favorite, well-liked (2)
たいそう（体操） gymnastics (5)
だいどころ（台所） kitchen (6)
ダイバー diver (7); ダイビング(する) *n.v.* diving; to dive (5)
タイプ(する) *n.v.* typing; to type (6)
たいふう（台風） typhoon (4)
たいへん(な)（大変[な]） *na-adj.* terrible, awful, impressive (4)
ダイヤ diamond (6)
たいよう（太陽） sun (4)
たいわん（台湾） *p.n.* Taiwan; たいわんじん（台湾人） Taiwanese person (*1*)
たかい（高い） *i-adj.* expensive, high (2)
だから *conj.* therefore, and so (4)
〜たがる *C1, intr.* to want to do… (*with conjunctive form of verb*) (6)
たくさん much, many, a lot (2)
タクシー taxi (2)
〜だけ only… (7)
たこ octopus (6)
たす（足す） *C1, tr.* to add (*GS2*)
だす（出す） *C1, tr.* to take out, put out; to mail, send (*GS1*)
〜たち（〜達） *pl.* suffix for humans (*1*)
たつ（立つ） *C1, intr.* to stand (*GS1*)
たっきゅう（卓球） table tennis, ping pong (5)
たてもの（建物） building (2)
たてる *C2, tr.* to set up (a plan), build (7)
たのしい（楽しい） *i-adj.* fun (2); たのしむ（楽しむ） *C1, tr.* to enjoy (5)
たのむ（頼む） *C1, tr.* to request, ask (6)
タフ(な) *na-adj.* strong, tough (2)
たぶん（多分） *adv.* perhaps, probably (4)
たべる（食べる） *C2, tr.* to eat (*GS3*); たべもの（食べ物） food; たべものや（食べ物屋） food store (6)
たまご（卵） egg; たまごりょうり（卵料理） egg dish (6)
たまに *adv.* once in a while (3)
たまねぎ（玉葱） onion (6)

ダメ(な) *na-adj.* not good (5)
ためし(試し) test, trial run (6); ためす(試す) *C1, tr.* to try (7)
〜たら if, when (7)
だれ(誰) who (*GS4*); だれか(誰か) someone; だれでも(誰でも) anyone; だれも everyone, no one (5)
〜だろう probably… (*with plain form of verb*) (4)
だんしがくせい(男子学生) male student (5)
たんじょうび(誕生日) birthday (3)
ダンス dance; to dance (5)
だんせい(男性) man (5)

ち/チ

ちいさい(小さい) *i-adj.* small (2)
チーズ cheese; チーズケーキ cheesecake (6); チーズバーガー cheeseburger (*GS5*)
チェス chess (5)
チェック check (*pattern*) (7)
ちか(地下) underground; ちかい(地階) underground floor (*GS3*); ちかてつ(地下鉄) subway (2)
ちかい(近い) *i-adj.* near, close (*GS3*); (近く) *adv.* near, close (3)
ちがう(違う) *C1, intr.* to differ (*GS1*)
チキン・ヌードル chicken noodle (6)
チケット ticket (5)
ちず(地図) map (2)
ちち(父) father (5)
ちゃいろ(茶色) brown; ちゃいろい(茶色い) *i-adj.* brown (7)
〜ちゃく(〜着) counter for jackets, clothes (2)
ちゃわん(茶碗) teacup, rice bowl (6)
ちゅうかりょうり(中華料理) Chinese food (6)
ちゅうごく(中国) *p.n.* China; ちゅうごくご(中国語) Chinese language; ちゅうごくじん(中国人) Chinese person; ちゅうごくりょうり(中国料理) Chinese dish (1)
ちゅうしゃじょう(駐車場) parking lot (2)
ちゅうしょく(昼食) lunch (6)
ちゅうもん(する)(注文[する]) *n.v.* order; to order (7)
チューリップ tulip (7)
ちょう(兆) trillion (2)
ちょうさ(する)(調査[する]) *n.v.* investigation, survey; to investigate, take a poll (5)
ちょうじょ(長女) oldest daughter (5)
ちょうしょく(朝食) breakfast (6)
ちょうなん(長男) oldest son (5)
ちょうみりょう(調味料) seasoning (6)
〜ちょうめ(〜丁目) district number in address (2)
チョーク chalk (*GS1*)
ちょきん(する)(貯金[する]) *n.v.* deposit (*money*), savings; to deposit, save (7)
チョコレート chocolate (*GS5*)
ちょっと *adv.* a little, a bit (*GS1*)

つ/ツ

ついたち(一日) first of the month (3)
つかう(使う) *C1, tr.* to use (*GS1*)
つかれる(疲れる) *C2, intr.* to become tired (3)
つぎ(の)(次[の]) next (*GS1*)
つくえ(机) desk (*GS1*)
つくる(作る) *C1, tr.* to make; to cook (*GS1*)
つくろう(繕う) *C1, tr.* to mend (7)
つけもの(漬物) pickle (6)
つける *C2, tr.* to wear, put on (7)
つたえる(伝える) *C2, tr.* to tell, convey (6)
つづく(続く) *C1, intr.* to continue (4)
つつむ(包む) *C1, tr.* to wrap; つつみがみ(包み紙) wrapping paper (7)
ツナサラダ tuna salad (6)
つま(妻) wife (5)
つまらない *i-adj.* boring (2)
〜つもりだ to intend to do… (*with nonpast, plain form of verb*) (6)
つゆ(梅雨) rainy season (*June and July*) (4)
つゆ(露) dew (4)
つよい(強い) *i-adj.* strong, powerful (4)
つり(釣り) fishing (4)
つれていく(連れていく) to take, accompany (2)

て/テ

で *part.* with; at; by means of (2)
〜ていく to do and leave (6)
〜ている to be …ing (4)
〜てください please do… (2)
〜てしまう to complete… (6)
Tシャツ T-shirt (5)
ディスコ disco (3)
ていりゅうじょ(停留所) bus stop (2)
テークアウト take out food (6)
デート(する) *n.v.* date; to go on a date (*GS2*)
テープ tape (*GS1*); テープ・レコーダー tape recorder (7)
テーブル table (*GS1*)
でかける(出かける) *C2, intr.* to go out, leave (3)
てがみ(手紙) letter (*GS3*)
できる(出来る) *C2, intr.* to be able to, can; to be completed (5)
でございます polite form of です (7)
デザート dessert (6)
デザイン(する) *n.v.* design; to design; デザイナー designer; デザイナー・ブランド designer brand (7)
てじな(手品) magic, sleight of hand (5)
でしょう *pol.* probably (4)
です *pol.* to be (1)
てつがく(哲学) philosophy (1)
てつだう(手伝う) *C1, tr.* to help, assist (3)
テニス tennis (*GS2*)
では *conj.* then (*GS1*)
ではありません negative of です (1)
デパート department store (*GS2*)
てぶくろ(手袋) glove(s) (7)
〜てみる to try to do… (6)
でも *conj.* but (4)
でる(出る) *C2, intr.* to leave, go out (3)
テレビ TV (*GS3*); テレビゲーム video game (5)
てんいん(店員) store clerk (7)

てんき（天気） weather; てんきず（天気図） weather map; てんきよほう（天気予報） weather forecast (*4*)
でんき（電気） electric light, electricity (*GS1*); でんきてん（電気店） electric appliance store (*7*)
でんごん（する）（伝言［する］） *n.v.* message; to leave a message (*3*)
でんしゃ（電車） electric train (*2*)
てんじょう（天井） ceiling (*GS1*)
てんのう（天皇） emperor; てんのうたんじょうび（天皇誕生日） emperor's birthday (*3*)
てんぷら（天麩羅） tempura; てんぷらや（天麩羅屋） tempura restaurant (*6*)
でんわ（する）（電話［する］） *n.v.* telephone; to make a phone call (*GS2*); でんわばんごう（電話番号） telephone number (*1*)

と／ト

と *part.* with; and (*GS3*)
と quotation marker (*6*)
〜ど（〜度） counter for temperature (*4*); counter for frequency (*2*)
ドア door (*GS1*)
〜という（〜と言う） to say that...; (A) という (B) (B) called (A) (*6*)
ドイツ *p.n.* Germany; ドイツご（ドイツ語） German language; ドイツじん（ドイツ人） German person (*1*)
トイレ rest room, bathroom, toilet (*2*)
〜とう（〜頭） counter for large animals (*2*)
どう *dem. adv.* how (*1*)
どうか somehow (*5*)
とうきょう（東京） *p.n.* Tokyo (*3*)
どうして how; why (*1*)
どうぞ please, go ahead (*GS1*)
とうふ（豆腐） tofu (*bean curd*) (*6*)
とうめい（な）（透明［な］） *na-adj.* transparent (*7*)
どうも *inf.* indeed; thanks (*GS1*)
とお（十） ten (*2*); とおか（十日） tenth day (*3*)
とおい（遠い） *i-adj.* far away (*GS3*)
〜とおもう（〜と思う） to think that ... (*6*)
とおり（通り） avenue (*2*)
とかす *C1, tr.* to comb (*3*)
〜とき（〜時） when ... (*7*)
ときどき（時々） *adv.* sometimes (*3*)
とくい（な）（得意［な］） *na-adj.* good at and like; forte (*5*)
とくぎ（特技） special talent (*5*)
どくしょ（する）（読書［する］） *n.v.* reading books; to read (*5*)
どくしん（独身） single, unmarried person (*5*)
とくに（特に） *adv.* especially (*GS2*)
とけい（時計） clock, watch (*GS3*); とけいてん／とけいや（時計店／時計屋） watch shop (*7*)
どこ *dem. pron.* where (*GS3*)
どこか somewhere (*5*)
どこでも anywhere, everywhere (*5*)
どこも everywhere; nowhere (*with negative*) (*5*)
とこや（床屋） barbershop (*5*)
とし（年） age (*1*)
どしゃぶり（土砂降り） downpour (*of rain*) (*4*)
としょかん（図書館） library (*1*)
としより（年寄） aged people (*5*)
とじる（閉じる） *C2, tr.* to close (*box, drawer, etc.*) (*GS1*)
どちら *pol.* where, which (of the two) (*GS4*); どちらか either; どちらでも whichever; (*5*) どちらのほう which one; (*4*) どちらも both; neither (*with negative*) (*5*)
どっち *coll.* which one (*1*)
とても *adv.* very (*GS3*)
どなた *pol.* who (*1*); どなたか *pol.* someone; どなたでも *pol.* anyone; どなたも *pol.* no one (*with negative*) (*5*)
となり（隣） next to; next-door (*2*)
どの *dem. adj.* which (of more than two) (*1*)
とぶ（飛ぶ） *C1, intr.* to fly (*3*)
とほ（徒歩） by walking, on foot (*2*)
トマト tomato (*6*)
ともだち（友だち） friend (*GS3*)
どようび（土曜日） Saturday (*GS4*)
ドライ・クリーニング dry cleaning (*7*)
ドライブ（する） *n.v.* drive; to drive (*3*)
トランプ card game (*5*)
とり（鳥） bird (*2*); とりにく（鳥肉） chicken meat (*6*)
とる（取る） *C1, tr.* to take (*5*)
とる（撮る） *C1, tr.* to take (a photo) (*7*)
どれ *dem. adj.* which thing (of more than two) (*GS4*); どれか one of them; どれでも any of them; どれも all of them; none of them (*5*)
トレードマーク trademark (*7*)
トレーナー sweatshirt (*7*)
ドレス dress (*7*)
どんな *dem. adj.* what kind (*GS4*)

な／ナ

ない *i-adj.* not there, to not exist (*2*)
ナイフ knife (*3*)
ナイロン nylon (*7*)
なか（中） in, inside (*2*)
ながい（長い） *i-adj.* long (*2*)
ながそで（長袖） long sleeves; long-sleeved (*7*)
なかなか *adv.* rather, quite (*5*)
〜ながら while ...ing (*with conjunctive form of verb*) (*6*)
なく（泣く） *C1, intr.* to cry (*3*)
なげる（投げる） *C2, tr.* to throw (*5*)
なし（梨） pear (*6*)
なぜ why (*1*); なぜか somehow (*5*)
なつ（夏） summer (*4*); なつやすみ（夏休み） summer vacation (*6*)
など and so on (*6*)
なな（七） seven (*GS2*); ななじゅう（七十） seventy (*GS5*); ななつ（七つ） seven (*2*); なのか（七日） seventh day (*3*)
なに、なん（何） what (*GS4*); なにいろ（何色） what color (*1*); なにか（何か） something (*5*); なにご（何語） what language; なにじん（何人）

what nationality (*1*); なにも（何も） anything, nothing (*3*); なんかい（何階） how many floors (*GS2*); なんがつ（何月） what month; なんさい（何歳） how old (*1*); なんじ（何時） what time (*GS2*); なんじかん（何時間） how many hours (*3*); なんでも（何でも） anything (*5*); なんど（何度） how many degrees (*4*); なんとか（何とか） in some way, somehow (*5*); なんども（何度も） many times (*6*); なんにち（何日） what day, how many days; なんねん（何年） what year, how many years (*3*); なんねんせい（何年生） what year in school (*1*); なんぷん（何分） what minute, how many minutes (*3*); なんようび（何曜日） what day of the week (*GS4*)
ナプキン napkin (*6*)
なべ（鍋） pan, pot (*6*)
なま(の)（生[の]） raw (*6*)
なまえ（名前） name (*GS1*)
ならう（習う） *C1, tr.* to learn (*6*)
なる *C1, intr.* to become, turn into (*4*)
なるほど I see; of course (*4*)

に／ニ

に（二） two (*GS2*); にがつ（二月） February (*1*); にじゅう（二十） twenty (*GS2*); にじゅうよっか（二十四日） twenty-fourth day (*3*)
に *part.* (indirect object) at, in (*GS3*)
にあう（似合う） *C1, intr.* to be suited, fit (*5*)
におい（臭い） smell (*6*)
にがい（苦い） *i-adj.* bitter (*6*)
にがて(な)（苦手[な]） *na-adj.* clumsy at and dislike; weak point (*5*)
にぎやか(な) *na-adj.* lively (*2*)
にく（肉） meat (*2*); にくや（肉屋） butcher shop (*7*)
〜にくい *i-adj.* difficult to… (*with conjunctive form of verb*) (*7*)
にし（西） west (*4*)
〜にする to decide on… (*6*)
にちじょうせいかつ（日常生活） everyday life (*3*)
にちようび（日曜日） Sunday (*GS4*)
にほん（日本） Japan; にほんご（日本語） Japanese language (*GS1*); にほんしゅ（日本酒） Japanese saké (*6*); にほんじん（日本人） Japanese person (*1*); にほんぶよう（日本舞踊） Japanese traditional dance (*5*)
〜によると according to… (*7*)
ニュース news (*GS3*)
にゅうもん(する)（入門[する]） *n.v.* entry level, introduction; to begin (*5*)
にる（煮る） *C2, tr.* to boil, stew (*6*)
にわかあめ（にわか雨） rain shower (*4*)
〜にん（〜人） counter for people (*2*)
にんき（人気） popularity (*5*)
にんじん（人参） carrot (*6*)

ぬ／ヌ

ぬう（縫う） *C1, tr.* to sew (*7*)
ぬぐ（脱ぐ） *C1, tr.* to take off clothes (*3*)

ね／ネ

ね *part.* sentence-final emphatic particle (*GS1*)
ねぎる（値切る） *C1, tr.* to bargain, haggle over price (*7*)
ネクタイ necktie (*7*)
ネグリジェ negligee (*7*)
ねこ（猫） cat (*5*)
ねだん（値段） price (*7*)
ネックレス necklace (*7*)
ねぼう(する)（寝坊[する]） *n.v.* oversleeping; to oversleep (*4*)
ねむる（眠る） *C1, intr.* to sleep (*3*)
ねる（寝る） *C1, intr.* to sleep, go to bed (*GS3*)
ねんごう（年号） era (*3*)
〜ねんせい（〜年生） …year in school (*1*)
〜ねんまえに（〜年前に） …years before (*6*)
ねんれい（年齢） age (*1*)

の／ノ

の *part.* possessive marker (*GS2*); one (*pronoun*) (*7*); nominalizer (*5*)
ノート notebook (*GS1*)
のせる *C2, tr.* to put on, place (*6*)
〜のために for the sake of, for the purpose of (*6*)
〜ので because (*4*)
のどがかわく（咽が乾く） to be thirsty (*3*)
〜のはなしでは（の話では） according to… (*7*)
のべる（述べる） *C2, tr.* to state (*6*)
のむ（飲む） *C1, tr.* to drink (*GS3*); のみほうだい（飲み放題） all you can drink (*6*); のみもの（飲み物） beverage (*GS3*)
のり（海苔） seaweed (*1*)
のる（乗る） *C1, intr.* to ride (*3*)

は／ハ

は *part.* topic marker (*pronounced わ*) (*1*)
は（歯） tooth; はをみがく（歯を磨く） to brush teeth (*3*)
バーゲンセール bargain sale (*7*)
バースデー・ケーキ birthday cake (*4*); バースデー・プレゼント birthday gift (*3*)
パーティー party (*GS2*)
バーベキュー BBQ (*6*)
パール pearl (*7*)
はい *interj.* yes (*GS1*)
〜はい（〜杯） counter for glass- or cupfuls (*2*)
〜ばい（〜倍） counter for multiples (*2*)
はいいろ（灰色） gray (*7*)
バイオリン violin (*5*)
ハイキング(する) *n.v.* hiking; to hike (*4*)
バイキングりょうり（バイキング料理） all you can eat (*6*)
はいけい（拝啓） Dear… (*used at the beginning of a letter*) (*4*)
はいたつ(する)（配達[する]） *n.v.* delivery; to deliver (*7*)
パイナップル pineapple (*6*)
ハイヒール high heels (*7*)

はいる（入る） *C1, intr.* to enter (*3*)
はく *C1, tr.* to wear; to put on (*feet or legs*) (*4*)
はこ（箱） box (*2*)
はさみ（鋏） scissors (*7*)
はし（箸） chopsticks (*6*)
はじ edge (*2*)
はじまる（始まる） *C1, intr.* to start (*3*)
はじめに（初めに） first; first of all (*6*)
はじめまして nice meeting you (*GS1*)
はじめる（始める） *C2, tr.* to start (*GS1*)
パジャマ pajamas (*7*)
ばしょ（場所） place (*5*)
はしる（走る） *C1, intr.* to run (*GS1*)
バス bus (*2*)
バスケットボール basketball (*5*)
はずす *C1, tr.* to take off (*glasses, etc.*) (*7*)
パスタ pasta (*6*)
バスてい（バス停） bus stop (*2*)
バター butter (*6*)
はたち（二十歳） twenty years old (*1*)
はたらく（働く） *C1, intr.* to work (*3*)
はち（八） eight (*GS2*); はちがつ（八月） August (*1*); はちじゅう（八十） eighty (*GS5*)
パチンコ pachinko (*Japanese pinball*) (*5*)
はつおん(する)（発音[する]） *n.v.* pronunciation; to pronounce (*4*)
はつか（二十日） twentieth day (*3*)
はで(な)（派手[な]） *na-adj.* gaudy; bright; loud (*in color*) (*2*)
バドミントン badminton (*5*)
はな（花） flower (*4*)
はなし（話） story; talk; speech (*2*)
はなす（話す） *C1, tr.* to speak, tell, talk (*GS3*)
バナナ banana (*2*)
はなみ（花見） (cherry) blossom viewing (*4*)
はなや（花屋） flower shop (*7*)
バニラ vanilla (*GS5*)
はは（母） mother (*5*); ははのひ（母の日） Mother's Day (*7*)
パパ papa (*5*)
パパイア papaya (*6*)
ハム ham (*6*)
はめる *C2, tr.* to wear, put on (*rings, etc.*) (*7*)
はやい（早い／速い） *i-adj.* early, fast, quickly (*GS3*); （早く／速く） *adv.* early, fast, quickly (*4*)
はらう（払う） *C1, tr.* to pay (*7*)
バランス balance (*6*)
はり（針） needle (*7*)
はる（春） spring (*4*); はるがっき（春学期） spring quarter, spring semester (*5*); はるさめ（春雨） spring rain (*4*)
はれ（晴れ） clear skies, sunny weather; はれる（晴れる） *C2, intr.* to get sunny (*4*)
バレーボール volleyball (*5*)
はん（半） thirty minutes; half (*GS2*); はんぶん（半分） half (*7*)
～ばん（～番） number... (*GS2*); ～ばんめ（～番目） number... (*5*)
パン bread (*6*); パンや（パン屋） bakery (*7*)
はんがく（半額） half price (*7*)
ハンカチ handkerchief (*7*)
ばんぐみ（番組） program (*TV, radio*) (*5*)
ばんごう（番号） number (*GS2*)
ばんごはん（晩ごはん） dinner, supper (*GS2*)
ハンサム(な) *na-adj.* handsome (*2*)
はんそで（半袖） short sleeves; short-sleeved (*7*)
ばんち（番地） number (*in address*) (*2*)
パンツ briefs (*7*)
パンティー panties; パンティーストッキング pantyhose (*7*)
ハンティング hunting (*5*)
バンドエイド Band-Aid (*7*)
ハンバーガー hamburger (*GS3*)
ハンマー hammer (*7*)

ひ／ヒ

ピアス pierced earrings (*7*)
ピアニスト pianist; ピアノ piano (*5*)
ピーマン green pepper (*6*)
ビール beer (*GS2*)
ひがし（東） east (*2*)
～ひき（～匹） counter for small animals (*2*)
～びき（引き） reduced ...% (*7*)
ひきにく（ひき肉） ground meat (*6*)
ひく（引く） *C1, tr.* to subtract, draw (*GS2*)
ひく（弾く） *C1, tr.* to play (*a musical instrument*) (*5*)
ひくい（低い） *i-adj.* low; short (*2*)
ひげ beard, facial hair; ひげをそる *C1, tr.* to shave facial hair (*3*)
ピザ pizza (*GS2*)
ひさしぶり it's been a long time; after a long absence (*GS1*)
ビジネス(する) *n.v.* business; do business (*3*)
びじゅつ（美術） art (*1*); びじゅつかん（美術館） art museum (*2*)
ひだり（左） left side (*2*)
ビデオ video (*6*); ビデオ・ゲーム video game; ビデオカメラ videocamera (*5*)
ひでり（日照り） drought (*4*)
ひと（人） person (*1*)
ひどい (*i-adj.*) terrible (*GS1*)
ひとつ（一つ） one (*2*)
ひとり（一人） one person (*2*); ひとりで（一人で） by oneself (*5*)
ビネガー vinegar (*6*)
ひま(な)（暇[な]） *na-adj.* free, not busy (*3*)
ひゃく（百） hundred (*GS5*); ひゃくまん（百万） million (*2*)
びょういん（病院） hospital (*2*)
びよういん（美容院） beauty parlor (*7*)
びょうき（病気） sickness, illness (*3*)
ひらがな hiragana (*GS1*)
ひる（昼） noon, noontime (*GS2*)
ビル building (*1*)
ひるごはん（昼ごはん） lunch (*GS2*)
ひるま（昼間） daytime (*4*)
ひろい（広い） *i-adj.* wide, spacious, big (*2*)
ピンク pink (*7*)
ピンポン table tennis, ping pong (*5*)

ふ／フ

ファーストフード　fast food　ファーストフード・レストラン　fast food restaurant　*(6)*
ファクシミリ　facsimile　*(1)*
ファスナー　zipper　*(7)*
ファッション　fashion　*(5)*;　ファッション・ショー　fashion show　*(7)*
フィッシュバーガー　fishburger　*(GS3)*
フィット（する）　*n.v.*　fit; to fit　*(7)*
フィルム　film　*(5)*
ブーケ　bouquet　*(7)*
ブーツ　boots　*(7)*
ふうふ（夫婦）　married couple;　ごふうふ（御夫婦）　*pol.*　married couple　*(5)*
プール　swimming pool　*(1)*
ふえる（増える）　*C2, intr.*　to increase　*(6)*
フォーク　fork　*(3)*
フォーマル（な）　*na-adj.*　formal　*(7)*
ふかめる（深める）　*C2, tr.*　to deepen　*(5)*
ふく（服）　clothes　*(3)*;　ふくそう（服装）　clothes, dress; appearance　*(7)*
ふく（吹く）　*C1, intr.*　to blow (*wind*)　*(4)*;　ふく（吹く）　*C1, tr.*　to blow (*musical instrument*)　*(5)*
ふじんふくてん（婦人服店）　women's wear store　*(7)*
ふたつ（二つ）　two;　ふたり（二人）　two people　*(2)*
ぶたにく（豚肉）　pork　*(6)*
ふつう（普通）　usual, ordinary　*(6)*
ふつか（二日）　second day　*(3)*
フットボール　football　*(5)*
ぶつりがく（物理学）　physics　*(1)*
ブティック　boutique　*(5)*
ぶどう（葡萄）　grape　*(6)*
ふとる（太る）　*C1, intr.*　to get fat　*(6)*
ふとんや（布団屋）　futon store　*(7)*
ふぶき（吹雪）　snowstorm　*(4)*
ふべん（な）（不便［な］）　*na-adj.*　inconvenient　*(2)*
ふまじめ（な）（不真面目［な］）　*na-adj.*　not serious, lazy (*person*)　*(4)*
ふゆ（冬）　winter　*(4)*;　ふゆやすみ（冬休み）　winter vacation　*(6)*
フライパン　frying pan　*(6)*
ブラウス　blouse　*(5)*
ブラジャー　brassiere　*(7)*
ブラジル　*p.n.*　Brazil;　ブラジルじん（ブラジル人）　Brazilian　*(1)*
プラモデル　plastic model　*(7)*
フランス　*p.n.*　France　*(1)*;　フランス・パン　French bread　*(7)*;　フランスご（フランス語）　French language;　フランスじん（フランス人）　French person　*(1)*
ブランチ　brunch　*(3)*
プリン　pudding　*(6)*
プリント　print (*pattern*)　*(7)*
ふる（降る）　*C1, intr.*　to fall (*rain and snow*)　*(4)*
ふるい（古い）　*i-adj.*　old　*(2)*
ブルー　blue　*(7)*
フルーツ・サラダ　fruit salad　*(6)*
フルート　flute　*(5)*
ブレザー　blazer, jacket　*(7)*
ブレスレット　bracelet　*(7)*
プレゼント　present, gift　*(3)*
フレンチフライ　French fries　*(GS3)*
プロ　professional　*(5)*
ブローチ　brooch, pin　*(7)*
プログラマ　programmer;　プログラミング（する）　*n.v.*　programming; to do programming　*(5)*;　プログラム（する）　*n.v.*　program; to program　*(7)*
ブロッコリ　broccoli　*(GS2)*
プロポーズ（する）　*n.v.*　proposal; propose marriage　*(7)*
〜ふん（かん）（〜分［間］）　counter for duration in minutes　*(2)*
ぶんか（文化）　culture　*(1)*;　ぶんかのひ（文化の日）　Culture Day　*(3)*
ぶんがく（文学）　literature;　ぶんがくぶ（文学部）　literature department　*(1)*
ぶんかつばらい（分割払い）　installment payment plan　*(7)*
ぶんぼうぐ（文房具）　stationery　*(GS3)*;　ぶんぼうぐや（文房具屋）　stationery store　*(7)*

へ／ヘ

へ　*part.*　toward, to (*pronounced* え)　*(GS3)*
ペア　pair　*(GS1)*
ヘアースタイル　hairstyle　*(5)*
へいきん（平均）　average　*(4)*
へいじつ（平日）　weekday　*(3)*
へいせい（平成）　Heisei era　*(3)*
へえ　*interj.*　oh (*exclamation of surprise*)　*(3)*
ベーグル　bagel　*(7)*
ペキン　*p.n.*　Beijing　*(4)*
ベジタリアン　vegetarian　*(GS5)*
へた（な）（下手［な］）　*na-adj.*　poor at, not skilled at　*(5)*
ペット　pet　*(5)*
べつに（別に）　*adv.*　separately; not particularly (*with negative*)　*(6)*
へや（部屋）　room　*(2)*
ベルト　belt　*(7)*
ヘルメット　helmet　*(7)*
ペン　pen　*(GS1)*
へん（な）（変［な］）　*na-adj.*　strange, weird　*(2)*
べんきょう（する）（勉強［する］）　*n.v.*　study; to study　*(GS2)*
ベンチ　bench　*(2)*
べんとう（弁当）　box lunch　*(6)*
ペンパル　pen pal　*(1)*
へんぴん（する）（返品［する］）　*n.v.*　returning merchandise; to return merchandise　*(7)*
べんり（な）（便利［な］）　*na-adj.*　convenient　*(2)*

ほ／ホ

ほう　direction, way (*used in comparative constructions*)　*(4)*
ほうがく（法学）　law　*(1)*
ぼうし（帽子）　cap, hat　*(7)*
ほうせきてん（宝石店）　jewelry shop　*(7)*
ほうちょう（包丁）　cleaver, big cutting knife　*(6)*
ボーイフレンド　boyfriend　*(2)*

ポータブル portable (*7*)
ボート boat (*5*)
ボーリング bowling (*5*)
ボール ball (*2*)
ボールペン ball-point pen (*GS1*)
ぼく（僕） *pron., m., inf.* I (male); ぼくたち（僕たち） *pron., m., inf., pl.* we (male) (*1*)
ボクシング boxing (*GS2*)
ポケット pocket (*7*)
ほしい（欲しい） *i-adj.* to want; ほしがる（欲しがる） *C1, tr.* to want (*6*)
ボタン button (*7*)
ポップコーン popcorn (*6*)
ポツポツ raining in big, scattered drops (*4*)
ボディーガード bodyguard (*5*)
ポテト potato (*6*); ポテトチップ potato chip (*7*)
ホテル hotel (*2*)
〜ほど as much as, about (*3*)
ほとんど *adv.* almost; ほとんど...ない almost never... (*3*)
ポリエステル polyester (*7*)
ポルトガルご（ポルトガル語） Portuguese language (*1*)
ほん（本） book (*GS1*); ほんや（本屋） bookstore (*6*)
〜ほん（〜本） counter for long, often cylindrical, items (*2*)
ホンコン（香港） *p.n.* Hong Kong; ホンコンじん（香港人） Hong Kong native (*1*)
ぼんさい（盆栽） bonsai (*5*)
ほんとう（本当） real, true (*GS2*);（本当に） *adv.* really, truly (*4*)

ま／マ

まあまあ so-so, not bad (*2*)
マーガリン margarine (*6*)
マージャン mah-jongg (*5*)
〜まい（〜枚） counter for thin, flat items (*2*)
まい〜（毎〜） every (*3*); まいあさ（毎朝） every morning (*GS3*); まいしゅう（毎週） every week; まいつき（毎月） every month (*3*); まいにち（毎日） every day (*GS4*); まいばん（毎晩） every night (*3*)
〜まいどり（〜枚撮り） counter for film exposures (*7*)
まえ（前） front (*2*)
まぐろ（鮪） tuna (*6*)
まご（孫） grandchild (*5*)
まさか *interj.* that can't be... (*3*)
まじめ(な)（真面目[な]） *na-adj.* serious (*2*)
まず first of all (*3*)
まずい *i-adj.* not tasty, bad (*4*)
また *adv.* again (*GS1*)
まだ *adv.* not yet, still (*3*)
まち（町） town (*2*)
まちがいでんわ（間違い電話） wrong number (telephone) (*3*)
まちがう（間違う） *C1, intr.* to make a mistake (*3*)
まつ（待つ） *C1, tr.* to wait (*GS1*)
まったく（全く） *adv.* totally (*5*)
まで *part.* up to, until (*2*)
まど（窓） window (*GS1*)
マトン mutton (*7*)
マフラー scarf (*7*)
ママ mama (*5*)
まめ（豆） bean, pea (*6*)
まもなく（間もなく） soon, before long (*7*)
マラソン(する) *n.v.* marathon; to run a marathon (*5*)
まるい（丸い／円い） *i-adj.* round (*2*)
まわり（回り） around (*location*) (*2*)
まん（万） ten thousand (*2*)
まんいん（満員） full capacity (*train, etc.*) (*6*)
まんが（漫画） cartoon (*7*)
まんなか（真ん中） middle (*2*)
まんねんひつ（万年筆） fountain pen (*1*)

み／ミ

ミンチ ground meat (*6*)
ミーティング meeting (*GS2*)
みえる（見える） *C2, intr.* can be seen (*5*)
みがく（磨く） *C1, tr.* to brush, polish; to wipe clean (*3*)
みかん mandarin orange (*6*)
みぎ（右） right side (*2*)
みじかい（短い） *i-adj.* short (*4*)
ミシン sewing machine (*7*)
みず（水） water (*unheated*); おみず（お水） water *pol.* (*6*)
みずぎ（水着） bathing suit, swimwear (*7*)
みずたま（水玉） polka dots (*5*)
ミステリー mystery novel (*3*)
みせ（店） store, shop (*7*)
みせる（見せる） *C2, tr.* to show (*3*)
みそ（味噌） miso; みそしる（味噌汁） miso soup (*6*)
みぞれ sleet (*4*)
みち（道） street (*2*)
みっか（三日） third day (*3*); みっつ（三つ） three (*2*)
みつける（見つける） *C2, tr.* to find, discover (*6*)
みどり（緑） green (*7*); みどりのひ（緑の日） Greenery Day (*3*)
みな、みんな（皆） all, everyone;（皆さん） everyone (*5*)
みなみ（南） south (*1*); みなみかぜ（南風） south wind (*4*)
みぶんしょうめいしょ（身分証明書） ID (identification) (*3*)
ミュージカル musical show (*5*)
みりん sweet cooking sake (*6*)
みる（見る） *C2, tr.* to see (*3*)
ミルク milk (*3*)

む／ム

むいか（六日） sixth day (*3*)
むかい（向かい） across from, facing (*2*)
むこうがわ（向こう側） the other side (*2*)
むじ（無地） plain (*no pattern*), solid color (*7*)
むしあつい（むし暑い） *i-adj.* sultry; hot and humid (*4*)
むす（蒸す） *C1, tr.* to steam (*6*)
むずかしい（難しい） *i-adj.* difficult (*2*)

むすこ（息子） son; むすこさん（息子さん） *pol.* son (*5*)
むすめ（娘） daughter; むすめさん（娘さん） *pol.* daughter (*5*)
むっつ（六つ） six (*2*)
むら（村） village (*2*)
むらさき（紫） purple (*7*)
むらさめ passing rain (*4*)
むり(な)（無理[な]） *na-adj.* impossible, very difficult (*5*)
むりょう（無料） free of charge (*6*)

め／メ

〜め（〜目） suffix making ordinal numbers …th (*2*)
めい（姪） niece; めいごさん（姪ごさん） *pol.* niece (*5*)
めいし（名刺） name card (*GS1*)
めいじ（明治） Meiji era (*3*)
めいわく(な)（迷惑[な]） *na-adj.* annoying; めいわく(する)（迷惑[する]） *n.v.* nuisance, trouble; to cause trouble, bother (*5*)
メーカー maker (*1*)
メーター、メートル meter (*4*)
メールオーダー mail order (*7*)
めがね（眼鏡） eyeglasses; めがねてん／めがねや（眼鏡店／眼鏡屋） optician's; めがねをかける（眼鏡をかける） to put on, wear glasses (*7*)
メキシコ *p.n.* Mexico; メキシコじん（メキシコ人） Mexican person (*1*)
メニュー menu (*GS2*)
メモリー memory (*7*)
メロドラマ soap opera (*5*)
メロン melon (*6*)
めん（綿） cotton cloth (*7*)
めんせき（面積） area, size, floor space (*2*)

も／モ

も *part.* too (*3*)
もう *adv.* already; never (*with negative*) (*GS1*); *adv.* more (*2*)
もうしこみしょ（申込書） application form (*5*)
もうしぶんない（申し分ない） satisfactory, good enough (*7*)
もうしわけない（申し訳ない） be very sorry (*7*)
もくようび（木曜日） Thursday (*GS4*)
もしもし *interj.* hello (*on the telephone*) (*2*)
もちろん（勿論） of course (*2*)
もつ（持つ） *C1, tr.* to have, own, hold (*3*)
もっと *adv.* more (*4*)
モデル fashion model (*7*)
もの thing; item (*2*)
もよう（模様） pattern (*7*)
もん（門） gate (*3*)
もんだい（問題） question; issue, problem (*4*)

や／ヤ

〜や *part.* and so on (*3*)
やおや（八百屋） vegetable store, greengrocer (*7*)
やきとり（焼き鳥） yakitori (chicken shish kebob) (*GS4*)
やきゅう（野球） baseball (*GS3*)
やく（焼く） *C1, tr.* to broil, grill, bake (*6*)
やさい（野菜） vegetable (*GS1*); やさいサラダ（野菜サラダ） vegetable salad (*6*); やさいジュース（野菜ジュース） vegetable juice (*7*)
やさしい *i-adj.* easy; lenient (*2*)
やしょく（夜食） evening snack (*6*)
〜やすい *i-adj.* easy to… (*with conjunctive form of verb*) (*7*)
やすい（安い） *i-adj.* inexpensive, cheap (*2*)
やすみ（休み） day off, rest; やすみのひ（休みの日） day off; やすむ（休む） *C1, intr.* to take a rest (*3*)
やっきょく（薬局） pharmacy, drugstore (*7*)
やっつ（八つ） eight (*2*)
やはり after all (*4*)
やま（山） mountain; やまのぼり（山登り） mountain climbing (*4*)
やめる（止める） *C2, tr.* to stop, quit (*3*)

ゆ／ユ

ゆうがた（夕方） evening (*GS2*); ゆうごはん（夕ごはん） dinner (*3*); ゆうしょく（夕食） dinner, supper (*6*); ゆうだち（夕立） evening shower (*4*)
ゆうこうに（有効に） effectively (*5*)
ゆうびんきょく（郵便局） post office (*2*)
ゆうめい(な)（有名[な]） *na-adj.* famous (*2*); ゆうめいじん（有名人） celebrity (*6*)
ゆか（床） floor (*GS1*)
ゆき（雪） snow (*4*)
ゆっくり *adv.* slowly (*1*)
ゆでる cook in boiling water (*6*)
ゆびわ（指輪） ring (finger) (*7*)
ゆめ（夢） dream (*7*)
ゆるい *i-adj.* loose (*7*)

よ／ヨ

よ *part.* sentence-final particle (*emphasis*) (*2*)
ようか（八日） eighth day (*3*)
ようき(な)（陽気[な]） *na-adj.* cheerful, lively (*4*)
ようし（養子） adopted child (*5*)
ようじ（用事） errand (*3*)
ようしょく（洋食） Western cuisine (*6*)
〜ようとおもう（〜ようと思う） to intend to do… (*6*)
ようひんてん（洋品店） Western clothing store (*7*); ようふう（洋風） Western style (*6*); ようふく（洋服） Western clothes (*7*)
ヨーグルト yogurt (*6*)
よか（余暇） free time (*5*)
ヨガ yoga (*5*)
よく *adv.* often, well (*1*)
よこ（横） side (*2*)
よしゅう(する)（予習[する]） *n.v.* preparation for class; to prepare for class (*GS1*)
よっか（四日） fourth day (*3*); よっつ（四つ） four (*2*)

ヨット　yacht　*(5)*
よてい(する)（予定[する]）*n.v.*　plan; to plan, schedule　*(6)*
よぶ（呼ぶ）*C1, tr.*　to invite　*(6)*
よむ（読む）*C1, tr.*　to read　*(GS3)*
よやく(する)（予約[する]）*n.v.*　reservation; to reserve　*(6)*
〜より　more than…　*(4)*
よる（夜）night　*(GS2)*
よろしく　please do as you see fit　*(GS1)*
よわい（弱い）*i-adj.*　weak　*(4)*
よん（四）four　*(GS2)*;　よんじゅう（四十）forty　*(GS5)*

ら／ラ

ラーメン　ramen (*Chinese-style wheat noodles*)　*(GS3)*;　ラーメンや（ラーメン屋）ramen restaurant　*(6)*
らいげつ（来月）next month　*(3)*
らいしゅう（来週）next week　*(3)*
ライス　rice (*cooked*)　*(6)*
ライトブルー　light blue　*(7)*
らいにち(する)（来日[する]）*n.v.*　coming to Japan; to come to Japan　*(7)*
らいねん（来年）next year　*(3)*
ラグビー　rugby　*(5)*
ラケット　racket　*(5)*
ラジオ　radio　*(GS2)*;　ラジカセ　radio cassette　*(1)*
ラップ　rap　*(2)*
ラップトップ・コンピュータ　laptop computer　*(4)*
ラフ(な)　*na.adj.*　rough　*(4)*
ラム　lamb　*(6)*
ランゲージ・ラボ　language lab　*(1)*
ランニング　running　*(5)*

り／リ

りくじょうきょうぎ（陸上競技）track and field　*(5)*
リポーター　reporter　*(6)*
リボン　ribbon　*(7)*
リモコン　remote control　*(7)*
りゅうがくせい（留学生）foreign student　*(7)*
りょう（寮）dormitory　*(1)*
りょうしゅうしょ（領収書）receipt　*(7)*
りょうしん（両親）parents;　ごりょうしん（御両親）*pol.*　parents　*(5)*
りょうり(する)（料理[する]）*n.v.*　cooking, cuisine; to cook　*(GS1)*
りょくちゃ（緑茶）green tea　*(6)*
りょこう(する)（旅行[する]）*n.v.*　trip, travel; to travel　*(5)*
りんご　apple　*(6)*

れ／レ

れい（零）zero　*(GS2)*;　れいか（零下）below zero　*(4)*
れいぞうこ（冷蔵庫）refrigerator　*(6)*
れいとうしょくひん（冷凍食品）frozen food　*(6)*
レインコート　raincoat　*(4)*
れきしがく（歴史学）history　*(1)*
レコード　record　*(3)*;　レコードてん／レコードや（レコード店／レコード屋）record store, music store　*(7)*
レジ　cash register, cashier　*(7)*
レシート　receipt　*(7)*
レシピー　recipe　*(6)*
レジャー　leisure　*(5)*
レストラン　restaurant　*(2)*
レスリング　wrestling　*(5)*
レタス　lettuce　*(6)*
レバー　liver　*(4)*
レモン　lemon　*(6)*
レンジ　oven, range　*(6)*
れんしゅう(する)（練習[する]）*n.v.*　practice, exercise; to practice, to exercise　*(2)*

ろ／ロ

ろく（六）six　*(GS2)*;　ろくがつ（六月）June　*(1)*;　ろくじゅう（六十）sixty　*(GS5)*
ロシア　*p.n.*　Russia;　ロシアご（ロシア語）Russian language;　ロシアじん（ロシア人）Russian person　*(1)*
ロック　rock and roll　*(GS2)*
ロッククライミング　rock climbing　*(5)*
ロブスター　lobster　*(6)*
ロマンス　romance　*(2)*

わ／ワ

〜わ（〜羽）counter for birds　*(2)*
わ　*part., f.*　sentence-final emphatic particle　*(4)*
わあ　*interj.*　wow!　*(GS3)*
ワープロ　word processor　*(1)*
ワイシャツ　dress shirt　*(7)*
ワイン　wine　*(GS2)*
わかい（若い）*i-adj.*　young　*(2)*
わがまま(な)　*na-adj.*　selfish, egoistic　*(5)*
わかる　*C1, intr.*　to understand　*(GS1)*
わしょく（和食）Japanese cuisine　*(6)*
わすれる（忘れる）*C2, tr.*　to forget　*(5)*
ワセリン　Vaseline　*(7)*
わた（綿）cotton tufts, plant　*(7)*
わたし（私）*pron.*　I, me　*(GS1)*;　わたしたち（私たち）*pron., pl.*　we　*(1)*;　わたしの（私の）*pron.*　my　*(GS1)*
わふく（和服）Japanese-style clothes　*(7)*
わらう（笑う）*C1, tr.*　to laugh, smile　*(3)*
わりびき(する)（割引[する]）*n.v.*　discount; to discount　*(7)*
わる（割る）*C1, tr.*　to divide　*(GS2)*
わるい（悪い）*intr.*　bad　*(2)*
ワンピース　dress　*(7)*

を

を　*part.*　direct-object marker　*(GS1)*

English-Japanese Glossary

Abbreviations used in this glossary are explained at the beginning of the Japanese-English Glossary.

A

about, approximately　～くらい、～ぐらい　*(4)*
academic major; major in　（専攻[する]）　せんこう(する)　*n.v.*　*(1)*
academic subject　（学科）　がっか　*(2)*
accessory, jewelry　アクセサリー　*(7)*
according to…　～によると;（～の話では）　～のはなしでは　*(7)*
across from　（向かい）むかい　*(2)*
action movie　（アクション映画）　アクションえいが　*(2)*
activity; engage in activity　（活動[する]）かつどう(する)　*n.v.*　*(5)*
add　（足す）たす　*C1, tr.*　*(GS2)*
address　（住所）じゅうしょ　*(1)*
administration office　（事務室）じむしつ　*(1)*
adopted child　（養子）ようし　*(5)*
adult　（大人）おとな　*(6)*
advertisement　（広告）こうこく　*(7)*
aerobics　エアロビクス　*(3)*
Africa　アフリカ　*p.n.*　*(6)*
after…　（後）あと;　after that　（その後）そのあと　*(3)*
after all　やはり　*(4)*
afternoon　（午後）ごご　*(GS2)*
again　また　*adv.*　*(GS1)*
age, year　（年）とし　*(1)*
age　（年齢）ねんれい　*(1)*
aged people　（年寄り）としより　*(5)*
ahh　ああ　*interj.*　*(2)*
air pressure　（気圧）きあつ　*(4)*
all　（全て）すべて　*(5)*;　（全～）ぜん～　*(7)*;　（全部）ぜんぶ　*(5)*
all day long　（一日中）　いちにちじゅう　*(GS3)*
all items　（全品）　ぜんぴん　*(7)*
all of them　どれも　*(5)*
all the way　ずっと　*adv.*　*(4)*
all you can drink　（飲み放題）　のみほうだい　*(6)*
all you can eat　（バイキング料理）　バイキングりょうり　*(6)*
almost　ほとんど　*adv.*　*(3)*
a lot, much, many　たくさん　*(2)*
already　もう　*adv.*　*(GS1)*
although　けど　*conj. coll.*;　けれども　*conj.*　*(7)*
always　いつも　*adv.*　*(2)*
A.M. (morning)　（午前）ごぜん　*(GS2)*
amateur　アマ　*(5)*
America　アメリカ　*p.n.*;　American　（アメリカ人）　アメリカじん　*(1)*
amount of money　（金額）きんがく　*(7)*
and (*emphatic*)　し　*(7)*
and　と　*part.*　*(GS3)*
and so on　や　*part.*　*(3)*
and so on, etc.　など　*(6)*
and, and then　そして　*conj.*　*(3)*
and then, after that　それから　*(3)*
announcement　（知らせ）しらせ　*(5)*
annoying　うるさい　*i-adj.*　*(2)*　（迷惑[な]）めいわく(な)　*na-adj.*　*(5)*
answer　（答）こたえ　*(5)*;（答える）こたえる　*C2, intr.*　*(3)*
anthropology　（人類学）じんるいがく　*(1)*
antique　（骨董品）こっとうひん　*(5)*
any of them　どれでも　*(5)*
anyone　だれでも;　どなたでも　*pol.*　*(5)*
anything　（何でも）なんでも　*(5)*
anything, nothing　（何も）なにも　*(3)*
anytime　いつでも　*(5)*
anywhere　どこでも　*(5)*
apartment　アパート　*(GS3)*
appetizer　（前菜）ぜんさい　*(6)*
apple　りんご　*(6)*;　apple pie　アップルパイ　*(7)*
application form　（申込書）もうしこみしょ　*(5)*
appropriate, as you like it　よろしく　*(GS1)*
approximately (*amount, extent*)　～くらい、～ぐらい　*(4)*
approximately (*time*)　（頃）ころ、ごろ　*(GS3)*
April　（四月）しがつ　*(1)*
apron　エプロン　*(5)*
Arabic language　（アラビア語）アラビアご　*(4)*
area　（面積）めんせき　*(2)*
around (*location*)　（回り）まわり　*(2)*
art　（美術）びじゅつ　*(1)*; art museum　（美術館）　びじゅつかん　*(2)*
as much as, about　ほど　*(3)*
ask; listen　（聞く）きく　*C1, tr.*　*(GS1)*
ask; request　（頼む）たのむ　*C1, tr.*　*(6)*
ask; inquire　（伺う）うかがう　*C1, tr.*　*(5)*
asparagus　アスパラガス　*(5)*
aspirin　アスピリン　*(7)*
astringent　（渋い）しぶい　*i-adj.*　*(6)*

at, by　で　*part.*　*(2)*
at, in　に　*part.*　*(GS3)*
athlete　スポーツせんしゅ　*(5)*
attractive　きれい(な)　*na-adj.*　*(2)*
August　(八月)はちがつ　*(1)*
aunt　おば；おばさん　*pol.*　*(5)*
Australia　オーストラリア　*p.n.*　*(GS2)*
autumn　(秋)　あき；　autumn rain　(秋雨)　あきさめ　*(4)*
avenue　(通り)とおり　*(2)*
average　(平均)へいきん　*(4)*
awful, awesome, very　すごい　*i-adj.*　*(5)*

B

back　(後ろ)うしろ　*(2)*
bad　(悪い)わるい　*i-adj.*　*(2)*
bad at and dislike　(苦手[な])　にがて(な)　*na-adj.*　*(5)*
badminton　バドミントン　*(5)*
bag　(鞄)かばん　*(GS1)*
bagel　ベーグル　*(7)*
bakery　(パン屋)パンや　*(7)*
balance　バランス　*(6)*
ball　ボール　*(2)*
ball-point pen　ボールペン　*(GS1)*
banana　バナナ　*(2)*
Band-Aid　バンドエイド　*(7)*
bank　(銀行)ぎんこう　*(GS2)*
barbershop　(床屋)とこや　*(5)*
bargain, haggle over price　(値切る)ねぎる　*C1, tr.*　*(7)*
bargain sale　セール、バーゲンセール　*(7)*
baseball　(野球)やきゅう　*(GS3)*
basketball　バスケットボール　*(5)*
bath　(お風呂)おふろ　*(3)*
bathe　(浴びる)あびる　*C2, tr.*　*(GS3)*
bathing suit　(水着)みずぎ　*(7)*
bathroom　トイレ　*(2)*
BBQ　バーベキュー　*(6)*
be (copula, plain)　だ　*(3)*
be (copula, polite)　です　*(1)*
be … ing　いる　(*with te-form of verbs*)　*C1*　*(5)*
be able to, can　(出来る)できる　*C2, intr.*;
ことができる　(*with dictionary form of verb*)　*(5)*
bean　(豆)まめ　*(6)*
beard　ひげ　*(3)*
beautiful　(美しい)うつくしい　*i-adj.*　*(4)*
beauty parlor　(美容院)びよういん　*(7)*
because, and so　から　*part.*　*(1)*;　ので　*(4)*
become, turn into　なる　*C1, intr.*　*(4)*
beef　(牛肉)ぎゅうにく　*(6)*
beer　ビール　*(GS2)*
before long　(間もなく)まもなく　*(7)*
behind, back　(後ろ)うしろ　*(2)*
Beijing　ペキン　*p.n.*　*(4)*
believe　(信じる)しんじる　*C2, tr.*　*(3)*
belt　ベルト　*(7)*
below　(下)した　*(2)*
bench　ベンチ　*(2)*
best　(一番)いちばん　*(4)*
between　(間)あいだ；　between A and B
(AとBの間に)　*(2)*
beverage　(飲み物)のみもの　*(GS3)*
bicycle　(自転車)じてんしゃ　*(2)*
bill, invoice　(請求書)　せいきゅうしょ　*(7)*
biology　(生物学)　せいぶつがく　*(1)*
bird　(鳥)とり　*(2)*
birth date　(生年月日)せいねんがっぴ　*(1)*
birthday　(誕生日)たんじょうび　*(3)*
birthday cake　バースデー・ケーキ　*(4)*;　birthday gift
バースデー・プレゼント　*(3)*
bit, a bit　(少し)　すこし　*adv.*　*(3)*;　ちょっと　*adv.*
(GS1)
bitter　(苦い)にがい　*i-adj.*　*(6)*
black　(黒)くろ／(黒い)くろい　*i-adj.*　*(7)*
black-and-white photo(graphy)　(白黒写真)
しろくろしゃしん　*(5)*
black tea　(紅茶)こうちゃ　*(6)*
blazer, jacket　ブレザー　*(7)*
bloom　(咲く)さく　*C1, intr.*　*(4)*
blouse　ブラウス　*(5)*
blow, play (*a musical instrument*)　(吹く)　ふく　*C1, tr.*
(5)
blow (*wind*)　(吹く)　ふく；　*C1, intr.*　*(4)*
blue　(青)　あお、ブルー；(青い)　あおい　*i-adj.*　*(7)*
boat　ボート　*(5)*
body　(体)からだ　*(4)*
bodyguard　ボディーガード　*(5)*
boil　(煮る)にる　*C2, tr.*　*(6)*
bonsai　(盆栽)ぼんさい　*(5)*
book　(本)ほん　*(GS1)*;　bookstore　(本屋)
ほんや　*(6)*
boot　ブーツ　*(7)*
boring　つまらない　*i-adj.*　*(2)*;　become bored, get
tired of　(飽きる)　あきる　*C2, intr.*　*(6)*
born (be born)　(生まれる)うまれる　*C2, intr.*　*(1)*
borrow　(借りる)　かりる　*C2, tr.*　*(7)*
both　どちらも　*(5)*
bottle opener　(栓抜き)せんぬき　*(6)*
bouquet　ブーケ　*(7)*
boutique　ブティック　*(5)*
bowling　ボーリング　*(5)*
box　(箱)　はこ　*(2)*
boxing　ボクシング　*(GS2)*
box lunch　(弁当)べんとう　*(6)*
boy　(男の子)おとこのこ　*(5)*
boyfriend　ボーイフレンド　*(2)*
bracelet　ブレスレット　*(7)*
brassiere　ブラジャー　*(7)*
Brazil　ブラジル；　Brazilian person　(ブラジル人)
ブラジルじん　*p.n.*　*(1)*
bread　パン　*(6)*
breakfast　(朝ごはん)　あさごはん　*(GS2)*;　(朝食)
ちょうしょく　*(6)*
briefs　パンツ　*(7)*
bright, well-lighted　(明るい)あかるい　*i-adj.*　*(4)*
broccoli　ブロッコリ　*(GS2)*
broil　(焼く)　やく　*C1, tr.*　*(6)*
broken (become broken)　(壊れる)こわれる　*C2, intr.*
(7)
brooch, pin　ブローチ　*(7)*
brothers　(兄弟)きょうだい　*(5)*
brown　(茶色)ちゃいろ；(茶色い)ちゃいろい　*i-adj.*
(7)

brunch　ブランチ　*(3)*
brush　（磨く）みがく　*C1, tr.*;　brush teeth　（歯を磨く）はをみがく　*(3)*
brush calligraphy　（書道）しょどう　*(5)*
building　（建物）たてもの　*(2)*;　ビル　*(1)*
bullet train　（新幹線）しんかんせん　*(3)*
bus　バス　*(2)*
bus stop　（停留所）ていりゅうじょ；（バス停）バスてい　*(2)*
business; do business　ビジネス（する）　*n.v.*　*(3)*
business hour　（営業時間）えいぎょうじかん　*(6)*
busy　（忙しい）いそがしい　*i-adj.*　*(2)*
but　しかし　*conj.*　*(3)*
but, and　が　*conj.*　*(3)*
but, even so　でも　*conj.*　*(4)*
butcher shop　（肉屋）にくや　*(7)*
butter　バター　*(6)*
button　ボタン　*(7)*
buy　（買う）かう　*C1, tr.*　*(3)*
by means of, at　で　*part.*　*(2)*
by the way, well…　さて　*conj.*　*(4)*

C

cabbage　キャベツ　*(7)*
cafeteria　カフェテリア　*(1)*
cake　ケーキ　*(6)*;　cake shop　（ケーキ屋）　ケーキや　*(7)*
calculation, bill; tally, calculate　（勘定［する］）かんじょう（する）*n.v.*　*(6)*
calculator　（計算機）けいさんき　*(7)*
calendar　カレンダー　*(4)*
calm (ocean, personality)　おだやか（な）　*na-adj.*　*(4)*
camera　カメラ　*(GS3)*;　camera shop　（カメラ店／カメラ屋）　カメラてん／カメラや　*(7)*
camping　キャンピング　*(5)*;　camp; go camping　キャンプ（する）*n.v.*　*(4)*
campus　キャンパス　*(1)*
can, be able to　ことができる　*(with dictionary form of verb)*　*(5)*
can be heard　（聞こえる）きこえる　*C2, intr.*　*(5)*
can be seen　（見える）みえる　*C2, intr.*　*(5)*
can opener　（缶切り）かんきり　*(6)*
Canada　カナダ　*p.n.*　*(GS2)*;　Canadian　（カナダ人）カナダじん　*(1)*
canned food　（缶詰）　かんづめ　*(6)*
cap　（帽子）ぼうし　*(7)*
car　（車）くるま　*(1)*
card　カード;　card game　トランプ　*(5)*
care; take care of　（世話［する］）　せわ（する）　*n.v.*　*(5)*
careful (be careful)　（気をつける）きをつける　*(4)*
carnation　カーネション　*(7)*
carrot　（人参）にんじん　*(6)*
cartoon　（漫画）まんが　*(7)*
case　ケース　*(7)*
cash　（現金）げんきん　*(7)*
cash register, cashier　レジ　*(7)*
casual　カジュアル（な）　*na-adj.*　*(7)*
cat　（猫）ねこ　*(5)*
catalogue　カタログ　*(7)*
catch a cold　（風邪をひく）かぜをひく　*(4)*
CD (compact disk)　シーディー　*(7)*
ceiling　（天井）てんじょう　*(GS1)*
celebrity　（有名人）ゆうめいじん　*(6)*
centigrade　（摂氏）せっし　*(4)*
certainly, at your service　かしこまりました　*(6)*
chair　（椅子）　いす　*(GS1)*
chalk　チョーク;　chalkboard　（黒板）こくばん;　chalkboard eraser　（黒板消し）こくばんけし　*(GS1)*
champagne　シャンペン　*(6)*
change (money)　（お釣り）おつり　*(7)*
change　（変える）かえる　*C2, tr.*　*(3)*
change clothes　（着替える）きがえる　*C2, tr.*　*(3)*
cheap, inexpensive　（安い）やすい　*i-adj.*　*(2)*
check (*pattern*)　チェック　*(7)*
cheerful, bright　（明るい）あかるい　*i-adj.*　*(4)*
cheerful (*mood*)　（陽気）ようき（な）　*(4)*
cheese　チーズ　*(6)*;　cheeseburger　チーズバーガー　*(GS5)*;　cheesecake　チーズケーキ　*(6)*
chef　シェフ　*(6)*
chemistry　（化学）かがく　*(1)*
cherry blossom　（桜）さくら;　cherry blossom viewing　（花見）はなみ　*(4)*
chess　チェス　*(5)*
chicken　（鳥肉）とりにく　*(6)*
child　（お子さん）おこさん　*pol.*　*(5)*;（子）こ　*(4)*;（子供）こども　*(5)*
China　（中国）ちゅうごく　*p.n.*　*(1)*
Chinese language　（中国語）ちゅうごくご;　Chinese cooking　（中国料理）ちゅうごくりょうり;　Chinese person　（中国人）ちゅうごくじん　*(1)*
Chinese food　（中華料理）ちゅうかりょうり　*(6)*
chocolate　チョコレート　*(GS5)*
choose　（選ぶ）えらぶ　*C1, tr.*　*(5)*
chopsticks　（箸）はし　*(6)*
church　（教会）きょうかい　*(2)*
circle, activity group　サークル　*(5)*
citizen　（国民）こくみん　*(3)*
city　（市）し　*(2)*
class　クラス　*(GS2)*
classical music　クラシック　*(GS2)*;（クラシック音楽）クラシックおんがく　*(5)*
classmate　クラスメート　*(1)*
classroom　（教室）きょうしつ　*(GS1)*
clean　きれい（な）　*na-adj.*　*(2)*
cleaning; to clean (*house*)　（掃除［する］）　そうじ（する）*n.v.*　*(3)*
clear weather　（晴れ）はれ;　clear up　（晴れる）はれる　*C2, intr.*　*(4)*
cleaver, big cutting knife　（包丁）ほうちょう　*(6)*
climate　（気候）きこう　*(4)*
clock, watch　（時計）とけい　*(GS3)*
close (*book, box, etc.*)　（閉じる）とじる　*C2, tr.*　*(GS1)*
close (*door, window, etc.*)　（閉める）しめる　*C2, tr.*　*(3)*
close, near　（近い）ちかい　*i-adj.*　*(GS3)*
clothes　（衣服）いふく　*(7)*;（服）ふく　*(3)*;（服装）ふくそう　*(7)*
cloud　（雲）くも;　cloudy　（曇り）くもり;　become cloudy　（曇る）くもる　*C1, intr.*　*(4)*

club　クラブ　(5)
coat　コート　(4)
cocktail　カクテル　(*GS2*)
coffee　コーヒー　(*GS2*);　coffeemaker　コーヒーメーカー　(6)
coffee shop　(喫茶店)　きっさてん　(2)
cola　コーラ　(*GS2*)
cold, flu　(風邪)　かぜ　(4)
cold　(寒い)　さむい　*i-adj.*　(*GS4*)
collect　(集める)　あつめる　*C2, tr.*　(5)
color　(色)　いろ　(7)
color photo(graphy)　(カラー写真)　カラーしゃしん　(5)
comb　とかす　*C1, tr.*　(3)
combine　(組み合せる)　くみあわせる　*C2, tr.*　(7)
come　(来る)　くる　*C3, intr.*　(3);　come to…　(に来る)　にくる　(7)
comedy　コメディ　(2)
coming to Japan; come to Japan　(来日[する])　らいにち(する)　*n.v.*　(7)
commemoration; commemorate　(記念[する])　きねん(する)　*n.v.*　(7)
commute　(通う)　かよう　*C1, intr.*　(6)
company　(会社)　かいしゃ　(3);　company worker　(会社員)　かいしゃいん　(5)
complete…　〜てしまう　(6);　be completed　(出来る)　できる　*C2, intr.*　(5)
computer game　コンピューターゲーム　(5)
computer science　コンピュータ・サイエンス　(1)
concert　コンサート　(5)
confectionery shop　(お菓子屋)　おかしや　(7)
consommé　コンソメ　(6)
continue　(続く)　つづく　*C1, intr.*　(4)
convenience store　コンビニエンス・ストア　(7)
convenient　(便利[な])　べんり(な)　*na-adj.*　(2)
conversation　(会話)　かいわ　(5)
convey　(伝える)　つたえる　*C2, tr.*　(6)
cook, make　(作る)　つくる　*C1, tr.*　(*GS1*)
cooking; cook　(料理[する])　りょうり(する)　*n.v.*　(*GS1*)
cook, chef　コック　(6)
cooking oil　クッキング・オイル;　cooking school　クッキング・スクール　(6)
cool　(涼しい)　すずしい　*i-adj.*　(*GS4*)
corner　(角)　かど　(6)
cosmetics　(化粧品)　けしょうひん;　cosmetics store　(化粧品店)　けしょうひんてん　(7)
cost　かかる　*C1, intr.*　(3)
cotton fabric　(綿)　めん　(7);　コットン　(1)
cotton plant, tuft　(綿)　わた　(7)
counters for noun categories: number of photos on film　(〜枚取り)　〜まいどり　(7);　age　(〜歳)　〜さい　(1);　birds　(〜羽)　〜わ;　books, notebooks　(〜冊)　〜さつ;　duration in minutes　(〜分)、(〜分間)　〜ふん、〜ふんかん　(2);　duration in months　(〜月間)　〜げつかん　(3);　flat, thin items　(〜枚)　〜まい　(2);　floors of a building　(〜階)　〜かい　(1);　frequency　(〜回)　〜かい　(*GS3*);　frequency　(〜度)　〜ど;　glassfuls or cupfuls　(〜杯)　〜はい;　hours　(〜時間)　〜じかん;　houses, buildings　(〜軒)　〜けん;　jackets, clothes　(〜着)　〜ちゃく;　large animals　(〜頭)　〜とう;　lessons, courses　(〜課)　〜か;　long and often cylindrical items　(〜本)　〜ほん;　machines　(〜台)　〜だい　(2);　months　(〜ヶ月)　〜かげつ　(1);　multiples (times)　(〜倍)　〜ばい;　people　(〜人)　〜にん;　shoes, socks　(〜足)　〜そく;　small animals　(〜匹)　〜ひき　(2);　counter for temperature　(〜度)　〜ど　(4);　weeks　(〜週間)　〜しゅうかん　(3)
country　(国)　くに　(1)
country and western music　カントリーウエスタン　(2)
cousin　いとこ; おいとこさん　*pol.*　(5)
cream, lotion　クリーム　(6)
cream color　(クリーム色)　クリームいろ　(7)
credit card　クレジット・カード　(2)
croissant　クロワッサン　(7)
crowded (get crowded)　(混む)　こむ　*C1, intr.*　(5)
cry　(泣く)　なく　*C1, intr.*　(3)
cucumber　きゅうり　(6)
cuisine　(料理)　りょうり　(*GS1*)
culture　(文化)　ぶんか　(1)
culture center　カルチャーセンター　(5)
curry　カレー　(6);　curry and rice　カレーライス　(2)
curtain　カーテン　(*GS1*)
customer, guest　(お客さん)　おきゃくさん　*pol.*　(2);　(客)　きゃく　(7)
cut　(切る)　きる　*C1, tr.*　(3)
cute, pretty　かわいい　*i-adj.*　(5)
cute　キュート(な)　*na-adj.*　(2)
cuttlefish　(烏賊)　いか　(6)
cycling; to cycle　サイクリング(する)　*n.v.*　(5)

D

dance　(踊る)　おどる　*C1, tr.*　(3);　ダンス　(5)
dangerous　(危険[な])　きけん(な)　*na-adj.*　(5)
dark, badly lighted　(暗い)　くらい　*i-adj.*　(4)
dark (*color*)　(濃い)　こい　(7)
dark blue　(藍色)　あいいろ;　ダークブルー　(7)
date; go on a date　デート(する)　*n.v.*　(*GS2*)
daughter, girl　(娘)　むすめ;　(お嬢さん)　おじょうさん　*pol.*;　(娘さん)　むすめさん　*pol.*　(5)
day after tomorrow　あさって　(4)
day before yesterday　おととい　(*GS4*)
day off　(休暇)　きゅうか;　(休日)　きゅうじつ;　(休み)　やすみ;　(休みの日)　やすみのひ　(3)
daytime　(昼間)　ひるま　(4)
Dear… (*used at the beginning of a letter*)　(拝啓)　はいけい　(4)
December　(十二月)　じゅうにがつ　(1)
decide on…　〜にする　(6)
deepen　(深める)　ふかめる　*C2, tr.*　(5)
delicious, tasty　おいしい　*i-adj.*　(3)
delivery; deliver　(配達[する])　はいたつ(する)　*n.v.*　(7)
department (*academic*)　(学部)　がくぶ　(1)
department store　デパート　(*GS2*)
deposit; to deposit　(貯金[する])　ちょきん(する)　*n.v.*　(7)

design; to design　デザイン(する)　*n.v.*;　designer デザイナー;　designer brand　デザイナー・ブランド (*7*)
desk（机）つくえ (*GS1*)
dessert　デザート (*6*)
dew（露）つゆ (*4*)
diamond　ダイヤ (*6*)
dictionary（辞書）じしょ (*GS1*)
die（死ぬ）しぬ　*C1, intr.* (*4*)
diet　ダイエット (*6*)
dietician（栄養士）えいようし (*6*)
differ（違う）ちがう　*C1, intr.* (*GS1*)
difficult（難しい）むずかしい　*i-adj.* (*2*);　be in difficulty, have trouble　こまる　*C1, intr.* (*4*)
difficult to…　〜にくい　(*with conjunctive form of verbs*)　*i-adj.* (*7*)
dining hall（食堂）しょくどう (*2*)
dining out; to dine out（外食[する]）がいしょく(する) *n.v.* (*6*)
dinner, evening meal（夕ごはん）ゆうごはん (*3*);（夕食）ゆうしょく (*6*);（晩ごはん）ばんごはん (*GS2*)
dirty, filtly（汚い）きたない　*i-adj.* (*2*)
disco　ディスコ (*3*)
discount; to discount（割引[する]）わりびき(する) *n.v.* (*7*)
discourtesy; be discourteous, excuse oneself（失礼[する]）しつれい(する)　*n.v.* (*GS1*)
discover（見つける）みつける　*C2, tr.* (*6*)
disgusting（嫌[な]）いや(な)　*na-adj.* (*4*)
dish（皿）さら (*6*)
dislike（嫌い[な]）きらい(な)　*na-adj.* (*GS2*)
district number（〜丁目）〜ちょうめ (*2*)
divide（割る）わる　*C1, tr.* (*GS2*)
diving; to dive　ダイビング(する)　*n.v.* (*5*);　diver ダイバー (*7*)
do（致す）いたす　*C1, tr., pol.* (*4*);　する　*C3, tr.* (*GS3*)
do and come　〜てくる (*6*)
do and leave　〜ていく (*6*)
dog（犬）いぬ (*2*)
door　ドア (*GS1*)
dormitory（寮）りょう (*GS5*)
down（下）した (*2*)
downpour of rain（土砂降り）どしゃぶり (*4*)
draw（描く）かく　*C1, tr.*;　draw a picture（絵を描く）えをかく (*5*)
dream（夢）ゆめ (*7*)
dress, clothing（服装）ふくそう (*7*)
dress　ドレス、ワンピース (*7*)
dress shirt　ワイシャツ (*7*)
drink（飲む）のむ　*C1, tr.* (*GS3*)
driving; drive（運転[する]）うんてん(する)　*n.v.*; ドライブ(する) (*3*)
drizzle（時雨）しぐれ (*4*)
drop（落す）おとす　*C1, tr.* (*6*)
drought（日照り）ひでり (*4*)
drugstore（薬屋）くすりや (*7*)
dry cleaners（クリーニング屋）クリーニングや;　dry cleaning　ドライ・クリーニング (*7*)

E

early, quick（早い、速い）はやい　*i-adj.* (*GS3*);（早く、速く）はやく　*adv.* (*4*)
early summer rain（五月雨）さみだれ (*4*)
earring　イヤリング (*7*)
east（東）ひがし (*2*)
easy（簡単[な]）かんたん(な)　*na-adj.* (*5*); やさしい　*i-adj.* (*2*)
easy to…　〜やすい　(*with conjunctive form of verb*) *i-adj.* (*7*)
eat（食べる）たべる　*C2, tr.* (*GS3*);　I will eat now (*said before eating*)　いただきます (*6*)
economics（経済学）けいざいがく (*1*)
edge　はじ (*2*)
education (*academic subject*)（教育学）きょういくがく (*1*)
education（教養）きょうよう (*5*)
effectively（有効に）ゆうこうに (*5*)
egg（卵）たまご;　egg dish（卵料理）たまごりょうり;　egg salad　エッグサラダ (*6*)
egoistic　わがまま(な) *na-adj.* (*5*)
eight（八）はち (*GS2*);（八つ）やっつ (*2*)
eighth day（八日）ようか (*3*)
eighty（八十）はちじゅう (*GS5*)
either　どちらか (*5*)
electric appliance store（電気店）でんきてん (*7*)
electricity（電気）でんき (*GS1*)
electric train（電車）でんしゃ (*2*)
elegant　エレガント(な)　*na-adj.* (*2*)
elevator　エレベーター (*1*)
eleventh day（十一日）じゅういちにち (*3*)
embroidery; embroider（刺繍[する]）ししゅう(する) *n.v.* (*5*)
emperor（天皇）てんのう (*3*)
end, finish（終わる）おわる　*C1, intr.* (*3*)
engineer　エンジニア (*1*)
engineering（工学）こうがく;　engineering department（工学部）こうがくぶ (*1*)
England　イギリス　*p.n.* (*1*)
English language（英語）えいご (*1*);　English writing（英文）えいぶん (*5*);　English person（イギリス人）イギリスじん (*1*)
enjoy（楽しむ）たのしむ　*C1, tr.* (*5*)
enter（入る）はいる　*C1, intr.* (*3*)
entertainment（娯楽）ごらく (*5*)
entry level; begin（入門[する]）にゅうもん(する) *n.v.* (*5*)
envy; to envy, be jealous（嫉妬[する]）しっと(する) *n.v.* (*7*)
era（年号）ねんごう (*3*)
eraser（消しゴム）けしゴム (*GS1*)
errand（用事）ようじ (*3*)
especially（特に）とくに　*adv.* (*GS2*)
evening（夕方）ゆうがた (*GS2*);　evening shower（夕立）ゆうだち (*4*)
evening snack（夜食）やしょく (*6*)
event; item（種目）しゅもく (*5*)
every（毎〜）まい〜;　every day（毎日）まいにち (*GS4*);　every month（毎月）まいつき (*3*);

every morning （毎朝）まいあさ *(GS3)*; every night （毎晩）まいばん; every week （毎週）まいしゅう *(3)*
everyday life （日常生活）にちじょうせいかつ *(3)*
everyone （誰でも）だれでも、（誰も）だれも; （皆さん） みなさん *pol.* *(5)*; （皆）みんな、みな *(3)*
everywhere どこでも、どこも *(5)*
examination （試験[する]）しけん(する) *n.v.* *(3)*
excuse me, well… あのう… *(1)*
excuse me すみません *(GS1)*
exercise; to do exercise （運動[する]）うんどう(する) *n.v.* *(GS2)*
exist (*animate things*) いる *C1, intr.* *(2)*
expensive, high （高い）たかい *i-adj.* *(2)*
eyeglasses （眼鏡）めがね; put on eyeglasses （眼鏡をかける）めがねをかける *(7)*

F

face （顔）かお *(3)*
facing （向かい）むかい *(2)*
facsimile ファクシミリ *(1)*
fact こと *(5)*
fall (*rain and snow*) （降る） ふる *C1, intr.* *(4)*
fall, autumn （秋）あき *(4)*
Fahrenheit （華氏）かし *(4)*
family （家族）かぞく; （御家族）ごかぞく *pol.* *(5)*
famous （有名[な]） ゆうめい(な) *na-adj.* *(2)*
far away （遠い）とおい *i-adj.* *(GS3)*
fashion ファッション *(5)*; fashion model モデル; fashion show ファッション・ショー *(7)*
fast, early （早い、速い）はやい *i-adj.* *(GS3)*
fast food ファーストフード; fast-food restaurant ファーストフード・レストラン *(6)*
fat (get fat) （太る） ふとる *C1, intr.* *(6)*
father （お父さん） おとうさん *pol.*; （父） ちち *(5)*
favorite, greatly liked （大好き[な]） だいすき(な) *na-adj.* *(2)*
February （二月） にがつ *(1)*
female student （女子学生）じょしがくせい *(5)*
few （少ない） すくない *i-adj.* *(2)*; （少なく） すくなく *adv.* *(6)*
fifteenth day （十五日）じゅうごにち *(3)*
fifth day （五日） いつか *(3)*
fifty （五十） ごじゅう *(GS5)*
film フィルム *(5)*
find （見つける） みつける *C2, tr.* *(6)*
finish, end （終わる） おわる *C1, intr.* *(3)*
finish …ing 〜しまう (*with te-form of verb*) *C1, tr.* *(6)*
first （最初） さいしょ *adv.* *(7)*
first; first of all （初めに）はじめに *(6)*
first-class （高級[な]） こうきゅう(な) *na-adj.* *(7)*
first day （一日） ついたち *(3)*
first of all, to begin with まず *(3)*
first year (*in era*) （元年） がんねん *(3)*
fish （魚） さかな *(GS2)*; catch fish （魚を釣る） さかなをつる *(5)*; fish store （魚屋） さかなや *(7)*
fish burger フィッシュバーガー *(GS3)*
fishing （釣り）つり *(4)*
fit; to fit フィット(する) *n.v.* *(7)*
fitting room （試着室）しちゃくしつ *(7)*
five （五つ） いつつ *(2)*; （五） ご *(GS2)*
flood （洪水）こうずい *(4)*
floor （床） ゆか *(GS1)*
floor space （面積） めんせき *(2)*
flower （花） はな *(4)*; flower arranging （生け花） いけばな *(5)*; flower shop （花屋） はなや *(7)*
flute フルート *(5)*
fly （飛ぶ）とぶ *C1, intr.* *(3)*
fog （霧） きり *(4)*
food （食べ物） たべもの; food store （食べ物屋） たべものや; foodstuffs （食料品）しょくりょうひん *(6)*
football フットボール *(5)*
foreign languages （外国語） がいこくご *(1)*
foreign student （留学生）りゅうがくせい *(7)*
forget （忘れる） わすれる *C2, tr.* *(5)*
fork フォーク *(3)*
formal, ceremonious, stiff （堅苦しい） かたくるしい *i-adj.* *(7)*
formal フォーマル(な) *na-adj.* *(7)*
forty （四十）よんじゅう *(GS5)*
fountain pen （万年筆）まんねんひつ *(1)*
four （四） し、よん *(GS2)*; （四つ）よっつ *(2)*
four seasons （四季） しき *(4)*
fourteenth day （十四日）じゅうよっか *(3)*
fourth day （四日）よっか *(3)*
France フランス *p.n.*; French language （フランス語） フランスご; French person （フランス人） フランスじん *(1)*
free, not busy （暇[な]） ひま(な) *na-adj.* *(3)*; free time （余暇）よか *(5)*
free of charge （無料） むりょう *(6)*
French bread フランス・パン *(7)*
French fries フレンチフライ *(GS3)*
Friday （金曜日）きんようび *(GS4)*
friend （友だち）ともだち *(GS3)*
from から *part.* *(1)*
front （前） まえ *(2)*
frost （霜） しも *(4)*
frozen food （冷凍食品） れいとうしょくひん *(6)*
fruit （果物）くだもの *(GS1)*; fruit salad フルーツ・サラダ *(6)*; fruit store （果物屋） くだものや *(7)*
fry （揚げる） あげる *C2, tr.* *(6)*
frying pan フライパン *(6)*
full capacity （満員）まんいん *(6)*
fun （面白い） おもしろい *i-adj.*; （楽しい） たのしい *i-adj.* *(2)*
funny おかしい *i-adj.* *(2)*; おかし(な) *na-adj.* *(6)*
fur （毛皮）けがわ *(7)*
furniture store （家具屋）かぐや *(7)*
futon store （布団屋）ふとんや *(7)*

G

gambling; gamble ギャンブル[する] *n.v.* *(5)*
game, match; play a match （試合[する]） しあい[する] *n.v.* *(5)*

gardening （園芸）えんげい *(5)*
gas station ガソリン・スタンド *(2)*
gate （門）もん *(3)*
gather （集める） あつめる *C2, tr.* *(5)*
gaudy, brightly colored （派手［な］） はで（な） *na-adj.* *(2)*
general education subject （教養科目）きょうようかもく *(1)*
gentle (breeze) おだやか（な） *na-adj.* *(4)*
Germany ドイツ *p.n.*; German language （ドイツ語） ドイツご; German person （ドイツ人）ドイツじん *(1)*
get off, get down （降りる）おりる *C2, intr.* *(3)*
get up （起きる）おきる *C2, int.* *(GS3)*
gift ギフト *(3)*
girl （女の子） おんなのこ *(5)*
girlfriend ガールフレンド *(1)*
glass, cup コップ *(6)*
gloomy （陰気［な］）いんき（な）*na-adj.* *(4)*
glove （手袋）てぶくろ *(7)*
go （行く）いく *C1, intr.* *(GS3)*
go back, return （帰る）かえる *C1, intr.* *(GS3)*
go out, come out, leave （出る）でる *C2, intr.*; （出かける） でかける *C2, intr.* *(3)*
go to... （〜に行く） 〜にいく *(7)*
go to bed （寝る） ねる *C1, intr.* *(GS3)*
gold color （金色）きんいろ *(7)*
goldfish （金魚）きんぎょ *(5)*
golf ゴルフ *(4)*
good いい *i-adj.* *(GS1)*
good, satisfactory （結構［な］） けっこう（な） *na-adj.* *(GS5)*
good afternoon こんにちは *(GS1)*
good at, skillful （上手［な］）じょうず（な）*na-adj.* *(5)*
good at and like, forte （得意［な］） とくい（な） *na-adj.* *(5)*
good-bye さよ（う）なら *(GS1)*
good enough, OK （大丈夫［な］）だいじょうぶ（な） *na-adj.* *(GS4)*
good evening こんばんは *(GS1)*
good-looking, stylish かっこういい *i-adj.* *(5)*
good morning おはよう *(GS1)*
good night おやすみなさい *(GS1)*
goods （商品）しょうひん *(7)*
gospel music ゴスペル *(2)*
graduate student （大学院生）だいがくいんせい *(1)*
grandchild （お孫さん）おまごさん *pol.*; （孫）まご *(5)*
grandfather （祖父）そふ; おじいさん *pol.* *(5)*
grandmother （祖母）そぼ; おばあさん *pol.* *(5)*
grape （葡萄）ぶどう *(6)*; グレープ *(GS5)*
gray （灰色）はいいろ; グレー *(7)*
green （緑）みどり; グリーン *(7)*
greengrocer （八百屋）やおや *(7)*
green pepper ピーマン *(6)*
green tea （緑茶）りょくちゃ *(6)*
greeting; greet someone （挨拶［する］） あいさつ［する］ *n.v.* *(3)*
grill （焼く） やく *C1, tr.* *(6)*
grocery store （食料品店）しょくりょうひんてん *(7)*
guest, customer （お客さん）おきゃくさん *(2)*
guidebook ガイドブック *(7)*
guitar ギター *(5)*
gym （体育館）たいいくかん *(1)*; ジム *(5)*
gymnastics （体操）たいそう *(5)*

H

hail あられ *(4)*
hair （髪）かみ *(3)*; hairstyle ヘアースタイル *(5)*
half （半）はん *(GS2)*; （半分）はんぶん; half price （半額）はんがく *(7)*
ham ハム *(6)*
hamburger ハンバーガー *(GS3)*
hammer ハンマー *(7)*
handicrafts （手芸）しゅげい *(5)*
handkerchief ハンカチ *(7)*
handsome かっこういい *i-adj.* *(5)*; ハンサム（な） *na-adj.* *(2)*
hardware store （金物屋） かなものや *(7)*
hat （帽子） ぼうし *(7)*
hate, dislike intensely （大嫌い［な］） だいきらい（な） *na-adj.* *(2)*
have, hold （持つ）もつ *C1, tr.* *(3)*
he （彼）かれ *pron.* *(1)*
head （頭）あたま *(7)*
health （健康）けんこう; healthy （健康［な］） けんこう（な） *na-adj.* *(2)*
healthy, energetic （元気［な］） げんき（な）*na-adj.* *(4)*
hear, inquire （伺う）うかがう *C1, tr., pol.* *(5)*
hear, ask （聞く）きく *C1, tr.* *(GS1)*
heavy （重い）おもい *i-adj.* *(2)*
hello (*answering the telephone*) もしもし *interj.* *(2)*
helmet ヘルメット *(7)*
help, assist （手伝う）てつだう *C1, tr.* *(3)*
here ここ、こちら *dem. pron.* *(1)*
high heel ハイヒール *(7)*
hiking ハイキング *(4)*
history (*study of*) （歴史学） れきしがく *(1)*
hit （打つ）うつ *C1, tr.* *(5)*
hobby （趣味）しゅみ *(5)*
Holland オランダ *p.n.* *(2)*
Hong Kong （香港） ホンコン *p.n.*; Hong Kong native （香港人） ホンコンじん *(1)*
home うち *(GS5)*
hometown, native place （出身）しゅっしん *(1)*
homework （宿題）しゅくだい *(4)*
horseback riding （乗馬）じょうば *(5)*
hospital （病院）びょういん *(2)*
hot (*temperature*) （暑い）あつい *i-adj.* *(GS4)*
hot, spicy （辛い）からい *i-adj.* *(6)*
hot water （お湯）おゆ *(6)*
hotel ホテル *(2)*
house （家） いえ *(1)* うち *(GS5)*
household finance book （家計簿）かけいぼ *(7)*
housing, residence （住まい） すまい *(1)*
how どう *dem. adv.*; どうして *(1)*
how about いかが *(GS5)*
how many days （何日）なんにち *(3)*; how many degrees （何度）なんど *(4)*; how many floors

（何階）なんかい (*GS2*); how many hours （何時間） なんじかん (*3*); how many minutes （何分） なんぷん (*3*); how many years （何年）なんねん (*3*)
how much, how many いくつ (*1*); いくら (*cost*) (*GS3*)
how old いくつ; （何歳）なんさい (*1*)
however, but しかし *conj.* (*3*)
however much… いくら (*GS3*)
humidity （湿度）しつど (*4*)
hundred （百）ひゃく (*GS5*)
hundred million （億）おく (*2*)
hundred thousand （十万）じゅうまん (*2*)
hungry (get hungry) おなかがすく (*3*)
hunting （狩り） かり; ハンティング (*5*)
husband （夫）おっと; （御主人）ごしゅじん *pol.*; （主人）しゅじん (*5*)

I

I あたし *pron., inf., f.*; （僕） ぼく *pron., inf., m.* (*1*); （私）わたし *pron.* (*GS1*)
ice アイス (*GS5*)
ice cream アイスクリーム (*GS5*)
ice milk アイスミルク (*GS3*)
ice tea アイスティー (*GS2*)
ID (identification) （身分証明書） みぶんしょうめいしょ (*3*)
idea （考え）かんがえ (*6*)
idle one's time away, loaf ゴロゴロする *C3, intr.* (*5*)
if 〜たら (*7*)
immediately すぐ、すぐに *adv.* (*6*)
impossible （無理［な］）むり（な） *na-adj.* (*5*)
in, inside （中）なか (*2*)
in, at, to に *part.* (*GS3*)
in total （全部で）ぜんぶで *adv.* (*2*)
in-law （義理の）ぎりの (*5*)
inconvenient （不便［な］）ふべん（な） *na-adj.* (*2*)
increase （増える）ふえる *C2, intr.* (*6*)
indeed, thanks どうも (*GS1*)
ingredient （材料）ざいりょう (*6*)
ink インキ (*7*)
inquire, ask （伺う）うかがう *C1, tr.* (*5*)
inside うち (*GS3*)
inside, center （中）なか (*2*)
installment payment system （分割払い） ぶんかつばらい (*7*)
instant food インスタント・フード; （インスタント食品）インスタントしょくひん (*6*)
instant ramen インスタント・ラーメン (*6*)
intend to do… （〜ようと思う）〜ようとおもう (*with verb root*) (*6*)
intention つもり (*7*)
interesting, fun （面白い）おもしろい *i-adj.* (*2*)
interview; to interview インタビュー（する） *n.v.* (*6*)
introduction; introduce （紹介［する］） しょうかい（する） *n.v.*; self-introduction; introduce oneself （自己紹介［する］）じこしょうかい（する） *n.v.* (*1*)
introduction; beginning level （入門）にゅうもん (*5*)
investigation; investigate （調査［する］） ちょうさ（する） *n.v.* (*5*)
invite （誘う）さそう *C1, tr.* (*7*); （呼ぶ）よぶ *C1, tr.* (*6*)
iron (*appliance*) アイロン; use an iron アイロンをかける (*7*)
issue, problem （問題）もんだい (*4*)
Italy イタリア *p.m.*; Italian language （イタリア語） イタリアご; Italian person （イタリア人） イタリアじん (*1*)
Item, thing もの (*2*)

J

jacket ジャケット; jacket, suit coat （上着）うわぎ (*7*)
January （一月）いちがつ (*1*)
Japan （日本）にほん *p.n.*; Japanese language （日本語） にほんご (*GS1*); Japanese cuisine （和食） わしょく (*6*); Japanese person （日本人） にほんじん (*1*); Japanese playing game カルタ (*5*); Japanese sake （日本酒）にほんしゅ (*6*); Japanese traditional dance （日本舞踊）にほんぶよう (*5*)
Japanese-style clothes （和服） わふく (*7*)
jazz ジャズ (*GS2*)
jealousy; to be jealous （嫉妬［する］） しっと（する） *n.v.* (*7*)
jeans ジーパン、ジーンズ (*7*)
jewelry shop （宝石店）ほうせきてん (*7*)
jogging; jog ジョギング（する） *n.v.* (*5*)
joke （冗談）じょうだん (*7*)
juice ジュース (*GS2*)
July （七月）しちがつ (*1*)
June （六月）ろくがつ (*1*)

K

ketchup ケチャップ (*6*)
key （鍵）かぎ (*7*)
kilometer, kilogram キロ (*5*)
kimono （着物）きもの; kimono store （呉服屋） ごふくや (*7*)
kind, type （種類）しゅるい (*6*)
kind, nice （親切［な］） しんせつ（な） (*2*)
kiss; to kiss キス（する） *n.v.* (*5*)
kitchen （台所）だいどころ、キッチン (*6*)
knife ナイフ (*3*)
knit, crochet （編む）あむ *C1, tr.* (*7*)
knitting (*object*) （編み物）あみもの (*5*)
know （知る）しる *C1, tr.* (*3*)
Korean language （韓国語）かんこくご (*1*)

L

laboratory （実験室）じっけんしつ (*1*)
lamb ラム (*6*)
language （言葉）ことば (*4*)
language lab ランゲージ・ラボ (*1*)
laptop computer ラップトップ・コンピュータ (*4*)

large, big （大きい） おおきい *i-adj.* *(2)*
last month （先月） せんげつ *(3)*
last week （先週） せんしゅう *(GS4)*
last year （去年） きょねん; （昨年） さくねん *(3)*
late （遅く） おそく *adv.* *(3)*; be late （遅れる） おくれる *C2, intr.* *(4)*
late, slow （遅い） おそい *i-adj.* *(3)*
later （後で） あとで *(3)*
laugh （笑う） わらう *C1, tr.* *(3)*
laundromat コインランドリー *(3)*
laundry （洗濯） せんたく *(3)*
law （法学） ほうがく *(1)*
lazy （不真面目［な］） ふまじめ（な） *na-adj.* *(4)*
learn （習う） ならう *C1, tr.* *(6)*
leave （出る） でる *C2, intr.* *(3)*
left side （左） ひだり *(2)*
leisure レジャー *(5)*
lemon レモン *(6)*
lend, rent out （貸す） かす *C1, tr.* *(7)*
lenient, gentle やさしい *i-adj.* *(2)*
letter （手紙） てがみ *(GS3)*
lettuce レタス *(6)*
liberal arts （教養） きょうよう *(5)*
library （図書館） としょかん *(1)*
lie （嘘） うそ *(3)*
light (*not heavy*) （軽い） かるい *i-adj.* *(2)*
light (*electric*) （電気） でんき *(GS1)*
light, pale color （薄い） うすい *i-adj.* *(7)*
light blue ライトブルー *(7)*
light meal （軽食） けいしょく *(6)*
lightning （稲光） いなびかり; （稲妻） いなずま *(4)*
light rain （小雨） こさめ *(4)*
like, favor （好き［な］） すき（な） *na-adj.* *(2)*
like that そう *dem. adv.* *(GS1)*
like this こう *dem. adv.* *(4)*
limit （限る） かぎる *C1, tr.* *(5)*
linguistics （言語学） げんごがく *(1)*
liquor, sake （お酒） おさけ *(GS1)*; liquor store （酒屋） さかや *(7)*
listen, ask （聞く） きく *C1, tr.* *(GS1)*
literature （文学） ぶんがく; literature department （文学部） ぶんがくぶ *(1)*
little, a little （少し） すこし *adv.* *(3)*; ちょっと *adv.* *(GS1)*
live, reside （住む） すむ *C1, intr.* *(3)*
lively にぎやか（な） *na-adj.* *(2)*; （陽気） ようき（な） *(4)*
liver レバー *(4)*
lobster ロブスター *(6)*
lock, key （鍵） かぎ; lock up （鍵をかける） かぎをかける *(7)*
lonely （寂しい） さびしい *i-adj.* *(7)*
long （長い） ながい *i-adj.* *(2)*
look for （探す） さがす *C1, tr.* *(1)*
loose ゆるい *i-adj.* *(7)*
loud, gaudy （派手［な］） はで（な） *na-adj.* *(2)*
love （愛） あい *(7)*
low, short （低い） ひくい *i-adj.* *(2)*
lunch （昼食） ちゅうしょく *(6)*; （昼ごはん） ひるごはん *(GS2)*

M

machine （機械） きかい *(2)*
made in… （〜製） 〜せい *(7)*
magazine （雑誌） ざっし *(GS3)*
magic, sleight-of-hand （手品） てじな *(5)*
mah-jongg マージャン *(5)*
mail, post （出す） だす; mail a letter （手紙を出す） てがみをだす *C1, tr.* *(7)*
mail order メールオーダー *(7)*
make, fabricate （作る） つくる *C1, tr.* *(GS1)*
make (*a telephone call*) かける *C2, tr.* *(3)*
make a mistake （間違う） まちがう *C1, intr.* *(3)*
maker メーカー *(1)*
male student （男子学生） だんしがくせい *(5)*
mama ママ *(5)*
man （男） おとこ *(2)*; （男の方） おとこのかた *pol.*; （男の人） おとこのひと; （男性） だんせい *(5)*
mandarin orange みかん *(6)*
many （多い） おおい *i-adj.*; たくさん *(2)*
many times （何度も） なんども *(6)*
map （地図） ちず *(2)*
marathon; run a marathon マラソン（する） *n.v.* *(5)*
March （三月） さんがつ *(1)*
margarine マーガリン *(6)*
market （市場） いちば *(7)*
married couple （御夫婦） ごふうふ *pol.*; （夫婦） ふうふ *(5)*
mathematics （数学） すうがく *(1)*
matter こと *(5)*
May （五月） ごがつ *(1)*
meal （御飯） ごはん *(3)*
meal; to eat a meal （食事［する］） しょくじ（する） *n.v.* *(6)*
mean, bullying （意地悪［な］） いじわる（な） *na-adj.* *(4)*
meaning （意味） いみ *(4)*
meat （肉） にく *(2)*; ground meat （ひき肉） ひきにく; ミンチ *(6)*
meet, see (*a person*) （会う） あう *C1, intr.* *(GS3)*
meeting ミーティング *(GS2)*
meeting, conference （会議） かいぎ *(5)*
melon メロン *(6)*
memorize （憶える） おぼえる *C2, tr.* *(7)*
memory メモリー *(7)*
mend （繕う） つくろう *C1, tr.* *(7)*
menu メニュー *(GS2)*
merchandise （商品） しょうひん *(7)*
message; leave a message （伝言［する］） でんごん（する） *n.v.* *(3)*
meter メーター、メートル *(4)*
Mexico メキシコ *p.n.*; Mexican person （メキシコ人） メキシコじん *(1)*
middle （真ん中） まんなか *(2)*
milk （牛乳） ぎゅうにゅう *(6)*; ミルク *(3)*
million （百万） ひゃくまん *(2)*
miserly けち（な） *na-adj.* *(4)*
mystery (*novel*) ミステリー *(3)*
Monday （月曜日） げつようび *(GS4)*
money （お金） おかね *(2)*; （金） かね *(5)*
more もっと *adv.* *(4)*

more than… 〜より (*4*); (〜以上) 〜いじょう (*5*)
morning (朝) あさ (*GS2*); (午前中) ごぜんちゅう (*3*); A.M. (午前) ごぜん (*GS2*)
morning and evening (朝夕) あさゆう (*4*)
most, top, best (一番) いちばん (*4*)
mother (お母さん) おかあさん *pol.*; (母) はは (*5*)
mountain (山) やま; mountain climbing (山登り) やまのぼり (*4*)
movie (映画) えいが; movie theater (映画館) えいがかん (*GS2*)
Mr., Mrs., Ms. (〜様) 〜さま *pol.* (*4*); 〜さん (*GS1*)
multiply (掛ける) かける *C2, tr.* (*GS2*)
music (音楽) おんがく (*GS3*); listening to music (音楽鑑賞) おんがくかんしょう (*5*)
music store (レコード店／レコード屋) レコードてん／レコードや (*7*)
musical ミュージカル (*5*)
musical instrument (楽器) がっき (*5*)
mutton マトン (*7*)
my (私の) わたしの *pron.* (*GS1*)

N

name (名前) なまえ (*GS1*)
name card (名刺) めいし (*GS1*)
napkin ナプキン (*6*)
narrow, small (狭い) せまい *i-adj.* (*2*)
national holiday (祝日) しゅくじつ (*3*)
nationality (国籍) こくせき (*1*)
nearby place そば (*2*)
near, close to (近い) ちかい *i-adj.* (*GS3*); (近く) ちかく (*3*)
necklace ネックレス (*7*)
necktie ネクタイ (*7*)
need, want (要る) いる *C1, tr.* (*4*)
needle (針) はり (*7*)
negligee ネグリジェ (*7*)
neighborhood (近所) きんじょ (*2*)
neither どちらも (*5*)
nephew (甥) おい; (甥ごさん) おいごさん *pol.* (*5*)
never (一度も) いちども (*6*); もう (*with negative*) *adv.* (*GS1*)
new (新しい) あたらしい *i-adj.* (*2*)
news ニュース (*GS3*)
newspaper (新聞) しんぶん (*GS3*)
New Year's Day (元日) がんじつ (*3*)
next (次) つぎ (*GS1*); (次の) つぎの (*6*)
next-door (隣) となり (*2*)
next month (来月) らいげつ (*3*)
next to (隣) となり (*2*)
next week (来週) らいしゅう (*3*)
next year (来年) らいねん (*3*)
niece (姪) めい; (姪ごさん) めいごさん *pol.* (*5*)
night (夜) よる (*GS2*)
nine (九) きゅう、く; (*GS2*) (九つ) ここのつ (*2*)
ninth day (九日) ここのか (*3*)
ninety (九十) きゅうじゅう (*GS5*)
no いいえ (*GS1*)
noisy うるさい *i-adj.* (*2*)
none of them どれも (*5*)
noon (昼) ひる (*GS2*)
no one (誰も) だれも; どなたも *pol.* (*5*)
north (北) きた (*2*); north wind (北風) きたかぜ (*4*)
not at all (全然) ぜんぜん (*with negative*) (*3*)
notebook ノート (*GS1*)
not good ダメ(な) *na-adj.* (*5*)
notice, announcement (知らせ) しらせ (*5*)
not serious (不真面目[な]) ふまじめ(な) *na-adj.* (*4*)
not tasty まずい *i-adj.* (*4*)
not there, not to exist いない (*animate nouns*); ない *i-adj.* (*2*)
not very much あ(ん)まり (*with negative*) *adv.* (*2*)
not yet, still まだ *adv.* (*3*)
November (十一月) じゅういちがつ (*1*)
now (今) いま *adv.* (*GS2*)
nowhere どこも (*5*)
nuisance; cause trouble (迷惑[する]) めいわく(する) *n.v.* (*5*)
number… (〜番) 〜ばん (*GS2*); (〜号) 〜ごう (*2*); (〜番目) 〜ばんめ (*5*)
number (番号) ばんごう (*GS2*)
number (*in address*) (番地) ばんち (*2*)
number one; first; best (一番) いちばん (*4*)
nutrition (栄養) えいよう (*6*)
nylon ナイロン (*7*)

O

o'clock (〜時) 〜じ (*GS2*)
ocean, sea (海) うみ (*4*)
October (十月) じゅうがつ (*1*)
octopus たこ (*6*)
oden おでん (*6*)
of course (勿論) もちろん (*2*)
office オフィス (*1*)
often よく *adv.* (*1*)
oh… ああ *interj.* (*2*)
oh (*exclamation of surprise*) へえ *interj.* (*3*)
oil painting (油絵) あぶらえ (*5*)
old (古い) ふるい *i-adj.* (*2*)
older brother (兄) あに; (お兄さん) おにいさん *pol.* (*5*)
older sister (姉) あね; (お姉さん) おねえさん *pol.* (*5*)
oldest daughter (長女) ちょうじょ (*5*)
oldest son (長男) ちょうなん (*5*)
Olympic オリンピック (*5*)
omelet オムレツ (*GS3*)
on (上) うえ (*2*)
once (一度) いちど (*GS1*)
once in a while たまに *adv.* (*3*)
one (一) いち (*GS2*); (一つ) ひとつ (*2*)
one of them どれか (*5*)
one person (一人) ひとり (*2*)
oneself (自分) じぶん; by oneself (自分で) じぶんで (*6*)

oneself, alone （一人で）ひとりで (*5*)
one time （一度）いちど (*GS1*)
onion （玉葱）たまねぎ (*6*)
only ～だけ; しか (*7*)
onomatopoeia （擬声語）ぎせいご (*5*)
open （開ける）あける *C2, tr.* (*GS1*)
opera オペラ (*5*)
optician's （眼鏡店／眼鏡屋） めがねてん／めがねや (*7*)
or か *part.* (*1*)
orange オレンジ; orange color （オレンジ色） オレンジいろ (*6*); orange juice オレンジ・ジュース (*GS3*)
order; to order （注文[する]）ちゅうもん(する) *n.v.* (*7*)
ordinal （普通）ふつう (*6*)
origin, hometown （出身）しゅっしん (*1*)
other side （向こう側）むこうがわ (*2*)
out of stock （品切れ）しなぎれ (*7*)
outside （外）そと (*2*)
oven オーブン (*6*)
oven, range レンジ (*6*)
over （上）うえ (*2*)
overcoat オーバー (*4*)
oversleeping, oversleep （寝坊[する]）ねぼう(する) *n.v.* (*4*)
over there あそこ *dem. pron.*; あちら *dem. pron., pol.* (*1*)
own （持つ）もつ *C1, tr.* (*3*)

P

painful （痛い）いたい *i-adj.* (*7*)
painting （絵画）かいが (*5*)
pair ペア (*GS1*)
pajamas パジャマ (*7*)
pan for cooking （鍋） なべ (*6*)
panties パンティー; pantyhose パンティーストッキング (*7*)
papa パパ (*5*)
papaya パパイア (*6*)
paper （髪）かみ (*GS1*)
parents （御両親）ごりょうしん *pol.*; （両親） りょうしん *pl.* (*5*)
park （公園）こうえん (*2*)
parking lot （駐車場）ちゅうしゃじょう (*2*)
part （一部）いちぶ (*7*)
particularly, separately （別に）べつに *adv.* (*6*)
part-time job アルバイト (*3*)
party パーティー (*GS2*)
pass (*time*) （過ごす）すごす *C1, tr.* (*5*)
passenger （お客さん）おきゃくさん (*2*); （客）きゃく (*7*)
passion （情熱）じょうねつ (*7*)
pasta パスタ (*6*)
pastime （娯楽）ごらく(*5*)
pattern, design （模様）もよう (*7*)
pay （払う）はらう *C1, tr.* (*7*)
pea, bean （豆）まめ (*6*)
peaceful （静か[な]）しずか(な) *na-adj.* (*2*)
pear （梨）なし (*6*)
pearl パール (*7*)
pen ペン (*GS1*)
pencil （鉛筆）えんぴつ (*GS1*)
pen pal ペンパル (*1*)
pepper （胡椒）こしょう (*6*)
perhaps, it seems that おそらく *adv.* (*4*)
perhaps, probably （多分）たぶん *adv.* (*4*)
perhaps… (*conjecture*) ～かもしれない (*4*)
person （方）かた *pol.*; （人）ひと (*1*)
pet ペット (*5*)
pharmacy （薬屋）くすりや; （薬局） やっきょく (*7*)
philosophy （哲学）てつがく (*1*)
photo album アルバム (*5*)
photograph, photography （写真）しゃしん (*1*)
physics （物理学）ぶつりがく (*1*)
pianist ピアニスト (*5*)
piano ピアノ (*5*)
pickle （漬物）つけもの (*6*)
picture （絵）え (*5*)
picture postcard （絵はがき）えはがき (*7*)
pierced earrings ピアス (*7*)
pineapple パイナップル (*6*)
ping pong ピンポン (*5*)
pink ピンク (*7*)
pizza ピザ (*GS2*)
place （場所）ばしょ (*5*)
place, set on のせる *C2, tr.* (*6*)
plain （地味[な]）じみ(な) *na-adj.* (*7*)
plain (*no pattern*) （無地）むじ (*7*)
plan （予定）よてい (*6*)
plastic model プラモデル (*7*)
plate （皿）さら (*6*)
play （遊ぶ）あそぶ *C1, intr.* (*5*)
play (a musical instrument) （演奏する）えんそうする; （弾く）ひく *C1, tr.* (*5*)
please (do something) ～てください (*2*)
please, go ahead どうぞ (*GS1*)
please, give me… ～ください (*GS2*)
plug outlet コンセント (*6*)
P.M. （午後）ごご (*GS2*)
pocket ポケット (*7*)
police box （交番）こうばん (*2*)
police officer おまわりさん *coll.* (*2*)
polish （磨く）みがく *C1, tr.* (*3*)
political science （政治学）せいじがく (*1*)
polka dots （水玉）みずたま (*5*)
polyester ポリエステル (*7*)
poor at, unskillful （下手[な]）へた(な) *na-adj.* (*5*)
popcorn ポップコーン (*6*)
popularity （人気）にんき (*5*)
population （人口）じんこう (*2*)
pork （豚肉）ぶたにく (*6*)
portable ポータブル (*7*)
Portuguese language （ポルトガル語）ポルトガルご (*1*)
post office （郵便局）ゆうびんきょく (*2*)
pot （鍋）なべ (*6*)
potato （薯） いも、じゃがいも、ポテト (*6*)
potato chip ポテトチップ (*7*)

practice; to practice （練習［する］）れんしゅう（する） *n.v.* (2)
precipitation （降水量）こうすいりょう (4)
preparation; prepare （準備［する］）じゅんび（する） *n.v.* (3)
preparation for class; prepare for class （予習［する］） よしゅう（する） *n.v.* (GS1)
present, gift プレゼント (3)
pretty きれい（な） *na-adj.* (2)
price （価格）かかく; （金額）きんがく; （値段） ねだん (7)
print プリント (7)
probably 〜だろう (*with plain form of verb*); 〜でしょう *pol.* (4)
problem, question （問題）もんだい (4)
professional プロ (5)
professor, teacher （先生）せんせい (GS1)
professor's office （研究室）けんきゅうしつ (1)
program (*radio, TV*) （番組）ばんぐみ (5)
program; to program プログラム（する） *n.v.* (7)
programmer プログラマー; programming; to do programming プログラミング（する） *n.v.* (5)
pronunciation; to pronounce （発音［する］） はつおん（する） *n.v.* (4)
proposal; propose marriage プロポーズ（する） *n.v.* (7)
pudding プリン (6)
purple （紫）むらさき (7)
purpose, for the sake of 〜のために (6)
put on, wear: eyeglasses, etc. かける *C2, tr.* (7); the head かぶる *C1, tr.* (7); the torso （着る）きる *C2, tr.* (3); つける *C2, tr.* (7); the feet or legs はく *C1, tr.* (4); rings, etc. はめる *C2, tr.* (7)
put out, eject （出す）だす *C1, tr.* (GS1)
put something in （入れる）いれる *C2, tr.* (3)

Q

question; ask a question （質問［する］）しつもん（する） *n.v.* (GS1)
quick （早い、速い） はやい *i-adj.* (GS3); quickly （早く、速く）はやく *adv.* (4)
quiet （静か［な］） しずか（な） *na-adj.* (2)
quiet, plain (*color*) （地味［な］）じみ（な） *na-adj.* (7)
quit やめる *C2, tr.* (3)
quite なかなか *adv.* (5)

R

racket ラケット (5)
radio ラジオ (GS2)
radio cassette ラジカセ (1)
rain （雨） あめ (GS1); heavy rain （大雨） おおあめ (4)
raincoat レインコート (4)
raise or have a pet （飼う） かう *C1, tr.* (5)
rank, ranking （順位）じゅんい (5)
rap ラップ (2)
rarely ほとんど *adv.* (3)
rather なかなか *adv.* (5)
raw （生） なま; （生の） なまの (6)
read （読む）よむ *C1, tr.* (GS3)
reading books; read books （読書［する］） どくしょ（する） *n.v.* (5)
real （本当） ほんとう (GS2); really （本当に） ほんとうに *adv.* (4)
receipt （領収書）りょうしゅうしょ、レシート (7)
receive いただく(*humble*) *C1, tr., pol.* (4); （受ける） うける *C2, tr.* (5)
recently （最近） さいきん *adv.* (5)
reception office （受け付け） うけつけ (1)
recipe レシピー (6)
recommended item （おすすめ品） おすすめひん (6)
record レコード (3); record store （レコード店／レコード屋） レコードてん／ レコードや (7)
red （赤） あか; （赤い） あかい *i-adj.* (2)
reduced ...% （〜引き） 〜びき (7)
refrigerator （冷蔵庫） れいぞうこ (6)
relative （ご親戚） ごしんせき *pol.*; （親戚） しんせき (5)
remember （思い出す） おもいだす *C1, tr.* (6)
remember, memorize （憶える） おぼえる *C2, tr.* (7)
remote control リモコン (7)
rent, lend （貸す） かす *C1, tr.* (7)
rent, borrow （借りる） かりる *C2, tr.* (7)
repeat （繰り返す） くりかえす *C1, tr.* (GS1)
reporter リポーター (6)
request, ask （お願い） おねがい (GS5)
request （頼む） たのむ *C1, tr.* (6)
reservation; to reserve （予約［する］） よやく（する） *n.v.* (6)
reside （住む） すむ *C1, intr.* (3)
respond （答える） こたえる *C2, intr.* (3); response （答え） こたえ (5)
rest （休む） やすむ *C1, intr.* (3)
restaurant レストラン (2)
rest room トイレ (2)
return, give back （返す） かえす *C1, tr.* (7)
return, go back （帰る） かえる *C1, intr.* (GS3)
returning merchandise; return merchandise （返品［する］） へんぴん（する） *n.v.* (7)
ribbon リボン (7)
rice (cooked) （御飯） ごはん (3); ライス (6)
rice (uncooked) （米） こめ (6)
rice bowl （茶碗） ちゃわん (6)
rice dealer （米屋） こめや (7)
ride （乗る） のる *C1, intr.* (3)
right side （右） みぎ (2)
ring (finger) （指輪） ゆびわ (7)
rise, get up （起きる） おきる *C2, intr.* (GS3)
robust （丈夫［な］） じょうぶ（な） *na-adj.* (7)
rock and roll ロック (GS2)
rock climbing ロッククライミング (5)
romance ロマンス (2)
room （部屋） へや (2)
room number... （〜号室） 〜ごうしつ (5)
rough ラフ（な） *na-adj.* (4)
round （丸い、円い） まるい *i-adj.* (2)
rugby ラグビー (5)

run （走る） はしる *C1, intr.* *(GS1)*
running ランニング *(5)*
Russia ロシア; *p.n.*; Russian language （ロシア語） ロシアご; Russian person （ロシア人） ロシアじん *(1)*

S

safe （安全［な］） あんぜん（な） *na-adj.* *(2)*
sake (for the purpose of) 〜のために *(6)*
saké (*liquor*) （お酒） おさけ *(GS1)*
salad サラダ *(GS3)*; salad dressing サラダドレッシング *(6)*
salaried worker サラリーマン *(5)*
sale （売り出し） うりだし *(7)*
sales セールス *(7)*
salmon （鮭） さけ *(6)*
salt （塩） しお; salty （塩辛い） しおからい *i-adj.*; salty, spicy （辛い） からい *i-adj.* *(6)*
same （同じ） おなじ *(4)*
sandal サンダル *(7)*
sandwich サンドイッチ *(6)*
Saturday （土曜日） どようび *(GS4)*
sausage ソーセージ *(6)*
say （言う） いう *C1, intr.* *(6)*; *C1, tr.* *(GS1)*
scenery （景色） けしき *(6)*
schedule スケジュール *(3)*
school （学校） がっこう *(GS3)*; school year （学年） がくねん *(1)*
science fiction エスエフ *(5)*; science fiction movie （エスエフ映画） エスエフえいが *(2)*
scissors （鋏） はさみ *(7)*
seafood シーフード *(6)*
season （季節） きせつ *(4)*
seasonal word （季語） きご *(4)*
seasoning （調味料） ちょうみりょう *(6)*
seaweed （海苔） のり *(1)*
second day （二日） ふつか *(3)*
see （見る） みる *C2, tr.* *(3)*
see, meet (*a person*) （会う） あう *C1, intr.* *(GS3)*
see someone off （送る） おくる *C1, tr.* *(7)*
self （自分） じぶん *(6)*
selfish わがまま（な） *na-adj.* *(5)*
sell （売る） うる *C1, tr.* *(7)*
send （出す） だす *C1, tr.* *(GS1)*
sense センス *(5)*
September （九月） くがつ *(1)*
serious （真面目［な］） まじめ（な） *na-adj.* *(2)*
service; do gratuitously サービス（する） *n.v.* *(7)*
set up a plan, build （建てる） たてる *C2, tr.* *(7)*
seven （七） しち、なな *(GS2)*; （七つ） ななつ *(2)*
seventh day （七日） なのか *(3)*
seventy （七十） しちじゅう、ななじゅう *(GS5)*
several いくつか *(5)*
sew （縫う） ぬう *C1, tr.*; sewing machine ミシン *(7)*
shave （剃る） そる; shave facial hair ひげをそる *C1, tr.* *(3)*
she （彼女） かのじょ *pron.* *(1)*
shellfish （貝） かい *(6)*
shirt シャツ; long sleeves; long-sleeved （長袖） ながそで *(7)*; short sleeves, short-sleeved （半袖） はんそで *(7)*
shoe （靴） くつ *(GS3)*; shoe store （靴屋） くつや *(7)*
shooting; to shoot （射撃［する］） しゃげき（する） *n.v.* *(5)*
shop owner （主人） しゅじん *(5)*
shopping; to shop （買い物［する］） かいもの（する） *n.v.* *(GS2)*; ショッピング（する） *(7)*
shopping district, shopping street （商店街） しょうてんがい *(7)*
short （短い） みじかい *i-adj.* *(4)*
shorts ショートパンツ *(4)*
show （見せる） みせる *C2, tr.* *(3)*
show window ショーウインドー *(6)*
shower (rain) （にわか雨） にわかあめ *(4)*
shower シャワー *(3)*
shrimp えび *(6)*
shrine (Shinto) （神社） じんじゃ *(2)*
siblings （兄弟） きょうだい; siblings, brothers （御兄弟） ごきょうだい *pol.* *(5)*
sick （病気） びょうき *(3)*
side （横） よこ *(2)*
signature; to sign サイン（する） *n.v.* *(3)*
silk （絹） きぬ *(7)*
silver color （銀色） ぎんいろ *(7)*
simple （簡単［な］） かんたん（な） *na-adj.* *(5)*; シンプル（な） *na-adj.* *(7)*
sincerely (*used in a letter*) （敬具） けいぐ *(4)*
sing （歌う） うたう *C1, tr.* *(3)*; sing a song （歌を歌う） うたをうたう *(5)*
Singapore シンガポール *p.n.*; Singaporean （シンガポール人） シンガポールじん *(1)*
single person (not married) （独身） どくしん *(5)*
six （六つ） むっつ *(2)*; （六） ろく *(GS2)*
sixth day （六日） むいか *(3)*
sixty （六十） ろくじゅう *(GS5)*
size サイズ *(7)*
skating スケート; to skate スケートをする *(4)*
skiing スキー *(GS2)*; ski スキーをする *(4)*
skillful （器用［な］） きよう（な） *na-adj.* *(2)*; skillful （上手［な］） じょうず（な） *na-adj.* *(5)*; skillfully （上手に） じょうずに *adv.* *(4)*
skirt スカート *(7)*
sky （空） そら *(4)*
sleep （眠る） ねむる *C1, intr.* *(3)*; （寝る） ねる *C1, intr.* *(GS3)*
sleet みぞれ *(4)*
slender (person) スマート（な） *na-adj.* *(2)*
slipper スリッパ *(7)*
slow （遅い） おそい *i-adj.* *(3)*; slowly ゆっくり *adv.* *(1)*
small （小さい） ちいさい *i-adj.* *(2)*
smell （臭い） におい *(6)*
snack おやつ; （軽食） けいしょく; スナック *(6)*
sneakers スニーカー *(4)*
snow （雪） ゆき; heavy snow （大雪） おおゆき; snowstorm （吹雪） ふぶき *(4)*
snow boots スノーブーツ *(7)*

so, really　そう　*dem. adv.*　*(GS1)*
so-so, not bad　まあまあ　*(2)*
soap opera　メロドラマ　*(5)*
soccer　サッカー　*(5)*
sociology　(社会学)　しゃかいがく　*(1)*
socks　(靴下)　くつした　*(GS3)*
sofa, couch　ソファー　*(7)*
software　ソフトウエア　*(3)*
sold out　(品切れ)　しなぎれ　*(7)*
some　いくつか　*(5)*
someday　いつか　*adv.*　*(5)*
somehow　どうか; (何とか)　なんとか　*(5)*
someone　(誰か)　だれか;　どなたか　*pol.*　*(5)*
something　(何か)　なにか　*(5)*
sometime　いつか　*adv.*　*(5)*
sometimes　(時々)　ときどき　*adv.*　*(3)*
somewhere　どこか　*(5)*
son　(息子)　むすこ; (息子さん)　むすこさん　*pol.* *(5)*
song　(歌)　うた　*(5)*
soon　(間もなく)　まもなく　*(7)*
sorry, too bad　(残念[な])　ざんねん(な)　*na-adj.* *(GS4)*
sorry, excuse me　すみません　*(GS1)*
sound　(音)　おと　*(7)*
soup　スープ　*(GS3)*
soup or rice bowl　(お椀)　おわん　*(6)*
sour　(酸っぱい)　すっぱい　*i-adj.*　*(6)*
south　(南)　みなみ　*(1)*
South Korea　(韓国)　かんこく　*p.n.*;　South Korean person　(韓国人)　かんこくじん　*(1)*
south wind　(南風)　みなみかぜ　*(4)*
souvenir　おみやげ　*(4)*
soy sauce　(醤油)　しょうゆ　*(6)*
space heater　ストーブ　*(4)*
spacious, wide　(広い)　ひろい　*i-adj.*　*(2)*
spaghetti　スパゲッティー　*(6)*
Spain　スペイン　*p.n.*;　Spaniard　(スペイン人)　スペインじん;　Spanish language　(スペイン語)　スペインご　*(1)*
speak, talk, converse　(話す)　はなす　*C1, tr.*　*(GS3)*
special talent　(特技)　とくぎ　*(5)*
specialized subject　(専門科目)　せんもんかもく　*(1)*
specialty store　(専門店)　せんもんてん　*(7)*
speech　スピーチ　*(4)*
spend (time)　(過ごす)　すごす　*C1, tr.*　*(5)*
spicy　(辛い)　からい　*i-adj.*　*(6)*
spoon　スプーン　*(6)*
sports　スポーツ　*(GS2)*
sports car　スポーツ・カー　*(7)*
sportswear　スポーツウエア　*(7)*
spring　(春)　はる　*(4)*
spring rain　(春雨)　はるさめ　*(4)*
spring semester　(春学期)　はるがっき　*(5)*
stamp　(切手)　きって;　stamp collecting　(切手集め)　きってあつめ　*(5)*
stand　(立つ)　たつ　*C1, intr.*　*(GS1)*
start　(始まる)　はじまる　*C1, intr.*　*(3)*; (始める)　はじめる　*C2, tr.*　*(GS1)*
state, tell　(述べる)　のべる　*C2, tr.*　*(6)*
station　(駅)　えき　*(2)*
stationery　(文房具)　ぶんぼうぐ　*(GS3)*;　stationery store　(文房具屋)　ぶんぼうぐや　*(7)*
steak　ステーキ　*(GS3)*
steam (*in cooking*)　(蒸す)　むす　*C1, tr.*　*(6)*
stereo　ステレオ　*(5)*
stew　シチュー　*(5)*
stewardess　スチュワーデス　*(5)*
stir-fry　(炒める)　いためる　*C2, tr.*　*(6)*
stockings　ストッキング　*(7)*
stomach　おなか　*(3)*
stop　やめる　*C2, tr.*　*(3)*
store, shop　(店)　みせ　*(7)*
store clerk　(店員)　てんいん　*(7)*
storm　(嵐)　あらし　*(4)*
story; talk; speech　(話)　はなし　*(2)*
strange, funny　おかし(な)　*na-adj.*　*(6)*;　おかしい　*i-adj.*　*(2)*
strange, odd　(変[な])　へん(な)　*na-adj.*　*(2)*
strawberry　(苺)　いちご、ストロベリー　*(6)*
street　(道)　みち　*(2)*
strict　(厳しい)　きびしい　*i-adj.*　*(2)*
stripe　(縞)　しま　*(7)*;　ストライプ　*(5)*
stroll; to stroll　(散歩[する])　さんぽ(する)　*n.v.* *(GS2)*
strong, durable　(丈夫[な])　じょうぶ(な)　*na-adj.* *(7)*
strong, powerful　(強い)　つよい　*i-adj.*　*(4)*
strong, tough　タフ(な)　*na-adj.*　*(2)*
student　(学生)　がくせい;　student ID　(学生証)　がくせいしょう　*(1)*
study; to study　(勉強[する])　べんきょう(する)　*n.v.*　*(GS2)*
subtract　(引く)　ひく　*C1, tr.*　*(GS2)*
suburbs　(郊外)　こうがい　*(2)*
subway　(地下鉄)　ちかてつ　*(2)*
such as that　そんな　*dem. adj.*　*(4)*
sugar　(砂糖)　さとう　*(6)*
suit　(背広)　せびろ　*(7)*
suited (be suited, fit)　(似合う)　にあう　*C1, intr.* *(5)*
suit coat　(上着)　うわぎ　*(7)*
sultry　(むし暑い)　むしあつい　*i-adj.*　*(4)*
summer　(夏)　なつ　*(4)*;　summer vacation　(夏休み)　なつやすみ　*(6)*
sun　(太陽)　たいよう　*(4)*
Sunday　(日曜日)　にちようび　*(GS4)*
sunglasses　サングラス　*(7)*
sunny　(晴れ)　はれ　*(4)*
supermarket　スーパー　*(2)*
surely, certainly, undoubtedly　きっと　*adv.*　*(4)*
sushi restaurant　(寿司屋)　すしや　*(6)*
sweater　セーター　*(GS3)*
sweatshirt　トレーナー　*(7)*
sweet　(甘い)　あまい　*i-adj.*　*(2)*
sweets (cake and confections)　(お菓子)　おかし　*(6)*
swim　(泳ぐ)　およぐ　*C1, intr.*　*(3)*
swimming　(水泳)　すいえい　*(GS2)*
swimming pool　プール　*(1)*
swimwear　(水着)　みずぎ　*(7)*

T

table　テーブル　(*GS1*)
table tennis　(卓球)　たっきゅう　(*5*)
Taiwan　(台湾)　たいわん　*p.n.*;　Taiwanese (person)　(台湾人)　たいわんじん　(*1*)
take　(取る)　とる　*C1, tr.*　(*5*)
take, escort　(連れていく)　つれていく　(*2*)
take, require (*money, time*)　かかる　*C1, intr.*　(*3*)
take a bath　(お風呂に入る)　おふろにはいる　(*3*)
take (a photo)　(撮る)　とる　*C1, tr.*　(*7*)
take out, eject　(出す)　だす　*C1, tr.*　(*GS1*)
take a shower　(シャワーを浴びる)　シャワーをあびる　(*3*)
take care of　(世話する)　せわ(する)　*n.v.*　(*5*)
take off, remove (*glasses, etc.*)　はずす　*C1, tr.*　(*7*)
take out (*food*)　テークアウト　(*6*)
talk　(話す)　はなす　*C1, tr.*　(*GS3*)
talkative　おしゃべり(な)　*na-adj.*　(*4*)
tape　テープ　(*GS1*);　tape recorder　テープ・レコーダー　(*7*)
taste　(味わう)　あじわう　*C1, tr.*　(*6*)
tasting a sample; taste a sample　(味見[する])　あじみ(する)　*n.v.*　(*6*)
taste, flavor　(味)　あじ;　taste good　(味がいい)　あじがいい;　taste poorly　(味が悪い)　あじがわるい;　have no taste　(味がない)　あじがない　(*6*)
tasty　おいしい　*i-adj.*　(*3*)
taxi　タクシー　(*2*)
tea　(お茶)　おちゃ　(*GS3*)
tea ceremony　(茶道)　さどう　(*5*)
teach　(教える)　おしえる　*C2, tr.*　(*3*)
teacher, professor　(先生)　せんせい　(*GS1*)
teacup, rice bowl　(茶碗)　ちゃわん　(*6*)
telephone; to make a phone call　(電話[する])　でんわ(する)　*n.v.*　(*GS2*);　telephone number　(電話番号)　でんわばんごう　(*1*)
tell　(話す)　はなす　*C1, tr.*　(*GS3*)
temperature　(気温)　きおん　(*4*)
temple (Buddhist)　(お寺)　おてら　(*2*)
tempura　(天麩羅)　てんぷら;　tempura restaurant　(天麩羅屋)　てんぷらや　(*6*)
ten　(十)　じゅう　(*GS2*);　とお　(*2*)
tennis　テニス　(*GS2*)
ten thousand　(万)　まん　(*2*)
tenth day　(十日)　とおか　(*3*)
terrible　すごい　*i-adj.*　(*5*);　(大変[な])　たいへん(な)　*na-adj.*　(*4*);　ひどい　*i-adj.*　(*GS1*)
textbook　(教科書)　きょうかしょ　(*GS1*)
thank you　ありがとう　(*GS1*)
thanks to you　おかげさまで　(*GS1*)
that　あの　*dem. adj.*;　それ　*dem. pron.*　(*1*)
that much, that many　そんなに　*dem. adv.*　(*5*)
that (thing)　その　*dem. adj.*　(*1*);　that thing over there　あれ　*dem. pron.*　(*GS1*)
theatrical play　(演劇)　えんげき　(*5*)
then, if so　じゃあ　*interj.*;　では　*conj.*　(*GS1*)
then, therefore　それで　(*3*)
there　そこ、そちら　*dem. pron.*　(*1*)
therefore　だから　*conj.*　(*4*)
there is/there are (*inanimate things*)　ある　*C1, intr.*　(*2*)
they (female)　(彼女たち)　かのじょたち;　(彼女ら)　かのじょら　*pron., pl.*　(*1*)
they (male)　(彼たち)　かれたち;　(彼ら)　かれら　*pron., pl.*　(*1*)
thick, not thin　(厚い)　あつい　*i-adj.*　(*2*)
thin　(薄い)　うすい　*i-adj.*　(*7*)
thing, fact　こと　(*5*)
thing　もの　(*2*)
think (opinion)　(思う)　おもう　*C1, tr., intr.*　(*6*)
think　(考える)　かんがえる　*C2, intr.*　(*3*)
third day　(三日)　みっか　(*3*)
thirsty (be thirsty)　(咽が乾く)　のどがかわく　(*3*)
thirteenth day　(十三日)　じゅうさんにち　(*3*)
thirty　(三十)　さんじゅう　(*GS5*)
this　この　*dem. pron.*　(*1*)
this morning　(今朝)　けさ　(*2*)
this month　(今月)　こんげつ　(*1*)
this side　(こちら側)　こちらがわ　(*2*)
this thing　これ　*dem. pron.*　(*GS1*)
this time　(今度)　こんど　(*3*)
this week　(今週)　こんしゅう　(*3*)
this year　(今年)　ことし　(*3*)
though　けど　*conj., coll.*;　けれども　*conj.*　(*7*)
thought　(考え)　かんがえ　(*6*)
thread　(糸)　いと　(*7*)
three　(三)　さん　(*GS2*);　(三つ)　みっつ　(*2*)
throw　(投げる)　なげる　*C2, tr.*　(*5*)
thunder　(雷)　かみなり　(*4*)
Thursday　(木曜日)　もくようび　(*GS4*)
ticket　チケット　(*5*)
tight　きつい　*i-adj.*　(*2*)
time, counter for hours　(時間)　じかん　(*2*)
timetable　(時間割)　じかんわり　(*1*)
tire, become tired　(疲れる)　つかれる　*C2, intr.*　(*3*)
today　(今日)　きょう　(*3*)
tofu　(豆腐)　とうふ　(*6*)
together　(一緒に)　いっしょに　*adv.*　(*GS1*)
toilet　トイレ　(*2*)
Tokyo　(東京)　とうきょう　*p.n.*　(*3*)
tomato　トマト　(*6*)
tomorrow　(明日)　あした　(*3*)
tonight　(今晩)　こんばん　(*3*);　(今夜)　こんや　(*7*)
too　も　*part.*　(*3*)
tooth　(歯)　は　(*3*)
top　(上)　うえ　(*2*)
totally　すっかり　*adv.*　(*7*);　(全く)　まったく　*adv.*　(*5*)
touch　(触る)　さわる　*C1, intr.*　(*3*)
tough, durable　(丈夫[な])　じょうぶ(な)　*na-adj.*　(*7*)
tough, strict　きつい　*i-adj.*　(*2*)
town　(町)　まち　(*2*)
toy store　(おもちゃ屋)　おもちゃや　(*7*)
track and field　(陸上競技)　りくじょうきょうぎ　(*5*)
trademark　トレードマーク　(*7*)
trading company　(商社)　しょうしゃ　(*5*)
transparent　(透明[な])　とうめい(な)　*na-adj.*　(*7*)
travel; to travel　(旅行[する])　りょこう(する)　*n.v.*　(*5*)

treat to food （御馳走する） ごちそうする (*3*)
tree （木） き (*2*)
trial （試し） ためし (*6*)
trillion （兆） ちょう (*2*)
trouble; cause trouble （迷惑［する］） めいわく（する） *n.v.* (*5*)
trousers ズボン (*7*)
true （本当） ほんとう (*GS2*); truly （本当に） ほんとうに *adv.* (*4*)
trust （信じる） しんじる *C2, tr.* (*3*)
try （試す） ためす *C1, tr.* (*7*)
try to do… 〜てみる (*6*)
T-shirt Tシャツ (*5*)
Tuesday （火曜日） かようび (*GS4*)
tuition （授業料） じゅぎょうりょう (*5*)
tulip チューリップ (*7*)
tuna （鮪） まぐろ (*6*); tuna salad ツナサラダ (*6*)
turn into なる *C1, intr.* (*4*)
turn on (a switch) （入れる） いれる *C2, tr.* (*3*)
tutor （家庭教師） かていきょうし (*3*)
twelfth day （十二日） じゅうににち (*3*)
twentieth day （二十日） はつか (*3*)
twenty （二十） にじゅう (*GS2*)
twenty-fourth day （二十四日） にじゅうよっか (*3*)
twenty years old （二十歳） はたち (*1*)
two （二） に (*GS2*); （二つ） ふたつ (*2*)
two people （二人） ふたり (*2*)
TV テレビ (*GS3*)
type, kind （種類） しゅるい (*6*)
typing; to type タイプ（する） *n.v.* (*6*)
typhoon （台風） たいふう (*4*)

U

umbrella （傘） かさ (*GS3*); put up an umbrella かさをさす (*7*)
uncle おじ; おじさん *pol.* (*5*)
under （下） した (*2*)
underground （地下） ちか (*GS3*)
underground floor （地階） ちかい (*GS3*)
understand わかる *C1, tr.* (*GS1*)
underwear （下着） したぎ (*7*)
undress （脱ぐ） ぬぐ *C1, tr.* (*3*)
uniform （制服） せいふく (*7*)
university （大学） だいがく; university student （大学生） だいがくせい (*1*)
until now これまでに (*6*)
up （上） うえ (*2*)
up to, until まで *part.* (*2*)
use （使う） つかう *C1, tr.* (*GS1*)
usual （普通） ふつう (*6*)

V

vacation （休暇） きゅうか (*3*)
vanilla バニラ (*GS5*)
various （色々［な］） いろいろ（な） *na-adj.* (*2*)
Vaseline ワセリン (*7*)
vegetable （野菜） やさい (*GS1*); vegetable juice （野菜ジュース） やさいジュース (*7*); vegetable salad （野菜サラダ） やさいサラダ (*6*); vegetable store （八百屋） やおや (*7*)
vegetarian ベジタリアン (*GS5*)
very とても *adv.* (*GS3*)
very, awful すごい *i-adj.* (*5*)
very (much) （大変［な］） たいへん（な） *na-adj.* (*4*)
very sorry （申し訳ない） もうしわけない (*7*)
video ビデオ (*6*)
videocamera ビデオカメラ (*5*)
video game テレビゲーム、ビデオ・ゲーム (*5*)
village （村） むら (*2*)
vinegar （酢） す、ビネガー (*6*)
violin バイオリン (*5*)
visit; inquire （伺う） うかがう *C1, tr.* (*5*)
vivid （鮮やか［な］） あざやか（な） *na-adj.* (*7*)
volleyball バレーボール (*5*)

W

Wednesday （水曜日） すいようび (*GS4*)
Western clothes （洋服） ようふく (*7*)
Western clothing store （洋品店） ようひんてん (*7*)
Western cuisine （洋食） ようしょく (*6*)
Western-style style （洋風） ようふう (*6*)
wait （待つ） まつ *C1, tr.* (*GS1*)
waiter ウエター; waitress ウエトレス (*2*)
wake up （起きる） おきる *C2, intr.* (*GS3*)
walk （歩く） あるく *C1, intr.* (*GS1*)
walking, on foot （徒歩） とほ (*2*)
wall （壁） かべ (*GS1*)
wallet （財布） さいふ (*2*)
want （欲しがる） ほしがる *C1, tr.*; （欲しい） ほしい *i-adj.* (*6*)
want to… 〜たがる (*with conjunctive form of verb*) *C1, intr.* (*6*)
want to… 〜たい (*with conjunctive form of verb*) *i-adj.* (*6*)
ward (*in city*) （区） く (*2*)
warm （暖かい） あたたかい *i-adj.* (*GS4*)
wash （洗う） あらう *C1, tr.*; wash one's face （顔を洗う） かおをあらう (*3*)
watch (clock) shop （時計店／時計屋） とけいてん／とけいや (*7*)
water （お水） おみず; （水） みず (*6*)
watercolor （水彩画） すいさいが (*5*)
we (female) あたしたち *pron., inf., f., pl.* (*1*)
we (male) （僕たち） ぼくたち *pron., m., inf., pl.* (*1*)
we （私たち） わたしたち *pron., pl.* (*1*)
weak （弱い） よわい *i-adj.* (*4*)
weak point （苦手） にがて (*5*)
wear (see "put on") かぶる *C1, tr.*; つける (*7*); はく (*4*); （着る） きる (*3*)
weather （天気） てんき; weather forecast （天気予報） てんきよほう; weather map （天気図） てんきず (*4*)
week before last （先々週） せんせんしゅう (*GS4*)

weekday (平日) へいじつ (3)
weekend (週末) しゅうまつ (3)
weight lifting ウエート・リフティング (5)
weird (変[な]) へん(な) *na-adj.* (2)
well… あのう... (1)
well, see you じゃあ... *interj.* (GS1)
well (done) よく *adv.* (1)
well-lighted (明るい) あかるい *i-adj.* (4)
west (西) にし (4)
what (何) なに、なん (GS4); what (何) なん (GS1); what color (何色) なにいろ (1); what day (何日) なんにち (3); what day of the week (何曜日) なんようび; what kind どんな *dem. adj.* (GS4); what language (何語) なにご (1); what minute (何分) なんぷん (3); what month (何月) なんがつ; what nationality (何人) なにじん (1); what time (何時) なんじ (GS2); what year (何年) なんねん (3); what year in school (何年生) なんねんせい (1)
when (in questions) いつ (GS4)
when… (〜時) 〜とき (7)
where どこ *dem. pron.* (GS3); どちら *pol.* (GS4)
whether… 〜かどうか (7)
which (of two) どちら (GS4); which (of more than two) どの *dem. adj.* (1)
whichever どちらでも (5)
which one どちらのほう (4); どっち *coll.* (1)
which thing (of more than two) どれ *dem. adj.* (GS4)
while… 〜ながら (*with conjunctive form of verbs*) (6)
whiskey ウイスキー (GS2)
white (白) しろ (7) (白い) しろい *i-adj.* (2)
white-collar worker サラリーマン (5)
who だれ (GS4); どなた *pol.* (1)
why どうして、なぜ (1)
wide (広い) ひろい *i-adj.* (2)
wife (奥さん) おくさん *pol.*; (家内) かない; (妻) つま (5)
wind (風) かぜ; wind blows (風が吹く) かぜがふく (4)
window (窓) まど (GS1)
wine ワイン (GS2); red wine (赤ワイン) あかワイン (5) white wine (白ワイン) しろワイン (5)
winter (冬) ふゆ (4); winter vacation (冬休み) ふゆやすみ (6)
with, by で *part.* (2)
with (together) と *part.* (GS3)
withdraw (*money*) おろす *C1, tr.* (7)
without knowing it (いつの間にか) いつのまにか (5)
woman (女) おんな (2); (女の方) おんなのかた *pol.* (5); (女の人) おんなのひと (2); (女性) じょせい (5)
women's wear store (婦人服店) ふじんふくてん (7)
wood (木) き (2)
wool ウール (7)
word (言葉) ことば (4)
word processor ワープロ (1)
work (働く) はたらく *C1, intr.* (3)
wow わあ *interj.* (GS3)
wrap (包む) つつむ *C1, tr.*; wrapping paper (包み紙) つつみがみ (7)
wrestling レスリング (5)
write (書く) かく *C1, tr.* (GS1)
wrong number (*telephone*) (間違い電話) まちがいでんわ (3)

Y

yacht ヨット (5)
year before last おととし (7)
year in school (学年) がくねん (1)
years before (〜年前に) 〜ねんまえに (6)
yellow (黄色) きいろ (6); (黄色い) きいろい *i-adj.* (7)
yen (円) えん (GS3)
yes ええ、はい *interj.* (GS1)
yesterday (昨日) きのう (GS3)
yoga ヨガ (5)
yogurt ヨーグルト (6)
you あなたたち *pron., pl.* (1)
you あなた *pron., s.* (1)
young (若い) わかい *i-adj.* (2)
younger brother (弟さん) おとうとさん *pol.*; (弟) おとうと (5)
younger sister (妹さん) いもうとさん *pol.* (妹) いもうと (5)

Z

zero (零) れい、ゼロ (GS2)
zipper ファスナー (7)

Index

ability, describing, 315, 316–19, 329–333
academic subjects/ departments, 92, 94
accentuation, 13–14, 262, 331
accepting, 54, 220
adjectives, 131–133, 173, 236, 298
  comparatives and, 249–255
  conjoining, 275
  conjugation of, 133, 244–248, 386, 388
  demonstrative, 103–104
  irregular, 246
  kanji and, 73
  negative and, 132, 133, 244–246, 261
  nominalizing, 323–325
  nonpast tense of, 244–246, 261, 266
  past tense of, 244–246, 259–260, 261
  plain form and, 244–246, 261, 266, 275, 381, 396, 404
  predicate use of, 132–133, 244
  prenominal use of, 131–133, 244
  present or future and, 284–285
  questions and, 266
  ta-form and, 263
  te-form and, 273–277
adverbs, 133, 369, 417
  in affirmative sentences, 206, 417
  certainty and, 286
  comparatives and, 250–255
  indicating frequency, 38, 204–206, 235
  kanji and, 73
  in negative sentences, 205–206, 417
affirmative, 87
  adjectives and, 132, 133, 244–246, 266
  adverbs and, 206, 417
  interrogatives and, 306
  particles and, 326–328
  verbs and, 187–196, 201–204, 261–264, 415
age, 96–97, 98
agreement, expressing, 19–20, 232
although, 272–273
and, 68, 211, 224, 235, 274
animals, 58
anoo, 24
answering negative questions, 266–267
any, 306
apology, 3, 6, 7
apostrophe, 54
appreciation, expressing, 3
are, 24–25
asking about future, 39–40
asking about Japanese language, 295
asking for clarification, 20, 24–25
asking for opinion, 401–402
asking for personal information, 96, 99
asking how often, 38
asking how to say in Japanese, 10
asking location, 63–66
asking permission, 388
asking price, 68
asking someone to do something, 11, 232, 411
asking what someone wants, 389
asking what something is, 24–25
asking what's available, 67
asking why, 269
attention, attracting, 3, 24

birthdays, 184, 185
both, 333
bowing, 2
but, 216

Calpis, 406
campus, 105–106, 120–121
change in state, 354–356
chigaimasu, 25
Chinese characters, 14, 29, 75, 123–124
chotto, 67
cities/towns/neighborhoods, 138–139
  places about, 143–146
classroom expressions, 11–12, 15–16, 47, 78
clauses
  connecting independent, 272–273, 274, 278–279
  relative, 348–353
colloquial form, 133, 244, 246, 265, 403
comma, 74
commuting, 129, 137, 139
comparatives, 249–255
compliments, responding to, 362–363
conjecture, 283–289
conjugation
  of adjectives, 133, 243–248, 386, 388
  hiragana and, 73
  of verbs, 38, 53, 73, 185–191, 329–330, 415
conjunctions, disjunctive, 216, 272–273
conjunctive form, 193–194, 199–204, 219, 235, 275, 388, 398, 417, 422
consonants, 28
  double, 45, 60
  voiced vs. unvoiced, 27, 28
copula, 86–88, 244–246, 273–277
  plain form and, 396, 404
  te-form of, 275
counting/counter, 17–18, 129, 157–161, 175, 204–205, 326–327
  books and, 308, 327
  cameras and, 326
  comparatives and, 251
  glassfuls and, 327
  ordinal numbers and, 313
  times/degrees and, 381
countries/languages, 50

daily/everyday activities, 24, 34–35, 39, 191–192, 199–200, 206, 234
dakuten, 27
days/weeks, 40, 51, 55, 61, 106–107, 121, 180, 182, 183, 204–205, 214–215
declining, 55, 220, 232
demonstratives, 101, 102–104
deshita, 7
desire, expressing, 385–393
desu, 2, 4, 18, 41, 42
diacritical marks, 27, 59
dictionary form, 188–189, 261–262, 193, 329, 415
direction, 46, 209
disjunctive clauses, 272–273
disjunctive sentences, 216
distance, 256
doo itashimashite, 7
doomo, 7
doozo yoroshiku, 2

early, 251
eateries, 386
ellipsis points, 74

emotions, expressing, 20, 386, 387
emphasis, 58, 362
equative sentence, 252-253
every, 306
excuse me, 151
existence, expressing, 140-142, 147
experience, expressing, 380-382
explaining reasons, 264-266

family, 143, 259, 334-341, 363-364, 365, 367-368
father, 339-340
foods/beverages, 31, 48-49, 51, 53, 62, 78, 374-379, 433
  flavors/tastes of, 394, 433
  likes and dislikes for, 41, 71
  ordering, 69-70, 100
  preparation of, 408-409, 434
  seasonings in, 394
forecasting, 282
foreign loanwords, 14, 58
  in *katakana*, 72, 73
formal forms, 286
frequency, 38, 204-206, 235
fu, 28
future, 39-40, 284-285

gairaigo, 73
gender, 11
glide, 43, 45
go, 311, 312
goodbye, 8, 15
goro, 37
grammar, 53, 136-137, 299
  particles and, 46, 53, 207-213
  verbs and, 187-188, 194
gratitude, expressing, 6-7
greetings, 7-9, 15, 30, 61, 78, 104
  weather and, 56-57, 240

hai, soo desu, 18
hajimemashite, 2
handakuten, 27
hello, 8
hi, 28
hiragana, 2, 14, 15, 26-28, 30, 43-46, 47
  chart for, 27
  children's books and, 74
  as *hurigana*, 75
  katakana compared with, 58, 59
  mixed with *katakana* and *kanji*, 74
  origin of, 29
  potential form and, 329
  rooma-ji spelling vs., 29
  te-form and, 416
  rules of, 73
  verbs and, 186, 194
  volitional verbs and, 411
hobbies/pastimes, 304-305, 310-311, 341, 366-367
holidays/vacations, 213-214
home, 143
honorifics, 336
house, 143
however, 272-273
hurigana, 75

i-adjectives, 131-133, 244-245, 261
  change in state and, 354-356
  in expressing desire, 386, 388
  in expressing opinion, 398
  nominalizing, 323-325
  present or future and, 284-285
  questions and, 266
  te-form of, 274
iie, 7, 25
imperative form, 415
informal forms, 4-5, 38
intent, expressing, 410-415
interrogatives, 305-309
  comparatives and, 254
  particles and, 87-88, 110-114, 307-309
  words formed from, 369
intonation, 87
introductions, 2-6, 117-119, 363-364
  self-, 119
invitations/offers, 54-56, 220, 411

Japanese addresses, 145
Japanese books, 74, 76
Japanese communication, 92, 170
Japanese dictionaries, 28
Japanese family, 338
Japanese food, 48, 376, 384, 406
Japanese games, 311-312
Japanese holidays, 217-218
Japanese language, questions about, 295
Japanese letter writing, 291-292
Japanese names, 4
Japanese people, praise and, 320
Japanese politeness, 336
Japanese rain, 257-258, 282
Japanese schools, 75, 93
Japanese sports, 321-322
Japanese tea, 376
Japanese telephone numbers, 18
Japanese use of Celsius system, 242
Japanese women, 338
Japanese years (birthdays), 184
judo, 321

ka, 3, 4, 42, 54-56
kanji, 14, 15, 28, 29, 30, 47, 61, 176, 236, 299, 369, 435
  asking about, 295
  children's books and, 74
  introduction to, 75-79
  learning, 115-116
  lists of, 123
  mixed with *hiragana* and *katakana*, 74
  quoting and, 402
  repeating, 205
  rules of, 73
  te-form and, 416
  types of, 123-124
  verbs and, 194
karate, 321
katakana, 2, 14, 15, 30, 47, 58-60, 61
  as *hurigana*, 75
  foreign loanwords and, 72, 73
  mixed with *hiragana* and *kanji*, 74
  onomatopoeic words and, 73, 362
  origin of, 29
  rooma-ji spelling vs., 29
  rules of, 73
kekkoo desu, 69
kendo, 321
kilometers, 256
kissaten, 69
ko-so-a-do, 103, 396
kooban, 145
kore, 24-25
kudasai, 11

leave-taking, 8
leisure activities, 304-305, 313
likes and dislikes, expressing, 40-41, 71, 161-164
listening, 13
location, 63-66, 146-154
  on map, 170-171
  particles and, 209

mah-jongg, 311, 312
martial arts, 321-322
meals, 432-433
measurement
  distance, 256
  temperature, 242, 288, 381
meeshi, 5-6
menus, 67, 69-70, 425
midpoint, 74
modifiers, 348-349
months, 98, 121, 182, 204-205, 235
more/less than, 315

na-adjectives, 131-133, 244, 245, 368
  change in state and, 354-356
  in expressing opinion, 398
  nominalizing, 323-325
  present or future and, 284-285
  questions and, 266
  te-form and, 274
nai form, 412
name cards, 5-6
names
  Japanese, 4
  place and personal, 32
nationalities/languages, 83-85, 121
ne(e), 19-20, 41
negative, 25, 67, 141, 381, 387

adjectives and, 132, 133, 244-246, 261, 381
adverbs and, 38, 205-206, 417
conjugation and, 38
copula and, 87
of equative sentence, 252-253
interrogatives and, 306
particles and, 326-328
present or future and, 284
questions in, 141, 266-267
verbs and, 187-196, 201-204, 260-261, 415
Nihongo, 32
no, 18
no, saying, 25, 67, 87, 306
nominal verbs, 187, 312, 322-323
nominalizers, 322-325, 380
nonpast tense
of adjectives, 244, 266
of verbs, 38, 187-189, 192-196, 261-264, 344, 387, 388, 404, 412, 415
noun phrases, 323-325
nouns, 11, 16, 32, 49, 79, 173, 235, 298-299, 368
change in state and, 354-356
conjoining, 224, 275
inanimate vs., animate, 141-142, 147
kanji and, 73
modifiers and, 349
nonpast, affirmative, 266
particle connecting, 99, 224
possessive particle and, 90
present or future and, 284-285
sentence structure and, 36
topic particle and, 86
numbers, 17-23, 30-31, 66, 78, 155-161, 326-327
for age, 96-97, 98
approximate, 226
for days of month, 182, 235
in expressing existence, 142
large, 156-157, 175
ordinal, 313
telephone, 18-20
objects, 24-25, 46, 208, 210, 323
of desire, 387, 388
potential form and, 330
in sentence structure, 36
ohayoo, 7
okurigana, 194
onamae wa, 4
one time, 381
onomatopoeic words, 14, 58, 258, 362
katakana and, 73, 362
opinion, expressing, 386, 395-402, 429
or, 333

pachinko, 311, 312
part-time jobs, 181
particles, 53, 235, 326-328, 333, 387
connecting, 68, 99
direction, 46
in expressing existence, 141-142
grammar and, 46, 53, 207-213
hiragana and, 73
interrogatives and, 87-88, 110-114, 307-309
location and, 147
nouns joined by, 99, 224
possessive, 90
prepositions vs., 36
sentence-final, 19-20, 151-152, 386
subject, 207-211, 349
time and, 208-209, 347
topic, 46, 86, 207-211, 349
past, recent, 381
past tense
of adjectives, 244-246, 259-260
of verbs, 38, 51-53, 187-189, 201-204, 259-264, 285-286, 344-347, 380
people, 120
counting, 161, 175
older, 335, 336
period, 74
personal information, 91, 96, 99, 120
personal pronouns, 101-102
pitch accent, 13-14
places, 173, 208
plain form
adjectives and, 244-246, 266, 275, 381, 396, 404
copula and, 396, 404
female speakers and, 247
nominalizers and, 323
polite vs., 140-141, 244-246
probability and, 283
relative clauses and, 349
verbs and, 187-189, 259-264, 266, 380, 396, 404, 411, 415
plans, 412-415
plants, 58
please, 100, 278
police box, 144
polite form, 7-9, 15, 30, 61, 100, 335-336
adjectives and, 244-246
conjugation and, 38
copula and, 87
in declining invitation, 55, 220
demonstratives and, 103-104
personal pronouns and, 102
plain vs., 140-141, 244-246
questions and, 305
relative clauses and, 349
requests and, 296-297
telling time with, 37
verbs and, 187, 192-196, 201-204, 219, 411, 415
positional words, 147-150, 152-153, 175-176
possessive, 18, 90, 349
postpositions, 36
potential form, 328-333
praise, 320
prepositions (particles vs.), 36
present tense, 284-285
probability, 283-289
pronounciation, 26-28, 46, 137
asking about, 295
foreign loanwords and, 72
kanji and, 75
pronouns, 24-25, 323
personal, 101-102
possessive particle and, 90
topic particle and, 86
punctuation, 74
purpose, particles and, 209

question mark, 3
questions, 15, 30, 52, 53, 61, 265-269, 108-114, 122
informal, 4-5
echo, 42
either/or, 88
formal, 286
indirect, 286
about Japanese language, 295
negative, 141, 266-267
particle and, 87-88, 141-142
yes/no, 87-88, 141
quick, 251
quotation marks, 74, 86
quote marker, 403-404
quoting speech, 402-407
direct vs. indirect, 404

rain, 257-258, 282
relative clauses, 348-353
requests, polite, 296-297
restaurants, 68-70, 100, 386, 425-426, 429-430
rice, 378
romanization, 2, 26, 84
rooma-ji, 2, 29
roots, *kanji* and, 73

-san, 4
sankyuu, 7
sayo(o)nara, 8
seasons, 270-272, 282-283, 298
-sensee, 4
sentence-final particle, 19-20, 151-152, 386
sentence-final verb, 279
sentence structure, 36, 211
sentences, compound, 216
sequential actions/events, 199, 279-281
shitsuree shimasu, 8
shogi, 311, 312
simultaneous actions, expressing, 422-423
singular/plural, 11
skills/abilities, 315, 316-19, 329-333
some, 306
soo desu nee, 41

sore, 24–25
sound words, 362
speech fillers, 22, 41, 42
sports, 314–315, 321, 367
subject, 323
subject particle, 207–211, 349
subject-verb agreement, 35
suggestion, making, 69, 218–220, 222
sumimasen, 7, 24
sumimasen ga, chotto, 67
sumo, 321
superlatives, 252
surprise, expressing, 197
syllabaries, 14, 28, 58–60, 186
syllables, 14, 28, 45–46

ta-form, 263, 278, 380–382
te-form
  of adjectives, 273–277
  of verbs, 277–281, 342–344, 387, 416–421
tea, 376
telephone, talking on, 229–230
telephone numbers, 18–20
temperature, 242, 288, 381
tense, 38, 187–204, 279
thank you, 3, 7, 15
time, 20–23, 36–37, 47–48, 61, 180, 234, 345
  free, 181, 313
  counting, 129, 175,
  particles and, 208–209, 347
to be, 87
to be called, 402–403
to become, 354
to come, 187
to do, 187, 312, 416–421
to finish doing, 417
to say/tell, 402–403
to start doing, 417
to try, 416
too much, 398–400
topic particle, 46, 86, 207–211, 349
transitions, 272–273, 279
transportation, 172
two or three things, talking about, 306
typhoons, 256

uncertainty, 283–289

verb roots, *kanji* and, 73
verbs, 48, 236, 299, 369
  auxiliary, 342–344
  basic structure of, 185–190
  change in state and, 354–356
  Class 1/2/3, 186, 192–194, 260–264, 278, 329–333, 387, 411, 418
  communication, 404
  comparatives and, 250–255
  compound, 187
  conjugation of, 38, 53, 73, 185–191, 329–330, 415
  conjunctive form of, 193–194, 199–204, 219, 388, 398, 417, 422
  hiragana and, 73
  invitations and, 54–56
  irregular, 187, 411, 415
  kudasai with, 11, 30
  long vs. short form of, 330–331
  nai form and, 412
  nominal, 187, 312
  nominalizing, 323–325
  nonpast tense of, 38, 187–189, 192–196, 261–264, 344, 387, 388, 404, 412, 415
  past tense of, 38, 187–189, 201–204, 259–264, 285–286, 344–347, 380
  plain form and, 187–189, 259–264, 266, 380, 396, 404, 411, 415
  polite form and, 187, 192–196, 201–204, 219, 411, 415
  potential form and, 328–333
  present or future and, 284–285
  questions and, 266
  relative clauses and, 349
  sentence structure and, 36, 211
  sentence-final, 279
  subjects with, 35
  ta-form of, 278, 380–382
  te-form of, 277–281, 342–344, 387, 416–421
  tense of, 38, 51–53, 187–204, 279
  volitional, 219–220, 410–415
vocabulary. learning new, 122–123
volitional form, 219–220, 410–415
vowel, 28
  devoiced, 26
  double, 44–45, 60
  semi-, 43

want/wish, 386–393
weather, 56–57, 240–242, 256–259, 282–283, 288, 297
while, 422–423
word order, 211
word space, 74
writing, 14, 26–30, 43–46
  asking about, 295
  for children, 74
  horizontal vs. vertical, 43, 76–77
  of letters, 76, 291–292
  word space and punctuation in, 74

y, 43, 45
Yakitori, 51
years, 183–184
yes, saying, 87

Grateful acknowledgment is made for use of the following:

Photographs: *Page 1* © Hideaki Omura/Amana Corporation; *2* © John Burbank/The Image Works; *17* © Katsuyoshi Tanaka; *34* © Dennis Budd Gray/Stock Boston; *51* © SuperStock; *58* © Jose Fuste Raga/The Stock Market; *63 (top)* © Barbara Alper/Stock Boston; *(bottom)* © Fujifotos/The Image Works; *70* © John Burbank/The Image Works; *82* © Fujifotos/The Image Works; *93* © Sonia Katchian/Photo Shuttle Japan; *119* © Sonia Katchian/Photo Shuttle Japan; *127* © Fujifotos/The Image Works; *138* © Charles Gupton/Stock Boston; *144* © Fujifotos/The Image Works; *179* © Charles Gupton/Stock Boston; *218* © Hiroshi Mizouchi/Amana Corporation; *239* © Lou Jones; *257* © Robert Holmes; *271* © Keiki Haginoya/Amana Corporation; *294* © Fumihiko Murakami/Amana Corporation; *303* © Fujifotos/The Image Works; *311* © Barbara Alper/Stock Boston; *320* © Charles Gupton/Tony Stone Images, Inc.; *322* © Fujiphotos/The Image Works; *338* © Don Smetzer/Tony Stone Images, Inc.; *373* © Sonia Katchian/Photo Shuttle Japan; *376* © Charles Gupton/Stock Boston; *379* © Cameramann/The Image Works; *438* © Luxereau Christophe/Liaison Agency Inc.; *455* © Fujifotos/The Image Works; *491* © Sonia Katchian/Photo Shuttle Japan

Realia: *Page 55 Shufunotomo Zaiteku Kakeibo* 1987 (Tokyo: Shufunotomo sha, 1987); *68* Charles Jourdan, Hilton, Lasserre, Elnard; *70* Reprinted with permission of Café Terrasse Yókó; *76* From *Saibo Kogaku* 13, no. 9 (Tokyo: Shujunsha, 1994); *77* From *Shin-Cai-ron* by Yumiko Yamaoka (Tokyo: Computer Age Co.); *128* Teito Rapid Transit Authority; *243* Courtesy of *The Yomiuri Shimbum* and the Japan Meteorological Society; *359* Community Plaza Shinyuri; *374* Juujiya Food Center; *408 Shufunotomo Zaiteku Kakeibo* 1987 (Tokyo: Shufunotomo sha, 1987)

0 100 200 km

日本地図

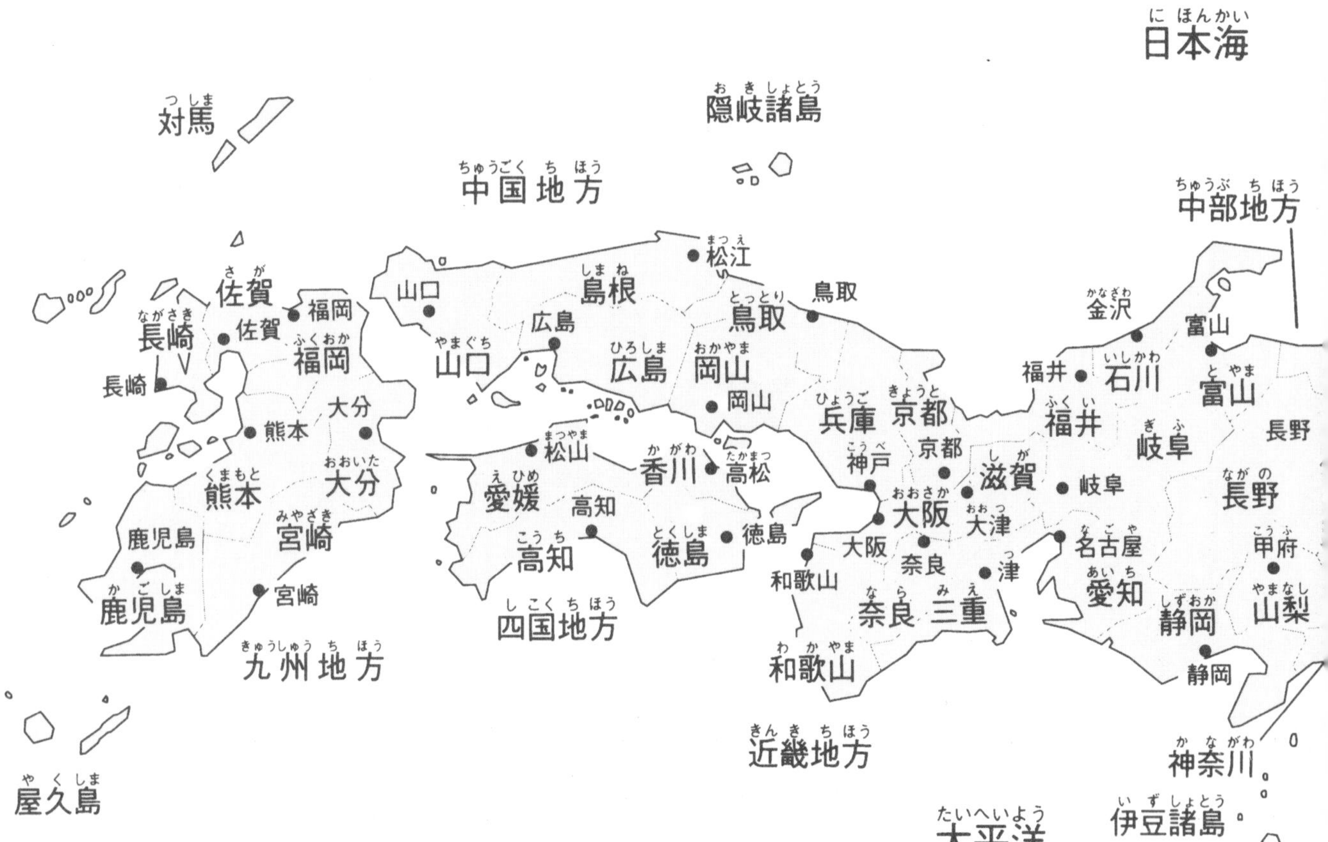